Attachment Disturbances in Adults

Attachment Disturbances in Adults

TREATMENT FOR COMPREHENSIVE REPAIR

Daniel P. Brown
David S. Elliott

WITH

Paula Morgan-Johnson
Paula Sacks
Caroline R. Baltzer
James Hickey
Andrea Cole
Jan Bloom
Deirdre Fay

W.W. NORTON & COMPANY
Independent Publishers Since 1923
New York • London

For information about permission to reproduce selections from this book, write to Permissions, W. W. Norton & Company, Inc., 500 Fifth Avenue, New York, NY 10110

For information about special discounts for bulk purchases, please contact W. W. Norton Special Sales at specialsales@wwnorton.com or 800-233-4830

Manufacturing by Versa Press
Production manager: Christine Critelli

ISBN: 978-0-393-71152-3

W. W. Norton & Company, Inc.,
500 Fifth Avenue, New York, N.Y. 10110
www.wwnorton.com

W. W. Norton & Company Ltd.,
15 Carlisle Street, London W1D 3BS

7 8 9 0

To all parents
who have devoted themselves
with careful attunement
to raising securely attached children,
which insures passage of secure attachment
down through the generations;
and with deep compassion,
for all those parents who were not able
to provide security of attachment,
and for all the insecurely attached children of the world.

Contents

Expanded Contents

Acknowledgments

This book would never have been written without the legacy of John Bowlby, the visionary ideal father figure of the attachment field, or without Mary Ainsworth, our ideal mother figure, who translated Bowlby's ideas into a research paradigm that has left its mark on the attachment field for generations.

The senior author, Dr. Brown, would like to acknowledge his special indebtedness to Mary Main and Erik Hesse, the masterminds behind the analysis of discourse from the Adult Attachment Interview, and to Deborah Jacobvitz for her deep patience in teaching him the Adult Attachment Interview coding system. Thinking about patients in terms of states of mind completely transformed his years of clinical practice and served to shape this book. He would also like to acknowledge the influence that Giovanni Liotti had on the way we have come to think about disorganized attachment, dissociation, and especially collaborative behavior. The chapter on collaborativeness in this book started from what Dr. Brown learned directly from Dr. Liotti on a visit to him in Rome in 2004 as well as from Dr. Liotti's talk on collaborative behavior at Harvard Medical School in 2005. Dr. Brown would like to express his gratitude to Clint Fuhs and Ken Wilber for convincing him to reflect on the profound positive mental health impact of the stages of post-formal adult metacognitive development, as these seminal talks served to shape the chapter on metacognition. Howard Steele receives our gratitude for his collaboration on our orphanage study and for masterfully carrying out the statistical analysis of the orphanage study findings.

Andrea Cole (along with the rest of us) also wishes to thank Dr. Steele for teaching her the Reflective Functioning coding system so that we could use the RF Scale in our orphanage study and also describe it in detail in this book. Dr. Brown would like to thank his friend and colleague Mark Schwartz for his graciousness in supplying a brief prepublication write-up of his data analysis of AAIs given to a large sample of inpatients with eating disorders.

The second author, Dr. Elliott, along with gratitude for all those who Dr. Brown acknowledges above, wishes to extend appreciation to two early mentors: Catherine Morrison, who first introduced attachment theory to him through her attuned and responsive clinical supervision, and Thomas Yeomans, who helped to open and deepen his integrative approach to all dimensions of the person. Dr. Elliott also wants to honor the founders, staff, and students of the Harmony Institute in St. Petersburg, Russia, for their enthusiastic embrace of the principles and practices of the attachment treatment methods described in this book. Dr. Alexander Badkhen and Dr. Mark Pevzner deserve particular appreciation for giving Dr. Elliott the opportunity to bring this and other material to the psychological treatment community in Russia, as does Marina Badkhen, who for almost 20 years has been a skilled and sensitive interpreter for Dr. Elliott during his teachings in St. Petersburg. Dr. Elliott's experiences in Russia have very much informed our thinking and practice. Special thanks goes to Patricia Crittenden for providing consultation about her model and methods of assessment and treatment and for reading early drafts of Dr. Elliott's writing about her work.

We all owe our gratitude to Deane Dozier for the many AAI transcripts she carefully scored for us in our attachment working group. Because the working group has been active for over 10 years, several of our dearly missed members were unable to contribute to the actual writing, but their input as part of the group over the years has certainly helped in shaping the outcome of this book. Olga de Armas and Robert O'Neil are integral members of our attachment working group.

The group also wants to acknowledge all the teachers who have taught one or more of us, as their teaching and inspiration have benefited us all as we have explored and discovered together. Drs. Anthony Bateman, Alexandra Harrison, and Howard Wishnie are three such valued teachers.

We all wish to thank and honor friends, colleagues, and family who have provided support for our work in various ways: Robbie Baltzer; Steve, Michael, and Erica Miller; Lonny Darwin; Linda Thörn Elliott; Boone Gross; Michael Hopper; Rob Jaskiewicz; John Kingston; Peter Kober; Gretchen Nelson; and Jeffrey C. Sacks.

Ben Yarling, our Editor at Norton, provided skilled, sensitive, and enthusiastic support and guidance that helped to shape the final form of the manuscript and bring it to fruition. It has been a pleasure to work with him. Elizabeth Baird and the Norton production team did fine work with the manuscript from the copyediting phase forward, and we are grateful for their precision and care.

And last but certainly not least, we all honor our patients, with whom we have shared exploration and discovery that has greatly contributed to this book.

A Reader's Guide

Attachment Disturbances in Adults: Treatment for Comprehensive Repair is intended to be a complete resource book for understanding attachment, its development, and the most clinically relevant findings from attachment research, and for using this understanding to inform systematic, comprehensive, and clinically effective and efficient treatment of attachment disturbances in adults.

We realize that readers approach this book from various backgrounds in attachment theory. Readers who have a strong background in the field of attachment may wish to read through certain chapters, such as the Part I "Foundational Concepts" chapters, primarily to find what we believe to be important and how we frame the state of the field, whereas other readers who are less familiar with the field may want to carefully read this entire first section.

Readers less familiar with attachment theory will get an overview of the seminal ideas in the history and development of the attachment field through a careful reading of Chapter 1, "Attachment Research: A History of Ideas." This chapter covers such foundational concepts as John Bowlby's ideas and work on the attachment bond, Mary Ainsworth's research on patterns of attachment, cross-cultural patterns of attachment, intergenerational transmission of attachment, attachment states of mind and internal working models of attachment, the development of metacognition, intersubjectivity, and nonverbal and verbal attunement and misattunement.

Likewise, readers who are less familiar with factors contributing to the development and change of patterns of attachment over time will want to pay particular attention to Chapter 2, "Understanding the Development of Attachment Bonds and Attachment Behavior Over the Life Course." In this chapter, we trace the origins of attachment behavior in infancy, show how stable prototypical patterns of attachment emerge during the second year of life, and illustrate how these prototypical patterns of attachment remain stable, change, or transform during the toddler, preschool and school years, and adolescence. We also focus on how attachment patterns appear in adult intimate relationships.

Part II, "Assessment," addresses issues pertaining to the assessment of attachment disturbances. Chapter 3, "Adult Attachment Prototypes and Their Clinical Manifestations," is designed for the reader who is less familiar with the specific clinically relevant prototypes of attachment: secure, dismissing, anxious-preoccupied, and disorganized/fearful. Emphasis is given to the specific patterns of attachment behavior, organization of self, and affect regulatory functions for each of these patterns of attachment. The main purpose of this chapter is to help clinicians appreciate how deactivating, hyperactivating, and disorganized attachment styles are likely to manifest in the treatment setting and outside of it in various relationships, so that clinicians can better identify and understand the appearance of these patterns.

Chapter 4, "The Assessment of Adult Attachment," is intended as an overview of attachment assessment for the clinician. We review in some detail the main interview-based and self-report measures of attachment to give the reader an overview of the available assessment tools. Furthermore, we make practical recommendations about what we consider to be the best approaches to attachment assessment for the clinician to use. This chapter also describes a number of instruments that are useful for assessing attachment behavior within the therapeutic relationship.

The contributions of early childhood attachment disturbance to adult psychopathology have been of great research interest. Chapter 5, "Attachment and Psychopathology," is designed as an overview of how patterns of insecure attachment are related to various psychiatric conditions such as anxiety disorders, affective disorders, somatic symptom disorders, posttraumatic stress and dissociative disorders, personality disorders, and addictive behaviors. This chapter also includes a summary of the research findings from our study of adults who were abused as children in an orphanage. This sample included children who were physically and sexually abused, many by the same abusers, and were either securely or insecurely attached at the period of their abuse. It was possible to separate out the relative and independent contributions of early attachment status and childhood abuse to adult psychopathology. These data strongly suggest that treatment of patients with complex trauma, personality disorders, and/or dissociative disorders should focus first on attachment repair before any phase-oriented trauma processing.

Part III, "Treatment," addresses treatment approaches to attachment disorders in adults. Those less familiar with the range of available attachment-based treatments should carefully read Chapter 6, "An Overview of Treatments for Attachment Disturbances." This chapter reviews a wide range of currently available attachment-based treatments. We have tried to present both the advantages and limitations of each approach as we have come to understand them. This overview of available treatments, along with a discussion of their underlying assumptions and limitations, serves as the rationale for why we developed a new treatment approach.

Chapter 7, "An Introduction to the Three Pillars of Comprehensive Attachment Treatment," is a must-read for the clinician. In this chapter readers are given an overview of what we believe to be the three essential ingredients (the "three pillars") of clinically effective and efficient attachment-based treatment. These include (a) systematically utilizing ideal parent figure imagery to develop a new positive, stable internal working model of secure attachment; (b) fostering a range of metacognitive skills; and (c) fostering nonverbal and verbal collaborative behavior in treatment. This chapter concludes with a discussion of how each pillar of treatment is interdependent with the other pillars, thereby forming an internally consistent, unified method of treatment.

Chapter 8 is a richly detailed instructional guide for using "The First Pillar: The Ideal Parent Figure Protocol." We show the clinician how to introduce the protocol, shape the imagery, and conclude the session. The chapter presents and describes three mutually enhancing approaches to shaping the ideal parent figure (IPF) imagery: one based on research findings about attachment, one based on the five primary conditions that promote secure attachment, and one based on a patient's descriptions of her or his early experiences with caregivers. Special attention is given to the wording of the imagery instructions, and these are richly illustrated with clinical vignettes. We also highlight the problems clinicians typically encounter when working with IPF imagery and provide guidance for avoiding these problems or resolving them when they occur.

Chapter 9 addresses "The Second Pillar: Metacognitive Interventions for Attachment Disturbances." This chapter presents four generations of the development of metacognitive approaches to treatment. The second generation has developed a treatment method, the increasingly popular *mentalization-based treatment*, (MBT). This approach serves to develop a general capacity for reflective function in patients, which in turn increases overall coherence of mind. There is impressive outcome data from MBT studies of patients with borderline personality disorder. The third generation, the modular or condition-specific approach, is less familiar to many. Yet the research that underlies this approach shows that patients with different diagnoses tend to have very specific metacognitive skills and weaknesses. Recognizing the specific metacognitive deficits of a given patient allows treatment to focus on developing the specific metacognitive skills that the patient is lacking. The chapter concludes with our own model and methods of fostering metacognitive skills. We have found that most existing metacognitive-based treatments are grounded only in preformal and formal stages of cognitive development and that no existing metacognitive-based treatments consider metacognitive skills that develop at more mature, advanced stages of adult cognitive development. In presenting our approach, we hope the reader will come to appreciate that there are a wide range of post-formal metacognitive skills that have very important implications for mental health.

Chapter 10 presents "The Third Pillar: Fostering Collaborative Capacity and Behavior." We review a variety of social anthropological findings that illustrate what distinguishes the human species from primates in the evolution of inherently collaborative behavior. This innate tendency toward cooperation and collaboration is strongly manifest in the nonverbal and verbal exchanges between a secure infant–caregiver intersubjective dyad. Evidence suggests that this innate nonverbal and verbal collaborativeness is impaired in insecurely attached individuals. Chapter 10 covers how to detect and address the main failings of nonverbal and verbal collaborativeness in adult patients with clinically significant attachment disturbances so as to enable such patients to develop healthy collaborativeness over the course of treatment.

Part IV, "Type-Specific Treatment," illustrates the very specific treatment protocols we have developed for each of the three insecure attachment prototypes. We show the reader that our attachment-based treatment is not only generic (the "three pillars") but that we also modify the methods within the generic structure according to what is most clinically effective for each of the three insecure prototypes. Chapter 11 is devoted to treating dismissing attachment, Chapter 12 to treating anxious-preoccupied attachment, and Chapter 13 to treating disorganized/fearful attachment. The approach to Chapter 13 is especially relevant to clinicians treating patients with borderline personality disorder and dissociative identity disorder. Each chapter has the same format: a review of the research findings on the etiology of that particular type of insecure attachment, specification of the necessary therapeutic stance, guidelines on how to tailor IPF imagery specifically for that kind of insecure attachment, and instruction on how to foster the metacognitive skills and collaborative behaviors specifically deficient in that kind of insecure attachment. Each chapter ends with a case illustration that includes transcripts excerpted from therapy sessions. The purpose of the transcripts is to show clinicians how all three pillars of treatment are included systematically as a consistent focus within and across treatment sessions.

Part V is devoted to "A Treatment Guide and Expected Outcomes." Chapter 14 includes an outline of a step-by-step treatment manual to assist the clinician in using the Three Pillars approach to attachment-based treatment. Chapter 15 gives an overview of the indicators of successful treatment and how to assess them. This chapter also presents a pilot outcome study we conducted using the Three Pillars treatment. Our data illustrate that this treatment can lead to the development of high coherence of mind and greater metacognitive capacity. Most important, after treatment all patients in the pilot sample had switched from pre-treatment insecure attachment to post-treatment earned secure status.

Appendix A, "The Core Self, Proactive Self-Agency, Self-Esteem, and the 'Best' Self," gives the clinician an overview of our approach to specifically enhancing self-development. We include this section because many adult patients with dismissing, anxious-preoccupied, or disorganized/fearful attachment show inhibited self-development, usually in several of its dimensions. Appendix A shows clinicians the methods for enhancing self-development in such patients. Appendix B, "Protocols for Developing Adult Secure Intimacy in Individuals and Caring Behaviors in Couples," addresses the issue of secure intimacy in adulthood. The overall goal of using IPF imagery is to help the patient develop a new, positive, stable internal model for secure attachment. However, the development of this new internal working model is largely based on the ideal parent figures associated with childhood. In Appendix B we illustrate for the clinician how to expand this new positive map into a model for secure intimacy pertaining to a dyadic adult romantic partnership, both for patients not in an intimate relationship and also for patients in a relationship who wish to improve the quality of secure intimacy in the relationship.

Attachment
Disturbances
in Adults

PART 1

FOUNDATIONAL CONCEPTS

CHAPTER 1

Attachment Research
A History of Ideas

The current understanding of the phenomena of attachment, including its development, its manifestations, and treatment of its insecure forms, has evolved through a series of seminal ideas. These ideas emerged from naturalistic observations, spontaneous insights, and organized research. This chapter presents what we consider to be the most important of those ideas along with the historical context and the thinking and activity that produced them. It is from the material we review in this chapter that our comprehensive treatment model and methods have been developed.

Maternal Deprivation

The history of the human attachment field begins with a number of studies from the 1930s that arose out of the child guidance movement. These studies entailed direct observation of disruptions to early attachment processes and highlighted the deleterious effects of such disruptions. For example, when pediatrician Harry Bakwin became director of the pediatric nursery at Bellevue Hospital in New York City in 1931, he was interested in the effects of institutionalization on infants. He noted that because of concerns about infection, hospital nursery staff were not allowed to hold the infants, and parents were not even allowed to visit. He observed that such children failed to thrive: They ate poorly and failed to gain weight, did not sleep well, showed arrested sucking and smiling responses, were largely unresponsive, and seemed unhappy. Ironically, they often sustained lasting infections that would not properly heal (Bakwin, 1942).

Loretta Bender, head of the Child Psychiatry Service at Bellevue during the same time period, found that young children at the Jewish Foundling Homes had very little interaction with others and lacked stimulation or play. Many of these children had developmental delays in speech and behavior. They seemed superficially affectionate toward anyone, but their ability to form consistent bonds with particular people seemed compromised. These children were often moved from one foster home to another, and they failed to develop lasting attachment bonds to foster parents (Bender & Yarnell, 1941; Karen, 1998). At the Angel Guardian Home, the directors believed that it was wrong to let a child form an attachment to someone who was not going to be a lasting parent figure, and so it was institutional policy to intentionally discourage attachment behavior (Karen, 1998). Consequently, these children were transferred from one home to another within the system every six months. By age five, most of these children had failed to develop attachments, appeared to lack feelings for others, and seemed aimless and distractible in their play. Bender noted that "emotional deprivation" contributed to the development of psychopathic personalities in these children.

René Spitz (1945) observed that infants who had extended stays at hospital pediatric units often exhibited arrested physical, cognitive, and emotional development. Many failed to thrive, and more than a third of the children in these institutional settings died despite adequate nutrition and medical care. Spitz used the term *hospitalism* to characterize the patterns and effects of institutional deprivation of nurturing and social contacts. In 1947, Spitz released a film, *Grief: A Peril in Infancy*, which documents a foundling home staffed with only six nurses for 45 children. With such a low caregiver–child ratio, Spitz considered the children to be deprived of sufficient maternal nurturance, and the film chronicles the progressive effects of maternal deprivation lasting a period of months. The children developed "anaclitic depression," or a pattern of physical, social, emotional, and cognitive impairment, and they became progressively more unresponsive.

Several other films documenting the effects of maternal separation were made sometime later by James Robertson, a colleague of John Bowlby. In England during World War II, Robertson's participation in evacuating children during bombings and resettling them after the war gave him rich experience of the effects of separation from maternal caregivers. The children's distress of separation was painfully obvious to him, which may be why he chose the visual medium of film to present the effects of separation. The first two films (Robertson, 1953, 1962) focus on the effects of *hospitalism*, while later films highlight children's experiences of foster care. In the first film, *A Two-Year-Old Goes to Hospital* (1953), Robertson documented the progressive reactions of Laura, a two-year-old girl, during an eight-week hospitalization that necessitated separations from her parents. Laura's parents visited her every other day. Initially, whenever Laura's parents departed, she panicked and demonstrated protest and clinging behaviors; during subsequent visits, Laura was withdrawn and unresponsive. This film graphically illustrates the problematic effects of even a short separation and disruption of continuity between a child and parents. Subsequently, through a study of children undergoing prolonged hospitalization for tuberculosis, Robertson identified three progressive stages in children's experience of separation from parents: First is *protest* (crying, clinging) when the parent leaves; then, when the child realizes that the mother is not returning, *despair* emerges; finally, as separation becomes extended, *detachment* appears, indicated by indifference to caregivers and parents alike.

Interest in the effects of separations due to foster care paralleled the study of hospitalized children and children in orphanages. Being moved from one foster care situation to another began to appear important in the development of psychopathology. Robertson's later films focused on children in foster care and were produced while he and his wife were temporary foster parents to four children whose mothers had been hospitalized. These films illustrate anxious behaviors in the foster home following separation from the birth parents and a combination of clinging and rejection during visits by the father. Much earlier, David Levy (1937) wrote about a case of an eight-year-old girl at a child guidance center in New York who was placed in a series of foster homes before being adopted. The adoptive mother found her to be superficially related but actually incapable of genuine affection. Levy concluded that this child was suffering from *primary affect hunger,* which Karen (1998) describes as not merely "hunger for affection, but rather for the full spectrum of human feelings, even including hostility, that arise from daily interaction with a mother" (p. 15). Later, Levy observed a group of children who experienced significant disruptions in parental care during their formative years and found that they had difficulty forming attachments to subsequent foster or adoptive parents. Karen (1998) summarizes Levy's descriptions of these children:

> Children shifted around, adopted after several years, often pleasant and affectionate on the surface, indeed indiscriminately affectionate, but seemingly indifferent underneath; lacking pride; and displaying incorrigible behavior problems that often included sexual aggressiveness, fantastic lying, stealing, temper tantrums, immature or infantile demands, and failure to make meaningful friendships. (p. 17)

As a way of understanding the behavioral and developmental problems observed in children in institutional and foster care, more and more researchers began to focus not on separation per se but on the effects of *maternal deprivation* during separation. Karen (1998) summarizes this seminal idea:

> It's the *depriving* separation that's so calamitous, where the child never has a chance to develop a true attachment; where there's no alternative mother figure to take up where the first mother left off and perhaps keep her memory alive; or where there are, early on, a series of short-term mother figures and thus repeated losses, all of which cause a bitterness and mistrust to develop and the shutting down in the child of his natural tendency to reach out for love and connection. (p. 58)

Bowlby (1951) consolidated the diverse research findings on maternal depriva-tion in an important monograph for the World Health Organization titled "Mater-nal Care and Mental Health." This work was based on a 1948 United Nations study of children separated from their parents, orphaned, or left homeless in their native country, as contrasted with children left homeless as a result of war or children who became political refugees. Bowlby wrote that "the quality of the parental care which the child receives in his earliest years is of vital importance for his future mental health" (p. 11). This assertion reflected his thinking from his first study on the influence of the early emotional environment on the devel-opment of the child, in which he wrote that the "general colour of the mother's emotional attitude to her child" is critical to the child's subsequent development (1940, p. 157). Further specifying the ideal quality of care, he wrote:

> For the moment it is sufficient to say that what is believed to be essential for mental health is that the infant and young child should experience a warm, intimate, and continuous relationship with his mother (or permanent moth-er-substitute) in which both find satisfaction and enjoyment. (1951, p. 11)

According to Bowlby, too little of that experience constitutes maternal depri-vation and adversely affects the child's developing mental health. Maternal depri-vation is most obvious when a child and his or her mother are separated, whether due to institutionalization or some circumstances of foster care, but Bowlby high-lighted that a child living at home with a mother who is unable to provide suffi-cient care may also experience maternal deprivation. He was critical of the early child guidance concept of a "broken home," because he believed that disruption of the parent–child attachment bond, not the disruption of the home per se, is the essential cause of mental health problems.

Bowlby's report lists several problems in the parent–child dynamic that may contribute to mental health problems in the developing child: an unconsciously rejecting attitude by the parent, an excessive demand for love and reassurance by the parent, or a parent who gets unconscious vicarious gratification from the child's acting out. Bowlby reviewed the findings of Bakwin, Bender, Spitz, Levy, and others and concluded that "the causative factor is maternal deprivation" (1951, p. 21). Based on the common finding in the studies of delinquent and psy-chopathic children (e.g., Bowlby, 1944) that these children experienced "frequent separations" or "prolonged separations occurring before about two and a half years of age and without a substitute figure being available" (1951, p. 26), Bowlby concluded that "prolonged deprivation of the young child of maternal care may have grave and far-reaching effects on his character and so on the whole of his future" (p. 158).

The Development of the Concept of the Attachment Bond

In 1951, Bowlby discovered Konrad Lorenz's 1937 article, "The Companion in the Bird's World," and realized an immediate connection between the biological process of imprinting in Lorenz's ducks and the intensity of the attachment bond in humans. Bowlby noted:

> The way in which attachment behaviour develops in the human infant and becomes focused on a discriminated figure is sufficiently like the way in which it develops in other mammals, and in birds, for it to be included, legitimately, under the heading of imprinting. (1969, p. 223)

Considering the sources of the imprinting process, Lorenz had determined, on the basis of his observation that many young birds are not fed by their parents but rather feed themselves, that the strong imprinting bond that develops between the baby and mother duck occurs independent of parental feeding of the duckling. Likewise, Bowlby believed that the intense bond between the human infant and his or her mother is not due simply to feeding behavior (Bowlby, 1988, p. 25).

In light of Lorenz's identification of species-specific instinctual patterns of birds, Bowlby began to study human infant–mother interactions to look for possible instinctual patterns. His first discovery of such instinctual patterns in human infants included a wide range of caregiver-signaling behaviors: rooting, sucking, grasping, looking, reaching, following, calling, crying, babbling, smiling, and protesting when left alone. Bowlby called these "fixed action patterns" (1969, p. 66) and believed they were all innately designed to attract and keep the mother nearby. He coined the term *attachment behaviors* to describe this set of innate fixed action patterns in human infants. He stated:

> Attachment behaviour is any form of behaviour that results in a person attaining or maintaining proximity to some other clearly identified individual . . . [It is] a fundamental form of behaviour with its own internal motivation distinct from feeding and sex. (1988, pp. 26–27)

The goal of such attachment behavior is proximity to the caregiver. Bowlby concluded, "The child's tie to his mother is a product of the activity of a number of behavioural systems that have proximity to mother as a predictable outcome" (1969, p. 179).

Bowlby's (1977) concept of the importance of the attachment bond was further strengthened by Harlow's research on attachment in primates (Harlow, 1958). Baby rhesus macaque monkeys were separated from their mothers and raised individually in cages with both a cloth and a wire-mesh surrogate mother monkey. Either the cloth or wire surrogate was fitted with a feeding nipple, allowing the infants to feed as needed. The monkeys showed a strong visual preference for the cloth mother monkey and spent considerable time clinging to it, even if the wire surrogate had the nipple and provided food. When placed in an unfamiliar environment with a variety of objects, the infant monkey would rush and cling to the surrogate cloth mother. This study provided strong evidence that soft contact is more important than feeding for the development of attachment.

Similar to the phenomena of imprinting in animals, Bowlby noted that attachment in human infants is highly specific and "is directed towards one or a few specific individuals, usually in clear order of preference" (1979, p. 154). He saw attachment behavior as essentially "care seeking" (Bowlby, 1988, p. 121) and as primarily associated with forming, maintaining, reacting to disruption of, and reestablishing attachment bonds. Bowlby saw that in any species, infant attachment to the mother serves the function of "maintenance of proximity" (Bowlby, 1979, p. 156), prompting the young to stay close to the mother, which serves the immediate goal of protection and the larger goal of survival of the species (Bowlby, 1969, p. 224).

Bowlby proposed that attachment in human infants evolves in four stages: (a) indiscriminate orientation, (b) orientation toward a specific caregiver, (c) proximity-maintaining behavior, and (d) goal-corrected partnership (1969, p. 267). The last stage, goal-corrected partnership, involves the baby's and mother's mutual dynamic interchange toward meeting as best as possible their respective needs and goals. In their dynamic interchange, both infant and mother engage in "goal-corrected" behavior, which Bowlby defined as behavior that is "constantly corrected by reference to whatever discrepancy exists between current performance and set-goal" (1969, p. 69).

The development of Bowlby's newly emerging theory was best represented by his publication of *The Nature of the Child's Tie to His Mother* (1958). His descriptions of the phenomena and importance of infant attachment and its relational aspects was in direct contrast to the then-prominent psychoanalytic drive theory, which emphasized the primacy of individual drives such as hunger, sex, and aggression. To Bowlby, a psychoanalyst himself, the innate attachment processes were at least as important, if not more so, than sexual and aggressive drives in the development of the personality. Furthermore, the new concept of attachment behavior served as an explanatory model for the earlier observations of infants' reactions to maternal deprivation. In the attachment model, protest, despair, and detachment were reinterpreted as attachment behaviors designed to maintain proximity to the caregiver.

Bowlby made a clear distinction between attachment and dependency. He stated that while "dependence is maximum at birth and diminishes more or less steadily until maturity is reached, attachment is altogether absent at birth and is not strongly in evidence until after an infant is past six months" (1969, p. 228). He later wrote:

The concept of attachment differs greatly from that of dependence. For example, dependence is not specifically related to maintenance of proximity, it is not directed towards a specific individual, it does not imply an enduring bond, nor is it necessarily associated with strong feeling. (1979, p. 156)

In reference to proximity-seeking, Bowlby (1973) suggested that the mother's availability and responsiveness are essential for the strengthening of the attachment bond. If the infant seeks proximity and receives a welcoming or accepting response, then attachment behavior is reinforced; in contrast, if the infant finds the mother to be repeatedly unresponsive, then the attachment behavior is deactivated.

Bowlby became interested in the interplay between attachment behavior and *exploratory behavior* in infants (Bowlby, 1969/1982, 1973, 1988). He observed that the more an individual has a secure emotional bond with the caregiver, the more there is a natural tendency to explore progressively farther from the caregiver. Children with a secure attachment bond alternate between episodes of attachment behavior, such as proximity-seeking, and exploratory behavior, progressing in the direction of increased exploration and autonomy. But if the child experiences a threat, exploratory behavior becomes inhibited and a series of predictable attachment behaviors emerge. Ainsworth, Blehar, Waters, and Wall (1978) summarize this interplay:

> Exploratory behavior is antithetical to attachment behavior in that it leads the infant toward interesting features of his environment and thus usually away from the attachment figure. If, however, the baby is alarmed, attachment behavior as well as wary/fearful behavior tends to be activated. (pp. 255–256)

Ideally, when an exploring baby becomes alarmed and manifests proximity-seeking attachment behavior, the mother responds with retrieving behavior, in which "the young are brought . . . close to the mother" (Bowlby, 1969, p. 240).

Patterns of Attachment

Mary Ainsworth's thinking about attachment was influenced by her first mentor, William Blatz, whom she met in 1929. Blatz's personality theory centered on the idea that children derive a sense of emotional security from their parents (Karen, 1998). This idea found its way into Ainsworth's concept of *secure base*: When a caregiver provides an infant with stable and consistent availability for protection, responsiveness, support, and comfort, the infant develops a sense of security in connection to that caregiver, and that security is the "base" from which the infant explores. The greater the felt sense of security and confidence in the availability of the caregiver, the greater the infant's exploration. If the infant ventures too far and becomes fearful or becomes insecure about the caregiver's availability, he or she will likely return to the caregiver and then, once reassured, will resume exploration. These concepts of secure base and the interplay between attachment behavior and exploratory behavior were not only important for understanding attachment, but they also set the foundation for subsequent thinking about the role of the therapist in treating attachment disorders: The common approach to treating attachment disturbances focused on the therapist providing a secure base for the patient's exploration in psychotherapy.

In 1950, Ainsworth moved to England and worked directly with John Bowlby for three and a half years. She also worked with James Robertson on his studies of children suffering from maternal deprivation. Robertson used methods of direct observation of family bonds prior to separation and of infant reactions during separation periods. Ainsworth saw the value of "direct observation in the natural environment" (Karen, 1998, p. 132), and in 1954 she started her first major research project, using direct observation of infant–parent interactions in Uganda. She made very detailed and comprehensive observations of maternal behaviors, such as breast-feeding, bathing, potty training, physical comfort and holding, and discipline, as well as infant behaviors such as crying and protest.

From these careful observations, Ainsworth developed a list of attachment behaviors characteristic of securely attached infants. These include smiling, cooing, other vocalizations, crying, greeting, following, searching, burying the face in the mother's lap, and seeking proximity with the mother when anxious. From seeing progressive exploratory behavior in some children as they got older, Ainsworth developed the concept of secure base. She observed that when mothers provided the conditions that support secure attachment behaviors, over time their children showed increasingly more complex exploratory behaviors, with periodic returns to the mother for contact and reassurance.

Ainsworth's first delineation of the development of the attachment bond included five phases: In the first, or undiscriminating phase, the infant shows no preferential response to the caregiver. In the second phase, differential responsiveness appears and the infant shows a clear preference for the primary attachment figure. In the third phase, the child is able to manifest attachment behaviors at a distance—for example, crying when the mother leaves the room and clapping or cooing when she returns. In the fourth or active initiative phase, the child shows distinct proximity-seeking behaviors such as approaching, sinking into the mother's lap, and crawling after the mother. The fifth phase is indicated by the appearance of stranger anxiety (Ainsworth, 1967).

Ainsworth's direct observations of infant–parent interactions in Uganda also led her to make the first rudimentary delineation of different patterns of attachment. She noted, for example, that some of the babies in her sample, left unattended in their cribs for long periods of the day, appeared non-attached. They failed to show crying and protest when the mother left or greeting behaviors when the mother returned. Ainsworth also noted that some of the babies cried excessively and were very clingy. She considered children who consistently showed these characteristics to be insecurely attached.

In the early 1960s, Ainsworth started a second direct observational study of child–mother interactions, this one of American mothers and infants, in Baltimore. In this study she hoped to collect further data on the distinct *patterns of attachment* she had initially observed in Uganda. In this naturalistic, observational study of babies in their familiar home environment (1967), Ainsworth observed that the American infants showed most of the same attachment behaviors that their Ugandan counterparts did. Of particular interest to her were the several differences: The American infants showed less secure-base behavior, had less protest when their mothers left the room, and demonstrated less stranger anxiety. Ainsworth came to attribute these differences to cultural differences in parenting in Ugandan and American home environments. She explained:

> Now, the Ganda babies are much more used to having their mother with them all the time. Whereas the Baltimore babies were used to having their mothers come and go, come and go, and they were much less likely to cry when their mother left the room. So when they were happily exploring it wasn't clear if it was because the mother was there or not. (Karen, 1998, p. 146)

The Baltimore babies were more familiar with brief separations from their mothers, and Ainsworth surmised that their threshold for experiencing threat and resulting distress was higher. She then devised a method for having infants and mothers interact in an unfamiliar setting rather than in the comfort and familiarity of their home environments. Her hypothesis was that differences in patterns of attachment might be amplified in the unfamiliar setting. She described the idea for this method as follows:

> We'll have the mother and baby together in a strange environment with a lot of toys to invite exploration. Then, we'll introduce a stranger when the mother's still there, and see how the baby responds. Then we'll have a separation situation where the mother leaves the baby with the stranger. How does the baby respond to the departure? And when the mother returns, how does the baby respond to the reunion? But since the stranger was in the room during the first departure, maybe we'd better have an episode in which the mother leaves the baby entirely alone. Then we could see whether the return of the stranger would lessen whatever distress has occurred. Finally, we'll have another reunion with the mother. We devised this thing in half an hour. (Karen, 1998, p. 147)

Though devised in just half an hour, this experimental method has become perhaps the best-known and most widely used standardized laboratory paradigm in the study of infant–caregiver attachment: the Strange Situation. The standardized paradigm includes the following sequence of eight distinct episodes:

1. The infant and his or her mother are introduced to an unfamiliar playroom, in which a large array of toys are strewn around the room to encourage exploratory behavior in the child.
2. The mother and infant are observed for three minutes.
3. In the next three-minute sequence, a stranger enters and is at first silent, then converses with the mother, then initiates interaction with the infant. This episode ends when the mother leaves the room.
4. The stranger is in the room with the baby for three minutes (first separation), or less if the baby becomes overly distressed.
5. In the next three-minute sequence, the mother returns and comforts the infant (first reunion) and the stranger leaves.
6. After the mother leaves a second time the infant is alone for three minutes (second separation).
7. The stranger returns and focuses on the infant for three minutes.
8. The mother returns and comforts the infant (second reunion) while the stranger leaves.

The entire sequence is designed to assess infants' attachment behavior and exploratory behavior as well as to see the interplay of these behaviors in conditions of being with the mother, being with a stranger, and being alone in an unfamiliar environment. Ainsworth et al. (1978) hypothesized that under conditions of a secure base, when the mother is present, attachment behavior would show low activation while exploratory behavior would show high activation; conversely, under conditions of separation and reunion, attachment behavior would show high activation and exploratory behavior would show low activation (Ainsworth et al., 1978, p. 22). Ainsworth et al. also designed the Strange Situation Procedure to provide circumstances for detecting individual differences in patterns of attachment, which they believed represent "differences in the way infant–mother attachment has become organized" (1978, p. xi). Ainsworth et al. recognized, however, that the Strange Situation allows for observing the immediate effects of only brief separations (minutes) on attachment and exploratory behaviors, in contrast to the effects of major separations lasting weeks or months that were observed in the earlier studies of maternal deprivation.

Patterns of Attachment by Ainsworth and her associates (1978) describes in detail the first systematic controlled laboratory study, using the Strange Situation procedure, of infant–mother attachment behaviors and patterns. The study emerged directly from the differences observed between Ugandan and American infants and investigated the interplay between attachment and exploratory behavior in an unfamiliar situation. Ainsworth et al. state that the study addressed "the hypothesis that infants and young children tend to explore an unfamiliar environment in the mother's presence, but slow down or cease exploration in her absence" (p. x), and that it was designed to assess "distress upon being separated" (p. x) and the "infant's responses to a stranger" (p. x).

The study observed 106 white, middle-class, one-year-old infants and their mothers in the Strange Situation (SS). Ainsworth et al. stated:

> The intrinsic design of the strange situation was dictated by the hypothesis that 1-year-olds who are attached to their mothers will use her as a secure base from which to explore an unfamiliar environment when she is present . . . It was expected, however, that attachment behavior (crying and search) would be activated by the mother's departure and/or absence in the separation episodes, at the expense of exploratory behavior, which would thus decline. It was further expected that relevant forms of proximity- and contact-seeking behavior would be activated in the reunion episodes (at least initially), also at the expense of exploratory behavior. (1978, p. 80)

Infants and their mothers were observed in the SS through a one-way mirror. Videotaping was not done. Observers recorded what was happening every 15 seconds. Twelve specific behaviors were coded: locomotion (avoidance locomotion, exploratory locomotion, proximity locomotion); body movement (walk, creep, crawl, hitch); body posture; hand movements; visual regard (directed toward a person or a toy); location (how close or far away from the mother); adult contact behavior (e.g., the adult picking up or holding the infant); baby contact behavior (e.g., the infant clinging, touching, clambering, resisting contact, or protesting being held or released); crying; vocalization directed to the mother or elsewhere; oral behavior; and smiling (at the mother or at the stranger). Four dimensions of interactive sequences were coded: proximity- and contact-seeking behavior (e.g., purposefully approaching the adult through creeping, crawling, or walking; signaling a desire to be picked up; initiating activity to achieve physical contact); contact-maintaining behavior (e.g., actively resisting release); avoidance (e.g., persistently ignoring the mother while focusing on toys, turning away, looking away); and resistance (e.g., pushing away, resisting being picked up, striking out, squirming, rejecting toys).

The data were compiled to assess both the frequency of specific behaviors and the nature and degree of interactive sequences. The normative results largely confirmed the main hypotheses, showing activation of exploratory behavior and deactivation of attachment behavior under the conditions of a secure base, and activation of attachment behavior at the expense of exploratory behavior under conditions of separation, absence, or reunion. For example, exploratory locomotion and exploratory manipulation of toys as well as maintaining contact at a distance were significantly higher when the infant was alone with the mother in the SS playroom. Crying, proximity-seeking, searching, and contact-maintaining behaviors were lowest when the infant was alone with the mother and highest during separation and reunion.

Ainsworth et al. also examined whether the infants could be classified according to different patterns of attachment behavior. They had hypothesized "that differences in early social experiences will lead to differences in the development and organization of attachment behavior" (p. 95). Discriminant function analysis revealed three major patterns of attachment behavior in the one-year-olds that correctly classified 82% of the sample. Group A infants were characterized by avoidance of the mother, especially during the first and second reunion episodes of the SS. Ainsworth et al. describe this pattern as "conspicuous avoidance of proximity to or interaction with the mother in the reunion episodes" (p. 109). These infants also showed significant resistance to physical contact with the mother. In contrast, securely attached infants showed significantly greater proximity-seeking and contact-seeking in these same episodes. Avoidant infants, however, showed strong exploratory behavior. Ainsworth et al. state that these infants "maintain exploration at a relatively high level across separation and reunion" (p. 319). Overall, Group A babies showed heightened exploratory behavior and inhibited attachment behavior.

Group B infants fit the paradigm of secure attachment. In comparison with the other two groups of infants (considered insecure), Group B infants showed significantly greater exploratory behavior when the infant and mother were in the room together (SS Episode 2); greater proximity- and contact-seeking behavior toward the mother than the stranger when the mother and stranger were both present with the infant (Episode 3) and also healthy protest behavior after the mother left (Episode 4); continued exploratory behavior in the presence of the stranger (Episode 4); less crying and more exploratory behavior than Group C when left alone (Episode 6); and less resistance and greater proximity- and contact-seeking in both reunions (Episodes 5 and 8). Overall, Group B babies showed a balanced interplay of exploratory and attachment behavior in the SS.

Group C infants were characterized by "conspicuous contact- and interaction-resisting behavior," especially during the reunion episodes (pp. 111–112), but also showed strong resistance to contact with the stranger. These Group C infants cried significantly more than infants from other groups during Episode 2 of the SS, in which the infant is with the mother in an exploratory context. According to Ainsworth et al., such crying "reflects inability to use the mother as a secure base from which to explore" (p. 113). These infants also cried significantly more during separation episodes, during Episode 6 when they were left alone, and also during the two reunion episodes. The authors state that the difficulty in being comforted upon reunion:

in part reflects extreme distress in the separation episodes, after which it takes a while to settle down, and in part reflects the ambivalence toward the mother . . . [The infants show] simultaneous occurrence of both resistant and proximity- and contact-seeking behavior. (p. 114)

These infants also showed "moderate to strong seeking of proximity and contact and seeking to maintain contact once gained" (p. 112). They also displayed greater contact-maintaining behavior—becoming more clingy—than the other groups when the mother left the playroom. The patterns that Group C infants display were characterized as *ambivalent*.

Mary Main (1979a, 1979b) investigated exploratory behavior in the SS and found that Group C babies had significantly less exploratory behavior in general and showed significantly less interest in a given toy during an exploratory episode. Group C babies had a significantly lower developmental quotient than babies from the other groups. Overall, Group C infants were chronically anxious in relation to the mother and showed heightened attachment behavior and inhibited exploratory behavior.

The Ainsworth et al. (1978) study also addressed the interesting question of subgroups within each of the respective groups—A, B, and C—and found notable differences even though the sample sizes were small. The data allowed initial classification of infants along a continuum:

A1   A2   B1   B2   B3   B4   C2   C1

This classification suggests that from B3, considered the prototype of a securely attached baby, there are gradations of avoidant and ambivalent patterns. Along a continuum, B1 babies are closer to A babies in their avoidance, and A1 babies are more avoidant than A2 babies, who are closer to the B classification; B2 babies are closer to B3 babies, but are still somewhat avoidant; B4 babies are considered securely attached but closer to C babies in manifestation of ambivalent behavior. C1 and C2 babies are more ambivalent than B4 babies, with C1 babies being more resistant and C2 babies being more passive (the continuum model does not work as well for C1 and C2 distinctions).

Considering specific behavior in the Ainsworth et al. (1978) SS study, A1 babies showed less proximity-seeking and stronger avoidance than A2 babies in the reunion episodes. A1 babies' mothers were more rejecting and interfering, whereas A2 babies' mothers were inaccessible for long periods. B1 infants were identical to B2 infants except for less proximity-seeking in the second reunion episode. B1 and B2 infants' mothers were inconsistently sensitive in response to their babies. B3 babies showed an almost complete lack of avoidance and resistance, and they cried less than all other groups and subgroups. B3 babies' mothers were the most sensitive to their babies' signals when compared with all other mothers. B4 babies were more anxious than the other three B subgroups but more positive and less resistant than Group C babies; they also showed less exploratory behavior relative to other groups and subgroups. C1 babies showed strong resistance in reunion episodes, and their mothers were interfering and controlling. C2 babies were significantly more passive than all other groups and subgroups and showed very weak exploratory behavior relative to other groups and subgroups; C2 babies' mothers were inaccessible and ignoring.

Ainsworth and her associates (1978) also wanted to know whether the infants in their study behaved the same way at home in their natural environment as they did in the unfamiliar environment of the SS. A subsample of 23 infants were observed in their homes once every three weeks for four hours for approximately 50 weeks. The observers used the same coding system as the one they used for the SS. The results are as follows:

> In summary, Group B infants at home were conspicuous for little crying, infrequent separation distress, frequent positive greetings (and infrequent negative or mixed greetings) upon reunion, frequent initiation of close bodily contact, positive response to it once achieved, and yet positive response to cessation of such contact. In addition, B babies tended to have better-developed modes of communication than non-B babies, to be more compliant to the mother's wishes, and to be less frequently angry. In contrast, the infants of both A and C groups were characterized by relatively more crying in general, more separation distress, disturbances related to close bodily contact with the mother, and more anger . . . B babies have relatively secure attachment relationships with their mothers in comparison with A and C babies . . . A and C babies . . . differ in the ways in which they manifest their anxieties. . . We have also suggested that the source of the disturbance is different for Groups A and C. Whereas in C babies the source of the disturbance lies in the discrepancy between what they want and what they expect to receive, in A babies there seems to be a more basic conflict between the kind of comfort and reassurance that they want and are prompted to seek, and a fear or at least an avoidance of just that. (p. 131)

The data from the home study confirmed that the same three patterns of attachment manifested in both the unfamiliar SS setting and the familiar home environment.

Ainsworth and her colleagues also examined whether particular maternal behavior could be associated with the three patterns of attachment. They observed the mother's responsiveness to crying (e.g., crying and how long the mother ignored it); whether the mother acknowledged the baby upon entering the room; the quality of touch the mother demonstrated when picking up the baby (e.g., affectionate, abrupt, careful, inept, routine); whether the physical contact was pleasant or unpleasant (e.g., rough handling, force-feeding, overstimulating, uncomfortable holding); the quality of face-to-face interactions (e.g., pacing, silent, unsmiling, routine); the frequency of verbal commands and discipline-oriented physical interventions; the timing and amount of feeding and the synchronization of feeding to the baby's intake pace; and general maternal characteristics (e.g., sensitivity/insensitivity to the baby's signals, acceptance/rejection, cooperation/interference, and accessibility/ignoring).

There were several notable findings: (1) Group B babies' mothers were more affectionate during physical contact, tender when holding their babies, more and more quickly responsive to their babies' crying; and more sensitive, accepting, cooperative, and accessible to their babies. (2) Group A babies' mothers were more rejecting of their babies, showed less positive feelings and more anger toward their babies, were less affectionate in picking up their babies, had greater aversion and aberrant reactions to physical contact with their babies, were abrupt and interfering when picking up their babies, gave more verbal commands, and delivered more physical interventions for discipline. (3) Group C babies' mothers showed significant delay in responding or unresponsiveness to their babies' crying, were more involved in routine activities when holding their babies, and struggled when feeding their babies. Overall, Group C mothers were notably insensitive to their infant's signals. The authors concluded that "different patterns of infant strange-situation behavior are associated with different constellations of maternal behavior" (p. 301).

Ainsworth and her associates also reviewed studies that focused on changes in attachment behavior and exploratory behavior from ages one to four, as observed in the SS. Two-year-olds were similar to one-year-olds in the SS except that they showed stronger proximity-seeking, but they did not need to maintain contact as strongly. Three-years-olds were not very disturbed by separation episodes and maintained a high level of exploratory behavior throughout the SS. Four-year-olds were even less disturbed by separation than three-year-olds and had even stronger exploratory behavior than three-year-olds. The goal-corrected partnership between mother and child increased from age one to age four.

Disorganized Attachment

Another significant emergence in the understanding of attachment was the identification of a fourth primary classification group. Ainsworth and her associates, and many researchers since their pioneering studies with the SS, found that a percentage of children did not fit the three patterns of attachment that they identified—avoidant, secure, and ambivalent. During the early era of this research, these children were generally seen as unclassifiable and their data were ignored. But in the 1970s, Main (1973, 1979a) developed a scale to assess disorganized and disordered attachment behaviors in babies in the SS. Main and Weston (1981) exposed one-year-old babies to a silent, immovable, masked clown in the presence of their mothers. A week later, the children and mothers participated in the SS, and 13% of the children were found to be unclassifiable. That discovery led Main and her associates to reexamine over 200 unclassifiable cases from previous SS studies. From this sample, they established criteria for a fourth primary classification, which they called *disorganized/disoriented* (D). Using this new coding system, the interrater reliability for identifying disorganized attachment from the SS is approximately 80% (Lyons-Ruth & Jacobvitz, 1999).

In general, babies classified as insecure, disorganized/disoriented type (D), were seen as lacking a coherent and consistent strategy for dealing with separation stress in the SS and/or as showing contradictory attachment behaviors (Main & Solomon, 1986, 1990). For example, such babies alternate between avoidant and ambivalent behaviors over time or show contradictory avoidant and ambivalent behaviors at the same time. In addition, during the SS such babies display misdirected and interrupted movements, mistimed and anomalous behaviors, freezing, pervasive indices of fear and apprehension, and outright signs of disorganization and disorientation (Lyons-Ruth & Jacobvitz, 1999).

Patricia Crittenden (1992b) presented a view different from Main's in respect to interpretation of observed disorganized behaviors in children. Whereas Main sees these behaviors as indicating a lack of a consistent and coherent attachment strategy, Crittenden suggested that there is an underlying organization to the "disorganized" child's behavior (1985a, 1985b; Crittenden & Ainsworth, 1989). She argued that, especially for maltreated children, behavior that is usually labeled as disorganized represents "a separate pattern—that is, another organization of the behaviors identified by Ainsworth as relevant to the assessment of security of attachment" (Crittenden & Ainsworth, 1989, p. 442). This form of organization emerges in maltreated children, who learn that their proximity-seeking "will be ignored, rebuffed, or possibly punished," as a way of "resolving the conflict between the child's need for proximity to the mother and his expectations of his mother's reactions to his behavior" (p. 442). In other words, beyond infancy, "older children who have had to cope with major inconsistencies eventually integrate that information into their set of expectations and develop an organized pattern of responding" (Crittenden & Ainsworth, 1978, pp. 442-443). Inherent in this construct is that what may appear as disorganized behavior actually reflects a specific and organized *strategy* for maximizing need-fulfillment in the context of specific relational circumstances.

Crittenden labeled this emerging organization "A/C" to indicate the presence of *both* insecure patterns in a potentially predictable relationship with each other. Any subtype of the A and C patterns can be combined into an A/C pattern. Crittenden later refined and expanded this category of organization by describing an "AC" pattern, in which the A and C strategies are blended and simultaneously manifest rather than alternate as in A/C (see Crittenden & Landini, 2011, pp.

229–235). Subsequent to her 1989 paper with Crittenden, Ainsworth specifically continued to utilize the Main and Solomon D categorization for disorganization (Ainsworth and Eichberg, 1991). Since that time there has been considerable research on (Solomon & George, 1999) and clinical applications of (Steele & Steele, 2008a) the concept of attachment disorganization. Landa and Duschinsky (2013) highlight that Ainsworth supported *both* Main's and Crittenden's understandings of disorganized behavior, seeing them as complementary rather than in conflict, with their differences based largely on interpretation of what constitutes *organized vs. disorganized*, and differences in populations studied. Fonagy (2013) suggests that "in the same way that light can be seen as either waves or particles, the consequences of attachment trauma can be seen as adaptation [Crittenden's perspective] that also reflects the absence of an organised strategy [Main's perspective]" (p. 179).

Consistent with Crittenden's view that organization can be seen in what has been described as disorganized, in her classification system "the notion of disorganization and [the adult disorganization] category of "Cannot Classify" [CC] have been eliminated" (Crittenden & Landini, 2011, p. 8). Crittenden and Landini further state that

"... having only one category (unresolved/disorganized/Cannot Classify) for all cases of severe problems limits greatly the power of the M&G [Main and Goldwyn Adult Attachment Interview classification] method to address the array of individual differences that typify psychopathology" (p. 366).

As we explain in Chapter 4, we agree that there are limitations to the traditional CC category. But we do not think it is necessary to drop the original CC category and its extensive research tradition. Rather, our approach emerged from the spirit of the original AAI scoring manual that mentions the possibility of "potential subcategories of CC" (Main, Goldwyn, & Hesse, 2002) derived from the more recent applications of the AAI to various clinical populations. In our Chapter 4 discussion of the AAI scoring system, we identify and describe nine subcategories of CC from our experience of applying the AAI to clinical populations with severe psychiatric disturbances. For our purposes, we advocate expanding and refining the CC scoring system rather than dropping it.

Regardless of the differences in interpretation of observed disorganized behaviors, the patterns that are most commonly named as disorganized attachment have multiple causes. In their original work, Main and her associates were struck by the presence of *pervasive fear* in disorganized babies. With respect to maternal behavior in the SS, mothers of disorganized babies were observed at times to be distinctly frightening to their children (e.g., looming in the child's face, talking too loudly, approaching the child too quickly or too suddenly, threatening the child, or being outright abusive). Additionally, these mothers at times appeared frightened of their own children (e.g., displaying deadpan expressionlessness, freezing behavior, and backing away from their own children in apparent fear).

This combination of *frightening and frightened maternal behavior* presents an impossible dilemma for the baby: the object of proximity-seeking and contact-seeking is simultaneously the source of fear. Normally when a baby is frightened, he or she seeks contact and proximity with his or her mother for comfort; in disorganized babies, the mother *is the source* of the baby's fear, which leaves the baby with the continuous conflict of wanting to approach yet needing to avoid at the same time. Main refers to this conflictual state as "fear without solution."

Independent of frightening/frightened maternal behavior, a mother's extreme *misattunement* to the infant and disrupted affective communication have also been found to be significantly correlated to disorganized attachment in infants. Lyons-Ruth and Jacobvitz (1999) state that such "mothers may show a particularly impaired ability to engage in well-attuned affective communications with their young children" (pp. 531–532).

Maternal dissociative behavior has also been found to be a strong predictor of disorganized attachment in children (Schuengel, Bakermans-Kranenburg, & van IJzendoorn, 1999). Main and Hesse (1990) believe that dissociative states and maternal frightening/frightened behavior may be interrelated: Mothers who are prone to significant dissociative episodes are more likely than less dissociative mothers to engage in frightening/frightened behaviors when they are dissociated. Main and her associates found that parents of disorganized children often have unresolved trauma or loss in their histories. In a study of dissociation in mothers, mothers with unresolved status for trauma or loss were significantly more dissociated than mothers with resolved status for previous trauma or loss (Hesse and van IJzendoorn, 1999). Particular behaviors of the child may trigger unresolved trauma or loss in the parent and thereby activate fear and/or dissociation in the mother in ways that are sudden and out of context for the child. In such contexts, the child is likely to become frightened of the mother and to experience her as both the source of caregiving and the source of fear.

Main and others also discovered a close affinity between the behavioral signs of disorganized attachment and a range of dissociative behaviors and experiences in the children themselves. Children classified as disorganized exhibit a wider range of observable dissociative behaviors and experiences throughout childhood than do normal children (Carlson, 1998; Liotti, 1992). Longitudinal studies examining the fate of early attachment disorganization over time have shown that children disorganized from 12 to 18 months are significantly more likely than secure children to have dissociative experiences and to manifest dissociative behaviors throughout childhood and into adolescence (Ogawa, Sroufe, Weinfield, Carlson, & Egeland, 1997).

In addition, early disorganized behavior is associated with controlling behavior in attachment relationships during later childhood and adolescence. Controlling behavior may manifest directly as manipulative, bossy, or aggressive behavior toward peers and adults. It may also appear indirectly as compulsive caregiving (Crittenden, 1992b). Describing children with controlling behavior, Main and Cassidy (1988) state, "[They] seem to attempt actively to control or direct the parent's attention and behavior and assume a role which is usually considered more appropriate for a parent with reference to a child" (p. 418). They found that 84% of children classified as disorganized at one year were seen as controlling by six years of age.

The Stability of Attachment Patterns Over Time

Bowlby considered the prototypical patterns of attachment from 12 to 18 months to be "a property of the relationship [with the caregiver]" (1988, p. 127). However, through a process of "internalization" and linking the attachment behaviors with what he called "internal working models," these patterns of attachment become relatively stable patterns over the course of childhood, adolescence, and adulthood. Bowlby stated, "As the months pass . . . the inner organization of attachment with its working model of attachment figure, becomes ever more stable. As a consequence not only does it resist change but it does so increasingly" (1969/1982, p. 365).

Alan Sroufe and his colleagues used the Strange Situation Procedure to study the stability of patterns of attachment over time. In "Attachment as an Organizational Construct" (1997), Sroufe and Waters described the conceptual foundation for what would become an important longitudinal research program on attachment, the Minnesota Longitudinal Study of Parents and Children (see Sroufe, Egeland, Carlson, & Collins, 2005). Sroufe and Waters considered the attachment behaviors observed in the SS as the manifestation of a central organizing principle in the developmental processes of the child. The Minnesota study researchers embarked on a long-term plan of research to investigate the stability of attachment patterns over time, the effects of early attachment on personality development, and how parenting style affected attachment status. In an early study, Waters (1978) found that 48 of 50 babies tested at 12 months showed the same pattern of attachment at 18 months. Other studies have concurred. From 12 to 18 months, the stability of secure attachment was found to be 75%, and the test/retest measurement of disorganized attachment was 67% from 12 to 18 months. From 18 to 24 months, the test/retest measurement of secure attachment was 75% and disorganized attachment was 81% (Barnett, Ganiban, & Cicchetti, 1999; Vondra, Hommerding, & Shaw, 1996). The overall stability of attachment classification from 18 months to 20 years is as high as 72% to 77% (Solomon & George, 1999).

Attachment and the Organization of Development

With respect to changing patterns over time, in the Minnesota Longitudinal Study Sroufe and his associates (2005) found that at 18 months, secure children were less distressed by separation and less in need of physical contact in the SS.

Secure two-year-olds were more autonomous in their exploratory behavior than they had been six months earlier in the SS, and secure three-and-a-half-year-olds were more comfortable around peers than insecure children. A picture had begun to emerge from this longitudinal research, showing how the patterns of attachment change form as a child grows older.

Sroufe and his colleagues investigated the organization of, continuity of, and change in development from birth to adulthood. They stated that the guiding principle of their research was "an 'organizational perspective' on development" (Sroufe et al., 2005, p. 38), which means that *Development is defined by changes in organization of behavior over time*" and that "organization of behavior is central to defining individual differences" (p. 39). Central to their work was the idea that "early experience plays a critical role in the development of the person" (p. 8). The seven areas the study addressed were prenatal factors, being born into poverty, age-by-age assessment, comprehensive measures across domains, normal versus maladaptive development, developmental context, and assessment of early relationships (p. 12).

The study included 179 young, expectant mothers of low socioeconomic status who were followed, with their children, until their children's adulthood. Many of the mothers came from homes where alcoholism, domestic violence, child abuse, and maltreatment were common. The study assessed physical abuse, sexual abuse, physical neglect, psychological unavailability, and verbal abuse in this high-risk sample. The SS was given to all infants at 12 months and again at 18 months, and these same participants were administered the Adult Attachment Interview (described in Chapter 4 of this book) at age 19 and again at age 26. At 12 months, 22% of the babies were classified as resistant (Ainsworth's ambivalent) and 20% were classified as avoidant. The category of disorganized attachment was not available at the time of the assessment but was assessed post hoc from videotapes of the SS. The Sroufe study essentially replicated the earlier work of Bowlby and Ainsworth:

> Overall, our longitudinal data affirmed Bowlby's (1969/1982) hypothesis that differences in quality of care lead to differences in quality of attachment, as well as Ainsworth's findings . . . that attachment relationship quality is related to caregiver responsivity at various points in the first year. (Sroufe et al., 2005, p. 97)

This longitudinal study included intensive direct observations of children in a research preschool setting as a way of studying the effect of early attachment status on the development of the personality. For example, the "salient issues" (Sroufe et al., 2005, p. 66) at each period of development were guided self-regulation in the toddler years, self-reliance in the preschool years, competency in the school years, individuation in adolescence, and emancipation in the early adult years. Secure preschool children were more ego-resilient, had greater self-esteem, and had more positive peer relationships than insecure children.

Sroufe and his associates (2005) observed that during the preschool years, one of three types of avoidant patterns emerged, with some children being characterized as bullies, shy loners, or daydreamers. Two patterns of ambivalent attachment were seen during this period: the impulsive child with poor concentration and the fearful, clingy child. Longitudinally, securely attached children were likely to grow up into securely attached adults and insecure children were likely to retain their insecure status into adulthood unless they were exposed to healthy attachment figures with whom they could earn security of attachment. Insecure attachment was significantly correlated with the later development of depression. Insecure children who were frequently distracted from exploratory play behavior by their mothers in the SS were significantly more likely as adults to show attention deficits.

Ambivalently/resistantly attached children were significantly more likely than other children to manifest a clinically significant anxiety disorder diagnosis as an adult. Avoidantly attached children were significantly more likely than other children to manifest externalizing problems and conduct disorders in later childhood and adolescence. Disorganized children had a wide range of dissociative experiences and behaviors throughout childhood and adolescence but tended to grow out of these behaviors as adults unless they had been abused as children, in which case they continued to manifest significant dissociative experiences as adults. Disorganized attachment in infancy was strongly correlated with the emergence of psychopathology in early adulthood. An early history of disorganized attachment, aggravated by a subsequent history of sexual abuse, was significantly correlated with the emergence of self-injurious behavior.

Counterpoints

Despite the growing interest in and body of evidence pertaining to attachment, there were of course detractors who raised challenges to some of the findings and interpretations. Michael Lamb and his associates (Lamb, Thompson, Gardner, Charnov, & Estes, 1984) criticized Ainsworth's research with the SS for its small sample size and expressed concern about making generalizations with respect to patterns of attachment. He also questioned the reliability and validity of the SS observations because none of the research used video-recordings. Notwithstanding Lamb's criticisms of these methodological limitations, the findings based on the SS have been replicated or partially replicated many times.

Jerome Kagan (1984), a strong critic of attachment theorists, does not believe that maternal sensitivity and other environmental factors are important components of the child's developing personality. Rather, he believes that the effects of parenting on child development are unstable and transient, not lasting. Kagan does not believe that stable patterns of attachment exist, and correspondingly challenges the contention that the SS properly assesses such patterns. He asserts that organized states of mind do not emerge based on the quality of early attachment relationships and that the primary factors in the development of personality are *hereditary*, including *temperament*.

Kagan's position found support in Stella Chess and Alexander Thomas's (1982) New York Longitudinal Study, which investigated the effects of early infant temperament on subsequent development. Chess and Thomas assessed the level of activity of the infant, the rhythmicity of the sleep-wake cycle, approach versus withdrawal patterns, the reactivity level, the threshold of responsiveness, mood, distractibility, and attention span. Infants were classified into four groups according to temperament: difficult babies, slow-to-warm babies, easy babies, and "cannot classify" babies with a mixture of temperament qualities. The researchers found that temperament made a significant contribution to development and that parenting style did not significantly correlate with whether the baby was easy or difficult. Central to Chess's work is the notion of "poor fit" between parent and infant temperaments.

There are two compelling arguments in response to Kagan and Chess. First, Sroufe's Minnesota Longitudinal Study addressed the nature–nurture argument by including data on heredity and temperament and also on the quality of early attachment by administering the SS twice, once at 12 months and again at 18 months. The quality of early attachment and maternal behavior accounted for a much greater portion of the variance than did temperament. Likewise, Belsky and Isabella (1988) found that the mother's temperament, but not the infant's temperament, was significantly correlated with the infant's pattern of attachment in the SS. The hereditary components of personality traits and temperament certainly influence the infant–parent relationship, but this fact does not negate the data that indicate the powerful role of the early attachment relationship in the organization of development. From the available data, it is clear that *both* temperament and the early attachment relationship contribute to later development and to the emergence of psychopathology in adulthood. Second, the four prototypical child patterns of attachment—secure, avoidant, ambivalent/resistant, and disorganized—are a robust finding across many studies. Furthermore, the data consistently reveal that these patterns remain relatively stable across time unless altered by unusual life circumstances such as divorce, family dysfunction, or extreme stress (Weinfield, Whaley, & Egeland, 2004).

The Role of the Father

Although much attachment research focus was placed on the relationship between the infant and his or her mother, Main and Weston (1981) conducted a comparative study of toddler attachment to both mothers and fathers. Using the SS, they found comparable rates of secure and insecure attachment to both mothers and fathers, but there was no significant correlation between the two: A toddler could show secure attachment toward one parent but not to another. Goossens and van IJzendoorn (1990) conducted a meta-analysis of eight studies on infant–father attachment. They found a small but significant effect size (0.13) regarding paternal sensitivity associated with secure attachment, an effect size smaller than maternal sensitivity as associated with secure attachment. An important factor pertaining to fathers as secure attachment figures is that many fathers are less involved with their babies than are mothers (Lamb, 1997). However, when this is not the case and fathers are actively involved with their babies in positive ways, fathers easily become secure attachment figures.

There is some research suggesting that the father's role in secure attachment may be different from that of the mother, with the mother's role being more focused on the infant's proximity- and contact-seeking behaviors and the father's role being more focused on encouraging exploratory behavior (George & Solomon, 1999). The father's role in the quality of toddler play has consistently been found to be associated with father–child secure attachment (Belsky, Gilstrap, & Rovine, 1984; Grossmann & Grossmann, 1991). Howes (1999) summarized the research data: "Fathers who express more positive feelings about their infants and their role as parents, and who assign a high priority to time spent with the infants, have more secure infants" (p. 679).

Cross-Cultural Studies of Attachment Patterns and Maternal Behavior

Interest in the universality of attachment patterns of behavior developed early in the history of the field. Cross-cultural study of attachment behavior began with Ainsworth's comparison of children and their mothers in Uganda with children and their mothers in Baltimore, Maryland. As noted above, the main difference between the two groups was that Ugandan children were more used to having their mothers with them all the time, whereas American children were used to having their mothers come and go. Nevertheless, in both groups children became attached to their mothers, and the three main patterns of attachment, A, B, and C, were observable in both the Ugandan and the American samples.

Subsequent to Ainsworth's research, a number of cross-cultural studies of attachment patterns in children have been published. Among the Gusii of Kenya, older children take care of the babies for most of the day, mostly playing with the children, while mothers care for their children at night and also provide most of the physical care. A study using a modified version of the SS found that 61% of the babies showed secure attachment to their mothers and 54% showed secure attachment to nonmaternal caregivers (Kermoian & Leiderman, 1986). The study did not include insecure classifications. Several cross-cultural differences were observed in SS behavior: Gusii babies were greeted with a handshake at reunion rather than a hug as in the American sample; exploratory behavior also differed in that American babies tended to manipulate toys with their hands whereas the Gusii babies tended to explore the environment visually.

Hausa men in Nigeria typically have four or five wives, so the babies have four to five caregivers in addition to their biological mother. The children remain in close physical proximity to one or more caregivers at all times, as babies are not allowed to explore the wider environment because of physical danger. While this study did not use Ainsworth's three-way classification, the study demonstrated secure attachment to multiple caregivers and also highlighted the principle that a secure base of attachment protects the baby from physical danger (Marvin, Van-Devender, Iwanaga, LeVine, & LeVine, 1977).

True (1994) studied parents and infants of the Dogon culture in Mali. Because of a high infant-mortality rate from starvation, children are breast-fed on demand, and grandparents and siblings serve as multiple caregivers. True used the SS and a four-way classification system that included disorganized attachment as a category. A total of 69% of the children were classified as secure, 8% were classified as resistant, 0% were classified as avoidant, and 23% were classified as disorganized. Possible unresolved loss in the mothers, due to the high incidence of infant mortality, may account for the relatively high disorganized attachment rate (this link in general is addressed in a later section of this chapter).

!Kung bushmen mothers feed their children on demand, and as part of a hunting and gathering society, the mothers often carry their children in a sling to keep them in close proximity. By the second or third year of age, the children spend more time with mixed-age peers than with their mothers. This dense social network clearly facilitates secure attachment and healthy peer adjustment (Konner, 1977). Similarly, the Efe rain forest pygmies have a close social network, with children having multiple caregivers. Nevertheless, children still showed a preference for and a stronger attachment bond to their biological mothers (Morelli & Tronick, 1991).

Study of Israeli kibbutz children offers a unique circumstance in that kibbutz children typically sleep apart from their parents in a communal setting after spending time with their families in the afternoon and evening. Sagi et al. (1985) found that secure attachment in the communal group was lower (56%) than in non-kibbutz Israeli children in day care (75%) and lower than in Western studies (65% to 70%). In the kibbutz sample, ambivalent/resistant attachment was over-represented (37%) and avoidant attachment underrepresented (7%). However, non-kibbutz Israeli children raised at home by their parents showed very high rates of secure attachment (80%), somewhat high rates of resistant attachment (17%), and very low rates of avoidant attachment (3%; see also Sagi et al., 1995; van IJzendoorn, Sagi, & Lambermon, 1992).

Grossmann and Grossmann (1991) conducted a study of attachment in Northern Germany. The findings of this study are unusual in that two-thirds of the sample of babies were found to be insecure, with half being avoidant. The Grossmanns interpreted the results as being related to the high value placed on early independence in Northern German culture. They observed that the parents in this study became progressively less responsive to their children when the children were about six months of age. The Grossmanns conducted a second study (Grossmann, Grossmann, & Waters, 2005) in Southern Germany and found the rates of attachment patterns to be comparable to those in the American studies.

Studies of attachment in Asian populations have also examined attachment patterns associated with cultural and maternal caregiving circumstances. China formerly had a one-child-only policy, and interdependence is favored over independence (van IJzendoorn & Sagi, 1999). Using the SS, Hu and Meng (1996) found a distribution of patterns of attachment similar to that of Western culture: 68% secure, 16% avoidant, and 16% resistant. Avoidant babies seemed remarkably indifferent to their mothers during reunion episodes. Mothers of the avoidant babies generally worked outside the home and were less involved in the care of their babies when at home, whereas the ambivalent/resistant babies generally had stay-at-home mothers. However, there may be an important difference in attachment patterns between rural and urban Chinese mothers: Many rural mothers work day and night in large factories and their babies are "warehoused" in large, multiple-caregiver settings, in contrast to urban Chinese mothers who spend significant time with their children. Warehoused children who rarely see their mothers show high rates of avoidant attachment (J. Yu, personal communication with D. Brown, 2010).

Japanese parenting is characterized by encouraging dependence of the child on the mother. Nevertheless, Japanese mothers were able to clearly distinguish secure attachment from dependency. In a study using the SS in a Tokyo sample, the distribution of attachment patterns was similar to that found in Western studies: 61% securely attached, 18% resistant, and 13% avoidant. In this study, mothers who felt supported by their husbands were more likely to raise securely attached children than mothers who felt unsupported (Durrett, Otaki, & Richards, 1984). In a study of attachment in Sapporo, Keiko Takahashi (1986) found 68% of the children to be securely attached, 32% to be resistant, and 0% to be avoidant. The low incidence of avoidant attachment may be an artifact of research observation, in that the mothers were observed to be self-conscious and unnatural in the SS in a way that may have masked rejecting behaviors and aversion to physical contact.

Pleshkova and Muhamedrahimov (2010) assessed family-reared infants in St. Petersburg, Russia, with the Strange Situation procedure and found that only 6.2% could be considered secure (B) in relation with their mothers. They state:

We found a considerably lower proportion of infants with a secure pattern of attachment than has been found in other countries—within ABC+D system characteristics . . . as well as within the Dynamic-Maturational Model [see discussion later in this chapter]. We think this is an indicator of how unstable and threatening the immediate social environment has been for infants and their parents during Soviet and post-Soviet times. (p. 358)

Overall, cross-cultural studies offer compelling evidence in support of the universality of attachment patterns A, B, C, and, from those studies that included it, D. Of note is that exposure to multiple caregivers does not seem to adversely affect the attachment relationship or the quality of the attachment bond with the primary caregiver.

Intergenerational Transmission

Generally speaking, attachment status tends to be transmitted down through the generations. Main and her associates found a strong correlation between the parent's pattern of attachment on the Adult Attachment Interview (AAI) and the baby's pattern of attachment in the SS (Main, Kaplan, & Cassidy, 1985; see also Fonagy, Steele, & Steele, 1991). Summarizing Main's findings, Bowlby stated that "Main found a strong correlation between how a mother describes her relationships with her parents during her childhood and the pattern of attachment her child now has with her" (Bowlby, 1988, p. 133).

He concluded that across studies, the pattern of attachment of the parent on the AAI significantly predicted the pattern of attachment of his or her baby in the SS. In a study that looked at three generations, the attachment status of the grandmother on the AAI significantly predicted the pattern of attachment of both the mother and also the mother's baby (Benoit & Parker, 1994, as cited in Hesse, 1999; see Wallin, 2007, p. 37). Despite these findings, van IJzendoorn (1995) noted that a "transmission gap" remains because available research has not offered an adequate explanation of how the pattern of attachment of the parent often becomes the pattern of attachment of the child. According to David Wallin (2007), the missing ingredient relates to *metacognitive capacity*, which is described in a later section of this chapter.

Main and her associates explored another possible factor in the intergenerational transmission of attachment patterns. In developing the Adult Attachment Interview, they discovered that some adults show remarkable temporary states of disorganization when describing a previous history of trauma or loss. This disorganization is specific to a given description of trauma or loss and not to each description of trauma or loss on the AAI. Furthermore, this temporary, event-specific disorganization contrasts with the presence of pervasive disorganization across the transcript, as is characteristic of adults with disorganized attachment on the AAI (the CC—"cannot classify"—category). Main and her associates coined the term "Unresolved, disoriented" (Ud classification) for discrete, temporary disorganization occurring in response to specific AAI topics and inquiries (Main & Goldwyn, 1994). Adults with unresolved status for a given trauma or loss often show lapses in the organization of their discourse in relation to that trauma or loss and also often have deficits in metacognitive monitoring. The three types of phenomena that receive the highest scores for Ud status on the AAI (thus indicating unresolved trauma or loss) are extreme, persistent irrational beliefs about the loss or trauma that are not tempered by reasoning; extreme psychological manipulations, such as dissociative compartmentalization; and severe, persistent clinical symptoms of trauma or grief that last beyond when they could reasonably be expected to resolve. Main and Hesse (1990) found that unresolved status was associated with dissociation of memories from awareness, current disorganization from partially dissociated memories, and coexisting but contradictory dissociated memories.

Main and her associates (Main & Hesse 1990, 1992) found that unresolved status for trauma or loss in adult parents was significantly associated with disorganized attachment in their babies as assessed with the SS procedure. They reasoned that since the trauma or loss is unresolved and dissociated by the parent, certain experiences involved in raising a young child (e.g., washing a baby's genitals) can trigger and activate the mental and emotional states associated with the trauma or loss, resulting in temporary states of disorganization in the parent. Such temporary disorganization negatively affects the responsiveness of the parent toward the child. Additionally, unresolved status is associated with the parent acting in frightening and frightened ways toward his or her baby. The cumulative effect of the parent's intense shifts in state and lapses toward disorganized states of mind is vulnerability of the child to developing multiple, contradictory internal working models (see discussion on IWMs later in this chapter) of the caregiver and the associated development of disorganized attachment in the child. In support of this theory, the Minnesota Longitudinal Study (Sroufe, 2005) found that 40% of the parents who had been abused as children maltreated their own infants, and another 30% provided marginal care to their infants. The 30% of parents who had been abused but were nonabusive with their children were significantly more likely to have received emotional support from a nonabusing adult, to have participated in psychotherapy to treat the abuse background, and/or to have developed a satisfying intimate relationship with a partner as an adult (pp. 95–96).

Stovall-McClough and Cloitre (2006) studied 60 treatment-seeking women with a history of childhood sexual abuse, 57% of whom were identified as unresolved regarding abuse or loss by the AAI. Unresolved status strongly predicted a diagnosis of posttraumatic stress disorder and mildly but significantly predicted dissociative symptoms. Furthermore, the women who had unresolved as compared to resolved status were significantly more likely to parent a child with disorganized attachment. However, women with unresolved status of childhood abuse who were effectively treated with psychotherapy were more likely to raise secure children.

Consideration of intergenerational transmission benefits from recognition of the base rates for adult attachment pattern classification. Bakermans-Kranenburg and van IJzendoorn (2009) examined over 200 studies that assessed various populations with the Adult Attachment Interview. When they combined the AAI results from North American mothers without identified clinical histories (*n* = 748), they found the following distribution of three-category attachment classifications: 58% secure (F); 23% dismissing (Ds); and 19% anxious-preoccupied (E). Using a four-category classification system, with unresolved (U) and cannot classify (CC) categories combined (*n* = 700), they reported 56% F, 16% Ds, 9% E, and 18% U/CC. The AAI data from North American fathers indicated that the distribution was not significantly different from that of mothers for the three-category classification (*n* = 439), but when the U/CC category was included (*n* = 374), there were significantly more dismissing classifications (24% vs. 16%).

Samples from European countries did not differ statistically from what Bakermans-Kranenburg and van IJzendoorn considered the norm (i.e., the data from North American mothers, given that the AAI was developed using a similar population) when using the three-category differentiation. Adding the U/CC category resulted in a slightly higher rate of dismissing attachment in the European studies. Bakermans-Kranenburg and van IJzendoorn highlight the impressive similarity of the rates of the adult classifications across cultures, stating that "the few [AAI] studies conducted in non-European countries like Japan and Israel (in Hebrew), or in non-English languages such as Dutch, Swedish, German, and Italian, do not result in strongly deviating attachment representation patterns" (2009, pp. 247–248).

While these findings highlight that the base rate norm from North American mothers can be used as a general understanding of the distribution of attachment pattern classifications, it must be remembered that there is significant deviation from this distribution in clinical populations (as reported by Bakermans-Kranenburg & van IJzendoorn, 2009, and many others; see Chapter 5), and in some countries (e.g., Russia; see Pleshkova & Muhamedrahimov, 2010).

The Organization of States of Mind: Internal Working Models

Bowlby began to think about humans' mental representations of attachment behavior through learning of Lorenz's work with other species. He discovered in Lorenz's work that digger wasps make an internal mental map of their environment to enable them to better navigate their environment (Karen, 1998). According to Bowlby (1969/1982), an animal makes a "schematic representation of the topography of the environment in which it is living" (p. 71). The honeybee, for example, initiates the seeking of honey using a visually controlled system that (1) directs the bee to fly toward what appears to be a flower, (2) compels the bee to smell and settle on the flower, and (3) drives the bee to touch and locate the area where it can suck the honey. This behavioral system is organized into a series of "chains" that link each goal-corrected behavior toward the final goal (p. 75).

Consequently, Bowlby began to wonder how infants might also develop internal maps for the quality of attachment with their caregivers. While the development of an internal representational world was already familiar to Bowlby from his background in psychoanalysis, Bowlby adopted the term *internal working model* from information-processing theory (Craik, 1943). Similarly, Bowlby used it to refer to infants' construction of an inner model of their relational reality (Bowlby, 1973). Bowlby describes an internal working model (IWM) as follows:

> In the working model of the world that anyone builds, a key feature is his notion of who attachment figures are, where they may be found, and how they may be expected to respond. Similarly, in the working model of the self that anyone builds a key feature is his notion of how acceptable or unacceptable he himself is in the eyes of his attachment figures. On the structure of these complementary models are based that person's forecasts of how accessible and responsive his attachment figures are likely to be should he turn to them for support . . . whether he feels confident that his attachment figures are in general readily available or whether he is more or less afraid that they will not be available—occasionally, frequently, or most of the time. (p. 203)

Bowlby came to believe that patterns of attachment behavior can be explained by the operation of internal working models, which represent either secure or insecure experience with attachment figures. In the case of insecure IWMs, through a process of defensive exclusion of aspects of experience, a child may form multiple, contradictory, or distorted IWMs that create disruptions to attachment behavior. Moreover, particular forms of IWMs can cause an entire behavioral system to become "deactivated" (Bowlby, 1980a, p. 66). For example, attachment behavior becomes deactivated in avoidant babies and exploratory behavior becomes deactivated in resistant babies.

While IWMs of securely attached babies are more flexible and adaptable, IWMs of insecurely attached babies are more rigid, distorted, contradictory, and relatively resistant to change:

> These models of a parent and self in interaction tend to persist and are so taken for granted that they come to operate at an unconscious level . . . [They] persist in a more or less uncorrected and unchanged state even when the individual in later life is dealing with persons who treat him in ways entirely unlike those that his parents adopted when he was a child. (Bowlby, 1988, p. 130)

However, through exposure to a healthy attachment figure in later childhood or an effective attachment-based psychotherapy, an insecure IWM can be changed into a stable, secure IWM. Main refers to such change as the establishment of "earned security" (Main & Goldwyn, 1984a; Main, Goldwyn, & Hesse, 2002).

Bowlby's ideas about the cognitive structure of attachment behavior came to fruition in the work of Mary Main, who trained with Mary Ainsworth. Influenced by linguistics, Main began to see that the observed differences in attachment behavior in the SS between babies with different patterns of attachment were a reflection of different patterns of cognitive organization. Karen summarizes Main's thinking:

> The child's early attachment experiences . . . cause him to establish an internal model that organizes and directs not only his feelings and behavior "but also attention, memory, and cognition," to the extent that such mental functions are related to attachment. As a result, people with different attachment histories not only have different patterns of behavior but different "patterns of language and structures of mind." (1998, p. 215)

Main conceived of IWMs not so much as representations but as "a set of conscious and/or unconscious rules for the organization of information relevant to attachment" (Main et al., 1985, p. 67). She went on to say that

> secure versus the various types of insecure attachment organizations can best be understood as terms referring to particular types of internal working models . . . that direct not only feelings and behavior but also attention, memory, and cognition . . . Individual differences in . . . internal working models will be related not only to individual differences in patterns of nonverbal behavior but also to patterns of language and structure of mind. (Main et al., 1985, p. 67)

The Dynamic-Maturational Model of Attachment

Also interested in patterns of organization of mind in relation to attachment, Patricia Crittenden, who like Mary Main trained with Mary Ainsworth, developed a way of understanding attachment patterns that has built upon and expanded the work of Bowlby, Ainsworth, Main, and others. Her model, known as the Dynamic-Maturational Model (DMM) of attachment and adaptation (Crittenden, 1995, 2000a, 2000b, 2008, 2015), very much emphasizes consideration of the organization of mind in response to experience. Fundamental to her DMM approach are considerations of children's experiences of danger and threat and the information-processing strategies for coping that develop over the course of early as well as later childhood through the interplay of maturation and experiences with attachment figures.

Crittenden's theory, assessment, and treatment approaches are predicated on the principle that children, when they experience danger or threat, develop strategies for coping according to (1) the degree to which their attachment figures provide protection and comfort and (2) their maturational level at the time that coping strategies are required. According to her model, variation in attachment behavior reflects variation in patterns of information processing that underlie the child's (and ultimately the adult's) ongoing, environmentally and developmentally influenced attempts to cope with danger and threat of danger. Whereas Main and her colleagues have fruitfully focused on *state of mind with respect to attachment*, the DMM brings attention to these attachment-related patterns of information processing, which Crittenden's assessment methods attempt to specify.

Crittenden sees the two primary functions of attachment as *protection* from harm, or death, in order to ensure *reproduction*:

> The Dynamic-Maturational Model of attachment and adaptation defines attachment as three-entwined components: (1) relationships focused on protection and comfort; (2) patterns of mental processing of information about danger and sexual opportunity; and (3) strategies for self-protection, reproduction and protection of progeny. (Crittenden & Landini, 2011, p. 10)

> Attachment is seen in the DMM, not as a stable property of the individual (as in "attachment disorder"), but as a strategy—or range of strategies—used, mostly non-consciously, to attempt to keep safe within relationships and to produce the next generation. (Pocock, 2010, p. 3)

In Crittenden's view, "maladaptive behavior is the result of earlier attempts to protect oneself and one's progeny" (2008, p. 246). When parents do not provide adequate protection, a child processes the experience of danger or threat according to his or her zone of proximal development, or "the set of competencies that are emerging for a given individual at a specific moment in time" (Crittenden, 2008, p. 17; see Vygotsky, 1978). The goal of the processing is always to preserve the central functions of attachment—most immediately, self-protection—and "distortions in the way information is processed preserve the function under conditions of threat" (Crittenden & Landini, 2011, p. 34).

Crittenden highlights two primary forms of information-processing distortion, both involving relative omission of a category of information: omitting *affective* information and privileging cognitive, contingency- or consequence-based information; and omitting *cognitive* information and privileging affective, experiential, intensity-based information. Such patterns of including/excluding particular domains of information serve the goal of protection by disposing the child or adult to relate to available information in ways that through experience have been most associated with better outcomes when facing danger or threat of danger. Crittenden states that "patterns of attachment reflect learned patterns of mentally managing cognitive and affective information so as to predict and adapt to dangerous circumstances and opportunities for reproduction" (Crittenden & Landini, 2011, p. 36).

The particular ways that experience is processed lead to specific strategies for coping, for "eliciting needed caregiving from the parent[,] and for reducing possible rejection or harm" (Crittenden, 2008, p. 21). Repeated over time, these strategies and their underlying pattern of information processing create *dispositional representations* (DRs) "that reflect individuals' interpersonal expectations" (Crittenden & Dallos, 2014, p. 54). To Crittenden, the concept of DRs is more precise than Bowlby's "internal working models," "both because it clarifies the 'disposing to action' function of representation and because it emphasizes the transient, in-process quality of represent*ing* (as opposed to the retained and static quality of models)" (Crittenden, 2008, p. 92).

The "disposing to action function" of DRs leads to particular, relatively consistent patterns of attachment behavior and response, and the "transient in-process quality" reflects Crittenden's view that the information-processing patterns activated by experience change over time because of the interaction of both organismic maturational factors and new experiences.

Crittenden aims to honor the complexity inherent in her developmental and information-processing perspectives on attachment patterns by identifying "a wider array of [attachment] strategies than Ainsworth found in infancy" (Crittenden, 2008, p. 248). She takes as a starting point for her categorization system Ainsworth's (1973; Ainsworth et al., 1978) distinction among avoidant (A), balanced or secure (B), and ambivalent (C) strategies. Regarding a classification approach, Crittenden suggests:

> It could retain the Ainsworth patterns of infancy or be revised to reflect adult organizations that coalesce only after infancy (see Crittenden & Ainsworth, 1989). Describing such organizations is at the heart of the DMM method. From the three Ainsworth ABC patterns of infant attachment, an expanded DMM set of classifications is offered to address organizations of thought and behavior beyond the range described by Ainsworth. These classifications identify strategies that infants cannot yet organize. (Crittenden & Landini, 2011, p. 18)

A foundation of Crittenden's expanded system is the differentiation between *cognitive* and *affective* forms of information processing that underlie the A and C strategies:

> Ainsworth's three basic strategies form the core of the classificatory system, with the notion of cognition and affect functioning as information about when and where there might be danger constituting the explanation for the

universality of the three patterns . . . [T]he DMM is inherently a two-category model that includes gradations between the two processes. The two processes are drawn from information processing and refer to transformation of sensory stimulation into two basic forms of information. One is temporally ordered "cognitive" information; this is the basis for the Type A organization. The other is based on the intensity of stimulation and yields the construct of "affect"; this is the basis of the Type C organization. Type B is their balanced integration. Types A and C are construed as psychological opposites, with Types B and AC being their integration. (Crittenden & Landini, 2011, p. 40)

People using Type A strategies "tend to omit feelings from processing and to act in accordance with expected consequences" (Crittenden, 2005, p. 4). Forming an expectation of a consequence is the result of a disposition to process experience according to its perceived temporal contingencies (i.e., the sequence of experienced phenomena), which Crittenden identifies as a *cognitive* strategy of information processing (Crittenden, 2008, p. 19). People using Type C strategies "do the opposite: they act in accordance with their feelings with little attention to consequences" (Crittenden, 2005, p. 4). Such feeling-based action results from a disposition to process experience according to its intensity and the resulting autonomic nervous system responses, which is an *affective* information-processing strategy.

The Type B strategies involve using a mix of *both* cognitive and affective information, depending on the demands of the context, in a balanced, integrated way that does not distort or omit any information. Types A/C and AC, which replace Main and Solomon's (1990) Type D and the CC classification, are "classifiable, organized strategies" (Crittenden & Landini, 2011, p. 230) that also involve using both cognitive and affective strategies, but in alternating, less integrated ways (A/C) or in a blended way (AC) that integrates, to varying degrees, "false, denied, and delusional affect and cognition" (Crittenden & Landini, 2011, pp. 230–231).

Every strategy is considered to "reflect learned patterns of mentally managing cognitive and affective information so as to protect and adapt to dangerous circumstances and opportunities for reproduction" (Crittenden & Landini, 2011, p. 36). Though adaptive from this perspective, any tendency to privilege or exclude available information will "distort information in ways that often lead to heightened expectation of danger and, thus, to the use of self-protected behavior under safe circumstances" (Crittenden & Landini, 2011, p. 35). Such behavior is characteristic of insecure attachment.

Crittenden's model of information-processing strategies that underlie attachment patterns can be applied across the developmental spectrum. By specifying particular variants of affect-focused and cognition-focused strategies, Crittenden describes 11 possible patterns of attachment in infancy, 13 at preschool age (reflecting maturing out of the possibility of two infancy patterns and into four new possible patterns), 15 by school age, 17 by adolescence, and 22 by adulthood (see Crittenden, 2008, pp. 16–88). These include subcategories of Types A, B, C, and, in adulthood, the blended pattern AC. In addition, across the developmental spectrum, any A and C strategy can operate in an alternating pattern as A/C.

To illustrate the developmental maturation aspect of the classification system, at infancy there are three possible variants of the A (cognition-privileging) and C (affect-privileging) patterns, whereas at adulthood there are eight possible variants of each, reflecting the developmental potential for greater cognitive and affective capacities at adulthood. Similarly, at school age, approximately 6 to 12 years, there are six possible variants of C patterns but only four possible variants of A patterns, reflecting findings that affect development outpaces cognitive development at this age range.

> Because maturation increases the range of mental and behavioral responses, the need for and use of self-protective organizations of thought and behavior may change with development, even when circumstances themselves are unchanging. This can result in a change of pathways as well as the organization of new strategies. (Crittenden & Landini, 2011, p. 37)

Identification of States of Mind

Concepts consistent with information processing have also been central to Mary Main's work with the Adult Attachment Interview (AAI) and her differentiations of attachment types. She and her colleagues place great emphasis on *coherence of state of mind*; they have found, for example, that secure adults describe early attachment relationships in an organized, coherent manner. Main and Goldwyn (1998) define coherence as "a connection or congruity arising from some common principle or relationship; consistency; [or] connectedness of thought, such that parts of the discourse are clearly related, form a logical whole, or are suitable or suited and adapted to context" (p. 44).

Operationally, Main and her associates apply Grice's (1975) categories that define cooperative, rational discourse: namely, truthful in *quality*, succinct but complete in *quantity*, *relevant*, and clear and orderly in *manner*. "Discourse is judged coherent when a subject appears able to access and evaluate memories while *simultaneously* remaining plausible (consistent, or implicitly truthful) and collaborative" (Hesse, 1999, p. 404). Secure adults richly and accurately describe memories of early attachment relationships with sufficient detail. They stay on topic. Their discourse about attachment depicts a singular working model for each attachment figure. Insecure, dismissing adults do not describe early attachment relationships in a very coherent manner. Their descriptions of early attachment figures are rarely supported by evidence, and when they do provide illustrative memories, they are often overidealized and unrealistic or they lack sufficient memory detail. These descriptions may be too succinct to provide a clear picture of early attachment figures. Insecure, preoccupied adults are exceedingly verbose. Their descriptions of early attachment relationships are filled with irrelevancies, passive speech, and jargon, and their descriptions are often excessively long and meandering. Insecure, disorganized adults present a contradictory mixture of discourse showing characteristics of both dismissing and preoccupied speech.

Overall, dismissing, preoccupied, and disorganized adults show low coherence of discourse in describing their early attachment experiences on the standardized Adult Attachment Interview (described fully in Chapter 4). On a 1 to 9 scale to indicate coherence of discourse in response to the AAI questions, insecure individuals generally score below 3 and secure individuals generally score above 7. Thus, the way a person organizes or cannot organize his or her thoughts and discourse about early attachment relationships is considered to be a primary indicator of secure versus insecure attachment. In essence, Main and her colleagues associated each of the four adult attachment types with very specific organization or patterns of state of mind.

Hesse (1999) stated that the discovery that attachment patterns are represented by states of mind inferred through discourse patterns opened a new era in attachment research in which focus could be placed on *how attachment is represented as a state of mind*. The new focus allowed researchers to go beyond studying young children's nonverbal behavior as coded from the strange situation to exploring older children's and adults' representations of attachment through states of mind.

Three Generations of Metacognition

In a seminal article, John Flavell (1986) defined metacognition as "thinking about thinking." A more comprehensive definition is direct perception of one's own state of mind or the state of mind of the other. In this definition, "state of mind" includes not only *thinking* but any cognitive or affective experience. Research on metacognition in the attachment field began with Mary Main (1991). Using the Adult Attachment Interview, she discovered that secure adults, as compared to insecure adults, tended to have a greater capacity to reflect on their attachment experiences and to see the "*merely* representational nature" of their own beliefs and feelings about attachment experiences (p. 129).

Main and her associates identified several kinds of metacognitive thinking in AAI discourse. For example, when a respondent says, "It *seemed* as if my mother was angry when I was growing up," he or she is recognizing an "appearance–reality distinction" in that the respondent understands that the way it seemed may not have been how it actually was. The statement "It seemed to me that my mother was angry, but my sister didn't see it that way at all" reflects understanding of "representational diversity" in that the respondent is aware that two siblings can develop very different representations for the same attachment experience. When a respondent says, "I used to think my mother was angry when I was growing up, but I don't see her that way anymore," he or she is showing understanding of "representational change," recognizing that representations of early attachment experiences may significantly change over time.

These examples illustrate the relative nature of all representations, highlighting that representations are just that—merely representations. AAI transcripts characterized by frequent examples of metacognitive statements are likely to be secure transcripts. High scores on the metacognitive scale of the AAI are significantly correlated with coherence of transcript and coherence of mind. While the metacognitive scale on the AAI reflects the first attempt to articulate and codify the presence of metacognitive thinking when reflecting on attachment experiences, the scale never developed beyond the identification and inclusion of the three types—appearance–reality distinction, representational diversity, and representational change.

Peter Fonagy, Anthony Bateman, and their associates in the area of metacognition (hereafter referred to as the London School) greatly advanced research on metacognition and attachment with their work on *mentalization*. Mentalization is defined as

> making sense of the actions of oneself and others on the basis of intentional mental states, such as desires, feelings, and beliefs. [It] entails the recognition that what is in the mind is in the mind. It reflects the knowledge of one's own and other's mental states as mental states. (Bateman & Fonagy, 2004, p. 58)

Reflective function "refers to the psychological processes underlying the capacity to mentalize" (Fonagy et al., 1998, p. 4), and *reflective functioning* is the operationalization of mentalization. Peter Fonagy, along with Mary Target and Howard and Miriam Steele, developed the Reflective Functioning Scale (RF-S, Fonagy et al., 1998) that can be applied to an AAI transcript or a therapy transcript. The RF-S measures reflective functioning across four broad domains: (1) awareness of mental states, including awareness of the relativity of all knowledge systems and the limitation of knowledge; (2) awareness that behaviors are associated with underlying states of mind, including reflection on the causes of behavior, awareness that feelings about a situation may differ from behavior, and reflection on how mental states affect the interpretation of others' behavior and also how others interpret one's own behavior; (3) awareness of the developmental aspect of mental states, which includes taking a transgenerational perspective, putting one's own behavior into a historical context, and being aware of the familial-contextual aspects of experience; and (4) awareness of mental states in relation to the interviewer, including acknowledgment of separateness of states of mind, emotional attunement to the interviewer, and acknowledgment of perceptions and beliefs about the interviewer.

On the AAI or in a therapy session, an individual with highly developed reflective capacity is likely to make many metacognitive statements of the nature mentioned above, such that these statements pervade the discourse. The RF Scale spans from minus 1 to plus 9, and transcripts of individuals with high reflective capacity are likely to score between 7 and 9. On the other hand, Fonagy and his associates claim that they never found a patient with a personality disorder or a dissociative disorder diagnosis that scored 3 or above on the RF Scale. Based on this observation, Fonagy and his associates developed an entire approach to psychotherapy for patients with personality and dissociative disorders called *mentalization-based treatment* (MBT). Outcome research on MBT has demonstrated that when psychotherapy systematically focuses on the development of mentalization capacity and the capacity to reflect on one's own and the other's state of mind, there is significant improvement in reflective functioning. Further, overall coherence of mind, as measured on the AAI, significantly improves, and many such MBT-treated patients no longer meet diagnostic criteria for a personality disorder.

The third generation of research on metacognition emerged from the work of Antonio Semerari and his associates (Semerari et al., 2003) at the Third Center of Cognitive Psychotherapy, Rome (hereafter referred to as the Rome School). Semerari and his colleagues differ from the London School in that they do not consider metacognition to be a single, general function that resembles reflective capacity but instead identify a range of distinct metacognitive abilities. They take what they call a *modular view of metacognition*. Semerari and his associates identified four discrete categories of metacognition: (1) *metacognitive identification*, which refers to the capacity to become aware of one's state of mind; (2) *metacognitive mastery*, which refers to the capacity to become aware of one's state of mind in a way that has a regulatory effect on this state; (3) *metacognitive relating* of states, behaviors, and motivations; and (4) *metacognitive integration* or organization, which refers to awareness of the degree of organization or disorganization of one's state of mind.

Semerari et al. (2003) coded therapy session transcripts of patients with a diagnosis of either borderline or narcissistic personality disorder for each of these four metacognitive capacities. They found significant differences in metacognition between each diagnostic group. For example, borderlines scored adequately on metacognitive identification but had a primary deficit in metacognitive mastery. Narcissists showed the opposite: They scored adequately on metacognitive mastery but had a primary deficit in metacognitive identification of others' and their own states of mind. Giovanni Liotti, from this same research group, demonstrated a primary deficit in metacognitive organization in both borderline and dissociative disorder patients (1999). According to the Rome School, the main implication of the findings is that metacognitive deficits may be *condition-spe-*

cific and that metacognitive-based psychotherapy may need to address very specific metacognitive deficits in a patient with a specific diagnostic condition.

Intersubjectivity

Ainsworth and her associates laid the foundation for a generation of research on
parental *attunement* with her discovery that maternal responsiveness, or lack
thereof, can predict secure and insecure attachment as assessed in the Strange
Situation. Secure infants clearly signaled distress upon separation and then relief
of distress upon being comforted in reunion episodes, and responsive mothers
correctly identified their infants' signals and responded appropriately. Avoidant
babies failed to communicate their distress and/or their mothers failed to recognize their babies' distress cues. Ambivalent babies communicated ongoing exaggerated distress in reunion episodes, and irrespective of the mother's response,
this distress was not relieved.

Researchers began to discover that these interactions were not simply about
maternal responsiveness but that the *interaction* between mother and baby as
either a secure or insecure dyad was of equal significance. Bowlby's concept of
goal-corrected behavior also implied that collaborative interaction and contingent reinforcement of signaled behaviors was of great importance. These findings
and their interpretations opened the door for a new wave of research on attunement and misattunement.

A contemporary of Bowlby, Donald Winnicott, was an English pediatrician
and psychoanalyst who developed his ideas through his treatment of children. In
The Child and the Family (1957), Winnicott presented the idea that the mother's
attuned presence acts as a "holding environment" for the child. A "good-enough
mother" consistently and attentively holds her child—physically while comforting, feeding, and bathing the child, and also *emotionally* in all contexts. The
cumulative consequence of "good-enough" holding is that the child becomes able
to develop a physical representation of bodily experience and also a representation of mind. The concept of holding conveys a careful attunement by a mother
toward her infant. Additionally, Winnicott was interested in and wrote a great
deal about *play*. He suggested that a child's play is a central ingredient to the
development of the sense of self (1971). A mother who is consistently encouraging and reassuring in response to her baby's spontaneous expressions is likely
to raise a child who develops a healthy and stable sense of self. Conversely, the
child of a mother who consistently rejects or discourages his or her spontaneous
expressions is likely to develop a fragile and/or false self (Winnicott, 1960).

Tronick, Adamson, Als, and Brazelton (1975) conducted one of the first experiments demonstrating reciprocity in infant–mother interactions using what has
become known as the *still face experiment*. This method entails video-recording the interactions of a one-year-old child with his or her mother. Initially, the
child and mother greet each other, and then the child playfully interacts with his

mother for several minutes. Typically, the mother and child respond with reciprocal exchange of spontaneous facial expressions, hand gestures, and vocalizations. Next, the mother is instructed to maintain a nonresponsive, expressionless face for the next 3 minutes. The baby initially responds by trying to reengage the mother with hand gestures, pointing, smiling, and vocalizations. As these infant-elicited attachment behaviors fail to evoke any response from the mother, the baby shows a progressive decrease in spontaneously initiated behaviors, a muted smile, protest sounds, averted gaze, distress, crying, and decreased motor coordination. This experiment strongly illustrates the importance of the reciprocal nature of infant–caregiver attunement and the profound negative effects of even a brief misattunement in an otherwise secure infant–mother dyad.

Andrew Meltzoff (1985, 1990; Meltzoff & Moore, 1998) developed a theory of innate *intersubjectivity*. He sees intersubjectivity as arising initially from the infant's perception of the mother's behavior and believes that such perceptual acuity is present at least shortly after birth. His theory is derived mainly from studies of *imitative behavior* in infants. For example, he discovered that neonates at 42 minutes of age imitated the mother's facial expression. Infants were then given a pacifier to inhibit the infant's spontaneous imitation of the mother's facial expression, and the mother either opened her mouth wide or stuck her tongue out. When the pacifier was removed several minutes later, the child made progressively more accurate imitations of the mother's facial expression that he or she had seen just minutes before. By six weeks, the baby was able to imitate the mother's facial expression seen on the previous day when exposed to a neutral expression of the mother's face. By nine months, imitative behavior can be deferred for longer and longer durations. Meltzoff reasoned that such infants must be creating a mental representation of the mother's facial expression, a mediator of imitative behavior. Imitative behavior is also based on the *perception of correspondence* between the infant's own behavior and that of the mother. The subjective representation of that correspondence results in a sense of *fundamental relatedness* between self and other.

Colwyn Trevarthen (1979) developed his theory of intersubjectivity by conducting a micro-analysis of videotaped recordings of infant–mother interactions. In contrast to Meltzoff's innate theory of intersubjectivity, Trevarthen views intersubjectivity as a consequence of the interactions between infant and mother over time. He argued that what is innate is the infant's ability to *detect contingency effects*—that is, to detect effects that are or are not contingent on the infant's behavior toward the mother. Such *dyadic, mutually regulated communication* and *cooperation* is characterized by mutual imitative behavior, emotional empathy, and reciprocal nonverbal and verbal communication. Reciprocal communication entails both the infant and the mother matching each other's response with respect to the timing of the response, the form of the nonverbal or verbal communication, and the intensity of the response.

Intersubjectivity entails a process by which the infant fits her or his intention, attention, and behavior to that of the other in a mutually regulated interactive sequence. This process requires accurate perception of and adaptation to the expressions and behavior of the other. It does not entail passive imitation but rather translation, deliberate reproduction, mirroring, amplification, and embellishment.

Daniel Stern (1971, 1985) also conducted detailed microanalyses of infant–mother interactions on videotape and discovered the back-and-forth sequences of the infant's and mother's respective responses to each other. Stern used technology that was sufficiently sensitive to observe the minute, carefully synchronized patterns between infant and mother (Karen, 1998, p. 347). Like Trevarthen, Stern sees intersubjectivity less as something innate and more as a phenomenon arising out of the reciprocal interactions between infant and mother over time. It begins with the infant's acute awareness of the other, and, through mutually regulated interactions, infant and mother both learn the rules of interactions and represent and interpret the meaning of each other's behavior. Stern's work is notable for its emphasis on dyadic *affect attunement*.

Additionally, Stern emphasizes that an important developmental shift occurs between 9 and 12 months. With the maturation of cognition, there is a shift away from mutually regulated overt behaviors to mutually regulated subjective states in infant and mother alike. By the end of the first year of life, the baby begins to develop the capacity for symbolic thinking and thereby is able to make a neural representation of subjectivity and intersubjectivity. In other words, by this age, the child has begun to develop a theory of one's own mind as well as of the mind of the other. The baby discovers his or her own mind and the mind of the other, and also that subjective experiences can be communicated and shared through the ongoing dyadic communication of intention, attention, and emotion.

The relation between the attachment system and intersubjectivity is best described as follows:

> Stern believes that attachment and intersubjectivity are separate and complementary motivational systems. The attachment system balances our related needs for the security of physical proximity and the learning that exploration makes possible. The intersubjective system is driven by our need to know and be known by others. If attachment exists to foster felt security, intersubjectivity exists to promote the experience of psychic intimacy and belonging . . . While it is possible to be attached without intersubjective relatedness . . . and intersubjectively related without attachment, . . . it is generally true that attachment and intersubjectivity are mutually enhancing. (Wallin, 2007, p. 54)

According to Karen (1998), "well-synchronized mother–infant interactions predict secure attachment" (p. 350).

Attunement, Misattunement, and Synchronization of Expression

Beatrice Beebe's (2005) research on intersubjectivity has focused on synchronized, coordinated timing of interactional patterns and rhythms between infant and mother—what she refers to as *forms of intersubjectivity*. Using real-time video-recording analysis of infant–mother interactions, Beebe and her associates have studied nonrandom rhythmic patterns of nonverbal dyadic exchanges (orientation, gaze, looking, head movements, gestures, postural mirroring, facial expression, and touch) and verbal dyadic exchanges (tone and pitch, vocal rhythm, vocal timing, turn-taking) (Jaffe, Beebe, Feldstein, Crown, & Jasnow, 2001).

The opposite of carefully synchronized and mutually regulated interactions between infant and mother is misattunement. Karen (1998) describes several circumstances of misattunement in insecure infants:

> Those [mothers] whose babies tended to be ambivalently attached to them misattuned to a broad spectrum of the baby's emotional expression, but were extremely attentive and well attuned when the baby was afraid. They were, in effect, training him to see fear as a primary means of achieving a sense of relatedness to another person. Mothers whose babies tended to be avoidantly attached to them, on the other hand, were most likely to misattune to the infant when he was expressing a negative feeling, especially toward them, or when he was seeking comfort or reassurance. Such mothers excelled, however, in attuning to their baby's exuberance, especially when he was mastering some new toy or game. (pp. 354–355)

Beebe and Frank Lachman (2014) have also researched intersubjectivity with adult patient–therapist dyads. For example, they present a compelling case study in which Beebe empathizes with a disorganized patient's communicative expressions and feelings of loss by utilizing a questioning intonation to introduce the possibility that the patient could respond. In treating Dolores, who initially could not look at Beebe because of her intense fearfulness, withdrawal, and dissociation, Beebe videotaped her own face while conducting a number of sessions and watched the videotapes with Dolores afterward. In the videotapes, Beebe was seen to make use of facial expression, self-touch, and other forms of nonverbal communication to mirror the patient's verbal rhythms, facial expressions, and body language, thus providing attuned gestural responses. By matching her responses to the patient's, Beebe tried to model and enhance the expressions of affect the patient would experience and convey if she were more securely attached. Beebe summarizes the process below:

> Since Dolores initially did not make much use of the facial-visual channel of communication, the early phases of the treatment were carried through

my rhythms of voice and body rather than my face. My contingent coordination with her rhythms constituted the process of how I reached for her, how I tried to sense her state, and she could come and sense mine. Both Stern (1985) and Trevarthen (1998) argue that matching of communicative expressions simultaneously regulates both interpersonal contact and inner state. Dolores gradually came to sense a "comforted" inner state as she became more aware of how I matched her and coordinated with her. Thus correspondences of expressions through time, form, and intensity provided a powerful nonverbal mode of therapeutic action. My coordination simultaneously gave me a greater feeling of "being with" her. (Beebe & Lachman, 2014, p. 87)

Another way of describing Beebe's verbal technique is by saying she used "motherese" in attempting to evoke new capacities for attachment-oriented communication in Dolores. One of our three pillars of attachment treatment includes making use of such dyadic verbal communicative expressions as matching, coordination of tone, pitch, and vocal rhythm. Our integration of these methods into treatment is described fully in Chapter 10.

Conclusion

With this overview of what we see as the seminal ideas that have emerged so far in the history of the attachment field, we have attempted to set the context for our focus throughout the rest of this book. Our treatment model and methods reflect our particular integration of what we consider to be the most important ideas and understandings about the origins, manifestations, and treatment methods of attachment disturbances in adults. The next chapter reviews what is known about the developmental factors that contribute to the emergence of the attachment bond in children.

CHAPTER 2

Understanding the Development of Attachment Bonds and Attachment Behavior Over the Life Course

Developmentally informed treatments for attachment disturbances are based on an understanding of what an attachment bond is and how it forms. Out of the rich and complex interplay of an infant's internal maturational processes and the interpersonal behavioral dynamics with his or her primary caregiver, an attachment bond emerges and is shaped and consolidated over time. That bond, whether secure or insecure, creates and is reflected by an internal representation, or internal working model, of the attachment relationship and has a profound influence on the child's continued development. Later strengths and problems in areas of self-experience, affect regulation, and capacity for intimacy in relationships can often be traced to what happened during the early processes of attachment bond formation. The treatment model presented in this book is founded on the developmentally essential factors for the formation of secure attachment, and the treatment methods integrate those factors in ways that can reshape an adult's internal representation of insecure attachment into one that is secure and can repair the problems that occur in the domains of self, affect, and relational functioning.

This chapter presents an overview of the current understanding of the normative factors and dynamics that contribute to the formation of a secure attachment bond and the related developmental achievements. The emphasis is on the interplay of infant attachment behavior and caregiver responses. Though the attachment bond is stably established by approximately the third year of life, continued maturation and later experience during childhood, adolescence, and adulthood result in changes in ways that the attachment bond manifests. The latter part of this chapter reviews those changes.

When considering any developmental process, it can be useful, for conceptual understanding, to impose a stage or phase structure on the linear sequence of developmental emergence. Mary Ainsworth (1972; Ainsworth, Blehar, Waters, & Wall, 1978) gave slightly different names to John Bowlby's earlier description of four phases in infants' development and strengthening of the attachment bond with caregivers: (1) initial pre-attachment, (2) attachment-in-the-making, (3) clear-cut attachment, and (4) goal-corrected partnership. The developmental factors that contribute to the emergence of these phases and the features characteristic of each phase are detailed below. Though typical age ranges for the phases are indicated, it must be kept in mind that, as with any developmental sequence, there can be great temporal variation in their unfolding.

Phase 1: The Pre-attachment Phase (Birth to 2–3 Months)

Infants are entirely dependent on caregivers for their survival, and so any behavior that increases the chance that attention and care will be provided is adaptive. Bowlby (1969/1982) believed that attachment behaviors, or behaviors that orient toward and promote proximity to potential caregivers, have been evolutionarily hardwired into the nervous system. During the first weeks of life, before the infant can seek out or even recognize a caregiver, automatic, reflexive behaviors occur to attract a caregiver's attention and to provide information that ideally will guide the caregiver to meet the infant's immediate needs and ensure his or her ultimate survival.

Bowlby's view was that "at birth or very soon thereafter, every sensory system in the infant is working . . . [and] there is much evidence that the sensory systems are structured so that the baby is particularly likely to respond to behavior from humans in general" (Marvin & Britner, 2008, p. 275). The earliest signs of nonverbal communication to humans emerge within just a few hours after birth in the form of tongue protrusion, mouth opening, lip protrusion, smiling, and showing surprise (Nagy & Molnar, 1994). Meltzoff and Moore (1977) found that as early as 42 minutes after birth, infants are able to imitate the nonverbal behavior of their caregiver. Bowlby further believed not only that infants have innate responses to humans, but also that their response patterns are organized in ways that promote and maintain human contact: "In a complementary way, a baby's signal and motor systems are especially adept at eliciting interest and caregiving from other humans, so that proximity, physical contact, nutrition, and warmth are the predictable outcomes" (Marvin & Britner, 2008, p. 275). During this phase, the largely automatic behaviors of the infant may be seen as casting a net to establish recognition of and rudimentary connection with a caregiver. The adaptive nature of these innate and early-appearing sensory and behavioral patterns is clear: As proximity and need-gratification are fundamental to survival, until the infant develops both the motor skills that allow self-initiation of proximity to a caregiver and the communication skills to directly indicate the presence of needs, he or she must behave in ways that increase the likelihood that a caregiver will be near and will provide essential caregiving functions.

Ainsworth et al. (1978) stated that the initial pre-attachment phase entails "orientation and signals without discrimination of figure" (p. 23). Immediately after birth, human infants show a capacity for visual orientation and basic tracking of moving objects, human or not. Over the first weeks of life, the infant becomes more adept at head-turning and focusing his or her gaze, and increasingly he or she responds to others, especially to whomever is consistently nearest, with orienting responses of the head and eyes.

The primary pre-attachment behaviors, emerging from the innate *attachment behavioral system* (Bowlby, 1969/1982), are *crying, babbling, reaching, grasping, clinging,* and *smiling.* These behaviors are not learned but occur reflexively in response to internal and/or external conditions and ideally attract the attention, proximity, and beneficial response of the caregiver. Jude Cassidy (2008) highlights Bowlby's view that the attachment behavioral system functions in a "goal-corrected" manner: "Unlike certain reflexes that, once activated, maintain a fixed course (e.g., sneezing, rooting), the attachment behavioral system enables the individual to respond flexibly to environmental changes while attempting to attain a goal" (p. 5).

The attachment behaviors operate on and attempt to influence external conditions, but the fundamental purpose of these behaviors is the elimination of states of inner tension.

Crying is an automatic response to conditions experienced by the infant as noxious, and functions as an alerting signal (Ainsworth et al., 1978) to the caregiver to come to the infant and act to diminish the discomfort that triggered the crying. If the caregiver responds with behavior that soothes the infant, the crying behavior has been successful and is terminated. The largely reflexive and caregiver-independent gross motor movements of reaching, grasping, and clinging are physical expressions of the desire and need for physical proximity and/or comfort and may or may not be paired with crying. Especially soothing even shortly after birth are soft vocalizations from caregivers who respond with physical acceptance of the infant's rudimentary forms of reaching, grasping, and clinging.

Smiling is also one of the earliest attachment behaviors and is, like crying, a signaling behavior (Ainsworth et al., 1978). The earliest smile is not yet a social smile in response to a preferred caregiver but an automatic facial display pattern (Tomkins, 1968), a reflexive response of the striate muscles that control facial expression that is triggered when the infant sustains interest or joy in what is occurring in the moment. This facial display pattern is an amplified, external expression of the infant's internal experience and ideally cues the caregiver to maintain the conditions that elicited the smile.

In addition to smiling, several other automatic facial displays are also amplified expressions that function as cues to the caregiver. A facial pattern of *surprise* often indicates initial overwhelm from internal or environmental conditions. If such conditions are prolonged, the facial display becomes one of *fear;* if the conditions are reduced or modified by the caregiver to create an optimal, balanced level of stimulation that the infant can bear, the expression shifts to what might be described as *contentment*. An expression displaying *frustration* or *anger* indicates the infant's experience of his or her interest being disrupted. Restoration of the interesting conditions or soothing in some other form will likely then elicit a positive reflexive display, such as *smiling* or *contentment*.

The automatic facial displays function not only to promote engagement with a caregiver and to cue her or him regarding immediate physical needs. They also cue a caregiver to modify the environment in ways that benefit other developmental needs. For example, the infant's visual perceptual system isn't fully developed until about the third month (D. P. Brown, 1993), and its optimal development depends on an ever-changing array of stimulation, neither too much nor too little. The infant depends on the caregiver to provide an environment that includes such stimulation. In the same way that facial displays cue the attuned caregiver to respond to the infant's immediate physical needs, they can guide the caregiver to modify the visual environment to maximize the development of the perceptual system. Responding to the infant's expressions of smiling, surprise, fear, frustration, anger, and contentment, the caregiver makes changes to the visual environment that reduce negative and promote positive facial displays.

The dynamic interplay between the infant's pre-attachment behaviors and the caregiver's responses serves not only to maximize the conditions for the infant's momentary well-being and perceptual development, but also to build and shape the caregiver's attunement to the infant and thereby to *build the relationship*. The main interchanges between infant and caregiver during this pre-attachment phase involve each adapting to the other's rhythms of sleeping, waking, feeding, and elimination to create a best-fit dyadic correspondence (Sander & Julia, 1966). The internal conditions and experience of the infant during these interchanges produce a behavioral display, ideally the caregiver notices and responds, and the caregiver's response has impact on the infant, whose subsequent display reflects the impact of that response. The repetition of this reciprocal, contingent pattern of display-response-display gives the caregiver ongoing opportunity to learn about what best meets the infant's needs, in the moment and in general. As the attuned caregiver more and more "gets it right," there will be fewer and less intense appearances of attachment behaviors, such as crying, and more displays of interest, contentment, and smiling. Overall, patterns of interaction become more consistent and stable.

Infants' nonverbal imitative capacity, present from within the first hour after birth (Meltzoff & Moore, 1977) and growing steadily during the first months of life, can also be seen as contributing to the emerging relationship between infant and caregiver. Imitation itself reflects a relationship, as it is a response to the perception of behavior of an attended-to other. If that other is attentive and attuned and contingently responds to the infant's imitation, then the resulting dyadic exchange reinforces the infant's behavior, his or her attention to the other, and the relationship between them. According to Meltzoff and Moore (1977), this coordinated nonverbal interchange constitutes a kind of presymbolic communication between the infant and caregiver. Thus, both the innate imitative capacity and, as described earlier, the operation of the automatic facial display patterns are hardwired contributions to the emerging relational dynamics of nonverbal intersubjective communication (Trevarthen, 1979) and mutual, collaborative exchange (Tomasello, 2009).

Several infant nervous system maturations during this phase support the early attachment bond of the infant to the caregiver. During the third and fourth weeks of life, the infant begins to show a clear visual preference for the human face (Stechler & Carpenter, 1967; Wolff, 1969) and thus more frequently and for longer periods looks at humans who are near. By the fourth week, the infant develops head orientation toward others, and shortly thereafter shows preferential orientation toward the primary caregiver (Izard, 1971) and direct eye-to-eye contact and a smiling response to that contact (Stern, 1985). The primary caregiver will thus experience being looked at by the infant more often, which, along with the reward of learning the contingencies that result in positive facial displays, can have the effect of a net that "captures" and increases the caregiver's motivation for presence and attention to the infant and his or her needs. For the infant, preferred orientation toward the primary caregiver and experience-based expectation and anticipation that the caregiver will contingently respond are fundamental developmental achievements during this phase, which "come to an end when the baby is capable of discriminating among people and, in particular, of discriminating his mother figure from others" (Ainsworth et al., 1978, p. 24).

Phase 2: Attachment-in-the-Making (2–3 to 6–9 Months)

During approximately the third month after birth, the infant whose nervous system is not impaired and who has had good-enough caregiving shows signs of differentiating between familiar caregivers, especially the primary caregiver, and others. For example, whereas earlier, smiling was the infant's response to internal conditions, now the infant smiles in response to the most familiar caregivers. The more that reciprocal patterns of interaction are repeated with a particular caregiver, the more likely it is that the infant will begin to show a preferential orientation toward that caregiver. Ainsworth et al. (1978) referred to Phase 2 as "orientation and signals directed toward one (or more) discriminated figure(s)" (p. 24). Marvin and Britner (2008) state that this phase is "operationally defined in terms of the infant differentiating between the most familiar caregivers and others in directing his or her attachment behavior," and they highlight Bowlby's identification of "13 relatively complex patterns of behavior that are differentially displayed toward one figure, usually the mother" (p. 276).

Seven of these patterns are likely to be seen during Phase 2 in relation to a particular or possibly several close caretakers (e.g., the infant's mother and father): visual-motor orientation, termination of crying, smiling, vocalization, greeting (with vocalization and/or smiling and/or reaching), climbing and exploring, and, toward the end of this phase, crying when the caregiver leaves. The other six patterns that Bowlby identified are likely to emerge during Phase 3 (Ainsworth et al., 1978, p. 26; Marvin & Britner, 2008, p. 276).

The Phase 2 patterns result from the significant sensorimotor advances that occur from about three to six months. Simple behaviors that appeared earlier become more complex and link with other behaviors as the underlying behavioral systems develop and integrate. Many behaviors become less reflexive and are increasingly under the infant's control (Marvin & Britner, 2008). The differentiation and recognition of primary caretakers, together with the new possibilities for dynamic interaction that the sensorimotor developments enable, contribute to the infant's "attachment-in-the-making" (Ainsworth et al., 1978, p. 23), building during Phase 2 toward a primary attachment bond between the infant and a particular caregiver. The infant begins to regularly orient toward and greet the primary caregiver with verbalizations, with the newly emerged social smile, and with deliberate reaching. By four months, the visual and motor systems are linked and coordinated in a way that allows a visual stimulus to activate a motor, reaching response; by five months, the infant has linked reaching and grasping, allowing him or her to not only deliberately reach out to the caregiver but also to grab hold (Marvin & Britner, 2008).

Facial displays continue to be automatic and reflexive at times, as they will be throughout life, but the infant also develops increasing control over the musculature of the face and becomes able to deliberately create facial expressions. Through visual-motor integration and the infant's capacity for imitation, he or she becomes able to recognize and match the caregiver's facial display, and between four and six months the capacity for deliberate, reciprocal exchange of facial displays between infant and caregiver emerges (Sroufe & Waters, 1997). Beebe and Lachmann (2014) filmed second-by-second face-to-face communication between four-month-old infants and their caregivers. A microanalysis of these infant–caregiver interactions revealed "a continuous, reciprocally coordinated process, co-created moment-to-moment" (p. 4). Repetitive patterns of mutual nonverbal matching in secure infant–caregiver dyads, and repetitive patterns of mutual nonverbal mismatching in disorganized dyads, are already fully in place by four to six months, and these patterns will later appear as part of prototypical attachment patterns identified with the Strange Situation procedure (p. 17).

Although during Phase 1 there is also dyadic communication through imitation-based matching, the infant depends on the caregiver to initiate interaction and is limited to *automatic* imitative responses. During Phase 2, the infant begins to seek and initiate interaction, begins to develop greater control of his or her behaviors, and is more able to make *deliberate* responses during the interaction. Malatesta and Haviland (1982) see such mutual exchange as initial intersubjective communication, and Trevarthen (1998) considers the dynamic nonverbal interactions between infant and caregiver to be a kind of protoconversational play. Contributing to these relational capacities are several self-observational and self-developments. Stern (1985) suggests that a rudimentary "core self" and "emergent relatedness" develops between the second and sixth month (pp. 26, 28), resulting from the infant's growing awareness of the links among perceptions, actions, and affective expressions. Lewis and Brooks (1978) also highlight the emergence of self-awareness as the basis for the early sense of self. They suggest that early self-awareness develops between the fourth and eighth month and is based on the growing perception of internal bodily states and their changes and redundancy. D. P. Brown (1993) points to the relational contribution to such perception, stating that the infant's awareness of his or her experience is promoted by sufficient caregiver attunement to and mirroring of the infant's affective expressions. Of note here is that self-developments are promoted by relational dynamics, and then those very self-developments contribute to further refinement and development of relational dynamics.

The sense of self is emerging during this period, but it is not yet differentiated from caregivers. Internal working models (IWMs) are forming, but they are based on linking and continuity of internal experience rather than recognition of caregivers as being separate from that experience. It is not until Phase 3 that the infant comes to differentiate self from others (see, e.g., Mahler, Pine, & Bergman, 1975) and thereby develops separate, distinct IWMs of caregivers and self (Marvin & Britner, 2008, pp. 277–278).

Phase 3: Clear-Cut Attachment (6–9 Months to 36 Months)

Ainsworth et al. (1978) characterized Phase 3 as a period of "clear-cut attachment" that can begin as early as six months. The earlier patterns of attachment behavior activation and satisfaction and the emerging and increasingly complex reciprocal interactive facial displays, gestures, and vocalizations between the infant and his or her primary caregiver culminate at Phase 3 in a unique bond, the primary attachment relationship. Marvin and Britner (2008) highlight research that indicates that most infants select one caregiver as the primary attachment figure. Though infants usually establish attachment relationships to a variety of caregivers,

> not all attachment figures are treated by the infant as equivalent . . . [A]ttachment behavior tends, especially when an infant is distressed, hungry, tired, or ill, to be focused on a particular person when both that person and other attachment figures are available. (p. 280)

During Phase 3, the infant's continuing maturational developments and the responses of the primary attachment figure contribute to the consolidation of this attachment bond and the development of the IWMs that shape the attachment prototypes and the resulting attachment patterns throughout life. Between 12 and 18 months, a child's attachment patterns become quite stable. Hamilton (2000) found that 77% of adolescents given the Adult Attachment Interview (AAI) at ages 17 to 19 years retained the same corresponding three-way attachment categorization that was identified at 12 months. Waters, Merrick, Treboux, Crowell, and Albersheim (2000) reported a 64% correspondence between 12-month three-way classification and AAI classification at 20 to 22 years, and when categorization was simplified to secure or insecure, there was 72% concordance. Sroufe, Egeland, Carlson, and Collins (2005) reported data from the Minnesota Longitudinal Study showing that 18-month (though not 12-month) ABC infant classifications predicted AAI categories at 26 years (though not at 19 years). This association was primarily based on the very strong association between autonomous (B) and later AAI secure status. In this study, disorganized infant attachment modestly predicted AAI insecurity at 19 years, and did so more strongly at 26 years.

A major advance in attachment behavior occurs with the infant's acquisition of locomotion, first in the form of crawling, which develops between 7 and 11 months, and then walking, during the second year. Ainsworth et al. (1978) characterize Phase 3 as "maintenance of proximity to a discriminated figure by locomotion as well as signals" (p. 25). They state, "Once locomotion has been acquired, the child is able to seek proximity to his attachment figure(s) on his own account" (p. 6). The infant becomes able to maintain proximity with the caregiver not only by nonverbal communicative exchange, but also by means of locomotion. Locomotion also sets the foundation for new infant exploratory behavior. By means of locomotion, the infant is able to move away from the attachment figure to explore the immediate environment as well as to return to him or her as needed. Such behavior is an early sign of a secure attachment bond.

Ainsworth identified several new, ambulation-enabled contact-seeking and contact-maintaining attachment behaviors that appear by the end of the first year: (1) preference for approaching the attachment figure, especially upon reunion or when distressed; (2) following the attachment figure when she or he leaves the room; (3) using the attachment figure as a secure base for exploration (i.e., "making exploratory excursions from the mother, returning to her from time to time, and terminating exploratory behavior and attempting to regain proximity if she moves off"); and (4) flight to the attachment figure as a safe haven when alarmed (Marvin & Britner, 2008, pp. 277–278). Two other new attachment behaviors are often, but not necessarily, paired with the preference for ambulation to the attachment figure: burying the face in the attachment figure's lap and clinging to the attachment figure when frightened, ill, or distressed.

In a "good enough infant–caregiver system" (Sander, 1975), the infant's manifestations of the primary attachment bond contribute to the strengthening of that bond and to interpersonal conditions that promote important developmental advances. As the infant shows preferential attachment behavior toward the primary attachment figure and is more and more attentive and responsive to her or him, the capable caregiver is delighted and is drawn to become even more attentive and responsive to the infant. The attachment-promoting behaviors of the caregiver continue, but in response to new capacities and expressions from the infant, the caregiver modifies those behaviors in ways that make them relevant and beneficial to the infant's developmental advances. From the caregiver's continuing interest and engagement, now enhanced by the infant's greater relational expression, she or he carefully attunes to the familiar and also newly emerging expressions of the infant. When the infant makes a spontaneous affective display, the caregiver responds, usually with exaggerated sounds, gestures, and affective facial expressions. The infant begins to recognize the cause-and-effect relationship between expressions and responses and becomes able to take initiative to intentionally elicit desired responses from the caregiver. This "infant eliciting behavior" enhances the infant's experience of the availability and responsiveness of the caregiver. In this dynamic, each cues and elicits responses from the other in a kind of expressive, affective dance. The caregiver mimics, exaggerates, and amplifies the infant's verbalizations and gestures, which serve to validate, reinforce, and strengthen the infant's developing affective experience (D. P. Brown, 1993).

Through this mutual responsivity (Field, 1978) and reciprocal affective display, the infant receives mirroring feedback that reinforces early affect experience. Further, as the caregiver expresses herself or himself in ways that are not yet available to the infant, whose affect system was initially limited to the rudimentary, stereotyped reactions of the automatic facial display system (Tomkins, 1962), the infant has the opportunity to experience and mimic new affective possibilities and range. Imitative capacity continues to serve the infant's development and at this phase imitation can be deferred for longer and longer durations (Meltzoff & Moore, 1977), which allows the infant to express imitated affect expressions during a wider range of circumstances.

Several maturational events are preconditions for the expansion of the infant's affect range and depth and allow the infant to maximally benefit from the dynamic interchange with the caregiver. By the beginning of Phase 3, the infant's autonomic nervous system, which regulates heart rate, respiration, digestion, perspiration, salivation, and other physiological functions, becomes more organized and stable (Izard, Porges, Simons, & Hayes, 1991; Lewis, 1971). This greater consistency of internal visceral experience enhances the infant's self-observational capacity and, in conjunction with emerging cognitive developments, supports greater clarification and identification of affective states as they occur.

The infant's greater awareness of internal affective states and the shifts among them, combined with the clear differentiation of attachment figures from others, with deepening experience with a primary attachment figure, and with several cognitive advancements, contributes to the emergence of the "eighth month anxieties" (D. P. Brown, 1993, p. 16). Prior to five or six months of age, infants' expressions of fear are limited to the automatic facial displays and are not particularly synchronized with internal visceral experience or with specific stimuli. But at around eight months, facial expressive and/or autonomic fear reactions appear in response to strangers, to some separations from attachment figures, to some novel or unfamiliar objects or surroundings, and to looming visual stimuli (Marks, 1987). Marvin and Britner (2008) note that "during the last quarter of the first year infants increasingly are more wary of unfamiliar adults than they are of unfamiliar nonhuman objects" (p. 279). They also point to findings showing that most infants develop person permanence before permanence of objects (Bell, 1970). The development of person and object permanence beginning at around eight months of age implies that the infant has and is able to respond to some sort of internal image that can be held and compared against what is present in the immediate external environment. Operation with such images supports comparative evaluations of familiar and unfamiliar people, places, and objects. Though wariness and stranger and separation anxiety emerge in response to autonomic and cognitive advancements, their presence further contributes to the experiential bond with the primary attachment figure by intensifying the infant's differential sense of safety with her or him.

Significant integration and differentiation processes occur from about 9 to 12 months (Greenspan & Lourie, 1981). With object permanence, the infant is able to search for hidden objects or anticipate a whole object in response to seeing part of it (Piaget, 1981). Facial displays and internal visceral experience become synchronized, facilitated by attuned engagement and responsiveness from the caregiver:

> Interpersonally, the integration of affective expression and experience constitutes the outcome of careful mirroring of the child's internal state upon the care-giver's recognition of an affective display. When the mother says to the child, "Don't be frightened," the mother acknowledges the child's affective display and simultaneously draws attention to the child's internal visceral experience. As this empathic response is repeated during many infant–care-giver interactions, synchronization of affective expression and experience is increased. (D. P. Brown, 1993, p. 18)

An important cognitive development during this period also contributes to this synchronization. The caregiver's earlier and ongoing attunement and mirroring and the dynamic reciprocal affective display pattern begins the process of the infant's clarification and differentiation of affective states; but before about nine months of age, the infant has not developed the cognitive capacity for these states to be well differentiated. Between 9 and 12 months, the cognitive developmental milestone of the ability to group and categorize develops (Inagaki, 1989). With the emergence of categorical cognition, the continuing interpersonal mirroring has an even greater effect on promoting differentiation among affective states, and also on greater linkage of those internal states to external expressions. Subsequent affective experience becomes more differentiated and is grouped into categories, leading to experiential identification of discrete emotional states, such as happy, sad, mad, and scared. Through and during continued interaction, the infant gets better at recognizing and now categorizing his or her affect states, and the infant's affective displays become less automatic and stereotyped and more autonomous and directly related to discrete states of experience. As such, they serve as better, more accurate means of social communication.

THE CAREGIVER'S ROLE IN PHASE 3 DEVELOPMENTAL ACHIEVEMENTS

Before describing the next significant attachment-related developmental emergence, a brief review of the normative, healthy developmental achievements up to 12 months and some consideration of the factors that support this development are warranted. Recognition of these factors is an important component of understanding the significance of the next developmental emergence. By the end of the first year, the infant in a good-enough infant–caregiver system has the capacity for a wide range of genuine affective experiences (Kagan, 1978). Self-awareness has continued to refine and expand, as the development of categorical cognition allows the infant to form a "categorical self" (Lewis & Brooks, 1978), from which rudimentary categories of self-experience begin to emerge. Stern (1985) refers to this appearance as the emergence of the "subjective self" and adds that the infant soon "discover[s] that there are other minds out there" (p. 27). At around this time, this infant is likely to show some secure base behavior, which Ainsworth et al. (1978) described as the hallmark of attachment: The infant leaves the caregiver to explore the immediate environment, becomes afraid, returns to the "secure base" of the caregiver, experiences comfort and reassurance, and again leaves the caregiver and returns to exploration of the immediate environment.

These emergent capacities are dependent on both the infant's maturational processes and the caregivers' ways of being with the infant, and, as noted already, these two factors are interdependent; each influences and shapes the other. Several of the newborn infant's innate behaviors engage caregivers and shape their responses in ways that promote the infant's safety and development, and caregivers' responses contribute to the maturation of the infant's various systems and capacities, which in turn yield new infant behaviors that further engage a particular caregiver, who responds and provides experiences that foster further maturation. The foundations of affect and self-development, as well as the formation of an attachment bond, occur through this dynamic.

Many studies have examined the relative contribution of caregiver behavior in the development of a secure attachment bond. Jay Belsky and Pasco Fearon (2008) extensively reviewed the available evidence and concluded that though "associations between rearing and attachment are only modest in magnitude" (p. 304), "it is indisputable that Ainsworth's core theoretical proposition linking maternal sensitivity with attachment security has been empirically confirmed" (p. 300). They describe Ainsworth's proposition as follows:

> At the core of Ainsworth's extension of Bowlby's attachment theory was the contention that a sensitive, responsive caregiver is of fundamental importance to the development of a secure as opposed to an insecure attachment bond during the opening years of life. According to Ainsworth, a caregiver capable of providing security-inducing, sensitive, responsive care understands the child's individual attributes; accepts the child's behavioral proclivities; and is thus capable of consistently orchestrating harmonious interactions between self and child, especially those in which the soothing of distress is involved. (p. 295)

Based on our review of the literature pertaining to caregiver behavior that fosters attachment security, we have identified a set of behaviors and qualities of being that includes, specifies, and expands upon the components of maternal sensitivity. This set can be divided into two categories: *General factors* are the minimum, foundational conditions within which the *five primary behaviors that promote secure attachment* occur. Ideally, these factors and behaviors are present from the infant's birth and continue into early childhood and beyond. The general factors are *physical presence*, *consistency* of beneficial caregiving factors and behaviors, *reliability* of caregivers' availability and provision of caregiving, and *interest* in the infant and his or her individuality. The five primary behaviors that promote secure attachment are behaviors that provide *protection* of the infant; *attunement* to the infant's behavior, inner state, and current developmental capacities; *soothing* and *reassurance* when the child is upset; *expressed delight* in both what the child does and, most important, the infant's unique being; and *unconditional support and encouragement* for inner and outer exploration. These five primary caregiver behaviors are important particularly for the experiences that they foster in the infant. For example, while protective behavior ensures the physical protection of the infant, even more important for attachment security is the infant's *felt sense of safety* with the caregiver; similarly, soothing and reassurance is an immediate response to states of distress, but more important is the infant's experience over time of a *felt sense of comfort* with the caregiver. These five caregiver behaviors and the corresponding infant experiences are described further in Chapter 7.

These caregiver behaviors and ways of being promote the infant's sense of attachment security and provide the experiential, relational foundation for the emergence of a secure attachment bond. Two significant cognitive developments in the infant lead to the structuralization of these relational experiences into the foundation of the attachment bond, the formation of an internal working model, or map, of the attachment relationship. The first cognitive advance, already addressed, is the capacity to categorize experience, which allows the infant to link newly distinct affect states to particular caregivers. The other is the development of *representational cognition*, the capacity to *symbolically represent* the qualities of the caregiver relationship internally.

THE DEVELOPMENT OF REPRESENTATIONAL COGNITION

Between about 12 and 20 months, the infant's cognitive system develops the capacity to link experiences to thought-based symbols (D. P. Brown, 1993). The first sign of this capacity is the infant's looking at particular objects when someone speaks the words that symbolically represent those objects. The emergence of expressive language indicates the presence of at least rudimentary representational cognition, as language itself is a representational system. According to Tomasello (2010), verbal linguistic communication evolves from infants' earlier presymbolic use of nonverbal gesturing and pointing to specific objects to the use of specific words as symbols to indicate those objects after about 12 months (p. 151). This shift is supported by the development of the cognitive capacity for internal, symbolic representation.

Less visible during this period is the development of internal, symbolic representations of self and of others. While rudimentary internal representations are present earlier, allowing differentiation of caregivers, object permanence, and the eighth-month anxieties, the earlier representations develop from presymbolic experiential and imitative memory impressions of infant–caregiver interaction. These presymbolic impressions form simple image-based schemas (Greenspan & Lourie, 1981; Lewis & Brooks, 1978), and "at that point, the internal 'experiments' the child conducts take place as image sequences, in which images serve as activating and terminating conditions for other images" (Marvin & Britner, 2008, p. 284). During the second year of life, there is a large storehouse of these impressions and image-based imitative action-memory sequences and schemas. With the emergence of representational cognition, these become the material for the formation of internal symbolic representations of self and others.

In Margaret Mahler's object relations model of separation-individuation (Mahler et al., 1975), the rapprochement subphase, beginning at about 15 months, entails the development of separate internal representations of self and of others. By the end of the second year of life, the normally-developed child has established distinct and stable self and other representations that are in dynamic relationship internally. The internal representations of attachment relationships are what Bowlby (1969/1982) named "internal working models" of attachment, and what we call "attachment maps." Understanding the nature of these representations, and especially the ways of modifying or remapping them, is particularly valuable, as the nature of the IWMs or attachment maps is what determines attachment behavior during childhood and throughout adult life.

Of great import for understanding internal working models of attachment is consideration of what forms the content of the infant's object representation of the primary attachment relationship. Obviously, central to this representation are the infant's various experiences with the attachment figure. In a good-enough infant–caregiver system, the representation of the caregiver will include the caregiver's protectiveness, attunement, soothing, delight, and support, and also the infant's *affective experience* in response to those behaviors and ways of being. D. P. Brown (1993) highlights the integration of affect with the newly developing self and other representations:

> The symbolic self representation and object representations and the previously developed capacity for differentiated affective experience are synthesized into a common line. From this point in development and thereafter, affective states become associated with the inner experience of self and object representations. (p. 20)

Affective states become embedded in a dynamic web of internal representations of self and other, giving the representations an affective component. The infant now carries internal representations of the self, of the attachment figure, of the relationship, and of the *experiential quality of the relationship.* Feelings about the self and others become linked to their internal images, and the infant gains the ability to represent the affective *quality* of interactions.

The quality of the interactions—the feelings associated with the relationship between the infant and the caregiver—are fundamental components of the attachment map. In aggregate over time, experiences and feelings such as safety, comfort, soothing, availability, reliability, and stability will tend to create an attachment map in which these qualities are prominent. Such an attachment map is considered secure. When over time an infant has experiences of the caregiver as unsafe, agitating, unreliable, unattuned, rejecting, and confusing, these qualities will be prominent in the resulting attachment representation. This type of map is considered insecure.

Formed and shaped by experiences with the attachment figure, the representations develop an independent functional existence, as they remain and can be related to by the infant when the attachment figure is not present. The infant can have experiences and feelings about the self, about the attachment figure, and about their relationship in response to the internal representations, not only in response to immediate, direct contact with the attachment figure. Further, the representations function as symbolic models of the self, others, and the relationship, and as such set up expectations about interactions.

INTERNAL REPRESENTATIONS, AFFECT TOLERANCE, AND AFFECT SELF-REGULATION

The ability to fully experience a range of differentiated affects results from the maturational and relational dynamics of the early Phase 3 period. As described above, the stabilization of the autonomic nervous system, the intensification of the infant–caregiver relationship and their reciprocal affective displays, and the emergence of categorical cognition all contribute to the infant's ability to *have* various and distinct emotional experiences. But the capacity to experience a range of emotions is independent of the ability to *tolerate* and *self-regulate* them. Affect tolerance and self-regulation are dependent on the ability to evoke representations of soothing, which is dependent both on sufficient experience of being soothed when distressed and on the formation of internal representations of those soothing experiences (D. P. Brown, 1993; Mikulincer & Shaver, 2008).

Max Schur's (1955) notion of the "hallucinatory breast" is an example of an internal representation that provides soothing. An infant feels the tension of hunger as distress, and when he or she is fed through the mother's breast, that distress is soothed by receiving milk and by the comfort of being held close to the mother's body. Repeated experiences of this soothing, combined with the development of representational cognition, lead to internal representations of the breast and associated feelings of soothing. The infant is then better able to tolerate and self-regulate hunger distress, because when the mother is not immediately available, he or she can evoke the representation of her breast (Schur's "hallucinatory breast") and the associated feelings of soothing, comfort, and satiety.

A child's use of "transitional objects" (Winnicott, 1953) is another example of how representations can support affect tolerance and self-regulation. A blanket, doll, or any other object selected by a child becomes a symbolic representation of the experience of soothing and comfort. It is not the caregiver, but it is associated with the caregiver and the soothing and comforting that the child experiences from her or him. It is more immediately available than the caregiver, and the child can use it as a tool for affect tolerance and self-regulation. Gradually, the experience of soothing and comfort both from caregivers and from the use of the transitional object become internalized and form internal representations of soothing and comfort. When these representations are present and stable, the child lets go of reliance on the transitional object.

The presence of an internal representation or internal working model of an attachment figure who is present, protective, attuned, comforting, and soothing is a foundation of the capacity for affect tolerance and regulation. According to D. P. Brown (1993),

In a good enough child–care-giver system, the child repeatedly experiences the care-giver's soothing, affect-modulating responses. As the child's representational capacity matures, he or she is able to sustain an internal representation of the care-giver's soothing function for longer and longer durations. The child intentionally returns to the care-giver as a secure base when necessary. Repeated experiences of the care-giver's soothing coupled with the maturation of representational capacity results in internalization of the soothing function. (pp. 21–22)

Heinz Kohut (1971) and Marian Tolpin (1971) use the term "transmuting internalization" for the gradual process of replacing the affect-modulating function of the caregiver with an internal self-soothing structure. Tolpin describes this process as involving "bit-by-bit accretion of psychic structure" (p. 319) and indicates its importance not only for the development of affect self-regulation but also for the structuralization and cohesion of the self.

The more able, reliable, and consistent the caregiver is at accurately attuning to the infant's distress states and their likely sources, and the more able, reliable, and consistent she or he is at providing soothing and comfort, the stronger and more stable will be the infant's internal representations of that experience and the better the infant will become at affect tolerance and self-regulation as well as self-organization. The converse is also true: Consistent failures in good-enough attunement and provision of soothing lead to impaired affect experience, tolerance, self-regulation, and self-organization. As described in Chapter 5, insecure attachment and adult personality disorders are associated with problems in each of these domains.

THE EMERGENCE OF PROTOTYPICAL ATTACHMENT PATTERNS

Although the attachment bond gradually develops and strengthens during the first year of life, the nature of the bond, secure or insecure, remains quite malleable until the infant develops the capacity to symbolically represent the qualities of the attachment relationship internally. It is interesting that the period up until about 12 months appears to be a "sensitive period" for the formation of attachment. Marvin and Britner (2008) highlight Bowlby's suggestion that "the readiness to become quickly attached remains intact at least through the end of the first year" (p. 280). Attachment bonds can and certainly do form after the first year, but evidence suggests that such later-forming bonds tend to be more complicated in their development and less adaptive than bonds that form by or soon after the end of the first year (Marvin & Britner, 2008). As the capacity for internal, symbolic, mental representation begins to form at about 12 months, the infant's experiences with the attachment figure during the first year and from then on begin to become structured as internal representations. This structuralization creates relative stability of the representations. Once the attachment representations are formed, they can be modified, but any modification requires changing of the existing representations rather than the simpler process of spontaneous coalescing or cohering of experience into the initial representations. This process explains the malleability of the attachment bond during the sensitive period of the first year of life and the relative stability of the attachment prototypes once they emerge during the second year.

The attachment prototypes are the main forms of internal working models or attachment maps that are created by the internal representation of the infant's experiences with caregivers, particularly with the primary attachment figure. Each prototype describes a typical pattern of behavior that is likely to occur with close others and also reflects an underlying set of expectations about the behavior of close others. Ainsworth et al.'s (1978) three prototypes of infant attachment—avoidant (A), secure (B), and ambivalent/resistant (C)—and Mary Main and Judith Solomon's (1986) addition of disorganized/disoriented (D) attachment all emerge as observable, consistent patterns of attachment behavior starting at around one year of age.

Using the Strange Situation procedure (SS), Ainsworth et al. (1978) found that the A, B, and C prototypes of attachment are very stable from 12 to 18 months. Likewise, 62% of the children in the Minnesota Longitudingal Study received the same SS attachment classification at 12 months and again at 18 months (Sroufe et al., 2005). A small number of children in this study changed from secure to insecure between 12 and 18 months.

> Mothers of infants securely attached at 12 months but insecure at 18 months demonstrated similar caregiving skills in infancy but differed in affective and personality characteristics compared to mothers of stably secure infants. Both groups were observed to accommodate to newborn cues and needs; however, declining security was related to low ratings of maternal joy, pleasure, and gratification, as measured in feeding interactions at 6 months. Thus, whereas specific caregiving skills, such as pacing and timing, may contribute to the formation of attachment, affective behavior appeared to be influential in maintaining adaptive relationships. (Sroufe et al., 2005, pp. 103–104)

Most of these mothers had three to five children already when the infant being studied was born. These mothers likely felt affectively engaged with the young infant at first, but over the first year became less so, coming to just "go through the motions" with the new child in the context of having many other children to whom to attend. Relevant here is Bowlby's oft-quoted statement about the optimal infant–caregiver emotional environment: "The infant and young child should experience a warm, intimate, and continuous relationship with his mother (or

permanent mother substitute) in which both find satisfaction and enjoyment"
(1951, p. 11).

Some children in the Minnesota study changed from insecure at 12 months
to secure at 18 months:

> Mothers in these relationships had often been young and relatively imma-
> ture, and initially responded negatively to pregnancy. Over the course of
> the first year, maternal negative attitudes became more positive, and moth-
> ers became more skillful at caregiving . . . Thus, as their mothers matured
> and took to the caregiving task, the infants began to thrive. (p. 104)

These findings are good news about the possibility of developing secure
attachment in just a few months after initial insecurity. Even so, it is important to
recognize the relative stability of attachment prototypes over time.

Attachment Behavior During the Toddler Period (18 to 36 Months)

The emergence of a prototypical attachment pattern during the second year, based
on the establishment of an underlying internal working model, is a milestone of
attachment-related development. Normative research indicates that from then
until about three years, there occur no significant internal structural changes
in attachment dynamics. Marvin and Britner (2008) state, on the basis of their
review of studies of developmental changes in attachment behavior during the
first several years of life, that "from 1 until about 3 years of age the organization
of the youngster's attachment to the caregiver remains relatively unchanged" (p.
287). Although the internal organization of attachment is fairly stable during this
period, based on the stable internal working model, there are visible changes in
attachment behavior that arise from other developmental advances.

The Strange Situation procedure was designed for use with younger children, but studies have also looked at the behavior of two- and three-year-olds in
this protocol. While the same prototypical attachment patterns are observable at
these ages, some behavioral changes are notable. According to Marvin and Britner (2008), the toddler years are characterized by a marked increase in exploratory behavior as the child makes use of his or her more developed motor and
cognitive abilities. In the Strange Situation, toddlers, as compared to one-year-
olds, show greater and more extensive exploratory behavior and shorter physical
contact need during reunion episodes before resuming exploration away from
the caregiver. Moreover, the toddler shows greater skill in monitoring the caregiver's location, behavior, and attentiveness during exploratory episodes. Karen
(1998) reports that even by 18 months, infants who have secure attachment are
less distressed by separation episodes than when they were younger and do not
need as much physical contact during reunion episodes. However, Marvin and

Britner (2008) report that two-year-olds are as distressed as one-year-olds at separations that they don't initiate, but that they engage in more verbal calling and active search than crying. Marvin and his colleagues (Marvin, 1972; Marvin, VanDevender, Iwanaga, LeVine, & LeVine, 1977) reported that two-year-olds showed attachment behavior in the SS similar to that of one-year-olds, except that the toddlers cried less during reunion episodes, and although the two-year-olds showed a greater need of proximity after the stranger entered the room and at reunion, physical-proximity-seeking decreased and was partially replaced by verbal expressions. Sroufe et al. (2005) state that the major developmental issue during the toddler years is "guided self-regulation" (p. 66), which involves increasing self-regulation but continued dependence on the caregiver for cues, feedback, and support.

During the period from 18 to 36 months, verbal communication becomes increasingly complex (Marvin & Britner, 2008). The secure child develops elaborate affective concepts and fantasies and develops some skill in verbalizing affective states (D. P. Brown, 1993). Cooperative behavior also increases. For example, secure 18-month-olds show altruistic behavior in the form of opening a cabinet door when their mothers' hands are full (Tomasello, 2009).

Three-year-olds show important changes in the SS as compared to younger children. According to Ainsworth et al. (1978), three-year-olds "seemed little disturbed by the first separation episode, and maintained exploratory behavior at a high level until Episode 6, when they were left alone" (p. 200). They were much less distressed than younger children by brief separations and required less physical contact and physical proximity during reunion episodes. Marvin and Britner (2008) state, "By age 3, a child's locomotor skills have developed to the point where he or she can assume much of the responsibility for gaining and maintaining proximity to the attachment figure under most conditions" (p. 283).

Attachment Behavior During the Preschool Years (3 to 5 Years of Age)

Sroufe et al. (2005) describe the major developmental issue during the preschool years, from about age three to age five, as increasing self-regulation independent of the caregiver. Other important related issues include greater self-agency with support from the caregiver, greater self-direction and self-management, and increasing peer competence. Secure (B) and ambivalent (C) three-and-a-half-year-olds as compared to avoidant (A) same-age children have more positive peer relationships (Cassidy, Kirsh, Scolton, & Parke, 1996). In the Strange Situation, four-year-olds as compared to younger children are less disturbed by separation and maintain a high level of exploratory behavior (Ainsworth et al., 1978; see also Ainsworth, 1990).

During the preschool years, the ongoing developmental processes interact with the attachment patterns that developed earlier to produce greater differentiation of attachment subtype behavior. Crittenden (2008) suggests that during this period, children begin to show the capacity for coy behavior (e.g., half-smile with teeth covered, sideways glance, chin down and to the side, toes and knees together; p. 26) and for false-positive affect, both of which reflect newly available strategies for avoiding punishment, rejection, or aggression and for eliciting nurturance. Although Crittenden identifies these strategies as deceptive and coercive, she emphasizes that preschoolers "are not capable of intentional deception" and "merely use a behavior that functions to meet their immediate needs, given their parents' behavior" (p. 27).

The Preschool Assessment of Attachment (Crittenden, 1992a, 1992b), based on observing Strange Situation behavior, differentiates six preschool attachment patterns: secure/balanced, defended, coercive, defended/coercive, anxious-depressed, and insecure/other. Cassidy and Marvin (1992) identify five preschool types of attachment patterns from SS observations: secure, avoidant, ambivalent, controlling/disorganized, and insecure/other.

Sroufe et al. (2005) observed that the four attachment prototypes first observed in one-year-olds are associated with specific "preschool profiles" (p. 142). Children earlier identified as having the avoidant (A) subtype become hostile/mean, emotionally insulated, asocial, and disconnected during the preschool years. Ambivalent/resistant (C) children show anxious, overstimulated, and passive-dependent patterns by three and a half years (p. 142). Disorganized (D) children, who previously failed to show any definable attachment prototype, show signs of organization in the form of controlling behaviors (Solomon & George, 1999). The most problematic preschool behaviors were found in disorganized children, who by 36 months showed more defensive aggression toward peers and more disruptive behaviors at preschool than did secure and other insecure attachment types (Solomon & George, 1999). They also showed more anxiety about school performance and lower self-esteem than other same-age children in preschool (Lyons-Ruth, Alpern, & Repacholi, 1993).

Phase 4: Goal-Corrected Partnership

According to Marvin and Britner (2008), during the third year of life children "come to realize that others have their own feelings, goals, and plans" (p. 285), and "research suggest[s] that the *organization* of the attachment system changes significantly between the ages of 3 and 5 years" (p. 282). They cite findings showing that three-year-olds, when learning that their mother was about to initiate a separation, would either accept or protest her departure but would not engage in setting up a shared plan regarding the departure and reunion; in contrast, four-year-olds would engage in negotiation with their mother to establish a shared plan and then would not be distressed by the separation. Marvin and Britner attribute this shift to changes in the dynamics of the internal working models that result from developments in the child's information-processing capacities between three and a half and five years of age. "No longer limited to sequential processing through a chain-linked network of thoughts-images-plans, this older preschooler can now comprehend two or more of these images as component parts of yet a higher-order image-goal-plan" (p. 285).

This capacity to hold multiple components of higher-order conceptualizations, including relationships, is the foundation for Bowlby's (1969/1982) and Ainsworth's (1972) Phase 4, labeled "goal-corrected partnership." Ainsworth et al. (1978) draw from Marvin's (1972, 1977) work to differentiate Phase 4 from Phase 3. They state that around the end of the third year, the child "becomes increasingly capable of inferring his mother's plans and goals, and of coordinating them with his own, both conceptually and behaviorally" (Ainsworth et al., 1978, p. 204). The four-year-old child is able to "understand his mother's perspective, and consequently to realize that she has plans of her own, to infer something of what they are, and therefore to be able to communicate with her more effectively in his attempts to get her to accept a mutual plan compatible with his own" (p. 205). The child can now actively engage with his or her attachment figure to identify and take action toward mutually negotiated goals.

Marvin and Britner (2008) state that the four-year-old's new organization of attachment behavior results in interactions with attachment figures based more on physical orientation, eye contact, nonverbal expressions, affect, and personal conversations and less on physical proximity and contact.

> An older preschooler has come to organize attachment behavior in a new way—one that enables the child to realize that he or she and an attachment figure have a continuing relationship, whether or not they are in close proximity. (p. 287)

Increasingly, the secure child's internal working model of the attachment relationship represents the attachment figure as available independent of proximity—when the attachment figure is not physically present, the child can call upon the representation for reassurance and soothing, and has trust that the actual attachment figure will be available in conditions of upset and need. This attachment map supports the four-year-old child's growing comfort with exploring the physical and interpersonal world, behavior that promotes self-development, including interactions with nonfamiliar peers and adults.

Attachment Patterns in School Age Children (5 to 7 Years of Age)

Several studies have investigated similarities and differences between attachment patterns in the Strange Situation at one year and again at six years of age. Main and Cassidy (1988) modified the SS to develop a reunion paradigm for six-year-olds. It consists of a one-hour separation period during which the child reviews photos of various parent–child separations and then a sandbox free-play period before the caregiver returns. The Main and Cassidy study did not include ambivalent (C) children in the original sample. The other three groups—A, B, and D—showed an 84% concordance rate in attachment prototype classification over the five-year span. Main and Cassidy also found some important differences in the attachment patterns of one- and six-year-olds. The main difference was that six-year-olds primarily used language, not physical proximity, to express the need for attachment at reunion episodes. For example, secure six-year-olds tended to initiate conversations about separation and reunion. When avoidant six-year-olds experienced reunion, they looked at their caregivers only very briefly, spoke in a limited way, and tended to continue to play with toys. Disorganized/controlling six-year-olds assumed a parental role and attempted to control or direct the parent's attention and behavior. Two subtypes of controlling behaviors emerged in this group: Punitive disorganized children embarrassed and humiliated the caregiver upon reunion; caretaking disorganized children were overly acquiescent and attempted to direct parental behavior during reunion. The authors noted a link between disorganization and later controlling behaviors, highlighting the "transformation of disorganized into controlling reunion behavior" (p. 422).

Wartner, Grossmann, Fremmer-Bombik, and Suess (1994) used Main and Cassidy's reunion protocol for six-year-olds and included in their German sample children with either an A, B, C, or D classification from observations of SS behavior at 12 or 18 months. They found a comparable 82% concordance rate in attachment prototype classification over the five-year span, and the behaviors of the children across the two study periods were similar to what Main and Cassidy reported for their American sample. Wartner et al. reported that for children classified as secure at both study periods, the main difference between reunion episode behavior at 12 to 18 months and six years of age was that at age six there was less physical-proximity-seeking at reunion but greater verbal expression whereby the child and caregiver talked about what happened during separation. Avoidant six-year-olds turned away from the caregiver at reunion and showed little or no interaction or communication, very similar to how they behaved at reunion in the earlier assessment. Only one of the study subjects was classified as ambivalent at age six. The concordance rate of disorganized attachment from the first assessment to six years was 75%, lower than the concordance for the other attachment prototypes but still impressive.

In this same study, observations of the preschool behavior of the children at age five revealed that the children who were identified as secure at age six initiated play, become more concentrated during play, were more friendly, had fewer peer conflicts, were more competent in conflict management, and had fewer behavioral problems compared to six-year-olds in the insecure categories.

Interestingly, when children's overall preschool behavior was classified as "competent" or "incompetent" based on ratings of various elements,

> the majority of children classified as secure [were] found in the competent group, the children classified as disorganized [were] almost equally distributed among the competent and incompetent groups, and the children classified as avoidant were overrepresented in the incompetent groups. (Wartner et al., 1994, p. 1021)

Disorganized six-year-olds did show more odd and aggressive behaviors than other children. Judith Solomon and Carol George (1999) suggest that at this age, disorganized children engage in power struggles and are likely to manifest high levels of behavior problems. According to Teti, Gelfand, Messinger, and Isabella, 1995), disorganized attachment in early years becomes behavioral disorganization in later childhood.

Attachment During Middle Childhood (7 to 12 Years of Age)

During the years of middle childhood, approximately from ages 7 to 12, children experience more and longer separations from their parents because of their participation in school and other activities. Kathryn Kerns (2008) notes that "by middle childhood children have a clear preference for peers rather than parents as playmates" (p. 367). Ideally, they adapt to these separations by coming to use peers and adults other than their parents as a secure base. Children become less reliant on the physical proximity of parental attachment figures and more reliant on them for their general availability, particularly during times of distress (Marvin & Britner, 2008). More and more, the child takes on the function of self-protection rather than relying solely on parental attachment figures for protection. However, there is indication that despite this greater reliance on self and others, "even 11- and 12-year-old children show a strong preference for parents over peers . . . when asked about situations likely to invoke the need for an attachment figure" (Kerns, 2008, p. 368).

According to Sroufe et al. (2005), secure middle childhood children show significantly higher school and peer competence than insecure children. Insecure avoidant children in this age range show less contact-seeking, and insecure anxious-resistant children seek undue guidance, reassurance, and nurturance from adults. Cassidy et al. (1996) found that peer perception in middle childhood is affected by the way a child perceives the parental attachment figure in early childhood. For example, if an avoidant child perceived the parents as rejecting in early childhood, he or she is more likely at this age to perceive peers as having hostile intent. Cassidy et al. state, "The representation of the parent generalizes to the representation of peers" (1996, p. 901). Kerns (2008) raises the question of whether at this age children develop the unitary, integrated internal working model of attachment relationships that she notes that Main, Kaplan, and Cassidy (1985) described as a "state of mind with respect to attachment," or if they continue to operate from representations of distinct attachment figures. She suggests that children who have consistent experiences with different attachment figures may form a "general, internally consistent representation of attachment relationships" (Kerns, 2008, p. 368), whereas this development may not occur until adolescence in children who have had "very different experiences with different attachment figures" (p. 368).

Attachment Patterns During Adolescence

The majority of adolescents retain their prototypical IWMs of attachment from earlier childhood. According to Joseph Allen and Deborah Land (1999), adolescent attachment behavior is characterized by "the emergence of a single overarching attachment organization, which predicts future behavior with offspring and with marital partners" (p. 320). The major shift of adolescence is the development of formal operational thinking. Formal operational thinking

> lets the individual begin to construct, from experiences with multiple caregivers, a more overarching stance toward attachment experiences . . . [The adolescent is able to] compare relationships with different attachment figures both to one another and to hypothetical ideals . . . to represent multiple divergent attachment experiences. (p. 320; see also J. P. Allen, 2008)

The adolescent is able to manage the goal-corrected partnership with each parent as an attachment figure with "increased sophistication" (p. 320). The adolescent progressively becomes more and more independent, yet still turns to parental attachment figures in times of extreme stress (p. 321). Allen (2008) adds that the goal-corrected partnership of the adolescent and his or her parents is characterized less by coordination and more by negotiation (p. 420). He adds, "The issue is primarily one of developing a new balance between attachment behaviors (and cognitions) regarding parents and the adolescent's exploratory needs" (p. 421). There will come a time, however, that the late adolescent will become more and more autonomous and actively avoid seeking parents as a secure base at times of stress. Allen and Land emphasize that "adolescent autonomy-seeking behavior can be viewed as part of the exploratory system" (1999, p. 321). Peer relationships take on a primary role in supporting this developing autonomy and exploratory behavior:

> By midadolescence, interactions with peers have begun to take on many of the functions that they will serve for the remainder of the lifespan—pro-

viding important sources of intimacy, feedback about social behavior, . . . and ultimately attachment relationships and lifelong partnerships. (p. 322)

Allen (2008) adds that dependencies are transferred more and more from parental to peer relationships, and that "by midadolescence, interactions with peers have begun to take on many of the functions they will serve for the remainder of the lifespan" (p. 422).

Adolescence is also characterized by the initial attempts at romantic intimate attachments. According to Allen and Land, these romantic relationships often have the same fundamental characteristics as early child–caregiver attachment relationships with respect to (1) proximity-seeking, (2) secure base, (3) safe haven, and (4) separation protest. By late adolescence, certain long-term peer and intimate relationships serve the same functions as early childhood attachment relationships, especially for adolescents with secure attachment (1999, p. 323). Throughout adolescent identity formation and the shift to greater autonomy, parental attachment figures nevertheless still serve as a secure base for the adolescent's separation:

> A central function of the adolescent's attachment relationship with parents may be to provide an emotional secure base from which the adolescent can explore the wide range of emotional states that arise when he or she is learning to live as a relatively autonomous adult. (p. 330)

Several studies have investigated the manifestations of insecure attachment in adolescence. Allen and Hauser (1996) found that of the four attachment prototypes, adolescents with dismissing attachment showed the least autonomy as well as the least relatedness in interactions with parents. They believe that the dismissing adolescent's disengagement from parental attachment figures may interfere with the normal developmental task of renegotiating the parent–adolescent relationship. Becker-Stoll and Fremmer-Bombik (1997) found that dismissing attachment in adolescence was significantly associated with externalizing symptoms. Kobak and Sceery (1988) found that dismissing adolescents were lower on ego-resilience, were more distant and alone, expressed greater hostility, and had lower levels of family support than adolescents of other attachment prototypes. Adolescents with anxious-preoccupied attachment showed greater autonomy-inhibiting behaviors than other groups and were more enmeshed with their parents throughout adolescence. Enmeshment with parents at age 14 predicted anxious-preoccupied attachment at age 25 (Allen & Hauser, 1996). Preoccupied adolescents showed a persistence of involving anger from conflicts with fathers 10 years earlier, a tendency to overly personalize these arguments, and an inability to withdraw from these conflicts. Involving anger was significantly associated with an internalizing coping style and with depression (Allen &

Hauser, 1996). Kobak and Sceery (1988) found that preoccupied adolescents were less ego-resilient, were significantly more anxious, had higher levels of distress, and needed more family support than other adolescents. In contrast, secure adolescents were more ego-resilient, less anxious, and less hostile with peers than insecure adolescents.

Attachment in Adult Intimate Relationships

According to Hazen and Zeifman (1999), certain adult romantic relationships constitute a type of attachment relationship in that they meet the criteria of proximity-seeking, providing a secure base, providing a safe haven, and manifesting separation distress (p. 336). However, in mutual adult relationships, some of these attachment behaviors and functions become oriented toward different purposes. For example, proximity-seeking includes the goal of closeness for physical comfort and soothing but also includes goals based on sexual attraction (p. 348). Also, an adult's experience of having been protected as a child influences caregiving behaviors toward his or her partner and their children, which contributes to the intergenerational transmission of attachment patterns.

The main difference between early child–parent attachment and adult romantic attachments is that childhood attachments are one-sided, whereas in adult secure romantic attachment each partner mutually experiences the other as a secure base. In adult relationships, the goal-corrected partnership entails mutual attachment regulation. According to Hazen and Zeifman (1999), the stages through which a romantic relationship becomes a deep attachment bond include pre-attachment, attachment-in-the-making (falling in love), clear-cut attachment (loving), mutual goal-corrected partnership, and emotional interdependence.

Internal working models of adult attachment are far more complex than the IWMs of early attachment prototypes in that they include elements both of early attachment prototypes and core conflictual relationship themes (Luborsky, 1977; Luborsky & Crits-Christoph, 1998; see Chapter 7) accumulated across a lifetime of relationships. Karen (1998) states:

> Kobak has found that in marriages people don't always act the way their Berkeley adult attachment category would predict. As a result he believes that "adult romantic style may be more the product of adult romantic experience than of childhood relationships." (p. 388)

Adult romantic IWMs are more diverse and flexible than childhood attachment prototypes, at least for those with secure attachment. Those with significant attachment disturbance show less diversity and flexibility and are more likely to manifest a prototype of insecure attachment across a number of adult romantic relationships. For example, after a bad romantic relationship, even the most secure adult is likely to modify internal relational maps in a negative way; after a long-term positive and satisfying romantic involvement, he or she is likely to modify the internal relational maps in a positive way. It is probable that secure adults are more able to update and modify internal relational maps than insecure adults. Feeney (2008) points to the work of Collins and Read (1994), who suggest that adult relational models are complex and hierarchically arranged:

> A set of generalized models lies at the top of the hierarchy, with models for particular classes of relationships (e.g., family members, peers) at an intermediate level, and models for particular relationships (e.g., father, spouse) at the lowest level. Models higher in the hierarchy apply to a wider range of others but are less predictive for any specific situation. (p. 463)

Healthy, secure adults, as compared to insecure adults, have more complex internal relational maps that can be flexibly applied and readily updated by ongoing intimate relationship experiences. People with the greatest attachment disturbance show less flexibility and updating and manifest a similar set of deactivating, hyperactivating, or both deactivating and hyperactivating strategies across most adult relationships. Treating such individuals is the subject of the rest of this book.

PART II

ASSESSMENT

CHAPTER 3

Adult Attachment Prototypes and Their Clinical Manifestations

Appropriate treatment of patients with attachment disturbances must be based on recognition of their particular attachment patterns and dynamics. Formal assessment methods, including the Adult Attachment Interview, are presented in Chapter 4. In this chapter, the main features of each adult attachment prototype are described. We include fundamental etiological factors and also behavioral, experiential, and some assessment-response characteristics of adults with secure attachment and of those with one of the insecure types. Although the AAI is not described in detail until Chapter 4, we include here the relevant patterns of response typical of each attachment type to contribute to the reader's overall sense of how each type manifests.

Securely Attached Adults

Secure attachment in the infant–caregiver bond develops largely as a function of *consistent maternal responsiveness* (Ainsworth, Blehar, Waters, & Wall, 1978) and *contingent matching* (Gergely & Watson, 1996). Securely attached adults report more positive and stronger bonds with their parents (Collins & Read, 1990; Feeney & Noller, 1990; Hazen & Shaver, 1987). Overall interactions with family-of-origin members are generally positive (Diehl, Elnick, Bourbeau, & Labouvie-Vief, 1998). Many but not all secure adults report having had less childhood adversity than insecure individuals (Mickelson, Kessler, & Shaver, 1997).

Secure children in the Strange Situation and secure adults on the AAI find a healthy balance between attachment and autonomous exploration. According to Main and Goldwyn (1998), a secure adult, as indicated by his or her discourse on the AAI, "appears to value attachment relationships and regard attachment-related experiences as influential, but seems relatively independent and objective (autonomous) regarding any particular experience or relationship, and is free to explore thoughts and feelings during the course of the interview" (p. 160).

Secure adults' AAI discourse also indicates that they feel comfortable with attachment and can acknowledge a need to depend on others at times. AAI secure (F) characteristics include a clear valuing of attachment, ease with the topic of attachment, the capacity to talk about attachment themes and experiences with highly coherent discourse, metacognitive monitoring, and fresh speech. Speakers who fit the F category show a strong personal identity and are able to see and articulate how early attachment experiences had an effect on their personality development. They are comfortable with their own limitations and imperfections and can talk about failures of their own parents with a sense of proportion and context, and sometimes with forgiveness and compassion (Hesse, 1999; Main & Goldwyn, 1998).

On the basis of self-report studies of adult romantic attachments, Collins and Read found that "a person with a secure attachment style [is] comfortable with closeness, able to depend on others, and is not worried about being abandoned or unloved" (1990, p. 648). An adult with a secure romantic attachment is likely to experience his or her romantic partner as a secure base for exploration (Fraley & Davis, 1997).

Secure adults are likely to seek emotional support from their partners when distressed (Simpson, Rholes, & Nelligan, 1992) as well as to provide support to a distressed partner (Crowell, Trebaux, & Waters, 1999). When problems arise in relationships, they show an enhanced capacity for self-reflection and greater problem-solving ability; secure-adult relationships tend to be more stable and satisfying than those of insecure adults (Lopez, 2009) and are characterized by greater longevity, trust, commitment, and interdependence (Feeney, Noller, & Callan, 1994).

In general, Bartholomew and Horowitz (1991) found that secure adults

> obtained uniquely high ratings on the coherence of their interviews and the degree of intimacy of their friendships. They also received high ratings on warmth, balance of control in friendships, and level of involvement in romantic relationships . . . [The] secure prototype correlated highly with ratings of coherence . . . intimacy . . . balance of control in friendships . . . level of involvement in romantic relationships . . . self-confidence . . . and warmth. (p. 229)

With respect to attachment, secure adults are readily able to access trust-related memories (Mikulincer, 1998). In fact, secure individuals have greater access to both positive and negative memories than insecure individuals (Lopez, 2009). With respect to sense of self, secure adults are more ego-resilient and less anxious than insecure individuals (Kobak & Sceery, 1988). According to Mikulincer (1995), "secure people have a highly differentiated and integrated self-structure" (p. 1210), and they describe themselves mostly in positive terms but also are able to acknowledge negative self attributes. Overall, they have a coherent, positive sense of self (Obegi & Berant, 2009).

In psychotherapy, secure in contrast to insecure adults are predisposed to experiencing the therapist as a secure base (Obegi & Berant, 2009, p. 62). As compared to insecure patients, secure patients are much more likely "to report positive working alliances and to perceive their therapists as emotionally responsive and accepting" (Mallinckrodt, Coble, & Gantt, 1995; Obegi & Berant, 2009). In therapy, secure patients explore therapeutic issues in greater depth than insecure patients. Mallinckrodt, Porter, and Kivlighan (2005) say:

> Clients who are able to establish a secure attachment with their therapist early in brief treatment are able to achieve greater depth in their experience of sessions, together with a perception of smoothness that may go hand in hand with a sense of safety. (p. 97)

Mallinckrodt et al. (1995) found that security of attachment was significantly positively correlated both with perceiving the therapist as a secure base and with greater depth of exploration in treatment. Such patients have higher self-disclosure in therapy than insecure patients (Mikulincer & Nachshon, 1991).

A summary of possible manifestations of adult attachment security appears in Table 3.1. Each of these characteristics may be more or less present in any particular person.

Dismissing Insecure Adults

Avoidant attachment in children and dismissing attachment in adults is largely the outcome of *consistent and repetitive rejection of the child's attachment behaviors* by the primary attachment figure. Such rejection results in deactivation of the attachment system (Ainsworth et al., 1978; Cassidy & Kobak, 1988; Mikulincer, Shaver, & Pereg, 2003). Active rejection by a caregiver goes beyond the caregiver's simply being unresponsive to the child. According to Obegi and Berant (2009), the child's "natural instinctual tendency to seek proximity and protection when distressed [is] met with punishment, distancing, or neglect . . . [and the child learns to] suppress . . . attachment behavior in order to receive adequate or minimal care" (p. 37).

Marvin and Britner (2008), referring to Ainsworth et al.'s (1978) findings, describe the less actively rejecting parental behaviors that contribute to avoidant patterns in infancy. They say that "parents of infants who are later 'avoidant' tend to terminate their infants' cries less often and hold them less during the first months of life" (p. 277). They continue:

> In such a case, an infant is left in a "painful" state for considerable periods of time. The context is then ripe for the infant eventually to develop alter-

TABLE 3.1. Possible Manifestations of Adult Attachment Types

Secure Attachment
Seeks emotional closeness with others
Able to establish emotional intimacy
Comfortable with mutual dependence
Comfortable being alone
Positive self-image and other image
Warm and open with others
Accepts criticism without significant distress
Strong sense of self
Self-esteem
Self-observational skills
Self-reflective skills
Able to trust in relationship
Relationships tend to be stable, lasting
Open with others about feelings
Positive feelings about relationships
Balanced experience of emotions—neither too little nor too much
Values attachment

Dismissing Attachment
Avoidance of getting close or being intimate
Discomfort with closeness
Ambivalence
Dismissing behaviors
Aloofness and contempt
Mistrust about depending on others
Difficulty getting close
Preference for remaining distant
Fear of closeness
Lack of emotion or minimization of emotional expression
Discomfort with opening up, especially about private thoughts
False self
Pulls away if someone gets close
Illusion of self-sufficiency
Alexithymia

Anxious-Preoccupied Attachment
Excessive worry about relationships
Worry that one's partner won't care as much as he or she does
Obsessive preoccupation with and rumination about the relationship
Excessive need for approval
Ignoring signs of trouble in the relationship

Fear of scaring people away

Fear of abandonment/rejection/criticism

Resentment when partner spends time away from the relationship

Angry withdrawal

Frustration if partner is not available

Feels extremely upset/depressed when receives disapproval

Easily upset, with intensified displays of distress or anger

Jealousy

Fear of being alone

Compulsive caretaking

Submissive, acquiescent, suggestible

Seeks attachment at the expense of autonomy

Work, school, or friends get less attention than the relationship partner

Compulsive care-seeking

Partner describes self as "smothered" or "suffocated"

Eager to be with partner all the time

Needs excessive reassurance

Clinging, demanding, nagging, sulking

Desire to merge

Attempts to win favor or impress

Forces responses from partner

Self-centeredness, showing off, center of attention

Disorganized/Fearful Attachment

Disorganized Internal World
- Dysregulated psychophysiological state
- Affect dysregulation (too much or too little)
- Lapses in self-observation or monitoring
- Discontinuous self-states and affect states
- Cognitive distortion, confusion, and drive-dominated thinking

Disorganized Behavior
- Impaired self-agency and goal-directed behavior
- Inhibition of exploration and play

Disorganized Attachment Behavior
- Activation of contradictory attachment strategies
- Controlling behaviors
- Submissive or excessive caretaking behaviors
- "Stable instability" in relationships
- Defensive aggression and helplessness
- Inability to elicit desired responses

native links in its behavioral chains, in which some behavior on the part of the infant terminates its distress (e.g., turning its focus in a rather forced manner of exploration). (p. 277)

The activation of alternative behavior chains and alternative systems to manage distressing affect contributes to the process of deactivation of the attachment system. Dismissing adults function with a deactivated attachment system and rely on non-attachment-related systems for coping and adaptation. They often manifest exaggerated exploratory behavior with a manner of "I don't need any help" pseudoindependence. As a consequence, adults with dismissing attachment are unlikely to seek social support and are highly likely to engage in distancing coping behaviors (Lopez, 2009).

With respect to the state of mind of the dismissing adult as reflected in AAI discourse, Hesse (1999) says:

> The speaker's state of mind seems to indicate an attempt to limit the influence of attachment relationships in thought, in feeling, or in daily life. There is an implicit claim to strength, normality, and/or independence, and parents are often presented in positive to highly positive terms that are either unsupported or contradicted . . . potential negative effects of parenting or other untoward experiences are denied or minimized, or (rarely) attachment figures or attachment-related phenomena are derogated . . . [Dismissing attachment is] an organization of thought that permits attachment to remain relatively deactivated. (p. 401)

Examples of dismissing (Ds) characteristics of discourse on the AAI include a high degree of unrealistic idealization with respect to one or both parents; emphasizing parental activities over quality of the early relationship; giving a positive endorsement to negative parental behaviors; a clear tendency to minimize negative experiences; a strong tendency to dismiss or derogate attachment; an inability to access attachment-related memories; remoteness from emotions when answering questions that typically evoke attachment-related emotions; rare mention of hurt, distress, or vulnerability; and emphasis on the self as strong, independent, or normal.

From self-report studies of adult romantic attachments, it is well established that in relationships, dismissing adults engage primarily in deactivating attachment strategies. According to Mikulincer, Shaver, Cassidy, and Berant (2009), dismissing adults "tend to be vigilant about becoming needy, intimate, dependent, or emotional; they tend to deny vulnerability, emphasize their personal strengths, avoid threats, and resist becoming dependent on anyone" (p. 298).

Hazen and Shaver (1987) found that "avoidant lovers were characterized by fear of intimacy, emotional highs and lows, and jealousy" (p. 515). According to Collins and Read (1990), "an avoidant individual was uncomfortable with closeness and intimacy, not confident in others' availability, and not particularly worried about being abandoned" (p. 648). Avoidant individuals score low on measures of emotional expressiveness and warmth and low on all measures reflecting closeness in personal relationships (Bartholomew & Horowitz, 1991). Even though they tend to characterize relational experiences more negatively, they typically report less relational distress than secure individuals (Collins, 1996). Their frequent negative moods are related to emotional cutoff (e.g. suppression) (Wei, Mallinckrodt, Larson, & Zakalik, 2005).

As a consequence of deactivating the attachment system, adults with dismissing attachment report fewer emotional memories than secure adults (Mikulincer & Orbach, 1995), and they have poor immediate recall of information regarding attachment-related experiences (Mukulincer & Shaver, 2007). With respect to recall, Fraley, Garner, and Shaver (2000) report that "avoidant individuals encoded less information about the interview than did non-avoidant adults" (p. 816).

> Our findings suggest that the relatively poor recall of emotional experiences on the part of avoidant adults is due to defenses of a preemptive nature. In other words, avoidant adults appear to be less attentive to emotional events while those events are occurring; consequently, they encode less of the information available to them . . . Avoidant individuals appear to be particularly good at turning their attention away from troubling attachment-related thoughts and at the same time defusing the autonomic arousal associated with such thoughts. (pp. 823)

Dismissing adults simply turn their attention away from what is uncomfortable in relationships. Mikulincer, Dolev, and Shaver (2004) found that when asked to suppress thoughts about a painful relationship breakup, they showed no rebound under low cognitive load but showed rebound of suppressed thoughts of separation under high cognitive load. In other words, turning away from painful relationship thoughts and emotions required active cognitive effort, indicating an active denial process, which broke down under conditions of cognitive stress. Such denial also tends to suppress autonomic response associated with emotional arousal (Fraley & Shaver, 1997, p. 1087). In addition to poor recall, dismissing adults often have few words to describe attachment-related experiences. They are often alexithymic (Mallinckrodt & Wei, 2005, p. 239). They are also lower in self-disclosure than secure individuals (Lopez, 2009, p. 107).

In a study of romantic relationships,

> the dismissing group scored uniquely high on self-confidence and uniquely low on emotional expressiveness, frequency of crying, and warmth . . . [and were] also rated as being low on elaboration and caregiving . . . [Dismissing] correlated positively with self-confidence . . . [and] negatively with elaboration[,] . . . emotional expressiveness[,] . . . frequency of crying[,] . . .

warmth[,] . . . caregiving . . . and with all scales signifying involvement in close relationships—self disclosure[,] . . . intimacy[,] . . . level of romantic involvements[,] . . . reliance on others[,] . . . and use of others as a secure base. (Bartholomew & Horowitz, 1991, p. 229)

Most relationships were characterized by hostility and coldness (Horowitz, Rosenberg, & Bartholomew, 1993). Such adults are seen as cold, aloof, and dominating (Batholomew & Horowitz, 1991). Mikulincer, Shaver, and Pereg (2003) summarize the relationships of those with dismissing attachment as having the following qualities:

Denial of attachment needs; avoidance of closeness, intimacy, and dependence in close relationships; maximization of cognitive, emotional, and physical distance from others; and strivings for self-reliance and independence . . . low levels of intimacy and emotional involvement in close relationships, suppression of painful thoughts, repression of negative memories, lack of cognitive accessibility to negative self-representations, projection of negative self-traits onto others, failure to acknowledge negative emotions, and denial of basic fears. (pp. 85–86)

Waldinger et al. (2003) found that dismissing adults retain a wish for closeness but are more concerned with bolstering a strong autonomous self:

Those classified as insecure-dismissing on the AAI told stories about relationships that contained wishes for autonomy with significantly greater frequency than insecure-preoccupied individuals . . . [but] insecure-dismissing individuals express wishes for closeness as frequently as their secure and insecure-preoccupied counterparts. (pp. 90, 94)

With respect to sense of self, dismissing adults like to see themselves as strong, independent, and not needing relationships. Mikulincer (1995) found that they have a differentiated but less well-integrated self-structure than secure adults. He states:

[They have] a highly positive and differentiated self-structure that was not pervaded by emotional experience . . . [They show] low accessibility to negative self-aspects . . . [and a] positive self-view . . . [that] appears to lack balance, integration, and inner coherence . . . [There is] inability to integrate different aspects of the self. (p. 1212)

Mallinckrodt, Daly, and Wang (2009) found that dismissing adults tend "to inflate their self-esteem defensively in the face of attachment threats" (p. 239), and tend to "project unwanted self traits onto others" (p. 239). Mikulincer and Horesh (1999) add:

> Avoidant persons tend to under-evaluate the perception of self–other similarity . . . [T]o perceive themselves as dissimilar from others may result from projection onto others of traits that they do not want to possess . . . [The] avoidant person's perceptions of others are constructed around defensive projection. (pp. 1030–1031)

Despite their tendency to present a normal, positive self-image, dismissing adults generally have a more negative self-image than secure adults (Mikulincer, 1995).

With respect to psychotherapy, Lopez (2009) states that dismissing adults are "proportionately underrepresented within clinical samples" (p. 109). They are unlikely to seek therapy voluntarily unless an acute emotional crisis forces the issue of treatment. In therapy, they are far less self-disclosing than secure or anxious patients (Mikulincer & Nachshon, 1991). According to Lopez, therapy with dismissing patients at first has a superficial quality. They tend to explore others' rather than their own problems and often use therapy to convince themselves that they are OK. Their disclosures tend to be intellectualized rather than emotional, and they rarely explore their own issues and dynamics. Mikulincer and Nachshon (1991) add that dismissing patients are less likely to be responsive to therapist disclosures (p. 61).

Mikulincer and Shaver (2007, p. 42) describe the profile of the dismissing adult as including "denial of attachment needs," "compulsive self-reliance," and "dismissal of threats and of the need for attachment figure availability." "Deactivating strategies involve inhibition of the primary attachment strategy, proximity seeking." According to Mikulincer and Shaver, dismissing individuals have "two main goals in relationships: 1. Gaining whatever they need while maintaining distance, control, and self-reliance, and 2. Ignoring or denying needs and avoiding negative emotional states that might trigger attachment-system activation." They

> exclude from awareness thoughts or feelings that imply vulnerability, neediness, or dependence, which results in ignoring important information about psychological or physical threats, personal weaknesses, and attachment figure responses. This in turn lowers the accessibility in memory of threatening attachment-related thoughts . . . Attention is diverted from threatening and attachment-related information. (p. 42)

See Table 3.1 for a list of possible manifestations of adult dismissing insecure attachment. Again, each of these characteristics may be more or less present in any given person.

Anxious-Preoccupied Insecure Adults

Ambivalent/resistant attachment in children and anxious-preoccupied attachment in adults is the outcome of a prolonged pattern of *inconsistency of responsiveness from the attachment figure* and of *over-involving the child in the caregiver's state of mind*. Such experience produces hyperactivation of the infant's attachment system. According to Mikulincer, Shaver, and Pereg (2003), "These caregivers tend to be inconsistently responsive to their infant's needs, being sometimes unavailable and at other times intrusive, overprotective and interfering with their children's engagement in exploration" (p. 98).

Shaver and Mikulincer (2009) concur that anxious attachment is "rooted in parental anxiety and inconsistency" (p. 37). Ambivalent children in the Strange Situation and anxious-preoccupied adults in relationships show diminished exploratory behavior and a hyperactivation of attachment behavior (e.g., clinginess). In relationships, they predominately use hyperactivating strategies (Cassidy & Kobak, 1988). Mikulincer, Shaver, and Pereg (2003) describe their hyperactivating strategies as follows:

> [They] include a strong approach orientation toward relationship partners, attempts to elicit their involvement, care, and support through clinging and controlling responses, and cognitive and behavioral efforts aimed at minimizing distance from [them] . . . [and] efforts at closeness . . . aimed at establishing not only physical contact but also perceived self–other similarity, intimacy, and "oneness." (p. 84)

With respect to state of mind on the AAI, anxious-preoccupied adults show

> an excessive, confused, and unobjective preoccupation with particular attachment relationships or experiences . . . Descriptions of early relationships may seem vague and uncritical, or else angry, conflicted, and unconvincingly analytical . . . [S]ome [individuals] . . . seem fearfully preoccupied with and overwhelmed by traumatic experiences. (Hesse, 1999, p. 401)

Preoccupied (E) discourse characteristics on the AAI include passive vague discourse that fails to convey clear meaning, canned speech, preoccupation with past anger and resentments that invades the present, excessive use of psychological jargon, discourse that frequently wanders off topic and contains numerous irrelevancies, excessive uncertainties and oscillations in point of view, excessive self- or other-blame, a weak or undeveloped sense of self, and frequent shifts in orientation for past/present, parent/self, or self/child.

Anxious-preoccupied adults often show numerous entangled and disappointing relationships wherein they tend to fixate on themes of rejection and abandonment by others. In such relationships they show an excessive need for reassurance and a limited capacity for self-soothing. From self-report studies of adult romantic attachments, it is well established that in relationships, anxious-preoccupied adults engage primarily in hyperactivating attachment strategies. Bartholomew and Horowitz (1991) state:

> The *preoccupied* group was opposite to . . . the *dismissing* [group] in almost every respect . . . [They] scored uniquely high on elaboration, self-disclosure[,] emotional expressiveness, frequency of crying, reliance on others, and caregiving. They were also rated high on level of romantic involvement and low on coherence and balance of control in friendships . . . [An anxious-preoccupied orientation was] correlated positively with [the] presence of elaboration[,] . . . emotional expressiveness[,] . . . level of romantic involvements[,] . . . disclosure[,] . . . [the] tendency to rely on others[,] . . . use of others as a secure base[,] . . . caregiving[,] . . . [and a] tendency to cry frequently . . . and in the company of others[,] . . . and [was] negatively correlated with balance of control in friendships[,] . . . coherence[,] . . . and self-confidence. (pp. 229–230)

Similarly, Farber and Metzger (2009) report that anxious individuals score "high on measures of self-disclosure, emotional expressiveness, frequency of crying, crying in the presence of others, reliance on others, and use of others as a secure base" (p. 59). According to Hazen and Shaver (1987), "the anxious/ambivalent subjects experienced love as involving obsession, desire for reciprocation and union, emotional highs and lows, and extreme sexual attraction and jealousy" (p. 515). Mikulincer, Shaver, and Pereg (2003) describe them as having

> [an] overdependence on relationship partners . . . [and] a tendency to detect threats in nearly every transaction . . . They also intensify negative emotional responses to threatening events and heighten mental rumination on threat-related concerns, keeping them active in working memory, . . . [they] foster anxious, hypervigilant attention to relationship partners and rapid detection of possible signs of disapproval, waning interest, or impending abandonment . . . [and] score relatively high on attachment anxiety. (pp. 84-85)

Collins and Read (1990) state, "An anxious person [is] comfortable with closeness . . . [and is] fairly confident in the availability of others, but [is] very worried about being abandoned and unloved" (p. 648). Such people tend to over-evaluate threat in close relationships (Mikulincer, Shaver, & Pereg, 2003) and are unable to suppress painful emotions centering around fear of abandonment or rejection (Mallinckrodt et al., 2009, p. 238). Nelson (2009) adds that anxious-preoccupied adults "tend to be vigilant about possible neglect, rejection, or abandonment, and to be hypersensitive to signs of danger and lack of care" (p. 298), and that they need excessive reassurance in close relationships. They are also more likely to infer rejection and hostile intentions from others than secure adults and to appraise themselves more negatively in the face of threat (Mikulincer, 1998). Relative to secure adults, they are more likely to perceive conflict and to anticipate conflict escalation (Campbell, Simpson, Boldry, & Kashy, 2005). They report significantly greater distress than secure adults in the context of intimate relationships and have a tendency to exaggerate their distress and intensify negative emotions in close relationships. According to Mallinckrodt et al., (2009), anxious-preoccupied adults "have negative beliefs about their ability to cope with distress and expect that others will be inconsistently responsive and available" (p. 238). They seek, but devalue, social feedback (Lopez, 2009). According to Mikulincer and Shaver (2003), they tend to "disclose indiscriminately to those who are not prepared for intimate interactions and also tend to be unresponsive to their partner's disclosures" (in Farber and Metzger, 2009, p. 59).

With respect to access to attachment-related memories and emotions, anxious-preoccupied adults remain preoccupied with past hurts. They tend to ruminate about the past and engage primarily in emotion-focused coping (Wei, Heppner, & Mallinckrodt, 2003). They have strong emotional reactivity and pervasively negative moods (Wei, Vogel, Ku, & Zakalik, 2005). According to Wei, Mallinckrodt, Larson, and Zakalik (2005), people "with higher levels of attachment anxiety were more likely to report increased needs for reassurances from others, and, in turn, this . . . increased their vulnerability to depressive symptoms" (p. 374). Regarding this depression vulnerability, Wei et al. (2006) concluded that both maladaptive perfectionism and ineffective coping mediated depression in both anxious and avoidant individuals.

Anxious-preoccupied adults score low on measures of self-confidence (Bartholomew & Horowitz, 1991) and have a weak or poorly developed sense of self (Hesse, 1999). They have a less differentiated self-structure (Mikulincer, 1995, p. 1210) and show poor self–other differentiation (Mikulincer et al., 2009, p. 311). Mikulincer and Horesh (1999) add, "Anxious-ambivalent persons tend to over-evaluate the perception of self–other similarity" (p. 1030). According to Mikulincer (1995), they

> exhibited a negative, simple, and less integrated self-structure . . . pervaded by negative self-attributes and affects . . . [and] characterized by low differentiation and low integration of self-representations . . . Their difficulty in regulating distress was manifested in the high accessibility of negative self-attributes and the excessive use of affective criteria in organizing self-relevant information. (p. 1213)

In psychotherapy, preoccupied adults show a tendency to merge with the therapist to "reduce the fear of being unloved" (Mikulincer & Nachshon, 1991, p. 329). According to Mallinckrodt, Gantt, and Coble (1995), they extensively focus on the therapist and the therapist's other patients (Farber and Metzger, 2009, p. 59). Anxious-preoccupied patients have a weaker working alliance than do secure patients (Mallinckrodt et al., 2005, p. 88). Their tendency to have an intense level of anxiety in psychotherapy can interfere with progress over the course of treatment (Reis & Grenyer, 2004, p. 420). Preoccupied anxiety tends to impede progress not in the beginning but later in therapy.

Mikulincer and Shaver (2007) summarize the profile of the anxious-preoccupied adult as follows:

> The main goal of hyper-activating strategies is to get an attachment figure, perceived as unreliable or insufficiently responsive, to pay more attention and provide protection or support these strategies are exaggerations of the primary attachment strategy . . . [D]istinguishing features . . . consist of over-dependence[;] . . . excessive demands for attention and care; strong desire for enmeshment or merger; attempts to minimize cognitive, emotional, and physical distance from a partner; and clinging and controlling behavior designed to guarantee a partner's attention and support . . . [T]hese strategies can easily encourage intrusive, coercive, and aggressive behaviors toward a relationship partner that promote relationship dysfunction, partner dissatisfaction, and eventual rejection or abandonment—ironically and tragically, the very outcomes most dreaded by attachment-anxious people. (p. 40)

Table 3.1 includes a list of possible manifestations of adult anxious-preoccupied insecure attachment.

Disorganized/Fearful Insecure Adults

Disorganized attachment in children and disorganized or fearful attachment in adults* is the outcome of *frightening and frightened parental behavior* and *unresolved trauma or loss in a parent* (Main & Hesse, 1990, 1992), which leads to the parent being *present but not present* to the child and thereby *repetitively unresponsive*. Adults with disorganized/fearful attachment are more likely to report that one or more parent had a drinking problem (Brennan, Shaver, & Tobey, 1991) and/or to report physical or sexual abuse (Shaver & Clark, 1994). They manifest

---

* This form of insecure attachment in adults is variously referred to as "disorganized" and "fearful"; we prefer to use the former but acknowledge the latter by including it throughout this book when appropriate by context.

contradictory deactivating and hyperactivating attachment styles, in different circumstances at different times, or sometimes simultaneously. Such individuals show a strong propensity to dissociate in the face of attachment-related threats (Lopez, 2009).

With respect to state of mind as reflected by discourse on the AAI, adults with disorganized attachment show very low coherence of discourse/mind. Their responses indicate multiple, contradictory attachment patterns with no obvious single, dominant attachment style. Combinations of dismissing and preoccupied patterns are common, which leads to a "cannot classify" (CC) classification. Unresolved/disorganized (Ud) status with respect to loss or trauma is also common.

Paralleling the AAI findings, self-report studies of adult romantic attachments consistently report that disorganized/fearful adults engage in both deactivating and hyperactivating attachment strategies in relationships. According to Bartholomew and Horowitz (1991),

> the fearful group was rated significantly lower than the secure and preoccupied group on self-disclosure, intimacy, level of romantic involvement, reliance on others, and use of others as a secure base when upset . . . [This group] rated as uniquely low in self-confidence and as low on both balance-of-control scales . . . [N]egative correlations [were found] with self-confidence[,] . . . coherence[,] . . . and with all measures indicating closeness of relationships—including self-disclosure[,] . . . intimacy[,] . . . involvement in romantic relationships[,] . . . capacity to rely on others[,] . . . and use of others as a secure base . . . The fearful rating was also negatively correlated with balance of control measures for both friends . . . and romantic relationships . . . [The fearful group showed] lack of assertiveness . . . Only the fearful style was consistently associated with social insecurity and lack of assertiveness. (pp. 230, 234, 240)

Horowitz, Rosenberg, and Bartholomew (1993) also report that fearful adults tend to become passive, unassertive, or socially inhibited in relationships. According to Lopez (2009), disorganized/fearful adults manifest "persistent themes of interpersonal distrust, vulnerability, and passive withdrawal . . . and their efforts to recall and recount these painful experiences may exhibit fragmented and dissociative qualities . . . [They show] combined impairments in affective self-regulation and social competencies" (p. 110).

As a consequence, disorganized/fearful adults tend to have less satisfying relationships than other insecure or secure adults. In close relationships, they show a "confusing vacillation among detached, dependent, and controlling postures" (p. 110). They also tend to report a greater level of interpersonal conflict than other insecure or secure adults.

With respect to access to attachment-related memories and emotions, disorganized/fearful individuals show both a preoccupation with past hurts and an inaccessibility of past memories and emotions of early attachment relationships. Disorganized/fearful adults tend to show high levels of dissociative behaviors and symptoms (Main & Hesse, 1992) and, associated with this, diminished emotional expressiveness (Searle & Meara, 1999). Compared to other insecure or secure adults, they score lower on measures of self-disclosure, intimacy, reliance on others, and the use of others as a secure base (Bartholomew & Horowitz, 1991). The self is poorly developed and often fragmented, and dissociated self-states are common in this group. Disorganized/fearful adults have chronic low self-esteem (Lopez, 2009, p. 107).

In psychotherapy, disorganized/fearful patients present a confusing combination of dismissing and preoccupied attachment behaviors, with dismissing behaviors predominating earlier and preoccupied predominating later in treatment. According to Mallinckrodt et al. (2005), fears of rejection and withdrawal are significantly negatively correlated with session exploration. They add:

> Avoidant-Fearful attachment is negatively associated with both . . . depth and smoothness . . . [C]lients with strong themes of avoidance or anxiety in their romantic relationships also tend to exhibit considerable avoidance in their therapeutic attachments, which also appears to involve reluctance to self-disclose in therapy, a tendency to mistrust the therapist, and strongly negative feelings about psychotherapy. Avoidant attachment to one's therapist is also associated with clients' experiencing sessions as both shallow and rough. (pp. 95–96)

According to Reis and Grenyer (2004),

> "Fearful-avoidant" attachment similarly involves an intense distrust of others, behavioral avoidance of relationships and a view of self as unlovable and unworthy of care . . . [I]ndividuals reporting high levels of fearful attachment showed significantly less improvement following 16 sessions of psychotherapy . . . The negative view of self and others does not appear to be associated with major depression, but also impedes a positive response to therapy . . . Clients who fearfully avoid open interaction with others may be expected to find this early period more difficult as it requires a degree of disclosure that they may not initially be comfortable with. (pp. 415, 420)

According to Cyranowski et al. (2002), having disorganized/fearful attachment interfered with making a positive, timely response to treatment (p. 211), and it took much longer to stabilize such patients in treatment than it did other patients (p. 208).

Mikulincer and Shaver (2007) summarize the profile of disorganized/fearful adults as follows:

> [They] have trouble choosing decisively between deactivating and hyperactivating strategies . . . [T]hey enact both strategies in a haphazard, confused, and chaotic manner . . . This mixed attachment strategy . . . resembles the "disorganized" attachment pattern sometimes observed in Ainsworth's Strange Situation . . . [Because of these individuals'] failure to achieve any of the goals of the major attachment strategies: safety and security following proximity seeking, . . . [there is a] defensive deactivation of the attachment system . . . or [there is an] intense and chronic activation of the attachment system until security-enhancing proximity is attained . . . [These] fearfully avoidant individuals are relatively inhibited and unassertive, and . . . their lives may have been scarred by physical or sexual abuse or other attachment-related traumas . . . "[F]earful avoidants" are the least secure, least trusting, and most troubled of adolescents and adults . . . [F]earfully avoidant people have especially negative representations of their romantic partners . . . [They] are cognitively closed and rigid. (pp. 42–43)

Table 3.1 provides a list of possible manifestations of adult disorganized/fearful attachment.

To summarize the most basic patterns of each attachment prototype: Securely attached adults show a balance between healthy attachment behavior (e.g., proximity-seeking) and healthy exploratory behavior. Dismissing adults show a deactivation of attachment behavior, at least in close relationships and sometimes in all relationships, and an exaggerated form of exploratory behavior, independent of a secure base, that emphasizes a strong, independent pseudo-self. Anxious-preoccupied adults show a hyperactivation of attachment behavior and a general inhibition of exploratory behavior. Disorganized, fearful adults show a contradictory mixture of both deactivating and hyperactivating attachment styles and strongly inhibited exploratory behavior, except that exploratory behavior is possible when these individuals are sufficiently dissociated.

CHAPTER 4

The Assessment of Adult Attachment

Mary Ainsworth pioneered the structured assessment of childhood attachment with her development of the Strange Situation procedure (Ainsworth, Blehar, Waters, & Wall, 1978). As described in Chapter 2, this method and modifications of it have been used to further our understanding of the developmental processes involved in the various manifestations of childhood attachment bonds. Solomon and George (2008) review the SS and other methods of assessment and classification of attachment in children and suggest that there are "several reasonably well-validated measures available that are appropriate for children across the span of early childhood" (p. 408). Our focus in this book is the understanding and treatment of insecure attachment patterns as they manifest in adults, and effective treatment of an adult attachment disturbance depends on its accurate identification in each particular patient. This chapter reviews interview-based and self-report-based methods available to clinicians for assessing and identifying adult attachment patterns. Interview-based methods typically demand more resources from clinicians and patients than do self-report-based methods, but they also yield richer and more comprehensive detail about attachment patterns and dynamics. Circumstances in which one type or the other is preferred are discussed later in this chapter.

Interview-Based Assessment

THE ADULT ATTACHMENT INTERVIEW (AAI) AND SCORING SYSTEM

The assessment of attachment in adults has its roots in the Adult Attachment Interview (AAI; George, Kaplan, & Main, 1996; Hesse, 2008). The development of the AAI was based on the observation that both attachment behavior and *state of mind with respect to attachment* are relevant to understanding parent and child response to the Strange Situation. By asking the adult interviewee for descriptions of his or her attachment-related childhood experiences, the AAI elicits patterns of language, including coherence, narrative consistency, and productivity, that are indicative of the states of mind produced by the focus on childhood attachment experience. Hesse (1999) states that the AAI is "an interview-based method of classifying a parent's state of mind with respect to attachment" (p. 395). The original work with the AAI showed that classifications of parents' attachment-related states of mind are highly related to their infants' Strange Situation attachment behavior: The correspondence between parents' AAI primary attachment classification and their infants' Strange Situation-based classification assessed five years earlier was 75% (kappa = 0.61), and the correspondence between subcategories of attachment was 46% (Main & George, 1985; Main & Goldwyn, 1994).

While the original work matched three AAI classifications with three Strange Situation categories (Main & George, 1985; Main & Goldwyn, 1994), at present there are five primary AAI classifications, and four are considered parallel to the classifications derived from the Strange Situation assessment. *Secure* or *autonomous* is the same in both systems of assessment, the AAI *dismissing* category matches the *avoidant* Strange Situation category, and the AAI *preoccupied* category matches the *resistant* or *ambivalent* category in the Strange Situation. The *unresolved/disorganized* AAI category was originally thought to match the *disorganized/disoriented* Strange Situation category, and a fifth AAI category, *cannot classify*, "has no empirically established correspondent infant strange situation [category]" (Main, Goldwyn, & Hesse, 2002, p. 7). In our opinion, as is described later in this chapter, the AAI Cannot Classify category significantly overlaps with the disorganized/disoriented pattern from the Strange Situation. Table 4.1 presents Wallin's (2007) comparison of classifications from the AAI and the Strange Situation along with characteristic AAI adult verbal behavior and Strange Situation infant behavior.

According to Main, Kaplan, and Cassidy (1985), an AAI attachment classification, or type, reflects a "set of conscious and/or unconscious *rules* for the organization of information relevant to attachment" (p. 77). Wallin (2007) suggests that an attachment type represents the rules about attachment that guide attachment behavior, or "rules to live by" (p. 35). Each attachment type represents a different organization or set of rules that are activated when attachment-relevant experience arises. The specific organization or set of rules can be considered the foundation of the operative internal working model of attachment.

The AAI protocol is structured to bring into relief individual differences in what are presumed to be deeply internalized strategies for regulating emotion and attention when speakers are discussing attachment-related experiences (Hesse, 2008, p. 555). By eliciting attachment-relevant experience, the AAI activates the internal working model, which creates a state of mind, which in turn produces particular language patterns, which are then interpreted to identify the attachment-related organization or internal working model.

TABLE 4.1. AAI Discourse for Each Adult Attachment Type and Corresponding Infant Strange Situation Behavior

Adult State of Mind With Respect to Attachment	Infant Strange Situation Behavior
Secure/autonomous (F) Coherent, collaborative discourse. Values attachment but seems objective regarding any particular event/relationship. Description and evaluation of attachment-related experiences is consistent, whether experiences are favorable or unfavorable. Discourse does not notably violate any of Grice's maxims.	**Secure (B)** Explores room and toys with interest during pre-separation episodes. Shows signs of missing parent during separation, often crying by the second separation. Obvious preference for parent over stranger. Greets parent actively, usually initiating physical contact. Usually displays some contact-maintaining behavior by the second reunion, but then settles and returns to play.
Dismissing (Ds) Not coherent. Dismissing of attachment-related experiences and relationship. Normalizing ("excellent, very normal mother"), with generalized representations of history unsupported or actively contradicted by episodes recounted, thus violating Grice's maxim of quality. Transcripts also tend to be excessively brief, violating the maxim of quantity.	**Avoidant (A)** Fails to cry on separation from parent. Actively avoids and ignores parent on reunion (i.e., by moving away, turning away, or leaning out of arms when picked up). Little or no proximity- or contact-seeking, no distress, and no anger. Response to parent appears unemotional. Focuses on toys or environment throughout procedure.
Preoccupied (E) Not coherent. Preoccupied by past attachment relationships and/or experiences. The speaker appears angry, passive, or fearful. Sentences are often long, grammatically entangled, or filled with vague usages ("dadadada," "and that"), thus violating Grice's maxims of manner and relevance. Transcripts are often excessively long, violating the maxim of quantity.	**Resistant or ambivalent (C)** May be wary or distressed even prior to separation and undertake little exploration. Preoccupied with parent throughout procedure. May seem angry or passive. Fails to settle and take comfort in parent on reunion; usually continues to focus on parent and cry. Fails to return to exploration after reunion.
Unresolved/disorganized (Ud) During discussions of loss or abuse, the individual shows striking lapses in the monitoring of reasoning or discourse. For example, the individual may briefly indicate a belief that a dead person is still alive in the physical sense, or that this person was killed by a childhood thought. The individual may lapse into prolonged silence or eulogistic speech. The speaker will ordinarily otherwise fit the Ds, E, or F category.	**Disorganization/disoriented (D)** The infant displays disorganized and/or disoriented behaviors in the parent's presence, suggesting a temporary collapse of behavioral strategy. For example, the infant may freeze with a trance-like expression, hands in air; may rise at parent's entrance, then fall prone and huddled on the floor; or may cling while crying hard and leaning away with gaze averted. The infant will ordinarily otherwise fit the A, B, or C category.

Source: Wallin, 2007. Used by permission.

The brilliance of the AAI is that it gives clinicians and researchers a way of reliably and validly assessing adult attachment status through language—namely, by examining *how* attachment experiences are described during a semi-structured interview. Hesse (2008) states, "The central task the interview presents to participants is that of (1) producing and reflecting on memories related to attachment, while *simultaneously* (2) maintaining coherent, collaborative discourse with the interviewer" (pp. 554–555).

Of note is that historical accuracy of the described attachment experiences is not considered to be important, and that "organization of one person's attachment to another specific person is not what the AAI assesses" (Hesse, 1999, p. 421). Rather, the interviewee's statements and the evaluation of those statements allow for the identification of his or her overall, in-the-present state of mind with respect to attachment, which is considered to reveal the operative internal working model that applies to all of that person's attachment-related experience (e.g., Hesse, 2008, p. 555).

Administration of the AAI

Administration of the AAI obtains the information that is then evaluated according to a detailed coding system (Main et al., 2002). The interview is considered semi-structured in that its 20 primary questions are asked verbatim and follow-up probes are done within specific guidelines, but the interviewer may also be flexible with probes in order to obtain the most relevant and beneficial information for the assessment. The interview typically takes between 45 and 75 minutes to administer and is audio-recorded to allow for later verbatim transcription. The following overview of the AAI question categories and questions is presented for informational purposes only and does not qualify the reader to administer the AAI. It is very important that anyone wanting to administer the AAI receive supervised training by a qualified trainer, as without such training an interviewer will likely fail to elicit both the content and the states of mind that are essential for valid assessment of attachment status.

The interview begins with an open question about the family background of the interviewee, or speaker, while he or she was growing up—such as who was in the speaker's family, where they lived, and what the parents did for a living. This question is designed to gather basic background information but also to establish rapport. The second question asks the speaker to describe the nature of his or her early childhood relationship with each parent. For the third and fourth questions, the speaker is asked to generate five adjectives or words that best describe his or her early childhood relationship with his or her mother, then father. The adjectives are about the *relationship*, not about who the parent was as a person. Then the speaker is asked which parent he or she felt closer to and why. The next set of questions explores how emotional upset, illness, and physical injury were handled by the parents from the perspective of the speaker. Then, significant separations from the parents during childhood are explored as the speaker is asked to reflect on how separations were experienced and how the speaker perceived his or her parents' response to the separation. The next set of questions explore certain emotionally charged experiences, such as feeling rejected or threatened or being abused by parents and/or by others. Experiences of loss of a parent or of other important family members are also explored. The next set of questions require the speaker to reflect on early childhood experiences with parents, to consider the influence of these experiences on his or her adult personality, and to contemplate why his or her parents might have behaved as they did. Then, after exploring experiences of closeness with other adults, the speaker is asked to reflect on childhood losses of parents or other close or important people as well as on any possibly traumatic experiences.

The next questions ask the speaker about how the behavior of surviving parents has or has not changed from childhood to adulthood and about the speaker's current relationships with them. The speaker is then asked to reflect on what he or she may have learned from his or her childhood experiences, and the last section explores the attachment relationship between the speaker and his or her own children. If the speaker does not have children, he or she is asked to imagine having a child and answer the questions according to that imagined relationship.

A sampling of specific questions from the AAI appears in Table 4.2.

TABLE 4.2. Sample Questions From the Adult Attachment Interview

1.	To begin with, could you just help me get a little bit oriented to your family—for example, who was in your immediate family, and where you lived?
3–4.	Could you give me five adjectives or phrases to describe your relationship with your mother/father during childhood? I'll write them down, and when we have all five I'll ask you to tell me what memories or experiences led you to choose each one.
8.	Did you ever feel rejected as a child? What did you do, and do you think your parents realized they were rejecting you?
13.	Did you experience the loss of a parent or other close loved one as a child, or in adulthood?
15.	What is your relationship with your parents like for you currently?

Note: This table is meant only to present a sample of AAI questions and is not a full set of questions from which the interview can be conducted. Administering and scoring the AAI requires careful training, as described elsewhere in this book. These selected questions are published with the consent of the authors Mary Main and Erik Hesse.

Source: George, Kaplan, & Main, 1996. Used by permission.

AAI Analysis and Coding

The verbatim transcript of the interview is analyzed and coded by someone trained to apply the Main et al. *Adult Attachment Scoring and Classification System* (2002). This system includes numerous rating scales, which are of two major types: experience scales, which rate types of parental behavior described during the interview; and, most important, state-of-mind scales, which rate aspects of the speaker's language to infer inner states activated in relation to attachment themes. All scales use a 9-point Likert scale.

The five experience scales address the degree to which each parent is described as *loving, rejecting, involving, neglecting,* or as exerting *pressure to achieve.* According to the scoring manual, a high score on the *Loving* scale is given when a parent is described as actively loving and deeply accepting of the child. Descriptions of the parents showing the child physical affection and of responding to the child's individuality also contribute to higher scores. Descriptions of parents as consistently unsupportive of the child and unresponsive to the child's individuality contribute to lower scores. Scoring a parent as *Rejecting* is based specifically on descriptions of her or him rejecting the child's attachment behaviors, such as by actively turning away when the child sought contact. *Involving* or role-reversing pertains to the extent to which the parent involved the child in his or her state of mind rather than being attentive to and regulating the child's state of mind. Normally, a parent is carefully attuned to the state of mind of the child, and this attunement, among other functions, helps to regulate the child's emotional state. Involving parents consistently expect the child to involve himself or herself in their state of mind, needs, or care in a way that interferes with the child's emotion regulation and self-development. *Neglect* has a very specific meaning in the AAI: It refers to a parent's being inattentive and unresponsive to the child despite being physically present and potentially available. *Pressure to Achieve* pertains to the degree to which the parent shows a consistent pattern of pushing the child to succeed or demanding that the child take on adult responsibilities. Although the scores on particular experience scales do not in themselves determine attachment status on the AAI, the parental behaviors that these scales assess are typically associated with particular attachment types. For example, high Loving scores are associated with secure attachment, high Rejecting scores with dismissing attachment, and high Involving scores with preoccupied attachment.

The scales that have the most weight for determining AAI attachment status are the state-of-mind scales. These scales are designed to assess the current state of mind of the interviewee with respect to attachment (Main et al., 2002). The most important state-of-mind scales, from a mental health perspective, are the *Coherence of Discourse* and *Coherence of Mind* scales, because high coherence is associated with secure attachment and mental health and low coherence is associated with insecure attachment, which in kind is associated with relationship disturbance and psychopathology. Overall coherence of the AAI transcript is defined in terms of the overall consistency of the transcript, the extent to which it makes clear sense of the reader, and the degree to which the speaker's discourse about attachment themes is related in a sensitive way to the questions and context of the interview (Main et al., 2002).

Determination of coherence includes consideration of the degree to which the speaker's discourse meets or violates Grice's (1975) maxims. *Quality* of speech is assessed by its apparent truthfulness and by the consistency of what is said and the evidence offered to validate what is said. For example, in the context of the AAI task of coming up with adjectives to describe the relationship with each parent, a speaker's speech *quality* is considered high when he or she gives clear examples from memory that back up the given adjectives. *Quantity* of speech is assessed by consideration of the amount of speech appropriate in response to each AAI question. Speakers with dismissing attachment tend to offer too little speech, often giving clipped, brief responses with little or no detail, or saying, "I don't know" or "I don't remember"; speakers with preoccupied attachment tend to violate the maxim of *quantity* by saying *too much*, going on and on with unnecessarily long responses. *Relevance* pertains to how consistent a speaker's response is to the question or prompt and how well he or she stays on topic. *Manner* is violated when a speaker is vague, uses jargon (e.g., "you know, stuff like that"), uses contentless words as stand-ins for meaningful speech (e.g., "blah, blah, blah"), and/or does not finish sentences or statements.

An AAI transcript is scored as highly coherent when attachment experiences are consistently described in an accurate manner with ample and sufficient evidence; when there is enough but not too much detail; when the speaker stays on track, with descriptions that are clear and fresh with little jargon; and when the speaker is consistently collaborative with the interviewer. Secure interviewees also show evidence of *Metacognitive Monitoring*, whereby they show awareness of their own approach to the interview process and the way they think about the questions. Such individuals consistently monitor their responses to the interview for logical contradictions, personal biases, reaction tendencies, and the fallibility of memory. They also make a distinction between how early childhood relationships and attachment experiences might have *seemed* to them and what might have actually occurred.

The *Idealization* state-of-mind scale is particularly relevant to the determination of dismissing attachment status. Idealization pertains to the speaker's attempt to fabricate an account of excellent parenting throughout childhood and/or a false view of an unrealistically happy childhood. However, the evidence the speaker supplies during the AAI is either insufficient to support this unrealistically positive view or is contradictory to it (Main et al., 2002). Dismissing interviewees typically show high idealization. They present a highly idealized yet unsupported view of their primary attachment figure(s) as a way of distancing themselves from opening to or exploring attachment themes during the interview. Likewise, *Insistence on Lack of Memory* or recall with respect to attachment-related experiences is also a sign of dismissing attachment, especially if the reported lack of memory serves to block further exploration of the topic (Main et al., 2002). For example, a dismissing speaker may present very positive adjectives describing his or her early relationship with an attachment figure but, when asked for specific memories to support those adjectives, may indicate not having any, or may report only vague, nonspecific memories. Another state of mind scale relevant to dismissing attachment is the *Derogation* scale. Derogation is indicated when the speaker actively and directly derogates attachment experiences as a way of outrightly dismissing or minimizing them (Main et al., 2002).

There are two state-of-mind scales especially pertinent to preoccupied attachment. The *Involving Anger* scale is scored when the speaker not only indicates past and/or present anger toward an attachment figure but also then speaks at excessive length about it, with "run-on, grammatically entangled sentences" (Hesse, 2008, p. 565), poor ability to focus the anger, excessive detail about parental offenses, and attempts to elicit the interviewer's agreement. Passages exemplifying involving anger may include a back-and-forth canned exchange between the speaker and a parent that seems to have been replayed in the same, unmetabolized way many times. The *Passivity* scale pertains both to the frequency and magnitude of vague, incomplete, odd, or irrelevant passages as well as to confusions in voice, such as oscillating between self/other or parent/child perspectives (Main et al., 2002).

The AAI explores important losses of family members and other close persons as well as traumatic or abusive experiences in childhood. Ratings are made on several scales to assess temporary disorganization of state of mind when the interviewee is describing an important loss or traumatic or abusive childhood experience. These "lapses in the monitoring of reasoning or discourse" pertain to "temporary alterations in consciousness or working memory" that occur when the interviewee is exploring the trauma or loss experience (Hesse, 2008, p. 570). For example, with respect to loss, a primary sign of temporary disorganization of state of mind is significant failures of monitoring of reasoning, such as speaking as though the deceased person is still alive, expressing the belief that the interviewee somehow caused the death, and becoming confused or disoriented about the time and place of the death or funeral. Other indications of temporary disorganization include unusual attention to detail about the death or funeral, prolonged silence about the topic, incomplete exploration of the topic, and/or invasion of the loss into other parts of the interview. Such lapses in discourse are given weight in an overall rating of *unresolved/disorganized* (Ud) state of mind with respect to loss.

With respect to trauma or child physical or sexual abuse, the main signs of temporary disorganization of state of mind are, as for loss, significant failures of the interviewee's monitoring of reasoning, such as denial of the abuse, thinking that the interviewee caused the abuse to happen to him or her, thinking that the abuser still has influence over the victim's mind, and blocking the topic from consciousness. Other signs include unfinished exploration of the topic, odd associations, and having intrusive images enter the mind while describing the trauma or abuse. Lapses in discourse about trauma and abuse are given weight in the overall rating of *unresolved/disorganized* (Ud) state of mind with respect to trauma or abuse.

AAI Attachment Classifications

The scores on each of these state-of-mind scales have a central role in the determination of the main AAI attachment type. The *secure/autonomous* (F) AAI type corresponds to the secure/autonomous (B) type in the Strange Situation (SS). The secure individual shows high coherence of discourse, explores attachment themes with fresh speech, clearly values attachment, shows some signs of metacognitive monitoring, and is thoughtful, reflective, and forgiving of parental limitations. The *dismissing* (Ds) AAI type corresponds to the avoidant (A) SS type. The dismissing adult attempts to downplay the influence of attachment relationships in thought, feeling, and relationships by presenting the picture of a strong, normal, and independent sense of self along with a highly and unrealistically idealized view of one or both parents. Dismissing individuals typically minimize negative experiences and emotions and usually show poor *quality* and *quantity* or speech (Grice, 1975). The *preoccupied* (E) AAI type corresponds to the resistant/ambivalent (C) SS type. Preoccupied adults give excessively lengthy descriptions of attachment experiences that rarely stay on topic and are filled with numerous vague and meaningless passages in the transcript. A lot of the discourse is filled with psychological jargon and canned speech and therefore lacks freshness. The fourth AAI category, *unresolved/disorganized* (Ud) with respect to loss or trauma/abuse, corresponds to the disorganized/disoriented (D) category from the SS (Main et al., 2002).

An advantage of the AAI scoring approach is that it honors the continuous rather than discrete nature of attachment patterns by allowing for subclassifications within each of the three main attachment classifications. For example, a given interviewee may receive a main categorical classification as secure. The prototype of secure attachment is an F3 classification. However, a person may be secure with some degree of dismissing attachment (F1 or F2) or secure with some degree of preoccupied attachment (F4 or F5). Across the F1 to F5 spectrum, the overall coherence of transcript is high, but variations in discourse patterns warrant inclusion of some dismissing (Ds) or preoccupied (E) elements. Likewise, an interviewee may be determined to have insecure dismissing (Ds) attachment, with low coherence of the transcript, but may show more or less of the various dismissing characteristics, with Ds1 being more severely dismissing, Ds2 representing derogatory dismissing, and Ds3 representing less severe dismissing with some signs of valuing attachment. Interviewees who are insecure preoccupied (E) may vary more in terms of the nature of the preoccupation, whether it be high passivity (E1), angry preoccupation (E2), or fearful preoccupation (E3). The spectrum of main classification and subclassifications is as follows:

Ds1 Ds2 Ds3 F1 F2 F3 F4 F5 E1 E2 E3
Dismissing   Secure   Preoccupied

According to the scoring manual (Main et al., 2002), a fifth category, "Cannot Classify" (CC), is used when "no single state-of-mind with respect to attachment is predominant" (p. 189), either because a main attachment type is absent or because there is evidence of multiple, contradictory attachment types. The manual further indicates that "'CC' has as yet no empirically established corresponding infant Strange Situation behavior pattern." (p. 7). We have a somewhat different view. In our opinion, *both* the unresolved/disorganized (Ud) and cannot classify (CC) types are associated with the disorganized/disoriented (D) category derived from Strange Situation procedure coding, and CC *is actually a form of disorganization*. The main difference between the Ud and CC AAI categories pertains to pervasiveness of disorganization, not to disorganization per se. In other words, if an AAI interviewee shows significant disorganization *specifically limited* to exploration of one or more specific loss or traumatic events, the discourse would yield a high Ud score but not qualify for CC; if an interviewee shows disorganization across the entire AAI transcript, and not only in conjunction with discourse about loss or trauma, then the CC classification would be used. We think that the reason that the CC category is underdeveloped in the AAI manual is that until recent years the AAI was not used extensively to assess clinical populations with severe psychopathology, and it is in this population that there are likely to be enough exemplar transcripts to validate the CC category as we see it. The AAI scoring manual makes brief mention of "potential subcategories of CC" (p. 189) that include transcripts with a lack of an apparent attachment strategy, show contradictory attachment strategies, show an inability to respond to the interview, or show pervasive fear. Hesse (2008) describes two very different types of CC transcripts. Those with "contradictory strategies CC" show a mixture of dismissing and anxious-preoccupied attachment strategies. Those with "low coherence CC" show pervasive disorganization and low coherence (p. 572). However, the developers of the manual have not yet administered the AAI extensively to clinical populations, and so the goal of establishing norms for a more complete subtyping of CC has not yet been met.

We have administered the AAI to a variety of clinical populations and have discovered that the CC category is frequently represented in clinical samples. Furthermore, we have identified nine different subtypes of CC transcripts, described below. Whether our view of CC corresponds to the disorganized/disoriented (D) category of the SS remains to be answered empirically. The main point, however, is that CC classification, as indicated by *pervasive disorganization*, is frequently found in patients with personality and/or dissociative disorders, both associated with and also *independent of* unresolved/disorganized (Ud) classification with respect to specific loss or trauma. Our orphanage study, described in Chapter 5, provides data that support that CC, or pervasive disorganization throughout an AAI transcript, is very characteristic of personality and dissociative disorder patients.

Through our work with various clinical samples, we have identified nine different subtypes of CC, the first five of which reflect the various ways that contradictory or multiple attachment strategies may appear on the AAI:

1. The most frequent CC pattern is the presence of a dismissing strategy in response to the request for five adjectives pertaining to one parent and a preoccupied strategy for the other parent (i.e., Ds for one parent and E for the other parent).
2. Sometimes in describing the five adjectives and other evidence for the same parent, the interviewee oscillates back and forth between two contradictory attachment strategies for the same parent (e.g., both Ds and E in relation to the same parent).
3. With patients who have dissociative identity disorder and some borderline patients, the patient oscillates back and forth between different attachment strategies depending on which alter personality state or ego state is present at that point in the interview.
4. In individuals with early childhood experiences of multiple foster parents, adoptive parents, and/or orphanage staff, it is not uncommon to find multiple, contradictory attachment strategies across multiple caregivers, depending on which caregiver the interviewee is talking about at the moment.
5. An interviewee may begin the AAI interview with a single coherent strategy but by the end of the interview have switched to a very different strategy.

The other four subcategories of CC classification pertain to various ways that extremely low coherence of transcript is manifest:

6. The AAI manual makes reference to an AAI transcript characterized by pervasive fear associated with extreme experiences. Such a transcript typically shows very low coherence of discourse throughout the text.
7. Some disorganized interviewees refuse to cooperate or are unable to do the interview, so the transcript does not provide sufficient information to get

a coherent picture of attachment patterns. An example of this kind of CC subtype is when the interviewee provides only one or two adjectives per parent and provides almost no supporting evidence.

8. Some AAI transcripts, despite cooperation by the interviewee, show an apparent lack of *any* attachment strategy whatsoever.

9. Some CC transcripts are characterized by extreme incoherence throughout the interview and, as such, do not make much sense.

Our further differentiation and specification of the CC category and its sub-types allows it to be used as a fifth category with a practical meaning different than simply a "not any of the other four" category. From a clinical perspective, given the level of psychopathology that many clinicians commonly face, it is very important that those who use the AAI as an assessment tool score it using the full five-way classification system. Since the AAI was originally tested in nonclini-cal samples, a trend has developed in AAI research to score it using either the three-way or four-way classification system. Many clinically important research studies, notably those on assessing attachment status in borderline or other per-sonality disorder patients, use either the three-way or four-way classification. Such studies often report that borderlines have predominantly preoccupied attachment, but that finding is likely, to some degree, an artifact of not having the CC category available and thus having to fit transcripts into the available cat-egories. In our experience, many borderlines have disorganized (CC) status with multiple, contradictory attachment strategies. For this reason, we believe that the five-way classification system is necessary, especially when assessing attachment state of mind in patients with more severe psychopathology, such as personality and dissociative disorder patients.

Incorporating the AAI Into Clinical Practice

We recommend using the AAI and its scoring system for assessing attachment in adults in clinical populations. The AAI specifically assesses state of mind with respect to attachment, which is especially pertinent to detecting and under-standing the nature of the patient's internal working model(s) for attachment. The main advantage of using the AAI is that it provides the clinician with consider-able information, from many scoring scales, about a patient's state of mind with respect to attachment. The main disadvantage of using the AAI is that it requires a considerable time investment in training in order to develop interviewing and scoring reliability and validity. A typical training course offered by Mary Main and Eric Hesse or other trainers they have authorized consists of a two-week intensive class with limited enrollment. The class is devoted to learning all of the experience and state-of-mind scales and to learning the criteria for determin-ing the main attachment strategy and the subclassifications. Following the two-week intensive, trainees are given approximately 30 practice AAI transcripts, for which the scoring is illustrated for some and no scoring is given for others. After this practice period is completed, the student is given 36 more transcripts over a three-year period. The student fills out all the scoring information across all parental and state-of-mind scales and assigns an attachment classification for each protocol using the four-way classification system. To achieve scoring certification, the trainee must show equal or greater than 80% inter-judge agreement between his or her three- and four-way classification of each transcript and the classifications of the same test transcripts scored by Mary Main and Eric Hesse. The high training standards are designed to maintain the reliability and validity of the use of the AAI, and available evidence indicates that this goal is being well maintained: According to Hesse (1999), the inter-judge agreement on the main AAI attachment classifications across all published studies is 82% (p. 408).

Many clinicians hesitate to receive training in the AAI because of the time commitment. This is unfortunate, because taking the full training is an intensive way to learn to think about state of mind with respect to attachment on the basis of the way the patient talks about attachment. Although we strongly favor the full training, there is another way for clinicians to use the AAI. It is much easier to learn to administer the AAI than it is to learn to score it, although those who know how to score it probably administer it better than those who only know how to administer it. A clinician may administer the AAI, have the audio recording of the interview transcribed verbatim, and then send the transcript to a fully trained and certified AAI scorer. For a scoring fee, this scorer then sends the clinician a several-page, detailed report on the AAI scoring results. Many clinicians in our network follow this practice and have found it very useful as a way to incorporate an AAI assessment into their work with patients.

THE AAI Q-SORT SCORING SYSTEM

An alternate way to score the AAI is by using the Q-sort methodology (Kobak, 1989/1993; Waters & Deane, 1985). Instead of using the 9-point Likert experience and state-of-mind scales, Kobak created a list of 100 items, derived from the AAI scales, "that describe different aspects of interview transcripts including information-processing features, emotion regulation, and working models of self and parents" (Dozier & Kobak, 1992, p. 1475). This set of 100 items is referred to as the "Q-set." The items are printed on cards that coders sort into nine piles from most to least characteristic of the interviewee's discourse during the interview:

> The Attachment Q-set consists of 100 behaviorally descriptive items that are sorted into nine piles according to a predefined distribution . . . Items most characteristic . . . are placed at one end of the distribution (Piles 9, 8, and 7), and those most uncharacteristic . . . are placed at the opposite end (Piles 3, 2 and 1). Items that . . . are neither characteristic nor uncharacter-

istic . . . are placed in the center piles . . . Q-sort descriptions can be scored at the level of individual items and also in terms of broadly defined constructs, e.g. scoring security, dependency, sociability. (Vaughn & Waters, 1990, p. 1966)

The Q-set items can be seen as associated with particular attachment prototypes. For example, items that are related to secure attachment include "Is comfortable with the interview and responds in a clear, well-organized fashion" and "The relationship with the other was relaxed and comfortable." An example of an item most related to dismissing attachment is "Provided only minimum responses," and an item least related to dismissing attachment is "Is preoccupied with negative effects of early attachment experience on self." An item most characteristic of preoccupied attachment is "Has fears of loss or abandonment by parent," and least characteristic is "Mother or father was psychologically available."

Analyzing the sorted Q-sets of descriptive features allows for classification along two *continuous* dimensions related to attachment organization: security/insecurity and deactivating/hyperactiving. Continuous assessment has certain advantages over discrete, prototypical assessment and classification, especially in the context of statistical evaluations. In the standard AAI scoring system (Main et al., 2002), the 12-subclassification spectrum allows recognition that there is often overlap, or continuity, among attachment patterns, and the Q-sort approach operationalizes this continuity even further. It is possible to derive three-category differentiation of an interviewee's primary attachment strategy (secure, dismissing, or preoccupied) from the Q-sort data (Kobak, Cole, Ferenz-Gillies, Fleming, & Gamble, 1993), and according to Crowell et al. (1999, p. 440), there is an 80% overlap between AAI and Q-sort classifications. However, for the purposes of most clinicians, the traditional AAI scoring approach of using the ratings on the AAI scales to determine the main prototype and subtype of attachment state of mind is most practical.

THE DYNAMIC-MATURATIONAL MODEL (DMM) METHODS OF ASSESSMENT

Patricia Crittenden's Dynamic-Maturational Model (DMM) of attachment and adaptation, described in Chapter 1, is the basis for the comprehensive system of assessment of attachment status that she and Andrea Landini have published as a manual (Crittenden & Landini, 2011). They claim that the DMM assessment system is an advance over the George, Kaplan, and Main (1996) AAI and the Main and Goldwyn (1984a, 1994) classificatory system.* They state that "its roots are in the groundbreaking work of Main and Goldwyn" (Crittenden & Landini, 2011, p. 17),

---

* Crittenden and Landini primarily cite the 1984 and 1994 versions of Main and Goldwyn's AAI scoring and classification system.

and the DMM methods are similarly based on discourse analysis of responses to interview questions pertaining to early experiences. But Crittenden's structured interview, the DMM-AAI, is based on the AAI and includes questions designed to elicit a wider range of information, including "anger from and toward parents, dangerous experiences and abuse, adolescence, adult attachment, sexuality, and the use of one's parents as models for raising one's own children" (Crittenden & Landini, p. 7). The DMM discourse coding system includes many more and different subcategories of the traditional A, B, C, and D subtypes. Crittenden and Landini (2011) state that the DMM is "offered to address organizations of thought and behavior beyond the range described by Ainsworth" (p. 18), which includes additional attachment strategies and the resulting patterns that may emerge during preschool, school, adolescent, and adult years, and also in extreme situations. They take the perspective that maturation over time creates the potential for new attachment strategies, which results in "expanding the array of patterns" (p. 35) that may manifest. The DMM techniques for analyzing and classifying AAI discourse (from either the standard AAI or from Crittenden's adaptation of it, the DMM-AAI) "expand Main and Goldwyn's classificatory procedures by clarifying and augmenting them rather than being in conflict with them" (Crittenden & Landini, 2011, p. 46).

Crittenden developed her system of assessment to reflect what she considers integral to understanding patterns of attachment behavior and their underlying dynamics, particularly the variation in attachment-related information processing strategies. She believes that what have been the state-of-the-art methods for assessing adult attachment—the George, Kaplan, and Main (1996) AAI and the Main and Goldwyn AAI scoring and classification system—do not address this dimension of attachment. She offers the DMM methods as an expansion and updating of the traditional methods, upon which they are based.

Crittenden and Landini (2011) suggest that the expanded assessment and classification system is particularly beneficial when considering clinical populations. They highlight that Main and her colleagues developed and validated the AAI and its scoring system using a narrow demographic population of nonclinical, upper-middle-class mothers and their infants, whereas she and her colleagues developed the DMM methods "from AAIs from more than 20 countries, including AAIs with normative adults, adults in outpatient treatment, adults in psychiatric hospitals, and prisoners in correctional facilities" (Crittenden & Landini, 2011, p. 18). This broader sampling yielded a larger set of coding classifications that "permits greater differentiation among individuals with psychological disorders" (p. 332). In Crittenden's system, there are 22 possible classifications of adult discourse patterns, 12 possible forms of "unresolved loss," and 14 possible forms of "unresolved trauma" (see Crittenden & Landini, 2011, pp. 236–253, 386–387). As described in Chapter 1, Crittenden does not find value in the use of D and CC classifications, which she believes indicate a lack of recognition that the presence of multiple and seemingly conflicting attachment patterns actually reflects an organized strategy that developed to cope with experiences with attachment figures. In the DMM system, such strategies are identified as particular combinations of discourse patterns that appear in the interview transcript.

The DMM-AAI

Crittenden refers to her modification of the AAI as the DMM-AAI (Crittenden, 2007). The DMM-AAI maintains the overall sequence and progression of questions and the importance of careful administration of the interview that Main and her colleagues emphasize for the AAI (Crittenden & Landini, 2011, pp. 16–17). However, consistent with the importance Crittenden places on developmental factors and greater specificity of mental processes, the DMM-AAI includes more questions than the AAI so as to elicit information from and about more memory systems (procedural, imaged/perceptual, connotative, and source memory systems in addition to the semantic, episodic, and working memory systems emphasized by Main and her associates) as well as about anger from and toward parents, dangerous experiences, adolescent experience, sexuality, use of one's parents as models for one's own parenting, and other "salient issues of adulthood (i.e., self-regulation regarding protection and reproductive opportunities, spousal functioning, and parental functioning)" (Crittenden & Landini, 2011, p. 12). The DMM-AAI is unpublished, like the George, Kaplan, and Main AAI, but also like the AAI, it is made available to qualified researchers and clinicians by the author.

DMM Classification Methods

Crittenden and Landini's 2011 text is a coding manual for the DMM classification system. It provides, in much detail, explanations and descriptions of each of the identified patterns and of how to recognize them from transcripts of discourse obtained, ideally, from the DMM-AAI. Like Main et al.'s (2002) method, the DMM system evaluates the coherence of discourse and identifies information pertaining to the constructs and historical presence of parental *rejection, neglect, role reversal, pressure to achieve* ("performance" in the DMM) and *involvement*.* However, in notable contrast to the AAI evaluation method, the DMM coding approach does not use rating scales to indicate the relative presence or absence of these in a speaker's discourse; rather, all transcript information is considered in the context of how it appears through the content and patterning of speech. Crittenden emphasizes that the process of classification of the prominent attachment strategy is a task of complex pattern recognition. Information from many sources is taken into account and integrated into a coherent, descriptive shorthand of the patterns that appear.

---

* The DMM also brings focus to several other constructs pertaining to a speaker's history as they appear in the discourse in response to the DMM-AAI questions and inquiries: parental comfort, protection, and deception; danger; and sexuality.

The overall DMM classification of the transcript includes an indication of the primary information processing strategy used (or strategies, in a combination pattern); the differentiation of strategies used in relation to different attachment figures (e.g., $A3_M/C3_F$); the presence of any of the forms of unresolved trauma or loss; and the presence of any modifiers that indicate disruptions in the functioning of the primary attachment strategies (e.g., depression). An overview of the major DMM classifications appears below.

DMM Classification of Attachment Strategies

Crittenden's differentiation of attachment classifications emphasizes the relative prominence of two primary information-processing strategies that people may use in their attempts to adapt to experiences of threat and danger. One strategy involves omitting affective aspects of experience and focusing on and acting from cognitive, contingency- or consequence-based information; the other involves omitting cognitive information and privileging affective, experiential, intensity-based information. Crittenden's five B, or Balanced, categories reflect information processing that includes both forms of information, to varying degrees. The DMM B categories generally correspond to Ainsworth's (1973; Ainsworth et al., 1978) B category and to Main and Goldwyn's (1984a; Main et al., 2002) F category, with slight modifications.

> Speakers who are classified as balanced (B) tend to describe their childhood experiences using both sources of information: (1) cognition (i.e., temporal and causal order, realistically identifying complete and causal relations) and (2) affect, including both positive and negative feeling states. (Crittenden & Landini, 2011, p. 20)

The B3, "comfortably balanced," category "is the exemplar for the balanced strategy" (Crittenden & Landini, 2011, p. 123) and is based on Ainsworth's B3 infant pattern and Main and her colleagues' F3 pattern. B3 speakers

> display the widest range of mental, behavioral, and discourse strategies. That is, B3 speakers use all the strategies *when* they are appropriate and *without* mental confusion regarding the underlying true information . . . B3 transcripts have an assortment of discourse markers and display aspects of many classifications but are differentiated from other strategies by (a) the breadth of styles of mental processing of information and (b) the ultimate balancing and integration of these into a psychologically sound perspective on the speaker's experience. (Crittenden & Landini, 2011, p. 125)

B1 and B2 speakers are as above, but slightly emphasize cognitive information, as these patterns are closer to the A patterns, and B4 and B5 speakers slightly emphasize affective information, as they are closer to the C patterns. Of note is Crittenden's use of odd and even category numbering to indicate different tendencies within each of the cognitive-privileging strategies (A, which B1 and B2 lean toward) and affective-privileging strategies (C, which B4 and B5 lean toward). In general, the odd-numbered strategies are oriented outward and place focus on the attachment figures, while the even-numbered strategies are oriented inward and place focus on self-experience. In B1 and all the odd-numbered A strategies, there is a tendency to *idealize the attachment figure*, and in B2 and all the even-numbered A strategies, there is a tendency to *negate the self*. In B4 and all the even-numbered C strategies are gradations of *fear and desire for comfort*, whereas in B5 and all the odd-numbered C strategies, the discourse includes gradations of *angry affect and its expression*.

Adults using Type A strategies present positive, idealized descriptions of their parents in response to questions from the AAI. In response to the five-adjectives or descriptive-words questions, Type A speakers (especially those using the low-numbered A strategies, A1 and A2) present words that reflect idealization and mental stereotyping in the service of maintaining idealization. Chosen words are often similar positive qualities and may be synonyms of each other, the same or very similar words may be used when describing the mother and the father, and the words are often accompanied by absolute enhancers like *always* and *never*—all of which reflects defensive splitting between good and bad parental attributes in semantic memory. Because episodic memory is compromised by this splitting and the processes that maintain it, Type A speakers often have difficulty recalling examples from their experience that illustrate the descriptive words given. As they privilege cognitive, temporal information over affect, Type A speakers tend to make semantic generalizations "that are framed as if/then statements pertaining to responsibility or the consequences of failing to fulfill responsibility, for instance, '*If you were bad, then you were punished*'" (Crittenden & Landini, 2011, p. 140). They tend to dismiss their own perspectives, feeling states, and needs, and overall they "behave as if following the rule: *Do the right thing—from the perspective of other people and without regard to your own feelings and desires*" (Crittenden & Landini, 2011, p. 41).

As in Main et al.'s (2002) system, Crittenden's approach evaluates speakers' coherence using Grice's (1975) four maxims. Adults using Type A strategies tend to demonstrate moderate to low coherence. They tend to speak in an orderly *manner* but present insufficient *quantity* of speech, "particularly about the negative aspects of the attachment figure and positive aspects of the self" (Crittenden & Landini, 2011, p. 141); they show poor *quality* of speech in that they provide little evidence for their positive or idealized statements; and the *relevance* of their speech is compromised by their describing their childhood experience from others' points of view.

The A1 and A2 strategies are referred to as "dismissing attachment in the context of physical safety" (Crittenden & Landini, 2011, p. 20). Crittenden suggests that the A1 and A2 patterns result when children do not experience significant threat of physical danger but consistently do not receive the comfort they seek from parents or experience overt rejection of their attachment behavior:

> If the child is actually safe, but only partially comforted by attachment figures, only a mild distortion is expected (i.e., some mild dissociation of positive and negative characteristics [of parental behavior]). When, in addition, lack of comfort is accompanied by rejection . . . a simple defense against negative affect is often used. In this case, the good and bad qualities of the parent are split and only the good is acknowledged and display of negative affect is inhibited (i.e., dissociated). (Crittenden & Landini, 2011, p. 20)

Crittenden's A1 category generally corresponds to Ainsworth's (1973; Ainsworth et al., 1978) A1 and Main et al.'s (2002) Ds1, and her A2 category corresponds to Ainsworth's A2 and Main et al.'s Ds3. But her A3 to A8 categories are unique offerings, based on her readings of Bowlby (A3, A6) and of literature on child abuse (A4) and adult psychopathology (A7, A8) as well as on her own clinical observations (A5; see Crittenden & Landini, 2011, pp. 41–42).

Whereas the A1 and A2 strategies entail defense against negative affect regarding psychological discomfort in the context of actual physical safety, the A3 to A8 strategies (also referred to as the high-numbered or A+ strategies) reflect "dismissing in the context of danger" (Crittenden & Landini, 2011, p. 21). The A3 to A8 patterns result "when parents are the source of danger or fail to protect children from danger and if the danger is predictable and preventable" (p. 21). The high-numbered A strategies result from more severe and more chronic childhood experience of danger. As these episodes of threat and danger and the lack of protection are not inhibited from memory, full idealization of parents is not possible, so the defense against negative affect takes different forms.

Crittenden has found that A3 to A8 speakers' interpretations of problematic experience with their parents tend to take two primary forms: exonerating or justifying parents' actions or nonactions, and negating or denying oneself and one's attachment needs and feelings. As noted above in the description of Crittenden's B1 and B2 categories, the odd-numbered A strategies emphasize the former and the even-numbered A strategies emphasize the latter.

Pertaining specifically to affect, across the lower-to-higher A-strategy spectrum speakers show "increasing negation of negative affective response of all kinds up to lack of response to pain" (Crittenden & Landini, 2011, p. 42). As noted, A1 and A2 speakers simply inhibit negative affect. A3 and A4 speakers tend to "substitute false positive affect for inhibited negative affect," A5 and A6 speakers tend to "deny significance of physiological discomfort while continuing inhibition and falsification as needed," and A7 and A8 speakers tend to "deny perception of pain while sometimes adding delusional positive affects, and continuing inhibition and falsification as needed" (p. 42). Across the A1 to A8 spectrum, the forms of affect omission and coping response change and become more severe, and the high-numbered patterns are associated with more severe psychopathology.

Crittenden's eight Type C strategies have *affect*—feeling states and levels of arousal—as their basis and organization:

> *Affect*: Because, in the past, feelings have been more predictive of future danger and safety than have temporal contingencies, Type C speakers use affect to organize their psychological processes and self-processes and self-protective behavior. This is displayed in nonverbal indicators of high arousal (e.g., giggling, crying, smirking) and in images of scary, irritating, or comforting contexts.
>
> *Cognition*: Because, during childhood, the temporal order and the contingencies among events were unpredictable and, for high-numbered strategies, misleading, Type C speakers are confused about causation and tend to either not use or falsify cognitive information. (Crittenden & Landini, 2011, p. 186)

For Type C speakers, the three primary affect states that motivate behavior are *anger, fear*, and *desire for comfort*. Crittenden suggests that the organization of these conflicting affect states is managed by

> "splitting" the mixed feelings associated with arousal and displaying one part in an exaggerated manner that elicits a response from others while concurrently inhibiting display of the competing feelings. Once the other person has responded, the current display is maintained or reversed, contingent on the other person's behavior. The most frequent split is between the invulnerable display of anger and the vulnerable appearance of fear and desire for comfort. (Crittenden & Landini, 2011, p. 43)

In the DMM classification of the C strategies, the odd-numbered strategies indicate that a speaker's AAI discourse tends toward gradations of angry affect and its expression, whereas the even-numbered strategies reflect the relative prevalence of fear and desire for comfort.

In contrast with the Type A patterns, in which speakers tend to dismiss their own perspectives, feeling states, and needs, the Type C patterns all include *preoccupation with the self* and *dismissing others* in the context of relationships. Although Type C speakers place a lot of *focus* on others, such focus is in the service of their own feelings, wants, and needs. As such, Crittenden sees this strategy as *coercive*, in that the dispositions and resulting actions are designed to elicit comfort and protection from attachment figures. The fundamental strategy across all Type C patterns "can be thought of as fitting the following dictum: *Stay true to your feelings and do not negotiate, compromise, or delay gratification in ways that favor the perspectives of others*" (Crittenden & Landini, 2011, p. 43). Favoring their own perspectives, they distort information in order to avoid taking responsibility for their feelings, actions, and experiences.

> In the AAI, Type C speakers show several common discourse characteristics. Procedurally, Type C speakers talk about their pasts in the form of *involving discourse*, that is, in a rush of arousing words that capture listeners' attention without reaching a conclusion. In the high-numbered Type C strategies, few but intense words may accomplish the same function. In AAIs, interviewers are both caught up in the tales being told and also required to assist speakers to focus, come to closure, and move forward to the next topic. In addition, Type C speakers often expect interviewers to supply needed words and even thoughts, seek the interviewers' agreement with their perspectives, and, in the high-numbered strategies (C3–8), attempt to engage interviewers in a psychological collusion against others (or suspect interviewers of such collusion against themselves). (Crittenden & Landini, 2011, pp. 183–184)

Type C speakers' privileging of affective information and their difficulty with temporal and causal aspects of cognitive processing leads to several characteristic discourse patterns. They "often blur the boundaries of person, place, and time," such that "past events may be told in the present tense, stories from early childhood are mixed with recent episodes, and people from the past are spoken to as if they were present" (Crittenden & Landini, 2011, p. 184). Poor temporal and causal understanding results in deficits in semantic, or meaning-based, memory and expression; and descriptive words, including the five adjectives from the AAI, may be used in imprecise, vague ways. Strong feeling states are often too-readily accessible and become the basis for image-based descriptions of experiences. For example, "rather than naming feelings semantically (e.g., '*He was very angry*'), Type C speakers communicate with images (e.g., '*His eyes were popping out*')" (Crittenden & Landini, 2011, p. 184).

The coherence (Grice, 1975) of adult Type C speakers' speech usually ranges between low and very low. They tend to speak in a disorderly *manner* and present an excessive *quantity* of speech; the *quality* of their speech is low, as they tend to make generalizations without providing sufficient supportive evidence; and as they respond to questions with a mix of both relevant and irrelevant information, the *relevance* of their speech is low.

Crittenden describes the low-numbered Type C patterns, C1 and C2, as "preoccupied with relationships in the context of unpredictable care" (Crittenden & Landini, 2011, p. 22). As children, such speakers rarely experienced actual physical danger; the threat and danger they experienced was based on the unpredictability of their attachment figures' responses. Though attachment figures were available, "their unpredictable responses provided children with no confidence that they would be protected; . . . in such cases, children experience their parents as indecisively loving and are unable to explain why they continue to feel uneasy" (Crittenden & Landini, 2011, p. 22).

Ainsworth's (1973; Ainsworth et al., 1978) infant Type C category is characterized by mixed feelings of anger, fear, and desire for comfort. It is described as an ambivalent pattern, in which there is an alternation of anger with desire for comfort and fear. Ainsworth's C1 infant pattern, in which anger and resistance are prominent, is the basis for the DMM C1 pattern ("threateningly angry"), and Ainsworth's C2 infant pattern, in which infants are more passive, is the basis for the DMM C2 pattern ("disarmingly desirous of comfort"). Crittenden states that her C1 and C2 patterns are similar to Main and Goldwyn's (1984a, 1994) E2 preoccupied and angry pattern and E1 preoccupied passive pattern, respectively, except that these E categories include discourse patterns that Crittenden differentiates into the high-numbered DMM C patterns.

In Crittenden's model, C1 and C2 are considered to operate as a pair. "Type C speakers attempt to coerce comfort and protection from attachment figures by using exaggerated and alternating displays of anger and desire for comfort with some fear" (Crittenden & Landini, 2011, p. 22). Either threatening, angry expressions or affective comfort-seeking and fear will tend to be more prominent, and which of these feeling states will be expressed at any given time is determined by the behavior and responses of the attachment figure.

Like the high-numbered A strategies, the C3 to C8 patterns (also referred to as the C+ strategies) do not correspond with any of Ainsworth's (1973; Ainsworth et al., 1978) or Main and her colleagues' (Main & Goldwyn, 1994)* categories. Crittenden based these on her observations of preschool-age children's behavior (C3, C4) and on theory, clinical case histories, and study of AAI discourse (C5, C6, C7). She states that her C8 category "has been drawn from fewer examples than other strategies and is, therefore, both sketchy and in need of revision and elaboration" (Crittenden & Ladini, 2011, p. 225). This acknowledgment highlights Crittenden's perspective that her system is subject to continued development and refinement.

Crittenden refers to the high-numbered C strategies, C3 to C8, as *obsessive*. Whereas C1 and C2 speakers tend to oscillate between (a) fear and desire for comfort and (b) anger (with one being more prominent), speakers using the high-numbered C strategies "are consumed obsessively by a single perspective, largely to the exclusion of conflicting motivations" (Crittenden & Landini, 2011, p. 195). Angry invulnerability is prominent in the odd-numbered strategies, and desire for comfort and fear are prominent in the even-numbered strategies. Crittenden notes that in the Main and Goldwyn (1994) system, "the obsessive strategies are

---

* Crittenden refers only to the Main and Goldwyn (1994) classification manuscript in this instance.

often classified as fearfully preoccupied (E3), dismissing (Ds), unresolved/disorganized (U), cannot classify (CC), or even balanced/autonomous (B)" (Crittenden & Landini, 2011, p. 197).

In discourse from the AAI (and likely in behavior), the gradations of angry affect and its expression range from

> very slight irritated anger (B5) to mild anger (C1), to substantial anger expressed with overt aggression (C3), to obsessive directed anger that may be covertly enacted (C5), to overwhelming, unfocused rage that is directed toward unsuspecting victims who perceive no logical connection of themselves to the aggressor (C7). (Crittenden & Landini, 2011, p. 44)

The C3, C5, and C7 patterns include very little to no manifestation of fear and desire for comfort, as feelings of vulnerability are excluded from experience and expression. Such speakers "present with a pugnacious veneer of bravado to cover and deny their feelings of vulnerability and desire for comfort" (Crittenden & Landini, 2011, p. 195).

The even-numbered strategies, which privilege vulnerable affect and expression and inhibit and exclude anger, also exist along a continuum of gradation, and across that gradation, the two forms of vulnerability are differentiated:

> The gradient is from almost complete desire for comfort to the near exclusion of anger and fear (B4) to mostly desire for comfort with some minor fear (C2), to substantial fear mixed with equal desire for comfort (C4), to dominating fear that is expressed covertly (C6), to overwhelming, unfocused fear in response to people from whom there is no logical reason to expect attack. (Crittenden & Landini, 2011, p. 44)

Type C speakers engage in distortions of information that maintain their perspectives and dismiss those of others. C1 and C2 speakers use "passive semantic thought, which refers to failing to reach semantic conclusions" (i.e., vague, imprecise descriptions); C3 and C4 speakers additionally use "reductionist blaming thought, which refers to attributing responsibility to others by omitting information about one's own contribution"; C5 and C6 speakers engage in "rationalization of self, which refers to creating false, but persuasive, reasons that relieve the self of responsibility (thus making the self an innocent aggressor or victim)"; and C7 and C8 speakers show "denied self-responsibility or delusional states in which, coupled with denial of one's own causal contribution, one perceives oneself as having overwhelming power or being completely victimized" (Crittenden & Landini, 2011, pp. 44–45).

Types A/C and AC reflect the presence of combinations of the A and C strategies. "By combining the two self-protective strategies, A/C and AC speakers both double the range of possible defenses and also gain access, at different times, to all of the information" (Crittenden & Landini, 2011, p. 231). Crittenden suggests that these classifications allow for more clarity and specificity about the information-processing strategies that in the Main and Solomon (1990) model would be labeled as disorganized (D) or cannot classify (CC). Rather than considering the mixing of the A and C strategies as unclassifiable and indicative of internal disorganization, Crittenden sees them as "classifiable, organized strategies" (Crittenden & Landini, 2011, p. 230). Alternating (A/C) strategies, she says,

> may use any combination from both the low- and high-numbered patterns (e.g., A2/C1, A3/C2, A4/C6). Moreover, the alternation may reflect the use of specific strategies for different attachment figures (e.g., $A3_M/C3_F$) or it may indicate the use of specific strategies for different situations, for example, C1-2 for mild threats and A3-4 for serious threats. (Crittenden & Landini, 2011, p. 230)

The AC blended strategy involves a greater integration of the affect-privileging and cognition-privileging information-processing patterns than do the alternating A/C strategies. But in contrast to the fully balanced and integrated B3 strategy, in which accurate affective and cognitive information from and about experiences is processed with no or little information omitted, integration in the AC blended strategies involves some degree of omission and/or distortion of information. The AC gradient of increasing omission and distortion appears as

> integration of true affect or cognition with some omitted information (A1-2C1-2) to the integration of distorted information together with some omitted information (A3-4C3-4) to the inclusion of falsified and sometimes denied information (A3-6C3-6) to falsified, denied, and sometimes delusional information (A7-8C7-8). (Crittenden & Landini, 2011, p. 230)

Of note is that the most extreme of the AC patterns, A7-8C7-8, which Crittenden associates with psychopathy, can appear as B3.

> The presentation of psychopathic AC speakers is very like that of balanced speakers, that is, smooth, fluent, and engaging. Psychopathic AC speakers appear cooperative and have relatively few dysfluencies. However, while both B3 and psychopathic AC speakers seem very conscious and monitor what they say for coherence, psychopathic ACs are highly vigilant and non-spontaneous. (Crittenden & Landini, 2011, p. 232)

Although the A and C combination categories allow for specification of information-processing strategies that in Main et al.'s (2002) system would likely be categorized as disorganized (D) or cannot classify (C), Crittenden's system also allows that some transcripts may not be classifiable as fitting any of the B, A, C, or combination patterns of the DMM. Such transcripts are labeled "insecure other" (IO). Crittenden believes that, as with the D and CC categories, the discourse that currently would require an IO categorization likely has an underlying organization that simply has yet to be identified and understood. She recommends that "these transcripts . . . be set aside for periodic reconsideration. As other transcripts that are similar are identified, it may be possible to identify their organization" (Crittenden & Landini, 2011, p. 235).

As in the original Main et al. (2002) system, Crittenden's system also places importance on identifying from AAI discourse whether past traumas and/or losses have been resolved or not. Crittenden has brought more differentiation and specificity to the unresolved (U) category by identifying 26 possible subtypes. The primary differentiation is between *dismissed* and *preoccupying* forms of unresolved trauma and unresolved loss (see Crittenden & Landini, 2011, pp. 240–241). Crittenden suggests that the George et al. AAI (1996) is better at eliciting evidence for preoccupying lack of resolution than for dismissed forms, and that her modification, the DMM-AAI (2007), obtains information that can more clearly identify both forms as well as their subtypes.

In keeping with Crittenden's focus on specifying as clearly and completely as possible the operation of information-processing strategies reflected in AAI discourse, her coding system includes recognition of five "modifiers" that, when present, disrupt and render less effective the strategies established by a speaker. In general, modifiers are indicated when there are signs of particular strategies in the discourse (i.e., B, A, C, or A/C or AC) and also signs that those strategies are not fully or effectively functioning. The modifiers are *depressed* (Dp), *disoriented* (DO), *intrusions of forbidden negative affect* (ina), *expressed somatic symptoms* (ess); and *reorganizing* (R).

The *depressed* modifier is given when a speaker is aware both that the strategies that he or she is using are not resolving the problems to which the strategy is applied and that "the self and the actions of the self are irrelevant to outcomes" (Crittenden & Landini, 2011, p. 257). The *disoriented* modifier applies when a speaker whose primary strategies are combination patterns (i.e., A/C or AC) shows significant verbal inconsistencies, discrepancies, and disruptions. The speaker is unaware that his or her strategy is not functioning, and "the individual is oriented in conflicting directions around competing dispositions. The resulting behavior is nonstrategic, that is, neither self-protective nor comfort-eliciting" (Crittenden & Landini, 2011, p. 262).

Intrusions of forbidden negative affect are coded when a speaker who uses a high-numbered Type A strategy (i.e., compulsive dismissing) shows "a sudden and brief change from an inhibited state to a high and disinhibited arousal" that accompanies "unexpected use of language or forms of address that are unacceptable in the AAI context" (Crittenden & Landini, 2011, p. 265). *Expressed somatic symptoms* are nonverbal behaviors that disrupt the process and communication during the AAI and cannot be explained by any current medical condition. Examples include excessive coughing, scratching, or yawning; sudden or repeated bodily movements; falling asleep; and very slow speech. As some such appearances have no auditory component, the interviewer must make note of their appearance for inclusion in written transcripts. Crittenden highlights that videotaping of AAI administration provides for easy identification of these phenomena and the specific interview topics at which they appear. When *reorganizing* is present,

> speakers are changing from one strategy to another. In such cases, neither strategy functions fully and, thus, the classificatory criteria are mixed and not fully met. Often a non-B strategy is becoming more balanced through a reflective and integrative process. (Crittenden & Landini, 2011, p. 256)

Such speakers show signs of metacognitive function, such as recognizing discrepancies in their speech and attempting to remedy them, and "all use reflective statements" (Crittenden & Landini, 2011, p. 276).

Incorporating the DMM Into Clinical Practice

Some clinicians believe that the DMM system of assessment can be a valuable alternative or even supplement to the traditional AAI system. From a clinical perspective, a contribution of the DMM system is the greater number of classifications that finely differentiate and specify attachment strategies in terms of the degree and form of information-processing patterns developed as adaptations to experiences of threat/danger. Use of this system requires a shift from thinking about attachment in terms of the traditional prototypes to focusing on the specific adaptive strategies used in attachment contexts. It also requires understanding of and facility with the DMM, which is much more complex than the traditional AAI methods.

There is a practical, research-based consideration that pertains to the presence of many potential classification categories in the DMM system. For example, Crittenden and Landini (2011) describe a large number of subgroups of unresolved status with respect to trauma and loss, as compared to the AAI system. While we recognize the potential clinical usefulness of this greater differentiation and specificity of unresolved status, this large number of unresolved subgroups makes inter-rater reliability more challenging. Even with only two unresolved categories in the original AAI system (loss and trauma), it has been harder to establish as high inter-rater reliabilities using a four-way (including Ud status) as compared to a three way classification scheme (not including Ud status).

We see value in the simplicity of the AAI system's four prototypical primary attachment patterns along with unresolved classification, derived from the SS and AAI research, in contrast to the complexity of the many DMM categories. On the other hand, Crittenden and others believe that this greater complexity reflects a finer-grained understanding of what underlies the traditional prototypes and assists in individualizing treatment.

A significant practical limitation of the DMM assessment and classification method is similar to that of the Main et al. method: Extensive training is necessary to establish proficiency and reliability with the coding system. Crittenden and her colleagues provide such training, which entails three 6-day full-time segments over approximately six months, and an additional optional 6-day advanced topics segment. During and between these segments, trainees work with a standardized set of practice transcripts. While the coding manual is available to anyone, Crittenden believes that supervised, evaluated coding of at least 100 transcripts is minimally necessary for sufficient initial reliability and that maintenance of reliability over time requires regular coding and classification practice, periodic recertification, and actively avoiding conditions that decrease reliability (such as coding when tired, coding too many transcripts at a time, and being too confident about one's coding accuracy). As with the AAI method, clinicians who wish to use this system but who do not want to invest in the training process may hire qualified interviewers and/or coders.

Although the DMM offers a wide variety of clinically rich descriptive attachment categories, it is at present less well known and less frequently used than the traditional AAI approach. Farnfield et al. (2010) point out that there has been a "bias toward clinical rather than academic interest" in the DMM, and wider acceptance awaits further "testing by rigorous academic studies" (p. 324). Currently, the number of studies using the DMM and its assessment system is very small compared to the extensive traditional AAI literature. The research on attachment patterns in clinical populations has primarily used the AAI and the Main et al. scoring system, and thus provides a valuable domain of reference for clinicians wishing to consider their patients' attachment disturbances in the context of a large body of knowledge. Indeed, Bakermans-Kranenburg and van IJzendoorn's (2009) meta-analyses of over 200 adult attachment representation studies, spanning 25 years and including over 10,500 AAIs, led them to conclude that "the AAI and its coding system appear remarkably robust across countries and cultures" (p. 248). Though the DMM is becoming more widely known and used, and the amount of research applying it to clinical populations is growing, if a clinician wishes to draw from the most established research-based knowledge and determines that his or her treatment method does not require the specificity provided through the DMM system, then the well-established AAI approach, or other methods described below, is preferable.

Crittenden and Landini (2011) state, "We think that the last 25 years have generated enough data to indicate that the ABC+D model is not sufficiently fruitful to justfify continuing on that pathway" (p. 381). But more and more, the traditional

AAI has been used to assess a wide range of clinical populations, as exemplified by Steele and Steele's (2008a) *Clinical Applications of the Adult Attachment Interview*, as well as by the many studies on the AAI in relationship to adult psychopathology reviewed in this book. We believe that continued research and practice emerging from both models will lead to broader and deeper understanding about attachment in the years to come. Fonagy (2013) suggests that the field benefits from seeing and respecting the unique aspects and the strengths and limitations of each model and approach, as "Neither approach [alone] can hope to capture and encapsulate the phenomenal complexity" of attachment experience (p. 179).

Regarding treatment, Crittenden and Landini (2011) state, "no major new ideas or recommendations for differential treatment approaches have come from this [original AAI] model in more than two decades" (p. 377). We hope that our Three Pillars treatment, strongly derived from the original AAI and its classification system, fulfills this need.

THE CURRENT RELATIONSHIP INTERVIEW (CRI)

The AAI was designed to assess current state of mind with respect to attachment as related to the Ainsworth et al. (1978) prototypes of attachment derived from the Strange Situation research. The Current Relationship Interview (CRI) was modeled after the AAI but was designed to assess state of mind with respect to attachment in adult romantic partnerships (Crowell & Owens, 1998; Crowell & Waters, 1995). The manual states:

> The purpose of the interview is to reveal how participants mentally represent attachments in romantic relationships, as reflected in their manner of speaking about their relationships . . . [It] was developed to parallel the Adult Attachment Interview[,] . . . but the questions reflect the reciprocal nature of adult relationships. (Crowell & Owens, 1998, p. 3)

The CRI is intended . . ."to assess adult attachment within close relationships . . . [I]t explores the process by which a new attachment relationship may be integrated into an already existing representation of attachment, or by which a new representation develops" (Crowell, Fraley, & Shaver, 1999, p. 444).

Unlike from the AAI, Crowell and Owens (1998) state that

> [i]t is not uncommon in these [CRI] interviews to observe characteristics of several classifications. This is because the state of mind with respect to attachment in the current relationship is influenced by 1) the participant's state of mind based on past and present attachment experiences in their families of origin, 2) previous romantic relationships, and 3) the behavior of the [current] partner. (Crowell & Owens, 1998, p. 4)

The CRI begins by taking a thorough history of family relationships, and then previous romantic relationships and the current romantic relationship are explored. With respect to the interviewee's parents, attention is given to the quality of the parent's marriage, how loving or unloving the parents were to each other, the nature of conflict that occurred in that marriage, and how the interviewee was or was not exposed to such conflict. With respect to the interviewee's romantic relationships, attention is given to how each romantic relationship began, the intensity of the romantic involvement, and how the relationship ended. The current romantic relationship is explored in depth. The adjectives used to describe the current romantic relationship are evaluated according to whether or not they are supported by and not contradicted by the interviewee's statements. The degree of satisfaction in the current romantic relationship is assessed, from strong to moderate dissatisfaction to moderate to strong satisfaction.

Following the AAI, ratings using various experience scales and current-state-of-mind scales are made from examination of the interview transcript. The experience scales rate both the interviewee and the current partner using a 9-point Likert scale. First, both are rated on the degree to which they are *loving* in the current relationship. This rating includes assessments of whether the partner serves as a secure base and is cooperative, supportive, available, and responsive. The *Loving* score is lowered when there is evidence of physical or verbal aggression. Second, ratings are made along a number of negative behavior scales, some of which follow the AAI scales and some of which have been revised to make them relevant to a current adult romantic involvement. The rating of *Rejecting* behavior assesses "attempts to decrease attachment behavior" (Crowell & Owens, 1998, p. 11), whereas the rating of *Involving* evaluates "attempts to heighten attachment behavior within the relationships" (p. 13). The presence of *Controlling* behavior is rated by the degree to which each partner engages in "inhibiting exploratory behavior and undermining feelings of support and assurance" (p. 14). Controlling behavior may include insistence on the partner doing things one's own way, being "uncompromising and rigid," "discouraging independent activities," hovering and providing "excessive instruction," and not respecting the other's privacy (p. 15). The *Dependency* rating is determined by the degree to which the interviewee's life revolves around the partner, the interviewee or partner acts childlike and immature, or the interviewee manifests a tendency to give in to his or her partner or to try to excessively please the partner (pp. 16–17). The *Communication* scale assesses the quantity and quality of communication between the interviewee and partner. Honest, open communication and communication interested in the other earn high scores (p. 19).

Next, the relationship is assessed in terms of the degree to which it provides a *Safe Haven* in times of stress. As the manual states, "[a]ttachments between adults differ in an important way from those of parents and young children. In the adult attachment relationship, each partner at times fills a caregiver role and at times a care-seeking one" (Crowell & Owens, 1998, p. 19). The quantity and quality of both caregiving and care-seeking for interviewee and partner alike are assessed using 9-point Likert rating scales.

For classification purposes, the most heavily weighted scales pertain to coherence of discourse and state of mind with respect to attachment to the current romantic partner. Current state of mind with respect to attachment to the partner is assessed using a number of rating scales. The *Valuing of Intimacy* scale assesses "being close to a partner emotionally, trying to know the other person and to be known as honestly and clearly as possible. Activities such as talking to the partner about feelings, showing affection, or acknowledging insecurities are all intimacy-oriented" (Crowell & Owens, 1998, p. 24). The *Valuing of Independence* scale assesses "the frequency and force with which the participant expresses his or her need to lead a life independent of the partner" (p. 26). The *Angry Speech* scale is comparable to the *Involving Anger* scale of the AAI and assesses the degree to which the interviewee gets caught up in run-on, wandering, irrelevant, and passive speech following description of an offense. *The Derogation* scale assesses "cold, uninvolved derogation of the partner" (p. 29). The scale measuring idealization of the partner/relationship is comparable to the *Idealization* scale of the AAI. It assesses "the distortion in the representation of the partner/relationship . . . in a normalizing direction" (p. 31). The *Passive Speech* scale follows the AAI Passivity state-of-mind scale and assesses to what degree there is "a lack of focus, clarity or specificity" (p. 33). The *Fear of Loss of Partner* scale assesses "the extent to which the participant fears for the health and safety of the partner" (p. 36). Additional scales assess the possibility of unresolved/disorganized states of mind with respect to loss or trauma in a manner similar to the AAI system.

The CRI requires assignment of state of mind with respect to attachment for the current romantic partnership using a four-way system of secure, dismissing, preoccupied, and unresolved/disorganized. The CRI subclassification divides the secure group into S1, S2 and S3, with S2 being the prototype of secure attachment, S1 being secure with dismissing elements, and S3 being secure with preoccupied elements. Dismissing attachment is divided into D1, D2, D3, and D4 subcategories, from more extremely to less extremely insecure. Preoccupied attachment is divided into P1, P2, P3, and P4 subcategories, with P1 being passive, P2 being angry, P3 being enmeshed, and P4 being controlling. The P1 and P2 subclassifications are comparable to E1 and E2 in the AAI system, but the P3 enmeshed and P4 controlling categories are unique to the CRI.

We believe that the CRI is a very thorough and useful clinical tool for evaluating state of mind in a current partnership in a way that closely follows the AAI and that it is invaluable for individual and couples therapists with an attachment orientation to treatment. There is some reason to believe that the CRI is a better tool than the AAI to evaluate state of mind in current romantic relationships, as the AAI was designed to classify attachment prototypes comparable to the

Strange Situation prototypes for children, and adult romantic involvements are far more complex. For example, van IJzendoorn & Bakermans-Kranenburg (1996) conducted a meta-analysis of AAI classifications of 226 couples. The concordance rate for attachment status of each partner in a couple was 50–60% (kappa = 0.20), mostly accounted for by secure–secure pair bonds. As Crowell, Fraley, and Shaver (1999) state, "this finding suggests that factors other than attachment security are active in partner selection and maintenance." (p. 444)

Crowell et al. add, "Little relation between the broad construct of marital satisfaction and AAI classification has been found, but feelings of intimacy are related" (p. 444). These findings highlight the significant differences between attachment relationships in childhood and attachment relationships in adult romantic partnerships. Simpson and Rholes (1998) state, "Some authors . . . misinterpret the domain differences between the AAI, which focuses on adults' characterizations of their childhood relationships with parents, and [a] measure . . . which focuses on experiences in romantic relationships" (p. 29).

Further consideration of the significant differences between the AAI and related interview measures and measures of adult romantic attachment is the main subject of the section below on self-report assessment of adult attachment.

THE ADULT ATTACHMENT PROJECTIVE PICTURE SYSTEM (AAP)

The Adult Attachment Projective Picture System (AAP) is an assessment approach that measures *attachment coherence*, which George and West (2012) define as "the representational integration of attachment and caregiving, that is, coherence in relationship" (p. 51). The AAP does not entail an interview per se, but its assessment is based on the evaluation of the narrative structure and content of a participant's responses to a structured set of images. Essentially, it is a visual projective tool designed to elicit attachment-related themes.

The AAP stimulus set consists of eight cards displaying line drawings of various scenes, the first of which is considered neutral and the remaining seven of which are designed to evoke responses that reveal attachment style. The eight scenes are:

1. *Neutral* (two children playing with a ball);
2. *Child at Window* (a child gazing out of a window);
3. *Departure* (a couple standing by three suitcases);
4. *Bench* (a girl seated on a bench, her head between her folded arms and legs);
5. *Bed* (a child in bed reaching out to an adult figure sitting at the end of the bed);
6. *Ambulance* (a heavyset, elderly woman standing by a seated child with her unseen hand possibly touching the child's unseen arm, the child looking

out of a window at two people at the back of an ambulance carrying a figure on a stretcher);

7. *Cemetery* (a man, hands in pockets, looking down at a gravestone);

8. *Child in Corner* (a child standing in a corner with her/his arms out, palms facing outward, and head turned far to one side toward the back). (George and West, 2012, pp. 32–36)

According to the protocol, the participant is asked to describe the presented picture and then to imagine what led up to the scene and what will happen next. George and West note that in contrast to the AAI, the task of the AAP is not autobiographical, it doesn't take conversational form, and "the administration instructions release the interviewee from the constraints of interpersonal discourse" (2012, p. 51). Analysis of the responses focuses on "the overall patterns of story content and defensive processing elements in the entire set of responses to the attachment stimuli" (p. 94). Evaluation of defenses in relation to attachment is central to George and West's classification. They endorse George and Solomon's (2008) perspectives on Bowlby's (1980a) concept of *defensive exclusion*:

> Defensive exclusion characterizes all patterns of attachment . . . [B]oth attachment security and insecurity are associated with defense. For secure individuals, defense acts as a sorting mechanism—transforming and excluding attachment affect experience in order to support integration, flexibility, and sincere confidence in the self and attachment figures as agents of care and effectiveness. For insecure individuals, defense takes on more of an exclusionary role, akin to Bowlby's (1980[a]) original thinking. (p. 80)

Assignment of an interviewee to one of four possible attachment categories in the AAP classification system—secure, dismissing, preoccupied, or unresolved—is largely based on the degree and form of attachment-related defenses.

> Security is evidenced by the presence of internalized secure base and haven of safety in alone stories, and sensitivity or goal-corrected synchrony in the dyadic stories. Secure cases typically contain relatively little evidence of defensive processing; when present, defense helps the individual navigate and manage tension or distress. (p. 95)

Bretherton and Munholland (2008) note that in the AAP,

> a secure stance is indicated by coherent and constructively resolved narratives in which the distressed protagonists either receive care or (in response to "alone" pictures) rely on inner resources, such as reflecting on

and exploring feelings. The latter responses are coded as indicative of an "internalized secure base." (p. 121)

The relative degree of the major forms of defensive exclusion in the interviewee's responses—deactivation and cognitive disconnection—determines assignment to either of the organized-insecure attachment classifications. "If deactivation predominates in the story responses, the case is judged dismissing" (Brent & Munholland, 2008, p. 95). George and West (2012) state:

> Deactivation would be evidenced in individuals' AAP responses by specific story content and themes that exclude thoughts and affects that would activate their attachment systems. We should expect this response because the AAP pictures depict threatening events (illness, solitude, death, etc.), and deactivation works as an attempt to dismiss, divert, or neutralize distressing perceptions and affective reactions triggered by these scenes from consciousness . . . Deactivation enables the individual to complete the task of telling a story without being distracted by attendant attachment distress. (p. 82)

When cognitive disconnection predominates without the presence of deactivation, then the interviewee is classified as preoccupied. Stories of preoccupied interviewees are characterized by

> non-integrated "pieces" of attachment information. That is to say, the individual's ability to tell a story will be compromised by the inclusion of irrelevant information and affect as well as uncertainty leaving him or her unsettled and continually shifting back and forth. At the extreme, this uncertainty gives rise to the inability of individuals to make up their minds or complete their thoughts when telling their stories. (George & West, 2012, p. 86)

George and West apply Bowlby's (1980a) concept of *segregated systems* to the determination of an interviewee's unresolved status. According to their view, when affect and experience associated with unresolved loss and/or trauma becomes too intense, there is complete defensive exclusion of that material and it becomes "segregated" and inaccessible to consciousness; however, such segregation is brittle and is prone to breakdown, leading to states of mental dysregulation and attachment disorganization. During the AAP process, evidence of segregated systems can take two primary forms, *dysregulation* and *constricted immobilization*. Dysregulation appears in the picture responses in content and themes such as "fear and failed protection"; "helplessness"; "emptiness and isolation"; and "spectral, dysregulated thinking and obtrusions" (George & West, 2012, p.

92). Constricted immobilization reflects shutting down or blocking in the face of stimuli that evoke intense, unresolved experience and typically appears in the form of inability or unwillingness to respond to one or more picture.

Classification of attachment status based on the AAP has been shown to be highly related to AAI classifications. George and West (2012) report results from their study showing that a two-way classification, secure or insecure, yielded a kappa for AAP/AAI convergent validity of 0.89; using a four-way classification (F, Ds, E, and U) yielded a kappa of 0.84. This strong association with the AAI suggests that the AAP can be a valuable alternative to the AAI for determining attachment status. However, it has several limitations. As with the AAI, the time investment required for establishing scoring competence is quite significant. Unlike the AAI, the AAP does not provide information about attachment proto-type subclassifications. George and West argue that the attachment field "rarely specifies category subgroups in research or clinical applications" and that "new classification groups and subgroups have emerged from empirical need rather than theoretical relevance" (2012, p. 52). We differ from this stance on attachment subclassification and have found treatment-related value in knowing a patient's subclassification of major attachment prototype. The chapters in Part III of this book, which specify modifications within our treatment methods for the major attachment prototypes, include recommendations for working with patients with specific AAI subtypes of the organized-insecure attachment patterns.

Another current limitation of the AAP is that there is little research on its use in clinical populations. Some such research does exist and is growing, but at present the vast literature on AAI status and psychopathology and a smaller but growing literature pertaining to Crittenden's DMM categories and psychopathology (see Chapter 5) provide both researchers and clinicians with a wealth of information about these associations. Despite these limitations, we do see value in the AAP and respect it as a valid measure of the major attachment prototypes.

Self-Report Based Assessment

PEER AND PARENTAL ATTACHMENT IN ADOLESCENCE

Clinicians who wish to assess adolescent attachment to peers and parents can use the Inventory of Parent and Peer Attachment (Armsden & Greenberg, 1987). This 60-item self-report inventory is one of the most widely used to assess security of attachment in adolescents, and it evaluates parental and peer attachment in three broad categories: degree of mutual trust, quality of communication, and degree of anger/alienation. An example of a parent item in the degree-of-mutual-trust category is "My parents respect my feelings"; an item in the quality-of-communication category is "I like to get my mother's point of view on things I am concerned about"; and an item in the degree-of-anger/alienation category is "My mother expects too much of me." With respect to the peer items, an example in the degree-of-mutual-trust category is "I trust my friends"; an example in the quality-of-communication category is "My friends listen to what I have to say"; and an example in the degree-of-anger/alienation category is "Talking over my problems with my friends makes me feel ashamed or foolish" (Crowell, Fraley, & Shaver, 1999, p. 447). In studies using this measure, the quality of parent and peer attachments in adolescents was positively correlated with self-esteem, life satisfaction, and other measures of well-being (p. 445).

THE PROTOTYPE APPROACH—ROMANTIC ATTACHMENT

Forced Choice Prototype Self-Assessment

Hazen and Shaver (1987, 1990) used Ainsworth et al.'s (1978) three-way typology of attachment patterns in infancy—secure/autonomous, avoidant, and anxious/ambivalent—to develop a forced-choice self-report assessment of adult romantic relationships to differentiate respondents into one of the attachment prototypes. Hazen and Shaver (1987) state:

> We designed a "love quiz" to be printed in a local newspaper . . . A single-item measure of [each of] the three attachment styles was designed by translating Ainsworth et al.'s (1978) descriptions of infants into terms appropriate for adult love. The love-experience questionnaire . . . was based on the assumption that conscious beliefs about romantic love . . . are colored by underlying, and perhaps not fully conscious, mental models. (p. 513)

The instructions for this item are: "Think back across [your] history of romantic relationships and indicate which of the three best captures [the] way [you] generally think, behave, and feel in romantic relationships" (p. 513). The respondent then reads the three following prototypical descriptions of adult romantic relationship behavior and chooses the one that best fits his or her experience:

> *Secure.* I find it relatively easy to get close to others and am comfortable depending on them and having them depend on me. I don't often worry about being abandoned or about someone getting too close to me.

> *Avoidant.* I am somewhat uncomfortable being close to others; I find it difficult to trust them completely, difficult to allow myself to depend on them. I am nervous when anyone gets too close, and often, love partners want me to be more intimate that I feel comfortable being.

> *Anxious/Ambivalent.* I find that others are reluctant to get as close as I would like. I often worry that my partner doesn't really love me or won't

want to stay with me. I want to merge completely with another person, and this desire sometimes scares people away. (1987, p. 515)

The item was initially published as part of a 95-item questionnaire in a local newspaper, and data from the first 620 respondents were analyzed. The following self-reported prototype distribution was found: 56% secure, 19% anxious/ambivalent, and 25% avoidant. Results further showed that respondents described

secure lovers describe their most important love experience as especially happy, friendly, and trusting. They emphasized being able to accept and support their partner despite the partner's faults . . . The avoidant lovers were characterized by fear of intimacy, emotional highs and lows, and jealousy . . . The anxious/ambivalent subjects experienced love as involving obsession, desire for reciprocation and union, emotional highs and lows, and extreme sexual attraction and jealousy. (Hazen & Shaver, 1987, pp. 514–515)

Hazen and Shaver's single-item measure of adult romantic attachment style has the advantage of "brevity, face validity, and ease of administration" (Crowell & Treboux, 1995).

CATEGORICAL AND DIMENSIONAL MEASURES OF ADULT ROMANTIC RELATIONSHIPS

A limitation of the forced-choice prototype approach is that it is not possible to have more than one attachment classification (M. B. Levy & Davis, 1988). This limitation goes against research we have seen on the CRI that shows, at least with respect to adult romantic attachment, that some people show different attachment styles in different relationships. Additionally, requiring a forced choice of one attachment type does not allow for the detection of multiple internal working models of attachment. Therefore, some researchers interested in using self-report scales to assess adult attachment began to move in the direction of developing continuous rating scales (Feeney, 2008). Several of these are based on the Hazen and Shaver single-item prompt.

The Adult Attachment Scale (AAS)

Collins and Read (1990) point out that each Hazen and Shaver prototype "description contains statements about more than one aspect of relationships . . . [and that] respondents must accept an entire description that may not reflect their feelings on all dimensions" (p. 645). To develop "a more sensitive instrument to measure adult attachment styles . . . [in order to] examine in more detail the contents of these models" (p. 645), Collins and Read decomposed each of the Hazen and Shaver prototypes into component statements and formed the Adult Attachment Scale (AAS), which consists of 18 questionnaire items that are rated in a

Likert scale format. There are six questions for each of the three prototypes. An example of a question related to secure romantic attachment is "I am comfortable depending on others." Anxious attachment is exemplified by the statement "I often worry that my partner does not really love me." An item related to avoidant attachment is "I am somewhat uncomfortable being close to others." Instructions require respondents to rate themselves on each item along a 5-point Likert scale according to the "extent to which it describes your feelings about romantic relationships." A rating of 1 is made if the item is "not at all characteristic of me," and 5 is chosen when the item is "very characteristic of me."

Factor analysis of the AAS revealed three factors: closeness (being comfortable with closeness); dependency (being comfortable depending on others); and anxiety (being worried about being rejected or abandoned). These factors do not correspond well to the three Hazen and Shaver attachment prototypes. Collins and Read state, "Thus, the factor analysis did not provide three factors that directly correspond to the three discrete styles (secure, avoidant, and anxious) but, instead, appears to have revealed three dimensions (Close, Depend, and Anxiety) that underlie the styles" (1990, p. 647). They add, "In Ainsworth's infant typology, the three general styles are further broken down into eight substyles" (p. 661). In other words, Collins and Read's factor analysis shows that self-report questionnaires of adult romantic attachment need to address a wider variance of attachment style than can depicted by single-item or few-item assessments (Collins & Read, 1994).

Attachment Style (AS)

Simpson's (1990) criticism of Hazen and Shaver's single item is similar to that of Collins and Read (1990). Simpson says, "[The] meaningful individual difference variability that exists within each category cannot be assessed . . . [S]ome adults may be best characterized as a blend of two or more styles" (p. 973). Based on these criticisms, Simpson also decomposed the Hazen and Shaver prototype item and created a 13-item assessment tool. Items are rated along a 7-point Likert scale, with 1 meaning "strongly disagree" and 10 meaning "strongly agree." Sample items include "I find it relatively easy to get close to others," "I am nervous whenever anyone gets close to me," and "I often worry that my partner(s) don't really love me" (p. 973). Using this brief questionnaire, Simpson found that

> people who exhibit a secure attachment style tend to be involved in relationships characterized by higher levels of interdependence, trust, commitment, and satisfaction. Those who exhibit insecure styles . . . tend to have relationships defined by the opposite set of features. Moreover, the three attachment styles are strongly associated with different patterns of emotional experience within relationships. (p. 977)

Simpson notes that the relationships of people with a secure attachment style are characterized by more positive emotion and less negative emotion, whereas the relationships of people with an anxious or avoidant style show the opposite pattern.

The Adult Style Questionnaire (ASQ)

Feeney and Noller (1990) and Feeney, Noller, and Hanrahan (1994) decomposed the Hazen and Shaver prototype item into 65 items, and a principal component analysis was used to reduce the final set of items to a 40-item scale. The scale was created as "a measure suitable for young adolescents . . . with little or no experience of romantic relationships" (Feeney, Noller, & Hanrahan, 1994, p. 133). Factor analysis revealed both a three-factor and a five-factor solution. The three-factor result yielded factors close to the categories of secure, avoidant, and anxious. The five-factor solution is summarized as follows:

> The five-factor solution involves two factors that were previously part of Anxiety, and two factors that were previously part of Avoidance, plus the Confidence factor. Specifically, Anxiety breaks up into Need for Approval and Preoccupation with Relationships; similarly, Avoidance tends to break up into Discomfort with Closeness and Relationships as Secondary. (pp. 135–136)

Feeney, Noller, and Hanrahan conclude, "It is . . . possible to distinguish different types of insecurely attached individuals," especially in young adults who have little experience with romantic relationships (1994, p. 149).

The Relationship Questionnaire (RQ)

Brennan, Shaver, and Tobey (1991) found that fearful subjects tended to endorse both the avoidant and ambivalent Hazen and Shaver options. This pattern led to the development of an alternative prototype measure using four rather than three prototypes (Bartholomew & Horowitz, 1991; Griffin & Bartholomew, 1994). The four prototypes are secure, dismissing, preoccupied, and fearful. Three of the four type descriptions (secure, preoccupied, and fearful) are very similar to Hazen and Shaver's prototype wording. Respondents are instructed to read each prototype and "select one that best captures the way they approach close relationships." The descriptions read as follows:

> *Secure.* It is relatively easy for me to become emotionally close to others. I am comfortable depending on others and having others depend on me. I don't worry about being alone or having others not accept me.

> *Dismissing.* I am comfortable without close emotional relationships. It is very important to me to feel independent and self-sufficient, and I prefer not to depend on others or have others depend on me.

Preoccupied. I want to be completely emotionally intimate with others, but I often find that others are reluctant to get as close as I would like. I am uncomfortable being without close relationships, but I sometimes worry that others don't value me as much as I value them.

Fearful. I am somewhat uncomfortable getting close to others. I want emotionally close relationships, but I find it difficult to trust others completely, or to depend on them. I sometimes worry that I will be hurt if I allow myself to become too close to others. (Bartholomew & Horowitz, 1991, p. 244)

These four prototypes can be classified along two dimensions—*self versus other* and *positive versus negative*. Each prototype is characterized by a particular pattern of these dimensions: Secure represents the positive self and positive other; preoccupied represents the positive other and negative self; dismissing represents the positive self and negative other; fearful represents the negative self and negative other. According to Bartholomew and Horowitz (1991), "the two groups defined as avoidant of close relationships (the *fearful* and *dismissing*) both showed difficulties in becoming close to and relying on others, but they differed significantly on measures reflecting an internalized sense of self-worth" (p. 240). Bartholomew and Horowitz essentially divided Hazen and Shaver's avoidant category into fearfully avoidant and dismissing avoidant categories. However, it is important to note that their rendition of dismissing avoidance on the RQ differs from Hazen and Shaver's avoidant description and is closer to the dismissing category from the AAI scoring. Simpson and Rholes (1998) add:

> [The] three Hazen and four Bartholomew categories were significantly related . . . [There is] considerable evidence for convergences across various measures of adult attachment . . . The [RQ] dismissing category in turn, has no clear parallel in the Hazen-Shaver's classification system, although that system's avoidant category converges fairly well with Bartholomew's fearful category. (pp. 37–38)

Furthermore, the fearful category on the RQ was worded so as to be similar to the CC category on the AAI and the A/C combination in the Strange Situation.

As had been found by other researchers, Bartholomew and Horowitz (1991) discovered that respondents sometimes selected more than one prototype and that the variance of adult romantic attachment does not easily fit into a single category:

> None of the subjects in this project uniquely fit any one attachment prototype. Instead, most subjects reported a mix of tendencies across time and

within and across relationships. Many subjects were rated as showing elements of two, three, and occasionally all four of the attachment styles. Therefore a great deal of individual variability was lost when the four continuous ratings were collapsed into a simple, four-category classification. (p. 241)

Based on their research with the RQ and its comparison with many other self-report scales on attachment, Brennan, Clark, and Shaver (1998) conducted a factor analysis of 60 attachment subscales across existing measures. They found a two-factor solution, with the main factors being *avoidance of intimacy* and *anxiety about the romantic involvement*. From extensive factor analysis of the items across all these self-report scales, Simpson and Rholes (1998) concluded that "these two dimensions underlie virtually all self-report adult romantic attachment measures and appear crucial for capturing important individual differences in adult romantic attachment" (p. 67).

The Relationship Scales Questionnaire (RSQ)

Just as further research on Hazen and Shaver's self-report prototype item led to greater refinement of their idea, subsequent research on the RQ led to breaking the RQ prototype descriptions into various items and attempting to identify the underlying structure through factor or cluster analysis. A first attempt to deconstruct the RQ in this way led to the Relationship Scales Questionnaire (RSQ; Griffin & Bartholomew, 1994). The RSQ is

designed to yield a variety of attachment subscales. Included are items [from the Love Quiz, Relationship Questionnaire, and Adult Attachment Scale]. Each item is scored on a 5-point scale ranging from *not at all like me* to *very much like me*. (Griffin & Bartholomew, 1994, p. 439)

An example of a statement related to secure attachment is "I find it relatively easy to get close to others"; an item related to avoidant attachment is "I am nervous when anyone gets too close to me"; an example related to ambivalent attachment is "I find that others are reluctant to get as close as I would like"; and an item related to fearful attachment is "I worry that I will be hurt if I allow myself to become too close to others." Overall, the results using the RSQ failed to find clear evidence for attachment categories (Fraley & Waller, 1998).

Experiences in Close Relationships (ECR)

Obegi and Berant (2009) state, "By the mid- to late 1990s, researchers and clinicians new to the field were drowning in a sea of self-report measures of attachment" (p. 161). However, despite the proliferation of self-report measures, the underlying structure of adult romantic attachment was actually becoming increasingly clear.

Results from the multitude of factor analyses of data obtained from these measures showed "a fourfold, two-dimensional typology in adulthood [that] nicely matches what is emerging in the infant literature" (Brennan & Shaver, 1998, p. 839; see also Brennan, Clark, & Shaver, 1998; Brennan & Shaver, 1995). These two factors pertained to anxiety about and avoidance of adult romantic attachment:

> Since Hazen and Shaver's (1987) landmark article, the field has moved from classifying people with respect to three categories to scaling people with respect to two dimensions . . . The first, attachment-related anxiety, captures the extent to which people are insecure about their partner's availability, love, and responsiveness. The second, attachment-related avoidance, captures the strategies that people use for regulating attachment-related behavior, thought, and affect. (Obegi & Berant, pp. 163–164)

Repeated factor analyses of the pool of all items used in the various self-report measures of adult romantic attachment also identified the critical items that best indicated anxious and avoidant attachment. Based on this empirically derived set of items, Brennan, Clark, and Shaver (1998) selected 18 items that best tapped anxious adult romantic attachment and 18 additional items that best tapped avoidant adult romantic attachment. These items were constructed into the Experience in Close Relationships scale (ECR). Based on an additional analysis by Fraley, Waller, and Brennan (2000), some of the items were refined and replaced to develop the Experience of Close Relationships–Revised version (ECR-R).

An example of an avoidant attachment item is "I prefer not to show a partner how I feel deep down"; an example of an anxious attachment item is "I am afraid I will lose my partner's love." Both the ECR and the ECR-R items are scaled using a 7-point Likert scale, with 1 indicating "strongly disagree" and 7 indicating "agree strongly." The ECR-R has become widely recognized as one of the best and most empirically sound self-report instruments for assessing adult romantic attachment, and we highly recommend it.

Interview vs. Self-Report Assessment

Through extensive research, it has become quite clear that assessments of current attachment state of mind by the AAI and by self-report measures of adult romantic attachment are at best only very weakly correlated. Crowell, Fraley, and Shaver (1999) state, "The average correlation between the AAI and self-report measures of peer/romantic attachment is about .15." (p. 444). Their table reviewing all studies to date shows that these correlations range from −.12 to .30 across studies (p. 444). Similarly, no relation has been found between classifications and self-reports of the subjects' parents' behavior (Crowell, Treboux, et al., 1999).

These consistently weak correlations have at least three possible causes. First, the AAI interview and the self-report measures assess relatively independent phenomena: Whereas the AAI is used to evaluate state of mind, self-report measures are used to obtain conscious self-reporting of experienced security or avoidant or anxious relational behavior. Second, adult romantic involvement entails a much wider range of relational behaviors than those tapped by attachment-based AAI scales. Third, assigning a single main attachment type (or multiple types in the case of CC) from the AAI may better fit clinical populations whose attachment style is likely to be more rigidly defined and inflexible, whereas multiple attachment behaviors may exist especially in healthy adults who have developed greater range and flexibility of their attachment behaviors as relevant to the relationship at the time. In other words, healthy individuals are more complex than psychiatric patients. Therefore, we strongly recommend the use of the AAI and related measures, especially in clinical populations, and the ECR-R to assess the range of healthy secure, avoidant (deactivating), and anxious (hyperactivating) behaviors in adult romantic relationships. For the level of psychopathology we mainly treat, the treatment goal is to develop a single, stable, and positive state of mind with respect to attachment in contrast to multiple, contradictory states of mind, and we find the AAI and related measures well suited to this task. When the therapeutic goal is to create greater range and flexibility of intimate behaviors in our healthier patients, then certain self-report measures like the ECR-R along with a wider range of intimacy and relational measures is recommended. At least at this point, the ECR-R is the most suitable measure for detecting avoidant/deactivating and anxious/hyperactivating behaviors in adult romantic relationships.

Assessment of Attachment-Related Behaviors in Treatment

A number of assessment scales are especially useful to the attachment-based therapist as a way to assess the working alliance, the nature of the attachment to the therapist as a secure base, and the degree to which that attachment relationship has been developed as an internal working model by the patient.

THE WORKING ALLIANCE INVENTORY (WAI)

Horvath and Greenberg (1989) developed the Working Alliance Inventory (WAI). Working alliance is defined as "what makes it possible for the patient to accept and follow treatment faithfully" (Bordin, 1980, p. 2). The WAI consists of 36 items, 12 each designed to assess three broad areas of the working alliance in treatment: bonds, goals, and tasks. An example of an item evaluating the bond between therapist and patient is "My therapist and I understand each other"; an item assessing agreement about shared treatment goals is "My therapist and I are working on mutually agreed upon goals"; and an item addressing collaboration regarding therapeutic tasks is "My therapist and I agree about the things I will need to do in therapy to help improve my situation." Each of the 36 items is rated on a 5-point Likert scale, with 1 indicating "not related" and 5 indicating "very related" to the working alliance. Using this scale, Lyons-Ruth, Melnick, Patrick, and Hobson (2007) found that securely attached patients had a significantly higher working alliance than preoccupied or avoidant patients. The WAI can be given at various points in the overall treatment to assess whether the treatment approach is leading to a more effective working alliance in insecurely attached patients.

THE CLIENT ATTACHMENT TO THERAPIST SCALE (CATS)

The Client Attachment to Therapist Scale (CATS), as the name implies, directly measures the formation of an attachment bond by the patient to the therapist in therapy (Mallinckrodt, Gantt, & Coble, 1995; Woodhouse, Schlosser, Crook, Ligiéro, & Gelso, 2003). A panel of nine experienced therapists generated items pertaining to client attachment to the therapist. The initial pool of 100 items was reduced by factor analysis to the 36 best items. The three-factor solution consisted of three scales: Secure, Avoidant-Fearful, and Preoccupied-Merger. Examples of items from the Secure scale were "My counselor is sensitive to my needs" and "My counselor is a comforting presence to me when I am upset." Items from the Avoidant-Fearful scale included "I think my counselor disapproves of me" and "I don't like to share my feelings with my counselor." Examples of items from the Preoccupied-Merger scale were "I wish my counselor could be with me on a daily basis" and "I wonder about my counselor's other clients" (Mallinckrodt et al., 1995, p. 311). All 36 items were rated on a 6-point Likert scale, with 1 indicating "strongly disagree" and 6 indicating "strongly agree."

Various studies have shown that the CATS detects both hyperactivating and deactivating behaviors in treatment (Woodhouse et al., 2003, p. 396). Woodhouse et al. also found that more securely attached individuals were able to better tolerate the negative transference and the overall amount of transference in treatment (p. 404). Mallinckrodt and Jeong (2015) conducted a meta-analysis of 13 studies that employed the CATS. They found that attachment types is significantly correlated with anxiety and avoidance: CATS security is negatively associated with anxiety and avoidance, CATS avoidance is positively correlated with both anxiety and avoidance, and CATS preoccupation is positively correlated with anxiety but not avoidance. They also found that attachment types are significantly correlated with the working alliance: CATS security is positively correlated with the working alliance, CATS avoidance is negatively correlated with the working alliance, and CATS preoccupation is not significantly correlated with the working alliance. Furthermore, the CATS captured variance not accounted for by the WAI. Mallinckrodt, Porter, and Kivlighan (2005) state, "[The] CATS subscales predicted unique variance in session experience not accounted for by the WAI alone" (p. 85). They also found that "clients with strong avoidance and anxiety in romantic relationships also showed strong avoidance and anxiety in their therapeutic attachments" and that "security was associated with greater depth and smoothness of exploration in treatment" (p. 96).

THE THERAPIST REPRESENTATIONAL INVENTORY (TRI)

The Therapist Representation Inventory (Geller, Behrends, Hartley, Farber, & Rohde, 1992; Geller & Farber, 1993) presents a way to assess the development of internal working models of attachment to the therapist as a secure base. Geller and Farber (1993) state that the TRI is "a five-part measure designed to examine the content, form, and other phenomenological properties (duration, vividness, and frequency of recall) of patients' internal representations of their therapists and the therapeutic relationship" (p. 169).

The TRI consists of 50 items rated according to a 9-point Likert scale, with 1 indicating "not at all characteristic" and 9 indicating "highly characteristic." There are two subscales on the TRI: The Therapist Embodiment Scale (TES) consists of 12-items, and the Therapist Involvement Scale (TIS) consists of 38 items. An example of a TES item is "When I find myself experiencing my therapist[,] . . . I imagine a particular quality to the sound of my therapist's voice" (Geller & Farber, 1993, pp. 169–170). The TES taps items loading on three factors: imagistic, enactive, and conversational. An imagistic item is "I imagine my therapist sitting in his/her office"; an enactive item is "I am aware of a particular emotional atmosphere which gives me the sense that my therapist is with me"; and a conversational item is "I think of my therapist making specific statements to me" (p. 170).

The 38 items on the Therapist Involvement Subscale (TIS) each "[measure] salience of discrete affective-interpersonal themes that characterize patients' involvement with mental representations of their therapists" (Geller & Farber, 1993, p. 170). This subscale taps a variety of dimensions of therapist involvement: physical (e.g., "I imagine hurting my therapist in some way"); extra-therapeutic (e.g., "I imagine our talking to each other outside of therapy"); continuing therapeutic work in the absence of the therapist (e.g., "When I am faced with a difficult situation I sometimes ask myself what would my therapist want me to do"); doubting the efficacy of treatment (e.g., "I don't think my therapy will have a lasting effect on me"); strengthening contact with the therapist and missing the therapist. (e.g., "I rehearse what I will say to my therapist when we meet again"); and missing the therapist (e.g., "I doubt that anyone can replace my therapist in my life") (pp. 170–171).

Among the 38 TIS items are 24 items that specifically tap a variety of emotions that may be associated with the internal representation of the therapist (Geller & Farber, 1993, p. 200). These assess feelings such as comfort, relief, discouragement, anger, and anxiety when evoking the representation of the therapist. One important finding from the TRI is that patients tend to develop a more available visual or imagistic representation of their attachment-based therapist the longer they are in treatment. Rosenzweig, Farber, and Geller (1996) state:

> Clients who are in Phase 2 of therapy (between 13 and 36 months) tended to use visual imagery in evoking a representation of their therapist more often than clients who are in Phase 1 (between 1 and 12 months) of therapy (p. 201) . . . Those clients who make use of the therapist representation to continue the work of therapy feel comforted and safe when evoking this representation. (p. 205)

Over time, however, the visual representation of the therapist transforms into a more collaborative, conversational representation:

> The number of sessions attended appears to be significantly related to preferred mode of representation. The greater the number of sessions, the less frequent the use of a visual mode of representing one's therapist and the more frequent the use of Conversational-Conceptual mode. (Geller & Farber, 1993, p. 176)

While these clinically based assessment instruments lack the rigorous empirical tradition of, say, the ECR-R, nevertheless they are especially relevant to the assessment of various dimensions of the therapy relationship in attachment-based treatment. For that purpose, we recommend them.

CHAPTER 5

Attachment and Psychopathology

An Overview of Attachment and Psychopathology

In their comprehensive review of research involving attachment and psychopathology, Mikulincer and Shaver (2007) explore the nature of the relationship between psychopathology and attachment. Do problems with attachment *cause* psychopathology, and, if they do, what types of psychopathology? Ein-Dor and Doron (2015) describe what they perceive as the current limitations of what is known about psychopathology and attachment:

> Attachment theory . . . has difficulty simultaneously explaining the mechanisms by which attachment insecurities lead to multiple disorders, (i.e., the question of *multifinality* . . .), and why one individual with a particular attachment orientation develops one set of symptoms while another with the same attachment vulnerability develops another set of symptoms (i.e., the question of *divergent trajectories* . . .). (p. 347)

Ein-Dor and Doron (2015) classify psychological disorders as "internalizing" or "externalizing" in quality. Internalizing disorders are those characterized primarily by fear, such as anxiety disorders and PTSD, or distress or depression. Externalizing disorders are characterized by more outwardly observable phenomena, such as substance abuse or problems with impulsivity and aggression. Ein-Dor and Doron view problems with attachment, either anxious or avoidant, as "distal risk factors" for psychopathology. They posit that attachment problems make conditions ripe for a "dark triad of processes" that comprise the "proximal risk factors" that "link attachment anxiety with multiple psychopathological disorders" (p. 355).

In the case of attachment anxiety, the three processes of this "dark triad" are (1) maladaptive emotion-regulation processes, with a tendency to up-regulate negative affectivity; (2) a greater vigilance to threat-related cues and heightened empathic accuracy; and (3) a lower level of *perceived others' responsiveness*—that is, seeing others as less responsive and supportive and as less understanding of one's needs. The three proximal factors in avoidant attachment are (1) maladaptive emotion-regulation processes, with a tendency to down-regulate affectivity and employ distancing strategies; (2) compulsive self-reliance; and (3) lower levels of social support and perceived others' responsiveness (Ein-Dor & Doron, 2015, p. 358). Ein-Dor and Doron (2015) propose that it takes specific "moderators," interacting with the above proximal risk factors, to "foment psychopathology" (p. 360). They detail four main moderators: (1) living in an environment with a chronically "mild to moderate" level of threat, (2) experience of significant loss, (3) traumatic experiences, and (4) the kind of "modeling, observational learning, and reinforcement that increase the likelihood of conduct problems among people high on anxiety or avoidance" (pp. 360–362).

An illustration of Ein-Dor and Doron's theory, using the moderator of significant loss, is a person with an insecure attachment classification who suffers a significant relationship breakup, which triggers and/or exacerbates one or more of the proximal risk factors. For instance, in an anxiously attached person, the felt sense of loss and affective response might be more acute and intense and produce depressive symptoms. An avoidantly attached person might also experience depressive symptoms related to loss, but in reaction to a different kind or degree of loss that interacts with a proximal risk factor such as excessive self-reliance. The larger point is that a problematic attachment status and its concomitant proximal risk factors, *in the absence of a moderator*, do not necessarily result in psychopathology.

As one of the goals of their review of the research, Mikulincer and Shaver (2007, 2012) tried to answer three important questions pertaining to the attachment–psychopathology connection: (1) Can a specific type of attachment insecurity reliably link to a specific type of psychopathology? (2) Can we say that attachment pathology is or can be solely and directly responsible for psychopathology? (3) In what direction—unidirectionally or bidirectionally—are attachment and psychopathology linked? Mikulincer and Shaver believe that the data allow for the following conclusions:

> In our view, beyond disorders such as separation anxiety and pathological grief in which attachment injuries are the main causes and themes, attachment insecurities *per se* are unlikely to be sufficient causes of mental disorders. Other factors (e.g., genetically determined temperament; intelligence; life history, including abuse) are likely to converge with or amplify the effects of attachment experiences on the way to psychopathology. (2012, p. 12)

In our view, serious mental disorders result from multiple converging processes, and attachment insecurities act as catalysts of other pathogenic processes by reducing psychological and social resources, and weakening a person's resilience . . . Although attachment insecurities can contribute to psychological disorders, mental afflictions can also exacerbate attachment insecurity and lead to more severe attachment-system dysfunctions. (2007, p. 373)

Self-Report vs. Interview Assessment of Attachment

In this chapter, we explore what is known about the empirical associations between a disturbed attachment classification and the risk for certain types of psychopathology. We believe that when examining this connection, it is essential to consider that the relevant attachment classifications are established by interview or self-report measures. Hazen and Shaver (1987) authored the first measure of adult romantic attachment that assesses avoidant, anxious-ambivalent, and secure attachment styles through self-report. A number of limitations of their measure have been noted. Mikulincer and Shaver (2007) observe that the measure relies primarily on subjects' conscious perception of their experiences and feelings in romantic relationships and therefore reveals little about the presumably unconscious influences contributing to attachment patterns. The authors state, "Thus, the measure does not explicitly assess 'models' of anything . . . which is not very close to what Bowlby (1969/1982) meant by 'working models.'" Another limitation is that the measure is categorical and forced-choice in nature and hence does not acknowledge the reality and importance of significant individual differences within a category. Finally, as Mikulincer and Shaver point out, the test/retest stability of that measure was found by Baldwin and Fehr (1995) to be an inadequate 70%. Because this number did not decrease with increases in test/retest intervals, the authors concluded that "the instability was due to measurement error resulting from classification artifacts, not to 'true' changes in attachment security over time" (Mikulincer & Shaver, p. 86).

Developed from observing an individual's history of attachment, "internalized working models," or attachment representations, are an internalized set of assumptions regarding self and self-in-relation-to-others (Bowlby, 1980a). Self-report measures of romantic attachment are subject to response bias and represent the conscious perception of attachment-related style associated with particular relationships rather than assessing a single underlying representational model for *all* attachment relationships (Agrawal, Gunderson, Holmes, & Lyons-Ruth, 2004). Conscious perception and underlying representations are not necessarily well correlated. We maintain that interview-based assessment, such as with the Adult Attachment Interview (AAI), is the preferred assessment method over self-report measures. The AAI is able to access the adult's unconscious processes pertaining to emotional regulation (Jacobvitz, Curran, & Moller, 2002), and it identifies one's state of mind with respect to attachment as seen through the violations of Grice's maxims (described in Chapter 4 of this book). The AAI is able to glean the individual's specific attachment style by coding the forms of his or her AAI narrative as it *interacts* with the prompted and elicited content. The AAI has a way of "surprising the unconscious," whereas the limited nature of the self-report measure gives the unconscious the opportunity to defend itself, thus obfuscating accurate scrutiny into the person's true attachment style (Hesse, 1999).

Particularly important for clinical work, the AAI allows for a more detailed subclassification of attachment style, an element that self-report measures cannot provide. This detailed assessment is essential when forming a treatment plan for more complex cases, such as complex PTSD, borderline personality disorder, or dissociative disorders, or for "treatment-resistant" patients. It is not unusual for "treatment-resistant" patients to have made multiple attempts at finding appropriate treatment and suffered through shifting diagnoses, different recommendations for treatment strategies, and reactive medication management. These are the patients who as children needed to develop a mixture of attachment strategies due to the demands of interacting with conflicting parental attachment behaviors in one parent or between several caregivers. The difficult treatment ordeals these patients experience may be considered to reflect the presenting problems that the treatment plan must address. The five-way classification system that has been developed for the AAI allows for quite precise determination of attachment patterns, which is particularly helpful as the presenting psychopathology becomes more severe.

As is obvious from the above, in this book we give particular weight to the researcher/clinician-administered Adult Attachment Interview (AAI).* This assessment tool is capable of capturing the individual's attachment disposition and providing a nuanced view of any attachment disturbance. We believe that the AAI is the gold standard of measurement because of its ability to precisely discern an individual's internal state of mind with respect to attachment and to indirectly provide information about the internal working model(s) of attachment at the time of the interview. Thus, studies examining psychopathology and attachment using the AAI as the primary measure have, in our estimation, particular relevance to our therapeutic approach, and many of these studies on the AAI and psychopathology are reviewed in this chapter. At the same time, numerous other studies looking at attachment and psychopathology have exclusively or primarily used self-report measures to describe attachment style, attitudes, and behaviors. We do not want to ignore the findings from this domain of research. Further, we do believe that despite the depth and breadth limitations of self-report instru-

---

* As described in Chapter 4, we also find value in Crittenden's DMM-AAI (2007); however, our experience and most research to date is based on the original George, Kaplan, and Main (1996) AAI.

ments, their identification of aspects of a person's conscious perception of his or her attachment-related beliefs, attitudes, and behaviors can be useful, and self-report measures are of particular value when they identify hyperactivating and deactivating strategies of attachment behavior.

Our review does include studies using these measures, but it is particularly important to maintain perspective on the differences in what and how the interview and self-report instruments measure. There is considerable evidence that the AAI and self-report measures of attachment have little overlap. Roisman et al. (2007) note that the AAI comes from the developmental psychology tradition and relies upon inferences about a subject's attachment style gleaned from the interview. Self-report measures, such as the Adult Attachment Scale (AAS) and Experiences in Close Relationships (ECR) scale, have a social and personality psychology heritage and rely on the subject's conscious and deliberate endorsement of attachment-related attitudes and behaviors. Roisman et al. (2007) conducted the most comprehensive evaluation of the self-report and AAI comparison literature to date. They performed a meta-analysis of 10 studies "containing data on the convergence of the AAI with social psychological measures of self-reported attachment style" (p. 680). The overlap between AAI attachment status (secure versus insecure) and self-reported attachment style was found to be "trivial to small" ($r = 0.09$, $N = 1,221$; p. 682). A small effect ($r = 0.15$) was noted in the association between the AAI dismissing style and a self-reported avoidant style. Eagle (2013) notes the lack of convergence between the AAI and self-report measures (exemplified by the ECR), stating, "Apparently, an individual's conscious reports of attitudes and feelings towards his or her romantic partner tells us little about his or her implicit state-of-mind with respect to early attachment experiences" (p. 54).

Each section of this chapter reviews the association between attachment status and particular conditions of psychopathology. Because of the little overlap between self-report and AAI interview-based assessment of attachment, within each section we review the findings from self-report studies and then from AAI studies. When possible, we provide some integrative commentary about what, if any, consensus exists about the empirical connection between attachment status and that particular form of psychopathology. We also review studies that, in our opinion, provide findings suggestive of how attachment disturbance may contribute to psychopathology.

ATTACHMENT, EMOTIONAL DISTRESS, AND PSYCHIATRIC DISTRESS

Mikulincer and Shaver (2007) reviewed approximately 30 studies of nonclinical populations that examined possible correlations between attachment—anxious and avoidant—and neuroticism (from the five-factor model of personality). Neuroticism is also referred to as "negative affectivity"—"the extent to which a person is feeling upset or unpleasantly engaged rather than peaceful" (Clark & Watson, 1991, p. 321). The measures used to rate attachment were based on self-report (e.g., Adult Attachment Scale, Experiences in Close Relationships scale), as were the measures of neuroticism (e.g., Five Factor Personality Questionnaire). Mikulincer and Shaver report, "All of the studies, without exception, found significant correlations between attachment anxiety and neuroticism." The authors suggested that in both categories—anxious and avoidant—the data support the notion that previously learned attachment strategies in reaction to specific caregivers continue to exert a negative influence on individuals' emotional experiences.

Mikulincer and Shaver (2007) also conducted a separate review of 61 studies that examined the relationship between attachment orientation and psychiatric symptoms and negative affectivity. These studies are notable for measuring different qualitative aspects of attachment, including sense of security with peers and parents (e.g., Inventory of Parent and Peer Attachment [IPPA], Parental Attachment Questionnaire [PAQ]) and self-report measures of security and attachment style (e.g., Adult Attachment Scale). Instruments used to measure psychiatric symptomatology were also diverse, ranging from SCID (Structured Clinical Interview for DSM Disorders) interviews to self-report measures such as the Brief Symptom Inventory and Symptom Checklist–90. Mikulincer and Shaver noted that all studies in this review that used the IPPA or the PAQ "found secure attachment to parents to be associated with lower levels of negative affectivity and less severe psychiatric symptomatology" (p. 374). Breaking the data down further, an overwhelming number of the studies found significant correlations between an anxious form of attachment insecurity and psychiatric symptom/negative affectivity, whereas less than half found such correlations with the avoidant style.

ATTACHMENT AND ANXIETY DISORDERS

In their review of the research looking at attachment and anxiety disorders, Ein-Dor and Doron (2015) noted that anxious and preoccupied states as measured by both the AAI and by self-report measures correlate with more significant symptoms of anxiety. However, the authors observed that a less clear association is found between an avoidant classification style and anxiety symptoms, with approximately only 50% of studies finding a significant association. Ein-Dor and Doron cautioned that conclusions—especially regarding causality—derived from the research should be tempered by the largely cross-sectional versus longitudinal nature of the studies. Further, many of the cross-sectional studies included a potentially problematic mixture of more chronic cases with less chronic cases that likely had different levels of severity.

Doron, Moulding, Kyrios, Nedeljkovic, and Mikulincer (2009) investigated the relationship of insecure attachment as measured by the ECR to obsessive-compulsive disorder (OCD) symptoms as measured by the Padua Inventory–Revised

(PI) and the Obsessional Beliefs Questionnaire–Revised (OBQ). The results show a relationship between insecure attachment and elevated levels of OCD-related thinking style and symptoms, with attachment anxiety having a somewhat stronger relationship than attachment avoidance. The authors suggest that attachment anxiety and the corresponding "hyperactivation" of the attachment system may connect "with increased vigilance to intrusive thoughts, in particular those that are ego-dystonic . . . thereby increasing the need to act" (pp. 1040–1041). They suggest further that attachment-avoidant individuals, with their exaggerated emphasis on autonomy, may be more vulnerable to acquiring OCD-related dysfunctional beliefs about being able to control their thoughts and achieving an unrealistically perfectionistic standard of behavior.

Mikulincer and Shaver (2007) conducted a noteworthy study of Israeli college students who were divided into spider-phobics and nonphobics. Each group was exposed to three different visualizations designed to represent a secure, insecure, or neutral attachment experience. For example, the secure visualization involved imagining a supportive and caring partner, and the neutral scene involved a benign image of a pharmacy clerk. The subjects were then shown pictures of spiders along with neutral photos such as flowers. Spider-phobics showed less aversion to spider pictures following exposure to the secure attachment visualization compared with exposure to the neutral stimuli. Likewise, spider-phobics exposed to insecure attachment visualizations showed an increased aversion to spider pictures compared with neutral stimuli. Nonphobics did not show any statistically significant differences in their responses. Mikulincer and Shaver found significant correlations between anxious attachment and spider phobia as well as between attachment anxiety and phobic avoidance. They concluded, "Experimental and correlational findings indicate that attachment insecurities are involved in the generation of phobic symptomatology and that the restoration of attachment security can have healing effects on phobic people" (p. 383).

Dozier, Stovall-McClough, and Albus (2008) state, "Strategies that maximize the expression of attachment needs are expected to be associated with internalizing disorders, and strategies that minimize the expression of attachment needs are expected to be associated with more externalizing disorders" (p. 726). Using this paradigm, anxiety-related disorders would be considered internalizing disorders. Bowlby suggested that all anxiety disorders are related to the proximity and availability of the primary attachment figure, and Sroufe and Fleeson (1986) support that view: "The infant–caregiver attachment relationship is the womb from which the incipient person emerges. The first organization is dyadic, and it is from that organization, and not from the inborn characteristics of the infant, that personality emerges" (p. 67). Warren, Huston, Egeland, and Sroufe (1997) report that "a specific link was found between anxious/resistant attachment in infancy and anxiety disorders assessed 16 years later" (p. 642).

As part of their groundbreaking Minnesota longitudinal work covering three decades, Sroufe, Egeland, Carlson, and Collins (2005) conducted a comprehensive study of nearly 200 children born into poverty. Using Ainsworth's Strange Situation Procedure (SSP), the infants were assessed at both 12 months and 18 months. This study provided strong support for Bowlby's hypothesis: Secure attachment is strongly related to the development of emotion regulation, and secure attachment also supports the balance between safety, curiosity, and exploration. Bosquet and Egeland (2006) observed the original participants of the Minnesota study and examined the appearance and course of anxiety symptoms from infancy through adolescence. The subjects were assessed during the following periods: neonatal, 12 months, 18 months, 42 months, kindergarten, first grade, sixth grade, 16 years, and 17.5 years. The authors reported that insecure attachment in infants was associated with anxiety symptoms in adolescence, most likely due to the insecure internal working models of relationships.

E. K. Adam, Gunnar, and Tanaka (2004) found in their study of 100 middle-class mothers with two-year-olds that the mothers' observed parenting behaviors and their self-reports of emotional well-being correlated with adult attachment classifications using the AAI. The interviews with the mothers were scored using the Main and Goldwyn (1994) four-way classification system: dismissing (Ds), secure (F), preoccupied (E), and unresolved/disorganized (Ud). This study yielded two primary contributions: First, the development of a mother's internal working models created by *her* history of attachment relationships played an important role in her child's attachment experience; second, mothers classified as preoccupied on the AAI reported significantly higher levels of negative affect and anxiety and demonstrated angry and intrusive parenting behaviors that were demanding or role-reversing in style. Main and Goldwyn (1994) report similar findings of high levels of uncontained anger and speech in the AAIs of some preoccupied mothers.

In their study of mothers with anxiety disorders, Manassis, Bradley, Goldberg, Hood, and Swinson (1994) administered the AAI (using the four-way classification system) to 18 outpatient women who had anxiety disorders as determined from the Structured Clinical Interview (SCID; Spitzer, Williams, Gibbon, & First, 1993). Fourteen of the mothers had a primary diagnosis of panic disorder (two were additionally diagnosed with obsessive-compulsive disorder), three had generalized anxiety disorder, and one had a primary diagnosis of OCD. From the AAI, 14 (78%) of the mothers were determined to be unresolved (Ud) with respect to trauma or loss: Six were unresolved with respect to loss, two were unresolved with respect to trauma, and six were judged to be unresolved (Ud) with respect to both trauma and loss. To determine mothers' children's attachment classification, all of the children were administered the SS; 85% of the children were classified as insecurely attached, and 65% of the children determined to be disorganized. This high level of insecure attachment in the children led Mannasis and her colleagues to point out that "when treating adults with anxiety disorders, clinicians must be alert to the possible psychological difficulties in the children or in the parent–child relationship" (p. 1111). Manassis et al. emphasized that "helping anxious adults resolve the losses and traumatic experiences of the past may indirectly benefit their children by improving the parent–child relationship" (p. 1111). This study suggested that recognizing the prevalence of the unresolved attachment classification (Ud) in clinically anxious populations can both enhance the treatment planning and efficacy of the clinical treatment and indirectly benefit the insecurely attached children of the anxious patients.

Similarly, Fonagy et al. (1996) studied 82 nonpsychotic inpatients and 85 case-matched controls using the AAI scored with Main and Goldwyn's four-way classification system. Significantly more of the inpatient group (76%) than the control group received an unresolved classification (Ud), indicating disorganization related to either loss or trauma. A significant correlation was found between the unresolved classification (Ud) and the diagnosis of anxiety disorder. The study authors asserted that anxiety is related to the degree to which past experiences invade the present. However, they also proffered that "the direction of causality is unclear," and we are left with the question of whether or not anxiety is "an underlying mental state that results in disorganization and prevents an individual from resolving loss or abuse" (p. 28).

Ivarsson (2008) described a study by Ivarsson, Granqvist, Broberg, and Gillberg that investigated AAI patterns among adolescents with OCD. They interviewed 100 adolescents, 25 each with OCD, depressive disorder (DD), and OCD plus DD, and general population controls. The AAI was used to assess attachment classification, and the interviews were coded using the five-way classification system. Classification differed significantly across the groups: Adolescents with OCD showed a prevalence of dismissing traits, with 60% being classified as dismissing (Ds); 40% of the DD group was unresolved (Ud) with respect to loss or trauma and 28% were designated as cannot classify (CC); and subjects with both OCD and DD were classified as either dismissing or unresolved. Ivarsson and his colleagues concluded that attachment disturbances could be a possible contribution to OCD and should aid clinicians in understanding why OCD symptoms develop and are reinforced over time. They posited that a longitudinal study, similar to the Minnesota study, would be the ultimate test to correlate attachment classification and children with a high risk of developing OCD, such as children of adults with OCD and siblings of pediatric OCD patients.

Panic disorders are distinguished from other forms of anxiety disorders by their episodic sudden onset. The predominant symptoms of panic disorders are shortness of breath, heart palpitations, and chest pain; other symptoms may include nausea, vertigo, or feelings of derealization. Although some subjects in Manassis et al.'s previously mentioned study had panic disorder, there is little research that has measured the correlation between attachment classifications and panic disorder. The study that has focused most on this relationship was done by Zeijlmans van Emmichoven, van IJzendoorn, de Ruiter, and Brosschot (2003). Using the AAI four-way attachment classification system to examine 28 outpatients, the authors found that the majority of patients had panic disorder with agoraphobia and demonstrated more dismissing attachment: 43% (n = 12) were dismissing (Ds), 29% (n = 8) were preoccupied (E), and 11% (n = 3) were scored as unresolved (Ud).

If internal working models, or attachment representations, play an important role in the etiology of anxiety disorders, it follows that psychotherapeutic treatment focused on reshaping these representations would lessen the suffering of patients with these disorders. We propose that the Ideal Parent Figure protocol is a highly efficient method for reshaping internal working models by creating new, fresh, and positive attachment representations. This protocol is described in detail in Chapter 8 of this book.

Attachment and Affective Disorders

AFFECTIVE DISORDERS AND SUICIDALITY

Mikulincer and Shaver (2007) reviewed over 100 studies of nonclinical samples looking at attachment quality in adulthood and levels of depressive symptoms as measured by either self-report (e.g., Beck Depression Inventory, State-Trait Anxiety Inventory) or interview such as the SCID. The aggregate data showed a strong correlation between levels of secure attachment (determined variously across studies by assessments of attachment behaviors, subjectively felt attachment security, or attachment status from the AAI) and lower levels of depression. Mikulincer and Shaver (2007) noted that three studies showed no significant correlation between AAI classification and depression. Subjects classified as having an anxious attachment—whether identified as anxious-preoccupied (E) on the AAI or as having elevated levels of attachment anxiety on self-report attachment measures such as the AAS and ECR—showed consistently elevated levels of symptoms of anxiety and depression compared with securely attached subjects. In contrast, about 50% of avoidant subjects across studies showed elevated levels of anxiety and depression.

Ein-Dor and Doron (2015) noted that "more than 100 studies have examined the links between attachment dispositions and the severity of depressive symptoms" (p. 350). They noted in particular that across clinical settings and populations, those with either a dismissing or preoccupied classification on the AAI and people with self-reported attachment avoidance or anxiety showed more depressive symptoms.

Berant, Mikulincer, and Shaver (2008) conducted a seven-year prospective longitudinal study of 63 mothers of children born with congenital heart disease

(CHD). The authors investigated the interplay among the mothers' attachment style, mental health, and degree of marital satisfaction and their children's emotional vulnerabilities. Assessments were made at the study's start (T1), and at one year (T2) and seven years (T3). Regarding the mothers' mental health, neither the mother's attachment anxiety level nor the severity of the child's CHD at T1 "contributed uniquely to changes in mental health by Time 3" (p. 44). Women with avoidant (i.e., dismissing) attachment at the time of their child's CHD diagnosis had more symptoms than expected at T3. Mothers with a significantly higher level of avoidant attachment (i.e., 1 standard deviation above the mean) who had infants with CHD categorized as severe showed the most difficulty, while either a less severe form of CHD or a less pronounced avoidant style seemed to mitigate symptoms significantly. The mothers' attachment status was seen as related to children's later self-concept: "The higher the mother's avoidance or anxiety score at the time of diagnosis, the less positive her child's explicit self-concept 7 years later" (p. 47). Commenting on the interaction between attachment anxiety (but not avoidance) and severity of CHD, the authors concluded, "The mother's attachment anxiety seemed to predispose children who suffered from severe CHD to develop a less positive explicit self-concept" (p. 48).

Kobak, Sudler, and Gamble (1991) administered the AAI to a sample of adolescents and found that insecure attachment in general, and anxious-preoccupied attachment in particular, was significantly related to higher levels of depressive symptoms. The study also included direct observation of mothers and teens in problem-solving activities. Depressed teens perceived higher levels of maternal dominance and expressed higher levels of dysfunctional anger during these problem-solving episodes. Cole-Detke and Kobak (1996) studied 61 college women, all of whom were given the AAI as well as classified with the Q-sort method. Women with primarily hyperactivating (anxious-preoccupied) attachment strategies had significantly higher levels of depressive symptoms than those with deactivating, dismissing strategies.

Patrick, Hobson, Castle, Howard, and Maughan (1994) gave the AAI to 24 patients with borderline personality disorder and 8 patients with dysthymic disorder. Dysthymic patients, as compared to borderlines, had a significant representation of preoccupied attachment and unresolved status with respect to trauma.

In Fonagy et al.'s (1996) study of the AAI given to 82 nonpsychotic psychiatric inpatients and also to 85 matched healthy control subjects, there were 72 affective patients, including 21 bipolar patients, 21 dysthymic patients, and 30 patients with major depressive disorder (MDD). The authors report:

> Patients with MDD were significantly more likely to be secure than either bipolar or dysthymic patients (40% vs. 19% and 10% respectively) . . . Scores on the AAI Anger scale were significantly higher for the MMD group . . . than for the bipolar . . . and dysthymic groups." (pp. 26–27)

DeJong (1992) compared two groups of undergraduates, one with and one without a history of suicidality. The group with a history of suicidality had less secure attachment to their parents as measured by the IPPA. This group also showed less secure attachment compared to a third group of nondepressed students with no suicidality in their history. Similarly, K. S. Adam, Sheldon-Keller, and West (1996) gave the AAI to 132 inpatient psychiatric adolescents with and without a history of suicidal ideation. Of the suicidal group, 73% had unresolved attachment status with respect to trauma, but only 44% in the nonsuicidal group had unresolved status with respect to trauma. The authors found that both preoccupied attachment and unresolved status were significantly associated with suicidal ideation, while dismissing attachment meant low suicidal ideation. They concluded, "Preoccupied (E) attachment, in interaction with Ud attachment (Ud/E), also increases the probability of membership in the case group, whereas dismissing (Ds) attachment decreases the probability" (p. 269).

Riggs and Jacobvitz (2002) gave the AAI to 233 expectant mothers and fathers with a history of child abuse to examine the link between early attachment relationships and psychopathology. The AAI was administered to all participants and was scored using the five-way AAI coding system. Fifty percent of the sample had a secure attachment classification, 22% had a dismissing classification, 6% had a preoccupied classification, and 22% were classified as unresolved. In the unresolved group (52), 24 were classified as unresolved in relation to loss, 13 were classified as unresolved in relation to abuse, and 8 were classified as unresolved for both loss and abuse. Seven participants from the sample were coded as cannot classify (CC). Unresolved adults were considerably more likely to report emotional distress and suicidal ideation, dismissing adults were more likely to report criminal charges, and preoccupied adults were more likely to report suicidal ideation than either secure or dismissing adults. Subjects classified as preoccupied reported a significantly higher likelihood of suicidal ideation than those with other attachment classifications. Dismissing women had significantly lower levels of depression, "consistent with the idea that Dismissing adults minimize emotion and may express distress in other ways" (p. 202). Subjects with unresolved status for trauma or loss reported greater suicidal ideation, emotional distress, and substance abuse than those with resolved status.

ATTACHMENT AND BIPOLAR DISORDER

Berry, Barrowclough, and Wearden (2007) reviewed studies of attachment status in patients with psychosis—schizophrenia, bipolar disorder (type I), and psychotic depression. They reported that there are "higher levels of insecure attachment, dismissing attachment in particular, in samples with psychosis as compared to controls" (p. 458). In two of the studies, "individuals with a diagnosis of schizophrenia had higher levels of insecurity than those with affective diagnoses, including bipolar disorder and major depression (Dozier, 1990; Dozier, Stevenson, Lee, & Velligan, 1991)" (p. 462). Dozier (1990) gave the AAI to 42 psychotic patients, 25 of whom were diagnosed with bipolar disorder. Using the Q-sort method, patients with bipolar psychosis were found to have less secure attachment than schizophrenics. Dozier et al. (1991) described using the Q-sort method to assess AAI transcripts on 21 schizophrenics, 11 bipolar patients, and 8 patients with major depressive disorder. Dismissing attachment was associated with an externalizing/outward focus in bipolar patients. Psychotic patients with hyperactivating strategies reported greater symptom severity, but psychotic patients with dismissing strategies actually had more symptoms (Dozier & Lee, 1995).

In the Fonagy et al. (1996) study mentioned earlier, "patients with bipolar disorder were more likely to be classified as Ds (38%) than MMD (7%) or dysthymic patients (14%); . . . narratives of bipolar patients [were] characterized by derogation associated with a hypomanic or manic state and readily classified as Ds" (pp. 26, 28).

In our orphanage study, reported later in this chapter, a total of 14 of 45 subjects had a type II bipolar disorder diagnosis. There were no bipolar type I or psychotic bipolar subjects in the sample. Bipolar type II subjects were significantly more likely to have insecure than secure attachment on the AAI. Using the five-way classification system, most of their AAIs were scored as disorganized (CC); a pure Ds classification was rare in this sample. Thus, while most previous studies using the AAI identified the Ds classification as overrepresented in bipolar (mostly type I) subjects, we found an overrepresentation of disorganization (CC) in our bipolar type II subjects.

Attachment and Somatic Symptom Disorders, Factitious Disorders, and Malingering

SOMATIC SYMPTOM DISORDERS

Waldinger, Schulz, Barsky, and Ahern (2006) investigated the role of insecure attachment as it relates to adult somatization. The data set consisted of couples with abuse histories and couples with recent violence perpetrated by the male. All subjects completed the Somatic Symptom Inventory (SSI), an instrument drawn with items from the Minnesota Multiphasic Personality Inventory (MMPI) Hypochondriasis scale and the Hopkins Symptom Checklist (HSCL) Somatization scale (Lipman, Covi, & Shapiro, 1977). The attachment measure used was the Relationship Scales Questionnaire (RSQ; Griffin & Bartholomew, 1994). The data showed that 56% of women and 17% of men reported sexual abuse histories. Men reported more physical abuse (38% versus 26%), while women reported more emotional abuse (51% versus 36%). Women in the sample reported "significantly more trauma" (p. 131). The authors noted that "for both women and men, somatization scores were significantly correlated in the expected direction with the amount of childhood trauma reported" (p. 131).

> Study results support the idea that childhood trauma shapes patients' styles of relating to others in times of need, and these styles, in turn, influence the somatization process and how patients respond to providers . . . For women, childhood trauma influences adult levels of somatization by fostering insecure adult attachment. For men, the findings suggested that trauma and attachment are both important independent predictors of adult somatization. (p. 129)

Maunder and Hunter (2009) reviewed the main self-report and interview methods for assessing attachment, including the AAI, and argued that assessing attachment style is important in understanding symptom presentations in medical patients. They concluded that assessing attachment style "may allow clinicians to adapt medical care to the strengths and vulnerabilities that follow from particular patterns of adult attachment" (p. 128). Ciechanowski, Walker, Katon, and Russo (2002) studied a large sample of female primary care patients who were assessed for somatization. Attachment style was significantly related to symptom reporting and health care utilization. Women with an anxious-preoccupied or fearful attachment style reported significantly more physical symptoms than secure women. Anxious-preoccupied women had a significantly greater number of primary care visits and higher health care costs than other women, and fearfully attached women had the lowest number of health care visits. The authors concluded, "These results suggest that attachment style is an important factor in assessing symptom perception and health care utilization" (p. 660).

Waller, Scheidt, and Hartmann (2004) used the AAI to investigate attachment representations in patients with somatoform disorders. They characterized somatoform disorders as "the existence of multiple and variable physical symptoms without demonstrable pathophysiological processes" (p. 200). The aim of their study was to "apply the developmental perspective of attachment theory . . . to somatoform disorders" (p. 200). Their study included a sample of 37 subjects diagnosed with various forms of somatoform disorder (somatoform pain disorder, somatoform autonomic dysfunction, and somatization disorder) as compared to 20 control subjects. Subjects' AAIs were analyzed using the Q-sort method (Kobak, 1989/1993). Significantly more somatoform patients than controls were classified as insecure on the AAI: 48.6% of the patients were classified as insecure dismissing as compared to 25% of the controls, and 25.7% of the patients were classified as insecure preoccupied as compared to 15% of the controls. There were no significant differences between the subtypes of somatoform disorders with respect to attachment classification. Dismissing somatoform patients had significantly less frequent physician visits but a greater number of hospital admissions, whereas preoccupied somatoform patients had significantly more physician visits and less hospitalizations than dismissing patients. Somatization correlated positively with dismissing attachment, and the authors emphasize the "high proportion of insecure dismissing attachment in somatoform disorders" (p. 206). Somatoform patients with dismissing attachment tended to divert "attention from internal feelings of distress . . . [and repress] attachment-related affects" and in so doing had significantly higher "somatic attribution of symptoms" (p. 206). In other words, individuals with a dismissing attachment style minimize affects and convert affects into somatic symptoms.

Neumann, Nowacki, Roland, and Kruse (2011) gave the AAI to 15 patients diagnosed with somatoform pain disorder and 15 nonclinical control subjects. All 15 somatoform pain patients had insecure attachment. Compared with the controls, the patients had significantly lower parental loving scores and significantly higher parental rejection scores on the AAI parenting scales. On the AAI state-of-mind scales, somatoform patients had significantly higher scores on angry preoccupation. Overall coherence of transcript and mind was significantly lower, and unresolved status with respect to trauma was significantly higher in somatoform patients than in controls.

Pajuhinia and Faraji (2014) gave the AAI and Symptom Checklist-90 (SCL-90R) to 384 Iranian university students. Both dismissing and preoccupied insecure attachment were significantly positively correlated with vulnerability to somatization.

Scheidt et al. (1999) administered the AAI to 20 patients with idiopathic spasmodic torticollis and to 20 healthy control subjects. All subjects were also administered the Toronto Alexithymia Scale (TAS-20). The Q-sort procedure was used to analyze AAI classification. Dismissing attachment was significantly more prevalent in the torticollis group than in the control group. Alexithymia was also significantly more prevalent in the torticollis group than in the controls. The authors concluded that "alexithymia in adults is significantly interrelated with the mental representation of attachment" (p. 47).

Kozlowska and Williams (2009) studied attachment in 28 children with a diagnosis of conversion disorder using the Dynamic-Maturational Model (DMM) assessment system (Crittenden, 2000a, 2000b; Crittenden & Landini, 2011). Twelve children (43%) had an inhibitory attachment strategy (Type A), another 12 children (43%) had an excitatory attachment strategy (Type C), and the other 4 children (14%) had an alternating inhibitory/excitatory (Type A/C) attachment strategy. Attachment style was clearly related to the type of conversion symptom: Negative CD symptoms, such as loss of sensory or motor functioning, were related to an inhibitory attachment style, whereas positive CD symptoms, such as symptom exaggeration, exaggerated seizure-like activity, limb weakness, and astasia-abasia, were all related to an excitatory attachment style.

We acknowledge the continuing controversy about whether fibromyalgia is a somatoform disorder but report here a study by Waller, Scheidt, Endorf, Hartmann, and Zimmermann (2015), who used the AAI to assess attachment in 34 patients with fibromyalgia. Unresolved status with respect to trauma was unusually high (50%) in these patients.

FACTITIOUS DISORDERS

Factitious disorder as a diagnosis in the *Diagnostic and Statistical Manual of Mental Disorders* (DSM) originally emerged from a classic paper titled "Hysteria Split Asunder," published in 1978, just before the DSM-III replaced the previous DSM-II. In this paper, Hyler and Spitzer emphasized that the DSM-II concept of "hysteria," much like the idea of "insanity," was over-inclusive, diagnostically imprecise, and difficult to test empirically. They believed that "hysteria" could be divided conceptually into a variety of discrete diagnostic subgroups and that well-defined criteria could be established for each of these unique diagnostic entities. In essence, the over-general DSM-II category of hysteria was split into four individual categories for the DSM-III: (1) histrionic personality disorder (Axis II), (2) somatoform disorders (Axis I), (3) dissociative disorders (Axis I), and (4) factitious disorder (Axis I). According to this new classification approach, conversion disorder became a subtype of the generic somatoform disorders category, and somatoform and dissociative disorders were at least conceptually separated from each other, the former pertaining to physical symptoms and the latter to mental symptoms (relating to consciousness, identity, and memory). Factitious disorders were differentiated from somatoform disorders based on the *voluntary* production of physical symptoms in the former as compared to an *involuntary* experience of physical symptoms in the latter group. Like malingering, factitious disorders are voluntarily produced forms of deception; unlike malingering, factitious disorders are not obviously linked to environmental goals such as monetary gain or other incentives.

Hyler and Spitzer's project of "splitting hysteria asunder" was admirable in its goal of seeking greater conceptual clarity and empirical reliability and validity for each of the four diagnostic entities that had been categorized together simply as "hysteria." The problem with this enterprise, however, is that it virtually ignored the natural covariance between each of these four diagnostic entities. Given the increasing numbers of case reports and empirical studies that showed a clear comorbid association between factitious disorder and various personality disorders (such as borderline and histrionic personality) on the one hand and a comorbid association between somatoform disorders and dissociative disorders on the other, the interrelationship among these conditions, at least for certain patients, should not be ignored. Kihlstrom (1994), whose radical proposal was to return to the archaic diagnosis of hysteria, viewed the attempt to split hysteria asunder as a failure in that the naturally occurring comorbidity between somato-form, dissociative, and factitious disorders is obscured.

A factitious disorder is best defined as an "artificial production or simulation of a disease [or history]" (Folks & Freeman, 1985, p. 274). Comparable to malinger-ing, factitious behavior involves deliberate deception and, often, intentional self-harm. Symptoms are dramatically presented, and the production of symptoms and/or histories is even more exaggerated when the patient is being observed. According to Folks and Freeman, the three essential clinical features include pathological lying, recurrent simulated illnesses, and going from clinic to clinic assuming a sick role. Most experts agree that the basic motivation associated with factitious illness is the compulsive need to assume a sick role *in order to get attention or caretaking*. In fact, the goal of obtaining care differentiates factitious illness from other self-destructive behaviors (Eisendrath, 1984).

This need to assume a sick role to receive caretaking reveals the interrelation-ship between factitious behavior and attachment disturbance. There is a grow-ing consensus that factitious disorders arise from a "developmental disturbance" and that the relationships that factitious patients develop with caregivers is a reenactment of past developmental disturbances. The earliest psychoanalytic descriptions of factitious behavior stressed the pre-oedipal deprivation. Bursten (1965), for example, emphasized lack of parental affection in the early childhood histories of these patients. Spiro (1968) wrote:

> Early childhood deprivation and difficult relationships with aloof, absent, or sadistic parents may sensitize the latter patients to distorted learning stemming from traumatic early illness or hospitalization. The concept of mastery . . . offers the most useful explanation for the subsequent behavior. (p. 587)

According to Nadelson (1985), abnormal illness behavior arises from funda-mental problems in "attachment, bonding, and caretaking" (p. 182). Plassmann (1994) saw factitious behavior as an "attempt to cope with the early object losses in a narcissistic manner" (p. 14). In his sample of 22 factitious patients, 61% self-re-ported attachment problems, 24% had rape histories, 19% had incest histories, and 28% had suffered traumatic object loss. Although his study did not use the AAI, these data suggest that insecure attachment and unresolved status with respect to trauma and loss are likely important in the development of factitious behavior.

Arrested self and self-esteem development is also a primary feature in people with factitious behavior. In an important empirical study of 18 factitious patients, Ehlers and Plassmann (1994) found that nine had a coexisting borderline person-ality diagnosis and another six had a coexisting narcissistic personality diagno-sis. They found that 83% of the patients in the sample had significant evidence for "disorders of self-regulation" and concluded, "The overwhelming majority of patients suffering from factitious disorders therefore demonstrate a narcissistic pathology" (p. 70). This failure in self-development had several long-term consequences, including an unstable, protean sense of self and a vulnerability to self-fragmentation. Such self-pathology may serve to explain why the factitious patient can easily assume very different identities and personal histories over time and why, fundamentally, the factitious patient's identity is that of an impostor. Some experts have viewed factitious behavior as an adaptive attempt to prevent total fragmentation of an unstable sense of self by asserting and reinforcing false identities (e.g., Cramer, Gershberg, & Stern, 1971).

MALINGERING

Pianta, Egeland, and Adam (1996) gave the AAI and also the MMPI-2 to 110 women. Although the main purpose of the study was to examine the relationship between self-reported psychiatric symptoms on the MMPI-2 and attachment status, valuable data emerged about the relation of attachment to the validity scales on the MMPI-2. The women with dismissing attachment, as assessed with the AAI Q-sort method, "reported comparatively little psychiatric distress," [whereas the women with preoccupied attachment] . . . [were] highest on a range of indices of psychiatric symptoms" (p. 273). When the subjects' validity scales were examined, it was found that dismissing attachment was associated with minimization or a tendency toward a "fake" good profile on the MMPI-2 and preoccupied attachment was associated with exaggeration or a tendency toward a "fake" bad profile. All eight subjects who produced an invalid MMPI-2 profile had insecure attachment on the AAI Q-sort, with most being preoccupied and some having unresolved status for trauma or loss in addition to a preoccupied attachment status. Subjects with preoccupied attachment were also significantly more likely than others to score in the elevated range on the Response Infrequency (F) scale. The authors suggested that "they portray themselves in extreme psychological and emotional distress, possibly exaggerating their distress, and viewing themselves in need of sympathy and attention" (p. 277). On the clinical scales,

> the preoccupied group scored significantly higher than both the dismissing and autonomous groups on the Psychopathic Deviation, Paranoia, and Schizophrenia scales[,] . . . indicat[ing] . . . signs of impulsivity, insensitivity to others and social norms, suspiciousness, hostility, feelings of persecution, isolation, self-preoccupation, and inferiority. (p. 278)

In our opinion, significant elevations on the three F scales (Infrequency) and the Sc scale (labeled "Schizophrenia" and encompassing experiences of social and/or emotional alienation, poor ego functioning, and bizarre sensory experiences) of the MMPI-2 are common in subjects who have a history of dissociative coping with trauma, and the MMPI-2 profile is not necessarily invalid for these subjects. In such instances, it is important to carefully assess the raw and T scores on the F, F (back), and F (p) scale and also to use other tests to discriminate between random responding, exaggerated responding, and high levels of genuine dissociative pathology. We have found in a forensic context that significant elevations of F and Sc are more representative of disorganized (CC) status than preoccupied status on the AAI. Pianta et al. (1996) did not use the five-way classification, and thus many of their preoccupied subjects may have had a combination of preoccupied and dismissing attachment strategies on the AAI. Despite this limitation, Pianta and his colleagues noted that subjects with a combination of preoccupied attachment and unresolved status had elevation on the Sc scale and that this may be related to dissociation (p. 279).

Our orphanage study, described later in this chapter, evaluated 45 adult survivors of childhood sexual abuse. All subjects were given two psychological inventories designed to assess the probability of psychiatric symptom exaggeration and fabrication: the Malingering Probability Scale (MPS; Silverton & Gruber, 1998) and the Structured Interview of Reported Symptoms (SIRS; Rogers, Bagby, & Dickens, 2002). Subjects with insecure attachment as compared with secure attachment on the AAI, and subjects with low as compared to high coherence of transcript on the AAI, were significantly more likely to have elevated MPS malingering (MAL) scores as well as elevated SIRS total malingering scores across all eight SIRS malingering scales. In other words, insecure (mainly disorganized) attachment and low coherence of mind were significantly related to an increased probability of exaggerating or fabricating psychiatric and/or physical symptoms.

We believe that, as a result of an insecure attachment status, factitious individuals, and also certain individuals who malinger, exaggerate or fabricate psychiatric symptoms *based on a need to seek attention from caregivers*. Many of the factitious patients we have studied have insecure attachment and histories of chronic or prolonged physical illnesses in childhood. We believe that such patients discovered as children that unmet attachment needs could be partially satisfied by medical caretakers attending to their physical illnesses. Once this association was established, the person over time progressively, and ultimately compulsively, learned to produce physical or psychiatric symptoms in order to adopt a sick role and get unmet attachment needs satisfied by the responsiveness of the medical system (D. P. Brown & Scheflin, 1999).

Trauma-Related Disorders

POSTTRAUMATIC STRESS DISORDER

Pielage, Gerlsma, and Schaap (2000) investigated "the relationships between stressful events, attachment style and psychopathology" (p. 296) using the Relationship Questionnaire (RQ; Bartholomew & Horowitz, 1991), in which subjects were asked to endorse paragraphs reflecting "Secure," "Preoccupied," "Dismissing," and "Fearful " attachment patterns. Results indicated that secure attachment as measured by the RQ correlated negatively ($r = -0.22$) with the amount of experienced stressful events, while both fearful ($r = 0.40$) and preoccupied ($r = 0.23$) attachment styles correlated positively with the degree of stressful events experienced (p. 299). There was no significant correlation in the dismissing category. Concerning the presence of psychological symptoms, secure attachment was negatively correlated ($r = -0.21$), whereas fearful attachment was positively correlated ($r = 0.30$). The authors concluded:

> Our results suggest that fearful individuals' chronic sense of insecurity and distress, as reflected in their negative view of both self and others, makes them more prone to perceive and interpret events as stressful which, in turn, seems to increase their vulnerability to experience psychological symptoms. (p. 300)

With respect to the issue of insecure attachment and causality, the authors provided a caveat:

> Although attachment theory favors the interpretation that insecure attachment styles constitute a vulnerability factor for the development of psychological symptoms, in the absence of longitudinal data the reverse is equally likely: the experience of a relatively high degree of psychological symptoms might well lead individuals to endorse an attachment vignette that describes interpersonal experiences in terms of fear and distress. (Pielage et al., 2000, p. 301)

Such a possibility reflects a limitation of self-report measures, as we indicated at the beginning of this chapter.

Alexander (1993) studied 112 women who were victims of incest during childhood. Their attachment status was measured with the Relationship Questionnaire (RQ; Bartholomew & Horowitz, 1991), which required each subject to rate her similarity on a 7-point scale to each of four relationship types described (Secure, Preoccupied, Dismissing, and Fearful) and then to choose the one among the four that she believed to be the best fit for her primary attachment style. These subjects' endorsement of attachment styles was significantly different from Bartholomew and Horowitz's (1991) normative sample: 14% secure versus 49% in the normative group, 13% versus 12% preoccupied, 16% versus 18% dismissing, and 58% versus 21% fearful. With respect to posttraumatic symptoms, the proportion of the variance in the findings attributed to attachment status was most significant on the Impact of Event Scale's Avoidance scale (Horowitz, Wilner, & Alvarez,

1979), with subjects endorsing secure attachment showing the least avoidance. Alexander observed, "This finding is consistent with Main and Goldwyn's (1984) observation that adults assessed as securely attached had easier access to both positive and negative memories of childhood" (p. 359).

Whiffen, Judd, and Aube (1999) investigated whether the link between childhood sexual abuse and depression in women was moderated by, among other things, the quality of their adult attachment to their partners. A total of 60 partnered women completed a number of measures, including the Revised Adult Attachment Scale (RAAS; Collins & Read, 1990), whose 18 items were rephrased to focus the subject on her relationship to her romantic partner. The RAAS looks at three major areas: degree of comfort with intimacy with the partner, degree of confidence in being able to depend on the partner when needed, and degree of fear around being left or unloved. Whiffen et al. found no correlation in their sample between depressive symptoms and a history of sexual abuse. Women in the study with a more severe abuse history, compared with nonsurvivors, had an elevated level of attachment anxiety (fears about being abandoned and/or unloved) while still maintaining confidence in their partners' dependability in times of need (p. 950). The authors noted that this pattern is characteristic of an anxious attachment style, specifically referencing Bartholomew's (1990) framework of "a positive working model of others and a negative working model of self" (p. 950).

Ein-Dor, Doron, Solomon, Mikulincer, and Shaver (2010) studied two groups: 85 veterans who fought and were held captive and 72 veterans who had similar combat exposure but who had not been captives. The wives of all the veterans were also included as part of the study. The self-report attachment measure used was the Adult Attachment Styles Scale (Mikulincer, Florian, & Tolmacz, 1990), which contains 10 items rated on a 7-point scale, five measuring attachment anxiety and five measuring attachment avoidance. Self-report scales for PTSD symptoms were also given to the veterans and their wives to assess PTSD in the veterans and secondary traumatic stress (STS) in their wives. Among the veterans held captive, 24.8% showed clinically significant PTSD symptoms while 14.1% of their wives displayed significant secondary trauma symptoms. In the noncaptive control group, 3.8% of the men exhibited significant PTSD symptoms and none of their wives showed significant secondary symptoms. Regarding attachment, in both study groups, higher attachment anxiety in the veterans and their wives was correlated with the severity of PTSD and STS in the veterans and their wives, respectively; and only in the couples with a former captive soldier was avoidant status of the veterans and their wives associated with PTSD and STS.

Fraley, Fazzare, Bonanno, and Dekel (2006) investigated the relationship between adult attachment style and "psychological adaptation" (p. 538) in a sample of 45 subjects present at the World Trade Center terrorist attacks on 9/11. A large number of the sample had had direct exposure to graphic scenes. For example, 84% of the sample had "observed dead bodies during the attack" (p. 542) and

53% of the sample had seen people jumping from the towers. Study subjects were assessed 7 months and 18 months after the attacks. Attachment was measured by the Relationship Scales Questionnaire (RSQ; Griffin & Bartholomew, 1994). Concerning both PTSD and depression, insecure attachment was not related to the initial level of symptoms or any changes in symptom level during the measurement times. However, there were clear differences between the secure and insecure groups. Subjects with secure attachment "exhibited relatively modest initial levels of PTSD symptoms that decreased over time" (p. 545). In addition, secure individuals' PTSD symptoms were lower at both the 7-month and 18-month assessments than were those of study subjects rated as insecure (either preoccupied, fearful, or dismissing). Similarly, regarding depression, "prototypically secure adults exhibited a resilient pattern of low symptoms over time" (p. 545). Secure subjects' "depression levels were indistinguishable from the normative mean (CES-D = 9) observed for the same scale using community samples" (p. 545).

Wallis and Steele (2001) administered the AAI to 39 adolescents hospitalized on psychiatric units. The authors noted that "all 39 participants had experienced some form of childhood loss or abuse" (p. 263). Dismissing attachment and unresolved status with respect to trauma or loss were overrepresented in the sample: F, 10%; Ds, 51%; E, 28%; CC, 10%; and Ud, 59%. With respect to unresolved status, Wallis and Steele noted:

> The most common shared feature to the 39 interviews in the present sample was the remarkably high level of loss and trauma in the childhood histories of the adolescents studied. In examining the impact of resolution of loss and trauma in relation to attachment figures, this study is the first to demonstrate the widespread extent of these difficulties in a residential adolescent clinical sample . . . The present study raises important questions about the differential impact of varying types of traumatic experience for distressed adolescents. Those in the sample reporting experiences of loss alone (of an attachment figure) were more likely to have resolved this trauma as compared with others in the sample who experienced a combination of loss, physical abuse and sexual abuse (pp. 264–265).

Stovall-McClough, Cloitre, and McClough (2008) interviewed women between the ages of 18 and 65 who had histories of severe emotional, physical and sexual abuse. The women had been identified as possible study subjects by reporting abuse by a caregiver before the age of 18, having experiences of trauma-related symptoms and, with the hope of mitigating these symptoms, expressing interest in clinical treatment. Using the AAI, slightly over 50% of the women were classified as unresolved (Ud) regarding loss and/or abuse, with slightly over 40% of the women classified as unresolved regarding only abuse. Among the women who did not have an unresolved classification, the most frequent classification was anxious-preoccupied (E). Within this group, 19% were classified as passively preoccupied (E1), 38% as angrily preoccupied (E2), and 43% as fearfully preoccupied (E3). AAI transcripts that were coded as dismissive (Ds) constituted 12% of the clinical sample. Further differentiation of the dismissive category revealed no subjects with the idealizing type (Ds), 21% with the derogating type (Ds2), and 79% with the cognitively aware/emotionally restricted type (Ds3).

Schuengel, Bakermans-Kranenburg, and van IJzendoorn (1999) examined 85 nonclinical, middle-upper-class mother–infant dyads. The aim of the study was to test Main and Hesse's (1990) hypothesis that the presence of frightening behaviors exhibited by parents with unresolved loss is linked to the development of disorganized infant attachment. Frightening maternal behavior was categorized using three groupings: frightened behavior, threatening behavior, and dissociative behavior. The participants experienced trauma connected exclusively to the loss of a significant attachment relationship. The mother–infant dyads were assessed to identify maternal behaviors when the infants were approximately 11 months of age. When the infants were 12 months old, the mothers were administered the AAI to determine their attachment classifications. When the infants were approximately 15 months old, the Strange Situation Procedure was used to determine the attachment organizations of the infants. Of the 85 mothers who were administered the AAI, 20 were classified as having unresolved loss and 65 were classified as not having unresolved loss. Twenty-six of the infants were classified as disorganized according to their SS behavior, and 59 were classified as not disorganized. Interpreting their data, Schuengel and his colleagues found that "mothers with unresolved loss and an insecure representation of attachment had the highest scores for frightening behavior" and, conversely, that "mothers with unresolved loss and a secure representation of attachment had very low scores for frightening behavior" (p. 59). Further, frightening caregiver behavior forecasted disorganized infant attachment.

From their review of over 200 studies of adult attachment that included over 10,000 AAI administrations, Bakermans-Kranenburg and van IJzendoorn (2009) found that "adults with abuse experiences or PTSD were mostly unresolved" (p. 223). Stalker and Davies (1995) found that insecure attachment status, notably preoccupied attachment, predicts which survivors of childhood sexual abuse are more likely to have unresolved status with respect to the abuse. In a variety of studies examining mothers with unresolved states of mind, the mothers' frightened/frightening behavior was seen as an impingement on the mother–infant dyad. These studies repeatedly found a correlation among maternal unresolved attachment classification, maternal frightened behavior, and infant attachment disorganization (Iyengar, Sohye, Martinez, Fonagy, & Strathearn, 2014; Jacobvitz, Hazen, & Riggs, 1997; Lyons-Ruth & Jacobvitz, 1999; Madigan et al., 2006; Thalhuber, Jacobvitz, & Hazen, 1998). Data from these studies established a strong statistical link between unresolved loss and trauma in the mother (as measured by the AAI) and disorganized attachment in the infant (as measured by the SS).

Due to the intergenerational nature of attachment-related trauma, it is of vital clinical importance to provide treatment that not only moderates the individual's traumatic experiences and symptomology but also provides interventions aimed at decreasing the caregivers' frightened/frightening behaviors and increasing their sensitivity and attunement-focused behaviors when engaging with their children. Furthermore, we maintain that every individual, regardless of his or her attachment classification and its severity, can establish earned secure attachment.

ATTACHMENT AND DISSOCIATIVE DISORDERS

Nilsson, Holmqvist, and Jonson (2011) studied how attachment style and exposure to trauma relate to dissociative symptoms. The attachment measure used was a modified version of the Experiences in Close Relationships scale (ECR; Brennan, Clark, & Shaver, 1998), a 36-item instrument that yields two dimensions pertaining to attachment: avoidance and anxiety. A modification to the original ECR entailed having the subject endorse ECR items based on his or her closest relationship, regardless of whether it was romantic or not; another modification was that subjects were asked about whom they were thinking about when answering. Nilsson et al. state:

> The main finding in this study was that self-reported attachment style (both avoidance and anxiety) correlated substantially with dissociation, and more strongly than the number of self-reported potentially traumatic events The association between self-reported attachment style and the reported number of potentially traumatic events was rather weak. (p. 591)

The authors also tested the idea that secure attachment might provide some measure of protection against dissociative symptoms developing. To investigate, a subgroup of participants who had four or more different experiences of interpersonal trauma were examined for degree of dissociative symptoms. Specifically, the authors looked at "whether the individuals with many traumas but without clinical dissociation had a self-reported attachment style that differed from the style of those who reported dissociation" (Nilsson et al., 2011, p. 590). An analysis of the data showed that an anxious attachment style was more prevalent in the group with more trauma experience and more reported dissociative symptoms as compared with those with more trauma and subclinical levels of dissociation. The authors state, "The results of these analyses suggested that secure attachment might indeed protect against dissociation" (p. 591).

Coe, Dalenberg, Aransky, and Reto (1995) studied the relationships among adult attachment style, dissociative symptoms, and a history of violence in childhood in a sample of college students. The authors measured four types of dissociative experience identified by self-report: memory disturbance, absorption, isolation, and fragmentation. The overall data "provide support for the idea that insecure attachment is linked to increased levels of dissociation as well as to exposure to violence in childhood" (p. 150). Subjects with greater levels of secure attachment showed fewer dissociative symptoms of depersonalization and derealization and also reported lower levels of violence in childhood. On the other hand, "insecure attachment styles were predicted by higher levels of dissociation and reports of childhood exposure to violence" (p. 150). Additional findings related specific types of insecure attachment to specific types of dissociation. A fearful attachment style was significantly related to and predicted by memory disturbance and violence in childhood as well as by depersonalization and derealization symptoms. A preoccupied attachment style was significantly correlated with absorption, which is described by the authors as "a dissociative factor consisting of items reflecting high sensitivity and engagement with affective stimulation" (p. 150). Subjects with dismissing attachment, somewhat contrary to the authors' expectations, showed only a modest degree of dissociative isolation. Rather, it was the infrequent reporting of the dissociative absorption that predicted a dismissing attachment style: "Dismissing subjects reported their failure (refusal?) to become absorbed in emotion-laden events around them, rather than a complete lack of awareness of environmental events or affective experiences" (p. 150).

DEPERSONALIZATION/DEREALIZATION DISORDER (DRD)

Prior to the DSM-IV, depersonalization disorder (DPD) was a distinct condition that included derealization among its symptoms. For the DSM-5, this condition was changed to depersonalization/derealization disorder (DRD). DRD is defined by persistent or recurrent episodes of depersonalization, derealization, or both. Depersonalization is characterized by an alteration in the perception or experience of the self, or aspects of the self, so that one feels detached from, and as if one is an outside observer of, one's mental processes or body. Derealization is characterized by an alteration in the perception or experience of the world and one's surroundings such that one feels as if in a fog or dream.

Research conducted prior to DSM-5 demonstrated that DPD is a distinct disorder that can be differentiated from other dissociative disorders and other psychiatric conditions (Simeon et al., 1997). According to Sierra and Berrios (1998), DPD is characterized by a vigilant alertness and a profound inhibition of emotional feelings, including a diminished autonomic response to emotional stimuli and a blunted pain response. A subsequent factor analysis of DPD symptoms by Sierra and David (2011) identified symptom categories of emotional numbing, disembodiment, anomalous subjective recall and disruption of self-experience, and derealization.

In our orphanage study of adults who were sexually abused during childhood, the SCID-D identified 12 as having clinically significant depersonalization and 7 as having clinically significant derealization. An AAI primary classification of insecure (mostly disorganized) attachment was significantly associated with depersonalization ($p < 0.05$) and derealization ($p < 0.01$), whereas subjects with an AAI primary classification of secure attachment showed few of these symptoms. Apparently, secure attachment status protected children who were sexually abused from developing depersonalization or derealization in adulthood.

DISSOCIATIVE IDENTITY DISORDER (DID)

According to the DSM-5, dissociative identity disorder (DID) is defined by the existence of two or more alter personality states, loss of executive control when an alter personality state manifests over the host personality, and amnesia for a least some of the experiences/behaviors of alter personality states. Associated clinical features of DID typically include dissociative amnesia and depersonalization. Research has shown that somatoform symptoms are highly comorbid with DID. According to Nijenhuis, van der Hart, and Steele (2002), personality functioning in DID patients can be broadly classified into an apparently normal personality structure (ANP) concerned with everyday functioning at the expense of emotional processing, and a number of emotional personality (EP) states concerned with remembering and processing stressful emotional and traumatic experiences.

Steele (2003) gave the AAI to five adult female survivors of chronic ritual abuse with a confirmed or suspected diagnosis of DID who were treated at the Clinic for Dissociative Studies in London. Most of the early childhood caregivers "were cooperating in the perverse intent to abuse, disfigure, and ultimately destroy the developing personality of the child" (p. 355). Steele found that "the resulting profiles emerging from these Adult Attachment Interviews are remarkably similar" (p. 354). Using the five-way AAI classification system, all five women had unresolved status (Ud) with respect to trauma or loss on the AAI, and all also had "cannot classify" (CC) as the primary attachment classification. All showed "deeply divided states of mind concerning attachment" (p. 357). Steele notes:

> The surprising message of this paper is the co-occurrence in the same interview of so many incompatible attachment orientations. Usually an interview can be reliably assigned to one of the 15 Adult Attachment Interview subtypes. For the current sample, however, the same interview may qualify for membership in many different subtypes, including a mix of dismissing, preoccupied, autonomous, and unresolved subgroups. (p. 359)

The senior author of this book, Daniel Brown, has collected 60 AAIs of DID patients whose diagnosis was made using the SCID-D structured interview

(Steinberg, 1993). Using the five-way classification system, over 90% of the DID patients in this sample had cannot classify (CC) as their primary attachment classification, and over 90% had unresolved status (Ud) with respect to trauma or loss. Those few remaining subjects who did not show a CC classification had an anxious-preoccupied (E) classification (mostly E3) characterized by pervasive fear. Those few who did not show Ud status for trauma had addressed the trauma or loss in psychotherapy, which presumably resolved an earlier Ud status. These data strongly suggest that pervasive disorganization (CC), and specifically disorganization around the exploration of trauma or abuse (Ud), essentially defines the mind of the DID patient. In the context of attachment, we have come to understand each alter personality state as an expression of a specific unmet attachment need in a patient with severe disorganized attachment, and the switches from one alter personality state to another personality state as sequential manifestations of these unmet attachment needs (see Chapter 13).

In our orphanage study, only 3 of the total sample of 45 subjects met the full diagnostic criteria for DID. However, 17 met partial diagnostic criteria for DID in that they showed clear evidence of two or more distinct "parts," but they either did not show a loss of executive control and/or did not show amnesia across personality states. These subjects were given the diagnosis of dissociative disorder not otherwise specified (DDNOS). We pooled the data from the full DID and DDNOS subjects to create a group of 20 who had clinically significant dissociative "parts." There was a trend that fell just short of the 0.05 significance level for insecure (mostly disorganized) attachment to be associated with the DID/DDNOS distinct "parts" diagnosis. Not surprisingly, low coherence of transcript ($p < 0.01$) and low coherence of mind ($p < 0.035$) were significantly correlated with a diagnosis of DID/DDNOS in adulthood.

Farina et al. (2014) gave the AAI to 13 patients with various dissociative disorders, including DID and DDNOS, and to 13 healthy matched control subjects. As a measure of organization/disorganization of mind, the researchers used EEG coherence. As hypothesized, healthy control subjects immediately after exploring attachment themes in the AAI interview showed significant increases in cortical connectivity and EEG coherence, whereas patients with dissociative disorders did not show any changes in cortical connectivity or EEG coherence following exploration of attachment themes during the AAI. Healthy attachment has an organizing effect on states of mind, and in this case also on brain EEG coherence, which seems to be lacking in patients with clinically significant dissociative disorders. It should also be noted that 8 of the 13 subjects in the Farina et al. study were classified as CC using the five-way AAI classification system, but only 1 of the 13 met the full diagnostic criteria for DID.

The Minnesota Longitudinal Study of Parents and Children (Sroufe, 2005; Sroufe, Egeland, Carlson, & Collins, 2005) is the gold standard of studies of the various effects of childhood neglect and abuse. A total of 186 high-risk mothers (very young and involved in domestic abuse, drugs, or prostitution) and their infants were studied with multi-method assessment instruments at every phase of development from infancy through early adulthood over three decades. The Minnesota study also included assessments of attachment status using the Strange Situation Procedure at 12 months and 18 months of age and using the AAI in late adolescence and in early adulthood. Since many of these high-risk children were physically and/or sexually abused in later childhood, the study allowed for an assessment of the relative contribution of both early attachment disruption and later specific abusive incidents to the overall psychopathology emerging in early adulthood. This study clearly shows that *the combination of disorganized attachment aggravated by later childhood abuse* predicts the development of dissociative disorders in adulthood (Carlson, 1998; Ogawa, Sroufe, Weinfield, Carlson, & Egeland, 1997). Specifically, children found to have disorganized attachment at 12 and 18 months from the Strange Situation assessment showed a wide range of dissociative experiences throughout childhood and adolescence, which tended to decline during early adulthood. However, if a disorganized attached child was physically and/or sexually abused in later childhood, the older child tended to primarily use a dissociative coping style to deal with that abuse. The use of a dissociative coping style to handle abuse, in turn, changed the dissociation from a normal capacity to adaptively shift states to pathological, structural dissociation characterized by rigid compartmentalization. As a consequence, such a child does not show a decline of dissociative experiences over time but instead is likely to show the emergence of clinically significant dissociative conditions in adulthood, with the emergence of distinctive "parts" or alter personality states.

Liotti (1992) developed a three-pathway model to explain the development of dissociative disorders. He proposed (1) that exposure of the child to extreme frightened/frightening parental behavior during early childhood results in disorganized attachment in childhood and mild dissociative symptoms throughout childhood and adolescence, (2) that exposure of the child to frightened/frightening parental behavior in early childhood followed by subsequent physical and/or sexual abuse in later childhood results in DID in adulthood, and (3) that limited exposure to frightened/frightening parental behavior, or exposure offset by other healthy caregivers, results in high normal but not pathological dissociative experiences in adulthood.

Attachment and Addictions

ALCOHOLISM AND SUBSTANCE ABUSE

As characterized in the DSM-5, the core feature of substance abuse is an individual's continued use of the substance despite its negative impact upon his or her cognitive, behavioral, and physiological systems. A common feature of the excessive use of any substance is that it creates such an extreme direct stimulation of the brain reward system, that typical daily functioning is negatively impacted. Over time this leads to dependency, which involves increased tolerance, withdrawal symptoms upon discontinuing, and continued compulsive use to avoid withdrawal distress.

Kassel, Wardle, and Roberts (2007) investigated the relationship between attachment status and substance use in a college student population. The attachment measure was an 18-item Likert-style inventory adapted by Collins and Read (1990) from Hazen and Shaver's (1987) original categorical measure. Their measure yielded scores on three attachment categories: *close*, (i.e., comfort with closeness to others), *depend* (i.e., feeling confident others will be there in times of need), and *anxious* (i.e., having a lot of worry about being abandoned or not loved). The authors found that "all three attachment dimensions were also significantly related to self-esteem and dysfunctional attitudes; insecure attachment was associated with lower self-esteem and greater endorsement of dysfunctional attitudes" (Kassel et al., 2007, p. 1169). Students with anxious attachment smoked more tobacco, but those with the other two dimensions, *close* and *depend*, did not. No association was found between attachment and alcohol and marijuana. However, when stress-related use was assessed, the use of all three substances was significantly correlated with *anxious* attachment. Only stress-related marijuana use correlated with the other two attachment dimensions, *depend* and *close*. The authors concluded that "insecure attachment, specifically anxiety over possible abandonment (anxious attachment), proved to be significantly related to both frequency of substance use and stress-motivated use of substances" (p. 1173). Referring to the interactions with dysfunctional attitudes and problems with self-esteem, the authors suggest that

> A plausible etiological process linking insecure attachment and substance use is that insecurely attached individuals develop dysfunctional attitudes about themselves such that when these underlying insecurities are activated, they deplete the individual's self-esteem. Such low self-esteem enhances the likelihood of more drug use and, perhaps more importantly, more stress-motivated use of substances. (p. 1173)

J. P. Allen, Hauser, and Borman-Spurrell (1996) studied adolescents who had been psychiatrically hospitalized at age 14 as compared to demographically matched high school students without psychiatric histories. At age 25, insecure attachment was found to be significantly associated with the total number of incidents of hard drug use in later adolescence, namely, the use of heroin, cocaine, hallucinogens, amphetamines, and/or tranquilizers. Certain dismissing states of mind, namely, high derogation of attachment and lack of memory on the AAI, were significantly related to higher drug use, as was unresolved status with respect to trauma, although unresolved status with respect to loss was not.

In the Riggs and Jacobvitz (2002) study described earlier in the section on affective disorders and suicidality, adults classified as unresolved with respect to trauma, but not with respect to loss, were significantly more likely to report a history of alcohol or drug abuse, while those who were unresolved in relation to loss were more often reported to be involved in criminal behavior.

Rosenstein and Horowitz (1996) conducted a study examining psychiatrically hospitalized adolescents with affective disorder (55%), conduct disorder (13%), and combined affective disorder and conduct disorder (20%). All participants were administered the AAI, which was scored both using a four-category system (F, Ds, E, and Ud) and using the three-category system (excluding Ud). From the four-way scoring, 38% of the participants were classified as dismissing, 2% as autonomous (F), 42% as preoccupied, and 18% as unresolved. From three-way scoring, 3% were classified as autonomous, 47% as dismissing, and 50% as preoccupied. Dismissing attachment was linked to conduct disorders, both solely and together with affective disorders, and preoccupied attachment was linked to affective disorders. Adolescent substance abuse was most prominent in the dismissing classification group. Among the 24 participants classified as dismissing, 16 reported problems with alcohol or drug abuse; among the 28 identified as preoccupied, 10 reported problems with alcohol or drug abuse.

> Results showed that the dismissing group differed significantly from the preoccupied group by being more antisocial, narcissistic, and paranoid, with a trend for drug abuse . . . Adolescents using a dismissing attachment organization rely on an attachment strategy that minimizes distressing thoughts and affects associated with rejection by the attachment figure. Thus, psychiatric disorders, such as CD [conduct disorder] or SA [substance abuse], in which overt denial or downplaying of distress, coupled with actions that display those distressing affects, did occur in the context of a dismissing attachment organization. (pp. 248, 250)

Simonelli and Vizziello (2002) examined the attachment representations of 28 drug-addicted mothers. Their AAI assessments found that one woman (4%) was classified as securely attached, more than half had anxious-preoccupied attachment, and 39% were classified as unresolved. Most of the children of these mothers (81%) were classified as insecurely attached.

Barone, Borelli, Madeddu, and Maffei (2000) conducted a pilot study of alcoholics and drug abusers using the AAI to assess attachment status. Alcoholics and drug users showed an overrepresentation of insecure, largely dismissing attachment. Dismissing/derogating attachment was overrepresented in the AAIs of patients with borderline personality disorder with substance abuse/dependency (58%) and alcohol abuse/dependency (55%).

Savov and Atanassov (2013) noted affect dysregulation problems in drug addicts. They recognized that drug addicts are prone to failures in affect regulation and modulation, and have deficits in mentalizing.

Flores (2004) outlined an approach to addictions based on attachment treatment. He pointed out that "Substance abusers continue to substitute one compulsive, potentially addictive behavior for another until they are forced to face the gnawing emptiness and intolerable anxieties that drive their substance abuse" (p. 11). According to Flores, "unmet developmental needs" drive all addictions (p. 83), and all addictions are "misguided attempts at self-repair" (p. 219). He believes that "Those who develop dysfunctional or insecure attachment styles will be more vulnerable and more likely to turn to other sources of external regulation, like substances" (p. 219). The aim of attachment-oriented treatment of addictions, therefore, is the development of healthy internal working models for attachment and the associated healthy forms of affect regulation that can help addicts to detach from their objects of addiction.

Clinicians generally recognize that the abuse of alcohol and/or drugs is an attempt to temper internal conflict or overpowering emotions, and that the altered state of mind produced by substance abuse serves as a defense to block or limit the processing and/or reexperiencing of traumatic childhood events. The studies discussed above that address the relationship between attachment classification and substance abuse have significant clinical implications, highlighting the importance of considering early attachment relationships and current attachment patterns when treating patients with addictions and substance abuse disorders.

EATING DISORDERS

Illing, Tasca, Balfour, and Bissada (2010) investigated whether insecure attachment in women predicted the severity of eating disorder (ED) symptoms and/or treatment outcomes after completion of an intensive day hospital group-based program for eating disorders. The women met criteria for either anorexia nervosa, restricting type; anorexia nervosa, bingeing type; or bulimia nervosa. The attachment measure was the self-report Attachment Style Questionnaire (ASQ). A control group of women also completed the eating disorder and attachment measures. Women with an ED diagnosis showed a higher level of insecure attachment than the control group, with the diagnostic category of anorexia, bingeing type, scoring highest on measures of anxious and avoidant attachment. Women with higher degrees of attachment anxiety—specifically, an elevated score on the Need for Approval scale of the ASQ—had more severe eating disorder symptoms before treatment. Post-treatment results indicated that women with the highest levels of attachment anxiety (compared with other types of attachment insecurity) before treatment had the poorest treatment results. The authors suggest that "ED treatment models could be more effective if they specifically target attachment anxiety" (p. 657).

Shanmugam, Jowett, and Meyer (2012) looked at the links between attachment styles and disordered eating in young adult college and sports club athletes. Their attachment measure was the self-report Experiences in Close Relationships scale (ECR). They found a positive and significant association between their eating disorder measure and both anxious and avoidant attachment. The authors make several interesting points in their discussion:

> The current results further extend previous findings by demonstrating a multiple pathway between attachment styles and eating psychopathology. In particular, self-esteem, depression, and self-critical perfectionism were found to mediate the link between attachment styles and elevated eating psychopathology. This finding suggests that disordered eating is likely to manifest in athletes with an insecure attachment style by undermining their levels of self-esteem, depression, and self-critical perfectionism. This is in keeping with the traditional framework of attachment theory which postulates that whilst a secure attachment style is related to favourable cognitive and social development (Pierrehumbert, Miljkovitch, Plancherel, Halfon, & Ansermet, 2000), and positive affect and well-being (Mikulincer & Florian, 1998), an insecure attachment style is related to less favourable cognitive and social development, [and] negative affect and well-being (see Mikulincer & Shaver, 2007). (Shanmugam et al., 2012, p. 9)

Cole-Detke and Kobak (1996) administered the AAI to college women who had reported high or low eating-disorder symptoms. Subjects with dismissing attachment (67%) were significantly more likely than other attachment groups to report eating disorder symptoms when the depression level was statistically controlled. Women with *both* eating-disorder symptoms and depression were predominately anxious-preoccupied (53%). These patterns of insecure attachment represent "a strategy of diverting attention from attachment to outward appearance in order to win approval" (p. 288).

Fonagy et al. (1996) gave the AAI to nonpsychotic inpatients and matched healthy controls. Dismissing attachment, high idealization of parents, and low reflective functioning were significantly associated with eating disorders in inpatients. The authors state:

> The relationship between a diagnosis of eating disorder and a participant's idealization of his or her parents echoes the clinical observation that participants with eating disorders are perfectionists (Slade, 1982) whose eating disorder may stem from exaggerated standards that are also applied to parents. (p. 28)

Ward et al. (2001) administered the AAI to 20 anorexic patients and to 12 of their mothers. Nineteen (95%) of the anorexics and 10 (83%) of the mothers were classified as insecure on the AAI; 15 (79%) of the anorexics and 7 (70%) of the mothers had a primary classification of dismissing attachment. Reflective-functioning scores were very low for both anorexics and their mothers.

Zachrisson and Kulbotten (2006) administered the AAI to 20 anorexic women, whose attachment classification was scored using the Dynamic-Maturational Model (DMM) system. Their findings showed that insecure attachment and unresolved status with respect to trauma were overrepresented in anorexics, and that all 20 anorexics were insecure with either dismissing, preoccupied, and disorganized attachment. Anxiety levels were significantly higher in anorexics with dismissing attachment.

Barone and Guiducci (2009) gave the AAI to 30 subjects with clinically significant eating disorders and 30 matched nonclinical controls. Of the ED patients, 10 had anorexia, 10 had bulimia, and 10 had a binge ED. The majority of ED patients (90%) had insecure attachment, mostly of the dismissing type (47%). The frequency of cannot classify (CC) was low (16%). The ED patients, as compared to the healthy control subjects, had significantly greater parental rejection, involving, and neglect on the AAI parenting scales. ED patients as compared to controls had a significantly higher lack of recall regarding attachment experiences and significantly lower coherence of transcript and coherence of mind. The authors state:

> In ED subjects, the relationship with the mother appears to be the most problematic, since it conveys a loving and at the same time role-reversing, rejecting and neglecting stance associated with two problematic attachment states of mind; a stance toward idealization and a stance toward involving anger. (p. 413)

Unresolved status with respect to trauma was also overrepresented in this ED sample, but only in the bulimic and binge ED groups and not the anorexic group. The authors state, "Attachment disorganization appears to feature in bulimic and binge-eating patients but not in anorexics" (Barone & Guiducci, 2009, p. 414).

Mark Schwartz and Mike Rechtien administered AAIs to 75 inpatients with severe eating disorders upon admission at an eating disorder treatment facility. AAIs were scored with both the traditional AAI scoring system and also the DMM scoring system. Most of the 75 severe ED patients were given the cannot classify (CC) attachment classification from the five-way AAI classification system and an A/C classification from the DMM scoring system. According to Schwartz,

> this is representative of a form of disorganized attachment when scored by both the Main method and the Crittenden method. The latter proved to be extremely sensitive and highly predictive of clinical observations

by the treatment team . . . Using the AAI scoring to set treatment goals, therapy was then focused not on the addictive symptoms related to food but instead on repairing the attachment system by facilitating the client's "earned secure" attachment. Using the AAI on post-tests . . . indicated a movement away from disorganization with either the A or C strategy being assimilated in an organized way. This movement towards earned security of attachment strategy was accompanied by a marked decrease in the use of eating-disorder behaviors. (personal communication with D. Brown, July 2015)

Attachment and Personality Disorders

PERSONALITY DISORDERS IN GENERAL

Meyer and Pilkonis (2005) conducted a pilot study to investigate the relationship between attachment styles and personality disorders. Attachment style was assessed with the Experiences in Close Relationships (ECR) questionnaire (Brennan, Clark, & Shaver, 1998), which consists of items measuring two dimensions: attachment anxiety and attachment avoidance. The results showed positive correlations between the ECR Attachment Anxiety scale scores and avoidant, dependent, obsessive-compulsive, paranoid, schizotypal, histrionic, narcissistic, and borderline personality disorders. Particularly strong correlations were found for borderline and dependent personality disorders. No relationship was found between attachment anxiety and schizoid personality. Scores on the ECR Attachment Avoidance scale were correlated only with avoidant, paranoid, and schizoid personality disorders. Organizing their findings according to quadrants of the four attachment types, the authors reported that histrionic, borderline, and dependent subjects were found solidly in the preoccupied quadrant, while paranoid, obsessive-compulsive, narcissistic, and schizotypal subjects "were located at the border between preoccupied and fearful attachment" (p. 246). The dismissing quadrant contained only schizoid subjects, while avoidant types were in the fearful (i.e., disorganized) quadrant.

Dickinson and Pincus (2003) focused primarily on the question of whether there is validity in differentiating narcissistic personality into two subtypes: grandiose and vulnerable. The self-report attachment measure was the Adult Attachment Questionnaire (AAQ; Bartholomew & Horowitz, 1991), which requires subjects to endorse one of four descriptions of attachment styles that fit them best: secure, preoccupied, dismissing, or fearful. As the authors predicted, correlations were found between the groups' classification and endorsed attachment style. In the grandiose narcissism group, 60% were secure, 16% were dismissive, 13% were fearful, and 10% were preoccupied. In the vulnerable narcissism group, 50% were fearful, 27% were secure, 13% were preoccupied, and

10% were dismissive. The classification results for the control group were 53% secure, 23% fearful, 17% preoccupied, and 7% dismissive.

Alexander's (1993) study, described in the earlier section on attachment and posttraumatic stress disorder, also obtained data about the association of attachment status and personality functioning. She assessed attachment status using the self-report Relationship Questionnaire (RQ) and personality functioning with the Millon Clinical Multiaxial Inventory II (MCMI-II; Millon, 1987). The results showed significant correlations between attachment status and presence of a personality disorder. Fearful attachment accounted for most of the variance on the MCMI-II Avoidance scale, preoccupied and dismissing attachment were most associated with the Dependent scale, fearful and preoccupied attachment most significantly predicted scores on the Masochistic/Self-Defeating scale, and preoccupied attachment was most significantly associated with the Borderline scale. Summarizing her data pertaining to the relative effects of attachment status and abuse on personality, Alexander states that "basic personality structure, including more dysfunctional manifestations, was not associated with abuse characteristics but was instead predicted by adult attachment" (p. 358).

BORDERLINE PERSONALITY DISORDER

Individuals meeting the criteria for borderline personality disorder (BPD) suffer from a range of devastating behavioral problems, such as self-injurious behavior (69% to 75% prevalence, according to Kjellander, Bongar, & King, 1998) and a risk of suicide that is 400 times greater than in the general population (McGlashan, 1986). In addition, BPD negatively impacts the psychotherapeutic and psychopharmacological treatment efficacy for a number of Axis I disorders (Clarkin, 1996). Those who suffer from BPD are often difficult for clinicians to treat due to their rapidly shifting attachment strategies and extreme ambivalence in forming attachments. Given these phenomena, BPD can be seen as an important public health problem, and despite affecting only 1% to 3% of the population, it constitutes one of the most important sources of long-term impairment in both treated and untreated populations (K. N. Levy, 2005).

Lyons-Ruth, Melnick, Patrick, and Hobson (2007) examined women with borderline personality disorder who were more likely than those with dysthymia to manifest contradictory hostile-helpless states of mind (HH). Women with BPD and women with dysthymia were administered the AAI. In developing their hypothesis, the authors noted that in the absence of attuned parenting in early life, an individual may develop particular types of unintegrated idealized and denigrated representations of others and internalize these characteristics. With this developmental, internal-working-models perspective in mind, patterns of early relatedness that would have special relevance for adult BPD are the patterns associated with disorganized attachment. Research has shown that when parents display frightened and/or frightening behaviors as well as disruptive forms of affective communication with their infants, the infants may fail to develop an organized strategy for achieving comfort from their caregivers (Lyons-Ruth, Bronfman, & Parsons, 1999; Schuengel et al., 1999). The hostile-helpless (HH) coding system for the AAI that Lyons-Ruth and her colleagues used in this study differs from the Main, Goldwyn, and Hesse (2002) system for classifying unresolved states of mind. The HH coding system assesses the extent to which a person mentally *represents* and *identifies* attachment figures in contradictory and malevolent ways. Examples of hostile-helplessness include global devaluation of caregivers, identification with a hostile caregiver, a sense of special unworthiness, repeated references to a fearful affect, laughter at pain, references to controlling or punitive behavior toward caregivers, and ruptured attachment with a family member. In this study, all the women with BPD manifested hostile-helpless states of mind, whereas only half the women with dysthymia did. Fearfully preoccupied states of mind (E3) were significantly associated with references to having to provide caregiving to the caregiver in early childhood as well as the tendency to globally devalue the caregiver during the interview. The authors noted that the BPD study subjects showed little reflective functioning when talking about their caregivers.

Patrick et al. (1994) found that there was a significantly higher prevalence of preoccupied (E) classifications among BPD patients than among dysthymic patients, who had a significantly higher prevalence of dismissing (D) classifications. The authors also found that there were significantly more subjects with unresolved/disorganized (Ud) status in the BPD group than in the dysthymic group. An additional significant finding highlighted in this study was that the BPD patients tended to have a rare subtype of the E category: E3 (3% in low-risk populations). Preoccupied states have been linked to the use of multiple models of events that should have single mental representations. Unresolved (Ud) and unresolved/preoccupied with anger (Ud/E3) states of mind are associated with more pervasive disturbances of representations and with the more prominent limitations of metacognitive functioning that are often associated with BPD.

In a study by Rosenstein and Horowitz (1996), the authors sought to identify the quality of attachment in psychiatrically ill adolescents and their mothers and to explore the role of attachment in the development of adolescent psychopathology. Hospitalized adolescents were examined and their data were analyzed twice, using both the three- and four-way classification systems. The adolescents who only had borderline personality traits that did not satisfy diagnostic criteria did not have a preoccupied classification, whereas those diagnosed with BPD did. This finding was consistent with the Patrick et al. (1994) report. Additionally, a striking similarity was found between the adolescents' and their mothers' attachment classifications.

Fonagy et al. (1996) studied the patterns of attachment and psychiatric status with inpatients and participants in a control group using the AAI four-way classification system and the SCID-I and SCID-II. They found that the most specific and robust relationship was between BPD and attachment classification. The BPD patients' AAI interviews were differentiated by a combination of three characteristics: (1) They showed a higher prevalence of abuse and neglect (89%), (2) they had significantly lower ratings on the Reflective Self-Function (RSF) scale, and (3) they scored significantly higher on the Lack of Resolution of Abuse or Loss scales (89%). The RSF scale was a good predictor of infant–parent attachment security: Both mothers and fathers who were rated high in this capacity were three to four times more likely to have secure children. Patients in this study who were diagnosed with BPD reported parents who were less loving and more neglecting. The authors posited that individuals who had severe maltreatment in childhood may have responded by inhibiting their mentalizing function in order to defend against the realization that their caregiver wished them harm. They suggested that the initially defensive disruption of the capacity to depict feelings and thoughts in self and others becomes a core symptom in BPD, which makes it more difficult for these patients to work toward resolution of their traumatic stress. Fonagy et al. found that 75% of the BPD patients were preoccupied in their attachment style. Of particular interest was that 47% were fearfully preoccupied (E3), which reflected their fear of relationships. Interestingly, the authors made the observation that on Axis I, there was also a significant association between a diagnosis of anxiety disorder and the E3 subclassification (76%). However, the lack of a significant difference between the proportion of BPD patients with E3 who were classified as anxious and the proportion without E3 who were classified as anxious suggested that the association between E3 classification and BPD was not solely due to the association of the E3 classification with anxiety.

Barone (2003) used the AAI to compare nonclinical college students to participants with borderline personality disorder. She found major group differences in the distributions of AAI classifications: In the BPD group, unresolved and entangled/preoccupied (E) status were overrepresented whereas secure/autonomous (F) subjects constituted only a small percentage (7%). Interestingly, the author found that dismissing (Ds) classifications were evident in similar proportions in both groups (21%). An exploration of AAI subclassifications revealed some important qualitative differences between the two groups: BPD subjects with F classifications were generally high in the anger scores (F5), and those with Ds classifications had a trend toward angry derogation (Ds2) or high idealization (Ds1); BPD subjects with E classifications were mostly divided between an angry stance (E2) and a fearful overwhelmed stance (E3). Barone also found that the BPD group described fewer loving experiences from the mother and father and more rejecting and neglecting experiences from both parents. Also, the clinical group scored significantly higher on having had a role-reversing experience with their mothers during childhood. Another important finding was that the clinical group scored significantly lower on metacognition and significantly higher in terms of evidence of unresolved trauma. Barone was most impressed by the finding that the BPD group scored dramatically lower on ratings of coherence of transcript and coherence of mind.

Barone (2003) concluded her discussion by noting that when the borderline pathological condition and attachment security were associated, the main cues identifying the developmental issues of the disorder were related to the specific type of parental relationship described in the AAI—that of an actively reject-ing father and an unloving and neglecting mother, a combination of factors that may impair the security of BPD subjects and may be associated with a failure in resolving traumatic experiences. These findings help to identify the developmen-tal factors that can be considered to place a child at risk for developing borderline personality disorder.

Bakermans-Kranenburg and van IJzendoorn (2009) examined more than 200 adult attachment studies covering more than 10,000 AAIs administered over the prior 25 years. Their analysis showed that internalizing disorders—in particular borderline personality disorder—were strongly overrepresented by preoccupied and unresolved attachment classifications, and that disorders of a more external-izing type (such as antisocial personality disorder) were more associated with dismissing attachment as well preoccupied attachment. The authors described disorders with an internalizing orientation such as BPD as being associated with maximizing attachment signals.

Agrawal et al. (2004) reviewed 13 empirical studies that used either the AAI or self-report measures to examine the types of attachment found in individu-als with borderline personality disorder. All studies showed a strong associa-tion between BPD and insecure attachment. The types of attachment found to be most characteristic of BPD subjects were unresolved, preoccupied, and fearful. In each of these types, individuals showed a yearning for intimacy and, con-currently, a concern regarding dependency and rejection. Agrawal and his col-leagues concluded in their review that BPD attachments seem best characterized as unresolved with preoccupied features in relation to their parents, and fearful (self-report category) or, secondarily, preoccupied in their romantic relationships.

K. N. Levy (2005) offered a review of attachment theory and research as a means of providing a developmental psychopathology perspective on border-line personality disorder. He argued that a temperament-based theory of attach-ment (e.g., that physiological tendencies toward distress in infancy give rise to the development of anxious-resistant attachments characteristic of BPD) is not supported (Gunnar, Brodersen, Nachmias, Buss, & Rigatuso, 1996; Steven-son-Hinde & Marshall, 1999), although there may be an important intersection between attachment and constitutional factors that should be examined more closely (Depue & Lenzenweger, 2001; Derryberry & Rothbart, 1988; Posner et al., 2003). Levy reported that each study found an inverse relationship between scores of borderline characteristics and secure attachment. He also highlighted that although early interview studies suggested a strong relationship between BPD and preoccupied and unresolved attachments in particular, later studies suggested that BPD is not specifically related to one type of attachment pattern. Although most studies showed elevated rates of unresolved (Ud) attachment in BPD, Levy reported that the rates are generally in the 50% range, which is similar to the rates found in other psychiatric disorders, and that they have been found to be as low as 35%. Levy also pointed out that a number of newer interview studies have suggested that many BPD patients could be diagnosed with dismissing attachment (Barone, 2003; Rosenstein & Horowitz, 1996). He reported that BPD appeared not to be specifically related to a particular attachment pattern and suggested that there could be a range of functioning within each attachment pattern.

An important limitation of Levy's findings is that most of the studies he reviewed did not use the five-way classification system. We believe that borderline personality disorder is related to disorganized attachment (CC), wherein contradictory combinations of preoccupied (E) and dismissing elements (Ds) are common. Unless the classification system used allows for the combination classification of CC, scorers are forced to choose one or another attachment pattern, which may yield classifications that are artifacts of the limitation in the classification system rather than characteristic of actual attachment phenomena.

Crittenden and Newman (2010) conducted a study with 32 Australian mothers, 15 of whom had a diagnosis of BPD. They compared aspects of the functioning of mothers with borderline personality disorder to those of mothers without a psychiatric disorder using two different AAI classification systems: the Main and Goldwyn method (Ds, F, E, and U) and Crittenden's Dynamic-Maturational Model method (A, B, C, and A/C). Using the Main and Goldwyn classification method, none of the mothers with BPD were secure (F), while 35% of the comparison group of mothers were secure. All 15 mothers with BPD and 3 normative mothers had unresolved (Ud) status. Among the BPD group, eight had one of the dismissing classifications (Ds 1, 2 or 3) and seven had a preoccupied classification (six had E3 and one had E1). From the DMM classification, all in the BPD group were unresolved, and all had the combination A/C classification. The authors found that the DMM classifications discriminated between the two groups of mothers more effectively than did the Main and Goldwyn classifications.

Crittenden and Newman (2010) summarized their findings from the DMM analyses of the AAIs:

> We found that mothers with BPD recalled more danger, reported more negative effects of danger, and gave evidence of more unresolved psychological trauma tied to danger than other mothers . . . the AAIs of BPD mothers were more complex, extreme, and had more indicators of rapid shifts in arousal than those of other mothers. (p. 433)

The authors suggested that women with BPD experienced dangers during childhood that were beyond their ability to cope. Consequently, they engaged physiological and psychological adaptations that were partially effective initially, but became more maladaptive as the women got older.

Barone, Fossati, and Guiducci (2011) broke new ground by focusing on a range of Axis I comorbidities associated with BPD. The authors referenced the push toward reconceptualizing mental disorders as dimensional rather than categorical constructs (e.g., Widiger & Trull, 2007) and set out to identify the underlying syndromes that share phenomenological similarities. They summarized the previous 15 years of AAI investigations of BPD as showing a high prevalence and severity of the unresolved and preoccupied states of mind in borderline pathology (between 50% and 80%). Only a minority of studies showed no clear prevalence of the dismissing and preoccupied insecure strategies. Barone and her colleagues asserted that their investigation was the first to systematically compare the Axis I comorbidities of an Axis II BPD diagnosis in relation to both attachment categories and infer developmental pathways and states of mind. They sought to avoid the pitfalls of the prior body of research by controlling key variables, such as Axis I diagnosis and sample acquisition and size, and by using the AAI as the attachment assessment method in order to establish a reliable picture of attachment and states of mind in BPD. This study with a large sample size found that BPD is nearly always associated with insecure states of mind, particularly the E and Ds patterns. The authors state, "Insecure attachment was the rule, rather than the exception among BPD participants" (p. 466). Disorganization explained a large part of the typical functioning of patients with BPD. The authors found significant differences in attachment status among the four Axis I comorbidity groups: In BPD patients with comorbid mood disorders and anxiety disorders, there was overrepresentation of E and Ud classifications (E = 60% regardless of Ud/CC classifications; Ud/CC = 47.5%); the dismissing/derogating attachment style (Ds) was overrepresented in the substance abuse/dependence group (58%), the alcohol abuse/dependence group (55%), and the eating-disorders group (60%). Barone and her colleagues summarized the results as follows:

> Dismissing states of mind reflect attempts to minimize attachment needs and should therefore be associated with disorders which involve a strategy of turning attention away from one's own feelings and negative emotions (such as eating disorder, substance and alcohol abuse, and dependence), whereas enmeshed-preoccupied states of mind reflect the maximizing of attachment needs and should be associated with disorders which involve being absorbed in one's own feelings or emotions (such as depression and anxiety). (p. 463)

The following nine AAI coding-system dimensions were significantly associated with selected Axis I disorders among Barone et al.'s (2011) BPD participants:

neglecting mother, rejecting father, pressured-to-achieve father, involving angry mother, derogating mother, idealizing father, involving angry father, passivity of thought processes, and coherence of transcript. The authors asserted that their findings provided strong indication of the usefulness of assessing adult attachment mental states in order to customize treatment for BPD according to the Axis I disorder.

In our orphanage study (see p. 211), insecure attachment (mostly disorganized) as compared to secure attachment was significantly related to a mixed or borderline personality disorder (PD) in adulthood. Past or current trauma was not significantly related to a mixed or borderline PD diagnosis. These findings suggest that mixed and borderline PD are more related to early attachment disorganization than to trauma or abuse in later childhood or adulthood.

CONDUCT DISORDER AND ANTISOCIAL PERSONALITY

Timmerman and Emmelkamp (2006) examined the relationship between attachment styles and Cluster B personality disorders (i.e., antisocial, borderline, histrionic, and narcissistic) in Dutch prisoners (n = 192) and forensic inpatients (n = 39). A control group (n = 105) of normal subjects was drawn from the community. All subjects were assessed for attachment style with the Relationship Questionnaire (RQ). Results showed that subjects with a "criminal status (i.e., the prisoners and forensic inpatients)" (p. 53) were significantly different from normal controls in regard to frequency of secure attachment (less) and presence of a fearful attachment style (more). No differences were found with respect to preoccupied and dismissing attachment. The authors concluded, "None of the cluster B personality pathology variables were associated with the fearful attachment style and histrionic personality pathology was negatively associated with the dismissing attachment style" (p. 48). Furthermore, the presence of antisocial features correlated to dismissing attachment, while borderline pathology was associated with a preoccupied style.

Rosenstein and Horowitz (1996) conducted a study examining 60 adolescents psychiatrically hospitalized for affective disorder (55%), conduct disorder (13%), or a combined affective disorder/conduct disorder (20%). The remainder of the participants (12%) had other diagnoses. All participants were administered the AAI, and attachment status was determined using the four-way classification system: 38% of the participants were classified as dismissing, 2% as autonomous, 42% as preoccupied, and 18% as unresolved. Using the three-category coding system, 3% were scored as autonomous, 47% as dismissing, and 50% as preoccupied. Dismissing attachment was significantly linked to conduct disorders, and patients with both conduct and affective disorders were likely to be classified as dismissing. The authors concluded:

Adolescents using a dismissing attachment organization rely on an attachment strategy that minimizes distressing thoughts and affects associated with rejection by the attachment figure. Thus, psychiatric disorders, such as CD [conduct disorder] or SA [substance abuse], in which overt denial or downplaying of distress, coupled with actions that display those distressing affects, did occur in the context of a dismissing attachment organization. (Rosenstein & Horowitz, 1996, p. 250)

In the J. P. Allen et al. (1996) study mentioned earlier in relation to suicidality among psychiatrically hospitalized adolescents and demographically matched nonpsychiatric high school students, insecure attachment at age 25 was found to be significantly associated with self-reported criminal behavior when assessed in terms of the number of times the subjects reported engaging in any of 30 types of illegal behavior. More specifically,

Adults with dismissing attachment organizations reported significantly more criminal behavior than secure adults. Adults whose transcripts could not be classified displayed higher levels of criminal behavior and psychological distress and lower levels of self-worth than adults with secure classifications. (pp. 259–260)

The authors also discovered from the subjects' demographics and from the AAI that "young adult criminal behavior was associated with male gender, derogation of attachment relationships, and indices of lack of resolution of past trauma" (J. P. Allen et al., 1996, p. 258).

Fonagy and his colleagues (Fonagy, Target, et al., 1997; Levinson & Fonagy, 2004) gave the AAI to 22 prisoners who had been diagnosed with psychiatric disorders, to a matched clinical group of nonprisoners with comparable diagnoses, and to a group of healthy control subjects. Thirty-six percent of the prisoners, 14% of the clinical nonprisoner group, and 23% of the control subjects had dismissing attachment (Ds); 45% of the prisoners, 64% of the clinical group, and 14% of the healthy controls had preoccupied attachment; and 36% of the prisoners, 82% of the clinical group, and 0% of the controls had unresolved status (Ud) with respect to trauma or loss. Eighty-two percent of the prisoners had a history of childhood abuse as compared to 36% and 4% in the other groups. Parental neglect was also significantly higher in the prisoner group than in the other two groups. With respect to criminal behavior, Fonagy and his colleagues suggest that "disruptive behaviors may thus be viewed as strategies initially adopted by children who receive non-optimal care to maximize parental attention" (Levinson & Fonagy, 2004, p. 245). The prisoners also had the lowest scores on the Reflective Functioning Scale as compared to the other two groups. The authors offer an explanation of the link between low reflective functioning and criminal behavior: "Crimes, at least in adolescence, are often committed by individuals with inadequate mentalizing capacities" (p. 256).

Van IJzendoorn et al. (1997) administered the AAI to subjects incarcerated involuntarily on forensic psychiatric units after committing serious crimes such as murder or sexual offenses. The three-, four-, and five-way classification scoring systems for the AAI were each used. The distribution of attachment classifications for the 40 subjects using the five-way system were Ds = 9, F = 2, E = 8, and Ud/CC = 21. Secure attachment was "strongly under-represented" and disorganization (Ud/CC) was "strongly over-represented" in these forensic subjects (p. 453). With respect to personality disorder, the "total number of personality disorder symptoms was significantly related to attachment insecurity" (p. 456). Study subjects with dismissing attachment showed significantly fewer personality disorder symptoms, and those with disorganized attachment (CC) showed more personality disorder symptoms. With respect to the high percentage of CC classifications, the authors state, "The CC subjects have almost all been raised in institutional care, and they appear to show most personality disorders compared to the other attachment groups . . . CC subjects show a global breakdown of coherent discourse about attachment experiences" (p. 456). They add that sadistic and self-defeating personality disorders were especially prevalent in subjects with a CC classification combined with unresolved (Ud) status.

Frodi, Dernevik, Sepa, Philipson, and Bragesjo (2001) gave the AAI to 24 psychopathic criminal offenders in Sweden. All offenders were given the Hare Psychopathic Checklist (Hare, 1991; Hart, Cox, & Hare, 1997). AAI classifications were not significantly associated with the degree of psychopathy as determined from the Hare results. Dismissing attachment was overrepresented in this sample: 64% had a primary classification of dismissing attachment, and the other 36% had a Ud and/or a CC classification. From examining the AAI parenting scales, Frodi et al. found that subjects classified as CC made a distinction between emotional warmth by either the father as compared to the mother or vice versa, indicating contradictory attachment representations; subjects classified as Ds made no such distinction. Subjects classified as Ds as compared to those classified as CC had a "high degree of idealization (of the mother) and very poor recall of experiences in childhood, whereas the U/d/CC men, not surprisingly, scored high on lack of resolution of childhood trauma (primarily severe physical abuse)" (p. 280).

In the Riggs and Jacobvitz (2002) study mentioned several sections earlier, subjects with dismissing and/or unresolved status, as compared to those with preoccupied attachment, were significantly more likely to report criminal charges.

Conclusions About Attachment Status and Psychopathology

In our review of research about the relationships between attachment status and psychopathology, we have included studies that have relied on self-report measures of attachment status and studies that have relied on interviews, primarily the AAI. As we have stated, we see value in self-report measures, but believe that interview-based assessments, particularly the AAI and its scoring as a tool for identifying attachment patterns and states of mind relating to attachment, provide much more and more useful information for research and clinical applications. As such, we limit our discussion about the findings reported in this chapter to those obtained through use of the AAI.

In their first meta-analysis of 33 studies of more than 2,000 AAIs administered to adolescent and adult clinical populations, van IJzendoorn and Bakermans-Kranenburg (1996) concluded that clinical samples were characterized by "a strong overrepresentation of insecure attachment" (p. 8) in general, and specifically that "the U category was strongly overrepresented[,] . . . as was the E category" (p. 13). However, with respect to AAI primary attachment classifications as they relate to psychopathology, the authors stated, "The relations between oppositional and conduct disorders and Ds attachment, and between affective disorders and E attachment, are not clearly and convincingly supported by the available evidence" (p. 19). In a follow-up meta-analysis of over 200 studies with over 10,000 AAIs given to various clinical samples, Bakermans-Kranenburg and van IJzendoorn (2009) were able to draw the following conclusion:

> Disorders with an internalizing dimension (e.g., borderline personality disorders) were associated with more preoccupied and unresolved attachments, whereas disorders with an externalizing dimension (e.g., antisocial personality disorders) displayed more dismissing as well as preoccupied attachments. Depressive symptomatology was associated with insecurity but not with unresolved loss or trauma, whereas adults with abuse experiences or PTSD were mostly unresolved. (p. 223)

These conclusions are measured and robust. However, while it is very clear that insecure attachment in general, and unresolved trauma or loss in particular, is associated with a wide range of psychiatric psychopathology, it is also clear that even with this large AAI database, consistent relationships between specific types of insecure attachment and specific psychiatric disorders are harder to establish.

One limitation across this area of research has been the failure to use a five-way or even four-way classification model in many of the studies. Trying to force the best fit into a secure, dismissing, or preoccupied category obscures the fact that in forensic and psychiatric settings, cannot classify (CC) may be the best fit for the clinical case. Steele (2003) noted that during AAI administration, DID patients may switch among different alter personality states; each alter personality state has its distinct attachment style and may be contradictory to previous states that came forth during the interview. Without a CC classification, the presence of contradictory attachment patterns cannot be easily identified.

Schuengel and van IJzendoorn (2001) state, "It should be noted that in extremely disturbed individuals, the quality or type of attachment representation may not be adequately described by the current attachment concepts nor adequately established with the current coding system of the AAI" (p. 315). They estimate that across the main sample of their meta-analytic studies, "the percentage of CCs may be in the 10% to 20% range" (p. 317). They further note that CC is likely the primary classification in forensic and inpatient psychiatric settings. In our orphanage study (see p. 211), those subjects with extremely disrupted early parent–child attachment all had CC as the primary attachment classification. A total of 19 of 45 subjects (42%) in our sample had CC as the primary classification—a percentage considerably higher than the aggregate estimate advanced by Schuengel and van IJzendoorn (2001). Furthermore, Howard Steele and Valerie Sinason established a database from giving the AAI to patients with a dissociative identity disorder (DID) diagnosis and found a primary CC classification in over 90% of DID patients (the remainder classified as E). Unresolved (Ud) status is also very high in DID patients (H. Steele, personal communication with D. Brown, 2014).

The CC classification represents pervasive disorganization across the AAI transcript, not topic-specific disorganization as in the case of unresolved status (Ud). The CC classification represents the worst of early parent–child disorganized attachment and is strongly associated with mixed or borderline personality disorder and major dissociative disorders. Therefore, disorganized attachment over the course of development has major implications for mental health and needs to become a main focus of future research. In our opinion, such research would benefit from refining the CC category into a range of subtypes that can further differentiate the phenomena of attachment disorganization. Crittenden's categorization system (see Crittenden & Landini, 2011, and Chapter 4 of this book) includes subtypes of what has been described as disorganization, based on a variety of distinct combinations of the primary classification categories. In Chapter 4, we describe nine subtypes of CC that we have developed through our work with various clinical samples. We find clinical utility with these CC subtypes, but they have not been empirically validated.

As research into all forms of attachment disturbance continues, the forms and methods of use of interview-based assessment can be refined. The limitations of any instrument must be recognized and taken into account. Turton, McGauley, Marin-Avellan, and Hughes (2001) described a variety of issues and problems pertaining to giving the AAI to nonnormative samples: (1) When a person has had multiple transient caregivers throughout childhood, it becomes difficult to identify primary attachment figures for the AAI interview; (2) early loss of key attachment figures is prevalent and needs to be probed carefully in the interview so as to detect unresolved status; (3) violations of discourse are sometimes so extreme that it is hard to follow the interview; (4) derogation of attachment is sometimes extreme but appears "licensed" by descriptions of abuse and sadistic abuse by the caregiver; (5) dismissing derogation is often mixed with angry preoccupation; (6) idealization is high in certain cultural and ethnic settings independent of attachment status; (7) longing for attachment is strong in certain individuals with chronically negative parenting and should be seen as an example of secure valuing of attachment; (8) abuse by stepparents, foster care parents, caretakers, and non-family-members may be severe and frequent; (9) psychotic processes, use of medications, and institutionalization affects the validity of the AAI; and (10) E3 classification (fearful preoccupation) is overrepresented in psychiatric populations, but E3 and CC are rarely seen in training AAI protocols.

Despite these challenges to be considered, the AAI as an assessment instrument offers great promise for continuing to assist researchers in developing more and more recognition and understanding of the factors that underlie attachment dynamics and their relation to both well-being and psychopathology. The use of the AAI in the Minnesota study (Sroufe, Egeland, Carlson, & Collins, 2009), a study made uniquely strong by its use of a large sample size and its longitudinal nature, produced some of the strongest outcome data in the relatively short history of the field of developmental psychopathology.

For clinical work, we see the use of the AAI and an appropriate scoring system as especially important, because it allows for detailed subclassification of attachment patterns. It is essential to employ this aspect of the AAI when setting up the treatment plan for patients with more severe and complex difficulties, such as complex PTSD, borderline personality disorder, and dissociative disorders, and so-called "treatment-resistant" patients who have made multiple attempts to get appropriate treatment only to suffer through shifting diagnoses, different recommendations for treatment, and reactive medication management, sometimes over the course of many years. These are the patients who as children had to adaptively develop a mix of attachment strategies due to inadequate and/or harmful parenting behaviors. This mix of attachment strategies often underlies the disturbance presenting for treatment. We believe that use of the Main and Goldwyn five-way AAI classification system, or the DMM system from Crittenden, allows for more accurate and detailed identification of the important underlying patterns.

Equipped with these assessment methods, clinicians can apply the information obtained to engaging in methods of treatment that can efficiently repair attachment disturbances in patients and mitigate the passage of insecure attachment through the generations. The individual and societal toll exacted by attachment disturbances in our primary caregiving relationships is immense and too far reaching to even begin to calculate.

The Orphanage Study: Attachment and Complex Trauma

The development of the orphanage study occurred somewhat serendipitously. The senior author of this book, Daniel Brown, had conducted a large number of forensic evaluations of adult survivors of childhood sexual abuse over many years in the context of civil lawsuits against alleged offenders and/or third parties. At one point, Dr. Brown was asked to evaluate a number of adult survivors of childhood physical abuse (PA) and child sexual abuse (CSA) that had allegedly occurred at a Catholic orphanage in the greater New Orleans area in the late 1950s and 1960s as part of a lawsuit against the local Catholic diocese. The allegations of abuse involved two priests working at the orphanage and five staff members. Each of the priests had been previously accused of child molestation at least once, and the "solution" by the Church was to transfer all of these accused priests to work in the same orphanage. A number of the orphanage's staff members had also been accused of abuse at some point in their lives. Eventually what emerged at the orphanage was an organized "culture" of priests and staff who had been previously accused of sexual abuse and who therefore were all at high risk of reoffending in this new environment. Extensive physical and sexual abuse of many orphans occurred in that environment.

Most of the child victims had not reported the CSA at the time of its occurrence, and by adulthood all the victims had completely forgotten the sexual abuse but not necessarily forgotten the physical abuse. After three to four decades, the victims began to recover sexual abuse memories between 2004 and 2006, following national media exposure of priest sexual abuse and/or local media exposure of physical and sexual abuse at this specific orphanage. In the context of these lawsuits, many aspects of the abuse reported by a particular victim had been corroborated by other victims' reports, in that the physical and sexual abuse was often conducted in groups. The lawsuit was settled against the Church for most of the victims prior to going to trial. As part of a civil lawsuit against the orphanage and the archdiocese, between 2005 and 2006 Dr. Brown conducted a detailed forensic psychological assessment of each alleged victim. The assessment consisted of, on average, 16 hours of face-to-face interviewing and psychological testing.

There are two unique features of this sample. First, the sample represents victims not simply of individual offenders, but rather of an entire organized "culture" of child abuse—the majority of the staff at the orphanage allegedly participated in physical, sexual, and sometimes sadistic abuse of a group of children. The sample is unique in that all 17 subjects were abused in the same way, by the same group of offenders, during the same time frame. Second, all adult survivors who participated in the study were given the Adult Attachment Interview (AAI), which was scored according to the five-way classification system in order to determine their attachment prototype. About 60% of the 17 orphanage victims were determined to have insecure attachment, mostly of the disorganized type (Ud and/or CC status), from the AAI scoring. Many of these subjects came from chaotic family backgrounds, characterized by, for example, repetitive violence and alcoholism in the home and/or a parent running a drug ring and/or a prostitution network out of the home. The other 40% of the group came from large, loving Catholic families and were likely to have secure attachment status due to healthy parenting. However, because these families were often large and poor, the fathers often had to work multiple jobs to make ends meet. Many of these fathers worked at high-risk jobs such as on oil-drilling rigs. A common occurrence in these families was that the father had a serious industrial accident resulting in serious physical injury and disability or death; as a result, the mother was unable to afford to continue raising the children, and the family dissolved and the children were sent to the Catholic orphanage.

Thus, despite the very different backgrounds of the two groups of subjects, they were all abused—physically, sexually, and sometimes sadistically—by the same offenders. The main variable in the study was attachment status. The unique features of this sample allowed us the possibility of separating out the relative differential contributions of early attachment status on the one hand, and the effects of childhood physical and sexual abuse in later childhood on the other hand, to the subjects' overall adult psychopathology.

To increase the statistical power, we also examined a second mixed group of CSA victims. Group A comprised the 17 subjects described above, and Group B consisted of 28 adult subjects, all of whom were also adult survivors of sexual abuse. Dr. Brown had also conducted similar forensic examinations on each of these subjects as part of a lawsuit. All Group B subjects received exactly the same set of forensic instruments that were used for Group A. The main difference between Group A and Group B subjects was that all in Group A had been sexually abused by the same offenders, whereas those in Group B had all been abused by different offenders. A statistical comparison of Group A and Group B found few significant differences between the two groups, so that most statistical comparisons were conducted by combining Group A and Group B into a single pooled group of 45 subjects. The main significant differences between the orphanage Group A and the mixed Group B were that the mean unresolved score (Ud) with respect to trauma was significantly higher in the A versus B group, and that Group A versus Group B subjects were significantly more depressed and prone to panic attacks according to SCID-I findings. Given the severe "culture" of abuse at the orphanage, it is not surprising that the Group A survivors were significantly more dissociative, depressed, and vulnerable to panic than the Group B mixed survivors.

The age range across the combined 45 subjects varied from 16 to 75 years, with an average age of 44 years. The majority of the subjects were male (89%). Twenty-two percent of the subjects had never been married, 51% were married, and 12% had been separated or divorced. With respect to educational background, 27% had never finished high school, 36% had only completed high school, 27% had finished college, and 11% had completed a postgraduate degree. A total of 87% of the subjects were white, 9% were Hispanic, 2% were Asian, and 2% were Native American. The majority were Catholic (84%), because many of the lawsuits were against the Catholic church.

All subjects were given the same set of instruments: (1) Attachment status was assessed using the Adult Attachment Interview (AAI) and the Experience of Close Relationships scale (ECR; Brennan, Clark, & Shaver, 1998); (2) Axis I depression and anxiety conditions were evaluated using the SCID-I, the Beck Depression Inventory–1, the Penn State Worry Scale (PSWS; T. A. Brown, Antony, & Barlow, 1992), and the Body Sensations Questionnaire (BSQ; Chambless, Caputo, Bright, & Gallagher, 1984); (3) PTSD was assessed using the Trauma Symptom Inventory (TSI; Briere, Elliott, Harris, & Cotman, 1995) and the Clinician Administered PTSD Scale (CAPS; Blake et al., 1995, 2000); (4) dissociative conditions were evaluated using the SCID-D, the Dissociation Questionnaire (DQ; Vanderlinden & Vandereycken, 1997), and the Somatoform Dissociation Questionnaire (SDQ; Nijenhuis, Spinhoven, van Dijck, van der Hart, & Vanderlinden, 1996); (5) Axis II conditions were evaluated using the SCID-II and the Young Schema Questionnaire–III (YSQ-III; Young & Brown, 2001); and (6) other instruments included the Index of Self Esteem (ISE; Hudson, 1997), the Fear of Negative Evaluation scale (FNE; Watson & Freind, 1969), and the Social Avoidance and Distress Scale (SADS; Watson & Freind, 1969).

The main focus of the research was to determine how AAI-based attachment classifications were related to various diagnoses. Using Chi-square tests, the AAI secure/insecure status variable yielded a number of significant findings. The statistical analyses were done by Howard Steele, a collaborator on the study. Since the majority of insecure subjects on the AAI had disorganized status (Ud or CC classification) and many of the secure subjects also were disorganized with respect to trauma or loss (Ud), it was not possible to look at whether disorganized status alone was associated with certain diagnoses, as we lacked the power to detect this influence. Therefore, we looked at the broader distinction of secure versus insecure status against the background of trauma and unresolved mourning; that is, we asked if the effects of Ud/CC or unresolved mourning were less evident in the context of attachment security. Overall, our preliminary analyses focused on the relationship between certain AAI measures (secure vs. insecure, coherence of transcript, and coherence of mind) and various psychiatric diagnoses in adulthood. High coherence of transcript and high coherence of mind were significantly associated with less evidence of certain diagnoses.

With respect to a diagnosis of personality disorder, we divided the 45 subjects into a group of those that met sufficient SCID-II (First, Gibbon, Spitzer, Williams, & Benjamin, 1997) criteria for a mixed and/or borderline personality disorder and a group of those that did not. When insecure/secure attachment was cross-tabulated with SCID-II mixed PD or BPD, a significant Chi-square was observed ($p < 0.001$): Of the 25 subjects with mixed PD or BPD, 22 subjects had insecure attachment and only 3 subjects had secure attachment on the AAI. Of the 25 subjects in the total sample with a cannot classify (CC) primary classification, 17 had a mixed PD or BPD as compared to 8 subjects who did not ($p < 0.001$). Similarly, low coherence of transcript on the AAI was significantly related to a mixed PD or borderline PD on the SCID-II. Furthermore, when unresolved status with respect to trauma or loss (Ud) on the AAI was parceled out, the association between mixed PD or BPD and the CC classification was still significant. Thus, insecure attachment in general, and pervasive disorganized attachment in particular (CC), has a statistically significant relationship to the diagnosis of a mixed PD or BPD in adulthood.

The Young Schema Questionnaire-III has 232 items tapping various maladaptive schemes, categorized into 18 different schema domains. According to Jeffrey Young (personal communication with D. Brown, 2001) subjects who show high or very high scores on six or more of the 18 schema domains are likely to have a personality disorder diagnosis. Therefore, we divided our sample of 45 subjects into two groups—those subjects who had six or more of the 18 schema domains in the high or very high range and those subjects who did not. Using Chi-square tests, both AAI insecure attachment and low coherence of transcript were found to be significantly associated with a personality disorder as defined by having six or more YSQ-III maladaptive schemas. In the context of schemas, this finding indicates that the subjects with insecure as compared to secure attachment on the AAI were significantly more likely to have a greater number of negative, maladaptive schemas. In summary, a significant relationship between insecure attachment and a major personality disorder was found when either instrument to assess PD—the SCID-II or the YSQ-III—was used.

A relationship between insecure attachment (coupled with Ud status) and dissociative disorders was also confirmed. Using the SCID-D (Steinberg, 1993), we first looked at major dissociative disorders such as dissociative identity disorder (DID). Only 3 of the 45 subjects met the full diagnostic criteria for DID using the SCID-D. Therefore, we combined those subjects having either DID or DDNOS. Those with a diagnosis of DDNOS ($n = 17$) all reported distinctive "parts" of the mind but did not meet full DID criteria, either because they were co-conscious of their "parts" or did not show a loss of executive control. The common feature of the combined DID/DDNOS group was the existence of two or more distinctive alter personality states or "parts." There was a trend for insecure as compared to secure attachment to be related to DID or DDNOS, but it narrowly failed to reach the 0.05 significance level. However, low as compared to high coherence of transcript ($p < 0.01$) and coherence of mind ($p < 0.035$) were both significantly correlated with a DID/DDNOS diagnosis. In other words, both coherence of transcript and coherence of mind on the AAI were significantly lower for subjects with DID or DDNOS than for those without DID or DDNOS.

Depersonalization and derealization were significantly more prevalent in insecure subjects than in secure subjects. When AAI insecure/secure classification was cross-tabulated with the seven subjects who had a SCID-D diagnosis of derealization, a significant Chi-square was observed ($p < 0.01$). All seven subjects with a derealization diagnosis had insecure attachment, and all seven had unresolved status with respect to past trauma. Similarly, 12 subjects in the total sample had a SCID-D diagnosis of depersonalization, and 10 (83%) of these had insecure attachment. When insecure/secure classification was cross-tabulated for these subjects with depersonalization, a significant Chi-square was observed ($p < 0.05$) .

Using the SCID-I (First, Spitzer, Gibbon, & Williams, 1997), we identified those subjects with bipolar disorder. All bipolar subjects in the total sample ($n = 14$) had bipolar type II (hypomania) on the SCID-I, 11 with insecure and 3 with secure attachment on the AAI; none had type I bipolar disorder (classic manic depressive illness). When insecure/secure attachment was cross-tabulated with SCID-I bipolar type II diagnostic criteria, there was a significant Chi-square ($p < 0.037$).

Using a similar approach, when insecure/secure attachment was cross-tabulated with measures of self-esteem, fear of negative evaluation, and social avoidance and distress, in each case a significant Chi-square was observed. A logistic regression was computed, following a stepwise procedure, that showed that low self-esteem, fear of negative evaluation, and social avoidance/distress all shared some variance with each other and with insecure attachment, but that fear of negative evaluation was sufficient to predict insecurity 73% of the time ($p < 0.05$). Thus, individuals with insecure as compared to secure attachment are more likely to manifest a strong fear of negative evaluation by others.

We conducted similar analyses for other SCID-I psychiatric diagnoses. There were no significant statistical relationships between insecure attachment and major depressive disorder, dysthymia, panic disorder, or somatoform disorder. With respect to PTSD, insecure as compared to secure attachment was not significantly related to any of the 10 clinical scales on the TSI or the total trauma score on the CAPS. We also looked at whether alcohol and drug abuse or dependency was associated with attachment status. Findings for alcohol or drug abuse or dependency on the SCID-I were not statistically significantly related to insecure status or coherence of discourse on the AAI.

All subjects in the orphanage sample, assessed in the context of a civil lawsuit, were given the Malingering Probability Scale (Silverton & Gruber, 1998) and the Structured Interview of Reported Symptoms (Rogers et al., 2002). When insecure/secure attachment was cross-tabulated with the Malingering scale (MAL) on the MPS and with the total malingering score on the SIRS scale, significant Chi-squares were observed ($p < 0.05$). Similarly, subjects with higher malingering probability scores on either the MPS or SIRS had significantly lower coherence of transcript.

These findings linking psychopathology with insecure attachment can be seen to show the added vulnerability brought by insecurity and unresolved status (Ud) regarding past trauma or loss or, put the other way around, the diminished importance of unresolved status (Ud) when the underlying or overall pattern of attachment is secure.

The results of the orphanage study have important implications for the treatment of complex trauma. It is very common for patients diagnosed with "complex trauma" to have multiple, comorbid psychiatric diagnoses such as PTSD, panic, generalized anxiety disorder, major depression or dysthymia, a somatoform disorder, a dissociative disorder, a personality disorder, and/or multiple addictive behaviors. Herman (1992) initially defined complex posttraumatic stress disorder as a "spectrum of conditions rather than a single entity" that include "personality changes, alterations in affect regulation and meaning systems, consciousness, self-perception and relations with others." Further, she hypothesized that disorders of extreme stress not otherwise specified (DESNOS) have their origins in "a history of childhood trauma" (p. 125).

As the term "complex trauma," suggests, many have assumed that traumatic acts play a main role in the development of complex trauma disorders. For example, Roth, Newman, Pelcovitz, van der Kolk, and Mandel (1997) attribute complex trauma to "early trauma," such as sexual abuse prior to age 13 (p. 541). Van der Kolk, Roth, Pelcovitz, Sunday, and Spinazzola (2005) found that "early trauma," namely, sexual abuse prior to age 14, was significantly associated with the development of a complex trauma disorder.

The problem with etiologically attributing complex trauma simply to early childhood trauma is that it fails to account for the differential effects of early dysfunction in the infant–caregiver attachment system and specific abusive events, like sexual and/or physical abuse in later childhood. There has been a trend in the more recent literature to expand the definition of early trauma to include "trauma early in the life cycle" (van der Kolk et al., 2005, p. 389), but these attempts to push back the age of traumatization do not alter the fundamental assumption, namely, that complex trauma *is a result of early childhood trauma per se.* Roth et al. (1997), for example, say that "complex trauma is specific to trauma" (p. 541). This trauma-focused bias obscures the extent to which early attachment disturbance may account for complex trauma and/or multiple comorbidities, independent of or in combination with abuse. There is indication that attachment problems are being recognized as relevant to later trauma, as van der Kolk and Courtois (2005) have addressed "developmental trauma" (p. 385), which includes both "nonresponsive and abusive caregivers" (p. 386). Such recognition opens the door to reconsideration of the relative contribution of early attachment failure, not trauma per se, in the etiology of complex trauma.

An important exception to trauma bias in the complex trauma literature is Alexander's research (1993) on women survivors of childhood sexual abuse. In assessing attachment status, Axis I disorders including PTSD, and personality disorders, she found that childhood sexual abuse was significantly correlated with PTSD and other Axis I conditions, but that a personality disorder diagnosis was significantly correlated with early childhood attachment status in addition to the history of abuse. These findings suggest two separate pathways to complex trauma in adults, with insecure attachment contributing to personality disorders and abuse per se contributing to PTSD and other Axis I anxiety and affective conditions. However, this study was limited by the use of self-report inventories to assess attachment status.

We find support from various research findings for the presence of two pathways from early abuse toward different manifestations of trauma in adulthood. Evidence from prospective studies of physically and sexually abused children compared to demographically matched nonabused children have shown (1) that childhood abuse is causally related to the development of conduct and relational problems in adolescence and the emergence of circumscribed psychiatric conditions in early adulthood, such as PTSD (Widom,1999), depression, anxiety (Silverman, Reinherz, & Giaconia, 1996), somatoform symptoms (Putnam, 1998), and addictions (Silverman et al., 1996; Widom, Ireland, & Glynn, 1995); (2) that the emergence of multiple comorbid psychiatric conditions in adulthood as a consequence of abuse is common (D. P. Brown, 2001; Putnam, 1998); and (3) that the use of a dissociative coping style to handle the abuse predicts a greater severity and range of psychiatric conditions in adulthood (Putnam, 1998). Contributions from attachment research challenge the trauma-per-se view of the etiology of complex trauma. A large body of research from longitudinal studies has shown that early childhood insecure attachment is related to the emergence of significant areas of psychopathology in adolescence and adulthood (Putnam, 1998; Silverman et al., 1996; Widom, 1999). Childhood disorganized or resistant insecure attachment status is a risk factor for the development of personality disorders (Barone, 2003; Fonagy et al., 1996; Patrick et al., 1994; van IJzendoorn et al., 1997), anxiety disorders (Bosquet & Egeland, 2006; Warren et al., 1997), and addictions in adulthood (Widom, Ireland, & Glynn, 1995).

We referred to the Minnesota Longitudinal Study earlier in this chapter as "the gold standard" of prospective studies of childhood neglect and abuse. In addition to comprehensive, longitudinal assessments of attachment status, data were available about the physical and/or sexual abuse experienced over time by the children in the study. Such a database allowed for accurate assessment of the relative contribution of both early attachment disruption and later specific abusive incidents to the overall psychopathology as it appeared in early adulthood. The data clearly show that the *combination* of disorganized attachment aggravated by later childhood abuse predicts the development of dissociative disorders in adulthood (Carlson, 1998; Liotti, 1992; Ogawa et al., 1997). Main and Morgan (1996) also found that early attachment disorganization predicts a greater frequency and range of dissociative experiences in childhood and adolescence. Specific effects of disorganized attachment on the emergence and course of dissociative phenomena are detailed in the section on attachment and dissociative disorders above.

We see significant research support indicating that there are two lineages of long-term effects of trauma: simple and complex PTSD. Simple PTSD is typically associated with single or cumulative traumatic events per se, relatively uncomplicated by other factors, whereas complex trauma is the outcome of a *combination of early childhood insecure attachment aggravated by abuse or trauma in later childhood or adulthood*. Simple PTSD manifests mainly in Axis I psychiatric conditions like PTSD, affective and/or depressive symptoms, and sometimes addictive behaviors. In addition to the simple PTSD manifestations, complex trauma-related disorders can also include somatoform symptoms, a personality disorder, a major dissociative disorder or multiple dissociative symptoms, and often multiple addictive behaviors. Multiple comorbid psychiatric conditions are common in complex trauma disorders, and it is not uncommon to have 5 to 10 discrete DSM psychiatric diagnoses in such individuals.

In summary, simple PTSD is associated with single or cumulative specific trauma events, whereas complex trauma is primarily associated with insecure attachment aggravated by abuse or trauma in later childhood or adulthood. There is little support for the view that complex trauma is a function of early trauma per se or a function of multiple-event trauma or cumulative abuse (Terr, 1994). Rather, early childhood insecure attachment is a key ingredient in the eventual development of complex trauma, in combination with abuse or trauma later in childhood (Allen, 2001).

The findings of our orphanage study add further evidence to support the view that what has been called complex trauma is better viewed as early insecure attachment (mostly disorganized attachment) aggravated by physical and/or sexual abuse in later childhood. It is very clear from the study that Axis I conditions such as PTSD and depression, anxiety-spectrum conditions such as panic, and alcohol or drug abuse or dependency are significantly related to acts of physical and sexual abuse per se. It is also very clear from the orphanage study that a mixed or borderline personality disorder diagnosis, multiple dissociative disorder diagnoses, and a bipolar type II diagnosis are significantly related to insecure attachment and low coherence of discourse on the AAI.

These findings suggest that there are relatively independent contributions of attachment insecurity and traumatic acts to psychopathology in adulthood. Insecure attachment, especially disorganized attachment, is associated with a major disruption of most developmental lines, such as affect development, self-development, and the development of positive, unified internal working models for attachment. The long-term effects of insecure attachment on these developmental lines are likely to culminate in a mixed or borderline personality disorder diagnosis in adulthood. Additionally, our orphanage study, consistent with the Minnesota Longitudinal Study, strongly suggests that clinically significant dissociative symptoms and disorders are not a function of abuse per se but are the result of early childhood insecure, largely disorganized attachment aggravated by the effects of abuse in later childhood.

These findings have major implications for the *treatment* of complex trauma-related disorders. In our view, a consistent focus on trauma processing per se in patients with complex trauma-related disorders runs the risk of aggravating disorganization of mind, which is a feature of insecure attachment (and measured by low coherence of mind on the AAI). Dr. Brown had the opportunity to serve as an expert witness, largely for the defense, in the 1990s and 2000s in approximately 70 malpractice lawsuits against clinicians for allegedly implanting false memories of abuse in patients. The profile of many of these lawsuits was similar. The patient initially came to treatment for some issue other than abuse, such as relational disturbance, depression, or an eating disorder or other addiction. Over time the patient reported recovering memories of childhood sexual abuse, and various dissociative symptoms were observed. Eventually, the patient manifested alter personality states and was given the diagnosis of multiple personality disorder, or, more recently, dissociative identity disorder. Often treatment spanned over a decade, with multiple clinicians and multiple hospitalizations. At some point later in time, the patient encountered information pertaining to "false memory" claims and then established the belief that his or her abuse memories were false and had been iatrogenically created by the therapists. These cases often became expensive lawsuits involving multiple defendant clinicians and hospitals. In preparing for these cases, Dr. Brown often read crates of medical records spanning over a decade for each case as well as detailed deposition testimony of many defendant clinicians.

Immersion in this massive database allowed Dr. Brown to get a sense of the underlying essential clinical factors across many of the cases. As he saw it, contrary to plaintiff claims, most of the defendant clinicians were not using risky memory recovery techniques to zealously recover or suggest abuse memories in these patients. In fact, many of the plaintiffs were actually low on memory suggestibility when assessed. After the therapies, it appears that many plaintiffs were coached by attorneys and false-memory proponents into the belief that their abuse memories were false. This coaching, along with the promise of considerable money from the lawsuits, led the plaintiffs to substantially reinterpret their previous mental health treatment.

False-memory issues aside, these cases also illustrate something important for clinicians to learn with respect to treating patients with complex trauma. The defendant clinicians in most of these lawsuits were very likely to have engaged in systematic trauma processing of one sort or another, such as phase-oriented trauma treatment (D. P. Brown, Scheflin, & Hammond, 1999) or cognitive-behavioral exposure-based trauma processing. Both of these approaches, in our opinion, are well within the standard of care. So, if clinicians were not generally employing risky memory recovery techniques or iatrogenically implanting false abuse memories, where did these cases go wrong?

In our opinion, the available trauma-processing models of treatment in the 1990s and 2000s fail to consider the differential contribution of insecure, largely disorganized attachment to overall adult psychopathology. What Dr. Brown observed in many of these cases was that systematic trauma processing with patients who had disorganized attachment aggravated by abuse in later childhood *often led to further disorganization of mind*. While trauma processing per se may not have led to the development of false memories, as false-memory proponents would like us to believe, it was true that in many cases the patients *had gotten worse*, mainly by becoming more disorganized. The lesson to be learned is that trauma processing per se may be contraindicated for patients with disorganized attachment aggravated by abuse in later childhood. The findings from our orphanage study and also from the Minnesota Longitudinal Study remind us that the main etiological contribution to what has been called complex trauma is not trauma per se, but disorganized attachment. Based on all of this information, we began to rethink our approaches to the treatment of complex trauma.

We began to focus our treatment of these patients primarily on the treatment of the disorganized attachment component of their complex trauma, using the methods we have developed and outlined in the rest of this book. We found that by using this attachment-based treatment over time, our complex trauma patients were achieving high coherence of mind (on the AAI) and sometimes resolution of unresolved (Ud) status (on the AAI) *without having done any type of trauma processing*. Furthermore, once these patients had achieved high coherence of mind using the attachment-based treatment, it was easy to process the trauma with simple cognitive-behavioral exposure-based methods in a way that did not lead to disorganization of mind. It is our hope that trauma clinicians will use this book to reconsider their approach to the treatment of trauma patients when there is a clear history of disorganized attachment.

In the next section of this book, we address the treatment of attachment disturbances. Chapter 6 presents a review of the available attachment-based treatments. Chapter 7 describes the fundamentals of the model and methods of our Three Pillars approach to treatment, and Chapters 8, 9, and 10 detail the principles and practices of each of the Three Pillars.

PART III

TREATMENT

BACKGROUND AND THE THREE PILLARS MODEL OF COMPREHENSIVE ATTACHMENT REPAIR

An Overview of Treatments for Attachment Disturbances

As a foundation for the presentation of our treatment model and methods in the next section of this book, in this chapter we review treatment approaches and methods that are currently regarded as applicable to the treatment of attachment disturbances. Rather than exhaustively reviewing all available treatments, we have chosen those that we believe to be representative of the types and forms of treatments that have been developed since John Bowlby's and Mary Ainsworth's pioneering descriptions of attachment problems and their origins. By highlighting available treatments, their conceptual foundations, their methods, and their strengths and limitations, we show respect for the history of attachment-based treatments, provide information that may assist clinicians with their thinking about and practice with patients with insecure attachment, and prepare the reader for understanding the efficiency and strengths of our particular treatment model and methods.

Starting Points: Bowlby's Attachment-Based Psychotherapy

The origins of attachment-based psychotherapy go back to the work of Bowlby. In *A Secure Base* (1988), Bowlby outlined general principles for treatment of attachment problems. He saw the primary role of the therapist as providing a secure base from which exploration is encouraged, much like a mother serves as a secure base from which a child can explore (p. 152). According to Bowlby,

> The therapeutic alliance appears as a secure base, an internal object as a working, or representational, model of an attachment figure, reconstruction as exploring memories of the past, resistance (sometimes) as deep reluctance to disobey the past orders of parents not to tell or not to remember. (p. 151)

With the security of an attachment to the therapist, the patient is free to engage in exploration, in this case exploration of attachment themes, past and present. Consistent with Bowlby's training as a psychoanalyst, his focus of psychotherapeutic exploration was primarily on the influence of early experiences on the transference relationship (1988). But the context for that exploration framed the patient's *relationship* to the therapist differently than traditional psychoanalytic practice. Bowlby made explicit the kind of exploration that is specific to his approach to therapy and its relational context:

> [The therapist] provide[s] the patient with a secure base from which he can explore the various unhappy and painful aspects of his life, past and present, many of which he finds difficult or perhaps impossible to think about and reconsider without a trusted companion to provide support, encouragement, sympathy, and, on occasion, guidance. (p. 138)

Bowlby designed his attachment-based psychotherapy for patients who show "disturbances in [their] capacities to make secure attachments" (1988, p. 73). Such disturbances derive from outright threats not to love the child, threats to abandon the child, or threats of parental suicide, and also from an ongoing pattern of parental unresponsiveness or misresponsiveness through which the child develops a negative internal working model for what is expected of relationships. The ultimate goal of therapeutic work is to develop a more positive internal working model for attachment. Bowlby wrote:

> A therapist applying attachment theory sees his role as being one of providing the conditions in which his patient can explore his representational models of himself and his attachment figures with a view to reappraising and restructuring them in light of the new understanding he acquires and the new experiences he has in the therapeutic relationship. (p. 138)

Through such explorations of attachment experiences, feelings associated with attachment, and representations and expectancies about past attachment figures, the patient is able to reflect on the accuracy of past internal working models and develop more appropriate, positive models for healthy attachment.

Psychoanalytic Approaches

As a psychoanalyst, Bowlby received much attention from others in the psychoanalytic field in response to his thinking and practice pertaining to attachment problems. Not all of that attention was approving, as he was advocating a theoretical and practical conception of the therapeutic relationship that departed from the psychoanalytic strictures of the time. But his ideas and practices were incorporated in various ways into later psychoanalytically oriented attachment-based treatments (Slade, 1999, 2008; Tolmacz, 2009).

INTERPRETING DEFENSES AND WORKING THROUGH THE TRANSFERENCE

In *Remembering, Repeating, and Working Through Childhood Trauma* (1994), Lawrence Hedges advocates a classical psychoanalytic approach to working with patients with clinically significant attachment disorders. The core of his method involves interpreting resistance to and defenses against attachment as well as interpreting the pathological manifestations of attachment behavior in the transference relationship. His text focuses primarily on treatment of severely disturbed individuals, mainly psychotic patients. He considers psychosis to be related to maternal failure in the earliest months of life, which he calls the "organizing period" (p. 44). Thus, he sees psychotic patients as reenacting this organizing failure in the transference to the therapist—what Hedges calls the "transference of the organizing period" pertaining to the "failed mother" (p. 44).

The first work of treatment is to interpret the resistance to and defense against connection, such that the conflicts about human bonding emerge more clearly in consciousness and the wish for symbiotic merger become clear. Next comes transference interpretation using the here-and-now approach to the transference to the therapist. This process begins with identifying how the organizing transference manifests in treatment, allowing for its development, and thereby supporting the development of the patient's longings. Then Hedges advocates interpreting the painful experiences, "psychotic anxieties," and distorted memories (1994, p. 18) pertaining to maternal failure in the context of a solid working alliance. He states that as a consequence of working through the transference, the severely disturbed patient's mind becomes organized and a sense of self becomes consolidated (p. 109), reflexive mental states develop (p. 124), and a new template for relatedness develops (p. 276). The main work of treatment is to allow the organizing transference to develop. Consistent with the foundational theory of the psychoanalytic method, Hedges states, "Transference in all its variations . . . is the fundamental structuring mechanism of the human mind" (pp. 275–276).

MOURNING THE LOSS OF WHAT WAS NEVER GIVEN BY ATTACHMENT FIGURES

Malcolm West and Adrienne Keller (1994) developed an attachment-based approach to the treatment of patients with a personality disorder diagnosis. Their understanding of the etiology of personality disorders is based on Bowlby's observations on the effects of childhood loss and mourning. However, their definition of loss is not limited to *actual* loss of or separation from a parent, but rather on the experience of loss associated with *what was never present*—what the child needed from the attachment figure and what he or she never sufficiently received. The essence of West and Keller's treatment approach is to have patients acknowledge the

> loss of that which they have deeply desired but never fully experienced . . . A basic problem of insecurely attached individuals is that they have been unable to say goodbye to "lost" attachment figures; that is, they have been unable to forgive, forget, and reconcile themselves to the reality of unsuccessful past attachments . . . Attachment-based therapy strives to complete a delayed mourning process. (pp. 326–327)

West and Keller are critical of Bowlby's notion of defensive exclusion and prefer to speak of "defensive attachment patterns." The difference, in their view, is that defensive attachment patterns operate more to create distance and disconnection from a relationship rather than simply excluding disavowed feelings from consciousness. For patients with personality disorders, disavowal is accompanied by disconnection:

> When we speak of "defensive attachment patterns," we are referring essentially to an inauthentic style of relating. The forming and sustaining of meaningful attachments have a good deal to do with affective authenticity, in the sense of an openness to one's own feelings and a readiness to respond to another person's feelings. Inauthentic affective communication is a significant form of defense because it creates relational distance. (p. 320)

Following Bowlby's and Ainsworth's emphasis on the importance of secure-base experience, the foundation of West and Keller's treatment is for the therapist to become a secure base for the patient. They see the therapist as a "protective figure" (p. 322) who is able to "encourage exploration . . . against the background of safety" (p. 322). Therapeutic exploration in general focuses on "the various unhappy and painful aspects of [the patient's] life" (p. 322). In particular, West and Keller differentiate the target of exploration for patients with dismissing attachment from that of patients with anxious-preoccupied attachment. They suggest that dismissing patients with personality disorders develop their dismissing attachment style in response to repeated disappointments in and rejections by early parental attachment figures. Thus, exploration focuses on the "inability to feel anger and sadness . . . [and] the disappointment of relationships with parents" (p. 321). Anxious-preoccupied patients with personality disorders never got or get what they need from attachment figures, and so their attachment system becomes hyperactivated in a "persistent effort to recover lost relationships" (p. 321). Exploration focuses on such effort and the associated feelings.

As in classic psychoanalytic theory, West and Keller see intrapsychic conflict as playing a central role in the development of personality disorders. They call this conflict the "desire–fear drama." The desire part of the conflict pertains to "the longing for meaningful relatedness" (p. 323), while the fear part pertains to a regressive infantile longing for merger and the fear regarding one's "own vulnerability and anxiety about the other person's responsiveness" (p. 323).

> The therapist is portrayed as a reparative parental figure who provides relational experiences that were missing during the individual's childhood. At the same time, the individual's attachment to the therapist is conceived as a regressive infantile longing or as a symbolization of the earliest mother–child relationship . . . [This is the] conflictual situation—desire and fear. (pp. 322–323)

Also akin to classic psychoanalytic theory, as is obvious from the above passage, West and Keller see the main method of their attachment-based treatment as being interpretation of the transference. They say that the "inner attachment drama is close to the heart of the concept of transference" (1994, p. 325). The ongoing therapy becomes the "re-enactment of dangerous situations in transference . . . [and results in the] emergence of disavowed feelings" (p. 326). They add, "Our therapeutic approach to this desire–fear attachment drama is to separate the desire from the fear, leaving the desire component as an uninterpreted background against which the fear component may be examined" (p. 323). In other words, they leave the longing alone, as it is seen as a basic element of attachment-seeking. They interpret the fear in such a way that this longing for attachment can manifest as something healthy and not necessarily as regressive.

Although the primary method of West and Keller's treatment approach, transference interpretation, is drawn from classic psychoanalytic theory, the relational strictures regarding the role of the therapist are deferred in favor of the therapist being present in ways that provide a "corrective emotional experience" (p. 326). As West and Keller see it, this stance by the therapist during the vicissitudes of transference manifestations in treatment leads to new representations of attachment, and "new modes of action" develop (p. 324).

Attachment-Informed Psychotherapy

As adherence to strict psychoanalytic notions of transference and of the role of the therapist lessened within the field of psychotherapy, methods of treatment emerged that maintained the importance of aspects of intrapsychic functioning but also emphasized other dimensions of the person, such as cognitive and broader relational capacities and even extra-individual systemic factors. Several treatments embody the early synthesis of Bowlby's and Ainsworth's work with other psychological understandings. These are referred to as "attachment-informed" treatments to indicate that they have drawn from what we know about attachment and its development but also integrate later-developing concepts.

ATTACHMENT, INTIMACY, AND AUTONOMY

In *Attachment, Intimacy, Autonomy* (1996), Jeremy Holmes presents a method of treatment more akin to Bowlby's ideas than to a classic psychoanalytic approach, although he does include transference exploration. Holmes sees attachment theory as a useful "overall framework for thinking about relationships" (p. 3), but he also integrates findings from other areas of psychological study. His approach to therapy is well informed by the work of Bowlby, Ainsworth's explorations of patterns of attachment, Stern's and Trevarthen's notions on intersubjectivity, Main's work on narrative competence, and Fonagy's work on reflective capacity. We see Holmes's work as one of the first major psychotherapeutic syntheses of the wide range of research that is relevant to attachment (Holmes, 2004, 2010).

Holmes describes two goals of attachment-informed psychotherapy. With respect to the attachment system, the goal of treatment is *adult intimacy*; with respect to the exploratory system, the goal of treatment is *autonomy of the self* (Holmes, 1996, p. 19). Developing a secure-base experience with the therapist sets the foundation for developing a broader security of attachment and healthy self-autonomy:

> The aim of therapy is to transform insecure into secure attachment[,] . . . to move from clinging to intimacy, from avoidance to autonomy. In working for this the therapist tries to behave like a responsive, attuned parent-figure who is neither intrusive nor rejecting, rebuffing nor controlling, castrating nor seductive, overwhelming nor neglectful . . . [The therapist aims] to "be there," but also to push . . . away. (Holmes, 1996, pp. 70, 81)

Holmes likens the process of psychotherapy to Mary Ainsworth's Strange Situation:

> Therapeutic process is a microcosm of attachment and separation, with its rhythm of regular sessions punctuated by endings and breaks. This is analogous to the strange situation, in which the patient is subjected to minor stresses and their resolution and which can be examined in the "laboratory" of therapy. (1996, p. 32)

Treatment begins with the establishment of a secure base. Protest regarding the therapist's absence or misattunement and proximity-seeking in regard to the therapist serve as signs that the patient is developing a secure base in the therapist (Holmes, 1996, p. 59). The next step in treatment is to use that secure base as a starting point for exploration specific to dysfunctional attachment themes. The patient is encouraged to explore how patterns of clinging and/or avoidance are played out in the transference to the therapist (p. 81). Holmes advocates a therapeutic stance of interested nonreactivity. He says, "The stance of transference exploration is [that] the object is held and cherished but not controlled" (p. 84). The therapist shows a "capacity for detached reflection" (p. 86) "[by staying in] the present moment" (p. 87).

Holmes summarizes the dual focus of treatment—attachment and autonomy—and the therapeutic stance of nonattachment as follows:

> A robust sense of autonomy, which includes the notion of taking responsibility for one's feelings and actions, is based on the internalization of intimate relationships—a secure base. True intimacy, as opposed to dependency, requires the sense of a relationship in which the other's autonomy is respected—a state of emotional autonomy. Nonattachment, as opposed to isolation or denial, can be seen as an attempt to synthesize the apparently contrasting ideals of autonomy and intimacy at a higher level, and arises out of the experience of closeness to and respect for and from the other. (1996, pp. 196–197)

Ruptures and failures of empathy in treatment are seen as inevitable and, when worked through successfully, serve as the basis for a new internal working model of attachment. Holmes says, "The secure base is never entirely safe. Breaks, gaps, and losses are as intrinsic to the rhythm of life as are attachment and connectedness" (1996, p. 54). Over time the patient learns to "disengage from defensive attachments" (p. 62) and forms a new secure attachment pattern (p. 59), which becomes the template for healthy adult intimacy (p. 196). A central goal is the "development of a healing narrative" (p. 31), and through this newly established meaning system, the patient becomes more able to tolerate separation anxiety (p. 61), which leads to autonomy and, in the context of the therapy, independence from the therapist.

Holmes has recommendations for the differential treatment of patients with dismissing, anxious-preoccupied, and disorganized attachment patterns. For those who are dismissing, he says, "the first task is to establish some kind of emotional contact" (1996, p. 25). He says that those with

> ambivalent patterns (anxious-preoccupied) . . . are usually highly dependent . . . [and] become highly distressed around any separation . . . [so] The key issue here is the expression of appropriate anger at separation . . . [This kind of patient] needs to learn that she can protest and therapy will survive. (p. 25)

Holmes adds that patients with disorganized attachment "will go on to develop borderline personality disorder" (p. 26). Treatment entails unhooking such patient patterns of role-reversing *parentification* (p. 27) and moving beyond longing and loss (p. 30).

CLINICAL PATTERNS OF ATTACHMENT

In *Attachment and Adult Psychotherapy* (2000), Pat Sable presents a Bowlby-based approach to treatment of attachment disorders in adults. Like Holmes, she sees her approach not as an attachment-based treatment but rather as a treatment informed by an attachment perspective. She says, "Attachment theory gives us a way to think about our patients' experiences" (p. 88). She begins by setting forth some of the main points in Bowlby's theory of attachment that are relevant to understanding attachment in psychotherapy: Attachment is about safety and protection, attachment pertains to seeking both proximity with and the emotional availability of the therapist, and, since attachment behavior is "life-long" and "active throughout the life-cycle," the patient is capable of forming an attachment to the therapist (pp. 11–12, 29).

Sable believes a common factor across each distinct pattern of insecure attachment is that individuals do "not have sufficient confidence in the availability of their affectional figures" (2000, p. 101), which is associated with failed experiences with early attachment figures. She states, "A major feature of attachment-based treatment is affirming that clients' thoughts and feelings are based on real-life experiences with affectional figures" (p. 80). The main goal of her attachment-informed treatment is to modify dysfunctional internal working models (IWMs) of attachment. Sable reminds the clinician, "They are called 'working models' or representations because they are active, not static, and are capable of continually monitoring attachment-related experiences and updating expectations and plans accordingly" (p. 29). In other words, on a hopeful note, psychotherapy can fundamentally change IWMs.

The first step in attachment-informed psychotherapy is for the therapist to establish himself or herself as a stable attachment figure (Sable, 2000, p. 111). Unlike some of her psychoanalytic predecessors, Sable sees providing a secure base as something more than simply a transference reenactment. She says, "From a perspective of attachment, psychotherapy is a unique kind of attachment relationship, one that encompasses the past (transference), but is mostly focused on providing the opportunity to experience secure attachment in the present" (p. 332). This experience is "rooted in a new relationship" and serves as the basis for internalization of a new, healthy IWM (p. 332). Sable explains some of the unique features of the therapy relationship that contribute to its becoming a secure base:

> Being available with regular appointments, interested in and responsive to what is talked about, the therapist becomes a safe base from which to explore and understand one's attachment history . . . The therapist offers an emotional availability, a comforting presence, and regulation of affect, all of which increase the opportunity for attachment to develop . . . Therapists

promote the sense of safety for exploration by . . . remaining affectively attuned. (2000, pp. 239, 333, 336, 338)

Like Holmes, Sable emphasizes that establishing the therapist as a secure base does not foster a dependency relationship. As a secure base, the therapist serves as a trusted companion who supports the development of "greater self-reliance" (2000, p. 144).

The foundation of a secure base becomes the basis for exploration of early dysfunctional attachment experiences. Using Bowlby's terms, the exploration focuses on whatever it is about these experiences that has been defensively excluded:

> Only by establishing a secure base with the therapist is it possible to investigate and re-experience various unfortunate and unhappy aspects of one's life, some of which would be too difficult to think about and reconsider without empathy, support, and occasional guidance of a trusted companion . . . Through therapy, an individual can approach the thoughts and feelings that have been defensively locked away and begin to see them in a new light. (Sable, 2000, pp. 332–333)

Sable calls such exploration revisiting "ghosts in the consulting room" (2000, p. 335). This exploration entails the following processes:

1. *"Retriev[ing] memories [and feelings] that have been defensively excluded"* (Sable, 2000, p. 106).

Sable conceives of defenses as attempts to deal with unmet attachment needs (see 2000, p. 79).

2. *Validating emotions associated with early attachment experiences.*

Sable says:

> [The therapist helps the client] to understand that feelings of anxious attachment are basically an adaptive response to a signal of danger: separation, threat of separation, or unreliability in attachment relationships . . . [and] also [that the] fear of being alone [is] natural and adaptive. (2000, pp. 151, 188)

Sable draws upon Schore's work on affect regulation and states his principle that "the goal of attachment-focused treatment is to restructure strategies of affect regulation" (2004, p. 12).

3. *Mapping out past IWMs of attachment.*

Sable states:

Therapists help clients map out their attachment experiences so they can then ideally make more authentic relationships in the "real world" (2000, p. 345) . . . [T]herapy provided a temporary attachment relationship within which she could review current and past experiences in order to ascertain how certain representational models of herself and others were formed and maintained. (2000, p. 113)

4. *Correcting transference distortions and distortion in IWMs.*

When experiences were misconstrued, including experiences with [the] therapist (transference), [the client] was helped to recognize what may have caused these misconstructions . . . While remaining affectively attuned to the client's moods and needs, the therapist encourages the client to explore details of current affectional bonds and to examine whether expectations and unconscious biases have been brought to these close relationships, creating difficulty. (Sable, 2000, pp. 113, 338)

5. *Development of a coherent narrative.*

"It is through the process of experiencing an attachment relationship with the therapist, together with composing a historical narrative, that the person may be able to change working models to feel more confident and deserving of reliable relationships" (Sable, 2000, p. 345). The overall process of attachment-informed psychotherapy helps the patient "understand how working models have been generated and maintained" (p. 331) and in so doing helps the patient develop new healthy IWMs for adult attachment. "By identifying and affirming responses to this pattern of dysfunctional behavior, and clarifying the context in which it developed, clients can be helped to move away from abusive affectional ties and toward the capacity for healthier relationships" (p. 299). Ultimately, this process "leads to greater self-reliance" (p. 144) based on the patient's "confidence that the therapist [can] be relied on" (p. 151).

ATTACHMENT-BASED PSYCHOTHERAPY

Karl Heinz Brisch, in *Treating Attachment Disorders* (2012), presents a treatment approach that he characterizes as "attachment-based psychotherapy" (p. 97). His understanding and methods are rooted in the principles derived from Bowlby's and Ainsworth's theories and work. In addition to highlighting the therapist's role as an attachment figure, which includes maintaining sensitivity, emotional availability, flexibility around managing closeness and distance, and reliability as a secure base, Brisch advocates that the therapist "should encourage the patient to think about what attachment strategies he is presently using in his interactions with his important attachment figures" (p. 102), including the therapist. The patient's experiences within and outside the therapy are explored in detail, and the patient is "cautiously encouraged to compare his current perceptions and feelings with those experienced in childhood" (p. 102). Much reliance is placed on the patient's developing recognition and understanding of his or her attachment patterns:

> It should be made clear to the patient that his painful experiences with attachment and relationship, and the distorted representations of self and object that arose from those experiences, are probably inappropriate for dealing with current important relationships: in other words, that they are outdated. (p. 102)

Brisch suggests that the attachment-based goals for therapeutic change are met through the process of the therapist engaging as a good attachment figure as he or she helps the patient to establish greater awareness of his or her attachment strategies and their appropriateness for current life.

DYNAMIC-MATURATIONAL MODEL INTEGRATIVE TREATMENT

Patricia Crittenden's Dynamic-Maturational Model Integrative Treatment (Crittenden, 2015; Crittenden, Dallos, Landini, & Kozlowska, 2014) is informed by her view that attachment behavior reflects organized strategies for coping with and seeking protection from danger and for attempting to elicit protective behavior from caregivers. She sees maladaptive behavior as the result of repeated "exposure to unprotected and uncomforted danger" (Crittenden & Dallos, 2014, p. 56):

> Anxious attachment is not the problem; danger is the problem, and that is what we, as professionals, should focus on. Change the danger, not the child. Create an environment in which infants and children do not need to feel anxious and do not need the A and C strategies, and attachment will take care of itself. How do we do this? Through parents. (Crittenden, 2008, p. 21)

Emphasizing the family systemic contexts through which problematic attachment strategies emerge, Crittenden's treatment approach focuses on working not only with children or adults who exhibit attachment-related problems but also and especially with parents and, ideally, with complete families (Crittenden,

2008; Crittenden & Dallos, 2014; Crittenden et al., 2014). "Crucial to DMM . . . integrated treatment is that the family is the focus of treatment, even when some members might not attend the sessions or even be present in the family" (Crittenden & Dallos, 2014, p. 55). This approach aims to repair and modify the problematic dynamics within the individuals treated as well as within the parenting and family systems within which the individuals are embedded and which they co-create.

Regarding parents, Crittenden states that "treatment of parents who endanger their children should focus on the dangers the parents have experienced and the psychological and behavioral strategies they developed to cope with them" (Crittenden, 2008, p. 267). Parents who themselves have or develop more psychological and emotional resolution and balance are better able to respond with appropriate protection and soothing when their children experience danger, which helps their children to develop the balanced adaptive strategies that are associated with secure attachment. "Raising parents" (Crittenden, 2008) helps the parents who are treated and is preventive against the emergence or continuation of problematic strategies in their children.

Although one of the strengths of Crittenden's treatment model is its inclusion of multiple family members, the core principles of her treatment can be applied even when family members cannot or will not participate. No matter who is the focus of treatment,

> the central treatment issue becomes enabling the individual to generate and apply self-protective strategies at the right time and in the right context. That is, the goal is psychological balance . . . . The focus on protection clarifies the importance of creating in treatment an environment of safety in which new strategies can be learned without fear or threat. As opposed to symptom reduction, a DMM approach presumes that the patient's existing strategy is useful in some context and needs to be (1) repaired (if it is in a depressed, disoriented, or disorganized form), (2) freed of erroneous, distorted, and false information, and (3) applied with greater specificity. The combination of using existing strategies appropriately and developing a wider repertoire of strategies for other occasions should go a long way to making the individual's behavior adaptive in the present. Managing future challenges, however, means that the patient must learn to use reflective integration before the therapy can be considered complete and stable. (Crittenden, 2005, p. 8)

Of note is Crittenden's emphasis that changes in patients' abilities to respond effectively and beneficially to current circumstances is a necessary but insufficient indication of a fully successful treatment. She highlights the importance of patients' ability to carry their newly developed information-processing balance into future circumstances, stating that ..."the goal of treatment would be to change information processing in ways that promote adaptive and functional behavior, both in the current situation and in contexts not yet experienced or even envisioned" (2008, p. 302).

These statements about treatment goals refer to "long-term, ultimate objectives," which Crittenden differentiates from "more proximal goals" (Crittenden & Landini, 2011, p. 314). The proximal goals are established based on the specific presenting problems and the unique, dynamic interplay of the patient's intrapsychic, interpersonal, familial, and societal systems, all of which are identified through careful assessment and formulation based on Crittenden's DMM-AAI (see Crittenden & Landini, 2011).

Crittenden takes a realistic perspective on what the patient's current inner and outer conditions and resources allow for and adjusts the proximal, working goals accordingly: "Once we account for an individual's actual context, it could be that restoring a specific strategy to functionality might be sufficiently adaptive" (Crittenden & Landini, 2011, p. 315). As progress is made, and if the necessary choice, motivation, and resources continue to be available, the therapy can continue with the proximal goals being adjusted in the direction of the ultimate goals.

Regarding treatment methods and the process itself, Crittenden emphasizes that "good assessment, good formulation, and good therapeutic relationships" are essential to treatment (Crittenden, 2008, p. 307). These are the foundational steps of DMM integrated treatment (Crittenden & Dallos, 2014). Comprehensive assessment in the context of Crittenden's Dynamic-Maturational Model (see Chapter 4 of this text) yields information about which combination of the eight types of *dispositional representations* (DRs) underlie each patient's behavioral tendencies, and also about which information-processing patterns best characterize a patient's protective attachment strategies (i.e., the specific A, B, and C patterns and their combinations). The *functional formulation* draws from the information obtained during assessment and provides understanding of the nature, origins, and perpetuation of the particular intrapersonal, interpersonal, and familial problems that are presented for treatment.

In addition to individualized formulations for each patient, Crittenden suggests that her model can generate DR and information-processing strategy formulations that are characteristic, across patients, of particular diagnostic conditions, such as eating disorders, posttraumatic stress disorder, factitious illness by proxy, substance abuse, borderline personality disorder, and sexual offending (Crittenden & Dallos, 2014). Awareness of these generalized, condition-based formulations can facilitate the development of individualized formulations for specific patients, which then guide the selection of treatment tools for application to the particular problems presented.

Throughout their work, Crittenden and her colleagues provide highly detailed and specific guidance for assessment and formulation, which Crittenden sees as having strong empirical foundations, and she offers more general recommendations about the therapeutic relationship and the specific methods of therapy, which she sees as less empirically established. She is critical of manualized treatments and any approach that can result in fitting patients to techniques rather than vice versa, as doing so risks, at best, missing the unique needs of the patient, and at worst, doing actual damage based on a misfit between the technique applied and the patient's needs and capacities: "Having a set of techniques in the absence of good assessment and formulation and a comfortable relationship with the parent is like handing out weapons and hoping for the best" (Crittenden, 2008, p. 306). Crittenden's argument for individualization of treatment methods based on good assessment and formulation is consistent with parenting based on attunement to the unique characteristics, needs, and developmental stage of the child.

So, rather than recommending specific methods for achieving the goals as they are defined at any given point in treatment, Crittenden suggests that

> good treatment uses whatever techniques will best fit the goals of the treatment. That is, good therapists do not limit themselves to the techniques introduced by their school of therapy. Instead, they use everything that works when it is the best solution for the circumstances (when "circumstances" means the problem, the family members, and the therapist). These techniques include methods to elicit discovery, foster exploration, or encourage practice. (Crittenden et al., 2014)

They might also include medication, individual sessions, group sessions, inpatient hospitalization, or social service interventions (Crittenden, 2008, p. 267). Crittenden also notes that what matters is ". . . less the technique itself than the way it is used with respect to the parent(s) [i.e., patient(s)] and the therapist. Still, without judicious selection of techniques, the therapy may not be successful" (Crittenden, 2008, p. 301).

Crittenden and her associates (2014) describe six "general principles" of treatment that may be accomplished through various techniques chosen by therapists. Although the sequence of the six components in the list below (from pp. 158-160) reflects the likely steps or stages through which the treatment proceeds,

> it should be expected that progress through these "stages" will not be linear. The tasks will overlap, at times they will be revisited from a new perspective, and treatment will often be terminated before completion of them all. Whatever the reason, many families—and individuals—address this progression of tasks sequentially over time, often with different therapists. One might say they give themselves time for integration of the most recent accomplishments in treatment before moving forward. (pp. 160–161)

1. *Danger and safety.*

The therapist addresses the patient's experience of danger in the past, present, and future and works to establish an experience of safety, which might include assisting in ameliorating conditions of acute threat in the patient's present life. "Danger is the first concern . . . If the danger is substantial, it must be reduced before other aspects of the intervention are addressed" (Crittenden & Landini, 2011, p. 313).

Included in Crittenden's attention to patients' experiences of danger are the dangers associated with the therapy itself. Any intervention that challenges a patient's existing strategies and defenses will likely be experienced as dangerous or as a threat, "therefore creating 'resistance' to the intervention or to parts of it" (Crittenden & Landini, 2011, p. 313). Crittenden also considers the possibility that an intervention that effectively modifies information-processing strategies may be "dangerous" to some situations in the patient's life. She provides as an example "the risk that a marriage is maintained by active inattention to some information. Could treatment that made this issue explicit precipitate a divorce?" (Crittenden & Landini, 2011, p. 313). When the therapist is aware of and attentive to the patient's past, present, and potential future experiences of danger outside or within therapy and intervenes in appropriate ways at appropriate times, the therapeutic relationship is strengthened and the conditions for the best therapeutic outcomes are supported.

2. *Therapists as transitional attachment figures.*

The central treatment work of recognizing, exploring, and modifying the information-processing strategies associated with insecurity

> can happen only if the individual feels safe enough to suspend his or her self-protective strategy and engage in exploration. If the therapist is sufficiently informed about the individual's strategy to be able to function as a transitional attachment figure by making the treatment tolerably safe, then conscious work on information processing itself can begin. (Crittenden & Landini, 2011, p. 314)
>
> Therapists will be most effective at promoting adaptation when they function as transitional attachment figures who help to bridge the gap between the frightening perceptions of current conditions and a more accurate understanding of them. (Crittenden et al., 2014, pp. 158–159)

Crittenden suggests that the more problematic a patient's adaptive strategies, the more important the relationship with the therapist:

> People whose past history of being endangered and uncomforted has resulted in substantial distortions of information processing and close rela-

tionships are likely to need to form personal relationships with their therapists. Those relationships will have many of the characteristics of naturally occurring attachment relationships. (Crittenden, 2008, pp. 264–265)

The qualities that Crittenden identifies as increasing the likelihood of the patient experiencing the therapist as a transitional attachment figure and a secure base are *compassion, acceptance* (Crittenden et al., 2014, p 159), *attunement, sensitive responsiveness*, and "*genuine feeling, including especially comfort*" [italics added] (Crittenden, 2008, p. 306).

Crittenden makes an important point about the relational dynamic involved in the establishment of a secure base in therapy:

> A therapist can make him- or herself available as a secure base and can behave as a sensitively responsive attachment figure should, but actually feeling secure is the patient's contribution. Thus the connection between the therapist and the patient is the therapist's willingness to become a secure base and the patient's desire for one. (Crittenden, 2008, p. 305)
>
> Moreover, the progress of the relationship will itself be both the process and a goal of the treatment. (p. 264)

3. *Regulating arousal.*

Helping the patient to regulate arousal—to be neither too high nor too low nor too volatile—supports access to motivation, stability, and the mental processes that are important for the therapy process.

4. *Quieting traumatic responses to current conditions.*

"Unresolved traumas and losses require enough exploration to make them explicit and open to discussion" (Crittenden et al., 2014, p. 159). Effective exploration of unresolved traumas and losses as they relate to the patient's present circumstances has an important role in protecting against large fluctuations in the patient's arousal and, as in the third stage, in supporting the conditions that promote an effective therapy process. Such work can also highlight the ways that the strategies that emerged for coping with these early experiences are brought into current circumstances and relationships and are maladaptive in that context.

It is in reference to this component of treatment and the following one that Crittenden highlights the particular value of the formulation from her DMM-AAI assessment. Her approach aims to identify in fine detail the presence of unresolved traumas and losses. In addition to the general scoring categories of "Unresolved loss" and "Unresolved trauma," her coding system specifies 12 possible forms of the former and 14 of the latter in patients' discourse (see Crittenden & Landini, 2011, pp. 236–253, 386–387). Depending on which forms manifest, the therapist can tailor the focus and intervention accordingly.

> 5. *Increasing family members'* [i.e., patients'] *repertoire of protective strategies.*

This component of treatment involves helping patients "to acquire additional strategies that are better suited to their current circumstances than are their childhood strategies" (Crittenden, 2014, p. 160). Crittenden cautions that although the beneficial effects of regulating arousal and quieting traumatic responses usually lead to symptom reduction and the ability of current information-processing and attachment strategies to return to adequate functioning, problems are likely to recur when conditions call for strategies that are beyond the patient's repertoire. When new strategies are added to existing strategies that can be applied more adaptively, the patient is more resilient against conditions to which he or she has adapted poorly in the past.

Crittenden's functional formulation is again particularly relevant in this component of treatment.

> A functional formulation consists of two sets of hypotheses: those about the relation of past experience to current strategies and those about the relation of current conditions, including the strategy, to change processes. That is, the functional formulation gives meaning to the individual's past behavior, including how clinical symptoms were generated and are maintained, while narrowing and ordering the possibilities for treatment. The formulation leads to ideas about which interventions could enable the individual to pursue the goals of self-protection, reproduction, and protection of progeny more adaptively. The formulation also facilitates purposeful ordering of treatment actions. (Crittenden & Landini, 2011, p. 312)

Fundamental to the functional formulation is the identification of the patient's typical existing strategies of information processing and of the ways that these strategies are applied, effectively and ineffectively, in current life. Such identification allows for appropriate selection of a treatment focus and method:

> Each nonbalanced strategy implies a different pathway to a balanced state of functioning . . . For example, the speaker may need access to omitted information [e.g., Type A omission of affect] if more balanced functioning is to be achieved. Treatment strategies that promote discovery of discrepancies created by the omission are needed and, when successful, need verbal articulation. (Crittenden & Landini, 2011, p. 314)

Selecting appropriate interventions based on which strategies are overprom-inent and which are underrepresented not only helps to facilitate more balanced availability and use of the range of possible adaptive strategies but also protects against iatrogenic worsening of a patient's state. Crittenden notes some consider-ations regarding Type A and Type C strategies:

> Because they result from opposite processes, they are likely to be corrected by opposite forms of treatment. For example, a Type A individual might benefit from techniques that focused on feeling and somatic representa-tion of feeling, whereas this treatment might increase somatic symptoms of distress in a Type C individual. Similarly, a Type C individual might ben-efit from a behavioral approach emphasizing self-relevant contingencies, whereas this might expand the repertoire of compulsive behavior of a Type A person. (2005, pp. 7–8)

Crittenden also highlights the importance of paying attention to how patients' typical existing strategies will affect their ways of being in treatment:

> For a person using a compulsive Type A strategy, there will be an automatic component of obedience and deference to the treatment provider [resulting in appearance of progress that might not reflect actual progress], combined with inhibiting negative affect and accepting blame. For someone using a Type C strategy, there will be confronting or persuasive complicity with the therapist, combined with exaggerating negative affect and blaming others. Neither should be worrying to the therapist if the overall plan is clear, and if stages of the treatment are arranged so that full cooperation and straight processing of information are not needed until they are feasible. That is, the treatment should assume a transitional process that begins where the indi-vidual is and moves, always in the zone of proximal development, toward a more inclusive adaptation. (Crittenden & Landini, 2011, p. 314)

6. *Reaching coherence and resilience.*

This step promotes further resilience within current familiar circumstances and also in new, unfamiliar circumstances; it "can yield great personal rewards while yielding the greatest safety under the greatest range of conditions" (Critten-den et al., 2014, p. 160).

> The final step is reflective and integrative . . . Integration involves reconsid-ering one's experience, both past and present, from multiple perspectives to gain an understanding of what one has experienced, how one used that experience to develop self-protective strategies, the influence of change in

oneself (including maturation) and in one's context on the adaptiveness of one's strategies, and, finally, one's emerging ability to regulate the process of development in the future. The outcome of this iterative integrative process is greater flexibility, greater satisfaction in one's entire developmental progress, a more compassionate understanding of the limitations of important other people such as one's parents, and optimism that one could face new adversities and still protect oneself and one's loved ones. (Crittenden et al., 2014, p. 160)

As Crittenden emphasizes the importance of goal-setting and working within the patient's zone of proximal development (e.g., Crittenden et al., 2014, p. 161), she notes that the outcome and even the presence of this stage will vary according to the developmental level of the patient. "Because it involves complex cortical processing, full integration is not possible before late adolescence" (p. 160).

Crittenden refers generally to "reflective approaches to therapy" (Crittenden et al., 2014, p. 160) as the means for this integrative step. Although she does not provide recommendations for particular reflective approaches, throughout her work she praises the work of Fonagy and his colleagues on the constructs of reflective function and mentalization. "Fonagy's approach to reflective self-functioning is highly relevant to the method offered here and many ideas are borrowed from it" (Crittenden & Landini, 2011, p. 40). As she asserts that "good treatment uses whatever techniques will best fit the goals of the treatment" (Crittenden et al., 2014, p. 161), we assume that mentalization-based methods (e.g., J. G. Allen, Fonagy, & Bateman, 2008) are among those that are appropriate for this component of treatment.

Of note is that Diana Fosha also emphasizes the importance of, to use her term, *metaprocessing* with the patient during the later phases of treatment. "Focusing on the experience of transformation itself unleashes a transformational process, through which changes are consolidated, deepened, and expanded" (Fosha, 2009a, p. 187).

We respect the strengths of Crittenden's treatment model and its appropriateness for working with individuals, whether children, adolescents, or adults, and with any constellation of family members and even larger systems. Also, in emphasizing the importance of working at the "zone of proximal development" of each person in treatment, interventions are tailored to the individual's particular developmental needs and capacities, which not only promotes the resolution of the maladaptive strategies and behavior that are presented for treatment but also facilitates development itself.

For example, the parents might consider verbal episodes, while the toddler works through play enactments of episodes. For school-aged children, a crucial task is to connect preconscious DRs with verbal forms of representation;

this can permit children to think concretely and talk to others about their experience without having to re-enact it. (Crittenden & Dallos, 2014, p. 57)

Targeting Dysfunctional Attachment Representations and Internal Working Models

Bowlby's early recognition of the importance of internal working models, or representations of attachment relationships and experience, has centrally contributed to the developmental theories and methods for treating attachment problems. Several approaches work directly with patients' mental representations related to attachment.

WORKING WITH ATTACHMENT REPRESENTATIONS INDEPENDENT OF TRANSFERENCE

Michael Sperling and Lisa Sandow Lyons (1994) advocate a psychodynamically based approach to treating attachment disorders that does not focus on interpretations of transference reenactment of dysfunctional early childhood attachment experiences, but rather on identifying and modifying representations of attachment as they appear in the patient's experiences, both inside and outside the therapy context. Their view of attachment representations is informed by Mary Main and her colleagues' definition of internal working models of attachment: "a set of conscious and/or unconscious rules for the organization of information relevant to attachment and for obtaining or limiting access to that information, that is, to information regarding attachment-related experiences, feelings, and ideations" (Main, Kaplan, & Cassidy, 1985, pp. 66–67, as cited in Sperling & Lyons, 1994, p. 332).

Sperling and Lyons (1994) argue that interpretation of reenactments of early attachment experiences in the transference is unnecessary. Instead, they offer a treatment that "focuses directly on facilitating change in mental representations, particularly representations of attachment" (p. 331). The treatment is said to use an "interpersonal but non enactive transferential mode with regard to the therapeutic relationship" (p. 338). It focuses explicitly on identifying IWMs operative in the patient's past and current relationships so as to identify the main patterns:

A psychotherapy organized around an attachment-representational stance would vigilantly attend to the patient's report of current and past attachment experiences, attempting always to discern emergent representational patterns and the ways in which these patterns are used by the patient to give meaning to current events and the anticipation of future events. (p. 340)

Upon identifying the active representational patterns, the next step is to actively modify these IWMs through the therapist's narrative interpretations:

> The therapist tries to guide the patient in constructing defining relational narratives that serve to clarify particularly meaningful and/or conflictual aspects of attachment experiences. This clarity comes in large part from allowing the patient to develop a more conscious awareness of the idiosyncratic rules and expectations that govern his or her representations, and to use them as anticipatory markers against which new experiences can be compared and evaluated. (Sperling & Lyons, 1994, pp. 340–341)

Sperling and Lyons's (1994) method still relies on interpretations, but of patterns of experience rather than specifically on transference with the therapist. The therapist is actively involved in the identification and understanding of the patient's attachment representations, and "the interpretive process takes on a somewhat psychoeducational quality" (p. 341). Sperling and Lyons present this process as a way to develop new, healthy attachment relational narratives, or IWMs.

IMAGERY OF THE GOOD-ENOUGH THERAPIST TOGETHER WITH THE PATIENT

Elgan Baker, as early as 1981, reported an innovative approach to enhancing relatedness in psychotic and borderline patients (see also D. P. Brown & Fromm, 1986; Copeland, 1986), who commonly have attachment disturbances. Baker derived his method not from the attachment field but from British object relations theory. However, indicating integration of principles from attachment theory, Baker says:

> Object relations theory attempts to describe the development of the personality in terms of the internalization and organization of interpersonal relationships and experiences with significant others in the external environment. These internalizations form the basis for the structuralization of the ego and reciprocally serve to determine the quality and stability of the individual's involvement with the external world . . . Primitive forms of psychopathology are, then, conceptualized in terms of structural deficits in ego formation which result from difficulties in the accomplishment of these necessary developmental tasks. (1981, p. 137)

Baker developed a therapy method that combines the explicit cultivation of an attachment bond with structured hypnotic imagery of secure attachment. With respect to fostering the attachment bond through the interpersonal dynamic, Baker says:

In general, this involves a somewhat more active and nurturing role for the therapist, with greater gratification of the patient's dependency strivings in order to enhance attachment and a confrontive and sometimes intrusive approach to their attempts to avoid meaningful involvement with the therapist. (1981, p. 139)

While the psychotic transference clearly has the potential for "regressive aspects,"

the focus of this modulation of the regressive aspects of treatment is the maintenance of the "connectedness" to the therapist so that regression can be processed "in the service of the ego" . . . With this more active, directed and focused approach, much untoward regression can be avoided, and psychotherapy with psychotic patients is greatly enhanced. (Baker, 1981, p. 139)

According to Baker, "The therapist becomes a real object who can "hold" the boundaries of reality, much as Winnicott (1965) describes the quality of "holding" in the early interaction between mother and child" (1981, p. 140). Over time the therapist is "cathected," meaning that the patient forms a stable internal representation of the "good enough" therapist. The outcome of such internalization is "restructuralization," in which unstable boundaries between self and object are repaired and split self-representations and object representations become integrated (p. 140). Baker's method for creating such restructuralization, or new structuralization, is the systematic use of object relations imagery in the context of hypnotic states, combined with the therapist acting as a good-enough attachment object and providing a holding environment.

Introducing the relational-based imagery in a hypnotic state instead of in the waking state has several advantages. First, the hypnotic state is a heightened state of attentiveness. Since many severely disturbed individuals are highly distractible, the hypnotic condition reduces distractibility and enhances focus, allowing in Baker's method the efficient shaping of the relational imagery. Second, in the hypnotic state, there is a much greater inward orientation and less orientation to outside reality than in the waking state. Thus, for example, a patient with a hypervigilant attachment style to the state of mind of the other can relax that hypervigilance and focus on his or her internal needs and feelings. Third, hypnosis is a condition that entails greater access to internal emotions and memories, and so strong emotions and memories of dysfunctional early attachment experiences are more accessible than they would be in the waking state. Fourth, imagery is more vivid and more readily available in the hypnotic state than in the waking state, and so repetitive use of relational imagery in hypnosis accelerates the internalization process. Fifth, hypnotherapy occurs in the context of a highly structured relationship wherein the therapist can monitor, regulate, and control the unfolding process in such a way as to prevent regression.

Baker describes the seven steps of treatment:

1. The patient imagines himself or herself involved in some pleasant activity. The objective is for the psychotic patient to evoke a stable, nondistorted, positive representation of self through repeated imagining.

2. The patient opens his or her eyes to see the therapist carefully focused on his or her state. This reassures the patient that the therapist is still there as he or she continues the imagery process.

3. The patient repeatedly imagines the therapist as a benign and supportive presence.

4. The patient then undertakes a more complex task—imagining himself or herself and the therapist together with some degree of proximity. Emphasis is given to the patient imagining the therapist as *separate yet together* with him or her throughout a variety of activities and contexts. Gradually, the patient is told to imagine even greater proximity and closeness with the therapist, but in a way that preserves clear self/other boundaries. The patient is in charge of regulating proximity and distance in the imagery.

5. The patient is next asked to imagine himself or herself first in *parallel activities*, and then in more and more *coordinated interactions*. This is the most important step in the protocol because the therapist becomes internalized as a "good object."

6. Once a stable internal representation of the good-enough therapist has been established, the patient is invited to "externalize" malignant internal voices, threatening delusional figures, the abused or derived images of self, the crazy parent or self, and other disturbing representations. In other words, the patient does not repress nor reject such representations but imagines them outside the self. According to Baker, this process of externalization reworks significantly malignant or distorted representations, reduces splitting, and leads to the development of a new, integrated positive representation of a relationship.

7. As the patient becomes more stable, the work shifts to dynamic exploration of dysfunctional patterns of relationship and to integrating positive and negative images of the self and the other.

According to Baker, the foundation for the change process is internalization of the therapist as the "good object." He states:

> As the patient internalizes the therapist as a good object, free from distortion, this introject begins to provide a centering nucleus for strengthening the boundaries of the ego and restructuring internal object representations.

As the patient moves towards this enhancement of object relatedness, his attachment to the outer world strengthens, without fear of engulfment, and acute psychotic symptomatology begins to remit. (p. 145)

An important and unique contribution of Baker, which is not found in any of the psychoanalytically based attachment treatments, is the systematic and repeated use of attachment imagery in the context of a highly focused state, done in the context of careful patient–therapist dyadic communication. Another unique feature of Baker's approach is his refusal to develop canned or preestablished scripts for what to say to patients during the imagery. Baker believes that the attachment imagery must be co-created spontaneously and freshly each session as part of the ongoing dyadic exchange between patient and therapist. Overall, Baker stresses that the systematic introduction of positive relational imagery is an important, if not necessary, ingredient of attachment-based treatment.

New Forms of Attachment-Informed Treatment

In recent years, there have been several psychotherapeutic methods introduced for use with patients with attachment disturbances as well as more broadly. These approaches are integrative, as is Holmes's (1994) earlier work, and draw from a variety of research areas.

SCHEMA THERAPY FOR PATIENTS WITH PERSONALITY DISORDERS

In *Schema Therapy* (2003), Jeffrey Young, Janet Klosko, and Marjorie Weishaar set forth the broad outlines for an entirely new approach to treatment of patients with personality disorders, many of whom have attachment disturbances. Jeffrey Young served as the director in Aaron Beck's research about the cognitive distortions typically found in depression and anxiety disorders. However, when Beck, Young, and others started applying the triple-column technique (Beck, Rush, Shaw, & Emery, 1979) to patients with personality disorders and addictions, Young found that these largely cognitive-focused techniques brought little benefit. Therefore, he developed a new treatment largely based on emotion-focused or experiential methods. The construct of automatic negative self-talk was supplanted by a new concept of *schemas*. Young and his colleagues define schemas as "self-defeating emotional and cognitive patterns that begin early in our development and repeat throughout life" (p. 7). Each schema "revolve[s] around a childhood theme" (p. 28). These "Early Maladaptive Schemas" are composed of memories, emotions, cognitions, and body sensations that cohere into stable *patterns of expectation and experience* that become elaborated and reinforced and potentially last a lifetime. All schemas are relationally based; in various ways, they all are about self in relationship to others.

According to Young et al. (2003), the concept of maladaptive schemas is central to understanding the development of personality disorders (p. 7). Schemas are said to result from "unmet core emotional needs" (p. 9), and the presence of schemas that reflect the experiences pertaining to those unmet needs leads to maladaptive behaviors. Maladaptive behaviors are not schemas but the coping responses to schemas. Based on this conception, Young's treatment of personality disorders focuses "almost exclusively on Early Maladaptive Schemas" (p. 9).

Young developed a detailed questionnaire with 232 items. The questionnaire addresses 18 different schemas, categorized into five broad schema domains:

1. *Disconnection and rejection*: Abandonment, mistrust-abuse, emotional deprivation, defectiveness, and social isolation
2. *Impaired autonomy and performance*: Dependency, vulnerability, enmeshment and failure
3. *Impaired limits*: Entitlement, insufficient self-control
4. *Other-directedness*: Subjugation, self-sacrifice, and approval-seeking
5. *Overvigilance and inhibition*: Negativity, emotional inhibition, unrelenting standards, and punitiveness (see Young et al., 2003, pp. 38–39, for further detail).

The main goals of schema therapy are to identify the most salient maladaptive schemas and to heal them. Young et al. (2003) define schema healing as follows:

> Schema healing is the ultimate goal of schema therapy. Because a schema is a set of memories, emotions, bodily sensations, and cognitions, schema healing involves diminishing all of these: the intensity of the memories connected to the schema, the schema's emotional charge, the strength of the bodily sensations, and the maladaptive cognitions. (p. 31)

Treatment begins with a detailed assessment, the goal of which is to bring the salient maladaptive schemas into the patient's awareness. "The first goal of schema therapy is psychological awareness" (Young et al., 2003, p. 29). The "goal of treatment is to increase conscious control over schemas, working to weaken the memories, emotions, bodily sensations, cognitions, and behaviors associated with them" (p. 29).

The next task is to "understand the origins of these schemas in childhood" (Young et al., 2003, p. 64). It is important for the therapist to identify the adaptive function of even the most seemingly maladaptive schema. Then, the therapist and patient together endeavor to observe the operation of schemas in the therapy relationship, and even to deliberately "activate" schemas so that they can be seen and understood in the context of the collaborative therapy relationship (p. 52).

The role of the therapist is twofold. First, the therapist serves as an ally to actively "fight" against maladaptive schemas. "The therapist–patient relationship serves as a partial antidote to the patient's schemas. The patient internalizes the therapist as a 'Healthy Adult' who fights against schemas and pursues an emotionally fulfilling life" (Young et al., 2003, p. 46).

Second, the therapist serves as a parental model to provide "limited reparenting." It is this limited reparenting concept that defines schema therapy as a contemporary attachment-based therapy. Young sees the role of the therapist as being somewhat like that of a good parent, supplying the relational experience for developing positive, adaptive schemas:

> Limited reparenting involves supplying, within the appropriate bounds of the therapeutic relationship, what patients needed but did not receive from their parents in childhood . . . Like a good parent, the schema therapist is capable of partially meeting—within the limits of the therapy relationship—the patient's basic emotional needs [for] . . . 1. secure attachment; 2. autonomy and competence; 3. genuine self-expression of needs and emotions; 4. spontaneity and play; and 5. realistic limits . . . The goal is for the patient to internalize a Healthy Adult mode . . . The reparenting is "limited" in that the therapist offers an approximation of missed emotional experiences within ethical and professional boundaries . . . [L]imited reparenting is a consistent way of interacting with a patient that is designed to heal that patient's specific Early Maladaptive Schemas . . . Limited reparenting is especially valuable for patients who have schemas in the Disconnection and Rejection domain. (Young et al., 2003, pp. 47, 183, 201)

Equally important in schema therapy is the utilization of experiential techniques, primarily imagery and schema mode dialogues. These experiential techniques are said to "trigger the emotions connected to Early Maladaptive Schemas" (Young et al., 2003, p. 110) in a way that traditional cognitive therapy methods fail to do. First, the therapist introduces safe-place imagery. Once the patient establishes such imagery and reports feeling safe, he or she is instructed to "wipe out that image" (p. 80), and the therapist attempts to evoke a negative affect associated with early childhood experience and vulnerabilities: "Now picture yourself as a young child with one of your parents in an upsetting situation" (p. 80). After fully exploring the patient's thoughts and feelings and other aspects of the experience of this imagery, the therapist either continues with the parent imagery and prompts the patient to interact with the parents to express his or her wishes and needs or shifts to the "limited reparenting" process. Here, the parent images are let go, and the therapist asks the patient to imagine the therapist entering the imagery as a "Healthy Adult" and to re-imagine the scene as if it were happening the way the vulnerable child most needed it to. This imagery consists of the therapist reparenting the child. Young et al. (2003) summarize this approach:

> Limited reparenting is interwoven throughout the experiential work, especially imagery. When the therapist enters patients' images to serve as the

"Healthy Adult" and allows patients to say aloud what they needed but did not get from their parents as children, then the therapist is reparenting. The therapist is teaching patients that there are other ways a parent might have treated them. (pp. 202-203)

For example, for a patient with a maladaptive schema of emotional deprivation, the therapist encourages the patient to express what he or she most needed from the unresponsive parents-of-origin and then imagine getting a realistic response from the therapist while still "tolerat[ing] some deprivation" (Young et al., 2003, p. 203). The overall aim is for the patient to develop an internalized healthy adult representation, modeled after the therapist (p. 145). Young et al. (2003) explain further:

> [T]he therapist enters the images to take care of the child. The therapist does whatever a good parent would have done: removes the child from the scene, confronts the perpetrator, stands between the perpetrator and the child, or empowers the child to handle the situation. Gradually, the patient takes over the role of the Healthy Adult, enters the image as an adult, and reparents the child. (p. 335)

The other main experiential technique is working with dialogues and schema mode dialogues. For example, after establishing safe-place imagery, the patient pictures himself or herself with a parent in an upsetting situation, as described above. Then he or she is encouraged to carry on a dialogue with the parent about what he or she needed at the time from the parent. Additionally, the patient is encouraged to "consider how you would like your parent to change or be different in the image, even if it seems impossible" (p. 80). In most patients, the primary dialogues are between the representations of "Vulnerable Child, Healthy Adult, and Dysfunctional Parent" (p. 123).

In more severely disturbed patients, like those with borderline personality disorder, advanced techniques like *schema mode* therapy are used. Schema modes are

> the moment-to-moment emotional states and coping responses—adaptive and maladaptive—that we all experience . . . The predominant state that we are in at any given point in time is called our "schema mode" . . . schemas and coping responses tend to group together into parts of the self. For example, . . . the Vulnerable Child, . . . [t]he Angry Child mode, . . . [and t]he Detached Protector mode. (pp. 37, 41, 43)

There are 10 primary schema modes that fall into four broad categories: child modes (vulnerable/angry/impulsive/happy), maladaptive coping modes (compliant surrender/detached protector/overcompensator), dysfunctional parent modes (punitive/demanding), and healthy adult mode (p. 272). The goal of schema mode therapy is to access these schema modes and initiate a dialogue in a way that resolves conflicts among different modes or parts.

Central to schema therapy are behavioral homework assignments for practicing and rehearsing appropriate responses, which can directly replace maladaptive schemas (p. 46). These behavioral interventions also target self-defeating coping strategies. To replace these with more adaptive coping strategies, the therapist and patient make a list of the most problematic behaviors, coping strategies, and life patterns, which then become the targets for change. New healthy patterns are rehearsed in imagery, and then the patient is given the assignment to try them out in daily life.

Ultimately, the patient changes the most salient maladaptive schemas. Although Young and his colleagues (2003) do not use attachment language, the role of the therapist as an attachment figure is clearly central to the change process. "The therapist becomes a stable base upon which the patient gradually builds a sense of identity and self-acceptance" (p. 334). "Gradually, patients internalize these therapist behaviors as their own Healthy Adult mode, which then replaces the therapist in the imagery" (p. 335).

We see schema therapy as an attachment-informed approach to the treatment of patients with personality disorders that commands respect. In an outcome study comparing one year of Young's schema therapy with one year of Kernberg's transference-focused treatment for patients with borderline personality disorder, the treatment effect size for schema therapy was nearly double that of transference-focused treatment (Geisen-Bloo et al., 2006).

ACCELERATED EXPERIENTIAL DYNAMIC PSYCHOTHERAPY (AEDP)

In *The Transforming Power of Affect* (2000) and subsequent writings, Diana Fosha describes her innovative attachment-informed treatment, *accelerated experiential dynamic psychotherapy* (AEDP). The main focus of AEDP is on facilitating affect experience and transformation through the patient's engagement with the therapist as a good attachment figure. "The experience of vital affects in the context of an attached relationship is the primary agent of emotional transformation, in life and—a fortiori—in treatment" (p. 5).

Fosha's treatment model emphasizes the value of the patient's emotional experience with the therapist, so much so that AEDP aims "*to lead with* a corrective emotional experience" (Fosha, 2009a, p. 181).

> The patient needs to have an experience, a new experience. And that experience should be good. From the first moment of the first contact, and throughout the treatment thereafter, the aim and method of AEDP is the provision, facilitation, and processing and—through metatherapeutic

processing—consolidation of such experience. (D. Fosha, personal communication with D. Elliott, October 25, 2015)

A central concept in AEDP is *core affect*. Fosha defines core affect as

> that which is vital and spontaneous and comes to the fore when efforts to inhibit spontaneity (i.e., defensive strategies) are not in operation; *core affective experience*, refers to our emotional responses when we do not try to mask, block, distort, or severely mute them . . . The defining feature of core affect is that it has the power to engender a potentially healing state transformation when experienced in the absence of defenses and such blocking emotions as anxiety and shame. (Fosha, 2000, pp. 15–16)

The primary goal of AEDP is to increase the availability and stability of core affect:

> The aim of this work is to help clinicians effectively counteract the forces against experience (defenses), allay fears that fuel those forces (anxiety, helplessness, and shame, e.g.), and harness the power of core affective experience so that it can enrich and improve the individual's life. The facilitation of core affect enhances the patient's adaptation and helps him gain access to inner resources necessary to meet his unique needs, specifications, and life agenda. (Fosha, 2000, p. 15)

Such access to core affect promotes the emergence of *core states*. "The *core state* refers to an altered condition, one of openness and contact. Within it, the individual is deeply in touch with essential aspects of his own self and relational experience" (Fosha, 2000, p. 138).

Treatment begins with the establishment of the therapeutic holding environment: "To work their transformational magic, affects require the regulation of a reasonably intact self or relational holding environment. Affects develop in the transitional space between self and other" (Fosha, 2000, p. 22). The experience, expression, and communication of these core affective phenomena occurs in the context of a secure, emotionally facilitating dyadic relationship (Fosha, 2003, p. 233).

Fosha emphasizes qualities of the therapist's ways of being with the patient that will foster the development of this holding environment and the experience of the therapeutic relationship as a secure base. These qualities include empathic attunement; recognition, affirmation, validation, and valuing of the patient's experience; expressing care, compassion, and concern; authenticity and active use of the therapist's own affective experience; offering encouragement and being helpful (2000, pp. 220–225); and expressing delight in the patient (2009a, p. 181).

Fosha considers the holding environment and the secure-base experience themselves to be corrective emotional experiences for the patient, in large part because they reduce or "undo" the patient's sense of being alone with his or her painful experience (2009b). She also sees these as providing the sense of safety that is essential for the patient's willingness to explore his or her internal experiences and intersubjective experiences with the therapist (2000, p. 36).

Fosha has been especially influenced by research on intersubjectivity (e.g., Beebe & Lachmann, 1994), and so her attachment-based method of treatment centers on mutual communication, coordination, and dyadic regulation of nonverbal and verbal expressions of moment-to-moment affective states (2000, pp. 61–63). Therapist sensitivity, moment by moment, is seen as comparable to maternal sensitivity in a secure attachment dyad. In a working therapeutic dyad, both patient and therapist are in a "state of affective coordination with an other" (2000, p. 28). Just as maternal sensitivity and engagement promote the infant's affective development and emotion-regulation skills, the therapist's sensitivity and dyadic engagement help the patient to access, process, and regulate defensively excluded affects (2000, p. 40) and to develop the emotion-regulation skills that preclude the need for such defensive exclusion.

A primary task of the AEDP therapist is to attentively track moment-by-moment fluctuations in the patient's affective state. The therapist strives to recognize and maintain accurate attunement to fluctuations in voice pitch and rhythm, gaze, touch, and gesture as well as the timing of nonverbal and verbal expressions. From this attunement, the therapist tries to match and amplify the patient's ongoing affective displays and gives particular emphasis to facilitating the mutual, coordinated expression of facial displays of affect (Fosha, 2003, p. 237).

Following Beebe and Lachmann's (1994) principles, Fosha highlights three processes of dyadic interaction that support beneficial transformations: (1) *ongoing regulations*, which pertain to how moment-to-moment experience is received and responded to; (2) *heightened affective moments*, which pertain to the experience of intense emotional experiences in the relational context; and (3) *disruption and repair of ongoing regulations*, which pertains to how disruptions of coordination within the relational dyad are handled (2000, pp. 73–74). In AEDP, of particular importance is that these all occur in the context of the relationship with the therapist, and that highlighting the relationship itself is considered one of the essential components of transformation: "The patient's *experience* of the attachment relationship needs to be a major focus of therapeutic work" (2009a, p. 181). Such focus promotes the security-enhancing experience of "*existing in the mind and heart of the other*" (Fosha, 2000, p. 57).

In addition to these processes of dyadic interaction and the qualities of the therapist's ways of being with the patient, AEDP places emphasis on the patient's somatic experience (2000, p. 279) and on "metatherapeutic processing," or "metaprocessing" (2009a, pp. 186–188). Metaprocessing is direct, focused attention to and reflection on the experiences of affective transformation. Fosha suggests that "focusing on the experience of transformation itself unleashes a transformational process, through which changes are consolidated, deepened, and expanded" (2009a, p. 187).

With these principles and practices as the foundation of treatment, Fosha describes a characteristic sequence of AEDP process that leads to affect transformation and the development of attachment security. This "emotion-based transformational process" consists of "four states and three state transformations" (2009a, pp. 183–189):

State One. The patient comes to treatment in a state that includes some form of distress and symptoms that are troubling and disruptive to functioning and well-being. These are the "phenomena that need transforming" (Fosha, 2009a, p. 183). Underlying the presenting problems are dysregulated affects, inhibiting affects (such as anxiety and shame), and defenses. Fosha views defensive reactions as a failure of the caregiving environment "to provide responsive, helpful caregiving, which is incorporated in the individual's internal working model and reflected in his patterns of attachment " (2000, p. 41). She adds, "The aim of defenses always is to restore the feeling of safety and to eliminate aversive emotional experiences" (2000, p. 83).

Fosha emphasizes that along with the problematic affects and experiences in this first state are "glimmers—sometimes significantly more than glimmers—of transformance strivings and the patient's self-at-best" (2009a, p. 185). "Transformance" is defined as "the powerful motivational thrust that exists within us, a force toward healing" (2009a, p. 175), and its manifestation is indicated by the patient's immediate experience of "a felt sense of vitality and energy" (Fosha, 2008, p. 290).

Through dyadic attunement to the patient and his or her "vitality affects," or ongoing moment-by-moment fluctuations in affective states (Fosha, 2003, p. 236), the therapist provides the necessary holding environment that reduces defenses and inhibiting affects and supports transformation from the first state. Signs of this transformation include "green signal affects" that indicate greater openness to experience; "heralding affects," or early signs of core affective experience; and "transitional affects," a mix of emerging core affect and defensive caution (Fosha, 2009a, p. 185). "The full experience of a specific core affective phenomenon constitutes the first state transformation" (Fosha, 2003, p. 233).

State Two. When the patient feels sufficiently safe in the therapeutic dyad, he or she has "the sense that even intense emotions are welcome and can be dyadically handled, and emotional processing work can be launched" (Fosha, 2009a, p. 185). Therapeutic work throughout the second state involves "the processing of emotional experience" (Fosha, 2009a, p. 185), helping the patient to fully experience what was previously inhibited or excluded. Common here is the appearance of categorical emotions, or distinct feelings that arise in reaction to events, such as grief, anger, fear, sadness, joy, and disgust (Fosha, 2000, p. 139).

The dyadic support and affect regulation of these emotions and other core affective phenomena leads to experiences of relief, clarity, hope, and strength; resilience in the face of emergent affect; and "adaptive action tendencies" in response to affect, such as assertiveness and willingness to take action. These are all indications of the "second state transformation" (Fosha, 2009a, p. 186; see also Mikulincer & Florian, 1998).

State Three. The newly established ability to allow and regulate affect is experienced by the patient as a very significant change, a major transformation, and the focus of the work becomes "the processing of transformational experience" (Fosha, 2009a, p. 186). By bringing attention to the patient's experience of transformation and *metaprocessing* that experience, further transformation is facilitated.

Characteristic affects arise through this metaprocessing: *mastery affects*, such as pride, joy, and confidence about the progress being made; *emotional pain* from "mourning the self" for what it lost because of the phenomena that needed transformation; *tremulous affects* such as "fear/excitement, startle/surprise, . . . [and] even a feeling of positive vulnerability" that are part of the "crisis of healing change" (Fosha, 2009a, p. 188) as the patient adjusts to his or her new affective capacity and manifestation; *healing affects*, such as gratitude for the changes and feeling moved by them; and *realization affects*, "the 'yes!' and 'wow!' associated with new understanding" (Fosha, 2014).

The shifting from core affect to core state is indicative of the third state transformation. The patient begins to have experiences of "calm, clarity, and tremendous openness . . . [and a profoundly satisfying, deeply felt state of ease, flow, and relaxation" (Fosha, 2009a, p. 188) along with a sense of aliveness and vitality (Fosha, 2003, p. 233).

State Four. Within the AEDP model, transformation into the core state is associated with security of attachment (Fosha, 2009a, p. 189). At the fourth state, the culmination of the affect-transformation process, the core state is prominent and available and the patient manifests self and relational characteristics that are consistent with but also go beyond features of attachment security.

> The defining qualities of the core state overlap with qualities characteristic of resilient individuals and also with those cultivated by contemplative and spiritual practices—wisdom, compassion for self and others, generosity, vibrant well-being, equanimity, confidence, creativity, naturalness, enhanced initiative and agency, a sense of the sacred, more. (Fosha, 2009a, p. 188)

Fosha also states that "the affective marker for core state is the *truth sense*. The truth sense is a vitality affect whose *felt sense* is an *aesthetic experience of rightness*, the rightness of one's experience" (Fosha, 2009a, p. 189).

The unique contribution of Fosha's AEDP is its elaborately detailed description of thorough affect transformation in the context of a dyadic patient–therapist attachment relationship. In her model, all affective states, in an adequate holding environment, are the seeds for deeply transformative experience and development. We greatly respect the AEDP model and methods.

Intersubjectivity-Based Treatment

As noted above, Diana Fosha's thinking about treatment was very much influenced by the work of Beebe and Lachmann and others in the field of intersubjectivity, and she integrated principles from intersubjective theory and research into AEDP. Beebe and Lachmann themselves have presented an intersubjectivity-based treatment method. We believe that the attachment field's growing interest in the phenomena of intersubjectivity reflects recognition that the factors that are essential to an infant's developing secure attachment—particularly *maternal sensitivity* and *attunement* and the reciprocal dynamic interactions that can occur only in the presence of those—are fundamentally intersubjective phenomena.

INTERSUBJECTIVITY AND ADULT TREATMENT

In *Infant Research and Adult Treatment: Co-Constructing Interactions* (2002), Beatrice Beebe and Frank Lachmann present a model for treating adults for attachment disturbance based on their extensive research on intersubjectivity. They report on the findings of research using fine-grained analysis of video-recordings of moment-by-moment patterns of dyadic exchange between secure mother and infant dyads occurring in fractions of a second. They discovered a remarkably coordinated nonverbal communication pattern between infant and caregiver. What is apparent in these films is that the infant's communication is "contingent, i.e. predictable from, his own actions" (Beebe & Lachmann, 2014, p. 29) in a way that leads to a sense of self-agency and "effectance" (Beebe & Lachmann, 2002, p. 163). What is also apparent is that the caregiver is in the best sense responsive "through appropriate 'matches' or 'correspondences' in communicative expressions" (Beebe & Lachmann, 2014, p. 27). These behaviors are bidirectional and constitute a type of dyadic, co-constructed, reciprocally influencing exchange that is both self-regulating and interactive. In a secure dyad, the nonverbal behavior of the infant and caregiver becomes synchronized, rhythmic, and highly coordinated with respect to head orientation, gaze, display of facial affect, gesturing, touch, and vocalization. Beebe and Lachmann suggest that the moment-by-moment exchange is also represented within the infant mind in a presymbolic, procedural form. They say that infants will store models of how interactions unfold in the "dimensions of time, space, affect and arousal" (2014, p. 34).

Beebe and Lachmann discovered several salient patterns in their microanalyses of these split-second mostly nonverbal action sequences, which they characterize as reflecting the three "principles of salience" (2014, p. 37). With respect to secure, collaborative interactions, first, both infant and caregiver are engaged in self-regulation and ongoing interactive regulation. Second, during episodes of mismatch (i.e., asynchrony of nonverbal behavior), both infant and caregiver undergo a sequence of disruption and repair (i.e., resynchronization of nonverbal behavior). Third, when self-regulation and the interactive process are optimal for both infant and caregiver, there are extended sequences of intense moments of positive mutual engagement and heightened positive affect in both the infant and the caregiver (p. 38). In these exchanges, "both infant and partner can sense the state of the other, and can sense whether the state is shared or not" (p. 39). From these three principles of salience, Beebe and Lachmann say, primary intersubjectivity emerges.

Through their analysis of moment-by-moment video-recorded interaction sequences, Beebe and Lachmann discovered a significant difference between "collaborative" and "contradictory dialogues" (2014, p. 36). Contradictory interactions are characterized by significant nonverbal mismatching, the lack of contingent influence, the lack of coordination of expressions, or the absence of synchronization and timing of nonverbal and vocal rhythms. There is a huge difference between momentary missteps in a dance and failure to dance altogether. Rather than healthy rupture/repair sequences, contradictory dialogues are characterized by a sheer absence of responsiveness. As a consequence of this continuous failed self-exchange and interactive exchange, the infant develops the "expectation of misregulation," develops failed self-agency and ineffectance, and internalizes a presymbolic representation of dyscoordinated interaction and dysregulation.

Already in the first half year of life, infants who have experienced sustained contradictory dialogues have set a strong, largely nonverbal foundation for what will develop into one of the three patterns of insecure attachment by 18 to 20 months. For example, Beebe and Lachmann present a detailed analysis of the nonverbal exchange between a four-month-old infant and her mother in sustained contradictory interaction; they use this analysis to show how the origins of insecure, disorganized attachment assessed by the Strange Situation procedure at 18 months *are already present at four months*. The video-recordings reveal the infant and parent having mutually escalating overarousal cycles without attenuation or repair, and the infant having simultaneous and contradictory affects like a smile and whimper, disorientation, reduced touch, and ongoing disturbances in ability to be known. In the caregiver, the video-recordings reveal repeated mismatches of facial display and at times a lack of any facial display, excessive looming and intrusive posturing and touch, a significant reduction in or absence of affectionate touching, and an inability to read the infant's nonverbal expressiveness as a pathway to knowing the state of mind of the infant.

Beebe and Lachmann (2002, 2014; Beebe, 2004; Beebe, Knoblauch, Rustin, & Sorter, 2005) have applied their intersubjectivity research to psychotherapy with adult patients with attachment disturbances. Their approach primarily emphasizes attunement to the nonverbal exchange between patient and therapist. Using the nonverbal behavior categories derived from their coding of their video-recorded studies of infants and caregivers, Beebe and Lachmann suggest that the therapist make careful observation of where the therapist sits relative to the patient; head orientation; body posture; gaze; the nature of ongoing facial affect display and whether it is matched or mismatched, coordinated or uncoordinated; and the rhythm, pitch, tone, and timing of the verbal responses in both patient and therapist. The therapist's careful attunement to the patient's nonverbal behavior as well as to his or her own, moment to moment, allows the therapist to match the patient's nonverbal behavior and rematch it when their behavior becomes mismatched or asynchronous. This process parallels the way a mother in a secure dyadic system attunes to, matches, and rematches her infant's nonverbal behavior. Any patterns of distancing or hyperengaging nonverbal behavior in the patient, or excessive mismatching of the patient's behavior in the therapist, need to be brought into the awareness of both patient and therapist.

In their case studies (e.g., "Dolores," 2014), Beebe and Lachmann describe two methods of treating nonverbal intersubjectivity failures in insecure adult patients. First, after carefully attending to and identifying the pattern of dysregulated nonverbal behaviors in the patient, Beebe, as a therapist, offers sustained collaborative, noncontradictory nonverbal responsiveness to the moment-by-moment shifts in the dyadic therapeutic exchange. Beebe says:

> I tracked the shifts in rhythm and activation of her body and voice, "going with" each shift. I strained to catch her barely audible words, drastically lowered my level of activation, and frequently held my body (but not my face) perfectly still. My speech rhythm matched her slow pace; I tolerated very long pauses. Most of these adjustments were made out of my awareness. (Beebe & Lachmann, 2014, p. 84)

Because these nonverbal action sequences go so quickly and generally occur out of one's awareness, Beebe made a videotape showing only her own face during a therapy session with Dolores and then showed Dolores the results. The purpose of watching the videos together was for Dolores to see the earliest, micro-level, nonverbal exchanges between herself and the therapist, which revealed and highlighted to her how Beebe had affectively matched her experience and continuously expressed her understanding through nonverbal displays. Reviewing the videotape was an intersubjective method of bringing attention to the intersubjective dynamic during the therapy session and was thus doubly powerful in promoting the patient's experience of being known in the mind of the therapist.

Beebe and Lachmann's innovative approach reminds the clinician that, at least for treating attachment disorders in adults, awareness of the moment-by-moment nonverbal exchange between patient and therapist needs to be brought into the treatment. Diana Fosha's AEDP effectively integrates this principle into the treatment process, but regardless of the method used, we recommend that therapists treating patients with insecure attachment become familiar with these intersubjective principles and practices.

EXPLORATORY PSYCHOTHERAPY

In *Attachment Therapy With Adolescents and Adults* (2009), Dorothy Heard, Brian Lake, and Una McCluskey extend Bowlby's attachment-based treatment and the research on intersubjectivity into what they call "a comprehensive theory of attachment" (p. 18) and "a new attachment paradigm" (p. 3). One extension to Bowlby's thinking is their elaboration of behavioral systems other than the attachment system. These include collaborative interest-sharing with peers, affectional sexuality, the system of personal defense, and the external lifestyle system. In Heard and her colleagues' intersubjective theory and therapeutic recommendations, as in Beebe and Lachmann's approach, nonverbal emotive signals and body language play an important role. Heard and her associates define emotive nonverbal signals as

> information about the emotion the individual is feeling at the moment the nonverbal signal is sent . . . Gestures, facial expression, and tone of voice demonstrate the emotion a person is feeling . . . [N]onverbal signals only refer to what is happening "now" for the speaker. (pp. 28–29)

According to Heard et al. (2009), these nonverbal emotive signals constitute a kind of "protoconversation" between two people that reflects their intersubjectivity. The authors see intersubjectivity as a "mutually regulating" process that manifests through "intricate rhythmic patterns" of dyadic exchange (p. 34). The three, deepening aspects and levels of intersubjectivity are the "immediate sense of interpersonal communion within and between persons" (p. 31); that the participants in the dyad "[pay] joint attention to objects of reference in a shared domain of conversation" (p. 32); and that it is "reflective and recursive . . . in the sense of communicating understanding" (p. 32). During the sequence of dyadic exchange between infant and caregiver, in the best case, the caregiver shows affect attunement to the infant; in the worst case, the caregiver shows "purposeful misattunement." Overall, communication in an insecurely attached dyadic system is characterized by "true misattunement" between the infant and caregiver.

A unique feature of Heard et al.'s model is that the sense of self grows and develops not only as a function of attachment to a secure base, but also *apart* from the attachment relationship:

> In order for a person, whether a child or an adult, to remain in a state of wellbeing, it is necessary for the self to withdraw from time to time from interacting with other people in order to think things out and to make plans, to feel the present moment, and to let imagination have a free rein . . . [W]henever the self withdraws from the state of intersubjectivity it enters into the state of subjectivity[,] . . . to a state of being a secure self . . . A secure self during the state of subjectivity is able to be imaginative in a creative way[;] . . . the self can play. (2009, pp. 42–47)

Heard et al. (2009) see the secure self as complex. Each behavioral system serves a different function and both serves and reflects the self in different ways. For example, when the self senses a threat to well-being, the defensive or fear behavioral system is activated along with the defensive self. Similarly, the sense of threat activates the attachment system along with the care-seeking self. When mutual interests are pursued and shared by peers, the collaborative behavioral system is activated along with the interest in sharing the self (p. 53).

The full potential of the secure and autonomous self is the objective of what Heard et al. call "exploratory psychotherapy" (2009, p. 46). Exploratory therapy consists of two parts. The first is restorative, in that the patient as the care-seeker initiates a relationship with the therapist as the caregiver, typically because of a decrease of or threat to well-being. In the context of recognizing the various behavioral systems, the first task of therapy is to attenuate the fear system and allow for activation of the attachment system in relation with the therapist. Once a secure base has been established, this security becomes the basis for exploration of the self across each of the behavioral systems. Heard et al. highlight the importance of the secure base to therapeutic exploration:

> The first aim of an exploratory therapist is to enable any seeker of care, whose capacity to explore is overridden by his or her urgency to seek care, to regain at least some capacity to explore. The first key step is to find an invitation, acceptable to the client, to discover more about him or herself. (p. 125)

The quality of nonverbal dyadic exchange between patient and therapist is crucial in restoring the well-being that is the foundation for exploration of the potentials of the secure autonomous self. Heard et al. say, "It seems to be obligatory for caregivers to recognize empathically the emotional state of the care seeker, and then physically to communicate it, through emotive nonverbal signals, backed by some verbal messages" (2009, p. 124).

To this end, Heard et al. (2009) have made video recordings of patients and therapists and have done extensive microanalysis of the moment-by-moment exchanges between them. These video recordings are used to train therapists in nonverbal attunement so that they learn to offer the nonverbal conditions that support a secure base for exploration in treatment. Studying therapist and patient split-screen video recordings helps therapists become aware of effective and ineffective intersubjective caregiving. The training recordings highlight what Heard and her associates have identified as five typical care-seeking behaviors of patients during therapy sessions: (1) openness to discussing feelings, conflicts, or concerns; (2) avoidance of and reluctance to discuss issues; (3) discussing concerns in a way that gets tangled up with the caregiver's state of mind; (4) dismissal of the caregiver; and (5) being overwhelmed and disorganized when discussing issues. The authors also present five potential caregiving responses of therapists: (1) careful attunement and being exploratory; (2) misattunement followed by repair and learned attunement; (3) defection from exploration; (4) withdrawal and immobilization; and (5) becoming disorganized.

There are a total of 25 potential patterns of interaction based on all possible combinations of the above. Common nonverbal and verbal misattunements by therapists include interrupting the patient, failing to regulate the patient's state of mind, making a minimal or misattuned nonverbal response, avoiding facial displays of affect, manifesting a discrepancy between verbal and nonverbal responsiveness, ignoring the patient's nonverbal and verbal signs of fear activation that indicate that the patient is not ready to explore the topic, and missing the patient's immediate affect and pursuing some other issue. Through learning of these possibilities and experiencing them in manifest form, therapists learn to genuinely attune themselves to the patient so as to restore well-being, establish a secure base, and thereby "recovering the ability to explore" (p. 127).

Metacognitive Attachment-Informed Psychotherapies

In keeping with the expansion of understanding of the various behavioral systems and functions that are relevant to attachment, growing attention has been given in recent years to metacognitive functioning and its role in attachment. The research and practice in this area have shown the value of recognizing the metacognitive deficits associated with attachment disturbances and also the great benefit to patients of working in therapy to improve metacognitive functioning.

MENTALIZATION-BASED TREATMENT (MBT)

Peter Fonagy, Anthony Bateman, Jon Allen, and their colleagues (who we refer to as the London School or London group) developed an approach to the treatment of patients with personality and dissociative disorders that they call *mentalization-based treatment* (MBT; J. G. Allen & Fonagy, 2006; J. G. Allen et al., 2008; Bateman & Fonagy, 2001, 2003, 2004, 2008, 2009, 2012; Fonagy & Bateman, 2006). The central concept underlying MBT is *mentalization*. Mentalization is defined as follows:

> Mentalization entails making sense of the actions of oneself and others on the basis of intentional mental states, such as desires, feelings, and beliefs. It involves the recognition that what is in the mind is in the mind, and reflects knowledge of one's own and others' mental states as mental states. (Bateman & Fonagy, 2006, p. 185)

Mentalization is a metacognitive skill that normally develops over the first five years of childhood and is best supported in the context of a secure attachment relationship, in which the caregiver is continually attuned to the child's state of mind and also expresses her or his state of mind to the child. Bateman and Fonagy say, "It is a capacity that is acquired gradually over the first few years of life in the context of safe and secure child–caregiver relationships" (2006, p. 185).

There are several stages in the development of mentalization. Mentalizing capacity begins once the newborn discovers that the caregiver's responsiveness is contingent on his or her actions. As cognitive processes mature, the child develops a representation of the sense of self as an active agent (Bateman & Fonagy, 2004, pp. 59–62). Bateman and Fonagy say, "The infant's discovery of their high degree of contingent control over their caregiver's reactions positively arouses them and gives them feelings of causal efficiency" (2004, p. 68). Contingent mirroring by the caregiver entails the "capacity to incorporate into her expression a clear indication that she is not expressing her own feelings, but those of the baby" (Bateman & Fonagy, 2003, p. 193). The caregiver also "marks" the emotion by not only mirroring the infant's emotion but also by exaggerating when mirroring it:

> The infant internalizes the mother's empathic expression by developing a secondary representation of his emotional state with the mother's empathic face as the signifier and his own emotional arousal as the signified . . . [S]he signals in some way that what he is seeing is a reflection of *his own* feelings. (Bateman & Fonagy, 2004, pp. 65–66)

Through the processes of both contingent responsiveness and marking by the caregiver, combined with cognitive maturation, the child eventually develops the capacity to develop representations of emotions and thought. These are called second-order representations. The emergence of the capacity to reflect on emotions, beliefs, wishes, and needs is the foundation of mentalization. Bateman and Fonagy (2004) state, "The establishment of second-order representations of emotions creates the basis for affect regulation and impulse control and provides an essential building block for the child's later development of the crucial capacity for mentalization" (p. 68).

The older child utilizes pretend play as a means to understand that play is essentially a representation, and so the child eventually discovers that play states, thoughts, and emotions are all representations, and they are experienced as representations. Now the child has developed the capacity for true mentalization, through which he or she can reflect upon states of mind, both of self and other, as representations.

> In normal development the child integrates these . . . modes to arrive at *mentalization*, or reflective mode, in which thoughts and feelings can be experienced *as* representations . . . Mentalization [is] the capacity to think about mental states as separate from, yet potentially causing actions . . . Once mentalization occurs, the nature of affect regulation is transformed. It is no longer simply modulated. 'Mentalized affectivity' allows the individual to discover the subjective meanings of his own affect states. (Bateman & Fonagy, 2004, pp. 70, 123)
>
> Reflective capacity is defined as the capacity to apply mentalizing strategies in representing mental states of self or other. (p. 74)

Mentalization is most likely to develop in a child when two conditions are present: security of attachment and the caregiver's holding the mind of the child in mind. "Mentalization is a developmental achievement greatly facilitated by secure attachment" (Bateman & Fonagy, 2004, p. 72); "the child's capacity to create a coherent image of mind is critically dependent on an experience of being clearly perceived as a mind by the attachment figure" (2004, p. 64).

Individuals with insecure attachment are at risk for failure to develop mentalization capacity. Peter Fonagy, Mary Target, and Howard and Miriam Steele developed a rating scale to formally assess reflective functioning, or the capacity to apply mentalizing strategies, in adults: the Reflective Functioning Scale (RF-S; Fonagy et al., 1998). The numerical RF ratings span a range similar to the Adult Attachment Interview's range of 1 to 9, but a −1 was added for those individuals who engage in pseudoreflection. From their experience with administering the RF-S to inpatients and outpatients, the authors claim they never found a patient with a personality disorder (PD) or major dissociative disorder (DD) diagnosis who scored above 3 on the RF-S. In other words, PD and DD patients are remarkably lacking in reflective capacity (Bateman & Fonagy, 2003). It is this significant lack that contributed to the London group's development of MBT, which is an entire treatment focused on the development of mentalizing capacity.

> It is the guiding construct of our therapeutic approach that psychotherapy with borderline patients should focus on the capacity for mentalization . . . [T]he crux of the value of psychotherapy with BPD is the experience of other humans minds having the patient's mind in mind . . . The core of psychological therapy with individuals with severe personality disorder (PD) is the enhancement of reflective processes. The therapist must not only help the patient understand and label emotional states but also enable him to place them within a present context. (Bateman & Fonagy, 2004, pp. 141, 205)

Bateman, Fonagy, and their associates discovered that once mentalizing capacity develops in PD and DD patients, it has an *organizing effect on the mind*, creating what is known as coherence of mind. In turn, this increased coherence has a positive effect on the sense of self, relational security, and affect regulation:

> Treatment strategies target mentalization in order to foster the development of stable internal representations, to aid the formation of a coherent sense of self, and to enable the borderline patient to form more secure relationships in which motivations of self and other are better understood. (Bateman & Fonagy, 2003, p. 187)

Within the London School, there are two very different yet compatible approaches to developing mentalizing capacity in PD and DD patients. First, coming from the psychodynamic tradition, Jon Allen (2013) states that mentalizing is a consistent "stance" taken by the therapist, and that apart from this continuous stance, there are no mentalizing-specific skills for a therapist to learn. This approach is based on Elizabeth Meins's (1997) observations that caregivers who thought about their children in mentalistic terms and talked openly to their children about states of mind produced children who were not only securely attached but who also had very developed mentalization capacity. Like the best caregiver, "the therapist needs to develop and maintain a 'mentalizing therapeutic stance'" (Bateman & Fonagy, 2004, p. 253), which constitutes a kind of "mental closeness" (Bateman & Fonagy, 2003, p. 195). Essentially, this stance entails enabling the patient to discover his or her mind in the mind of the therapist:

> It is our belief that the relatively safe (secure base) attachment relationship with the therapist provides a relational context in which it is safe to explore the mind of the other in order to find one's own mind represented within it. (Bateman & Fonagy, 2004, p. 143)

Table 6.1 is Allen's (2013) excellent list of "tips for therapists on influencing mentalizing." This list describes ways that therapists, through their therapeutic stance and ways of being and responding, can either promote or undermine the patient's (and their own) mentalizing. We strongly recommend integrating these into clinical practice with patients with personality disorders and/or attachment disturbances. The integration of these "tips" contributes to the activity of the MBT therapist:

TABLE 6.1. Tips for Therapists on Influencing Mentalizing

Promoting mentalizing

- Maintaining an inquisitive, curious, not-knowing stance
- Offering interventions that are simple and to the point
- Promoting a level of emotional engagement that is neither too hot nor too cold
- Providing a secure-base experience that facilitates the patient's exploration of mental states—their own and yours
- Maintaining a balance between engaging patients in exploring mental states of self and others
- Engaging in a mirroring process in which your emotional responsiveness reflects the patient's mental state and feelings back to the patient
- Engaging in judicious self-disclosure about your interactions with the patient
- Validating the patient's experience before offering alternative perspectives
- Engaging the patient in viewing interactions and self-experience from multiple perspectives
- Letting the patient know what you are thinking so as to permit the patient to correct your distorted mentalizing
- Acknowledging when you do not know what to say or do and enlisting the patient's help in moving the process forward
- Acknowledging your own mentalizing failure and endeavoring to understand misunderstandings
- Acknowledging mistakes and actively exploring your contribution to the patient's adverse reactions
- Challenging patients' unwarranted assumptions about your attitudes, feelings, and beliefs
- Working with the patient--therapist relationship so as to help patients understand how their mind is working in the room at the moment

Undermining mentalizing

- Striving to be clever, brilliant, and insightful
- Offering complicated, lengthy interventions
- Presenting your ideas about the patient to the patient with a sense of certainty
- Attributing mental states to the patient based on your theoretical preconception
- Engaging in "psychobabble"
- Allowing prolonged silences
- Attributing the patient's experience of a relationship to a general pattern rather than exploring the experience and its basis in more detail
- Responding to the patient with intense reactive (nonmentalized) emotion

Source: Allen, 2013. Used by permission.

The experience of being understood generates an experience of security which in turn facilitates 'mental exploration,' the exploration of the mind of the other to find oneself therein . . . The . . . therapist . . . will continually construct and reconstruct in their own mind an image of the patient's mind. They label feelings, they explain cognitions, they spell out implicit beliefs. Importantly they engage in this mirroring process, highlighting the marked character of their verbal or non-verbal mirroring display. Their training and experience . . . further hones their capacity to show that their reaction is related to the patient's state of mind rather than their own. (Bateman & Fonagy, 2004, p. 142)

Exploration in therapy then essentially becomes exploration of a mind by a mind:

The therapist, in holding on to their view of the patient, and overcoming the patient's need to externalize and distort the therapist's subjectivity, simultaneously fosters mentalizing and secure attachment experience. Feeling recognized creates a secure base feeling that in turn promotes the patient's freedom to explore herself or himself in the mind of the therapist. Increased sense of security in the attachment relationship with the therapist . . . reinforces a secure internal working model, and through this . . . a coherent sense of self. (Bateman & Fonagy, 2004, pp. 143, 144)

The second approach to MBT was developed by Anthony Bateman, whose background is in the cognitive-behavioral tradition. Bateman developed a series of specific techniques to foster the development of mentalizing capacity. Consistent with the first approach, however, these techniques are introduced by a therapist whose stance embodies "*consistency, constancy, and coherence*" (Bateman & Fonagy, 2004, p. 187). Bateman and his associates describe four core strategies for developing mentalization: (1) enhancing mentalization, (2) bridging the gap between affects and their representation, (3) working mostly with current mental states rather than the past, and (4) keeping in mind the patient's deficits (Bateman & Fonagy, 2004, p. 203). *Enhancing mentalizing* in general entails adopting the mentalizing stance in therapy as described above, and in particular using this stance to mentalize about emotional states. *Bridging the gap between affects and their representation* entails the following steps: (1) identifying affect (Bateman & Fonagy, 2004, p. 204); (2) interpreting moment-by-moment changes in emotional state (Bateman & Fonagy, 2003, p. 198); (3) contingent mirroring and marking of affective states (Fonagy, Gergely, Jurist, & Target, 2002, p. 10); (4) understanding the immediate antecedents to emotional states (Bateman & Fonagy, 2003, p. 196); (5) clarifying and elaborating the meaning of affective states (Bateman & Fonagy, 2006, p. 193–194); (6) improving emotional control, which includes reflecting upon and understanding the intensity of emotional response (Bateman & Fonagy, 2004, p. 267); (7) placing feelings in context (Bateman & Fonagy, 2003, p. 198); and (8) learning to express feelings appropriately (Bateman & Fonagy, 2003, p. 197). The essential ingredient in this therapeutic process is what Fonagy and his associates call "mentalized affectivity":

> The aim of psychotherapy for these individuals is to regenerate the connection between the consciousness of an affective state and its experience at the constitutional level. We have labeled this "mentalized affectivity"—a term intended to indicate the capacity to connect to the meaning of one's emotions. The clinical emphasis on experiential understanding of one's feelings in a way that ensures "meaningfulness" is crucial because it serves to establish congruent connections between primary and secondary affect-representational structures. The focus on emotion ensures that the secondary representational structures used to think about or to reflect on affect are reconnected and that misconnections where displayed affect was tied to a different nonconscious affect state are corrected. (Fonagy et al., 2002)

The therapist and patient work with cognitive states in a similar fashion. They first identify the primary maladaptive beliefs that are operative for the patient. Then the patient is encouraged to reflect on his or her beliefs about these beliefs, and on the fears and wishes upon which these beliefs are based (the "aboutness" of the beliefs; Bateman & Fonagy, 2004, p. 253).

In keeping the focus on *current mental states*, the aim is for the therapist and patient alike to identify ruptures in the here-and-now, moment-by-moment process of the unfolding therapy. Bateman and Fonagy (2006) state:

> Stop and stand . . . interrupts the session to . . . [focus] on the moment of rupture so as to reinstate mentalizing in the patient and sometimes within [the therapist] . . . The principal aims are always the same: to reinstate mentalizing at the point at which it is lost, to stabilize mentalizing in the context of an attachment relationship. (2006, pp. 195, 198–199)

Another technique for maintaining focus on current mental states is called "mentalizing the transference," through which both the therapist and the patient collaborate in mentalizing "to highlight the underlying motive that underpins the patient's current mental state" (2006, p. 197).

Keeping in mind the patient's deficits refers to the obvious fact that PD and DD patients start with a remarkably underdeveloped mentalizing capacity, so that while mentalizing is consistently encouraged, it is neither expected nor demanded.

Once a genuine mentalizing capacity develops (which can be measured by use of the RF-S), the PD or DD patient is likely to manifest high coherence of mind as measured with the AAI. The long-term effects become the formation of a coherent sense of self, the capacity for second-order regulation of emotional states, and the capacity for secure intimacy. The outcome data on MBT are impressive (Bateman & Fonagy, 1999, 2001, 2008, 2009).

THE MODULAR APPROACH TO METACOGNITIVE DEVELOPMENT

The London School has generally conceived of reflective capacity as a unitary function that manifests in various ways. In contrast, those associated with the Third Center of Cognitive Psychotherapy, Rome, have conducted a clinical research program on PD and DD patients to show that metacognition is composed of at least six relatively independent functions, or "modules," of very specific metacognitive capacities. Furthermore, they have discovered that different psychiatric conditions are associated with very specific deficits in one or more of these metacognitive functions. In their model, metacognitive deficits are "pathology-specific" (Semerari et al., 2003, p. 256).

Similar to the London School, Semerari and his associates (who we refer to as the Rome School or group) recognize that impaired metacognition plays a major role in sustaining PDs and that problematic states of mind, dysfunctional interpersonal cycles, and impoverished self-narratives in PD patients all arise from these metacognitive deficits. However, the Rome School differs from the London School in the following ways: (1) In their view, metacognitive function has a modular structure, with discrete components or subfunctions; (2) for each type of psychopathological condition, there is a different type of metacognitive deficit profile; (3) psychotherapy, to be successful, needs to improve the specific deficient metacognitive subfunctions; and (4) specific metacognitive deficits are assessed using the Metacognition Assessment Scale (MAS; Semerari et al. 2003, p. 238).

The Rome School's research has identified six very specific metacognitive skills, or modules (Prunetti et al., 2008, p. 32):

1. *Identification*: the ability to distinguish, recognize, and define one's own inner states (emotions, cognitions).
2. *Differentiation*: the ability to recognize that the contents of representations are subjective events of a mental nature and, therefore, are different from reality (Semerari et al., 2003, p. 242). Differentiation also includes distinguishing fantasy from reality (Dimaggio, Semerari, Carcione, Nicolò, & Procacci, 2007, p. 15).
3. *Relating variables*: the ability to establish relations among separate components of a mental state and between components of mental states and behavior (Semerari et al., 2003, p. 242).
4. *Integration*: the ability to work out coherent descriptions of one's mental

state and processes (Semerari et al., 2003, p. 242). Integration also entails developing an integrated point of view as well as showing consistency from one state of mind to the next (Dimaggio et al., 2007, p. 18).

5. *Decentration*: the ability to comprehend another individual's mental state from a non-egocentric perspective (Semerari et al., 2003, p. 244).

6. *Mastery*: the ability to work through one's representations and mental states with a view to implementing effective action strategies in order to accomplish cognitive tasks or cope with problematic mental states (Semerari et al., 2003, p. 244).

The Rome group discovered that patients with different psychiatric diagnoses manifest different yet very specific deficits in metacognition (Liotti, 1999; Semerari et al., 2003). For example, patients with borderline personality disorder (BPD) were reasonably good at identifying mental states but generally poor at differentiation, integration, and mastery. Thus, popular approaches to the treatment of BPD that teach *mindfulness* as a core skill, such as dialectical behavior therapy (DBT; Linehan, 1993), may be too simplistic, in that mindfulness mostly pertains to identification of mental states and does not address deficits in differentiation, integration, and mastery. The Rome group also found that patients with narcissistic personality disorder (NPD) were relatively good at metacognitive mastery but generally poor at identifying states of mind in themselves and others. Patients with major dissociative disorders such as dissociative identity disorder (DID) were poor at metacognitive identification but even worse at metacognitive integration (Semerari et al., 2003, p. 256). This pathology-specific approach allows the clinician to construct "prototypical profiles of metacognitive malfunctioning" (Semerari et al., 2003, p. 240) and shape treatment accordingly.

In *Psychotherapy of Personality Disorders* (Dimaggio et al., 2007), the Rome group offers a broad outline of their metacognitive-based treatment. They start with "generat[ing] a good emotional atmosphere in sessions," which is free of the pitfalls of "submissiveness, desperation, pressing alarm and devitalization" (p. 32). They recommend three general ways to develop metacognitive skills: validation, therapist self-disclosure pertaining to mental states, and therapist sharing of experiences pertaining to mental states (p. 34). A central focus is on encouraging the patient to utilize metacognitive reflection on "problematic states" as they occur in the current treatment context (p. 73).

One of the members of the Rome School, Giovanni Liotti, has developed a major theory and coherent approach to treatment designed especially for patients with BPD and DID. Liotti sees both of these conditions as the long-term consequence of early childhood disorganized attachment, aggravated by abuse in later childhood (1999). The child with disorganized attachment faced the frightened/frightening behavior of the caregiver and so encountered the impossible dilemma in which "the source of the infant's safety, appears at the same time to be a source of danger" (p. 4). The resultant disorganized attachment is characterized by multiple, fragmented, and incoherent IWMs; multiple simultaneous transferences; and destabilizing states of mind associated with dramatic and multiple IWMs (pp. 4–7). Additionally, Liotti characterizes the destabilized, shifting mental states as "oscillating between construing self and the attachment figure as persecutor, rescuer, and victim of each other" (p. 4). As a consequence of this disorganization of mind, such patients show very poor metacognitive capacity, severe relational deficits, deficits in the integration of self, strong emotional dysregulation, and a range of dissociative experiences and behaviors (Liotti, Cortina, & Farina, 2008, p. 302). Liotti claims that nearly all the symptoms seen in BPD patients can be explained in terms of the manifestations of disorganized attachment (1999, p. 6).

A unique feature of Liotti's theory is his expansion of Bowlby's concept of behavioral systems. In addition to the fear system and the attachment system, Liotti's model includes the behavioral system of *cooperation and collaboration*; the behavioral system of *social rank*, from which dominance and submission derive; and the *sexual* behavioral system. These behavioral systems interact in complex ways. Any of the specific behavioral systems can become activated at any point in a treatment session. Liotti explains that since patients with PDs or DDs have an insecure attachment system, they typically activate *another* behavioral system when they experience threat rather than activating the attachment system. For example, when a borderline patient becomes intensely angry at the therapist, it is important that the therapist understand that the patient has likely defensively deactivated the attachment system and instead activated the ranking system; the emerging rage comes out of competition and any shame comes out of fear of submission, both of which are dimensions of the ranking system, not the attachment system. Likewise, eroticization of the treatment relationship entails deactivation of the attachment system and defensive activation of the sexual behavioral system. According to Liotti, this kind of shifting of systems within the therapeutic relationship can be carefully tracked within and across treatment sessions, and intervention can be designed to activate the behavioral systems that are therapeutic.

An extraordinarily important point for therapists treating patients with attachment disturbances to remember is Liotti's discovery that the activation of the attachment behavioral system in PD and DD patients early in treatment is strongly associated with a significant *decrease*, not increase, in mentalization, because it creates the "disorganization" that is central to these patients' experience and is the basis for describing their attachment pattern as "disorganized." Activation of their defensively deactivated attachment system brings into the patient's experience a variety of affects and cognitions that are usually defensively excluded, and these create disorganization and overwhelm. Elena Prunetti and her associates from the Rome group found that when a therapist validated the state of PD or DD patients early in treatment, such validation significantly decreased mentalization capacity:

> Following validation interventions, patients' responses revealed significantly higher rates of temporary metacognitive failure in comparison to the responses solicited by neutral intervention . . . [Validation activates emotional closeness to the therapist, which] . . . activate[s] the attachment system . . . [and results in] the disorganized IWM . . . also [being] activated . . . [which] may seriously hinder the patient's metacognitive abilities. (Prunetti et al., 2008, pp. 28, 33)

When such disorganizing activation of the attachment system occurs in treatment, mentalization is significantly increased if the therapist structures a response to activate and shift to the cooperative behavioral system. At that point, the provision of a compassionate, secure-base, empathic response from the therapist is essentially meaningless to the patient, but shifting the discourse to one that frames the patient and therapist as a team that is collaborating to make sense out of what just happened is likely to be of benefit. It is probable that many skilled therapists spontaneously shift to a collaborative mode as a way to handle patient disorganization and/or therapeutic ruptures without knowing why, but Liotti has brought this strategy and its basis explicitly into our metacognitive awareness.

A main thread throughout Liotti's work is that metacognitive shifts are both motivation- and context-specific. Mentalization deficits in PD and DD patients are associated with certain behavioral systems more than others, and such deficits occur within a given system in some contexts more than in others. For example, in the disorganized patient, moments of increased fear of loss or of closeness in treatment activate the attachment system at the expense of mentalization, but at times when the same patient is experiencing a secure base, mentalization capacity is increased. Liotti adds that in such contexts, "mentalization is highly regulated by the experience of threat or safeness" (Liotti & Gilbert, 2011, p. 9). In disorganized insecure patients,

> activation of brain areas mediating attachment behavior actually *inhibit* brain areas mediating mentalization . . . [A]ttachment processes may allow for the recovery of mentalization, in the presence of danger, through contact with an attachment figure that is able to provide help and guidance and activates a renewed *sense of safeness and soothing*. (Liotti & Gilbert, 2011, p. 10)

Clearly, the picture of enhancing metacognitive capacity in PD and DD patients becomes much more complex than simply providing a therapeutic secure base, because for those patients, the very same base is the source of fear as well as the source of security. This is why Liotti recommends that the therapist shift to the collaborative behavioral system at such times; once stability and safety are reestablished, metacognitive function is once again possible. Liotti says, "Social safeness . . . [is] . . . a key condition for the emergence of successful mentalization" (Liotti & Gilbert, 2011, p. 12). However, here "social safeness" is established through the cooperative behavioral system, *not* the attachment system.

To fully understand the importance of therapeutic strategic shifts from attachment to cooperation, it is necessary to lay a deeper foundation regarding Liotti's thinking about the collaborative behavioral system. In "The Intersubjective and Cooperative Origins of Consciousness: An Evolutionary-Developmental Approach" (2010), Cortina and Liotti lay out the conceptual groundwork for understanding the adaptive function of the cooperative behavioral system. Like other behavioral systems, they say, the cooperative behavioral system is an "inborn motivational system" necessary for group survival (Liotti, 1999, p. 6). Cortina and Liotti state:

> We think that superior cooperative and communicative abilities might have been key adaptations that helped early human nomadic hunter gatherer groups survive and prosper during the period in which our direct homo ancestors lived . . . These adaptations allowed for cooperation to take place at a new level of sophistication between kin and nonkin members, which in turn helped these more cooperative and cohesive groups compete favorably with less cooperative and cohesive groups . . . in order to offset selection at the level of individuals, that favors "selfish" individualists over cooperative altruists. (2010, p. 294)

While the cooperative behavioral system is innate, Cortina and Liotti believe that PD and DD patients rarely if ever had the experience of collaboration in their family of origin. They say, "Patients . . . rarely witnessed cooperation on equal grounds between their parents" (Liotti, 2005, p. 36). Therefore, attachment-based therapists explicitly introduce collaboration at the onset of and throughout treatment. Treatment necessitates "explicit agreement of goals and rules of therapeutic work . . . [which] is constructed at the beginning . . . [to establish a] joint formulation of a shared goal for the treatment" (Liotti, 1999, p. 6).

A therapist's openness regarding his or her thinking about the assessment and the treatment plan establishes the cooperative system and the foundation of treatment collaboration right from its onset (Dimaggio et al., 2007, p. 37). Furthermore, it is important that the therapist develop an ongoing stance of transparency regarding his or her impression of changes in symptoms and any need for altering the therapeutic course so that collaboration becomes an ongoing dimension of the treatment. To concretize and make explicit the cooperative and collaborative foundation of the treatment, it is helpful to provide a written treatment contract that has been mutually developed, agreed upon, and signed. Dimaggio et al. (2007) even suggest that at the end of a treatment session with a PD or DD patient, the therapist hand him or her a written, organized summary of that treatment session (p. 44–45), which also concretizes and makes explicit the experience of having worked collaboratively during the session.

Such interventions help to foster a cooperative, collaborative state of mind in the patient. Collaboration is built upon mutual understanding; as Liotti says, "to understand each other is the basic act of cooperation" (2005). Mutual understanding in turn fosters a foundation that leads to building a secure base within the treatment relationship:

> Cooperative motives, as attachment ones, involve feelings of safeness: individuals must feel safe enough to come into proximity long enough and to share and also not be cheated or exploited. Indeed sharing, working out what others want and giving it to them, then being appreciated in return, is a common source of pleasure and relationship building. (Liotti & Gilbert, 2011, p. 16)

In the sense of sharing, working mutually toward a common goal, appreciating and being appreciated, and experiencing pleasure as a response, therapeutic collaboration is like two musicians developing and playing a duet.

An additional development from Liotti's work is the management of the sometimes intense and confusing disorganized shifting of self- and other-states in severely disturbed BPD and DD patients by using parallel coordinated treatments—that is, a combination of both individual and group treatments, and often two primary individual therapists. Then, when a patient shifts to a problematic state that leads to a significant rupture with one therapist, the second therapist is less likely to be caught up in the state with the patient, so the patient and second therapist can collaboratively explore the nature of the rupture with the other therapist. Such a therapy structure can support the development of mentalizing capacity regarding the conditions that precipitated the rupture and lead to repair of the ruptured alliance. As Liotti et al. (2008) say,

> if . . . a second therapist is engaged in the therapeutic program[,] . . . the patient may feel that there is another source of help available, and this perception may reduce the emotional strain on the therapeutic relationship with the individual psychotherapist . . . [and] . . . promote metacognitive reflection . . . [This] leads to 1. modulation of attachment, 2. improving metacognition, and 3. increasing security of therapist and patient. (Liotti et al., 2008, pp. 306–308)
>
> The second therapist, thus, may provide an opportunity to examine each component of the conflict with the first therapist . . . [T]he second therapy can validate and support [the patient]. (Liotti, 2005)

The overall treatment program developed by Liotti is called Cognitive Evolutionary Therapy (CET), which is first done on an inpatient basis and then becomes an outpatient treatment. Prunetti, Bosio, Bateni, and Liotti (2013) describe a 20-hour- per- week, three-week-long inpatient version of this approach to therapy. They summarize the essential ingredients of CET:

> The therapist helps the patient to notice that they are able to reflect more skillfully on what is happening in their interactions when they are not under pressure by their unbearable interpersonal urges and encourages the patient to try out these methods during interpersonal exchanges in the hospital, and later in everyday life. Reaching a cooperative stance is one of the key goals of CET. (p. 265)

The work of Liotti, Semerari, Dimaggio, and others of the Rome School is of tremendous value in understanding and treating patients with personality disorders, dissociative disorders, and/or attachment disturbances. Clinicians need not initiate the full CET or multiple-therapist programs but can draw from the many practical therapeutic principles from the Rome group and integrate them into their therapeutic practices.

Beyond Mentalizing and the Representational Self: Mindfulness and Transcendence of Self

David Wallin, in *Attachment in Psychotherapy* (2007), extends mentalizing into the domain of mindfulness and also respects the research on intersubjectivity and nonverbal communication. The starting point for his suggested therapy for insecurely attached patients is implicit, nonverbal experience. He says:

> *Because our first relational experiences are mainly lived outside the domain of language, our crucial internalizations of early relationships register as representations, rules, and models that cannot be linguistically retrieved. For these hard-to-reach representations to later be modified . . . they must be accessed, that is, experientially engaged. In therapy, such representations in the patient often become accessible only as they are communicated through other-than-verbal channels . . .* [T]he foundations of our internal working models . . . are . . . nonverbal and unconscious . . . [W]e lack verbal access to many of the experiences that shape us most profoundly. (Wallin, 2007, pp. 113, 116, 117)

Wallin calls this nonverbal domain of implicit knowledge the "unthought known" (2007, p. 115). Such nonverbal states of mind tend to be reenacted in the transference, evoked in the mind and in the responsiveness of the therapist, and/

or embodied as bodily felt experience within the self and resonantly in the bodily felt states of the therapist. As Wallin states, "enactment, evocation, and embodiment are the primary means by which patients communicate what they know but have not thought" (p. 122).

Wallin's "crucible" for transformation of experience and the self is the provision of a secure base by the therapist. Drawing on Lyons-Ruth's research on healthy, collaborative communication between parent and child (1999), Wallin says that secure base is promoted by collaborative communication, which involves four essential elements: (1) fostering a collaborative dialogue that is inclusive of all domains of experience, (2) actively identifying ongoing ruptures and fostering repair; (3) upgrading the dialogue and the mentalizing to "higher levels of awareness" (Wallin, 2007, p. 198), and (4) providing a real relationship in which patient and therapist alike struggle with and fully engage each other.

Wallin describes a three-stage process of engaging ongoing experience in insecurely attached patients, the outcome of which is the development of a coherent self. He calls the three stages *embeddedness*, *mentalizing*, and *mindfulness*. The starting point of therapy with the insecurely attached patient is one in which he or she is deeply embedded in the vicissitudes of ongoing experience. Much of the ongoing experience remains implicit. The stance of the therapist—as well as the techniques used, such as contingent and marked mirroring—encourages reflective activity in the patient. Over time, the patient moves "from embeddedness to mentalizing" (2007, p. 139). At this point, the patient is said to "reflect on these mental states rather than simply experiencing them" (p. 150). Ongoing implicit experience has become explicit through a successive process of "interpretation, mentalizing, and narrative" creation (p. 155), and the "reflective self" develops (p. 148). Finally, the patient transitions from mentalizing to mindfulness. Wallin describes the difference between mentalizing and mindfulness as follows: "Rather than making sense of the *contents* of our experience, mindfulness directs our receptive awareness to the moment-by-moment *process* of experiencing" (p. 159).

Through mindfulness practice over time, there results a transition from a mentalizing focus to "a growing identification with awareness itself, rather than the shifting self states" (Wallin, 2007, p. 161).

> Mindfulness also offers something that mentalizing does not. For the *mindful* self is aware of the reflective self—and aware as well that reflecting upon experience is entirely different from being fully present to experience. Through repeatedly becoming aware of awareness, we *"shift the locus of subjectivity from representations of self to awareness itself."* (p. 165)

What emerges is "transcendence of the self" (p. 158) to a larger vision.

A Consensus-Based Model for Attachment Treatment

In designing "An Attachment Approach to Adult Psychotherapy," Brent Mallinckrodt and his associates (Mallinckrodt, Daly, & Wang, 2009) followed an interesting procedure. Rather than developing their own attachment-based treatment, they contacted therapists from the East Coast, Midwest, and West Coast of the United States and asked them to nominate individuals who they considered to be experts in attachment-based treatment of adult patients. These experts were then interviewed, and the interviews were transcribed. The material from the resulting 12 interviews was organized into different categories, and from this structure a model of attachment-based understanding and treatment was constructed. Mallinckrodt et al. say that the outcome was derived from what the experts seemed to agree upon and was "based on the most reasonable interpretation of the evidence" (p. 235).

The model is based on the consensus that, for adult patients who present with significant relational problems, "adult attachment theory offers a useful framework for case conceptualization and treatment of these maladaptive patterns" (Mallinckrodt et al., 2009, p. 236). For such patients, given the dysfunction in their relationships, the attachment system is likely to become readily involved, and thus such an approach to treatment is a good fit. The authors state that "when adults perceive a sufficiently great threat, their attachment system is activated in much the same way as in infancy" (p. 237). Such patients will see a therapist as a potential secure base and "use *security-based* strategies to seek comfort and emotional proximity with an attachment figure" (p. 237).

Drawing upon an extensive research literature, two main types of problematic attachment problems in adults can be identified, namely, those with *deactivating* attachment strategies and those with *hyperactivating* attachment strategies. Mallinckrodt et al. (2009) delineate the main clinical presentations of each type of patient. For example, those patients with deactivating strategies generally have inflated self-esteem, suppress attachment-related thoughts and feelings, show avoidant attachment, do not initially encode attachment-related material into memory, show reduced physiological arousal, project unwanted self-traits onto others, and have alexithymia regarding distress. Those with hyperactivating strategies generally have negative beliefs about their ability to cope with distress, expect that others will be inconsistently responsive and available, show anxious attachment, make an exaggerated appraisal of perceived threats, have pervasive fears of abandonment, are unable to suppress painful thoughts of separation, and are more alert to self-perceived weakness (p. 238). Each of these clinical features was derived from research using self-report inventories, and the two broad types of insecure attachment were identified with another self-report inventory, the Experience of Close Relationships scale (Mallinckrodt et al., 2009, p. 236).

Mallinckrodt et al. (2009) divide the attachment-based treatment into three phases: the engagement phase, the working phase, and the termination phase.

The engagement phase begins with the establishment of the therapeutic relationship as a secure base for exploration. Mallinckrodt and his associates state that therapy begins with "the process of helping a client form a secure attachment that he or she ha[s] rarely, if ever, known previously" (p. 241). The therapist joins with the patient "fighting as allies against pain . . . [T]his collaboration early in the work establishes a pattern quite different from anything the client may have known" (p. 249). According to Mallinckrodt et al., such joining helps in "promoting safety and engagement" (p. 247).

A central strategy of the engagement phase pertains to the therapist carefully regulating closeness and distance in the therapeutic relationship. The therapist is "continually monitoring therapeutic distance" (Mallinckrodt et al., 2009, p. 263). For example, a patient with a hyperactivating attachment style needs the closeness with the therapist, and so the therapist "reduces the therapeutic distance," at least early in treatment, but then increases the distance later. A patient with a deactivating attachment style needs more distance early in treatment, and then the therapist gradually *reduces* the distance in the therapeutic relationship over time (p. 243). Mallinckrodt and his colleagues correctly understand that patients with deactivating strategies *actually long for connection.* Therefore, therapists encourage such patients to "concentrate on the part . . . that deeply yearns for real connection, despite the fear of rejection or hurt typical of previous relationships" (p. 250).

Mallinckrodt et al. (2009) also recommend that the patient–therapist match be complementary in terms of attachment style. In other words, patients with a hyperactivated attachment style are likely to work better with a therapist with a deactivating style, and a patient with a deactivating style is likely to work better with a therapist with a hyperactivating style (p. 244).

The authors delineate a series of signs that indicate successful engagement of the insecurely attached patient. These "transitional markers" include that the client makes a commitment to change, reports some behavioral change outside the sessions, develops tolerance for deeper and more intense affect in sessions, and shows a capacity to "do the work" of therapy (Mallinckrodt et al., 2009, p. 251). They state, "Taken together, these transition markers can be considered indicators that a secure therapeutic attachment is in the making" (p. 253).

The main goal of the working phase

> is to develop a secure attachment in which clients are able to meet their needs consistently through security-based strategies of attachment, rather than relying on either hyperactivating or deactivating strategies to regulate affect or meet their interpersonal needs . . . This is the core feature of the corrective emotional experience. (Mallinckrodt et al., 2009, p. 255)

The specific goal for hyperactivated patients is to "reduce their need for reassurance from others" (p. 256). For deactivated patient, the goal is to "reduce their tendency to cut off emotional experience" (p. 257). The desired outcome for all patients is "a significant shift from insecure to secure attachment style over the course of therapy" (p. 257). "Secure attachment to a therapist provides a corrective emotional experience through which a client eventually comes to rely more on security-based strategies to regulate affect, and develops more effective social competencies to form satisfying attachments with others" (p. 263).

Mallinckrodt et al. (2009) warn that the termination phase signifies a major separation, and so reactivation of old dysfunctional attachment behaviors is expected at that time. They say, "Therapists should be keenly aware of any reemergence of the behaviors associated with hyperactivating and deactivation strategies when termination is approaching" (p. 259).

We see Mallinckrodt and his colleagues' consensus model of treatment as a useful integration of many of the preestablished principles of good treatment for attachment disturbances. Particularly valuable is the differentiation and focus on deactivating and hyperactivating attachment styles. This model, however, does not explicitly include the valuable contributions of several other theoretical and therapeutic models, particularly from the intersubjective and metacognitive fields.

Comprehensive Treatment of Attachment Disturbances

In the remainder of this book, we describe in great detail our "three pillars" of attachment treatment. We believe that this treatment model and its methods represent the best currently available way to think about and treat patients with attachment disturbances. Our integration of what we see as the most important published material relevant to attachment and its treatment, combined with our clinical experience, has produced an approach and set of methods for treatment that we find remarkably efficient at creating comprehensive attachment repair. The next chapter details the underlying principles and presents the overall framework of this approach.

CHAPTER 7

Introduction to the Three Pillars of Comprehensive Attachment Treatment

Attachment Disturbance as One Type of Relational Disturbance

Of all people who seek mental health treatment, about half present chief complaints that do not reflect psychiatric conditions like depression or anxiety disorders. Instead, their complaints pertain to difficulties with relationships or their sense of self (Beutler & Clarkin, 1990), which we consider indications of relational disturbance. As relational disturbance constitutes a good portion of the variance of reasons for entering psychotherapy, it is important to understand this category of difficulty and to recognize its various subtypes. In our view, not all relational disturbance is attachment related. We believe that there are three main types of relational disturbance, each with its own type, or map, of relational representation, and each with its own underlying cognitive structure that forms at different developmental stages.

The first type of relational disturbance results from attachment disturbance. The representational map for attachment, or internal working model, is the earliest to develop, forming between 12 and 20 months, concurrent with the development of symbolic or representational thinking (see Chapter 2). By the end of the second year, one of the four main types of attachment—secure, ambivalent/ resistant, avoidant, or disorganized—is stably established, both as an internal working model and as a resulting pattern of attachment behavior.

Relevant to the distinction among types of relational disturbance is that two memory systems develop during early childhood (Pillemer & White, 1989). The *behavioral memory system* is based on the infant's direct observation of others' behavior and immediate or delayed behavioral imitation of the observed behavior. This system is present in a rudimentary form in the first weeks of life (Trevarthen, 1979) and is reasonably well developed by nine months (Bauer, 1996). The *narrative memory system* begins to develop between

18 and 24 months and is not fully developed until the beginning of the fourth year (Pillemer & White, 1989).

The important implication of these two distinct lines of memory development is that internal working models and resulting attachment types are stably developed prior to the development of narrative memory. Therefore, it is not reasonable to expect that our adult patients with clinically significant attachment disturbance will remember early attachment experiences prior to the second year of life as detailed narrative memories, although some fragments of narrative memory may occur. Since behavioral, or reenacted, memory is the primary memory system operative during the first two years of life, attachment disturbance in adults is likely to be expressed primarily as reenactments in relationships, including transference reenactments in the treatment relationship. Although interpretation of transference reenactments has been a staple of many attachment-based treatments, the developmental timing of the two memory systems highlights that it is not reasonable to expect that interpretation of such reenactments will readily lead to insight. Interpretation assumes that significant attachment experiences are accessible through narrative memory, but if those experiences occurred prior to the development of this memory system, this assumption is not valid.

A second type of relational map develops between the third and fourth year of life. This period is characterized not only by the maturation of the narrative memory system but also by the development of complex emotional ideas, stable beliefs, and schemas; the elaboration of wishes, needs, and fantasies; and a complex structure of defenses through which aspects of problematic relational interactions become distorted or defensively excluded. These new capacities contribute to the emergence of a new form of relational representation, a second layer as it were, that is independent of the attachment representation formed earlier. This map has been referred to as the "core conflictual relationship theme" (CCRT; Luborsky, 1977; Luborsky & Crits-Christoph, 1998).

The CCRT is a relatively fixed and repeating pattern of a person's relational expectations and experiences. Based on a patient's account of his or her significant relationships, past and present (*relationship episodes*, RE), the therapist identifies the wishes, needs, and intentions (*wish*, W) that the patient typically enters relationships with, the ways that others in relationship with the patient commonly respond (*response from the other*, RO), and the ways that the patient usually feels and behaves in response to the others' responses (*response from the self*, RS). For example, on the basis of analyzing a series of a patient's relationship episodes, a resulting CCRT formulation might be:

> You go into relationships wanting to be appreciated for who you are (W), but instead you typically find that the man you're with is never satisfied (RO), and you then go into accommodation mode and feel not seen, discouraged, and depressed (RS).

CCRT maps are more complex and diverse than the four types of attachment maps and are highly stable by age five. Because narrative memory is functioning when CCRTs form, interpretations of CCRTs in psychotherapy are more likely to have benefit than are interpretations of attachment patterns. In response to a therapist's accurate interpretation of a CCRT, a patient is likely to report additional narrative memories supporting the interpretation. Evidence suggests that such identification and conscious recognition of dysfunctional CCRT patterns contributes to the diminishment of their effect as a map for relational functioning (Luborsky & Crits-Christoph, 1998).

Problematic and clinically significant CCRTs can be present whether or not a person has attachment disturbance. Studies of the attachment status of adults in the United States show that between 30% and 40% have insecure attachment. Most of the people in this group also have clinically significant CCRTs. Interestingly, of the 60% to 70% of American adults with a secure attachment type, many of these will show evidence of CCRT relational disturbance.

A third type of relational disturbance is trauma bonding. Trauma bonding occurs in a relationship characterized by a significant power differential in the context of intermittent experiences of fright and caring behavior (Carnes, 1997, p. 29). This relational experience may occur in a concentration camp, a hostage situation (Stockholm syndrome; Strentz, 1979; Symonds, 1982), a battering relationship (Dutton & Painter, 1981; Pence & Paymer, 1993), familial incest (de Young & Lowry, 1992), or destructive cult victimization (Hassan, 2000). Trauma bonding can occur in childhood, but unlike attachment representations and CCRT maps that only develop during childhood, trauma bonding maps can also develop in abusive relationships during adolescence and adulthood (Dutton & Painter, 1981). Some reports have suggested that trauma-bonded relationships reflect a reactivation of early attachment disturbance (Cogan & Porcelli, 1996; McClellan & Kileen, 2000), although even secure adolescents and adults are vulnerable to trauma bonding in extreme relational conditions. Therefore, trauma bonding can either be a reenactment of childhood insecure attachment, be acquired in adulthood, or both (J. G. Allen, 2001). In either case, trauma-bonded adults show a pattern of relational disturbance similar to fearful (i.e., disorganized) or anxious-preoccupied attachment (Henderson, Bartholomew, & Dutton, 1997).

Because not all relational disturbance is attachment related and the model and methods we present in this book are designed to treat attachment disturbance, it is essential that at the beginning of any treatment for relational disturbance, there is accurate determination of what underlies the patient's presenting relational problems. We typically begin treatment by assessing a person's attachment type using the AAI or some other measure (see Chapter 4) and also by collecting a history of relational episodes in order to develop a CCRT formulation. Whenever trauma or abuse is evident in the history, the therapist also determines whether trauma bonding is present. Then, it becomes necessary for the therapist and patient to decide together whether the relational disturbance is related primarily to attachment, CCRT, or trauma. Based on this determination, a very specific treatment plan is developed.

If the patient demonstrates secure attachment (F classification on the AAI) and problematic CCRTs or trauma bonding, then treatment focuses on latter issues. For cases in which there is significant insecure attachment of one type or another, or if problematic CCRTs or trauma bonding are also evident along with significant attachment disturbance, the initial treatment plan will first focus on the attachment patterns. Relevant CCRT themes and any trauma bonding are then addressed toward the end of treatment, once the patient shows evidence of earned secure attachment (e.g., a significant increase of coherence of mind). When there is primarily secure attachment with some degree of anxiety (F4 or F5 classification on the AAI) or some degree of dismissing attachment (F1 or F2 classification) and also CCRT conflict or trauma bonding, clinical judgment is needed as to whether to treat the attachment issues using the methods described in the rest of this book or to simply treat the CCRT themes or trauma bonding. The main criterion guiding this decision is whether the mild-to-moderate anxious or dismissing attachment has significantly interfered with the patient's relationships; in such cases, the attachment, CCRTs, and trauma bonding are likely to have considerable overlap. If such overlap is present, we follow the guideline that *treatment always starts with what formed earliest developmentally*. For example, in patients with significant CCRT conflicts along with secure overall attachment but with dismissing or anxious features that have disrupted their relationships, we recommend treating the attachment disturbance first and the CCRT patterns after that.

It is beyond the scope of this book to address treatments for CCRT problems or trauma bonding. Excellent resources for CCRT treatment include Luborsky, 1984; Strupp and Binder, 1984; Luborsky and Critt-Christoph, 1998; and Book, 1998. For expert accounts of trauma bonding treatment, see J. G. Allen, 2001; Hassan, 2000, 2009; Landenburger, 1989; and van der Kolk, 1989.

Treating Attachment Disturbance: The Three Pillars

We have been developing this treatment approach for adult attachment disturbances over the last 20 years. It started as the use of attachment-related imagery in the treatment of severely disturbed patients, and what evolved from this method was what we have termed the "Ideal Parent Figure" protocol. During the last 10 years, based on significant developments in attachment research, we added two more components of treatment: interventions that address the limitations of metacognitive capacity and interventions that address noncollaborative behavior in treatment. It is these three components that constitute what we call the "Three Pillars" of our attachment-based treatment for adults: (1) utilizing the Ideal Parent

Figure protocol to positively remap adult attachment representations, (2) fostering a range of metacognitive skills, and (3) promoting collaborative nonverbal and verbal behavior in the treatment relationship. An overview and rationale of each of these is presented below, followed by a more detailed description of the treatment methods in the next three chapters. In addition to the benefits that each treatment pillar brings to its particular domain of focus, applying each one also reinforces and benefits the others; this mutually enhancing interrelationship is explained at the end of this chapter.

THE FIRST PILLAR: THE IDEAL PARENT FIGURE PROTOCOL

Background and Core Assumptions

Our use of attachment-based imagery in the Ideal Parent Figure (IPF) protocol is based upon several key assumptions. First, as we reviewed in Chapter 2, attachment research suggests that innate infant–caregiver attachment behavior starts during the first weeks of life, but that the organization of an infant's specific and consistent patterns of attachment behavior (as seen, for example, in the Strange Situation), as well as the underlying representations and internal working model of attachment, do not develop until between 12 to 20 months, peaking around 18 months. This finding has important implications for treatment, namely, that *representation of attachment*, not attachment behavior per se, is ideally the main focus for treatment intervention. For this reason, we disagree with psychoanalytically oriented attachment-based treatments that primarily emphasize interpretation of reenactments of dysfunctional attachment behaviors in the transference relationship. Such treatments assume that insight about attachment patterns will lead to change in those patterns, but there is little evidence supporting such interpretation-based change. In addition to this developmentally inconsistent emphasis on attachment behavior, the interpretive method, as we have noted, is based on the incorrect assumption that narrative memory is operative when critical attachment-forming experiences occur.

We believe that the research on the development of attachment supports our method of directly introducing and consistently supporting patients' engagement with imagined positive, "ideal" parental attachment figures. Mental imagery is an internal representation, and we assume that utilizing this medium contributes directly and efficiently to the development of new, positive, internal representations and ultimately to a new, healthy internal working model of secure attachment.

A second assumption is that therapeutic techniques designed to reduce negative states of mind do just that, and that alone; reducing or eliminating a negative does not by itself create a positive. In other words, if what is required for patients with significant attachment disturbance is the development of a new, positive internal working model (IWM) or map for attachment, then interpreting and modifying dysfunctional IWMs will be inadequate as a treatment approach. Helping the patient see the distortions in his or her attachment representations does not lead to positive remapping. An effective approach, in our opinion, requires direct introduction of positive attachment imagery as the basis of creating a new, positive attachment map.

Our third assumption is that attachment-based treatments that mainly emphasize the therapist's role as a secure base, or as a limited reparenting figure, are problematic. Such methods assume that the experience of a therapist's secure-base behavior will be internalized by the patient and lead to a new, positive internal working model of secure attachment. While we do not dispute that such beneficial internalization can happen, we believe that relying on the adult patient–therapist dyad as the vehicle for it is inefficient, based on the time required and on developmental inconsistency pertaining to the nature of the dyad itself. Therapist secure-base behavior during psychotherapy sessions is certainly of value, but in a typical psychotherapy context of 50 minutes once or twice weekly, the patient's direct experience of being with the therapist as a secure base is for practical reasons quite limited. Any internalization of that experience that occurs will require an extended period of time with the therapist. Within our method of utilizing attachment-based imagery, the patient's experience of time with the ideal parent figures can be extended to far exceed the clock time of any particular session itself, thus making far more efficient use of the available time with the patient.

Regarding developmental inconsistency in the patient–therapist dyad, a patient's attachment map develops through experience with his or her parents or caregivers during childhood. We believe that remapping from insecure to secure attachment is much more efficient when the medium for that process is closer to the actual developmental circumstances that are central to the formation of attachment maps. The adult-to-adult experience of the psychotherapy relationship does not reflect those developmental circumstances. In the context of the Ideal Parent Figure protocol, the patient imagines being a very young child and then imagines adult parent figures who are ideally suited to helping the patient-as-child to feel, in the words of the therapist, "absolutely secure in the relationship with them." This experiential imagery is much more closely aligned with the formative conditions for attachment than is the adult patient–therapist dyadic interaction.

Also problematic with the model of therapist as secure base as a main component of treatment is that it requires the therapist to behave continuously as a secure base or "good enough" (Winnicott, 1965) parent figure. We believe that the therapist should take the stance of providing a secure base as much as is realistically possible given the limitations of the therapist's own attachment patterns, but we do not believe that this is the primary ingredient in effective treatment. Rather, the first pillar of our treatment is based on working with imagery of ideal parent figures who can provide a more effective and consistent model of a secure base than the behavior of any therapist will ever approximate. Therapist behavior is limited by who the therapist is and what his or her own attachment patterns are, whereas imagery creates new possibilities from the infinitely flexible capacity of imagination. Attachment imagery can thus be shaped and reshaped by the patient and therapist alike in an effort to find the most secure felt sense and "just right" experience in each imagined attachment scenario at any given point in the treatment.

A fourth, related assumption that underlies our use of attachment-based imagery is that although therapist-as-secure-base is not the most efficient means of remapping attachment representations, there is a type of therapist behavior that does significantly contribute to a new, positive internal working model. Careful studies of infant–caregiver interactions have revealed that infant development is mutually regulated and co-created (Beebe & Lachmann, 2014). This evidence requires clinicians to reformulate traditional notions about internalization. The traditional view assumes that the therapist provides a secure base through his or her therapeutic stance and behavior and that the patient internalizes this secure base as a new IWM. The reformulated view, which we advocate, is that a new, positive IWM is not merely a product of internalization of secure-base experience but is formed in large part through the dynamic engagement of co-creative interaction. In the IPF method, the therapist introduces attachment-based imagery in the form of ideal parent figures; then the patient and therapist together continuously explore, shape, and reformulate the imagery within the context of their interactions, which are much like the mutually regulated and co-created interactions of the infant and his or her caregiver. By collaboratively constructing and reconstructing, by continuously changing and refining the ideal parent figure imagery, the patient and the therapist co-create new, positive attachment experience and a new, positive attachment map.

In sum, we introduce and work with ideal parent figures directly through the medium of imagery on the basis of the assumption that attachment imagery, combined with a therapist's secure-base stance and collaborative, co-creative engagement with the patient's experience of the imagery, is much more effective than either interpreting dysfunctional attachment behavior or relying primarily on therapist secure-base behavior. In other words, we assume that the primary agent for fostering a new, positive internal working model or map is attachment-based imagery collaboratively engaged with from the therapist's best-available stance of secure base.

Ideal Parent Figures as the Medium for Attachment-Promoting Qualities

Through ideal parent figure imagery, the therapist can introduce and help the patient engage with a wide range of attachment-promoting caregiver qualities. In addition to bringing into the imagery the general qualities that promote secure attachment (described in the next section below), the therapist tailors the imagery frame to address specific patient-reported early experiences of failed attachment-promoting care. For example, when parental unresponsiveness, inconsistency, rejection, or failed contingency-matching have occurred in the patient's caregiver-of-origin experience, the therapist introduces ideal parent figures who embody the *positive opposites* of these—parent figures who are extraordinarily responsive, consistent, accepting, and matching of the child's behavior, respectively. Similarly, for a patient for whom a consistent lack of maternal protection was an important factor in the development of insecure attachment, the therapist suggests and co-creates an ideal maternal figure who is consistently protective of the child *"in just the right ways."* Repeated engagement with imagined parent figures who embody both the general and the specific developmentally absent attachment-promoting ways of being serves the overall treatment goal of positively remapping attachment.

A skilled therapist, like a good parent, knows how to be contingently responsive, that is, immediately responsive to the moment-to-moment experience and needs of the individual, unique patient. In the IPF process, contingent responsiveness is accomplished both through the therapist's overall stance and behavior and also through specific variation in the imagery that is introduced. For example, if the patient describes in the imagery an interactive mismatch between his or her child self and an ideal parent figure, the therapist is contingently responsive by recognizing the patient's need and immediately suggesting a specific change in the imagery. Contingent responsiveness is brought into the imagery itself by the therapist's suggestion that the ideal parent recognizes the mismatch and behaves in *"just the right way"* that corrects it and restores the felt sense of attunement. The specific way that the parent figure does this is left to the patient to imagine. Both the immediacy of the change and the specific variation suggested for the imagery are important for the patient's perception that both the therapist, in his or her behavior, and the ideal parent figures, in the imagery, are contingently responsive to the timing, rhythms, and content of the patient's experience, within and outside the imagery.

We also introduce qualities in the imagery that are specifically relevant to patients' specific insecure attachment subtype. For example, if a patient's attachment pattern is classified as dismissing, then ideal parent figures are introduced who are *"especially accepting and never rejecting."* If another patient has an anxious-preoccupied attachment pattern, the suggested imagery emphasizes parents with qualities of consistency and noninvolving focus on the child's, not their own, state of mind. For a patient who has a disorganized attachment pattern, in addition to the themes of acceptance and noninvolvement, the suggested imagery focuses on ideal parents who are consistently and fully present as well as calming and never frightening to the child.

The Five Primary Conditions That Promote Secure Attachment
We have found that there are five main areas of developmental experience relevant to attachment security that need to be addressed and strengthened during

treatment of patients with significant attachment disturbance. These areas can be considered as pairs of what a child or adult patient ideally experiences with parents or parent figures, and the parents' or parent figures' behavior that best promotes the development of such experiences. We refer to these linked pairs of child experience and parental behavior as *the five primary conditions that promote secure attachment*. They are (1) a sense of *felt safety*, promoted by parents' consistent and reliable *protection* of the child from danger and threat; (2) a sense of *being seen and known*, promoted by parents' consistent, reliable, and accurate *attunement* to the child; (3) the experience of *felt comfort*, promoted by consistent, reliable, and timely *soothing* and *reassurance*; (4) a sense of *being valued*, promoted by parents' consistent, reliable, and clear *expressed delight* in the child; and (5) a sense of *support for being and becoming one's unique, best self*, promoted by parents' consistent, reliable, *unconditional support and encouragement for exploration*. Note that *consistency* and *reliability* are components of each of the parental behavior categories. We consider these to be *general factors* common to and necessary for all categories, along with parental *presence* and *interest*.

When parents or parent figures behave in these ways and children or adult patients have the corresponding felt experiences, there are likely to be beneficial effects in several key self-functioning capacities that are characteristic of secure attachment: from soothing and reassurance, *emotion regulation*; from attunement and expressed delight, *self-esteem* and *metacognitive development*; from attunement and support for exploration, *self-development* and *metacognitive development*; and from the foundation of protection, all of these self-functions are supported. Each of the primary conditions that promote secure attachment is considered more fully below.

1. Felt Safety/Protection

Bowlby (1969/1982) believed that the primary function of attachment in both animals and humans, from an evolutionary perspective, is the protection of the species. The fawn stays close to the doe to be protected from predators. For human infants, maternal protectiveness results in the felt sense of safety in the world in general and, in particular, safety in the relationship with the mother. When failed protection occurs in a family system, such as when a child is physically or sexually abused, treatment often entails not only processing and integrating memories and feelings related to the abusive acts but also processing the memories and feelings related to the nonoffending parent or parents who failed to protect the child from the danger and abuse. Such processing and integrating of the failure of protection is often harder than integrating the experiences of abuse, because the need for protection is fundamental to life and all the functioning of the organism. A rupture at this deep level can be more devastating than the abuse itself. Although Bowlby highlights that parental protectiveness is built into the human (and many) species, it does not, unfortunately, always manifest and provide for the actual and felt protection needed by the child.

Parents who provide a secure base for their children are fiercely protective, but not overprotective, yet inevitable slight failures of protection are bound to occur. When a secure base is not present, larger protection failures are likely, which contribute to insecure attachment patterns. Using the IPF protocol to foster attachment repair and promote the experience of protection and secure base, we introduce parent figures who are deeply protective of the child, take all means to keep the child from harm, and when harm or abuse has occurred, are deeply responsive to the child's state of mind and needs for well-being. In other words, the therapist introduces and co-creates ideal parent figures who represent the positive opposite of parents whose protection failures were prominent.

2. Feeling Seen and Known/Attunement

Secure parents are likely to be carefully attuned to their child. There are three aspects of the child that an attuned parent will actively attend to and mostly accurately recognize: the child's immediate behavior, the child's inner state of mind, and the child's developmental range at any particular time. Such a parent will demonstrate his or her attunement to the child's behavior by being immediately responsive, by contingently matching the behavior, and/or by changing in response to the behavior. The attuned parent will also give voice to his or her best estimate of the child's emotions, needs, motivations, and ideas.

Attunement to the child's actual range of capacities relative to the child's developmental age allows the parent to work within and at times go slightly beyond that range so as to best foster the child's development. The attuned parent does not expect from his or her child abilities or behaviors that are too far outside the child's developmental range. Instead, such a parent engages the child in ways that support and reinforce the present capacities, and also introduces challenges that enable the child to go just a little bit beyond his or her immediate capability. Going too far beyond the present capacity would induce disorganizing anxiety (Meins, 1997) and arrest development, but providing "optimal frustration" (Kohut, 1977) promotes development. At each stage of development, attuned parents help their child to find what is called in the peak performance field "the right skill-to-challenge ratio," which promotes optimal functioning and development and can elicit in the child the state of "being in the flow" (Csikszentmihalyi, 1990) of his or her own experience (Meins, 1997).

Consider, for example, the developmental task of potty training. Parents will be far more contingently responsive and helpful to a child facing this task if they have the developmental knowledge that perceived sensation develops some months before sphincter control. Thus, a developmentally attuned parent does not assume when his or her child signals the sensation of a bowel movement that the child has physical control to move his or her bowels when and where the parent wishes. The parent who is not attuned in this way and does not have this knowledge is far more likely to engage the child in a power struggle, experience it as a personal failure, or humiliate the child when the child is unable to fulfill the parent-desired goal. This kind of nonattunement can be quite limiting to the formation of secure attachment maps in the developing child.

The overall experience of the secure child of carefully attuned parents is feeling deeply known and seen. For adult patients lacking this childhood experience, attachment repair is enabled through imagined ideal parent figures who embody qualities of attunement to the child's behavior and state of mind, effective contingent responsiveness, and alignment with developmental capacity. The objective of this IPF imagery is for the patient to incorporate the experience of consistent attunement and contingent responsiveness in all three areas into his or her newly developing, positive map of secure attachment.

3. Felt Comfort/Soothing and Reassurance

In addition to promoting attachment security, consistent parental soothing and reassurance contributes over time to the emergence of internal affect regulation. Marian Tolpin (1971) described that the child's developing internal structures for affect regulation result from the cumulative internalization of repeated soothing and comforting behavior by the parent. A parent whose behavior promotes secure attachment is responsive whenever the child is emotionally upset, and is responsive in particular ways by offering physical comfort, emotional soothing, and/or verbal reassurance. The resulting inner experience of this child is one of feeling soothed and what we call *felt comfort*. If the soothing parental response and the experience of felt comfort happens repeatedly over time, then, as the child develops the capacity for representational thinking, he or she will develop an internal representation of the soothing/comforting response. As this representation becomes more stable, the child needs the soothing parental behavior less because he or she can evoke from within the internal representation of soothing and felt comfort. Herein lies the beginning of the internal structures of mind for affect regulation.

Adult patients with insecure attachment typically show clinically significant affect-regulation deficits. Emotion-regulation repair and development is done by introducing ideal parent figures who provide physical comfort, emotional soothing, and/or verbal reassurance when the adult patient-as-child experiences emotional upset. The IPF imagery can be highly specific and individualized. For example, the therapist can say, *"These parents see that you're quite upset and know exactly what you're feeling. They really know what you most need right now and respond in just the right way to help you with these feelings."* The affect-regulatory goal of using IPF soothing imagery is that it will be incorporated into the newly developing positive map of secure attachment as soothing-related representations.

4. Feeling Valued/Expressed Delight

Consistently expressed delight by parents about and to the child not only promotes secure attachment but is also the foundation of healthy self-esteem development. Sander (1975) defined self-esteem in developmental terms as being the developmental linking of positive affect states to the self-representation. Adult patients who are narcissistically vulnerable, who have chronic self-esteem failure, were never able during childhood to link positive affect states directly to their self-representation. Older children and adults who lack self-esteem fail to experience a backdrop of positive feeling when they evoke their sense of self in everyday life, or they have a backdrop of largely negative feeling when they experience their sense of self.

When a child can count on parents to show delight in who he or she is, the experience of being valued and valuable emerges. Kohut (1971) asserted that in order to develop a sense of self-value and self-affirmation, every child needs the reinforcement of consistently experiencing being seen as "the gleam in the mother's eye." Parents who raise children with the healthiest self-esteem repeatedly express their joy to the child about almost everything the child does. More important, such parents delight not only in what the child does but also in the child's very being. Whenever their delight in being with their child is present, they do not inhibit or disguise it.

Such repeated expressions of joy and delight by parents becomes the developmental bridge for linking deeply positive emotional states to the child's self-representation. However, too many parents in modern Western culture become primarily focused on the job of parenting over the joy of parenting, and become preoccupied with what the child *does* rather than *who the child is*. So it is understandable that of the five primary conditions that support secure attachment, expressed delight is often lacking from an adult patient's experience. In the IPF method, self-esteem development is supported through ideal parent figures who express utter joy or sheer delight about the child's immediate behavior in particular and in his or her being in general.

5. Felt Support for Best Self/Unconditional Support and Encouragement

Parents of secure children who develop a strong, autonomous, and complex sense of self are champions of their children's best self-development. The child comes to know that the parents have a deep faith in him or her, in such a way that the child is free to explore, discover, succeed and fail, and, through such exploration, develop the best, strongest, and most unique sense of self. Winnicott (1971) said that play is the medium of self-development, and parents who facilitate their child's best self encourage free play and exploration and do not have agendas for the child. They do not need the child to develop in a preconceived way to fulfill their own needs, and they see themselves as co-explorers and supporters of who this unique child will become. They do not thwart but encourage the child's uniqueness and difference, and they are not threatened by the child's developing strength and assertion of self but actively encourage it, even if it means that conflict will ensue. Such parents provide encouragement and support for inner and outer exploration at each stage of the child's and adolescent's development so that the child can develop the best self possible.

Normal, healthy self-development is especially impaired in patients who have anxious-preoccupied or disorganized attachment patterns. These patients likely had involving parents who too often entangled them in their own states of mind—their own needs, emotions, and ideas. For adult patients with clinically significant self-pathology, ideal parent figure imagery is introduced such that parent figures provide strong support and encouragement for self-exploration and play and encourage the adult patient-as-child to discover and be his or her own uniqueness in the world. The goal of this form of IPF imagery is that the patient will incorporate the experience of support and encouragement into representations of his or her best self in the developing positive map of secure attachment.

Attachment-Based Imagery Over the Course of Treatment

Early in the treatment of a patient with insecure attachment, we focus the ideal parent figure imagery on the attachment-promoting conditions of safety/protection, being seen and known/attunement, felt comfort/soothing and reassurance, and feeling valued/expressed delight. At the middle to late stages of treatment, as the patient shows initial signs of developing a new, positive internal working model for secure attachment (e.g., seeking proximity to an ideal parent figure), the emphasis moves away from the earlier secure-base-promoting imagery and is placed instead on exploration-in-the-context-of-secure-base imagery. We shape the attachment-based imagery toward support for the child's various explorations, which first includes internal exploration of mind, such as curiosity about his or her inner states, and then external explorations. For example, the patient imagines exploring various new activities with the support and encouragement of the ideal parent figures, who are now experienced at least partly as a secure base.

The establishment of a secure base serves as the foundation for greater emphasis on the patient's self-development. A main goal at this phase of treatment is fostering further the development of a strong, autonomous, evolved sense of self, or what we call the "best self," which will serve as support for healthy exploratory behavior in the patient's life.

The therapist begins to use the IPF protocol less often and may instead introduce some or all of a developmental sequence of imagery protocols designed specifically to promote self-definition, self-organization, self-agency, self-esteem, self-in-relation-to-others, and self in expanded contexts from wider and wider perspectives (Kegan, 1982). At this point the patient is likely to use his or her metacognitive skills, which have been developing in parallel to secure base, to create a coherent life narrative about him or her self and life as a whole.

In the last phase of treatment, imagery of secure intimacy with a partner is introduced. The patient is asked to imagine a hypothetical relationship in the future that has all the best ingredients of secure intimacy on a number of levels. As with the earlier IPF imagery, patient and therapist co-create a positive map for secure intimacy that will serve in the future as a reference point for intimate relationships.

The fundamental purpose of utilizing attachment-based imagery as a main component of treatment is to efficiently foster the development of a new, unified positive internal working model, or map, of secure attachment that overwrites previous negative, fragmented, or multiple IWMs or maps. As the patient more and more uses the new, secure map as his or her basis of operation in everyday life, outdated insecure maps are eclipsed, and the patient's new map is increasingly reinforced by the ongoing positive experience of his or her relational life working more satisfactorily. Overall, effective treatment of a deactivated attachment system brings it back online and normalizes a hyperactivated attachment system.

THE SECOND PILLAR: FOSTERING A RANGE OF METACOGNITIVE SKILLS

Research using the Adult Attachment Interview (AAI) has shown that a fundamental difference between secure attachment and the three main prototypes of insecure attachment is the degree of coherence of discourse and the underlying coherence of mind (Main, 1984). Insecurely attached individuals show low coherence on the Main, Goldwyn, and Hesse (2002) AAI coherence scales (scores of 1 to 3), whereas securely attached individuals show high coherence on these scales (scores of 7 to 9). The coherence scales on the AAI are strongly correlated with metacognitive capacity, or the capacity to be aware of one's own and others' mind and mental activity *as mind and mental activity*, and to apply that awareness to various mental operations. Individuals who score high on the AAI Metacognitive Processes scale are highly likely to also have high coherence of discourse and a secure attachment pattern.

An important implication of this finding was explored by Peter Fonagy, Anthony Bateman, and others in the London School. They discovered that systematically fostering metacognitive capacity through specific treatment interventions significantly contributes to the development of high coherence and earned security in patients with clinically significant attachment disturbance, such as those with personality and dissociative disorders. Based on this finding, the London group developed an entire approach to treatment based on enhancing metacognitive development, namely, mentalization-based treatment (MBT). MBT entails recognition and exploration of one's own states of mind and the states of mind of others in the context of psychotherapy and begins with fostering curiosity about the states of mind of self and others. Bateman and Fonagy (2004) define mentalization as follows:

Mentalizing in psychotherapy is a process of joint awareness in which the patient's mental states are the object of attention and optimally patient and therapist are engaged in a process of representational redescription in which implicit information in the mind subsequently becomes explicit knowledge to the mind. The therapist should reduce excessive reliance on content and be more concerned with helping the patient to generate multiple perspectives. (Bateman & Fonagy, 2004, p. 280)

Fostering mentalization in a patient with low metacognitive skill requires the therapist to consistently hold and interact with the patient from a "mentalizing stance":

A therapist needs to maintain a mentalizing stance in order to help a patient develop a capacity to mentalize. Why is the patient saying this now? Why is the patient behaving like this? Why am I feeling as I do now? What has happened recently in the therapy or in our relationship that may justify the current state? (Bateman & Fonagy, 2004, p. 203)

Mentalizing entails "exploring a mind by a mind." The cumulative effect of systematic mentalizing efforts in MBT is the development of general metacognitive or *reflective* capacity in the patient. Fonagy and his colleagues developed the Reflective Functioning Scale (RF-S; Fonagy, Target, Steele, & Steele, 1998) to assess reflective capacity as it manifests in responses to AAI questions and queries. Reflective function "refers to the psychological processes underlying the capacity to mentalize" (Fonagy et al., 1998, p. 4), and reflective functioning is their operationalization of metacognitive capacity. Its overall strength is rated on the RF-S as somewhere between −1 and 9. According to research by the London group using the RF-S, MBT significantly contributes to the development of reflective function. Through MBT, a patient becomes more aware of his or her immediate mental state; learns to accurately mark, label and understand affective states and cognitive states, such as maladaptive beliefs and schemas; becomes sensitized to the limitations of knowledge and beliefs; learns to identify states of mind antecedent to behaviors; becomes able to contextualize states of mind; and becomes able to mentalize about others' states of mind and about the transference in the therapy.

In addition to fostering metacognitive capacity, the London group suggests how the process of mentalizing through MBT can lead to the development of new positive representations for intimate relationships:

Over a long period, frequent and diverse interpretations about the patient's perception of himself, the analyst, and their analytical relationship may enable him to attempt to create a mental representation both of himself and of his analyst, as thinking and feeling, together and independently. This can then form the core sense of himself with a capacity to represent ideas and meanings, and create the basis for the bond that ultimately permits new possibilities of separation and intimacy. (Fonagy, Gergely, Jurist, & Target, 2002, p. 480)

The London group's findings that mentalization-based methods contribute to reflective capacity, to increasing coherence of mind, and ultimately to earned security are consistent with other research showing that metacognitive function is associated with coherence of mind and that both are associated with attachment security. As such, we believe that methods that aim specifically to develop metacognitive, reflective capacity are an essential component of attachment-based treatment.

A limitation of the London approach is its assumption that reflective capacity is a unitary construct, and that all types of metacognition result from a single reflective function process. In contrast, researchers from the Third Center of Cognitive Psychotherapy, Rome (e.g., Dimaggio, Semerari, Carcione, Nicolò, & Procacci, 2007; Semerari et al., 2003) have found that there are specific metacognitive deficits that are associated with specific diagnostic conditions, suggesting that there is not a common pathway for all types of metacognition. For example, according to the Rome research, patients with borderline personality disorder are generally able to identify their internal states of mind but show deficits in the following capacities: metacognitive mastery, which supports self-regulation of internal states; differentiation of internal states and external reality; and the capacity to integrate internal states. In contrast, patients with narcissistic personality disorder generally show good metacognitive mastery over states of mind but low capacity to identify states of mind in themselves and others and low capacity to relate their own and others' behavior to underlying mental states. The Metacognition Assessment Scale (MAS) is a multi-category instrument that was designed to identify particular metacognitive strengths and deficits in each patient (Semerari et al., 2003).

Based on their recognition of such differences, the Rome school developed a very different approach to treatment, what they call *modular* and what we refer to as *condition-specific*. The aim of such treatment is to identify the specific metacognitive deficits presented by patients with particular diagnoses, or conditions, and then to consistently support the development of those particular deficient metacognitive abilities, or modules.

We agree with the Rome group that there are very specific metacognitive skills that are remarkably absent in patients of specific diagnostic groups, and that targeting those condition-specific metacognitive deficits for any given patient is a necessary component to treatment. We also agree with the London group that a consistent focus on metacognition in treatment is likely to improve general reflective capacity and reflective functioning. Our approach, like that of the Rome school, begins with an assessment of which specific metacognitive abilities are most lacking in a patient. Then, we foster the development of those specific abilities while simultaneously supporting the development of general reflective capacity. We find that patients can develop a general mentalizing skill at the same time that they acquire specific metacognitive abilities that they were missing, which highlights that there is merit to both the London general-function approach and the Rome condition-specific approach. By combining both approaches, our treatment leads to coherence of discourse and mind more effectively and efficiently than either approach does alone.

Based on findings that metacognitive development significantly contributes to coherence of discourse and mind *and* the development of earned security, we believe that fostering metacognitive skills in treatment is rightly a main component of the overall treatment of adult attachment disturbance. However, our assumptions and methods for developing metacognitive capacity go beyond both the London and Rome approaches. Neither of those approaches integrates the considerable research on adult post-formal-operational cognitive development, and so their range of potential metacognitive functioning is limited. Research on mature adult cognitive development shows that there is much more to metacognition than the formal operational first- and second-order representational mapping that is the focus of both groups' methods. In the model of cognitive development that is the basis of our metacognitive interventions, there are 12 stages, the fifth being formal operational thinking and Stages 6 to 12 being post-formal stages (Wilber, 2007). Therefore, our approach can identify and promote a much larger range of metacognitive skills, including those that are representative of higher levels of cognitive development. We have found that fostering the development of these more advanced metacognitive skills greatly contributes to overall mental health.

Higher-level post-formal cognitive development includes the capacity to conceptually grasp and operate on increasingly complex relationships: between all elements within a system, between one system and another in a supersystemic relationship, between groups of systems, and between systems and wider perspectives (Commons, Richards, & Armon, 1984). Inherent in the components of the Reflective Functioning Scale are several assumptions about knowledge that are operative only at less-developed (and admittedly more prevalent) levels of cognitive functioning. One is that all knowledge is relative and can be understood as such; however, because a supersystem perspective transcends relativism, this assumption breaks down at more-developed cognitive levels. Another is that knowledge is limited to representational knowledge; however, at the more mature stages of adult cognitive development, knowledge acquired through direct awareness supersedes knowledge acquired through representation. While what the RF-S identifies within its range and what the Rome school discerns with its

MAS are valid and will be suitable for most people assessed, neither reflects the potentials for metacognitive functioning that are indicative of the higher levels of cognitive development and of the greatest capacities for well-being.

From our expanded model of cognitive development, there are a wide range of metacognitive skills that we consider relevant to attachment-based psychotherapy. We work to strengthen overall mentalizing capacity and skills that are already present in a patient's functioning and also to promote the development and operational emergence of skills that are beyond those present when he or she came to treatment. Bringing together the metacognitive skills identified by the London and Rome groups as well as skills that are more advanced, we work from a full set of metacognitive potentials that we divide into three categories: basic, intermediate, and advanced.

Basic metacognitive skills

1. Awareness of the state of mind of self or other
2. Monitoring the accuracy of state of mind
3. Awareness of one's own influence on the other's state or behavior, and vice versa
4. Becoming aware of one's state of mind in such a way that it has a regulatory effect on that state
5. Awareness of one's own or another's action plans and goal-directedness
6. Meaning-making

Intermediate metacognitive skills

1. Recognition of how the past shapes one's experience
2. Appreciating the relativity of states of mind
3. Seeing beyond information given, more deeply into underlying assumptions and expectancies related to the information
4. Optimizing action plans in the face of accurate awareness of limitations
5. Fostering sensitivity to contextual effects on behavior
6. Perspective-taking, or the ability to consider something from another's point of view

Advanced metacognitive skills

1. Taking a wider, supersystemic perspective
2. Developing metacognitive awareness of past/present, self/other, or child/adult orientations
3. Awareness of the degree of organization or coherence of one's mind
4. Recognition of interdependence

5. Articulating ultimate concerns
6. Direct, nonrepresentational awareness of a wider reality
7. Highest-order metacognitive skills such as spacious freedom and wisdom

A fundamental assumption underlying our approach is that when treatment increases the patient's facility with overall mentalizing and a wide range of specific metacognitive skills, including those in the intermediate and advanced categories, he or she enjoys greater overall mental health and well-being. Although achievement of earned security and high coherence of discourse and mind on the AAI are important and measurable goals of the treatment of patients with personality and dissociative disorders, we also see great value in patients' advancement to and stabilization of higher levels of adult cognitive development through our metacognitively based treatment. Fostering the widest possible range of metacognitive skills is the second pillar of our comprehensive approach to treating attachment disturbance.

THE THIRD PILLAR: FOSTERING COLLABORATIVE NONVERBAL AND VERBAL BEHAVIOR

Gilbert (1989) and Tomasello (2009) have shown that the human species, as compared to primates, is uniquely cooperative and collaborative in three respects: in cooperative shared behavior, in nonverbal communication, and in verbal communication. Beebe and her associates, through microanalysis of video-recordings of infant–caregiver interactions, have shown that in securely attached children, nonverbal communication is highly collaborative even at a very young age (Beebe & Lachmann, 2014). Likewise, Tomasello has demonstrated that infants are inherently collaborative (2010). However, the considerable research showing collaborativeness between infants and caregivers has been done in the context of "good-enough" caregiving. Infants in a secure attachment caregiving system are likely to manifest behavioral, nonverbal, and verbal collaborativeness as a natural, innate expression of healthy, unimpeded development.

In contrast, infants in insecure attachment systems deactivate their natural tendencies toward collaborativeness in the face of caregiving inadequacies, such as unresponsiveness, inconsistency, overinvolvement, rejection, mismatches to contingent behaviors, and parental frightening or frightened behaviors. When such conditions are frequent and extreme enough, the child's behavioral, nonverbal, and verbal collaborativeness shuts down in relation to the attachment figures, and sometimes also in relation to shared interests with peers.

The effects of deactivation of collaborativeness are apparent in patients with insecure attachment, and especially in patients who have personality and dissociative disorders or psychotic disorders. For such patients, fostering a collaborative partnership is a main focus—the third pillar—of our attachment-based treatment. We have been strongly influenced by the pioneering work of Giovanni Liotti, who emphasizes that promoting "a collaborative state of mind" (2005) is a main goal of the overall treatment. Fostering collaborativeness is partly a function of the therapist's stance, an overarching perspective that guides the therapist's attention and intervention. In our approach, attachment-based therapists take the consistent stance that psychotherapy is a mutually regulated process of collaboration. From this stance and general goal, we also work to promote the manifestation of collaborativeness in therapy in the three specific domains relevant to the research on infant–caregiver interaction: behavior, particularly treatment-frame behavior; nonverbal communication; and verbal communication.

Specific therapeutic interventions and techniques are relevant to each of these areas. Regarding behavior, at the onset of treatment the therapist engages the patient in developing a collaboratively established, mutually agreed-upon treatment frame—a clear understanding of what is expected from both the patient and therapist during the course of therapy. Throughout the treatment, when the patient behaves in any way that goes against the treatment frame or interferes with the therapy, such as repeatedly missing or coming late to sessions or failing to pay fees, the therapist immediately and explicitly confronts the patient about this behavior as noncollaborative. The therapist also directly acknowledges his or her own ruptures to the treatment frame and any of his or her behaviors that interfere with therapy, such as missing or coming late to sessions or not giving sufficient notice about upcoming vacations. Direct engagement and discussion about such behaviors, whether they originate in the patient or in the therapist, highlights the importance of maintaining shared, collaborative responsibility and is in itself a collaborative process.

In insecure patients with personality disorders or severe disturbances such as psychoses or major dissociative disorders, it is likely that collaborative nonverbal behavior will be quite limited. Such patients can easily fail to establish a nonverbal expression of secure base in therapy, and the therapist's ongoing nonverbal responses to the patient are thereby filled with mismatches. In our approach, the therapist begins with careful observation and identification of the main patterns of mismatching and poor nonverbal communication between patient and therapist by paying attention to chair position, posture, head orientation, gaze, eye contact, facial affective display, self-touch, postural gestures, breathing patterns, and vocal rhythm, tone, and pitch. The therapist strives to increase nonverbal matching in these areas, and where the patient's nonverbal communication is most dysfunctional (e.g., never making eye contact), the therapist verbally brings the patient's attention to the pattern. Such pointing out enhances the patient's metacognitive awareness, both of the impaired nonverbal pattern of communication and of its antecedent states of mind (e.g., specific emotions, or underlying maladaptive schemas or negative self-talk). These methods will support the emergence of healthy patterns of nonverbal collaborativeness between patient and therapist, much as the mutually regulated collaborative nonverbal exchange gives rise to the implicit relational knowing (Stern, 1985) between infant and caregiver that Beebe and Lachmann (2014) describe in their work.

Our approach to understanding and working with verbal collaborativeness has been strongly influenced by Mary Main's work using the AAI. Poor verbal collaborativeness in adults with different types of insecure attachment often manifests through significant deviation from one or more of Grice's maxims of coherent, cooperative discourse (Grice, 1975). Insecure preoccupied adults frequently make irrelevant comments, wander off topic, lose track of the point, and use passive, vague, or jargon expressions in ways that make their verbal communications difficult to follow. Insecure dismissing adults do not express important points in sufficient detail and depth. In therapy, when patterns of noncollaborative verbal behavior appear, the therapist points these out to the patient and highlights that they limit the shared goal of mutual understanding and communication and explores their antecedent states of mind. Ultimately, the patient develops better metacognitive awareness of these patterns and their precipitants and thereby becomes better able to recognize them and replace them with more collaborative verbalization. The overall outcome is more consistently collaborative dialogue based on coherent, cooperative verbal expression throughout treatment and, more broadly, enhancement of collaborative verbalization capacity and behavior outside of therapy.

The Interdependence of the Three Pillars of Treatment

Like the process of negotiating the treatment frame and monitoring the treatment-frame behavior of both the patient and therapist, our methods for fostering nonverbal and verbal collaborativeness are inherently collaborative. As noted above, these latter methods also increase the patient's metacognitive awareness of his or her collaborative patterns. The beneficial effect that working on collaborativeness has on the patient's metacognitive development suggests that these dimensions are interrelated and can be mutually enhancing. We agree with Bowlby's (1969/1982) suggestion that the attachment system and the peer-collaborative behavioral system are independent systems, but we also consider those systems and the metacognitive system to be *interdependent*: In treatment, the process of engaging with each system activates and strengthens the other two systems. The six particular interrelationships are as follows:

1. ATTACHMENT IMAGERY PROMOTES METACOGNITIVE DEVELOPMENT

Engagement with ideal parent figure imagery promotes the development of various forms of metacognitive capacity. For example, a therapist asks a patient to imagine an ideal parent figure who is well attuned to the patient-as-child in such a way that the parent figure is accurately aware of the state of mind of the child. In this way, the ideal parent figure imagery highlights metacognitive awareness in the child's state of mind. Further, if the patient imagines himself or herself as a young child at a time when he or she was so emotionally upset as to evoke a temporarily disorganized state of mind, and then imagines a responsive ideal parent figure who, through a soothing approach, helps the child to affectively regulate the state of mind so that it becomes more organized, the patient is representing healthy attachment, building metacognitive awareness, and experiencing that awareness in a way that shifts the disorganized state of mind to an organized state of mind (i.e., metacognitive mastery).

2. METACOGNITIVE DEVELOPMENT PROMOTES ATTACHMENT

We teach our patients to be aware of their states of mind and their deactivation (dismissing) or hyperactivation (anxious-preoccupied) attachment patterns within the therapy relationship. We also make available and model our awareness of our own metacognitions about the therapy relationship, which gives the patient windows into the states of mind of the therapist. In the patient's engagement with attachment imagery, he or she experiences and comes to contextualize the strengths and limitations of attachment figures. Each of these metacognitively focused elements of treatment contributes to the development of secure attachment by supporting accurate and realistic internal representations of the therapist and of attachment figures as attentive, interested, and helpful.

3. COLLABORATIVENESS PROMOTES METACOGNITIVE DEVELOPMENT

The therapist states explicitly that the development of metacognitive skills is a collaborative goal of the therapy. For example, he or she might say, "A goal of our work together is that you become more aware of your thoughts and of the way your mind works; we'll see together that you can become more in charge of your inner experience and be more organized and clear in your states of mind and feelings." Developing a range of metacognitive skills becomes a mutually shared task of treatment to which both the therapist and patient contribute. The therapist's continued emphasis on collaboration and the patient's experience of two different minds working together contributes to the patient's metacognitive understanding of multiple perspectives.

4. METACOGNITIVE DEVELOPMENT PROMOTES COLLABORATIVENESS

By calling the patient's attention to noncollaborative treatment-frame behavior and noncollaborative nonverbal and verbal behaviors, the therapist promotes the patient's metacognitive capacity to serve the purpose of developing greater collaborativeness throughout treatment. When a patient is aware of the treatment-frame expectations, he or she can hold those expectations in mind in a way that promotes treatment collaboration and reduces disruptions in that collaboration. Similarly, when a therapist enhances the patient's awareness of noncollaborative nonverbal and verbal behavior, the patient is more likely to develop greater collaborative behavior in these domains. For example, a therapist might say, "You may not be aware of it, but you rarely make eye contact with me, and you often talk in a tone so soft that I can't hear what you're saying; probably others would have trouble hearing you too" or "You know, often when we talk, you go off topic a lot, and I also have the experience that there's not much space for me to respond to you." Presentation and discussion about these behaviors promotes the patient's metacognitive awareness of them and increases the likelihood of more collaborative behavior.

5. COLLABORATIVENESS PROMOTES ATTACHMENT

The patient's experience of a mutually respectful, collaborative relationship that focuses on support for his or her well-being promotes the development of a positive, healthy IWM or attachment map. Such experience occurs in the therapy relationship and also in the Ideal Parent Figure protocol, which is conducted in the context of the therapy relationship. Consequently, positive attachment representations are promoted by the collaborative therapy relationship, by the collaborative relationship with ideal parent figures in imagery, and by the collaborative process of engaging with ideal parent figures in the context of the therapy relationship. It is not uncommon for a patient to have resistance or difficulty early during the IPF process. When this happens, the therapist encourages the patient to stay with it, highlights the value of doing so, and works together with the patient to honor his or her difficulty and to find ways into the imagery experience. This collaborative stance of the therapist and the specific shared-goal efforts to resolve the difficulty help the patient to create ideal parent figure imagery that efficiently builds positive attachment representations.

Another example of how collaboration enhances attachment is the stance that the therapist takes when there is a rupture in the therapeutic alliance and the patient pulls back from the therapy or therapist. Liotti (2005) notes that it is very difficult to repair a rupture to the attachment relationship with the therapist from within the attachment relationship itself, because the patient temporarily loses a felt sense of safety and security in the therapy relationship. At those times, the therapist deliberately shifts focus from the attachment behavioral system to engage the collaborative behavioral system. For example, the therapist might say, "I know you're feeling awful and you don't want to be here anymore, but let's work on that as a team; let's both look at what happened and we can both figure out what happened together." As a collaborative team, both therapist and patient work cooperatively to understand what created the rupture and what will help to repair it. This collaborative intervention is itself part of the repair, and as the rupture is repaired, the attachment system is reengaged and enhanced.

6. ATTACHMENT IMAGERY PROMOTES COLLABORATIVENESS

As patients develop their positive attachment imagery in the Ideal Parent Figure protocol, they increasingly experience the attachment figures as attuned and responsive to their states of mind and needs. Repeated cycles of the parent figures recognizing, matching, and effectively responding to the child, followed by the child responding to the parents' responses, builds an experience of the relationship as mutually collaborative. Any imagined interactive play or shared-goal-directed behavior promotes the collaborative experience even more. These varied experiences of collaboration in the IPF relationships result in enhancement of overall collaborativeness and in the addition of collaborative elements to the newly developing, positive internal working model of attachment.

The Benefits of Three Pillars Treatment

We have found that actively including all three pillars in treatment—repeated engagement with ideal parent figure imagery, promoting a wide range of metacognitive skills, and fostering behavioral, nonverbal, and verbal collaborativeness—effectively and efficiently yields outcomes that are beneficial to patients with attachment disturbances. These outcomes include:

- formation of new, positive stable internal working models for healthy adult attachment
- manifestation of a range of metacognitive skills, including higher-order metacognitive skills utilized in everyday life
- achievement of some level of post-formal cognitive development
- manifestation of healthy behavioral, nonverbal, and verbal collaborative behaviors
- achievement of high coherence of discourse and mind on the AAI
- no longer meeting diagnostic criteria for a personality or dissociative disorder
- achievement of earned secure attachment
- capacity for secure intimacy in adulthood

These are the primary indicators of successful attachment-based treatment. In the next three chapters, we present each of the three pillars in more detail and show how to apply them toward establishing such success.

CHAPTER 8

The First Pillar

The Ideal Parent Figure Protocol

Overview: Positive Remapping

Using the Ideal Parent Figure (IPF) protocol, a therapist specifically, actively, and efficiently facilitates the development of a positive, stable inner working model, or map, of attachment relationships. The method is an imagery-based tool for remapping the terrain of attachment representations from insecure to secure. The therapist helps the patient to evoke and engage with imagery of positive attachment figures and of secure attachment experience with those figures, and repetition and elaboration of contact with this imagery establishes a new internal model, or map, of secure attachment.

As with any tool, skillful use yields better results, and every tool is used at least slightly differently depending on the particularities of the task. Each patient, while presenting common patterns specific to his or her insecure attachment subtype, also has unique patterns and needs. Skillful use of the IPF method emerges spontaneously from (1) familiarity with the tool, (2) recognizing the unique patterns and needs of the patient, and (3) understanding the caretaking qualities that promote secure attachment.

The IPF method differs from traditional attachment-based treatments in that the primary agent of change is the patient's relationship with his or her imagined attachment figures rather than the relationship with the therapist. However, the method is applied in the context of the therapeutic relationship, and the therapist's understanding and embodiment, in the relationship and in the application of the IPF protocol, of qualities that promote secure attachment will enhance the effectiveness of the imagery process.

The qualities that promote secure attachment are common to good psychotherapeutic relationships. The "general factors" are the minimum standards that a therapist must provide for any good therapy: *physical presence, reliability, con-*

sistency, and *interest* in the patient. Upon the foundation of the general factors, good therapy process often calls for the therapist's facility with the behavioral components of the five primary conditions that promote secure attachment, detailed in Chapter 7: providing *protection* when the patient is at risk in or out of the therapy session; applying interventions according to accurate *attunement* to the patient's behavior, state, and developmental level; being *soothing* and *reassuring* (in an attuned way) when the patient is affectively distressed; *expressing delight* or positive regard; and providing *support for inner and outer exploration*.

In working with the patient during the IPF protocol, the therapist is *present*, *reliable*, *consistent*, and *interested* in the patient's experience. He or she is also watchful for the need to *protect* the patient should any turmoil arise; is *attuned* to the moment-to-moment experience of the patient and adjusts the guiding of the protocol accordingly; guides the process and meets the patient's experience in a *soothing* and *reassuring* manner; *expresses delight*, through content and tone, in the patient's positive experiences with the imagined attachment figures; and embodies through the method itself *support for inner and outer exploration*.

Consistent with traditional attachment-based treatments (and with the other components of our comprehensive treatment model), the therapist's awareness and understanding of the qualities that promote secure attachment are valuable for guiding his or her ways of being with the patient. A great strength of the IPF method is that it builds upon this relational foundation by incorporating attachment-promoting qualities into the *content* of the work. In the context of the therapist's embodiment of these qualities, he or she facilitates their appearance in the patient's ideal parent figure imagery.

Throughout the IPF protocol, the therapist recognizes, mirrors, and enhances the qualities that promote secure attachment as they appear in the patient's imagery. For example, if a patient says about the imagined parents, "They help me to feel safe, that nothing bad will happen to me," the therapist might respond, "Yes. They are really there for you, to *protect* you from any harm." In this interchange, the therapist is *attuned* to the patient's experience of the parent figures as protective and mirrors and enhances the experience of that specific quality.

In another interchange, the patient describes being emotionally upset and says about the imagined mother figure, "She sees that I'm sad and she comes to me and hugs me." The therapist then mirrors and enhances the patient's felt experience of the mother's *attunement* to his state and of her *soothing* gesture:

> Really feel what that's like, that she's so tuned in to how you're feeling, and to what you feel as you feel her hugging you now.

Later in the protocol, the therapist draws from knowledge of the patient's unique attachment history to suggest specific attachment-promoting qualities if they do not appear spontaneously in the patient's imagery.

As is clear from above, practice of the Ideal Parent Figure protocol incorporates the principle of the therapist's stance as a good attachment figure. But from that interpersonal ground, it goes further by using specific methods that selectively and more efficiently develop and enhance the structural foundations of secure attachment. The remainder of this chapter presents, explains, and provides examples of the Ideal Parent Figure process. Of particular note is that this process neither offers nor condones preestablished scripts. It is most effective when the therapist's thorough understanding of the underlying principles leads to fresh expression and response during each session with each particular patient. Exemplars given in the sections below are not to be taken literally, but rather are offered as suggestions based on the purposes and goals of each component of the protocol.

The Foundational Protocol

SETTING THE THERAPEUTIC GROUND

Focus awareness inward. The therapist begins the IPF protocol by helping the patient to establish a calm, relaxed, inwardly focused state of awareness. Such a state increases the likelihood of greater vividness of imagery and decreases the interference of distractions. Ideally, attention is brought to the body, and a positive body feeling and focus is established. During the critical period of attachment formation, 12 to 20 months, identity is primarily body-based and memory is behavioral/enacted rather than mental/narrative. Thus, enhancing the patient's engagement with his or her immediate body experience establishes the most fertile ground for the evoked ideal parent imagery to take root as a new attachment representation. An example of how this state might be established is as follows:

> Take a few moments to settle comfortably into your chair [sofa], letting yourself move or shift or adjust the body in any way that supports your growing sense of comfort. That's right, whatever helps you feel more at ease, more relaxed, more at rest. And as you bring your attention even more to the felt sense of the body, notice that you don't have to make any effort at all to be supported there by the chair. You can let the chair do all the work. Notice how, as the muscles of the body realize that they don't have to make any effort to support the body, the muscles relax even more, let go even more, and you can feel even more at ease and relaxed.

It is often beneficial to go further and deeper from here. The decision about how much of this preliminary to provide should be based on the therapist's assessment of each patient's state and attachment status. For example, anxious-preoccupied patients, who tend to focus on others' experience more than on their own, and any patient who is agitated or distracted, will likely benefit from additional guidance toward self-focused, relaxed body awareness. Patients who are highly dissociative, such as patients with DID, who most often have disorganized attachment, will likely enter the preparatory state with little prompting.

Readers familiar with hypnosis will notice that the target state is quite similar to a hypnotic trance, which may be described as a calm, relaxed, inwardly focused state of attention. Therapists who have training in hypnosis may choose to deepen the ground state by applying body-focused hypnotic methods. But any guided focusing on calming, relaxing, and on body experience, such as progressive muscle relaxation, will be effective as a preliminary for the imagery work.

Deepen the inwardly focused state. For additional deepening, we like the simplicity and efficiency of a method originally formulated by Charcot (1886):

> And now, each time you inhale, let the eyes open fully, and each time you exhale, let the eyes fully and gently close. And as you do that, give close attention to the sensations, the sensations and feelings of the movements of the eyes and the movements of the breath. That's right, just like that.

The therapist continues to make supportive, focusing comments, watching closely and matching verbalizations to where the patient is in the cycle of eye movements and breath:

> Inhaling, opening the eyes . . . and exhaling, closing the eyes. Good. Just like that.

When the patient has settled into the pattern and shows signs of calming, the therapist enhances the focus on the calming and relaxation. In all "suggested phrasings" and clinical examples to follow, italicization indicates the therapist's vocal emphasis, which is explained in the section "Bring Attention to Experience and Amplify Positive States" below.

> And now, become *even more* aware of the exhalations. Each time you exhale, let the release of the breath bring a release of any tension, tightness, or stress that you'd like to let go of. *Really feel* the release, the letting go. Notice how each time you exhale, you can feel *even more* calm, *even more* relaxed, *even more* at ease . . .
>
> And soon it will feel natural to let the eyes remain closed, both on the exhalation and on the inhalation too. When it feels natural to let the eyes remain closed, they can remain closed, and you can become *even more* aware of the exhalations. *Even more* aware of the calming, the relaxing, the letting go that gets even more clear with each exhalation. And any tension, tightness,

or stress that you'd like to release just rides out on the exhaled breath, and drifts farther and farther away from you, harmlessly into the atmosphere.

As you become *even more* relaxed, more at ease, you've probably noticed that the breath gets a little longer, a little slower, all by itself, without any effort to make it so. And you might notice the space, the space at the end of each exhalation, before the beginning of the next inhalation. Even though this space is only a few moments in time, notice how still and quiet it can be. And you can relax *even more*, as you notice that stillness and quiet.

A final step for enhancing a positive body state and focus is a brief body scan:

And now, you can let the breath fade into the background of awareness. I'd like you now to look through the body, and find where in the body is the place that is *most* comfortable, *most* relaxed, *most* at ease. Look all through the body, and when you find the place that is *most* comfortable, *most* relaxed, *most* at ease, you can let me know where that is.

The patient indicates, verbally or by pointing, for example, the shoulders:

Yes. Really focus on the feeling in the shoulders. And notice what's there that lets you know how *very comfortable*, how *very relaxed*, how *very at ease* the shoulders are. And the *more* you're aware of that comfortable, relaxed feeling, the *stronger* and *clearer* it becomes. And soon that feeling will begin to spread, spread beyond the shoulders, bringing that *comfortable* and *relaxed* feeling beyond the shoulders to everywhere in the body. Notice how it's spreading now. Yes, that's right. *More and more* comfortable, *more and more* relaxed.

It bears emphasizing that the above method is simply an illustration of how a patient might be prepared for the subsequent ideal parent figure imagery. As long as the therapist understands the principle behind this preparatory phase, he or she is free to choose how much or how little of which method will best serve a particular patient.

FACILITATING THE CREATION OF IDEAL PARENT FIGURE IMAGERY

New, healthy, positive attachment representations will form from the patient's engagement with self-generated, affect-rich imagery of being a child in the presence of positive attachment figures behaving in ways that promote secure attachment. Care is taken to set up the conditions to best evoke such imagery. The therapist is flexible and aligns the process to the individual patient, but the wording for setting up the imagery frame can be more consistent across patients than is the subsequent work within that frame.

Evoke experience of a child-self state. The first step is to orient the patient's imagination to childhood.

> And now we're going to take a journey back, a journey back in time, a journey back in time to when you were a young child. So imagine now, going back in time, back to when you were a young child. You can begin to imagine yourself as a young child, and more and more feel yourself as a young child. More than just seeing yourself as a young child, more and more now you will actually feel yourself as a young child.

The therapist asks the patient to indicate when the child experience has been evoked. Such indication is valuable information for proceeding, and also highlights, ratifies, and deepens the experience for the patient.

> And when you are *feeling yourself* as a *young child*, you can let me know with a slight nod of the head.

Prompt for ideal parent figure imagery. When the patient nods, the imagination is invited to create ideal parent figures.

> Now, as a young child, imagine being with parents, but *not* the parents you grew up with in your family. Imagine now being with a *different* set of parents, parents who are *ideally suited* to *you* and to *your* nature. These parents are *right there* with you and *really know* how to be with you to help you feel so *safe* and *secure*. These parents *really know* how to be with you in *all the ways* that help you to feel *absolutely secure* in relationship with them.
>
> If you'd like, you can incorporate positive aspects from experiences you've had, but imagine ideal *fictional* parents, created entirely by your imagination, because you can change the imagination and keep changing it until you have it *just right*, with these parents having *all the qualities* that help you to feel *so safe* and *so secure* in relationship with them.
>
> These parents *really know* how to be with you, in all the ways that you most need. Notice the ways that they're being with you. Notice how you *feel* as they're with you in *all the ways* that you *most need* and in *all the ways* that are *so very right* for *you* and *your* well-being.

It is important that the therapist uses the word "imagine" rather than "visualize." When a patient is asked to *imagine*, he or she is free to draw from any or all sense modalities, whereas being asked to *visualize* limits what can be incorporated into the creation of the ideal parents. Many patients will spontaneously generate visual images, but using "imagine" in the guiding phrasing respects that for some people, the visual is not the primary imaginative domain.

And the more you imagine the details of being with these parents now, the more the *feelings* of security will become clearer and more and more vivid. You can *really feel* it, how that feels. And if there's anything you want to change about the ways that they're being with you, that might contribute to you feeling even *more* safe, even *more* comfortable, even *more* secure with them, with your imagination you can change what's happening in *any ways* you'd like. You can change anything about them or about being with them so that it feels *even more right* and beneficial for you now.

Inquire about the patient's imagery. The therapist then asks the patient to describe the experience of the ideal parents. This inquiry provides information about the patient's experience of the method and whether any modifications to the initial imagery are needed before proceeding.

As these parents become more and more clear to you, perhaps you wouldn't mind describing these parents and about the ways they're being with you. You can let the words to describe them and your experience of them just spontaneously arise, and as you speak, the sense of being with these parents can get *even more* clear and vivid.

Assess the adequacy of the patient's initial parent figure imagery. The patient's initial report about the imagery lets the therapist know how to proceed. Ideally, the patient would describe a multisensory experience of two parent figures who are not the patient's actual parents or people known to him or her and would describe these parent figures behaving in at least some attachment-promoting ways. As illustrated and described in the section below, "Principles and Practices for Framing and Responding to Patients' Experiences," the therapist would then respond by mirroring and enhancing the presence of the parent figures and their beneficial ways of being. However, because the presence of an attachment disorder indicates the absence of a positive internal working model or map of attachment, it is common for this ideal initial imagery scenario not to occur. If not ideal, *adequate* initial imagery would include:

1. At least one parent figure who is not one of the patient's actual parents or someone known to him or her
2. Contact with the parent figure(s) through some sensory modality (e.g., "I see them nearby"; "I don't really see them, but I feel that they're there"; "I hear the mother singing softly to me")
3. The absence of any overtly harmful frightening behaviors by the parent(s), such as yelling, criticizing, or ignoring

The patient may or may not at this point describe the parent or parents as engaging in specific attachment-promoting ways of being, but as long as there is some sense of their presence and there are no negative ways of being or behaviors reported, the work can proceed.

The more severe the attachment disorder is, the more likely it will be that the patient's initial imagery will require additional prompting and/or correction to establish at least adequate imagery. If no parent figures are imagined, or if they are vague and unclear, then more focus is placed on evoking the imagery by using phrases consistent with the initial framing and by encouraging the creativity of imagination and the possibility of experiencing ideal parent figures who are with the patient in ways that promote a sense of security. If the patient indicates that the images are of his or her actual parents, other relatives, or other people who the patient knows or has known, or if the parent figures exhibit harmful ways of being, the therapist provides guidance for letting go of these images and returning to the therapeutic task of creating fictional, ideal parent figures. Specific ways of providing that guidance, and of responding to the absence or inappropriateness of initial parent imagery, are described in the section below on common challenges (pp. 358–371).

A working assumption, validated by theory and by the authors' experience, is that every patient will initially or eventually create personalized imagery of parent figures behaving in ways that promote secure attachment in that patient. When the attachment system, present in every person regardless of how deactivated it might be, is activated by the therapeutic frame and the IPF method, positive attachment imagery emerges spontaneously from the innate sense of what is needed for the development of healthy, secure attachment.

CLINICAL VIGNETTES

Below are excerpts from clinical sessions with several different patients. These vignettes provide an illustrative introduction to some ways that adequate or better ideal parent figure imagery may manifest during early IPF sessions as well as to how a therapist might respond to support and enhance the imagery and the positive remapping process. Commentary about specific elements of each vignette is provided.

> *Patient:* They're very kind, and attentive. I really feel they're taking notice of me, which makes me feel cared for, and loved.
> *Therapist:* Notice what it is about their way of being with you that makes that *so clear* to you.
> *Patient:* Well, they're close by, and I notice that they're looking at me, and sometimes they're reaching out to me.
> *Therapist:* And you can be aware of how that affects you, how that affects your inner state.
> *Patient:* Well, I think I feel very calm, instead of worried. Because I know they're not going anywhere.
> *Therapist:* Yes, these parents *are fully with you* now, and you can feel

secure in their presence. They set aside their own concerns and issues, to *really be there* for you and for your needs as a child. They see your uniqueness, and they take you seriously. They want to be the best possible parents for you. Notice what happens.

Patient: I notice that I'm hugging them, and they're responding when I'm hugging them. They're just playing around and we're having fun together.

Commentary. This session was the third IPF session with the patient, who had disorganized attachment and unresolved trauma. Notice that already she was experiencing positive inner states in response to the imagined parents' ways of being with her. The therapist reinforced that experience by pointing her attention to the parents' ways of being, and after she responded with additional detail, the therapist pointed her attention again to her inner experience resulting from the positive parental ways.

It is very important to reinforce focus on the imagined parents' *ways of being* rather than on what they are *doing*. As noted in Chapter 2, positive qualities of being are much more important for attachment security than actions that the parents may take, even beneficial caretaking actions such as providing meals and reading bedtime stories. Such caretaking actions will promote security if they are done in the context of ways of being that communicate some combination of the five behavioral pillars for promoting secure attachment: protection, attunement, soothing, expressed delight, and support for self-development.

The patient noted the *proximity* of the parents ("they're close by") and indicated a sense of security about their presence ("because I know they're not going anywhere"). The therapist knew that the patient experienced her actual parents as preoccupied with their own issues and as uninterested in her or in being with her, and so the response emphasized the felt security of the imagined parents' presence and their ability to set aside their own issues and concerns to focus with interest on her and on good parenting. The beneficial effect of this intervention was proximity-seeking ("I'm hugging them") and experiencing the parents as responsive to her and playful in their manner, which brought a sense of "having fun together."

The fifth session with this patient included the following interchange:

Patient: Being with them feels very comforting, because of her demeanor. She's very caring, and nurturing. She's very caring and concerned about me. And he has a lot of energy, and a sense of humor.

Therapist: Notice what it is about her that lets you know how *caring* and *nurturing* she is.

Patient: She's pretty affectionate. Also, I can't hear exactly what she's saying, but she's asking me about my experience.

Therapist: Yes, she's *so very interested* in your experience, in you. And you can notice what that's like for you, that she's *so very interested* in you.
Patient: Well, I think I feel a lot of happiness inside. I don't feel tired or run-down, so I feel a kind of energy.
Therapist: Yes, *really feel* that happiness inside, *your own* happiness and the good energy that comes too. *Really feel it* in your body. And you can be really aware of how these parents are supporting you and your good feelings.
Patient: They're just very interactive. I'm running all around my backyard, and they're running around with me. And they're happy to be with me.
Therapist: Yes, they're *so happy* to be with you. And you can really take in what that says about you, that they're *so very happy* to be with you.

Commentary. Again, the therapist places focus on the qualities of being of the parents. "Notice what it is about her" is very different from "Notice what she does" in regard to the patient's experience of the mother as caring and nurturing. The patient's response can be interpreted as indicating her positive *felt sense* of the mother, as she describes her as "pretty affectionate" without mentioning any specific behaviors; further, the patient "can't hear exactly what she's saying, but she's asking me about my experience." The therapist reinforces this inquiry as a quality of the mother's being rather than focusing on the action itself by highlighting the mother's interest in her.

The therapist points to the patient's experience of the mother being interested in her and "marks" the positive experience by emphasizing the feeling, emphasizing that *it is hers*, and pointing her attention to how she feels it in her body. Because of the primacy of the body for identity and memory during the critical period for attachment formation, anchoring the emerging positive states in the felt experience of the body increases the likelihood that the positive states will be associated with the new attachment representations.

The last comment by the therapist mirrors the patient's positive experience of the parents and indirectly suggests that she can integrate that in support of her self-esteem.

As noted in the commentaries about the above two vignettes, the therapist's language oriented the patient's focus to the parent figures' *ways of being* rather than on what they were *doing*. Although in these sessions the patient did not describe any "doing-for," or *instrumental*, behaviors by the parents, it is quite common for patients to report parent figures engaging in such caretaking actions, which we describe as *instrumental love*.

The interchange below is an example of this kind of report and shows how the therapist both validated the positive caretaking action by the parent figure and refocused the patient's attention to the more important quality *from which the caretaking action was done*.

Patient: My mom helps me clean up my room, so it looks nice. She makes me something to eat, because I'm hungry.

Therapist: Yes, she's happy to do things *with you* and *for you*, and you can see from how she looks at you that she *cherishes* you whether she's doing something for you or not.

Commentary. The guiding principle is that although instrumental or caretaking behaviors are not in themselves problematic, they can be done with or without the parental qualities of being that promote attachment security. Whenever these behaviors are present in a patient's imagery, the therapist acknowledges and validates them and shapes the imagery so that the parent figures show a positive quality of being toward the patient.

The next vignette is from the first IPF session with the patient from the above example.

Patient: It's hard . . . I keep trying to make them different. I imagine something on the wall that's soft, like fur, and they like that and they show it to me. Maybe they pat it, and help me to pat it. And we look out the window, out to the backyard.

Therapist: You can make these parents just the way you'd like them to be. Deep down you know what you most need, and these parents have all those qualities that make you feel *so very secure* and *so very loved* for *who you are*. They wonder what you'll be interested in, and they like to help you find things that you'll enjoy.

Patient: They take me downstairs, and we just sit.

Therapist: Yes, you can just sit together without having to do anything in particular. Just by their way of being with you, these parents show you how much they *cherish* you, how *interested* and *attuned* they are to what *you* like, and to what *you* need.

Patient: I think they're just being reassuring . . . telling me "It's OK to be like that; you don't have to be different." They're not mad at me.

Therapist: These parents are *completely accepting* of who you are.

Patient: They understand.

Therapist: Notice what happens to your state of mind.

Patient: I feel more hopeful. That things will get better. It makes me feel a little encouraged.

Therapist: Yes. *Hopeful* and *encouraged*. And secure in feeling and knowing of their *acceptance* and *support*.

Patient: I'm not really sure I can trust them.

Therapist: They see that you're not really sure, and they understand that. They're very patient, knowing that as you're with them more and more, you'll get to see that they're there to *protect* you and to be *attuned* to you and your needs, and you'll see from your own experience how you'll choose to trust them.

Commentary. The first task of the therapist in this session was to help the patient to establish images of ideal parent figures. Her initial report indicated that it was taking some effort, but also that the patient was actively engaged toward the goal of creating this imagery ("It's hard . . . I keep trying to make them different"). It is quite common for the IPF imagery in the first several sessions to require more effort and to be less clear and vivid and detailed than during later sessions. Patients with insecure attachment have a deactivated attachment system, and in general, the stronger the deviation from balanced activation is, the harder it will be at first to establish clear and balanced imagery of parent figures with attachment-promoting ways of being.

As this patient was already collaborating with the therapist by applying effort toward the shared goal, the therapist provided simple support by expressing belief in the patient's ability to create the imagery: "You can make these parents just the way you'd like them to be." This phrase also reinforced that what the patient wanted was important and affirmed that at some level the patient knew how she would like the parents to be. The therapist's next phrase—"Deep down you know what you most need, and these parents have all those qualities that make you feel *so very secure* and *so very loved* for *who you are*" – explicitly points to that knowledge.

This patient's AAI had revealed her to have anxious-preoccupied attachment (E2). The therapist thus anticipated that in the imagery she would tend toward focusing more on the parent figures' states and needs than on her own. In her initial report about the imagery, she referred to "something on the wall that's soft, like fur" and indicated that the parents "like that and they show it to me. Maybe they pat it, and help me to pat it." While this interaction appears to be a positive one, it is the parents' preference ("they like that") and action ("they pat it") that are primary. The therapist chose to shape the parent figure imagery so that the patient would experience her own preferences as primary: "They wonder what you'll be interested in, and they like to help you find things that you'll enjoy."

Interest in and *attunement* to the child are among four general factors and five behavioral pillars that promote secure attachment. The therapist further emphasized and shaped the beneficial qualities of the imagined parents by stating that "they show you how much they cherish you, how interested and attuned they are to what you like and what you need." The patient then spontaneously reported experiencing the parents as having another of those qualities: "I think they're being reassuring."

It is notable that in this session, the patient reported about her imagined parents that "they're not mad at me," as during the assessment she had described her actual parents as frequently being angry with her. Although this description was spontaneous, much benefit occurs when the therapist shapes the IPF imagery with qualities that are *positive opposites* of problematic qualities that patients describe in their actual parents. This practice is described in more detail in the next section.

The therapist pointed the patient's attention to her own state of mind and then mirrored her positive states and suggested a felt sense of security ("and secure in feeling and knowing of their acceptance and support"). The patient indicated clearly that she did not yet feel a sense of security ("I'm not really sure I can trust them").

The therapist seamlessly incorporated the patient's experience of doubt into the imagery process by indicating that the parent figures were *attuned* to the patient's internal state and thereby recognized her experience ("they see that you're not really sure"). Beyond recognition, the therapist shaped the imagery such that the parent figures were *accepting of* and *patient with* both the patient's current experience and her process of development. The qualities of *protection* and *attunement* were then stated directly, as was validation of the primacy of the patient's own experience and learning over time ("and you'll see from your own experience how you'll choose to trust them"). Through this interaction, the patient likely experienced both the therapist and the ideal parent figures as attuned to and supportive of her actual experience.

The therapist's suggestion that the patient feel secure, although she did not at that time, may seem like a *lack* of attunement. But it had dual value as a test to find out if a feeling of security was present and as an expression of confidence in and gentle push toward realizing her developmental potential. Any sense by the patient of lack of attunement was likely resolved by the therapist's immediate validation of her actual experience. Her willingness and ability to assert her own experience against the therapist's suggestion was an important self-validation, in itself a sign of the possibility of security, especially given the patient's anxious-preoccupied attachment status.

Principles and Practices for Framing and Responding to Patients' Experiences

As there is wide variability in the type, degree, and manifestation of attachment insecurity, there is also great variability in how patients respond to the initial Ideal Parent Figure sessions, ranging from vivid and detailed imagery to imagining harmful or no parent figures. The above vignettes illustrate several possibilities of what patients might say and of how therapists might respond during early sessions of the IPF protocol; the commentaries explain aspects of the process that appear in these sessions and the rationale for the therapist's responses. If therapists keep in mind the principles that underlie the protocol and its application, they will be prepared to work effectively with any of the many ways that patients may engage (or not) with the method.

Particular challenges (such as imagining harmful or no parent figures) are addressed later in this chapter, and considerations pertaining to each of the insecure attachment subtypes are addressed in Chapters 11, 12, and 13. Below is a description of general guiding principles and also of principles for responding to patients and shaping their unique imagery and experience in ways that will best effect attachment repair.

GENERAL CONTEXT PRINCIPLES

Be with the patient as would a good attachment figure. The IPF method's fundamental agent of change is the patient's active engagement with ideal parent figure imagery. However, as already described, when a therapist's way of being with the patient embodies qualities common to good attachment figures, this relational stance both facilitates the imagery work and supports attachment repair through the patient's experience of the therapy relationship.

Any good-enough therapist will embody what we have termed the *general factors* of *physical presence, consistency, reliability,* and *interest* in the patient. Upon that foundation, the therapist's engagement with facilitating and guiding the IPF process makes quite easy the embodiment of the "five behavioral pillars" that promote secure attachment. Helping the patient to establish a calm, relaxed, inwardly focused state of awareness as the therapeutic ground for the protocol provides an experience of *soothing*, as does responding effectively to any discomfort that arises during the protocol. Communicating directly and indirectly that everything that arises is welcomed as part of the process provides *reassurance* that no matter what comes up, the patient is accepted and the therapist remains available. Being attentive to the patient's moment-to-moment experience and responding in ways that develop and maintain the experience of the IPFs indicates to the patient the therapist's *attunement*. Such attunement tends to reinforce itself and to engage the therapist's *interest*, which is communicated to the patient by frequent questions about what exactly he or she is experiencing and by the way the questions are asked and the answers met. *Expressed delight* is a quality of the therapist's verbal mirroring of the patient's reports of his or her ideal parent figures' positive ways of being. The therapist's interest in and openness to the patient's experiences with the IPFs and the active encouragement of engagement with them communicates *support for exploration* of the inner and outer world. Ideally, the aggregate of the ways that the therapist is with the patient during the protocol shows his or her dedication to the *protection* of the patient's well-being.

The patient's ideal parent figure imagery is the frame for developing attachment security. A frame is a context for something more central, and with this protocol, the imagery frame provides the patient with the opportunity to establish and deepen a relational experience that promotes attachment repair. At first, the therapist asks the patient to imagine parents "who are ideally suited to you and your nature," "who are right there with you and really know how to be with you to help you feel so safe and secure," and "who really know how to be with you in all the ways that help you to feel absolutely secure in your relationship with them." Notice that these phrases do not suggest specific qualities that the parent figures have, but instead implicitly ask the patient to access his or her own awareness, conscious and not, of what was and is most needed for creating attachment security. We know in general what the qualities of being are that promote secure attachment, but each patient will have unique needs for particular configurations and weighting of those qualities. By initially not hearing specific qualities named by the therapist, the patient is primed to access his or her unique needs, which will then be projected as qualities into the construction of the imagined parents, making them "ideal" for that particular patient. In this way, the patient's parent figures have as their foundation the qualities that come from the patient's deepest knowing of what was most missing during childhood and thus what in the present will best provide for attachment repair.

SHAPE THE PATIENT'S IMAGERY AND EXPERIENCE

Throughout the protocol, the therapist frequently asks the patient to describe the parent figures and his or her experiences of them. The therapist's responses to the patient's descriptions include *pointing the patient's attention* toward the attachment-promoting qualities of the imagined parent figures and *mirroring and enhancing* the patient's descriptions of those qualities. By recognizing and reinforcing these qualities, the patient's imagery and experience is shaped toward the inner conditions that most efficiently create attachment security.

Point the patient's attention to the attachment-promoting qualities of his or her imagined parent figures. Fundamental to this protocol is the patient's deeply felt experience of the imagined parent figures being and behaving in ways that promote attachment security. Ideally, then, the patient's attention stays primarily focused on those ways and on his or her felt experience in response. The therapist promotes this attentiveness by frequently making statements such as the following:

Notice the ways that they're being with you.

Notice how they're *being* with you now.

Notice the ways that they're being with you that feel *so very right* for you and for your well-being.

Notice the ways that they're being with you that help you to feel such a *clear* and *strong* sense of security with them.

Notice what effect their *ways of being* with you have on *your* inner state of being.

Notice how you feel as they're with you in all the ways that you *most* need and in all the ways that are *so very right* for you and your well-being.

Expressed throughout the protocol, these statements help the patient to stay on task. In addition to pointing attention to particular aspects of the imagery and the patient's experience of it, such statements reinforce the creative and generative aspect of the process, encouraging the patient to be curious and open to what will be produced by staying engaged with the imagery.

Mirror and enhance the patient's descriptions of the attachment-promoting qualities of the imagined parent figures. The therapist listens carefully to the patient's descriptions of the parent figures and chooses to reinforce anything that is consistent with qualities that promote secure attachment. At first, the imagery might be somewhat vague and the patient might be tentative about experiencing it and/or reporting it. Hearing the therapist use *the patient's same words and descriptions* with an affirming tone will ratify the imagery and strengthen the patient's confidence in the imagery and in the overall process. Mirroring also helps to keep attention on the beneficial qualities of the parent figures and the patient's immediate, felt experience of them.

It is very important that the therapist use the patient's words and phrases; then, building upon the patient's literal expressions, the therapist may incorporate other, closely related words and phrases that are consistent with the principle or spirit of what the patient says. Some examples are as follows:

Patient: They're both very interactive with me. The mother is reaching out to me; the father isn't, but he has his own ways of engaging with me. I feel they want to be doing what they're doing. I just feel they want to be with me.
Therapist: Yes, they *really want* to be with you, and they engage with you in their own ways. And you can *really take in* how good it feels that they want to be with you.

Another example:

Patient: The dad is standing. He has a nice smile. The mom is kind of soft, nice, and approving. They feel proud, not bad proud, just happy.

Therapist: They feel *so happy* and *proud* that they get to be *your* parents. Notice how that *feels* to you.

Patient: I feel happy too.

Therapist: Yes, you feel happy too. *Really feel* the happy feeling.

Another example:

Patient: I guess I see myself kind of with my face buried in my mother's stomach, standing waist high, face against her, her arms wrapped around my back.

Therapist: As you see yourself there, *really be there*, and you can feel the *contact*, the *support*, the *warmth*, the *support*.

Patient: It feels very safe. I can shut everything out, for at least a little while. It's safe. And it's just warm, not just physically. The emotional temperature is just right.

Therapist: Yes, you can shut everything out and *really feel* the *safety*, the *warmth*, and that *just-right* emotional temperature.

Another:

Patient: Well, I think they just express appreciation for things about me that are different. I see myself coloring a picture, and it's kind of crazy, but I feel it's accepted by them. I feel appreciated.

Therapist: These parents enjoy when you're creative, when you're expressing yourself in *your own* particular ways. *Really feel* that inside, being accepted and appreciated for who *you* are, in *all* ways.

Another:

Patient: The mother is the same way—very present, soft, loving. Moments of being still. Or being held, hugged. I'm just feeling . . . enveloped. Enveloped by . . . the warmth of their skin, their gentle but firm holding. Their deep presence.

Therapist: Yes. *Really feel* that deep presence, that warm, gentle, firm holding.

In several of the above examples, the therapist's first response was the statement "Yes." This simple and direct validation mirrors and reinforces both what the patient is experiencing and his or her engagement with the imagery task.

When the patient's description indicates that he or she is experiencing the ideal parent figures with specific sensory modalities, the therapist can make mirroring and enhancing statements based on those modalities. For example, if a patient reports that a parent figure is saying something to him or her, the therapist can say, "Notice her tone of voice, her tone that *really lets you know* that she's *right there* with you with *such affection* and *warmth*"; if a patient says that a parent figure is looking at him or her, the therapist can say, "Really notice *how* he's looking at you . . . you can see the *look in his eyes*, that tells you that he's *so caring,* and *so dedicated* to *protecting you* and helping you to feel *safe* and *secure.*"

Effective mirroring by the therapist contributes to the power of the imagery to create new, positive attachment representations. It also reproduces the beneficial developmental circumstance of a caregiver attuning to the child's experiences and providing direct, validating feedback about those experiences. Such feedback is made even more beneficial when the therapist "marks" the patient's experience with an affectively expressive tone. This "marked expressivity" is addressed later in this chapter.

SUGGEST ATTACHMENT-PROMOTING QUALITIES IN THE IMAGINED PARENT FIGURES

The therapist does not rely entirely on the patient to generate the qualities of the parent figures, as some patients at first have difficulty imagining any attachment-promoting qualities, even if they are able to imagine parent figures. After setting the imagery frame in a way that allows the patient maximal creative freedom to imagine and project ideal, attachment-promoting qualities onto the parent figures, the therapist mirrors and enhances what, if anything, the patient does generate, and then is free to suggest particular qualities in the parent figures. Such suggestion may include correcting for focus on parent figures' *doing* by pointing toward their qualities of *being* that underlie the doing; introducing qualities in the parent figures that are drawn from the general principles of secure attachment formation; and introducing qualities that are the positive opposites of the problematic aspects of the particular patient's experiences with his or her actual parents.

Correct for instrumental caretaking by suggesting underlying attachment-promoting qualities. Within the IPF protocol, the therapist often must mirror differentially between what the patient experiences and what among those experiences best supports the formation of secure attachment representations. For example, it is quite common for patients to describe the parent figures engaging in *instrumental actions*, such as cooking a meal, reading a bedtime story, or playing a game. Even though such actions may be with and for the child in the imagery, it should not be assumed that the actions are done with *qualities of being* that promote attachment security. Doing "all the right things" for a child can be partially or completely devoid of attunement, soothing, delight, support for exploration, and even some aspects of protection. Many insecurely attached patients had parents who objectively did "all the right things."

When a patient reports that the parent figures are *doing* something for him or her, the therapist acknowledges that action, mirroring that it's present, and then either points attention to or suggests positive, attachment-promoting *qualities of being* from which the figures are engaging in that doing. For example:

> *Patient:* We're in the kitchen and my mother is making dinner for me. She seems happy.
> *Therapist:* Yes. Notice what it is about her that lets you know how happy she is to be making dinner *for you.* She doesn't want to be anywhere other than there *with you* now, and she's happy to be making *for you* what she knows *you enjoy* so much.

In this example, the therapist mirrored both the action of the mother figure making dinner and the patient's sense that the mother was happy. The therapist also went beyond the patient's objective statements and suggested that the mother figure *was* rather than *seemed* happy, and that *the source* of her happiness was that she was "making dinner *for you,*" "there *with you* now," and "making *for you* what she knows *you enjoy* so much." This linking of the action, the affective state, and the relationship provided both mirroring and suggestive shaping of the imagery toward more attachment-promoting forms.

Here is another example:

> *Patient:* My mother is brushing my hair.
> *Therapist:* And you can feel from her that she's r*ight there with you,* s*oothing you* and brushing your hair *with such love* for you. You can *really feel* her *interest,* and her *caring,* and *her love* through the ways she's with you, whether she's doing something for you or just simply being with you.

In this example, too, the therapist mirrored the mother figure's action and then made suggestions that the action was done from and with specific attachment-promoting qualities of being.

Suggest that the imagined parent figures have qualities that are known in general to support secure attachment. In response to particular attachment-promoting qualities not being included in a patient's descriptions of the parent figures, the therapist includes suggestions of those qualities, drawing from the "four general factors" and the behavioral components of the "five conditions that promote secure attachment." Some possibilities, from each of these categories, are as follows, with key elements underlined:

General Factors

PHYSICAL PRESENCE

- These parents are <u>genuinely accessible</u> to you.
- You can count on these parents <u>to be with you</u> when you need them.
- This is a special relationship in which <u>they are reasonably available</u> to you <u>when you need them to be</u>.

CONSISTENCY

- These parents are <u>consistent</u> in their ways of being with you over time.
- These parents know what helps you to feel secure and safe, and they <u>consistently provide that for you every time you're with them</u>.
- <u>You come to know these parents</u> and their helpful ways of being with you.

RELIABILITY

- <u>You can count on these parents</u> to be with you in the ways you need, <u>every time</u> you're with them.
- Notice how <u>you can trust these parents</u> to find just the right ways to be with you, <u>every time you're with them</u>.
- You <u>can always turn to them</u> for understanding.

INTEREST

- These parents are <u>so very interested</u> in what you're interested in.
- You can feel how <u>interested</u> they are in what you're thinking and feeling.
- These parents are <u>happy to learn everything about you</u> that you want to share with them.
- Notice what it is about them that lets you know how <u>genuinely interested</u> they are in what you're experiencing right now.

Behavioral Conditions

PROTECTION

- These parents are so dedicated to you and to <u>protecting</u> you from any harm. More and more you can feel quite <u>safe</u> around them.
- When you're with them, you can feel the ways they <u>protect</u> you.
- You never have to worry about your safety, because these parents <u>watch out for you</u> and <u>protect you</u> whenever you need that.

ATTUNEMENT

- These parents are so very <u>attuned</u> to you and your needs. Notice what it is about them that lets you know how <u>attuned</u> they are to what you're feeling and needing right now.

Attunement to behavior

- These parents <u>notice what you're doing</u>, and <u>from what they see, they tune right in</u> to what you need.
- Whenever you get more quiet or more active, <u>these parents see that</u> and know that something has shifted in you.

Attunement to internal state

- <u>They can tell from the look on your face</u> what it is you might be <u>feeling inside</u>.
- And when you're feeling something, <u>these parents somehow tune right in</u> to that, and to what you need.

Attunement to developmental stage

- These parents <u>always know just how much is right for you</u>; they <u>never push you beyond what you're ready for</u>.
- <u>When you're ready</u> to learn more and to move ahead, these parents are right there to help you <u>take those next steps.</u>

SOOTHING AND REASSURANCE

- You can feel confident that <u>whenever you're upset, these parents are right there for you</u>, giving you the <u>soothing</u> and <u>reassurance</u> that will <u>help you in just the right ways</u>. They really know how to <u>comfort</u> you when you're upset.
- These parents <u>know just the right ways to help you when you're upset about something</u>. <u>You can always</u> count on them to <u>help you to feel better</u>.
- Notice the ways they're with you that <u>help you to calm down and feel so much better, so much more at ease</u>.
- They're able to <u>reassure you</u> when you're in doubt.
- These parents are capable of <u>accepting and containing your strongest feelings</u>, and they help you to accept them and contain them too, so that <u>you feel safe with all your feelings</u>.

EXPRESSED DELIGHT

- Notice how <u>delighted</u> these parents are that they get to be your parents. And as you're with them, <u>they'll let you know about their delight</u> about you simply being you, just as you are.
- You can feel that they <u>genuinely like you</u>, that they <u>delight in your very being</u>. And <u>they communicate their delight to you</u> in ways you can really take in.
- See what it is about them that makes it so very clear that they're <u>absolutely delighted</u> in who you are.

ENCOURAGEMENT FOR EXPLORATION

Inner exploration

- They help you to see that emotions are not dangerous but are natural ways of learning about yourself and are also ways of expressing unmet needs.
- In this special relationship, you experience them as especially attuned, capable of listening carefully, and able to validate your feelings.
- These parents help you to see yourself as the unique, deep, rich, and complex individual you are.
- Feeling such safety and security with them, you can begin to explore your inner experience in a creative way, bringing to your exploration an attitude of openness and discovery.
- No matter what you discover, you find that they are quite responsive and accepting of your inner experience, whether it's comfortable or uncomfortable to you.

Outer exploration

- With their support, you start to feel inspired to try new things.
- They encourage you to explore new ways of acting and doing things.
- With such secure feelings, you can become capable and competent in the world in so many ways.
- And with their encouragement, you can become more adventuresome and daring.
- They are happy to support you as you learn and explore and discover what you like.
- Isn't it wonderful to feel their support as you go off on your own to see what you find!

Notice that these suggestions are made in ways that do not impose *how* the imagined parents will manifest the qualities; instead, the presence of the qualities is suggested, and the patient's attention is pointed toward imagining the ways that the qualities will appear in the parent figures.

It can be particularly beneficial if the suggested qualities are linked to and build upon what the patient describes about the parents. For example:

Patient: I guess, they're just, smiling now, so happy to be around me [delight], putting their hand on my shoulder.

Therapist: Yes, they're so happy to be around you, and they express that to you in ways you can *really* take in. And putting their hand on your shoulder—it seems like such a simple touch, but notice *how deep* it feels, saying so much about how delighted they are to be with you. You can feel *so much* from that.

Here, the therapist mirrored the patient's experience of the parents being happy to be with him, using the same phrase as he did, and then suggested that they would *express* that happy feeling to him to highlight and possibly enhance the patient's experience of direct communication of the parents' *delight* in the child. The addition of "in ways you can really take in" is a suggestion of the parents being *attuned* to the patient's best ways of receiving their expressions.

Suggest that the imagined parent figures have specific qualities that are the positive opposite of the particular patient's experiences with his or her actual parents. During intake evaluation, inquiry into the patient's early recollections of his or her parents and the ways they were toward the patient during childhood yields information that can be fruitfully brought into the IPF sessions. Based on the principle that particular parental behaviors and ways of being impede the development of secure attachment, knowledge of which of those factors are relevant to a particular patient allows the IPF imagery to be developed and shaped so those factors are most effectively countered. When imagined parent figures embody the positive opposites of the developmentally disruptive ways of being of the actual parents, they will most effectively and efficiently create the new attachment representations that will result in earned attachment security.

Information about a patient's early experiences with parents can be obtained in several ways. The Adult Attachment Interview (AAI; George, Kaplan, & Main, 1996) was developed to specifically obtain information relevant to attachment status. Ideally, the therapist will be trained and qualified to administer the AAI and will do so with patients who present with relational disturbance. Alternately, the therapist can refer the patient to someone qualified to administer the AAI and obtain the transcript and scoring from that person. Questions 3 and 4 of the AAI each yield five adjectives that describe the patient's relationships with his or her mother and father (or primary caregivers), respectively, during early childhood. The adjectives chosen are revealing indicators of the nature of the parental relationships and the qualities of the parents that likely contributed to the attachment insecurity. Consider the following list of adjectives from a patient's AAI transcript:

Relationship with mother	Relationship with father
Anxious	Absent
Not accepting	Frightening
Cold	Irresponsible
Caretaking	Chaotic
Pressured	Playful

This information about the patient's experience of her actual parents is tremendously valuable as a guide for the therapist's shaping and suggesting of qualities of the imagined parent figures. Prior to the IPF session, the therapist establishes the *positive opposite* of the adjectives that reflect negative qualities. Positive opposites of the adjectives above are as follows:

Relationship with mother	Relationship with father
Calm	Present
Accepting	Safe; never frightening
Warm	Responsible
[Attuned caretaking]	Clear, predictable
Relaxed; accepting	[Attuned playfulness]

The bracketed words bear some explanation. In the AAI, after the patient names five adjectives for a parent, for each adjective the interviewer asks for specific memories that illustrate why that adjective was chosen. The patient's memory for "caretaking" revealed that she experienced her mother as *instrumentally caretaking*, providing food and shelter and transportation, but not in a caring, attuned way. So the positive opposite of that would be "attuned caretaking." The patient's memory for the description of the relationship with her father as "playful" was of the father being playful, but on his terms and not aware of the patient's state. So the positive opposite of that would be "attuned playfulness."

Often, some of the adjectives given reflect truly positive experiences with the parents. Such adjectives need not be modified. As is described in Chapter 11, on treating dismissing attachment, the adjectives given by patients with dismissing attachment are usually all positive. How to work with that circumstance is described in that chapter.

In IPF sessions with the above patient, when it was appropriate for the therapist to make specific suggestions of qualities of the imagined parent figures, the following statements were made (in no particular order and not all in one session). The relevant qualities are undelined. Note that although the AAI specifically asks for adjectives to describe the *relationship* with the parents, when the positive opposites are integrated into the IPF protocol, they can be applied as qualities of the relationships, qualities of how the patient feels in relationship to the parents, and/or as qualities of the parents themselves.

Notice how <u>calm</u> the mother is when you're with her, and how <u>calm</u> it feels when you're together.

This mother is so very <u>accepting</u> of who you are.

Notice what it is about this mother that brings that feeling of <u>warmth</u>.

This mother is always <u>attuned</u> to you and your needs, and provides for you what feels just right.

You can wonder what stands out to you most that shows you how <u>relaxed</u> and <u>accepting</u> she is of you.

This father is so very present with you, there for you much of the time, and when he's with you he's so <u>attentive</u> and <u>present</u> to you.

His way of being with you brings in you a feeling of <u>safety</u>. He feels so <u>safe, never frightening</u>.

You can count on this father to be <u>responsible</u>, providing for you what is so very important to you and your well-being.

Notice how <u>clear</u> and <u>calm</u> this father is when you're together.

And you can have fun being <u>playful</u> together, because it's so very clear that he's <u>attuned</u> to how you feel and what you want.

Many patients will immediately accept the suggestions of the positive opposites and will show their pleasure in interacting with parent figures who are embodying these qualities. But some patients may at first have difficulty recognizing the positive opposite qualities in the parent figures, as these qualities were absent from their early experiences. Such difficulty is heightened if there are defenses against feelings of longing for what was missing. But the therapist's persistent repetition of the positive opposites, interspersed with repetition of the positive parental qualities already named by the patient, will support the appearance and stability of them in the patient's imagery.

We highly recommend that therapists obtain AAI transcripts and scoring for every patient with relational disturbance. The richness of detail about childhood attachment experience that the AAI elicits is tremendously valuable for introducing and shaping the IPF imagery. In addition, when an AAI is given at the beginning of treatment, it can be given again during a later phase of treatment to assess progress in very specific areas. However, if the therapist is not qualified to fully administer the AAI and an AAI transcript is unavailable for a particular patient, an alternative way of obtaining parental relationship information is to explore it in detail during the initial evaluation. As part of history-taking, the therapist asks the patient to describe in a narrative way his or her early relationships with parents or other caregivers and probes to obtain as much detail as possible in order to get a sense of the parents' typical ways of being with the patient and the typical ways the patient experienced the relationships with the parents. In this way, it is possible to obtain sufficient information for establishing positive-opposite qualities to include in the development of ideal parent figures.

If during a patient's early childhood there was only one parent or caregiver, the therapist first focuses on the patient's experience with the single parent and then probes for the patient's experience as a child of *not having* the other parent. For example, such a patient might say that she felt "sad" and "empty" and "lonely." Transforming these into positive opposites and applying them to the ideal father figure might yield the following statement during an IPF session:

> Notice how this father is being with you in ways that bring you feelings of <u>happiness</u>, and <u>fullness</u>. And you <u>don't ever feel lonely</u> when you're together with this father.

This inquiry, for feelings pertaining to the absence of a father or father figure, is made even if the therapist has an AAI transcript for the patient, as the AAI would not have produced adjectives pertaining to a paternal relationship.

In support of the goal of obtaining information for tailoring the therapist's suggestions to the specific attachment-promoting needs of particular patients, any and all sources of information about the early relationships are valued. In preparation for the IPF sessions, the therapist integrates information obtained from all sources and formulates positive-opposite qualities that the ideal parent figures can be suggested to have.

CONTEXTUALIZE THE PATIENT'S EXPERIENCES WITHIN THE IPF FRAME

Once the imagery frame is established during an IPF session and the patient shows some engagement with the process, the frame becomes the context for all of the patient's experiences during that session. The therapist holds the larger context of overseeing and guiding the session, and within the context of the imagery frame constructed during that session, he or she responds to what arises in the patient *by referencing the parent figures' responses to what has arisen*. For example, in the initial IPF session, a patient expressed *fear* about seeing the parent figures:

> *Patient:* I don't know; this is kind of scary, seeing them there looking at me. I'm not sure I can do this.
> *Therapist:* Yes, and these parents understand how scary this can be for you. Notice how they show you that they understand that, and that they

won't rush you in any way. They find *just the right ways* to help you to feel safe, with this, and with them. And they help you to see that they won't let anything bad happen to you, that they'll do their best *to protect you* in *all circumstances.*

The goal is for the patient to experience the parent figures as beneficially responding to the entire range and focus of his or her experiences and states, from positive and comfortable to negative and uncomfortable. Through incorporation of all experiences into the frame, the frame itself and the effectiveness of the process is enhanced.

Patients' experiences will vary during the IPF process. Mirroring and enhancing positive experiences with the parent figures is a central aspect of the process. But no child has only positive experiences, and a patient with an attachment disorder will most certainly have some difficulty with or resistance to the process of experiencing positive parent figures from the perspective of a child. Several categories of difficulty that can be responded to from within the imagery frame are considered here: (1) separation or distance from the parent figure imagery, (2) decrease in engagement with or stepping out of the imagery frame, (3) mistrust or emotional distancing from the parent figures, and (4) uncomfortable affective states.

Separation or physical distance from the parent figures. Consider the following report from a patient in the first IPF session:

> *Patient:* I see parents there, but I'm separated from them by some gauzy, hazy material. I don't know how to get to them, and I feel alone even though they're there.

The "gauzy, hazy material" was likely a representation of the patient's resistance to contact with the parent figures. Instead of working with the patient to find a way to reduce that resistance, the therapist gave that task to the parent figures:

> *Therapist:* These parents understand that it sometimes can feel hard to have a felt sense of connection with them. And they know exactly how to help you get beyond the gauzy, hazy material, in a way that feels *just right* for you, and to *help you* to come to feel in *close connection* with them, so you don't have to feel so alone.

The patient then experienced the parents pulling aside the material, making a clear opening for her, and she had the clear sense that the parents were letting her choose whether to go to them immediately or not. She did go to them right away, and spoke of feeling supported and connected with them.

Another patient, whose father had been violent and whose mother had been passive and neglectful, at first did not see any parents. The therapist responded this way:

> *Therapist:* Through the powers of your imagination, you can create a set of parents who are *ideally suited* to you, who *really know* how to be with you in ways so that you feel *safe* and *supported.* You can have them be *any way that you'd like* and need them to be.
>
> *Patient:* I see them. But it's like we're in different worlds.
>
> *Therapist:* Tell me how it is you experience them.
>
> *Patient:* Well, it's like I'm in the city, and they're far away, like in the country.
>
> *Therapist:* Even though there's been that big distance between you, they know that it's important for you to be closer together, but only in a way that's *safe* and is *best* for *you.* So let's see what happens so that you can *all* be *together, safe* and sound.
>
> *Patient:* Now the upper part of my body is with them, but my feet are still in the city.
>
> *Therapist:* Okay, something has shifted, and you're *already closer together.* Let's see what happens next.
>
> *Patient:* (face showing release and an emerging smile) Now I'm with them, all of me. They're holding my hands, and smiling.

Through this interaction, the therapist was accepting of the patient's experience and pointed toward the possibility of being closer together. He did not suggest any specific *ways* for that to happen, but instead highlighted that the parents "know that it's important for you to be closer together, but only in a way that's *safe* and is *best* for *you.*" *How* that would happen was left to the frame and the parent figures in the frame: "Let's see what happens so that you can *all* be *together, safe* and sound." When the shift to being closer together happened, the therapist simply noted that "something has shifted," then highlighted the immediacy of greater closeness ("you're already closer together"), and then again indicated trust in the frame to continue the process ("Let's see what happens next").

Decrease in engagement with the imagery frame. Sometimes, after imagining interaction with parent figures, a patient will indicate decreased engagement not only from the parent figures but also from the imagery frame itself.

> *Patient:* They love each other, and they love me. It's a cohesive family unit. They provide for each other, and for me as well. Sometimes they spend time apart, but they come back together, and are happy to.

Therapist: Notice how *happy* they are to be *your* parents, and what it is about their way of being that lets you know about that happiness.

Patient: They support me. They guide me. Make sure I make the right decisions. They protect me, from others, sometimes, and sometimes from myself.

Therapist: They are *so attuned to you* that they recognize when you need something, and they do their absolute best to provide for your needs. And they know *just the right ways* to be with you so you feel *secure* and *safe.*

Patient: Yes.

Therapist: And you can notice what it is about them that makes it *so very clear* that they *cherish* you *so much.* Perhaps it's a gleam in their eyes. They delight in you being you.

Patient: They smile, they laugh, they pat me on the head . . . they're not real . . . they're . . . perfect . . . they're too perfect. This isn't real. They seem almost plastic. I can feel their love and can see their support, and love, and affection and caring about me, but it's—it's too good to be true. It's a sinking feeling. I can't do this anymore . . . this is just faking.

Therapist: They see, and they understand that it seems that way to you. They understand that at first it can be hard to really take in their deep and unconditional love. They protect you, and they protect you from yourself sometimes, and this is one of those circumstances in which they help to protect you from doubting too much, from doubting that what you most want and need is here for you. Notice how they respond to knowing that you feel this is fake and that it's too good to be true.

Patient: They brush it off; they put their arms around me, reassure me. They take it as a compliment that I experience them as too good to be true.

Therapist: Yes. They're *so happy* that their intention to be the *best possible parents* for you touches you as it does.

Patient: It feels complete, it feels whole, it makes me feel I'm part of something that is what was meant to be.

Therapist: Yes. It was meant to be that you be valued and loved for *exactly who you are. Really take that in.* Feeling *appreciated* and *valued* and *loved. Feel it* in your body.

Patient: It's still too perfect. This isn't real. I can't accept it.

Therapist: These parents recognize that it's still hard for you to accept. They're very patient, and it adds to their resolve to show you how much they value, and cherish you . . . Even amidst it being hard to accept, you have moments of really feeling and taking in the perfection of it . . . of feeling the *completeness* of it, the *wholeness* of it . . . of their *reassurance* and *support,* their *guidance* and their *protection.* And in those moments of perfection, you know that you're part of something that was meant to be.

Patient: They're wise. They understand. They've experienced it.
Therapist: Yes, they've been there, so they understand what you're going through, and they know how to support you in *all the right ways* for you.

At the beginning of this session, the patient was very engaged with the imagery and the process and generated a vivid, positive interaction with the parent figures. Then doubt emerged. It is notable that at first, even amidst doubt, he continued to experience the positive affect and ways of being of the parents:

This isn't real. They seem almost plastic. I can feel their love and can see their support, and love, and affection and caring about me, but it's—it's too good to be true.

Then he withdrew from the frame: "I can't do this anymore . . . this is just faking." The therapist maintained the presence of the frame by noting that the parent figures recognized and understood his doubt. Even though of course the IPF frame *is* "fake," the therapist supported the patient's return to suspension of disbelief by suggesting that the parent figures understood that "it seems that way" (i.e., fake) to him.

Toward the same goal of reviving the patient's engagement with the frame, the therapist incorporated what the patient had earlier said about the parents *protecting* him, *sometimes from himself*:

They protect you, and they protect you from yourself sometimes, and this is one of those circumstances in which they help to protect you from doubting too much, from doubting that what you most want and need is here for you.

By combining speaking from the frame with highlighting something that the patient had said about the parent figures when he was engaged with the frame, the therapist enhanced the possibility that the patient would reengage with the parent figure imagery and directly experience that engagement. He then invited such direct experience: "Notice how they respond to knowing that you feel this is fake and that it's too good to be true." This intervention was effective, as the patient himself incorporated his doubt and withdrawal into the imagery:

They brush it off; they put their arms around me, reassure me. They take it as a compliment that I experience them as too good to be true.

His reengagement, however, was short-lived. After the therapist's response to the patient's very significant experience of completeness, wholeness, and of being "part of something that is what was meant to be," the patient stepped back: "It's still too perfect. This isn't real. I can't accept it." Again the therapist pointed back to the frame, suggesting, in response to the patient's saying he "<u>can't</u> accept" the frame and the experiences within it, that the parents "recognize that <u>it's still hard</u> for you to accept." "Still hard" honors the patient's experience of difficulty and suggests that his difficulty does not mean that he cannot accept the frame and the positive experiences within it.

The frame was reinforced further by the therapist's incorporation and mirroring not only of the positive experiences the patient had expressed prior to the frame ruptures, but also his experiences of both engagement and disengagement with the frame:

> Even amidst it being hard to accept, you have moments of really feeling and taking in the perfection of it . . . of feeling the *completeness* of it, the *wholeness* of it . . . of their *reassurance* and *support*, their *guidance* and their *protection*. And in those moments of perfection, you know that you're part of something that was meant to be.

The IPF session ended with the patient feeling a supportive, loving connection with the imagined parents. During the next three sessions he also experienced intermittent withdrawal from the IPF frame, and each time the therapist's pointing to the parent figures' responses reengaged the patient with the frame. In subsequent sessions, he maintained his connection with the frame, but within the frame he several times indicated some wariness and mistrust about the parent figures.

Mistrust or emotional distancing from the parent figures. It is quite common for patients to be engaged with the IPF imagery frame but to experience guardedness or uncertainty about the parent figures' trustworthiness or reliability. One such expression was presented in the clinical vignette on pages 314–315:

> *Patient:* I'm not really sure I can trust them.
> *Therapist:* They see that you're not really sure, and they understand that. They're very patient, knowing that as you're with them more and more, you'll get to see that they're there to protect you and to be attuned to you and your needs, and you'll see from your own experience whether you'll choose to trust them.

The commentary about this interchange on page 316 explicates how the therapist "seamlessly incorporated the patient's experience of doubt into the imagery process."

Another patient was guarded against the imagined parents:

Patient: They're there, but I don't really want to open up to them. They kind of have to prove themselves to me first, that they won't make fun of me.

Therapist: Of course you need to take your time, to see for yourself whether you can really trust them to not make fun of you. They know that too, and they won't push you to open up before you're ready. Notice how it is they are with you, and notice how they are with you that begins to let you know that they *accept you* and *love you* for *who you are*, *no matter what* you open up to them about. And just when you're ready, you'll start to feel that sense of *trust* and *safety* with them.

Here, the therapist acknowledged and validated the patient's experience and indicated that the parent figures did the same. Using the patient's words and phrases ("make fun of," "to open up"), she suggested that the parent figures were attuned to and accepted the patient's guardedness and that they would *be* in some way that the patient would experience as promoting trust and a sense of safety. As always, the therapist did not suggest *how* the parent figures would be, but left it up to the patient's inner knowing of what was needed.

Uncomfortable affective states. As parents' reliable and effective soothing and reassurance when a child is affectively distressed promotes secure attachment, during IPF sessions the therapist watches for signs of distress in the patient and suggests that the parent figures "find just the right ways" to provide soothing and reassurance. The therapist aims to be attuned to the patient's changes of state, which will likely occur before the patient reports them or even before the patient is aware of them.

Nonverbal indications of a change of state might include a sudden frown or other facial expression shift, the appearance of tears, an increase in body movement, or a change in breathing rate or pattern. In the following example, the therapist brought a change she noticed into the IPF frame:

Therapist: These parents are so attuned to you, and they see now from the expression on your face that something has shifted in you. They have a sense of *exactly what you need* right now. Notice how they are with you that provides you with *exactly what you need* to help you with what's happening in you right now. They find *just the right ways* to *soothe* and *reassure* you about what it is you're feeling.

Here, the therapist did not know what the affective experience was but trusted the information from the patient's face and, in pointing to the parent figures' attunement, trusted that the patient's inner knowing of what she needed would appear in how the parent figures responded to her. The patient experienced both the therapist's and the parent figures' attunement as well as the soothing and reassurance that appeared in the imagery.

When the patient reports an affective shift, either within or outside the imagery frame, the therapist names the state that the patient has reported. For example:

> *Patient:* I'm afraid, I'm afraid now that they won't like me.
>
> *Therapist:* They see now that you've become afraid, afraid that they won't like you. They know how uncomfortable that you must feel, feeling that fear. And they find *just the right ways* to *reassure* you, that they like and love you *no matter what*. Notice now how they reassure you.
>
> *Patient:* They tell me that they love me.
>
> *Therapist:* Yes, and you can *really take that in*, that they love you *so much*, no matter what. *Really feel* what that's like as you take that in.
>
> *Patient:* I feel a little better, like they will like me.
>
> *Therapist:* Yes. They will like you, *no matter what*. And that feels better, doesn't it?
>
> *Patient:* Yes.

In the following example, the patient reported an affective shift and kept it in the IPF frame herself:

> *Patient:* I'm feeling angry at them. I want to see what they do.
>
> *Therapist:* Yes, let yourself feel angry, and see how they are with you as you feel that.
>
> *Patient:* They listen to why I'm angry. They don't laugh at me for being angry. They take my emotions seriously.
>
> *Therapist:* Yes, they take everything about you seriously, with *respect* and *care* and *concern*.
>
> *Patient:* They don't leave.
>
> *Therapist:* They *stay right with you*.
>
> *Patient:* I have the feeling that they're respectful of my feelings.

After the IPF session, the patient spoke of her childhood experience of her actual mother often laughing at her when she was angry and when she was upset about being teased.

If a patient is so emotionally upset that he or she is unable to respond to and within the imagined scene in the IPF frame, the therapist may suggest that the entire scene will change:

> *Patient:* No, it's just too painful. They can't help me.
>
> *Therapist:* They're so very present with you, and so patient and resourceful. They find *just the right way* to help you with these feelings.

Patient: No, they're not helping; they're just looking at me.

Therapist: And now this scene will fade away and a new scene will appear to you. In this new scene, you're still feeling upset, and this time your ideal parents are being with you in *just the right ways* for what you need right now. Notice how these parents are being with you in this new scene, in all the ways that help you with these painful feelings.

Patient: (pause of about 15 seconds) We're all together on the sofa now. My mother is pulling me close to her, and my father is telling me I'm going to be all right.

Therapist: Yes. What effect does that have on your emotional state?

Patient: Well, I feel more calm. Like maybe they can help me.

Therapist: Yes, more calm, and they help you feel better.

The therapist's action of suggesting a scene change reflects *attunement* to the patient's distress and her inability to receive relief from the current scene, *protection* from prolonged exposure to the distress and the lack of help, and *soothing* by pointing to a new scene in which the patient is able to experience some relief.

SUGGEST CHANGES IN SCENES OR NEW SCENES WITH THE IDEAL PARENT FIGURES

The creation of changes in scenes with ideal parent figures can be very beneficial, and not just in response to a patient having difficulty in a particular imagined scene. In an IPF session, after some time with a scene in which the patient experiences ideal parent figures in a positive way, the therapist may suggest either that something within the current scene will change or that a new and different scene will emerge. In either form, the therapist suggests that the patient will continue to experience attachment-promoting qualities from the parent figures, and that the change will highlight such qualities even more clearly and perhaps in different ways.

Such shifts reinforce the consolidation of representations of positive attachment experiences by generalizing them across various and changing situations and contexts. They also provide the patient with the opportunity to project additional attachment-promoting qualities onto the parent figures, either generated spontaneously by the patient or suggested by the therapist.

Changes within scenes. As the letting go of a scene and creating a new scene requires more imaginative effort and pliancy, it is best during early IPF sessions to only suggest changes within scenes. A possible wording for such a suggestion is as follows:

Therapist: And now <u>something in this scene will change</u>. Something will change so that you'll experience these parents as *even more* supportive of you feeling *absolutely secure* in your connection with them. As <u>something in the scene changes</u>, notice what it is that happens that brings you an *even clearer* sense of *comfort* and *security* with them. And when you're ready, you can tell me <u>what's different</u> and what that's like for you.

The open wording leaves the creation of the specific parental ways of being to the patient's knowing of what he or she most needs for building feelings of security. In the example below, the therapist suggested several attachment-promoting qualities that were positive opposites of the adjectives the patient used to describe his actual parents. So far in the IPF sessions, he had not included these in experiences of his imagined parent figures.

> *Therapist:* Keeping with you all the good feelings that you feel from being with these parents, now <u>something in the scene will change</u>, and you'll notice now how <u>calm</u> [tense] these parents are, and how <u>happy</u> [depressed] and <u>fully present</u> [distracted] they are with you. They're happy to put aside their own issues so they can be with you in all the ways that help you to feel *absolutely secure* in the relationship with them. <u>As something changes about the scene</u>, you'll find that you can *really take in* how it feels that they're with you in these ways.

Changes of scenes. After the patient has had several constructive IPF sessions and has been able to shift *within* scenes for additional positive experiences with the parent figures, the therapist may suggest changes *of* scenes. The format of the suggestions is similar to those above, with slight wording changes. In the example below, the patient is given the freedom to project specific qualities onto the parent figures in the new scene:

> *Therapist:* And now <u>let this scene fade away</u>, and as you continue to feel the good feelings of connection with these parents, <u>a new scene</u> is about to appear. <u>In this new scene, you're also with your ideal parents</u>, and they're being with you in ways that bring you *even more* feelings of security. Now <u>this new scene</u> is getting clearer and clearer. Notice how it is that they're being with you that helps you to feel *absolutely secure* in your relationship with them.

Specific qualities can also be suggested as appearing in the parent figures in the new scene:

> *Therapist:* As you continue to feel the benefits of being with these parents in the ways they're being with you, <u>this particular scene will now fade</u>

<u>away, and a new scene with your ideal parents is about to appear</u>. <u>In this new scene</u>, in which you're also feeling in close connection with these parents, they are *so very* <u>warm</u> [cold] and <u>easygoing</u> [strained] toward you. And something about them will let you know that you can begin to get a sense of how <u>trustworthy</u> [not trustworthy] they are in your connection with them.

Timing of suggesting scene changes. In addition to the principle that suggesting changes *in* scenes is done several times before suggesting changes *of* scenes, the choice of when during a session to suggest a change in or of a scene is based on several factors. The most obvious time to make a change, as described in the previous section, is when the patient is having difficulty that the parent figures are not able to help with. Otherwise, when the patient has been having positive experience with parent figures, the therapist mirrors and enhances that experience and watches for a natural lull in the intensity of or engagement with the process. It is important not to rush or to force a change, as it is beneficial for the patient to stay with the positive experience within a scene until its attachment-promoting benefit has peaked.

Recognition of that peak is based more on intuition than on objective factors. The more attuned the therapist is to the patient and the process, the more apparent it will be that a particular scene has largely fulfilled its purpose and that a change can be fruitfully introduced. Although facilitating scene changes is beneficial to the process, it is not essential in every session. When the therapist has the sense that the patient continues to be engaged and generative with the scene that first appears, he or she simply continues to mirror and enhance the positive qualities and felt experiences that the patient describes. Some patients in some sessions will create changes in or of scenes spontaneously, and again, the therapist simply supports the continuation of engagement with the process.

BRING ATTENTION TO EXPERIENCE AND AMPLIFY POSITIVE STATES

Central to the IPF method's contribution to attachment repair is the patient's direct, immediate experience of benefit from being with the imagined parent figures. To support such experience, the therapist actively and persistently points the patient's attention to his or her experiences of the parent figures' attachment-promoting ways of being. In the example below, the therapist suggests that the parent figures will be comforting, and then directly brings focus to how that feels to the patient:

> *Patient:* I'm crying, and they see that.
> *Therapist:* They begin by <u>comforting you</u>, <u>comforting you</u> in the ways you

need right now. You can feel the effect of them <u>comforting you</u>. How does that feel?

Patient: They're reassuring me that it's not stupid; they don't laugh at me.

Therapist: *Whatever* you experience matters to them. *Everything* about your state matters. They encourage you to talk about it. Notice the effect that has on your inner state.

Patient: It's more relaxed.

Therapist: It's *more relaxed*, yes. Feel what that's like in the body; *really* feeling more relaxed.

In this brief interaction, the therapist made sure that the patient's awareness of her inner state would be overdetermined. He stated the comforting as a fact ("You can feel the effect of them comforting you") and then asked her to report from her awareness ("How does that feel?"). He affirmed that her experience mattered—to the parent figures and, by implication, to him ("*Whatever* you experience matters to them. *Everything* about your state matters. They encourage you to talk about it"). He pointed her attention to her experience ("Notice the effect that has on your inner state" and "Feel what that's like in the body"), he mirrored her report ("It's *more relaxed*, yes"), and he encouraged *amplification* of the felt experience she reported ("*really* feeling more relaxed").

The more the patient is aware of positive inner states in relation to the parent figures and the stronger those positive states are, the more likely and efficient will be the introjection of the experiences with the parent figures to create new, positive attachment representations. Thus, the therapist both points the patient's attention to positive experience and uses phrases and phrase tone that will amplify that experience.

The value of amplifying the patient's experience is consistent with Gergely's research on "marked expressivity" (Gergely & Watson, 1996) and Fonagy, Gergely, Jurist, and Target's (2002) concept of "marked affectivity." When a child's or a patient's affective experience is mirrored with exaggerated content and tone, the experience is "marked" as having happened, as important, and as belonging to the self. For example:

Patient: I felt happy when that happened.

Therapist: *You* must have *really* felt happy when that happened. (Italicized words received tonal emphasis.)

This marking is especially beneficial when working with patients with anxious-preoccupied attachment, as they tend to focus on others' experience more than on their own. But such amplification of felt experience is valuable during IPF sessions with all patients. Developmentally, affective marking enhances awareness of and differentiation of affects (Gergely & Watson, 1996) and, as noted above, facilitates the introjection of positive attachment representations.

Phrasings for bringing attention to felt experience. The therapist can be creative with phrasings, guided by the simple goal of pointing the patient's attention to positive states he or she has in response to experiencing attachment-promoting qualities in the ideal parent figures. Some possibilities include:

- How does that feel? ("that" refers to how the parent figures are being)
- Notice what happens inside you as they . . .
- You can feel the effect of . . .
- Notice the effect that has on your inner state (or state of mind, or feelings).
- Feel what that's like.
- It's [*more relaxed*], yes. (patient's term in brackets)
- You feel that, don't you? (in response to a nonverbal indication of effect)
- That feels good, doesn't it? (in response to nonverbal positive signs)
- You can say what that's like inside as they . . .

Phrasings for amplifying positive states. Both the content and tone of expression will contribute to amplification of positive states mirrored by the therapist. Consistent with Stern's (1985) assertion that young children have strong responses to the tone of a caregiver's voice, the therapist can tonally "lean into" the amplification of words in phrases such as the following:

- *Really* feel what that's like.
- You can feel that [*happiness*] *even more* strongly now. (patient's term in brackets)
- *Yes. Really* feel that now. *Really feel that* all through your being.
- *Yes.* That feeling of [*joy*] gets *even more* clear now.
- And *soon* that [sense of *safety*] becomes *even* stronger.
- You might be *surprised* how *vivid* and *clear* that feeling of [*calm*] becomes.

Note the tonal emphasis on the patient's own words. When the patient hears his or her own words mirrored back in marked form, the states described by those words are validated and reinforced.

In practice, as in the example at the beginning of this section, the therapist integrates the attention-directing and experience-enhancing phrasings. But until the patient verbalizes something about the positive states, attention-directing is emphasized. Some attention-directing phrasings can include amplification, even before the patient reports on specific inner experience ("*Really* feel what it's like inside as they . . .").

Phrasings for stabilizing and extending positive states. When a patient is able to have positive states in relation to the imagined parent figures, both pointing to and amplifying those states contribute to their stabilization. The therapist may focus specifically on further stabilizing and extending the positive states with phrasing such as the following:

> **Therapist:** Focus on that feeling of [*safety*]. *Really* feel it now. As you tune in to that feeling of [*safety*] *more and more*, you're able to hold that feeling more and more continuously in your awareness.
>
> More and more continuously in your awareness, that feeling of [*safety*].
>
> Notice what it's like to begin to hold that feeling of [*safety*] continuously in your awareness.

ANCHOR POSITIVE STATES IN BODY EXPERIENCE

When a patient is aware of positive states in relation to the ideal parent figures, the attachment-repair process is served well by linking those states to felt body experience. As described in Chapter 2 on the development of attachment bonds and in this chapter in the section on setting the IPF therapeutic ground, during the critical period of attachment formation, 12 to 20 months, identity is primarily body-based and memory is behavioral/enacted rather than mental/narrative. Thus, in principle, the more the patient has positive body experience that is linked to interaction with the imagined parent figures, the more efficient will be the formation of new attachment representations.

When the therapist makes statements to bring the patient's attention to experience, as described in the previous section, he or she often points to body experience, as was done at the end of the first example in that section:

> **Patient:** It's more relaxed.
> **Therapist:** It's more relaxed, yes. Feel what that's like in the body, *really* feeling more relaxed.

Other phrasings might include:

- Notice what that feels like now in the body.
- And you can be *even more* aware of that [*peaceful*] feeling in the body.
- What's happening in your body as you're with these parents now?
- You can feel the effect of their ways of being with you in your body too.
- *Feel* it in your body.
- The *more* you feel the [*contentment*], the *more* you notice it in your body.
- You can *feel* that in your body too, can't you?

INTEGRATE METHODS FOR ENHANCING POSITIVE STATES

Once the patient is able to be aware of positive states in relation to the parent figures and has generated more experiential detail in response to having those states amplified, stabilized, extended, and anchored in body experience, the therapist can guide the patient in a way that integrates all of those elements. In the following interaction, the therapist applied all the state-enhancing elements to the patient's report of the parents being "comforting":

> *Patient:* It's comforting, being with them.
>
> *Therapist:* Yes. Focus on that sense of *comfort* now so you can *really* feel it. Become *even more* familiar with this feeling, and what it's like as you experience it in your body.
>
> And the *more* you do that the *more familiar* you'll become with feeling comfort. And the more familiar you are with this feeling, the more *continuously* you'll be able to *feel* it and hold it in your awareness.
>
> You can *really feel it* now, can't you? That *comfort*, that *comfort*.
>
> *Really* feel it, feel it *in your body* and through your *whole* being.
>
> And you'll be *so pleased* to notice that *more* and *more* you'll spontaneously feel this *familiar* feeling of comfort.
>
> And now the scene will change somehow, in whatever way will help you to feel that comfort *even more* fully, and *even more fully* in your body.

Concluding the IPF Session

Within a session, the therapist conducts the IPF protocol for as long as time is available. Toward the end of the available time, focus can shift even more to stabilizing and extending the positive states, anchoring the positive states in the body, and integrating all the positive state-enhancing elements. Then the therapist takes steps to end the session.

SUGGEST THAT POSITIVE STATES REMAIN AS IMAGERY FADES AWAY

When about 5 or 10 minutes remain for the session, the therapist suggests that the patient will retain all the good feelings and benefits from being with the parent figures while the scene fades away. One possible form of this suggestion is as follows:

> *Therapist:* And now, as you feel all of these positive feelings *even more* clearly, the scene is about to fade away. And you can keep all the positive feelings and benefits from being with these parents as the scene fades away.

CREATE A BRIDGE FOR A SMOOTH TRANSITION BACK TO THE THERAPY ROOM

The therapist then creates a bridge for conscious awareness to return fully to the room with the therapist. For example:

> *Therapist:* As I gradually count from five down to one, with each number you'll feel yourself more and more smoothly and comfortably returning to this room, here with me.

REORIENT THE PATIENT TO THE PRESENT

Equally if not more important than reorienting the patient to place is reorienting to time. During the IPF process, some patients have a very vivid experience of being a child, and it's important that that experience stays within the IPF process.

> *Therapist:* And when I reach one, your eyes will open and you'll feel alert and refreshed, here with me, and ready to continue your day, *this* day [day of week/month/day/year]. Five . . . four. . . three . . . two. . . and one, eyes open, refreshed, alert, ready to continue your day.

ALLOW BUT DON'T ENCOURAGE THE PATIENT TO SPEAK OF THE IPF SESSION EXPERIENCE

While it is best to let the resonance of the session experience be the primary post-session mode, some patients may have unpleasant feelings or thoughts, and it is important that the therapist know of any such experience so it can be addressed and soothed before the session ends. Thus, the therapist makes a general inquiry, such as the following:

> *Therapist:* Before we stop for today, is there anything you'd like to say about your experience of the session or about how you feel now?

NORMALIZE THE EXPERIENCE AND REASSURE THE PATIENT ABOUT ANY NEGATIVE EXPERIENCE

Most patients will report a very positive experience. But it is not uncommon for a patient to highlight something that they feel unsettled by or are self-critical about. If that happens, the therapist, as a good attachment figure, accepts the experience as it was, indicates that it is not at all surprising, and reassures the patient that what happened is an indication of why the IPF process is valuable and will be beneficial over time. The following post-IPF imagery interaction occurred with the patient whose doubt about the parent figures and the IPF frame was illustrated on pages 331-334:

> *Patient:* I could sense their presence, and I could actually feel myself with them, and I felt their positive attention, but I kept doubting it; I couldn't believe it was real. So maybe I wasn't doing something right.
>
> *Therapist:* Everything you did was exactly right. In fact, it's a *very* good sign that you could so clearly sense their positive presence for you. I think it's *completely* normal that you'd have some doubts along the way, because we're helping to create something that's new for you, that you haven't experienced before. That's why we're doing this in the first place. If you'd never have doubts, maybe we wouldn't be needing to do this at all. And sometime we won't need to do it anymore. So let's be patient with the process and we can accept whatever you experience.
>
> What I think is much more notable than you doubting the parent figures and imagery is that each time you did doubt them, you experienced *them* understanding and reassuring you, and each time that happened you reengaged with them. We're on exactly the right track with this.

Signs of Progress

Over the course of a series of IPF sessions, there will be various indications of development toward attachment security. Such development is a process that will vary in time and detail across patients. But the therapist will recognize particular signs that the process is under way. These signs can be categorized into three main types, roughly in order of when they are likely to appear during the course of IPF treatment: (1) engagement with the attachment-promoting imagery, (2) beneficial effects of positive attachment representations, and (3) manifestations of an internalized secure base.

SIGNS OF ENGAGEMENT WITH THE ATTACHMENT-PROMOTING IMAGERY

The presence of dismissing attachment in a patient indicates that his or her attachment system has been fully or partially deactivated, and anxious-preoccupied attachment indicates that the attachment system tends toward hyperactivation. When the attachment system is not fully active or is active in an unbalanced way, patients will in various ways have difficulty with engagement with available attachment figures, both in their lives and in the IPF process. In the IPF process, different patients will show different degrees and forms of initial engagement with the imagined parent figures and their attachment-promoting behaviors, depending on the degree of deactivation or imbalance of their attachment systems.

For patients whose attachment system has been largely or fully deactivated, the first indications of progress are reports of being with parent figures who show at least a few of the four general factors and/or five behavioral pillars that promote attachment formation. When the attachment insecurity is primarily of the anxious-preoccupied type, an essential quality from the parent figures is *interest* in the patient; if the dismissing type is primary, an essential quality is *physical presence*. In the example on page 331, the patient at first saw parents but said, "I see them, but it's like we're in different worlds" and "It's like I'm in the city, and they're far away." Consistent with his dismissing type of insecurity, the essential general factor of "physical presence" was not met. After a few short interventions by the therapist, the patient showed progress by experiencing being in their physical presence: "Now I'm with them, all of me. They're holding my hands, and smiling."

When a patient's attachment system is partially functioning, either initially or from the benefit of some treatment intervention, he or she will show some engagement with the ideal parent figures and their attachment-promoting behaviors. Progress from there will be indicated by increasing degrees and consistency of that engagement, within and across sessions.

Many of the examples that appear in this chapter illustrate patients' engagement with the ideal parent figure imagery. Signs of engagement include strong clarity and vividness of the imagined interactions, reports of close felt connection with the parent figures, and especially the appearance of experiences with the parent figures that elaborate upon the framing and suggestions offered by the therapist. An example of such a generative response is as follows:

> *Therapist:* She sees that you're upset, and knows *just the right way* to help you feel better.
> *Patient:* She sees that I'm upset, and she reaches out and touches my face. That feels so good. As she's touching my face, so gently, she looks at me and tells me how much she loves me. It's calming.

In this example, the patient incorporated the therapist's suggestions that the mother figure recognized the patient's upset; then, in her imagery, the mother figure *acted upon* her knowledge of how to help the patient feel better. The therapist had not suggested *how* the mother would help her to feel better, or even that she *would* help her to feel better, but simply that she *knew* how. The patient herself generated the mother figure's attachment-promoting behavior— soothing—which *did* help her to feel better ("That feels so good"). The patient continued to elaborate on the interaction, reporting first that the mother was touching her face "so gently" and then that she was looking at her and telling her that she loved her.

SIGNS OF THE BENEFICIAL EFFECTS OF POSITIVE ATTACHMENT REPRESENTATIONS

The activation of and engagement with attachment-promoting imagery is the necessary condition in which that imagery can have beneficial effects. Indications of such benefit are another sign of progress. In the previous example, the patient was engaged with her imagery to a sufficient degree that it brought her direct benefit: She said of the mother figure's soothing behavior, "It's calming," which is a clear sign that the mother figure's behavior had the effect of *emotion regulation*.

As a patient develops toward a stable internal experience of attachment security, from the IPF imagery there will be more and more reports of positive qualities and functions that are correlated with security. Manifestations in the imagery of *emotion regulation*, of a sense of *safety*, of *proximity-seeking*, of *self-esteem* and *self-development*, and of good *metacognitive function* and *organization of mind* all indicate progress. Examples of each of these categories of benefit appear below. Although these examples were chosen to illustrate single categories of benefit, it is most common for several categories to manifest together in patients' experience and descriptions.

Emotion regulation. Indications of emotion regulation, as in the example above, will primarily appear in the form of the patient reporting decreased feelings of emotional discomfort, agitation, or distress.

> *Patient:* They're both very calm, even though I'm distressed. They're affectionate; they reach out and put their hand on my hand. They're also inquisitive.
> *Therapist:* Notice what effect that being with them has on your inner state.
> *Patient:* I think because they're so calm, as they go on talking, I feel more calm inside, and less agitated. I also don't feel as lonely.

Another example:

> *Patient:* It makes me feel less angry. I can just look around, I don't have to be all pent up with the anger anymore.

Emotion regulation may also be manifested indirectly in the ways that the patient modulates the parent figures' behavior, as in the two examples below:

> *Patient:* Both are affectionate to me, *but not too much.*
> *Patient:* With her it's just warm, not just physically. Emotionally the temperature is *just right.*

Experience of safety. Following are several examples from different patients:

Patient: I guess I see myself with my face buried in my mother's stomach, standing waist high, face against her, her arms wrapped around my back. It feels very safe. I can shut everything out, at least for a little while.

Patient: My father is standing, and he's holding me. His arms are underneath me. I'm leaning against him, and my hands are on his shoulder. It feels soothing. I feel safe.

Patient: He's here and he's not going anywhere. So I can bring up whatever I want to talk about.

Patient: It feels so secure and safe. I'm feeling so relaxed and with deep trust.

Patient: Well, I feel very calm, instead of worried. Because I know that they're not going anywhere.

Proximity-seeking. Several examples follow.

Patient: I notice that I'm hugging them, and they're responding when I'm hugging them. They're just playing around and we're having fun together.

Another patient:

Patient: We're outside, on a hike. It's very invigorating. There's a sense of energy. I see myself falling behind a step or two, and then scampering to catch up . . . that scampering to catch back up, and be close to them, that driving energy.

Therapist: Yes, you can *really feel* that wanting to be close to them, how *good* and *safe* and *connected* you feel, and how *welcoming* they are as they see you scampering back up to be close to them.

Another patient:

Patient: I'm upset, so I go to them, and they put their arms around me.

Self-esteem. Following are several patient examples:

Patient: It means not having to perform. Not having to pretend to be interested longer than I am. And not having to pretend I want to do what perfect kids do. I can do what I want to do. It means that there's plenty of room for kids to be loved for who they are.

Patient: It's kind of like I'm okay, just being me.

Patient: They want to know what I see. They encourage me to look with my own eyes. The way I see things is the way they're most interested in. It's an authentic engagement with the world. I want to say things to the world.

Self-development. Examples from several patients follow.

> *Patient:* They're interested in the people I'm interested in. They don't feel that people are threats to them. They want to foster my own connections. They know how important that is.

Another patient:

> *Patient:* We're all outside together on a hike. Nice terrain, nice vistas. It's good to be outside with them, to be connected to nature, to them.
> *Therapist:* Yes, you can *really feel* that connection, to nature, to them, and how *good* that feels. Tune into their ways of being with you, that let you know how much they *value* you.

Another:

> *Patient:* They're trying to heighten my curiosity in the world, pointing out things. It's like being in a nice clear place and taking a deep breath. That's what they're trying to enhance in me, from being together.

Another:

> *Patient:* Well, I'm older now, my bike is broken, and we have to fix my bike. They give me all the tools, and they know how to fix the bike, but they know I want to learn. So they show me just enough. They use another bike as a model. They're not concerned about it being messy. They're interested in helping me to learn.

Another:

> *Patient:* They feel confident as parents; they trust themselves. I can ask for something if I need it. They teach me self-reliance. They're there, but not to force me to do anything, but to encourage me.
> *Therapist:* Yes. What effect does that have on your inner state?
> *Patient:* It makes me feel stronger, and also more generous. It makes me feel that sharing something isn't a kind of giving up. It's something different. Sharing myself isn't—it's not a loss of myself.

Metacognitive function. Here are a couple of patient examples:

Patient: I guess they're reading to me. And they're like letting me read along, and make out things that are happening in the story, and wanting to know what I think about the characters in the story, what might happen, and how the characters might feel.

Patient: It's mainly a mom. When I tell her about how the kids at school make me feel, she tells me that I'm beautiful, and I'm strong, and that I can make people happy. I have joy to give them. She's like Ingrid Bergman. My old mom, she was too hurt to make me feel better.

Organization of mind. Several examples follow.

Patient: I see a woman, and a man. The woman is very calm, even-keeled. The man is humorous, also pretty calm and stable. I see flashes of them taking me everywhere with them. The woman is very affectionate, she puts her hand on my back, and the man is kind of the same way. They seem really interested in me.

Therapist: And you can *really feel* and take in their ways of being with you. Their *calmness*, their *stability*, the ways that they're *so affectionate* to you. Notice what effect that has on your inner state.

Patient: Overall I just feel pretty content. A whole person— not all these fragments, scattered all over the place.

Another:

Patient: I see them both being energetic, but not over the top. I don't see too much different happening, I'm still talking with them, and they're listening to me. There's an even exchange between us. It makes me feel clear inside. What I'm saying is coming out clearly; it's not all jumbled.

In some of the above examples, patients reported direct experience of beneficial effects ("I feel safe"); in others, they described the imagined parent figures encouraging, facilitating, and supporting the development of particular benefits (e.g., "They're trying to heighten my curiosity in the world, pointing out things"). Both types of experience indicate benefit from the process. How the direct type indicates benefit is obvious; how the other type indicates benefit may initially seem less so. When the patient reports that the parent figures are intending or acting toward developing a quality or function in the patient, it is assumed that the developmental processes underlying that quality or function *within the patient* have been activated. Continuation of the IPF process will then promote its further development, likely leading to reports of *direct* manifestations of it in later sessions.

Although benefits in various categories and forms will appear throughout the course of IPF sessions, their *appearance* does not indicate that they are *stable*.

Therapists must continue to engage the patient in the imagery process over time until the indications of benefit are readily evoked, consistently appear, and are stable across imagery scenes and sessions.

MANIFESTATIONS OF AN INTERNALIZED SECURE BASE

When a secure base has developed and has been internalized through the IPF process, there will be several indications within the imagery: (1) consistency and stability of attachment-promoting qualities in the imagined parent figures, (2) consistency and stability of the benefits the patient experiences in response to those qualities, and (3) exploratory behavior by the patient. When in the imagery the patient begins to make excursions away from the parent figures, even if briefly, that is a sign that an internal representation of attachment security is forming. Greater frequency, consistency, duration, and physical extent of such excursions are indications of the presence of an internalized secure base. Other indications include going to the caregiver when distressed (safe-haven-seeking) and showing a preference for physical closeness and physical affection (proximity-seeking).

The examples below highlight several patients' exploratory behavior in the imagery. These excerpts were taken from sessions later in the course of the IPF process, ranging from 8 to 44 sessions.

> *Patient:* I guess I'm afraid that that it's going to go away.
> *Therapist:* This mother really understands that fear. Notice how she responds to you in a way that *reassures you*, in *just the right way*, in the way you need.
> *Patient:* She says that just because she has to go doesn't mean she isn't there.

Another:

> *Patient:* They're comfortable about who they are, so they can let me be who I am. They're not very fearful. They're letting me play with a cat.
> *Therapist:* Yes, they're with you in ways that support you in enjoying *who you are* and who you're *discovering yourself* to be. How does this affect your inner state?
> *Patient:* I'm able to—I have space to do what I want to do. I have a safety for exploring. I feel like they trust me. They're there to guide me, and help me, not form me.

Another:

> *Patient:* I feel safe enough. I feel I can express that, physically move to something new. It's a new feeling in myself, a kind of like courage, a feel-

ing like, being held in a space where you are just safe, and feel willing to stretch, and reach out into the world. I have this confidence, I have a knowing, that they'll watch me, in a way they trust, that they don't need to contain me, that they'll give me the space to move forward.

Another:

Patient: They're interested in the people I'm interested in. They don't feel that people are threats to them. They want to support my own connections. They know how important that is.
Therapist: They know how important that is. What effect does that have on your inner state?
Patient: It makes me feel I can venture farther. I'm not stealing myself from them. They think it's a healthy thing I want to go away. They're happy I can go away, and come back, and I'm my own person.

Another:

Patient: I can look around more. I'm walking. I can go to places I didn't want to go to before, to new places. I don't have to worry about things.

Another:

Patient: It's on the street, in a neighborhood where we live. I suggest walking together down the street. And we do. (Pause) And now I'm walking ahead, and I know they're there behind me, even though I can't see them. There's just a weird sense of the neighborhood expanding; no, not the neighborhood expanding, but the comfort expanding, into the world.

In the expression below, a patient highlights what he experiences as a very significant change in his experience of relationship with his ideal parent figures. This change is clearly the emergence of an internalized secure base:

It feels like a meeting has taken place among the three of us . . . it feels very *different* than before . . . it feels like a starting point, like I can start to do things, and they can start to guide me and help me in ways that are right. It feels like the connection has become fully established, rather than *becoming* established. Up until now it felt like I was *trying* to feel connection with them . . . now it feels like that's been established. Now it's about me being more active, because I have the trust and connection with them now . . . I can do things and return to them . . . for interpretation of what it is I'm doing . . . It's like a whole new approach to being in a way . . . fundamentally they're interested in me. I guess I can start to be me, with their guidance . . . they can help me with that . . . they can be supportive in ways I've never experienced before.

Reinforcing the Internalized Secure Base

When signs of a secure base are apparent in the patient's imagery, the therapist helps to extend, strengthen, and deepen that state by continuing to apply the principles of enhancing desired experiences. These include (1) mirroring, (2) bringing attention to felt experience, (3) amplifying positive states, (4) anchoring positive states in body experience, and (5) suggesting new scenes in which the desired state is also present. All of these appear in the example below:

Patient: We're on a beach, a rocky beach. I can go and get rocks, and come back and give them to them, and they receive them. They pay attention to them, to the details, so we can look at things together.

Therapist: Yes, you can go and get rocks, and then come back to them. Notice what it's like as you go off by yourself, *really feeling* that they're *there* for you. You can feel that secure feeling, can't you?

Patient: Yes.

Therapist: You can *really tune in* to that secure feeling now. *Feel* what that's like, as you experience the secure feeling right now. What's the secure feeling like?

Patient: Well, I feel like I can be myself, and do what I want. And even if I'm not with my parents, I know that they're there for me, if I need them.

Therapist: Yes, you can be yourself. And they're *there* for you, when and if you need them. . . . And now this scene fades away, and a new scene is about to appear. In this new scene, you're also with these parents, and you're feeling the secure feeling *even more strongly*. In this new scene, you're feeling the *secure* feeling *so* clearly, and you can be yourself, and do what you want, and you know deep down that these parents are *there for you* if you need them. As this new scene appears, you can say what's happening and what it's like for you.

Patient: Well, we're at a playground, and I'm playing with other kids. I know my parents are there, but they're letting me do what I want, playing, and I don't see them, but I know if I looked for them they'd be there.

Therapist: Yes. You can *feel* that they're there for you, while you're playing and enjoying yourself. Notice what you feel inside now.

Patient: I feel happy. And there's like a confidence too.

Therapist: You feel *happy*, and a *confidence* too. *Really feel* that *happy*

feeling, and that *confidence*. And as you feel that, notice how you feel that in your body. What's it like to feel so happy, and confident, in your body?
Patient: Well, there's an energy, a good-feeling energy. Like I can be me, and play. I'm safe there.
Therapist: Yes, you can be you, with that *good-feeling* energy, and you're *safe*. Feel that *even more clearly* in your body now. *Even more* in your body.

You can *really* feel it. Become *even more* familiar with this feeling, and what it's like as you experience it in your body. And the *more* you do that the *more familiar* you'll become with this *good-feeling* energy, being you, being *safe*. And the more familiar you are with this, the more continuously you'll be able to feel it and hold it in your awareness. . . . You can *really feel it* now, can't you?
Patient: Yes.
Therapist: This *safety*, this *safety*. *Really* feel it, feel it *in your body* and through your *whole* being.

When a patient is deeply immersed in the imagery, the sense of time can be expanded so that positive states can be experienced as having a longer duration than actual clock time. Time expansion (and contraction) is a common hypnotic technique and is very beneficial for supporting the development of familiarity and mastery of desired qualities. In the interaction with the above patient, the therapist introduced time expansion to reinforce the patient's experience of safety as follows:

> *Therapist:* And now, even though only a few moments of clock time will pass, it will seem like *much longer* time elapses, long enough for you to experience this *safety* in a way that makes it *so very familiar* to you. You have *all the time it takes* for this safety to become part of you, to experience it *more and more* as a foundation of who you are.

Working With Present Experience and Reducing the Frequency of IPF Sessions

As indications of internalized secure base appear more consistently and vividly in a patient's IPF experience, he or she will more and more frequently report signs of greater security in his or her current, day-to-day, between-sessions life. For example, a patient might say, "I find myself sometimes actually enjoying when she touches me" or "When he said he was mad at me, I wasn't as worried that he'd leave me" or "Finally I called a piano teacher and scheduled a first lesson." In response to these current life manifestations of security, the therapist delights in these new experiences and applies the same reinforcing methods that are used to support positive experiences in the IPF imagery: mirroring and amplifying the positive states and how they are experienced in the body. The IPF method of suggesting new scenes in which desired experiences are also present is modified to make it relevant to the patient's current life experience. After reinforcing the patient's specific experiences of greater security in the present, the therapist suggests that the patient imagine bringing that sense of greater security to other circumstances. For example:

> **Therapist:** Now, as you're *really connected* to this feeling, imagine feeling it in a different situation, some situation in which you'd really like to feel more *secure* and *comfortable*.
>
> **Patient:** Well, in classes I often want to say something, but I get too nervous and I just stay silent.
>
> **Therapist:** Yes, you've been wanting to express yourself in classes. Now *really tune in* to the *secure* feeling; *really tune in* to that feeling, and let me know when you're feeling it really clearly.
>
> **Patient:** I'm feeling it.
>
> **Therapist:** Good. Now, with this secure feeling *really* present, imagine being in class. And when you are imagining yourself in class, feeling *secure* and *comfortable*, let me know.
>
> **Patient:** Okay, I'm there.
>
> **Therapist:** Wonderful. Now, just feel yourself there in class, feeling *secure* and *comfortable*, coming to feel it *even more* clearly. And when you're ready, imagine yourself feeling ready to raise your hand to say something.

This process continues as the patient imagines each step toward the desired action in the context of an inner, felt experience of a secure base.

Working in this way with the patient's present experience allows for a gradual reduction in the frequency of using the IPF protocol. At this stage of the treatment, there are two ways in which the IPF protocol continues to be of benefit: reinforcement of the secure-base experience and working with present-day affective states. Secure-base experience results from the development of new, positive attachment representations, and the stronger and more stable those representations are, the stronger and more stable will be the secure base. It is common for signs of insecurity to reappear in response to circumstances that challenge the secure base until the new attachment maps are deeply established. Thus, there is value to continuing to include IPF sessions in the ongoing treatment, even if less consistently than earlier in the treatment. Revisiting the IPF protocol is called for whenever the patient presents with signs of less security, such as an increase in dismissive and/or anxious-preoccupied features. In this circumstance, the IPF protocol can be done in a general way, without bringing the specific manifesting insecure features into the imagery. Alternatively, the affects associated with those specific features can be emphasized and brought deliberately into the imagery.

For example, a patient came to a session and reported having strong anxiety that his girlfriend might end their relationship. After establishing that she had not given any signs of wanting to do so, and that on the contrary she had suggested that they spend more time together, the therapist discussed with the patient that his anxiety probably indicated that his security was being threatened by the possibility of greater closeness. They agreed to work with the anxiety in the context of an IPF session. First, after setting the initial conditions for the IPF process (i.e., focusing awareness inward), the therapist asked the patient to bring to mind his girlfriend's suggestion that they spend more time together in order to evoke the anxiety and allow him to feel it strongly in the present in the session. When the anxious state increased, the therapist initiated the IPF protocol:

> Now, feeing this anxiety as you do now, imagine yourself going back, going back in time, back in time to when you were a young child, and feeling much the same way, quite anxious.

Then, when the patient was imagining and feeling himself as a young child in that anxious state, the therapist suggested ideal parents who were attuned specifically to that state:

> And now, feeling yourself as a young child feeling quite anxious, you can imagine yourself being with parents, but not the parents you grew up with. You can imagine yourself being with a *different* set of parents, parents who are *ideally suited* to you and your nature, and to your feelings and needs right now. These parents recognize that you're feeling quite anxious, and they know *just the right way* to be with you so that you feel comforted and soothed. They know *just the right way* to be with you so that you come to feel safe and secure once again.

As this patient had previously established signs of an internalized secure base, he readily experienced imagery that provided him with soothing and came to feel comfortable, confident, and secure rather quickly. After reinforcing that state, the therapist brought the reestablished secure state back to the situation that had challenged it:

> **Therapist:** And now, very clearly feeling *comfortable*, *confident*, and *secure*, you can experience yourself coming back to your current adult self, bringing back with you this comfort and security. When you are back fully into your adult self feeling *comfortable* and *secure*, you can let me know with a slight nod of the head.
> **Patient:** (nods)
> **Therapist:** Good. *Really* feel how *comfortable* and *secure* you are. *Really*

feel it all through you. Now, imagine yourself with your girlfriend, feeling *comfortable*, *confident*, and *secure*, and she's saying to you that she'd like to spend more time together. And from your *comfortable*, *confident*, and *secure* state, feel what it's like now to hear that from her.

The patient reported a slight increase in anxiety but said that it was not too much. In the imagery, he spoke with his girlfriend to establish how and just how much they would increase their time together, and he established a plan that he felt comfortable, confident, and secure with; before the next session he presented that plan to his girlfriend, to which she happily agreed.

Any affect state can be addressed similarly with the IPF method. When a patient speaks of feeling anxious, sad, lonely, or angry, regardless of the circumstance that evoked the feeling and regardless of whether the patient currently feels the state in the session or has felt it sometime prior to the session, the feeling state can be brought into the IPF imagery in a way that helps with its regulation. Working with affects in this way facilitates the development of patients' capacity to regulate their affects internally, on their own, beyond the immediate, present state. Similar to the example given above, the therapist begins the IPF session by guiding the patient to focus attention inward; he or she then asks the patient to focus on the uncomfortable affect state, and to feel it even more strongly by imagining being in the circumstance that contributed to its emergence. For example:

Notice now how you feel the sadness now, how it is in your feelings and in your body. *Really tune* in to that, to exactly the ways you're feeling sad . . . Now, imagine yourself back several days ago, when you first started feeling this sadness. Imagine the circumstance you were in, and exactly what was happening when you started feeling more and more sad . . . You can put yourself *right back* there, and notice how the sadness gets *even more clear*, *even more strong*.

When the patient indicated that the sadness was very strong, the therapist initiated the IPF protocol:

Feeing this sadness as you do now, imagine yourself now going back, back in time, going back in time to when you were a young child, to when you were a young child, feeling much the same way, quite sad. Feel yourself going back, feeling yourself younger and younger, until you feel yourself as a young child, feeling sad.

Upon establishing the imagery and affective state within the imagery, the therapist suggested ideal parents who were attuned specifically to the patient feeling sad:

And now, feeling yourself as a young child feeling quite sad, you can imagine yourself being with parents, but not the parents you grew up with. You can imagine yourself being with a *different* set of parents, parents who are *ideally suited* to you and to your nature, and to your feelings and needs right now. These parents recognize that you're feeling quite sad, and they *really* get how difficult this is for you now. They *really* feel for you, and they know *just the right way* to be with you so that you feel *comforted* and *soothed*. They know *just the right* way to be with you that helps you with this feeling.

The therapist and patient explored and worked with the imagery such that the parent figures were accurately attuned to the patient's affect state and were with the patient in ways that alleviated that state. Using the IPF protocol in this way to facilitate affect regulation continues throughout the treatment, even after the use of it more generally has diminished because of consistent signs of an internalized secure base.

Common Challenges During the IPF Treatment Process

Therapists may face any of a variety of challenges as they implement the IPF protocol. These challenges can be divided into three categories: (1) difficulties that the patient has with aspects of the protocol, (2) difficulties that the therapist has with implementing the protocol, and (3) difficulties pertaining to the patient–therapist dyad in the context of the protocol. Therapists' understanding of these difficulties and of the challenges that they create, and their readiness to respond appropriately to them, will contribute to the effectiveness of the IPF method.

DIFFICULTIES THAT PATIENTS MAY EXPERIENCE WITH THE IPF PROTOCOL

There are three general principles of responding to difficulties that patients have during the implementation of the IPF protocol. The first is to be empathic. While most patients ultimately experience the IPF method as deeply positive and beneficial, the method asks them to engage with part of their history that was deeply problematic—their childhood experience with parents or caregivers who were unable to provide them what was needed for attachment security. The more painful their childhood experiences were, the more painful it will likely be initially for them to imagine themselves as a child and to imagine being with parent figures. Particularly during the first or first several IPF sessions, resistances based on such associations with a painful history are quite common. When a patient's difficulty is met with empathic, supportive responses from the therapist, with the verbal and nonverbal message that the therapist understands something of what it was like for the patient as a child, the patient is likely to feel attuned to and soothed and to feel that the therapy environment might just be a safe place for staying with the method, despite the initial discomfort.

Initial discomfort is not problematic; in fact, it is beneficial, as it indicates that the patient has accessed something of the source of the attachment dysfunction. Further, the discomfort itself provides the opportunity for the patient to experience being protected, attuned to, and soothed and comforted by the parent figures. Until the parent figures are imagined, the therapist provides this kind of response to any discomfort that arises.

Some patients, particularly those with dismissing attachment, will not initially experience any conscious discomfort but will have difficulty with engaging with the methods, such as difficulty imagining being a child or imagining any parent figures. In response, therapists are similarly empathic and supportive, based on understanding that the protocol asks the patient to visit problematic domains of personal history. Therapists can also draw from their experience that most patients find their way into the IPF imagery and come to experience it in very positive ways. It is rare for a patient to be unable to become engaged with and benefit from the method.

The second general principle for responding to patient difficulties during the protocol is to maintain a collaborative stance, modeling curiosity, interest, confidence, and patience during the shared task of establishing and engaging with imagined ideal parent figures. The therapist explicitly and implicitly highlights that he or she is there with the patient, able and willing to address and be with any difficulty that arises.

The third general principle is to contextualize patient difficulties within the IPF imagery frame. Several examples and ways of responding were already presented in pages 329–337. Once the patient has created some IPF imagery, any difficulty can be referred to the parent figures for response. For example:

> *Patient:* I don't trust them. I think they'll get mad at me. I don't want to imagine them anymore.
>
> *Therapist:* These parents understand that you're having a hard time trusting them, and that you think they'll get mad at you. They are very present with you and very patient, and they don't get mad at you at all. They understand that you're feeling like pulling away. They're *right here for you*, even if you pull away, and they don't get mad at you at all.

Keeping the experience within the imagery frame provides an opportunity for the patient's difficulty to be met in beneficial, nonrejecting, and nonpunitive ways by the parent figures, which contributes to the formation of new, positive attachment maps. This type of response also reinforces the frame itself, which contributes to its ongoing effectiveness as part of the attachment-repair process. When the therapist's contextualization of experiences within the imagery frame is done in the context of his or her empathic and supportive ways of being, many of the difficulties that patients may have with the IPF protocol are effectively met. Particular difficulties and additional beneficial therapist responses are described below.

Inability to experientially imagine being a very young child. As the first experiential imagery component of the IPF protocol is the patient's felt sense of being a young child, this is the first place where some difficulty might arise. It is not surprising when a patient initially cannot put himself or herself into a child-self state, because it is that state that experienced the circumstances that led to the attachment disturbance.

The therapist guides the patient toward the child state experience and asks the patient to nod "when you are feeling yourself as a young child." If the patient nods, the protocol setup proceeds; if he or she does not, the therapist asks the patient about the experience. The patient may indicate the absence of any child-state feeling, or may report an observing stance, in which the child self is being seen from a third-person perspective. In response to either, the therapist first encourages the patient to continue to try:

> Yes, even though it may be hard *at first*, you can continue to bring your awareness to feel yourself as a young child, as though you are actually experiencing yourself now as a young child. Notice what starts to happen, in your felt sense of yourself, that lets you know that you are *more and more* feeling yourself as a young child.

With gentle, empathic encouragement, many patients will find their way into the desired first-person child-self state. For patients who do not, there are several ways of responding. One is to simply continue, trusting that as the protocol setup proceeds, the patient will gradually and eventually come into an inner state that is receptive to the ideal parent figure imagery. For many patients, this approach is effective. Alternately, the therapist may call upon methods that involve *displacement* of the self, either for finding a solution that allows for the experiential child-state or for imagining a different child (the displaced self) who will go through the protocol. The first approach uses displacement to establish a possible solution:

> There are other people too who have *at first* had some difficulty really feeling themselves as a young child for this practice. I'd like you to imagine now, sitting in front of a television or computer screen, and you are about to watch part of a documentary about several people who *at first* had difficulty imagining themselves, *really feeling* themselves, as young children.

When you imagine yourself sitting in front of the screen, you can let me know with a slight nod of the head. (Patient nods.) Good. Now, the screen lights up, and the show begins. The first person is being interviewed, and [he/she—same gender as the patient] is telling the interviewer what it was that helped [him/her] to become more able to experience [himself/herself] as a young child. You can be *very interested* and *curious* about what this person found as the way to do this. And as [he/she] is speaking, you can tell me what [he/she] says.

This approach normalizes the difficulty and implicitly suggests that solutions can be found. After the patient reports what the first person says, then the therapist suggests that another person comes on the show. "This time it's someone who seems much like yourself," and the same prompts are given. A third person is then brought on, described as

someone who you can *really* relate to, and who has something to say that seems like it's *just what you need* to help you be able to imagine and *really feel* yourself as a young child. And as [he/she] speaks, you can tell me what [he/she] says.

The patient again reports what was observed, and then the therapist brings the displacement imagery to a close and encourages reflection on putting into practice what has come to the patient:

And now this documentary finishes, and as the credits are on the screen, you find yourself reflecting on what was most helpful to you personally. You can start to feel confident that you can yourself imagine being a young child. And when you have a sense that this is possible for you now, you can let me know with a slight nod of the head.

When the patient nods, the therapist guides the patient using the same phrasing as was used initially.

If the patient still is unable or indicates that he or she continues to observe the child-self from a third-person perspective, then another displacement method may be used. This method allows the observing, third-person stance and is based on recognition that experience with a displaced version of the self will still be of benefit because of the unconscious association between the displaced figure and the self. If the patient persists in having an image of himself or herself *as a child*, rather than as *being a child*, then the protocol simply continues in this context. The same language is used for creating and engaging with ideal parent figures, as though the patient were experiencing the child and parent figures from a first-person perspective. When a therapist says, "Now imagine yourself with parents who are ideally suited to you and your nature," the "yourself" and the "you and your" fit with either a first-person or third-person experience of the child-self. For most patients, a first-person experience, or some degree of it, will spontaneously emerge as the protocol proceeds in its usual form, either within a session or across a series of sessions. Even if it does not, engaging with ideal parent figures from a displaced self will still be of benefit.

When a patient cannot imagine himself as a child either in first or third person, and the therapist chooses to not simply proceed with the protocol as if the patient can, then a broader displacement may be created. He or she is asked to "imagine a scene in which you see a child who is much like you were" and the protocol proceeds as usual, except for substituting "he/him/his" or "she/her/hers" for "you/your/yours." If this approach is taken, after a session or two the therapist will begin the next IPF session with the usual form of encouraging direct experience of self-as-child; it is likely that after some experience with displacement, the patient will become more able and willing to bring himself or herself more directly into the protocol, in third person and eventually in first person.

Sometimes a patient will not imagine being a young child but will, from a first- or third-person perspective, imagine being an older child, teenager, or young adult. If this happens at the first or one of the early IPF sessions, the therapist encourages imagining being even younger:

> Yes, you feel yourself as a teenager now. And you can continue to feel yourself becoming younger and younger, until soon you're feeling yourself as a very young child.

Often this approach will be effective. If it is not, the therapist may simply continue with the protocol with the patient at the age he or she imagines being (especially if the imagined age is an older child or younger teenager). Or, the therapist may engage the patient in documentary-show displacement imagery (as described above) to find ways of imagining being younger (especially if the imagined age is an older teenager or young adult).

It is not uncommon for patients to imagine themselves at different ages during different IPF sessions. Particularly if a patient has in many IPF sessions imagined himself or herself as a very young child, imagining the self as older is likely a manifestation of the remapping process and its integration. In such a circumstance, the therapist accepts the older-age self and conducts the IPF protocol as usual.

Refusal to generate ideal parent figures. For the same reasons that a patient might have difficulty imagining being a young child, there can also be great discomfort about imagining ideal parent figures. There are two primary forms of such resistance.

Active resistance to the IPF protocol. The more painful the patient's experience of his or her own parents or caregivers was, the more likely it is that the task of imagining *any* caregivers, even framed as "ideal," will generate resistance. A patient who has initially agreed to participate in the treatment protocol may, upon reaching the step of imagining the parent figures, say that it is too hard or too painful and not want to continue. The therapist empathizes with the patient's experience and acknowledges that it can be hard *at first* to imagine parent figures (implicitly suggesting that it becomes easier). From this empathic, positive stance, the therapist incorporates the patient's difficulty as an indication of why it is so beneficial to continue. For example:

> I really understand that this is hard for you *at first*. And because it's hard for you now, that's all the more reason for us both to stay with this, so you can come to experience *something new* with parent figures; you can come to experience being with parent figures in a way that doesn't feel so hard. If you think you can't do it, that's *all the more reason* to try.

If a patient continues to resist engaging with the IPF process, the therapist may introduce the *inner child method* (Bradshaw, 1990). Particularly if the patient is feeling a strong sense of himself or herself as a child, this method can be very helpful as a transition to being able to imagine ideal parent figures. Instead of asking the patient to imagine parent figures, the therapist suggests that the patient-as-child is met by the patient-as-best-adult-self.

> Now imagine that as you're feeling yourself as a young child, you are joined by your best adult self who knows *better than anyone* who you are and what you need. No one understands you as well as your best adult self.

The patient is then encouraged to experience the adult self's ways of being with him or her that provide "what's most needed for your sense of security and well-being." After a session in this form, during the next session the therapist goes back to suggesting that the patient imagine ideal parent figures. If necessary, the inner child method is used again, and it is continued until the patient is willing to imagine parent figures.

Experience of being disloyal to or dishonoring the actual parents. Many patients resist or reject the IPF protocol at the point of being asked to imagine ideal parents. They say that the task of creating new parents feels like being disloyal to or fundamentally dishonoring their actual parents. The therapist empathizes with the patient's wish to honor his or her parents and emphasizes that there is no intention at all to dishonor or discredit the actual parents.

> What we're doing here is in *no way* critical of your actual parents; they did the *very best* that they could, given their own experiences as children. What we're doing here creates the possibility for you to have some very helpful inner experience that your parents weren't able to provide for you, despite their doing their best. We can imagine that your actual parents would want for you to have the kinds of experiences that will help you to feel the most secure and healthy that you can be.

If the patient has begun to imagine ideal parent figures and becomes troubled by a sense of disloyalty or dishonoring of his or her parents, the therapist can work with that experience from within the frame.

> These parents understand your concern and that you want to honor your actual parents. They know, like you do, that your actual parents had difficulties being parents because of the ways that they were parented. And these new, ideal parents would *never disrespect* your actual parents for their doing the *very best* that they could. . . . If these ideal parents were ever to encounter your actual parents, they would treat them with the *utmost kindness* and respect, and they would insist that they treat you in the same ways.

Difficulties pertaining to imagining ideal parent figures. This category describes patients' experiences that arise in the context of their willingness to imagine ideal parent figures, without any overt rejection or resistance to doing so. These experiences reflect subtle resistance, lack of any readily available models for positive attachment figures, or misunderstanding of the task of imagination. The therapist typically learns of these difficulties when he or she asks the patient to describe his or her experience of the ideal parent figures, such as, "And when you're ready you can describe these parents and their ways of being with you."

No parent figures are imagined. Despite apparent willingness by the patient to imagine parent figures, none become available. This is quite common during the first or even first several IPF sessions, especially for patients with dismissing attachment. It is not an indication of an inability of the patient to engage with the process; rather, it is best seen as a manifestation of the patient's deactivated attachment system. As the patient is willing to participate in the protocol, the therapist reassures him or her that sometimes it takes a while for the imagination to create ideal parent figures, and together, collaboratively, the therapist and patient stay with the task.

Some patients expect to *see* parent figures, despite the therapist not using explicit visual terms, such as "<u>See</u> these parents" or "<u>Picture</u> parents who are ideally suited to you." Not all patients have a strong visual imagination, and if those who don't are *looking* for indications of parent figures, they will likely not find any. This mismatch of expectation and dominant sensory mode can be corrected by highlighting the patient's *felt sense*:

> It may be that the first way you sense these parents is through the *feeling* that comes from their ways of being with you, their ways of being with you that feel *so very right*, so very *supportive* of your *deep sense* of *safety* with them. Notice what your felt sense is now, and how it might let you know that these parents are *right there* with you.

If the patient continues to have difficulty imagining parent figures, the therapist may use the inner child method, as described above. After a session that includes the patient engaging his or her child-self with his or her adult-best-self, the therapist returns to the attempts to evoke ideal parent figures.

Imagined parent figures are vague or distant. Either initially or after some period of not imagining any parent figures, the patient may begin to imagine them but without much clarity or closeness. The presence of any sense of ideal parent figures, even if vague or distant, is a sign that the attachment system is becoming engaged. To support further engagement, the therapist focuses on enhancing the clarity of the parent figures from within the imagery frame. The following example appears on page 331 in the section about this topic:

> *Patient:* I see them. But it's like we're in different worlds.
> *Therapist:* Tell me how it is you experience them.
> *Patient:* Well, it's like I'm in the city, and they're far away, like in the country.
> *Therapist:* Even though there's been that big distance between you, they know that it's important for you to be closer together, but only in a way that's *safe* and is *best* for *you*. So let's see what happens so that you can *all* be *together*, *safe* and sound.
> *Patient:* Now the upper part of my body is with them, but my feet are still in the city.
> *Therapist:* Okay, something has shifted, and you're *already closer together*. Let's see what happens next.
> *Patient:* Now I'm with them, all of me. They're holding my hands, and smiling.

The next example is also from that section:

Patient: I see parents there, but I'm separated from them by some gauzy, hazy material. I don't know how to get to them, and I feel alone even though they're there.

Therapist: These parents understand that it sometimes can feel hard to have a felt sense of connection with them. And they know exactly how to help you get beyond the gauzy, hazy material, in a way that feels *just right* for you, and to *help you* to come to feel in *close connection* with them, so you don't have to feel so alone.

Parent figures are the patient's actual parents, either in remembered or imagined "ideal" form. Patients who have issues of maintaining loyalty to their actual parents, who have ambivalent feelings toward them, or who misunderstand the imagery task are likely initially to bring to mind their actual parents, either as they are remembered or in idealized form. The distinction between memory and imagination is important here. Memory reflects what was, or the experience of what was, whereas imagination allows for possibilities different from what was. When a patient brings to mind actual parents, even in idealized form, he or she is drawing from memory of the actual parents. Engagement of memory related to the actual parents will at best limit the possibilities for experiencing secure attachment imagery; at worst, memory association to the actual parents will evoke and reinforce the problematic parental representations that contributed to insecure attachment.

Although the initial instructions for creating ideal parent figures emphasize forming "ideal *fictional* parents, created entirely by your imagination" (p. 309), the press of memory may supersede that prompt. If so, the therapist responds to the patient's invoking of his or her actual parents by again emphasizing the use of *imagination*:

Though it's not surprising that images of your actual parents have come to you, you can let those images of your actual parents gently dissolve away. What we're going to focus on now is using your imagination to create *completely new* parents, parents who are not your actual parents, but parents who are *ideally suited* to *you* and *your* nature. So call upon your imagination now, and let a *new* and *different* set of parents appear for you. You can use your *infinitely flexible* imagination to make these *completely new* parents exactly the way that's best for you and your well-being. Go ahead and shape and reshape these new parents until the ways they are feel *just right*.

It may be useful to address possible concerns about disloyalty or dishonoring of the actual parents by suggesting that the patient may draw from the best of what was and incorporate that into the creative process of imagining:

These *completely new* parent figures can have all the best qualities of your actual parents, who did their very best for you. And these new parents also have additional qualities that allow them to provide for you what you *most need* as a very young child, what you *most need* to feel *absolutely secure* in your relationship with them.

If resistance based on loyalty to or honoring actual parents continues, the therapist speaks directly to those issues, as on page 363–364 above.

Parent figures are people the patient has or had relationships with. This occurrence also reflects engagement of memory rather than imagination. Because most patients have had at least some positive experiences with others, it is not uncommon for a patient's imagined ideal parents to be people from his or her life. Although such people might have qualities that are more attachment promoting than the patient's parents, real people are inevitably more complicated than imagined ideal people. Any difficult experiences that the patient had with them are likely to limit the remapping power of the ideal parent figure method.

The therapist responds to the appearance of such people in the imagery in a way similar to how he or she would respond to the patient's imagining actual parents in ideal form:

> Though it's not surprising that images of these people you know have come to you, you can let the images of those people gently dissolve away. What we're going to focus on now is using your imagination to create parents who are *completely new*, parents who are not in the form of anyone you've actually known. These new imagined parents can have any or all of the best qualities of anyone you've known. Because it's your imagination, you can have these new parents be *just the way you'd like*, ideally suited to *you* and to *your* needs and to who you are. So call upon your imagination now, and let parents appear for you who are *completely new*. You can shape them until they are *just right* for you.

By repeatedly emphasizing the possibilities of imagination and by encouraging the patient to incorporate any and all known or imagined positive ways of being into the ideal parent figures, the use of memory can be corrected and the patient is likely to appropriately engage his or her imagination to create new and positive attachment figures.

Nonhuman ideal parent figures are imagined. Some patients who are open to the ideal parent figure process and who readily bring their imagination to the task may at first create ideal parent figures who are not human. For example, the parent figures might be cartoon characters, animals, or aspects of nature. Such forms suggest that the patient's attachment wounds make the prospect of allowing support from human attachment figures too threatening. As attachment security is best established in the context of human relationships, the therapist will prompt the patient to try to imagine human figures, but if the patient persists in imagining the nonhuman figures, the therapist continues with the protocol with those figures as they are. With each subsequent IPF session, the therapist makes specific reference to the parent figures as human:

> Now, as a young child, imagine being with human parents, but not the human parents you grew up with in your family of origin. Imagine now being with a *different* set of human parents, parents who are *ideally suited* to *you* and *your* nature. These parents are *right there with you* and *really know* how to be with you to help you feel *so safe* and *secure*. These parents *really know* how to be with you in all the ways that help you to feel *absolutely secure* in relationship with them.

At some point, the patient will begin to imagine human parent figures, and then may have difficulty in any of the ways presented in this section.

Only one ideal parent figure is imagined, or one is vivid and one is vague. It is not uncommon for a patient at first to imagine only one ideal parent figure or to imagine one clearly and the other not so clearly. When this happens, the "missing" parent figure is usually representative of the actual parent who the patient experienced as more abusive, neglectful, or absent. The therapist continues with the protocol, allowing the patient-as-child to focus on and engage with the one clearly present parent figure while also making gentle prompts to indicate the attachment-promoting presence of the other.

> Yes, this mother is *right there* for you, present for you in ways that feel so *very safe* and *supportive*. And even though you don't yet clearly sense the father, you can begin to get the feeling that this father is there for you too, in *all the right ways* that assure your *safety*, *comfort*, and *security*.
>
> Notice the ways that this mother is being with you that feel *so very right*. And when it also feels right for the father to join you both, he will be there with you too, in *just the way* you would want.

Whether during the first IPF session or later during a subsequent session, the patient will at some point begin to experience the initially absent parent figure.

Difficulties in the relationship with ideal parent figures. When the patient is able to imagine ideal parent figures, he or she begins to experience a relationship with each and both of them. Common difficulties in these relationships arise from the activation by the imagery of the patient's pre-treatment disturbed attachment representations, which create expectations or experience of these parent figures behaving in ways that the patient experienced with his or her actual parents. Generally, the therapist responds within the context of the IPF frame by suggesting that the imagined parents recognize and understand the patient-as-child's concerns and that they find ways to reassure and show him or her that they would never behave in those ways. For example:

> *Patient:* They seem nice, but I think they'll get tired of me and reject me, or that they'll make fun of me.
>
> *Therapist:* These parents understand that you feel afraid that they'll reject you or make fun of you. They know how much that being that way would hurt you, and so they would never do that to you. These parents are *dedicated* to being *right here* for you, and to helping you with whatever worried thoughts or fears that you have. Notice how they respond to you now, as they *really get* what your concerns about them are. They *really know* how to help you with this.
>
> *Patient:* They hug me and tell me that they love me like I am.

An exception to responding within the frame in this way occurs when the parent figures in the imagery become rejecting, neglectful, or abusive. If they become hurtful in any way, the therapist immediately calls for a change in the frame and for a new scene to appear with new ideal parent figures who are protective and not harmful. In the above example, the patient later in the same session reported that the parents had turned their backs on her and were being critical of her and laughing to each other about her.

> And now this scene dissolves away, and in a moment a *completely new* scene will come to you. In this new scene you'll be with a *different* set of parents, and these *new parents* will be *completely protective* of you and of your feelings. These new parents would *never* make fun of you or reject you. These *new parents* know how to be with you so you feel *completely safe* and *liked* and *loved* for exactly *who you are*. So go ahead and let yourself imagine being with these new parents, and when you're with them, you can let me know what it's like.

Difficulties that spontaneously break the imagery frame. The presence of a problematic attachment history and the resulting insecure inner working models of attachment make it likely that patients will have at least some difficulty with initially establishing ideal parent figures, with maintaining a positive experience with them, and with maintaining the imagery frame. In the following example, the imagery frame was broken by the patient's memories of his actual parents intruding upon what had started as a positive experience with imagined ideal parents:

> *Patient:* We're all at the dinner table, and they're both listening to what I'm telling them about my day at school. It's hard to believe that they're so interested, but I guess they are . . . My parents were never interested in what happened at school. And we hardly ever ate at the table; we were always watching TV when we ate, and didn't talk. That's when my dad was home at all. And when they weren't fighting. When I was a child, I didn't feel connected with them at all.
>
> *Therapist:* Even though memories of your actual parents come up, you can use those memories to help you to come back to your imagined parent figures, who are *so very different* from the memories of the ways your actual parents were. In fact, these *new parents* are in many ways the *positive opposite* of how your actual parents were. These new and different parents are *so happy* to sit with you at the dinner table as you all eat, and they're *so interested* in what happened during your school day. They're *so happy* to listen to you, and they're *so happy* with each other too. Let your imagination have these parents be *exactly as you'd like them to be*, and so different from memories you have. You can let those memories go, and *really enjoy* the new parents, who through the power of your imagination are exactly the ways you'd like them to be. You can feel *so very connected* to these parents.

Notice that the therapist stepped out of the frame to acknowledge the appearance of memories of the actual parents but did not support any engagement with them. She made reference to the break by indicating the possibility of coming "back to your imagined parent figures." Then she suggested that the memories would help the patient to return to the imagined parents, who in many ways embody "the positive opposite of how your actual parents were." The break from the frame was identified as memory, and then the frame was reinforced.

The therapist could also have responded by staying completely within the frame. For example:

> These parents understand that it was very different with your actual parents in the past. But now these *new parents* are with you, and now with them you're having a *very different* experience, a different experience that helps you to recognize that these parents are *so very attuned* to you and are *so very interested* in who you are. These parents are *really listening* to what you're telling them about your day at school, and they're *so happy* that you're all eating together and talking at the dinner table.

Another example of responding to a break from the imagery frame from entirely within the frame appears on pages 331–334. In this example, after several minutes of experiencing the parent figures in very positive, supportive ways, the patient abruptly doubted them and their reality and retreated from participating in the protocol:

> ***Patient:*** They smile, they laugh, they pat me on the head . . . they're not real . . . they're . . . perfect . . . they're too perfect. This isn't real. They seem almost plastic. I can feel their love and can see their support, and love, and affection and caring about me, but it's—it's too good to be true. It's a sinking feeling. I can't do this anymore . . . this is just faking.
>
> ***Therapist:*** They see, and they understand that it seems that way to you. They understand that at first it can be hard to really take in their deep and unconditional love. They protect you, and they protect you from yourself sometimes, and this is one of those circumstances in which they help to protect you from doubting too much, from doubting that what you most want and need is here for you. Notice how they respond to knowing that you feel this is fake and that it's too good to be true.
>
> ***Patient:*** They brush it off; they put their arms around me, reassure me. They take it as a compliment that I experience them as too good to be true.

The therapist effectively responded to the patient's experience by maintaining the imagery frame when the patient could not. Although the patient had stepped out of the frame and painfully rejected the imagery process as "just faking," the therapist stayed right with both the patient's experience and the imagery frame that had evoked the experience. Quite quickly the patient was able to reengage with the frame and with the parent figures as accepting and reassuring, and, quite remarkably, he himself incorporated his doubt back into the frame: "They take it as a compliment that I experience them as too good to be true."

Other forms of breaking from or reducing engagement with the imagery frame include *becoming affectively overwhelmed* or *becoming confused or disoriented* during the protocol. As with the example above, the therapist responds to these occurrences by maintaining the imagery frame for the patient and suggesting that the ideal parent figures respond empathically and effectively to the patient's shift of state. For example:

> These parents see that you're very upset right now, and they know *just the right ways* to help you with these feelings. They are with you in ways that help to *soothe* and *comfort* you, so that soon you'll start to feel these feelings becoming less overwhelming and more manageable. Notice how they are with you that feels so very *soothing* and *comforting*.

DIFFICULTIES THAT THERAPISTS MAY HAVE WITH THE IPF PROTOCOL

While therapists may certainly feel challenged by the difficulties that patients present, there are several common difficulties that therapists may have that are particular to their use of the IPF protocol.

Self-doubt about skill with the protocol. As with any therapeutic method, greater skill and greater confidence come with more training, study, practice, and experience. The in-depth presentation of the IPF method and its foundations in this book, along with the many illustrating clinical examples, provide sufficient introduction for a therapist to be able to bring it into his or her clinical practice. Initial or ongoing self-doubt can be addressed in several ways: (1) Reread this chapter several times, and refer to specific sections of it as issues and questions arise during treatment; (2) obtain supervision from qualified practitioners of the Three Pillars treatment approach detailed in this book; (3) take reassurance from the *collaborative* aspect of working with the IPF protocol, recognizing that when both patient and therapist understand that working with the protocol is a shared endeavor, any difficulties, lapses, or breaches, individually or relationally, are addressed and resolved together; and (4) recognize that although the IPF protocol has a basic structure, during and across sessions there are many opportunities for the therapist to revise and refine his or her application of it on the basis of the patient's responses and the therapist's ongoing learning and skill development.

Resistance to regular and consistent application of the protocol. Once this method is introduced to a patient, its benefits are most efficiently established by applying it during nearly every therapy session until signs of an internalized secure base are established. Resistance to doing so may come from self-doubt, or simply from greater ease and comfort with methods that are more familiar in the therapist's experience. The patient may have expectations about psychotherapy as "talk therapy" that align with the therapist's familiar methods, which would reinforce any tendency of the therapist to conduct the IPF protocol intermittently rather than regularly. Some flexibility is appropriate, of course; for example, in response to crises or other pressing issues brought in by the patient, the therapist may choose to forego the IPF protocol in a session or two and instead work more explicitly with the metacognitive and/or collaborative systems. But crises and pressing issues can often be effectively addressed by bringing the patient's experience of them into the IPF protocol, especially later in treatment, as described on pages 354–358 above in the section on working with present experience.

The goal of conducting the IPF protocol in nearly every session is served by the therapist's intention to do so, by collaboratively establishing with the patient an agreement that a period of treatment will proceed in this way, and by the therapist's and patient's monitoring of any internal resistance or deviation from this treatment frame. If the therapist (or patient) notices that a sequence of sessions without any IPF protocol is occurring, the therapist considers what factors may be operative, addresses those factors within himself or herself and possibly with the patient, and possibly reviews this chapter and/or obtains supervision.

Concern that the use of suggestion is manipulative or controlling. A factor that can contribute to some therapists' resistance to applying the IPF protocol is concern that it is too structured or directive, or that it is manipulative or controlling, especially for patients with abuse histories. Many therapists have training and experience with therapy methods that are nondirective and focus on supporting and responding to patients' immediate experience (e.g., Fosha, 2000). The use of suggestion is a central component of the IPF method, as is shaping of patients' experience. But suggestion is used to set an imagery *frame*, within which the patient is free to create fresh and unique forms, and the therapist's subsequent shaping of those forms is based on extensive research-based understanding of the conditions that support the development of secure attachment. As therapists develop more experience with what happens when patients engage with the IPF imagery frame and process, they recognize that rather than being manipulative or controlling, they are permissively establishing the conditions that allow for the activation of patients' own innate attachment system. When the attachment system is activated, the imagery frame is simply a context for its manifestation, and therapists' shaping of the imagery is simply support for its reinforcement.

Doubt about the IPF method because of lack of or inconsistent signs of progress. If a therapist expects a patient to form IPF imagery quickly and without difficulty, to show consistency of engagement with that imagery, or to show signs of an internalized secure base after just a few sessions, he or she may become discouraged and doubt the effectiveness of the method. A big challenge for therapists, particularly those who have not yet had much experience applying the IPF protocol, occurs when patients are unable to imagine any ideal parent figures for the first or first several sessions. As noted earlier in this section on common difficulties, it often takes more than one IPF session for a patient to begin to imagine ideal parent figures. Therapists who have had less experience with the method may interpret this lack of imagery as a sign that the method is not being effective or that it is not appropriate for the patient. On the contrary, patients who have the most difficulty initially are patients who likely have a strongly deactivated attachment system, making staying with the IPF process particularly beneficial for them. It is important for therapists to remember that any difficulty that patients have with imagined parent figures is to be expected, as the attachment map or maps that patients enter treatment with were formed by problematic experience with early caregivers. The IPF method helps patients to establish a new, positive attachment map that is based on the cumulative experience of usually gradually developing positive experiences with imagined ideal parent figures.

Those positive experiences might not be consistent or linear. A patient might feel very engaged with clear, vivid parent figures for several sessions, even initially, and then have a session or several in which there is more discomfort with or distance from the parent figures. Such an occurrence is not a sign of a problem with the protocol; rather, it is most likely an indication of the protocol having helped the patient to reach an element of his or her attachment map that is particularly problematic. Consistent underlying progress will not necessarily manifest as a positive experience in any single session or series of sessions. Therapists must be patient for the emergence of signs of an internalized secure base. Depending on the severity of the attachment disturbance, secure base signs may begin to appear after as few as 10 sessions or so, or they may still not be apparent after 40. As with a healthy parent who is attuned and responsive to the developmental level and needs of her or his child, the attuned therapist patiently continues the IPF work until the internalized secure base is established.

DIFFICULTIES PERTAINING TO THE PATIENT–THERAPIST DYAD

There are two primary forms of difficulty that may arise from particular dynamics within the patient–therapist dyad. One is collaborative avoidance of the IPF protocol, and the other is an affect-laden breach in the collaborative engagement with the protocol in which the patient not only breaks out of the imagery frame but also experiences a rupture in the relationship with the therapist.

Collusion to avoid the IPF protocol. The patient and therapist ideally form a collaborative dyad that engages the IPF protocol to reach goals that are mutually established early during treatment. However, just as the dyad can collaboratively support use of the protocol, it can also collaboratively *resist* its use. Because both the patient and the therapist may experience difficulty in relation to the IPF protocol—the patient because it challenges his or her deactivated attachment system, and the therapist because of self-doubt or concerns about the method—both may collude to avoid the regular and consistent application of the method. This collusion can compound, as the resistance of one will find support and reinforcement in the resistance of the other.

Signs of collusive avoidance may include the patient regularly bringing to sessions a series of crises or urgent issues that are presented for therapeutic discussion, which the therapist responds to by participating in such discussion rather than staying true to the agreed-upon nearly-every-session use of the IPF protocol. Often the therapist will feel some unease about not asserting the use of the protocol but will rationalize not using it by thinking that the patient has a more immediate need to talk. Ambivalence about the protocol may manifest itself in both the therapist and the patient agreeing at some point during a session to start it when only a short amount of time is left in the session.

The best prevention for collusive avoidance is to recognize that it may occur and to understand why. Ideally, part of the treatment-frame agreement pertaining to the IPF protocol is that both therapist and patient will collaboratively watch for manifestations of avoidance. The best remedy for avoidance if it does manifest is to identify it immediately and to address together the factors that are contributing to it.

The imagery frame breaks and the therapy relationship is ruptured. Patients' spontaneous breaks from the imagery frame that do not overtly involve the therapist are discussed in the above section on patient difficulties. When a break also includes a negative affect toward the therapist, such as anger or fear, the therapist does not respond from within the imagery frame. Further, the therapist does not respond from the attachment system at all, for, as mentioned in Chapter 7 (and as described more fully in Chapter 10), a rupture in the attachment relationship between the patient and therapist is best addressed in the *collaborative* behavioral system. The example below is from the 12th IPF session with a patient whose therapist had told her during the previous session that he was going on vacation after two more sessions.

> *Patient:* I'm really little. I'm in a lot of pain. I kind of see the parents, and they see that I'm in pain, and they want to help. I'm not sure they can help. They try.
> *Therapist:* Yes, they *really see* that you're in a lot of pain, and they want to help. Notice how it is they're with you that starts to feel helpful to you.
> *Patient:* I don't know . . . maybe there's nothing they can do. Maybe there's nothing anyone can do. I'm just a little girl, and everybody hates me.

At this point the patient opened her eyes and began to show very angry affect.

> *Patient:* And everybody still does! I know you hate me too. When you go away, you'll probably be relieved not to have to see me, and you'll probably make fun of me too. I really hate you! And I hate myself!

The therapist showed concern and acknowledged the patient's shift of state:

> *Therapist:* I get that you're feeling angry right now, and maybe other feelings too. Let's try to figure out together what happened.

> *Patient:* You know what happened! You're going on vacation and you'll be happy to get rid of me for a while.
>
> *Therapist:* Well, you're right about one of those things. I *am* going on vacation, as I told you last week. But I'm not at all feeling that I'll be happy about not meeting with you for a while. Tell me more about what it's like for you when you think of me going on vacation. I wonder if maybe it would have been better for me to give you more notice about my going away.

Their exploration of the patient's experience and of the rupture in the therapy relationship continued in a collaborative manner, with the therapist frequently making reference to the shared goals of understanding and resolving the breach. Through this process, both the collaborative and the attachment behavioral systems were restored. During the next session, the patient and therapist returned to the IPF protocol, and in the context of her ideal parents, the patient addressed feelings of abandonment and aloneness.

In addition to the common challenges of using the IPF protocol described in this chapter, there are challenges that are particularly relevant during the treatment of each of the specific types of insecure attachment. These challenges, pertaining to the IPF protocol and also to the other two pillars of treatment, are addressed in each of the subtype chapters.

Recognizing Successful IPF Treatment

In summary, the ideal parent figure protocol is an efficient, positive-focused method that integrates what is known about conditions that best support the development of secure attachment. In the context of a collaborative therapeutic relationship and the therapist's stance of embodying attachment-promoting qualities, a patient is first guided to shift his or her focus of awareness inward and onto a more relaxed body state, which is the ground for accessing the behavioral memory system, where attachment representations form. Then, the therapist invites the patient to engage his or her imagination to create an experience of being himself or herself as a young child. Supporting access to the behavioral memory system and evoking a felt sense of being a young child create the conditions that make it likely that the patient's innate attachment system will be activated at the deepest levels.

The introduction of ideal parent figures is the next step and further supports the activation of the attachment system. The patient and therapist work together to shape the imagery of those parent figures so that they come to feel "just right" to the patient. That "just-right" feeling occurs when the parent figures embody ways of being with the patient-as-child that meet his or her longings, wants, and needs for attachment security. The therapist is guided by knowledge of the general caregiver ways of being that support the emergence of an internalized secure base, and also by what was specifically missing in the particular patient's early childhood experience. Through the therapist's suggestion that the imagined parent figures embody those general and missing qualities, and by encouraging the patient-as-child to imaginatively access what only he or she knows is most deeply needed, the patient can have a full and rich attachment repair experience in mind, feelings, and body.

In addition to its effectiveness, a particular appeal of this method to patients and therapists alike is that it does not require focus on and processing of patients' painful childhood history. Rather, patients get to have new, positive, "ideal" experiences through the creative and evocative power of the imagination. Often, both patients and therapists are deeply moved by the beauty and tenderness and loving qualities and experiences that emerge in and through the imagery.

The account below is from a 57-year-old woman who had been in treatment for three years before the therapist learned the IPF methods and introduced them to her. Together they did the IPF protocol during six treatment sessions, and the patient thereafter did one session on her own using self-generated imagery. Rather quickly, there were profound changes in her experience, in her inner state, and in her relationships with others. She was so surprised and pleased that she wrote the following to her therapist:

> *Quite unexpectedly I liked this method.*
>
> *At the beginning I visualized a most simple situation: evening, I'm home alone, waiting for my parents to come from work. They came in, they are young, beautiful and they love me. We are glad to see each other. We talk. Nothing special, just simple conversation, but I feel that they are interested in me, they missed me and we are happy to be together.*
>
> *It seems to me that I have now more childhood memories than before. The pictures that I visualized during our sessions became a part of my real childhood memories.*
>
> *I took with me the feelings of warmth, light, safety and joy from these new memories. In these imaginary pictures I experienced a real joy of life, feeling that the world is beautiful. In my childhood I never felt this so vividly.*
>
> *When I was a little girl, I tried to manifest the emotion people expected from me, I tried to pretend to be imperturbable, older than I really was. I could not express myself freely, in a natural way. I could not feel the joy of life fully. As an adult person I can't feel it as well. But I can do it in my imagination! With ideal parents it was possible for my little girl to be herself. She has a right to express her feelings freely. She can feel a joy of being close to her beloved and appreciate this closeness. And it was wonderful.*
>
> *At the beginning of this work I felt guilty toward my real parents that I replaced them with ideal parents so easily, that I wanted to enjoy an ideal*

picture where there is not any stress or problems, where all my needs are met. But then I just concentrated on the process. I decided that I can allow myself to see from a new angle different pieces of my life, and my parents would not be hurt.

In the first two or three sessions I just imagined vivid pictures. Nothing special, just a feeling of closeness. Then I tried to invite my ideal parents into difficult moments of my childhood. And I felt that they did not reject me even when I was abusive, felt myself helpless or betrayed somebody. They could hear me, they empathized with me and helped me to deal with these situations. After that the situation does not look extremely awful and irreparable. I do not have to face these difficulties alone, wise adult people are with me. They are always ready to help me to understand the situation and to teach me how to behave. And I'll be able to deal with my trouble more successfully or understand myself better. I can confide to them my experience, they would not devaluate it. I think, to grow up each person needs to have an experience of making her or his own decisions but it is important as well to have a nearby wise adult person to ask for advice. I didn't have enough of such possibilities in my childhood. I did not dare to share with my real parents any of the difficult situations I reexperienced in my imagination with my ideal parents.

It is interesting that as the result of this work my negative feelings (resentment, anger) toward my real parents faded. In my imagination my ideal parents came to my real home. I realized that the sense of warmth and safety really existed in my childhood, these feelings just were buried under a lot of misunderstanding, resentment etc. My parents were demanding, they criticized me, but they also loved me! I'm sorry that they are gone. Probably we could talk in a different way than we used to talk.

When I came to therapy I had a strong feeling that I'm a bad, totally spoiled person and I should put all my efforts to hide this from people around, to pretend that I'm normal. Now this feeling is gone. My self-esteem grew up. I'm aware of my faults, but I can live my life.

She reported to her therapist in person that her relationships with her son, her friends, and her colleagues at work had become better. She said that she was not as demanding as had been usual for her, that she was blaming people less for not giving her what they could not give, and she was able to appreciate what was good in each relationship.

This patient's experience, after only six IPF sessions with her therapist, is of course highly unusual. Few patients will evidence such remarkable transformation in so few sessions. It is clear that this patient benefited from her three years of therapy prior to this work, which appears to have set the metacognitive and collaborative foundation for the IPF method to be so integratively powerful.

The IPF orientation toward positive relational experiences does not mean that experience with this method is always easy. When the attachment system has been deactivated or hyperactivated, difficulties of various sorts may and often do arise along the way toward reactivating or balancing it. But the difficulties themselves are expected and even welcomed, and both in and out of the imagery frame they are met in ways that further contribute to the development of attachment security. Despite the "common challenges," positive experiences with imagined new attachment figures begin to proliferate, and ultimately these experiences overwrite the old, insecure attachment maps and create a new, balanced and integrated map of earned secure attachment.

Although the IPF method focuses specifically on the attachment behavioral system, as described in Chapter 7 its activation also engages and strengthens the metacognitive and collaborative behavioral systems. The next two chapters detail the treatment pillars of developing a wide range of metacognitive skills and of fostering collaborative behavior, respectively. Treatment for attachment insecurity that includes, cultivates, and strengthens each of these three interdependent and mutually reinforcing systems not only best promotes attachment repair but also supports greater mental and emotional health and the greatest capacity for well-being.

CHAPTER 9

The Second Pillar

Metacognitive Interventions for
Attachment Disturbances

The History and Development of Metacognition

The history of the development of metacognitive interventions in attachment-based therapy can be roughly categorized into four historical generations of metacognition: (1) the zeitgeist of ideas leading up to Main and her associates at Berkeley developing a metacognitive monitoring scale for the Adult Attachment Interview (AAI), (2) the zeitgeist of ideas leading up to Peter Fonagy and his associates developing the Reflective Functioning Scale (RF-S) and mentalization-based treatment (MBT), (3) the research of Antonio Semerari, Giovanni Liotti, and their associates at the Third Center of Cognitive Psychotherapy leading up to the development of the modular approach to metacognitive psychotherapy; and at the same time (4) the research on higher cognitive development and its implications for understanding the full range of metacognitive skills.

FIRST GENERATION: THE APPEARANCE–REALITY DISTINCTION AND THE AAI

Interest in metacognition can be traced to a seminal paper by John Flavell from Stanford University in the *Amercian Psychologist* in 1979. Flavell stated, "Thus, the nature and development of metacognition and of cognitive monitoring/regulation is currently emerging as a . . . new area of investigation" (p. 906). He defined metacognitive knowledge as follows: "Metacognitive knowledge consists primarily of knowledge or beliefs about what factors or variables act and interact in what ways to affect the course and outcome of cognitive enterprises" (p. 907).

Later, Flavell (1986) defined metacognition as simply "thinking about thinking." Note, however, that his original definition is primarily a functionalist definition of metacognition in that it emphasizes thinking about thinking *in a way that functions to change cognitive operations*. His first description also emphasizes metacognitive strategies which [pertain] to knowledge of "what strategies are likely to be effective in achieving what goals" or solving problems (1979, p. 907). Since this original work, his pragmatic emphasis on metacognitive strategies as a way to metacognitively reflect upon and improve strategies for solving problems and reaching goals has had an enormous impact. For example, children are now taught to solve math problems by metacognitively monitoring the strategies they use to solve these problems.

Flavell's original work focused on how young children develop metacognitive capacity. He stated, "Young children are quite limited in their knowledge and cognition about cognitive phenomena, or their metacognition" (1979, p. 906). In the earliest investigation on the development of metacognition in childhood in North America, Flavell and his associates focused on one particular type of metacognition, namely, the appearance–reality distinction, which is recognition that experiences of reality are *representations*:

> The appearance–reality distinction is but one instance of our more general knowledge that the selfsame object or event can be represented . . . in different ways by the same person and by different people . . . [I]t is part of the larger development of our conscious knowledge about our own and other minds. (Flavell, 1986, p. 419)

Flavell and his associates developed a laboratory test to assess the development of the appearance–reality distinction in three- and five-year-olds (Flavell, Flavell, & Green, 1983). Children were given various objects that appeared one way but in reality were something else. For example, they were shown an imitation rock that looked like a stone but was made of a soft spongelike material, or they were shown a pencil that in reality was made out of rubber. In the appearance condition, for instance, the children were shown the rock or pencil and asked, "What does it look like?" Then, the experimenter squeezed the rock to show it was spongelike or bent the pencil to show it was rubber. In the reality condition, children were asked, "What is this *really, really*?" (Flavell, 1986). The researchers found that the ability to make an appearance–reality distinction increased with age from three- to five-years-old. Flavell et al. (1983) concluded that "some of the 3-year-olds did seem to have some grasp of the appearance–reality distinction . . . five-year-olds performed almost errorlessly" (pp. 102–103). The older children developed the capacity to know their constructions of reality *as constructions*, and thus as potentially limited or erroneous.

Alison Gopnik at the University of Toronto extended Flavell's research to investigate other variations on the theme of the appearance–reality distinction, namely, the study of *representational change* and *representational diversity* (Gopnik & Astington, 1988; Gopnik & Graf, 1988). Three- and five-year-old children were shown objects that looked one way but were really something else—in this case, the imitation rock as in the Flavell studies or a box labeled "Candy" that really had pencils inside. Then, the experimenter demonstrated to the children that the "rock" could be squeezed because it was soft, or that once the box was opened it had pencils and not candy inside. The children were asked what they thought the object was when they first saw it and then what they thought it was after the demonstration. The objective of the research was to see at what age the children changed their representation after the demonstration. They found that three-year-olds generally lacked representational diversity (that different children might represent the object differently) and representational change (that the same object could be represented differently before and after the demonstration). Gopnik and Astington (1988) concluded, "Children's understanding of representational change seems to develop between the ages 3 and 5" (p. 34).

In another experiment, Gopnik and Graf (1988) told children about objects hidden in a drawer. The children were either shown what was in the drawer, told but not shown what was in the drawer, or asked to infer what might be in the drawer from a clue. Immediately or after a delay, the children were asked how they knew about the content in the hidden drawer. Three-year-olds but not five-year-olds had difficulty identifying the *source* of their knowledge, especially after a delay. Gopnik and Astington (1988) interpreted these results as indicating that the development of *metarepresentational ability* occurs between the ages of three and five. They say that representational change is "a metarepresentational ability, an ability that requires children to construct representations of their own representations" (p. 27).

Harris, Donnelly, Guz, and Pitt-Watson (1986) extended the appearance–reality distinction in an investigation of children's ability to distinguish real from apparent emotions when hearing a story about a protagonist who hides emotions. Children were asked what the protagonist would be feeling. Four-year-olds had limited ability, but six-year-olds were quite capable of distinguishing real from apparent emotion.

The early research on the development of the appearance–reality distinction and its variations had a strong influence on Mary Main and her associates in their inclusion of a Metacognitive Monitoring scale on the Adult Attachment Interview (Main, Goldwyn, & Hesse, 2002). Main (1991) defines metacognition as "*thinking about thought* . . . being able to reflect on its validity, nature, and source" (p. 129), "the ability to step back and consider (one's own) cognitive processes as objects of thought and reflection" (p. 135). According to Main, metacognitive *knowledge* refers to reflecting on the nature of thought, and metacognitive *monitoring* refers to reflecting on its source and validity.

Main and her associates took a different perspective in their research on the development of metacognition in children. They looked at differences in metacognition based not only on age but also on attachment status. Their working hypothesis was that metacognitive capacities would be more developed in secure children as compared to insecure children of the same age. Main (1991) states, "Children who are securely vs. insecurely attached to primary attachment figures will differ with respect to both metacognitive knowledge and metacognitive monitoring" (p. 146). With respect to metacognitive ability and developmental age, Main reports that

> children under the age of 3 do not understand the *merely* representational nature of their own (or other's) thinking, because they are as yet unable to operate upon (or "metarepresent") it. Not having a metacognitive distinction between appearance and reality available, they are unable to imagine that some propositions are in fact without validity; that some individuals believe things which are not true; and that they themselves may have false beliefs at present or may have harbored false beliefs in the past. (pp. 129–130)

With respect to attachment status, Main predicted that children with insecure attachment, when compared to securely attached children of similar age, are less able to see their thoughts, beliefs, and mental models as representations and are less able to metacognitively view their thoughts, beliefs, and models as not reality and as potentially erroneous or distorted. Insecure children exhibited frequent "failures of corrective metacognitive monitoring" (1991, p. 135). Additionally, Main believes that these metacognitive deficits in insecure children make them likely to develop multiple, contradictory internal working models for attachment: "I suggest that difficulties with the 'appearance–reality' distinction and the dual coding of single entities will make a young child vulnerable to responding to unfavorable attachment experiences by developing 'multiple (conflicting or incompatible) models' of attachment" (p. 127).

In contrast, securely attached children show *coherence of mind* and construct a single internal working model (Main, 1991, p. 143). On the AAI, parents of secure as compared to insecure children had great access to attachment-related experiences and memories, showed better organization, had more coherent attachment-related discourse, were more able to monitor cognitive processes associated with attachment-themes, and were better able to monitor and correct possible distortions (p. 144).

With respect to the interaction of age and attachment status, Main (1991) cites several of her own studies to show how various aspects of metacognition develop with age. For example, secure as compared to insecure 21-month-old toddlers showed more spontaneous self-directed speech and used more self-correcting strategies to achieve a goal in a play episode. When six-year-olds were asked a series of questions like, "What is thought? Where are thoughts located? Do other people know what you are thinking when they can't see you?" secure but not insecure children showed that they understood the privacy of thought.

As noted above, Main and her colleagues incorporated their ideas about metacognition into the Metacognitive Monitoring scale on the AAI. The scoring manual of the AAI (Main et al., 2002) indicates three ways of recognizing metacognitive monitoring. The first pertains to the speaker's acknowledgment of the limitations of knowledge, that the way things *seem* to be is not necessarily the way they are in reality. Statements illustrating recognition of appearance–reality distinctions and related statements about representational change and diversity are scored as examples of metacognitive monitoring. For example, recognition of an appearance–reality distinction is indicated by the statement "It looked like I was ignoring him, but in fact I didn't see him because I didn't have my glasses on." Understanding of representational change is illustrated by the statement "I used to think that his thoughts were superficial, but now I realize that I just didn't understand the vocabulary that he was using." The speaker of the following statement clearly understands representational diversity: "I thought his parenting was in the secure range, but others who know him better might disagree with me."

Second, "fresh" comments illustrating monitoring of "reaction patterns" add to the metacognitive monitoring score (Main et al., 2002, p. 55). For example, if the speaker starts to give one answer to a question and then changes the answer a few moments later, it is likely an illustration of metacognitive monitoring. An instance of this would be, "When I first started answering this question, I didn't think that I'd learned anything from them, but now that I think of it, they taught me a great deal about how to manage my feelings when I was an adolescent." Third, examples of error monitoring, such as commenting on the fact that a belief or memory might be distorted or limited, increase the metacognitive monitoring score. An example of error monitoring is "You know, I don't really think that she cares about me, but she's stuck with me over the years, so maybe I'm wrong about that."

The scale produces a rating of the degree of metacognitive monitoring as follows: (1) none, (3) possible, (5) some monitoring, (7) marked monitoring, and (9) metacognitive monitoring characterizing the interview (Main et al., 2002, p. 60). In our extensive experience with the AAI, patients who have personality and/or dissociative disorders score very low on metacognitive monitoring, most secure individuals in the general population score in the moderate-to-middle range, and a smaller number of secure individuals and some individuals after having years of psychodynamic therapy score in the high range on this scale. Main states that while it is generally true that adults classified as secure on the AAI show evidence of metacognitive monitoring, it is also true that some secure individuals show no evidence of metacognitive monitoring on the AAI, and also that certain insecure individuals show some evidence of metacognitive monitoring on the AAI.

This first generation of work on metacognitive processes has several limitations. For example, the range and types of metacognition are poorly represented on the AAI. We now know that there is much more to the domain of metacognition than variations of the capacity for metacognitive monitoring. Main et al. stated

(2002) that the metacognitive monitoring scale is "still in draft" (p. 61), yet there has not been any substantial revision to the scale since the 2002 coding manual was developed. Further, Main states that the scale is limited to "self-monitoring" and does not address any metacognitive reflection on the state of mind of the other. The second-generation research by Peter Fonagy and his associates has addressed both of these issues.

SECOND GENERATION: INTERSUBJECTIVITY, MENTALIZATION, AND THE REFLECTIVE FUNCTIONING SCALE

The second generation of research, by Peter Fonagy, Anthony Bateman, and their associates from what we call the London School or group, evolved in a very different context. Their ideas about the development of mentalization and reflective function in childhood were heavily influenced by the developmental theory of mind research in general and by their collaboration with Gyorgy Gergely in regard to his social biofeedback theory of parental-affect mirroring. Through their work, not only did the recognition of types of metacognition expand, but also metacognition was seen as intersubjective and bidirectional—a mind being known in the mind of the other, *and* vice versa.

Just as Mary Main's 1991 paper was seminal in shaping the first generation of metacognitive work, Gyorgy Gergely and John Watson's (1996) article on social biofeedback was seminal in shaping the second generation of metacognitive work. Gergely and Watson present "a new theory of parental affect-mirroring and its role in the development of emotional self awareness and control" (p. 1181). In contrast to the first-generation research, the development of metacognitive capacity was not something studied as a developmental line *within* the child at successive ages, but as something that develops *between* a child and his or her caregiver that they co-create together. Gergely and Watson observed that somewhere between 9 and 12 months of age, children develop the capacity to detect the other's intention toward a goal and perceive the other as an intentional agent (p. 1182). This recognition of intentionality allows the child to represent beliefs, desires, and the emotions of others and is the "aboutness" of what is conceived of as the other's mind. Gergely and Watson are critical of Meltzoff and Gopnik's (1993) hypothesis that innate imitative mechanisms and imitation of the caregiver's facial display adequately explain the child's developing awareness of his or her internal emotional state. They argue:

> The mother plays a vital interactive role in modulating the infant's affective states . . . the quality of maternal interactions exert a strong regulative influence on the infant's affective state changes . . . Mothers are generally rather efficient in reading their infant's emotional displays and sensitive mothers tend to attune their own affective responses to modulate their infant's emotional states. (p. 1187)

Secure mothers with their spontaneous facial affect displays frequently match their infant's affect display and show increased coordination and synchronization of matches with facial display, gesture, and vocalization.

More important, Gergely and Watson (1996) see this interactive process as a kind of "training" for the infant via affective mirroring, in a manner not so very different from what happens in biofeedback training in adult patients. Both parental-affective mirroring and biofeedback training depend on contingency detection and amplification. Contingency detection and maximizing and marking are the keys to understanding the parent–child mirroring process. Contingency detection refers to the infant's discovery that the caregiver's response is in part the outcome of, or contingent upon, the infant's behavior. From this recognition, the child infers that he or she is an "active causal agent" (p. 1196). Marking refers to the caregiver's "producing an exaggerated version," or maximized version, of emotional expression (p. 1198). The following mother-to-infant expression is an example of such marking: "Oh *you* look *so very, very* uncomfortable. Let's see what we can do about that." According to Gergely and Watson, marking is critical to the child's learning that the momentary emotional display is about his or her internal state and not about the caregiver's emotional state. In this manner, the child is said to "decouple" the emotion from that of the caregiver and becomes "sensitized" to his or her immediate interoceptive cues so as to infer his or her own internal emotional state from those cues. Gergely and Watson state:

> The repetitive presentation of an external reflection of the infant's affect-expressive displays serves a vital "teaching" function that results in gradual sensitization to the relevant internal state cues as well as to the identification of the correct set of internal stimuli that correspond to the distinctive emotion category that the baby is in. As a result of this process the infant will eventually come to develop an awareness of the distinctive internal cues that are indicative of categorical-emotion-states. [This process is like what occurs in biofeedback training wherein] The internal state changes are mapped on to an *external* stimulus equivalent directly observable to the subject . . . parental affect-mirroring provides a kind of *natural social biofeedback training* for the infant and plays a crucial role in emotional development. (p. 1190)

Consistent marking produces an additional development with respect to mentalizing capacity. Gergely and Watson claim that "the infant will construct a separate representation" for the marked as compared to the actual facial affective display of the caregiver, and that this new representation "will come to function as *secondary representational structure*" (1996, p. 2000). This secondary, intersubjective representation is seen as the foundation of mentalization. Gergely and Watson summarize by saying that parental affective mirroring of affects serves four separate developmental functions: (1) sensitization to internal states, (2) building of secondary representations as representations; (3) regulation of child's internal emotional state, and (4) developing a generalized affective communication code based on the capacity to pretend, play, and know representations as representations (p. 1205).

Gergely and Watson (1996) also briefly discuss the developmental psychopathology implications of parental *"deviant mirroring styles."* When parents provide a congruent but unmarked form of affective mirroring, the emotion "is not going to be decoupled from the caretaker and will be attributed to the parent as his/her real emotion . . . and not become anchored in the infant . . . [and the] secondary representation . . . will not be established" (p. 1202). The following mother-to-infant expression exemplifies a lack of marking: "You're uncomfortable." Also, when the parent provides *marked but noncongruent* affective mirroring, the infant will develop a sense of the emotion as anchored in his or her internal state but will develop a "distorted secondary representation of his/her primary emotional state . . . and pathologically distorted self-representations" (p. 1198). An example of marked but noncongruent mirroring is a mother laughingly saying to her infant, "You're *so* uncomfortable." Fortunately, since Gergely and Watson state that "contingency detection is likely to be . . . active over the lifespan" (p. 1203), changing these forms of developmental pathology can be done through therapy or other beneficial experiences.

The London group's expanded understanding of the development of metacognitive capacity in children led to their concept of *reflective function* (RF). In essence, RF includes the processes of reflecting on the self and on the views of others and on contemplating the other's reflection on the self in ways which distinguish between inner and outer reality (Steele & Steele, 2008b). It is also described as "the mental function which organises the experience of one's own and others' behaviour in terms of mental state constructs" (Fonagy, Target, Steele, & Steele, 1998, p. 5). The RF construct draws from Dennett's thesis (1978, 1987) that beliefs and desires predict human behavior, as well as from the ideas of Sigmund Freud, Anna Freud, Melanie Klein, Donald Winnicott, John Bowlby, Daniel Stern, and others (Steele & Steele, 2008b). Fonagy and Target (1997) describe RF as "the developmental acquisition that permits the child to respond not only to other people's behavior but to his *conception* of their beliefs, feelings, hopes, pretense, [and plans]" (p. 679). This acquisition develops in part from:

> [a] caretaker with a predisposition to see relationships in terms of mental content [who] permits the normal growth of the infant's mental function. His or her mental state anticipated and acted on, the infant will be secure in attachment . . . [and] less reliant upon defensive behaviors to maintain psychic equilibrium. (Fonagy, Steele, Steele, Moran, & Higgitt, 1991, p. 214)

In order to assess and measure RF, Fonagy and his colleagues developed the Reflective Functioning Scale (RF-S) to be used either with AAI transcripts (Fonagy, Target, et al., 1998) or independent of the AAI with clinical session transcripts. Unlike the AAI Metacognitive Monitoring scale, the Reflective Functioning Scale assesses reflective capacity regarding the state of mind of both self and other and includes a wider range of metacognitive capacities than those focused on the appearance–reality distinction. Although reflective function is considered to be a unified process, the RF-S assesses four discrete categories or dimensions of reflective functioning. These categories are (A) awareness of the nature of mental states, (B) explicit effort to tease out mental states underlying behavior, (C) recognition of the developmental dimension of mental states, and (D) recognition of mental states in relation to the interviewer.

Each of these four categories of reflective functioning as they appear in the RF manual is described below. We include these here to specify the second-generation, more elaborated understanding of metacognitive capacities and also, most important, to provide for clinicians a guide of what to listen for that indicates the degree of reflective function present in their patients. The descriptions are adapted from the RF coding manual (Fonagy, Target, et al., 1998), and are followed by illustrative responses to Question 15 on the AAI (Main et al., 2002). Question 15 asks, "Were there many changes in your relationship with your parents between childhood and adulthood?" Since each of the four categories includes knowing representations *as* representations, responses that indicate such knowledge are weighted heavily in the scoring. The RF score given to each specific response is given in parentheses (scoring is explained below, following the examples).

A. Awareness of the nature of mental states (recognition of the characteristics of mental states in self and others):
   1. *Opaqueness of mental states.* Statements indicating uncertainty regarding a mental state, or uncertainty about which of the alternative mental states might be associated with a given behavior. Example: "I think that my relationship with my parents became closer in my early 20s, but I'm not sure." (4)
   2. *Mental states as susceptible to disguise.* Recognition that one's own and others' mental states can be disguised. Example: "I think that my relationship with my parents grew closer when I became a young adult, although my parents quickly became financially dependent on me, so it was hard to tell how they really felt." (5)
   3. *Recognition of the limitations on insight.* Awareness of limitations in one's ability to understand self and others. Example: "I think that my mother felt closer to me when I began to have children, but I'm not sure." (4)
   4. *Mental states tied to expressions of appropriate normative judgments.* Recognition of mental states as expectable responses to specific circum-

stances. Example: "When I was 18, I started to stay out past 10. She gave me the 'cold shoulder' on these occasions, I guess because she was angry and like many adults in my life, didn't understand that I had matured to adolescence." (3)

5. *Awareness of the defensive nature of certain mental states.* Statements indicating recognition that mental states can be modified to reduce negative affect. Example, "He seemed to ignore times when I was respectful, I guess because he believed in strict parenting." (5)

B. The explicit effort to identify mental states underlying a given behavior (identification of possible mental states that may account for behavior, and offering accurate or plausible links between mental states and behaviors in self and others):

1. *Accurate attribution of mental state to others.* Specific causal accounts of behavior in terms of mental states. Example: "My parents have changed very little over the years with respect to their views about child rearing; they treated my children not unlike the way they treated me, or this is how it seems to me." (6)

2. *Envisioning the possibility that feelings concerning a situation may be unrelated to the observable aspects or reality of the situation.* Recognition that affect may be inconsistent with the external situation. Example: "Even though I was incarcerated, I think that my parents and I sort of had a better relationship, you know, when I became an adult, because that is the way things go as you get older." (3)

3. *Recognition of diverse perspectives.* Explicit acknowledgment that different people may perceive a given behavior or situation differently. Example: "After I moved out of the house, I feel that I became the parent and my mother became the child. It was all about her creating a situation so attention was focused on her, or so it seemed to me. She would have disagreed." (6)

4. *Taking into account one's own mental state in interpreting others' behavior.* Recognition that one's interpretation of an event might have been distorted by what one was feeling or thinking at the time. Example: "Well, when he moved to the West Coast, after he divorced my mother, I certainly talked to my father less than when he was living with us. He didn't invite me to his wedding because I guess he assumed that I wouldn't have gone." (5)

5. *Evaluating mental states from the point of view of their impact on the self and/ or other.* Awareness of the role that one's own mental states might have had on behaviors. Example: "I think I was needy and demanding, and that probably was off-putting to him." (6)

6. *Taking into account how others perceive one.* Recognition of how others'

perceptions are influenced by their own or others' actions and reactions. Example: "I think other people saw me as pushy, but I just didn't have confidence." (5)

7. *A freshness of recall and thinking about mental states.* Spontaneous expressions indicating something currently thought or realized. Example: ". . . but as I think about it now, my father's refusal to talk about his past may have been to protect me, not to keep it secret from me as I used to feel. Does this make sense to you?" (7)

C. Recognizing developmental aspects of mental states (includes acknowledgment of the influence of one generation on the next, showing understanding of how mental states of others change, showing appreciation of family dynamics, and/or distinguishing between the thinking of a young child and an older person):

1. *Taking an intergenerational perspective, making links across generations.* Statements indicating recognition of intergenerational exchange of ideas, feelings, and behavior. Example: "When I turned 18, my parents came to me with problems that they were having with my younger sisters. I felt that I was betraying my siblings, but I went along with it, I think, because I yearned for approval from my parents. However, when I have children someday, I can't see myself going to the older ones with problems about the younger ones, or at least I hope I wouldn't do that." (8)

2. *Taking a developmental perspective.* Awareness that one's own and others' mental states and perspectives can change with age. Example: "I'd say that my relationship with my parents grew closer when I left home for college. Growing up, my parents rarely mentioned or demonstrated their feelings toward me. When I first left home, suddenly they began to bring up endearing stories about me as a child. When I was a child, it didn't seem to me that they were paying that much attention. But maybe that had to do with the fact that I stayed away from home whenever I could because I felt closer to my neighbors' parents than to them." (8)

3. *Revising thoughts and feelings about childhood in light of understanding gained since childhood.* Recognition that views of the social world and feelings and beliefs concerning it can change radically between childhood and adulthood. Example: "I used to think that all people were as wretched as my parents. I could give a damn about this whole topic now." (1)

4. *Envisioning changes in mental states between past and present, and present and future.* Recognition and/or anticipation of changes in one's own mental states or perspectives. Example of past-to-present change: "As a child I used to think . . . but as an adolescent I came to see . . ." (6). Example of present-to-future anticipated change: "I don't understand

how my mother tolerated my father's only being home from work on the weekends. Maybe when I've been married as long as they have, I'll understand." (6)

5. *Envisioning transactional processes between parent and child.* Recognition that parent and child have influence and impact on each other. Example: "I was a lazy son of a bitch and he kept at me about this, but I just behaved lazier and lazier." (2)

6. *Understanding factors that developmentally determine affect regulation.* Awareness that a small child is unable to regulate his or her own emotional state and is dependent on the caregiver to perform this homeostatic function. Example: "My mother's behavior remained erratic even during my adolescence. Perhaps this was why I was such a moody teenager." (3)

7. *Awareness of family dynamics.* Seeing the family as an interdependent system, where the mental states of the individual members interact and create attitudes and feelings that each individual member is affected by. (This is rare; when present, it indicates a high level of RF). Example: "I think he didn't understand the difference between children and adolescents and this is why he seemed to take my frequent experimentation with relationships as rejections of everything he and mom had taught me about social values." (7)

D. Mental states in relation to the interviewer (recognition of mental states as shown by interaction with the interviewer; indicates willingness to entertain mental states in the context of other relationships):

1. *Acknowledging the separateness of mind.* Recognition that the interviewer or therapist has a separate history, a unique set of experiences, and a different mental stance and thus may not necessarily share one's mental state. (Indicates high RF.) Example: "As you might have gleaned from the interview, as a child I had a terrible relationship with my mother, so it might be hard for you to believe that I let my mother move in with me to my first apartment when I turned 18, and we actually got along for reasons that I can't fathom." (7)

2. *Not assuming knowledge.* Efforts to help the interviewer understand by stepping outside the narrative and spontaneously clarifying confusing aspects. Example: "This may seem unusual to you, but there was a bigger change in my relationship to my stepmother than to my mother. I was very nasty to my stepmother as a child, thinking that she was the reason that my father had moved out of the house. As an adolescent, I was shocked to discover that my mother had had numerous affairs. In any case, once I learned about the affairs, I apologized to my stepmother and we have become very close. I'm still grateful at how easily she seemed to forgive me. I think that she understood that some of my

behavior toward her as a child had to do with my maintaining loyalty to my mother. You may find this to be too analytical, but this is actually why the relationship with my stepmother changed, from my perspective. Have I been clear enough for you to follow?" (9)

3. *Emotional attunement.* Recognition that the interviewer might be affected by the material that one provides; requires specific reference as to *why* the interviewer might be affected. Example: "My relationship with my mother changed drastically after my father died. My mother and I had fought a great deal prior to his death. Afterward, I think I tried to replace him and became very sweet to her and tried to take on the chores he used to do. I notice that tears are coming to your eyes and I wonder if you too lost a parent. If so, I imagine that this interview would be quite sad for you. If this is true, I regret it. I hope that what I've just said to you is not out of bounds." (8)

Scoring discourse with the RF-S was in part modeled after the scaling on the Metacognitive Monitoring scale of the AAI, which spans from 1 to 9. The RF-S, however, includes an additional anchor point (–1) to indicate active avoidance of mentalization, so that the scale ranges from –1 to 9, where a score of 9 indicates "exceptional" reflective functioning. The anchor points of the RF-S, together with the corresponding RF level descriptions, are as follows (Fonagy, Target, et al., 1998, pp. 37–40; Steele & Steele, 2008, p. 154):

–1: RF that is "distinctly anti-reflective or bizarre/inappropriate"
0: RF that is "disavowed or absent"
1: "Absent but not repudiated RF"
3: "Questionable or Low RF"
5: "Definite or Ordinary RF"
7: "Marked RF"
9: "Exceptional RF"

A score of –1 to 1 is consistent with disorganized attachment. A score of less than 3 is consistent with disorganized status or dismissing or anxious-preoccupied insecure status and is typically seen in individuals with borderline or antisocial personality disorder or a dissociative disorder (Fonagy, Target, et al., 1998). A score of 4 or 5 is associated with either insecure or secure status, and scores of 6 to 9 are associated with secure status. Less is known about typical RF-S scores for patients with Unresolved/disoriented (Ud) status on the AAI. However, Howard Steele has said that it is rare for someone with Ud status to score above a 5 on the RF-S (H. Steele, personal communication with D. Brown, 2012; and with A. Cole, 2015).

Exploring whether RF is a mediating variable between parental and infant attachment security, Fonagy et al. (1995) compared parents' RF score and attachment status with the attachment status of their infants assessed with the Strange Situation procedure at 12 and 18 months. They found that RF level differentiated whether the infants of insecure parents were secure or insecure: Parents with insecure status and high RF were more likely to have infants with secure status than were insecure parents with low RF.

Overall, one advantage of this second generation of research on metacognition is that reflective functioning goes beyond *self*-monitoring to include mentalizing about mental states of both self and other. Another important contribution of the RF concept that Fonagy and his associates have developed is that it is unitary and yet has a number of differentiated dimensions. In our opinion, the two fundamental factors operating across the four dimensions of RF (i.e., the nature of mental states, mental states associated with behavior, developmental aspects, mental states in relation to the interviewer) are (1) the capacity to recognize representations *as* representations or constructions, and therefore, as being relative and limited and (2) the capacity to take perspective and contextualize mental states.

The greatest value of this research on reflective function is that it is very relevant to effective clinical assessment and treatment. Using the RF-S, the London group has demonstrated that personality disorder (PD) and dissociative disorder (DD) patients generally score very low on RF, so much so that it justified developing an entirely new kind of treatment, *mentalization-based treatment* (MBT), which with PD and DD patients places persistent treatment focus on developing RF capacity. The outcome data on MBT with patients with borderline personality disorder has demonstrated the efficacy and clinical effectiveness of MBT (Bateman & Fonagy, 1999, 2001).

Despite the clear usefulness of the differentiation of metacognitive capacity into particular dimensions, and despite the clear value of applying these in MBT treatment interventions to develop reflective capacity, we believe that the concept of RF has an important practical limitation. As measured with the RF-S, a given individual has less or more reflective capacity, and hopefully develops significantly more reflective capacity through MBT. Because RF is seen as a unitary function, it does not account for the clinical observation that deficits in metacognition are often *pathology-specific*. Rather than different clinical conditions being characterized simply by different degrees of overall RF or metacognitive capacity, there is evidence that different clinical conditions are characterized by different metacognitive strengths and deficits. This limitation has been addressed in the research at the Rome Center of Cognitive Psychotherapy, which we see as the third generation of metacognitive research and understanding.

THIRD GENERATION: THE MODULAR, PSYCHOPATHOLOGY-SPECIFIC APPROACH

Antonio Semerari, Giancarlo Dimaggio, Giovanni Liotti, and their associates at the Third Center of Cognitive Psychotherapy, Rome, have further refined the understanding of metacognition and of its appearance in clinical populations. In contrast to the London group's view of reflective function as a unitary construct with various dimensions, the Rome group views metacognition not as unitary but as a number of independent capacities. They developed the Metacognitive Assessment Scale (MAS) and have used this instrument to assess metacognitive capacities in patients with borderline personality disorder (BPD), narcissistic personality disorder (NPD), and dissociative identity disorder (DID). Through this research, they discovered that patients with different diagnoses had "pathology-specific" deficits in particular metacognitive capacities but not others (Dimaggio, Semerari, Carcione, Nicolò, & Procacci, 2007). For each given psychiatric diagnosis, it became possible to construct a specific "metacognitive profile" for patients with that diagnosis. Knowing a patient's diagnosis, as well as having the result of the MAS for that specific patient, allows the therapist to orient the treatment toward cultivating whichever particular metacognitive capacity is deficient in that patient.

The Rome group describes six distinct metacognitive capacities. The descriptions of each are quoted and/or adapted from their work (Semerari et al., 2003), and examples are provided to illustrate what clinicians may hear as indications of each capacity.

1. *Identification*. Defined as "the ability to distinguish, recognize and define one's own [or the other's] inner states (emotions, cognitions). In the Metacognitive Assessment Scale the identification function is divided into two subfunctions: (a) the ability to recognize one's own representations (thoughts and images); and (b) the ability to recognize emotions" (p. 241). Examples: "I felt sad when I heard the news"; "She always thinks that she's treated unfairly"; "I'm angry"; "She was really happy when she saw me."

2. *Relating variables*. Defined as "the ability to establish relations among separate components of [one's own or another's] mental state and between the components of mental states and behaviour . . . Through RV a subject explains his/her own behavior in terms of causes and/or motivations" (p. 242). Examples: "I didn't answer the phone because I didn't want to speak to him" (p. 241); "He was angry at me because I hadn't helped him"; "I felt sad because I really wanted her to like me."

3. *Differentiation*. Defined as "the ability to recognize that the contents of representations [of one's own or another's mental states] are subjective events of a mental nature, and therefore, different from reality and without direct influence

on it . . . [It] acknowledges the subjectivity of our representations and recognizes the limits of the influence of our thoughts" (p. 242). Examples: "Giovanni is convinced that if he doesn't walk the same road every morning, a catastrophe will happen, but I know that it is one of his fantasies and not a premonition" (p. 244); "On the bus I think that everybody is looking at me, but they're probably just thinking about their own business."

4. *Integration.* Defined as "the ability to work out coherent descriptions of one's [own or others'] mental states and processes. It is the function we use to describe and discuss our inner scenario, [which] takes a narrative form and gives a sense of continuity" (p. 242). Poor integration is indicated by statements that are incomplete, confused, contradictory, or fragmentary. "Integration is divided into two items: (a) the ability to provide an integrated description of one's own mental state; (b) the ability to describe the changes over time in one's own mental states and give them a coherent narrative form" (p. 243). Example: "First I felt scared, but as I started to realize that the people there were friendly, I became less scared, and was aware of being excited."

5. *Decentration.* Defined as "the ability to comprehend another individual's mental state from a non-egocentric perspective. It enables us to recognize the hypothetical nature of our reading of other individuals' minds" (p. 244). Example: "She wasn't looking at me, and at first I thought that she was deliberately ignoring me. But then I realized that she was probably just thinking of her plans for tomorrow and not about me at all."

6. *Mastery.* Defined as "the ability to work through one's representations and mental states, with a view to implementing effective action strategies, in order to accomplish cognitive tasks or cope with problematic mental states" and "the overall definition we give to regulation and control activities" (p. 244). Awareness of one's state in a way that leads to regulation or change of that state. There are three levels of mastery, divided "according to the complexity of the metacognitive operations involved" (p. 244):

> First-level strategies: Calling upon coping methods
> (e.g., asking for help, medication, avoiding a situation)

> Second-level strategies: Inhibiting thinking, impulses, or behavior, or modifying attention

> Third-level strategies: Thinking through with rationality and perspective; mature acceptance of one's limitations; using awareness of others' states to regulate interpersonal difficulties

Semerari et al. (2003) and Dimaggio et al. (2007) reported the specific meta-cognitive deficits in patients with BPD and NPD and described how each of these patients manifest psychopathology-specific metacognitive deficits. BPD patients showed relatively normal metacognitive *identification* and the ability to think according to *relating variables* but showed significant deficits in metacognitive *differentiation* early on but not later in treatment, and severe deficits in metacognitive *integration* and *mastery* that didn't change much throughout the course of therapy. The following statements from a patient diagnosed with BPD illustrate the pattern of strength and deficit: "I was furious" (good *identification*); "I've been feeling this way since he didn't call me back" (good *relating variables*); "I know that I'm the only one of his girlfriends that he's ever blown off like this" (poor *differentiation*); "I hate him and I always have and I always will" (poor *integration*); "I might as well kill myself because there's nothing else I can do" (poor *mastery*). Given the BPD patient's relatively normal capacity for metacognitive identification of states, fostering core mindfulness in dialectical behavior therapy (DBT; Linehan, 1993) may not be a specific enough intervention for patients with BPD. The Rome group's findings highlight that effective treatment of BPD must include improving their metacognitive differentiation, integration, and mastery.

Patients with NPD, in contrast to BPD patients, showed an initial deficit in metacognitive *identification* and an even stronger deficit in *relating variables* that improved slowly over the course of treatment. *Differentiation* failures varied throughout the course of treatment, *integration* improved over treatment, and *mastery* was moderate. The following statements from a patient diagnosed with NPD illustrate this pattern of strength and deficit: "I don't have any feelings about her. I don't have any feelings, period" (poor *identification*); "I don't have a clue why this is so" (poor *relating variables*); "She's been sending me emails every day. I know she's trying to flatter me" (poor *differentiation*); "Don't ask me why, but I know she's madly in love with me" (poor *integration*); "I'm just going to label her emails as spam. No way am I going to write her back" (Level 1 *mastery*).

Overall, it is clear that BPD patients show the strongest deficits in *integration* and *mastery* but not in *identification* or *relating* of various mental states, whereas NPD patients show nearly the mirror opposite, with initially poor capacity to *identify* their own and other's mental states but better *differentiation*, *integration*, and *mastery*.

FOURTH GENERATION: BEYOND MENTAL CONSTRUCTIONS AND RELATIVISM OF MENTAL STATES

The work of the London and Rome groups has significantly advanced our under-standing of the nature of metacognitive functioning and of the treatment value of improving such functioning. Substantial research exists that shows that meta-cognitive development greatly benefits patients with personality disorders and/

or attachment disturbances. However, in our view, this third generation of meta-cognitive research and treatment remains limited in several ways. The reflective function concept constitutes, and is therefore limited to, *second-order intersubjectivity*, which is the ability to acknowledge representations *as* representations, or as constructions of mind. In other words, research on RF belies and is limited to a constructivist theory of mind. The Rome group expands the concept of metacognition beyond constructivism to include recognition of the *relativism* of mental states. However, neither approach accounts for developmental levels of mind that are beyond constructivism and relativism.

To develop a more complete picture of metacognition relevant to the clinical treatment of adults, it is necessary to consider the entire trajectory of life span development, and especially the types of metacognition characteristic of mature adult development. We do not assume that metacognitive development stops after early childhood. More important, we have found that the types of metacognition that develop after childhood are especially relevant to overall mental health.

Wallin (2007) has raised the possibility of bringing a more advanced understanding of mind into the treatment of patients with attachment disturbances. He presents the notion of *tertiary subjectivity*, wherein through practices of mindfulness, the patient may transcend the constructed mind and reach a direct, nonconceptual knowing of states of mind. Yet even Wallin's ideas do not go far enough. Ken Wilber's Integral theory (Wilber, 2000, 2007) articulates levels of knowing beyond constructivism and relativism, where all of the relative "maps" of mind reflect a transcendent "metamap" that accurately describes reality free of the limits of constructivism and relativism. It is our contention that each level of mind is associated with specific types of metacognition. Developing and strengthening these later-occurring levels of metacognition is, in our view, more strongly related to coherence of mind and well-being than simply fostering reflective capacity, and what patients discover in this domain goes beyond relativism into the domain of wisdom. We suggest that our understanding and integrating of these more advanced metacognitive possibilities into the treatment of attachment and other disturbances heralds the fourth generation of the field of metacognition.

The Spectrum of Adult Development

The stages of adult development have been articulated by a number of researchers in response to Piaget's theory (Piaget, 1963) of the stages of child and adolescent intelligence. Specifically, these researchers have identified stages of mature adult development that include and go beyond the cognitive developmental line and its stage of formal operational thinking, which is the last stage of Piaget's model, which he described as developing during adolescence. Such stage-model works include Commons, Richards, and Kuhn's (1982) attempts to extend Piaget's model beyond formal operations to systematic and metasystematic reasoning; Loevinger and Wessler's (1970) stages of ego development and the extension of these stages by Cook-Greuter (1990); Kohlberg's stages of moral development (1981); Kegan's work on the stages of self-development (1982); Labouvie-Vief's work on mature adulthood (1990); Sternberg's (1984) work on wisdom; and Wilber's (2000, 2007) integration of all of these into a full-spectrum model across many developmental lines that includes the highest stages of mature adult development as described in the great spiritual traditions. The consensus among researchers on mature adult cognitive development is best stated by Commons, Richards, and Armon (1984): "There is a great deal of development potential beyond formal operations . . . collectively labeled 'postformal [cognitive development]'" (p. xv).

Sternberg (1984), in his research on wisdom, has described three stages in cognitive development. First-order relations are relations between primary elements. Second-order relations are relations between relations. Third-order relations are a type of "higher order relational thinking" that constitute "advanced reasoning process" (p. 91). None of these "higher-order" cognitive processes are mentioned in any of the research from the first three generations of metacognition.

Commons, Richards and Armon (1984) and Commons, Sinnott, Richards, & Armon (1989) present a model for the stages of post-formal reasoning, intended as an extension of Piaget's stages of intelligence that stops at adolescent formal operational thinking. According to their research, fifth-order or *systematic* thinking constitutes complete and exhaustive operations between members of the same class (p. 97). The next, sixth-order stage in the development of intelligence is *metasystematic* thinking. Metasystematic thinking is characterized by "relationship of one system to another system [to define a] supersystem" (p. 97). The highest, seventh-order stage is called *cross-paradigmatic* thinking, which defines relationships "between families of systems . . . [that] relate fields that appear independent of each other" (p. 97).

Labouvie-Vief (1982, 1990) describes two post-formal stages of adult cognitive development. Each stage represents a "broad reorganization of the information-processing system" (1990, p. 56). In her model, formal operational thinking is *intrasystemic*. The first stage of cognitive development transitioning formal operational thinking is *intersystemic*, defined as thinking characterized by the "expansion of context" (1982, p. 175) and awareness that "highlight[s] meanings that go beyond the information given" (1990, p. 56). The next stage is called *autonomous*. This stage goes beyond "the logic of formal systems to the logic of self-regulating systems" (1982, p. 176) and extends creativity and generativity across generations.

Kegan's (1982) model emphasizes the stages of self-development. He describes each stage as a "succession of qualitative differentiations of the self from the world, with a qualitatively more extensive object with which to be in relation to created each time." (p. 77). In each successive stage, the self "emerges from its embeddedness" (p. 85) to a more expanded context. Ken Wilber often describes what changes across Kegan's stages as being that "the subject of one stage becomes the object [of the subject] of the next" (Wilber, 2000, p. 34). Kegan's stages, and the corresponding Piagetian stages, are (0) the incorporative self/sensorimotor, (1) the impulsive self/preoperations, (2) the imperial self/concrete operations, (3) the interpersonal self/early formal operations, (4) the institutional self/full formal operations, and (5) the interindividual self (post-formal thinking). The latter stages reflect the emergence of self-in-relationship to broader and broader contexts, such as self-in-relationship to society and self-in-relationship to the broader spiritual dimension of life.

Loevinger (1976) presented a nine-stage model of ego development that ranges from the earliest, *presocial/symbiotic* stage to an *integrated* stage, which is a post-formal stage that she states "is the hardest stage to describe . . . Because it is rare, one is hard put to find instances to study" (p. 26). Suzanne Cook-Greuter (1985/2013, 1990, 1994, 1999, 2000) has built upon the foundation of Loevinger's model and has further researched, defined, and described the stages that Loevinger initially laid out. We focus here on Cook-Greuter's descriptions of the post-formal stages of ego development and emphasize the cognitive correlates of each of those stages.

The transition from formal to post-formal ego development is indicated by Cook-Greuter's *individualist* stage (the sixth stage in her model, but labeled 4/5 to indicate that it is a stage of transition between Stage 4, the formal operational *conscientious* stage, and Stage 5, the post-formal *autonomous* stage). At the *individualist* stage, the person becomes aware of the importance of point of view or perspective, expectancies, and context in the construction of thought. Truth is seen more as relative than as absolute. Cook-Greuter (1990) states,

> People come to see themselves as contributing meaning to external events and facts. They realize that, by necessity they are participant observers who distort as they observe . . . [and] realize that not only the meaning of objects but the objects themselves are human constructs. (p. 96)

At the *autonomous* stage (the seventh stage in her model, labeled as 5), the person operates fully from post-formal thinking and perspective. Cook-Greuter describes cognitive functioning not as formal operations but as "metasystematic." Relationships between conflicting systems in thought are superseded by the development of a broader and more encompassing system. Pertaining to the self, such individuals "focus on discovering and actualizing their overall, long range potential" (1994, p. 122). Cook-Greuter states, "Metasystematic integrates several different conflicting frameworks of the self into a coherent new theory" (1990, p. 89).

The *construct-aware* post-autonomous stage (the eighth in the sequence, labeled 5/6) is where the individual develops a perspective on the limits of representational knowledge. Regarding thinking and cognition, Cook-Greuter says that construct-aware individuals become aware of the linguistic bias inherent in the construction and distinction of objects. They realize that the objects themselves are inventions, arbitrary but useful for orientation. This includes an ever-growing awareness of the processes and mechanism of thinking itself. (1990, p. 83)

Crook-Greuter also explains that

too much thinking gets in the way of genuine experience . . . [This stage is characterized by] heightened awareness that the mental habits of thinking, expecting, defending, and fearing are problematic in themselves . . . a more critical stance towards these automatic processes [develops]. (1994, pp. 127–128)

Pertaining to the self sense,

the ego no longer *unconsciously* organizes coherent meaning from experience, but becomes aware of itself as an organizer and as a temporary, though necessary and useful construct. This stage is therefore referred to as ego-aware or construct aware [stage] . . . Now, concepts can be seen for what they are; potentially effective but nevertheless arbitrary codifications, representations, summaries of the flux of sensory data . . . [Such individuals] want to be liberated from the bondage of rational "thought" . . . [They] realize that their self-identity is always and only a temporary construct . . . an attitude of complete openness. (1994, pp. 131–133)

The time frame for the growth of the self expands across the lifetime and down the generations. Cook-Greuter says, "One thinks of oneself as a separate individual with a unique mission . . . [who] becomes more conscious of growth and change over time" (1994, pp. 128, 131).

At the *universal* or *unitive* stage (the ninth in the model and labeled as 6), there is a "change to a concept of field (vision)[,] . . . [a] quantum leap in experience and outlook . . . that contains within itself many possible theories and models of possible definitions of self and of reality" (Cook-Greuter, 1990, p. 97). People functioning from the unitive stage yearn "to transcend their own rational, ever-watchful, conscious egos" (p. 92). Because of direct "attunement awareness" (p. 94) instead of representational thinking, there is an "immediate witnessing of the ongoing process" (1994, p. 133). Regarding self-experience, this stage is the "*natural outcome* of the completed journey of the self through the stages" (p. 140). It is characterized by a "global, transpersonal, or ego-transcendent experience" wherein the individual

experiences himself and others as part of ongoing humanity, embedded in the process of creation . . . Integrated persons have the ability to look at themselves and at others in terms of the passing of ages, of near and far in geographical, social, cultural, historical, intellectual, and developmental dimensions. They can take multiple points of view and shift focus instantly and effortlessly. (1990, p. 93)

This multiperspectival capacity brings awareness that one's center is no longer the ego, the personal self, but is beyond that, is a higher Self, integrated with a higher Unity. Cook-Greuter states, "The affirmation that one is *nothing* is at the core of this new self-perception. [The self is] No-'thing.'" Through this "ego-transcendent self-view . . . [t]he self is created and experienced anew at every moment" (1994, pp. 133–135). "The self in its moment-to-moment transformation . . . [is no longer reified]" (1994, p. 138).

An overall assumption in Cook-Greuter's stage model of ego development is that at the highest stages, the individual transcends the limitations of representational thinking to direct awareness of ultimate, not relative, truth. She says, "The basic tenet of constructivist-developmental psychology is that the more differentiated and objective, that is, the less distorted one's self-view, the closer to truth one gets" (1994. p. 119).

In *Integral Psychology* (2000) and *Integral Spirituality* (2007), Ken Wilber presents a comprehensive model of multiple lines of human development that also includes the highest stages described primarily by the great spiritual traditions, East and West. Wilber reviewed nearly 100 models of developmental sequences, ranging from ancient to modern, including intellectual/cognitive, self, moral, and spiritual developmental lines. By laying all these developmental sequences alongside each other and aligning them according to their common elements, he found a structural coherence that he believes reflects a universal framework for all developmental lines. By *structure*, Wilber means relatively enduring patterns that organize experience and behavior, and he believes that there is a regular, orderly, and universal sequence through which these patterns evolve for each developmental line.

To indicate the structural levels of any and all of these lines, Wilber (2007) uses the metaphor of 12 bandwidths of light, from lowest vibrational energy to highest: infrared, magenta, red, amber, orange, green, teal, turquoise, indigo, violet, ultraviolet, and clear light. The higher vibrational energies reflect higher, or later-developing (at least as potential), structural stages. For the intellectual/cognitive line, Piaget's stages of intellectual development align with the first five bandwidths, so that formal operational thinking corresponds to the fifth, orange stage. Adopting terms used by Clare Graves and Sri Aurobindo, Wilber (2007) identifies the first post-formal cognitive stage as being in the sixth stage-structure position and indicated by green, pluralistic, or relativistic and early-vision logic. At the seventh position, teal, cognition involves systemic thinking and middle-vision logic; the eighth, turquoise, reflects higher systemic thinking and late-vision logic; the ninth, indigo, is global and ego-transcendent, corresponding to an awakened or what Wilber calls an illumined mind; the 10th, violet, represents a level of mind wherein all dimensions are present simultaneously; the 11th, ultraviolet, and the 12th, clear light, represent the highest attainments, namely, the enlightened mind.

A UNIFIED MODEL OF THE DEVELOPMENT OF COGNITION AND METACOGNITION

We have found it useful to think of the development of cognition and metacognition according to the structural model described above. Here we describe more fully the spectrum of such development, with descriptions of the main changes at each stage. The three lowest levels (infrared, magenta, and red) represent an egocentric orientation to the world. These stages correspond to sensorimotor (infrared) and preoperational (magenta, red) stages in Piaget. The fourth stage (amber) corresponds to Piaget's concrete operational thinking. The fifth stage corresponds to Piaget's formal operational thinking. Each of these first five stages corresponds to Loevinger's and Cook-Greuter's symbiotic, impulsive, self-protective, conformist, and conscientious stages of ego development.

The fourth and fifth stages represent an ethnocentric orientation to the world. With the development of the fourth stage, concrete operational thinking, the child becomes increasingly sensitive to what others are thinking and attempts to conform to the norms of the peer group. At this stage the child develops an internal sense of "mind." The range of internal emotional states greatly expands, and emotions are now experienced less in connection with external events and more as internal states associated with the self. Fantasy involvement reaches a peak in these years. The ability to pay attention stabilizes. The metacognitive skills that develop at the fourth stage pertain primarily to the immediate awareness of the content of one's own mind and the capacity to represent the state of mind of the other. Meaning-making is largely based on social approval and the manifest content of experience.

The fifth stage is marked by the development of formal operational thinking. Greater appreciation of primary elements within a system develops, and deductive reasoning begins to emerge. At this level of cognitive development, the adolescent is able to think in terms of an infinite number of possibilities. The main metacognitive skills relevant to this stage include efficacy and mastery, awareness of latent meaning, the ability to understand the connection between an action and short- and long-term consequences, and the capacity to project long-term goals.

The sixth stage is the first post-formal-operational stage. Cook-Greuter refers to this stage as the *individualist* stage. Commons et al. (1990) refer to it as the *systematic* stage, and describe it as allowing for complete and exhaustive operations within the same class of cognitive objects. Labouvie-Vief (1990) says that this level is characterized by intersystemic relationships. The cognitive structure of this stage provides for a range of metacognitive operations: heightened sensitivity to context; the capacity to accurately become aware of underlying assumptions, schemas, and expectancies that go beyond the information given; the relativity of all states and therefore an appreciation for the limitation of all knowledge systems; the capacity to take perspective and to understand how point of view influences experience; and the capacity to optimize options in the face of limitation.

The seventh stage is Wilber's first integral stage and Cook-Greuter's *autonomous* stage. According to Labouvie-Vief, cognitive development shifts from logical systems to systems of self-regulation. Commons et al. refer to this stage as *meta-systematic*, which pertains both to the capacity to think in terms of relations between one system and another and also to the emerging capacity to think in terms of some overarching supersystem with interdependent relationships between elements within the system. Similarly, Sternberg (1984) refers to the skills that emerge at this stage position as "higher order relational thinking." A number of new metacognitive skills appear at this stage: a growing awareness of interdependence; the capacity to develop a wider system of meaning or purpose which supersedes all other goal strivings; definition of a unique purpose in life and its trajectory of actualization; awareness of generativity and intergenerationality; the capacity to resolve internal conflict or contradiction between goal strivings by developing an ultimate concern; and the ability to directly perceive the degree of organization or disorganization of state of mind. Moreover, this stage is also characterized by a heightened awareness of mental habits and recognition of the limitations of conceptual thought as a vehicle of knowledge.

The eighth stage is comparable to what Cook-Greuter calls the *construct-aware* stage. Commons et al. (1990) refer to it as the *cross-paradigmatic* stage because thinking can consider relations between families of systems and can operate on larger fields of cognitive objects. The central characteristic of this stage is the discovery that *conceptual knowledge interferes with knowing via direct experience or awareness*. Thought as a mode of knowledge becomes problematic and is eventually superseded by direct knowing through immediate awareness, much akin to Gendlin's notion of "experiencing" (1997, 1982). The main types of metacognition that emerge at this stage are immediate knowing through awareness; transcendence of thought as a mode of knowing; the appreciation that the self is a central organizer that is merely a temporary mental construction, yet useful as an organizing perspective in daily life; and an appreciation of the supersystemic order to life that is best characterized as pluralistic harmony, wherein everything is ordered and everything influences everything else, leading to recognition of the interconnection of all humanity.

The ninth stage, which Cook-Greuter calls *universal* or *unitive*, is characterized by ego-transcendence. In the Eastern spiritual traditions, this stage is characterized by the merging of individual (or "infant") consciousness with the universal (or "mother") consciousness. The individual becomes aware of a vast oceanlike field of consciousness, or unbounded wholeness. This oceanlike awareness, not ordinary personal self or ego mind, now becomes the center of one's experience, identity, and action. The very high level metacognitive skills that emerge at this stage include the disappearance of reactivity of mind within this vast domain of spacelike awareness (called "spacious freedom"); the ability to take simultaneous, multiple perspectives, including perspectives on perspectives; instantaneous, automatic monitoring of states of mind; a nonreified, flexible albeit immediate sense of self that effortlessly fits context; and spontaneous compassion for shared humanity.

The last three stages (violet through clear light) are beyond the scope of this book.

Clinical Applications: Methods for Promoting Metacognitive Skills in Patients

BASIC METACOGNITIVE SKILLS: THE PRE-FORMAL AND FORMAL LEVELS

Awareness of the State of Mind in Self and Others

Helping patients become more aware of their own internal experience is a foundational therapeutic skill. Many patients, especially patients with major dissociative disorders and narcissistic personality disorder, remain remarkably unaware of their own internal state of mind and the state of mind of others. Our therapeutic goal with such patients includes fostering greater awareness of general mood states, specific emotional states, automatic negative self-talk, and underlying assumptions, beliefs, schemas, needs, and motivations. With respect to specific emotional states, we frequently say to a patient:

> Notice what you are feeling at this moment . . . The more you focus on this, the more the specific feeling will become clearer and clearer . . . and as it becomes clear, just the right words will come to you that best describe that feeling.

To support recognition of negative self-talk, we might say, "Notice what you are saying to yourself when . . ." For clinicians trained in hypnosis, the television subtitles method is a useful way of fostering greater awareness of automatic negative self-talk (D. P. Brown & Fromm, 1986). For example, if a patient is depressed, the clinician might say:

> Imagine watching a video scene about a person who is depressed, much like you have been. As the scene unfolds, you'll discover exactly what that person experiences when he or she is depressed. Now look at the bottom of the screen . . . soon subtitles will spontaneously appear on the screen, much like when watching a foreign film . . . but here the subtitles will be

about all the things that person is saying to himself or herself when he or she is depressed like this . . . and you can read off the subtitles as they appear, as if you were reading all the thoughts that are going through that person's mind.

To enhance awareness of underlying maladaptive beliefs and schemas, the clinician might say, "What were the assumptions you were making about . . . ? What is the underlying belief?" Regarding wishes and needs: "What did you hope to accomplish?" "What did you most want from this?" For adaptive function: "In the best sense, what does this do for you? What did you hope this would accomplish, in the best sense?" By frequently considering such inward-focusing questions, patients become increasingly capable of observing their internal state of mind.

Many contemporary psychotherapists and some approaches to therapy, notably dialectical behavior therapy (DBT; Linehan, 1993), incorporate mindfulness as a core skill. As part of DBT, borderline patients learn mindfulness meditation to develop a kind of continuous, nonreactive awareness of whatever the immediate content of their experience is. When mindful, patients have greater awareness of their immediate felt experience without needing to think about or defensively react to their experience. Learning to "be with" their inner states can also lead to explorations of their meaning.

We have found it useful to use a simple self-rating scale to help patients to metacognitively reflect on the *degree to which they are or are not present to their own experience.* For example:

On a 1 to 10 scale, with 1 being completely *unaware* of your current state of mind, and 10 being completely *aware* of your current state of mind, and 5 being *somewhat aware* of your current state of mind, give me a number that best reflects the degree that you are aware of your current state of mind right now.

Similarly, for the patient with concentration difficulty:

On a 1 to 10 scale, with 1 being *completely distracted*, and 10 being *fully concentrated*, and 5 being *somewhat concentrated*, give me a number that best reflects the degree to which you are able to maintain concentration on the task at hand right now.

Or:

Give me a number that best reflects the degree to which you are *completely focused* on one thing at this moment, as compared to apportioning your attention to that thing and also to the background noise of thought or external perception.

The overall objective is for the patient to develop more continuous and more complete focus on the immediate circumstance or task at hand, over and against his or her habit of getting distracted, becoming nonaware, and dividing attention between the circumstance and nonrelevant stimulation, internal or external.

Since NPD and DID patients have poor ability to be aware of their emotional states, it is very beneficial when working with them to reinforce any awareness they do show by *affectively marking* those states. For example, whenever a patient reports having felt fear in a situation, the therapist might say, "*You* must have felt *very* afraid." Saying "you" with verbal emphasis locates the experience of the emotion within the patient, and adding the intensifier "very," again with verbal emphasis, marks the emotion in such a way that the patient is more likely to recognize it as an internally felt state of mind and not as something attributed to the other person. The clinical example below further illustrates marking of affective states:

> **Patient:** I was scared when my co-worker betrayed me to my boss. I never thought he would do that. It reminded me of when I was a kid. My mother would betray me and tell my father when she thought I did something wrong. Then he would hit me, whether I deserved it or not.
>
> **Therapist:** *You* must have been *very* scared and felt *really* betrayed by your co-worker. I also imagine that *you* were *very* scared of what the consequences might be.

The capacities to take perspective and be empathic in relation to others are important metacognitive skills and are especially lacking in patients with personality and dissociative disorders. The clinician uses structured inquiry to help patients develop these skills by asking such questions as the following: "What do you think motivated her to act like that?" "From his perspective, what do you think he had in mind when he . . . ?" "What is your best estimate of what she was feeling at the time?" "What do you think the unmet need was that kept driving her to act that way?" "What do you think the underlying assumptions or beliefs were that caused him to act like that?" The therapist takes a consistent stance, wondering out loud about the state of mind of the other, and thereby models for the patient how to wonder about and offer the best estimate of the other's motivations, needs, feelings, and underlying beliefs. Over the course of the treatment, the patient learns to wonder about and perceive the state of mind of others more consistently and more accurately.

Enhancing patients' capacity for *mentalization* helps to increase awareness not only of their own state of mind, but also of the state of mind of the other. We agree with Jon Allen (2013) that mentalization is best fostered by the stance of the therapist. If the therapist frequently wonders out loud about the state of mind of the patient and also appropriately discloses his or her own thoughts and feelings relevant to the ongoing therapeutic process, the patient is more likely over time to show increasing curiosity toward his or her own as well as the therapist's state of mind and that of others outside the treatment context. This process is accelerated when the therapist repeatedly gets the patient to wonder about his or her own and others' feelings, thoughts, needs, and motivations in specific situations, and also about what others might expect of him or her. In Chapter 6, we presented Jon Allen's (2013) excellent list of "tips for therapists on influencing mentalizing" and noted that we strongly recommend that therapists take guidance from the items on this list and integrate them into their practice (see Table 6.1, page 266).

The clinical example below illustrates how the therapist not only reinforced the patient's mentalizing strengths but also helped the patient to identify both her own state of mind and the state of mind of her mother:

> **Patient:** My mother wanted me to come to the beach house this weekend because we hadn't seen each other for a while. She said when I don't visit her, she feels rejected and wonders if she has done something wrong. I used to fight with her about her inability to see me as an adult and tell her she was self-centered. We would always end up in a long back-and-forth argument and then not speak to each other for a while. I braced myself for a fight, but then I thought about how lonely she must be since my father died. Instead, I told her that summer is my really busy work season, and, although it would be much more fun to be with her at the beach house, I can't take any time off right now. I asked her if one night we could get together for dinner in the city, and I told her I would take a weekend in September to come and stay with her at the beach house. Our conversation ended up on a positive note, and we said good-bye pleasantly. In the past, one of us would always hang up on the other because it would get so out of control.
>
> **Therapist:** That's a real shift! You were able to explain the reality of the responsibilities in your life, *and* at the same time have compassion for how lonely she must be feeling. I notice that as I heard you tell me about this I felt happy for you inside. You also came up with a compromise that both you and your mother felt good about. How did you feel after your phone call? How do you imagine your mother felt? I wonder what this means for your relationship in the future?

Metacognitive Monitoring

It is important to help patients increase their *accuracy* of their assessments of their own states of mind. Patients with a tendency toward poor accuracy of self-assessment may manifest this weakness in several ways (from less to more severe): making source-monitoring mistakes (i.e., confusing what was read or told by someone with a memory of an actual experience); confusing fantasies or dreams with memories of actual experience; being unaware of serious logical contradictions in beliefs; passive influence (e.g., thinking that speech, thought, emotions, or behavior is controlled by some outside force); serious lapses in reality-testing (e.g., an extreme belief, such as thinking that a deceased sadistic abuser is still able to control or harm the patient years later); and confusing inner speech with an actual perception (e.g., a dissociative or psychotic patient hearing voices).

Fostering an objective, scientific, and critical attitude can help the patient critically evaluate the accuracy of a reported memory. For example, one of the authors saw a female patient who was estranged from her husband; the patient developed an idea that her husband might have sexually abused their daughter. Her daughter had not reported anything of the sort, nor were there any symptoms or changes in her behavior that might indicate abuse. The patient herself had a sexual abuse history. On the Gudjonsson Suggestibility Scale (1984), she scored one and a half standard deviations above the mean for total suggestibility. She was given feedback conveying that because of her high suggestibility, she was at risk of incorporating outside, nonrelevant information into beliefs about her daughter being abused. In treatment, rather than focusing on that risk, she was encouraged to develop an objective, critical attitude about the evidence at hand. Over the next six months of treatment, she slowly developed the conviction that no abuse had occurred and that she had let her perception be influenced by her own history of childhood sexual abuse. She stopped being preoccupied with the thought that abuse had happened and was able to work out a cooperative custody arrangement with her estranged husband. The daughter was subsequently raised by both parents sharing joint custody, and there were no further claims or evidence of abuse as she grew up.

Experiments with nonpathological, highly hypnotizable subjects show that such subjects respond to hypnotic suggestions to hallucinate an object that is not actually present (i.e., a *positive* hallucination, in contrast to a *negative* hallucination, which is *not* experiencing something that *is* present). Such subjects are able to create the positive hallucination by suspending reality-monitoring in the hypnotic state (Kuzendorf, 1980). For patients who show deficits in reality-testing (e.g., who report voices), in therapy we want the opposite to happen—to activate and strengthen their reality-monitoring function. We would ask the patient to use a scale to estimate the degree to which the "voice" is perceived as an external voice or as an internal state of mind, and we would get the patient to wonder about and explore the source of the voice. For example:

> Now what I'd like you to do is tell me the degree to which you perceive this voice as external to you versus it being an internal state of your mind. With

1 being completely external to you, and 10 being completely an internal state of your mind, and 5 being right in the middle between external and internal, tell me a number that indicates how you're perceiving the voice now.

The patient might say "3," and the therapist then will say something like:

Okay, so you perceive the voice as not completely external to you, but more external than internal. Let's wonder together now where that voice might be originating from. Is there anything around you or near you that could be the source of the voice?

For the same reality-testing goal, with hypnosis we often utilize an inner-wisdom technique (J. van der Linden, personal communications with D. Brown, 2007):

Allow yourself to connect directly with your own inner wisdom, the wisdom of your unconscious mind. This inner wisdom is capable of accurately detecting the source of this voice. Your inner wisdom knows better than you do on a conscious level of thought whether this voice is a product of internal thoughts or memories, or whether it is a voice of an actual external person. The more you reflect on this, the more your inner wisdom will inform you more accurately about this.

Repeated appeals to the patient to activate his or her own inner reality-monitoring capacity help patients to develop a reasonably accurate differentiation of inner experience and external phenomena. Eventually, the hallucinated voices are seen as inner thoughts (Havens, 1986), and patients replace the experience of passive influence with self-awareness and self-efficacy.

Errors in the monitoring of contradictory and extremely irrational beliefs are best handled using a cognitive dissonance model of treatment. The therapist introduces the language of parts. Take, for example, the belief that a deceased abuser is still active in the victim's mind and capable of controlling his or her mind or behavior:

There is a part of you that strongly believes this abuser is alive in your mind and still controlling and abusing you. There is another part of you that knows that this is impossible and that the abuser has died and no longer has any influence on you whatsoever. There is a deep conflict within you between the part that believes this is true and the part that knows it is not true. Now, allow yourself to access other parts of mind that have a perspective on what might resolve the deep conflict between the part that does and does not believe this.

By heightening the dissonance between parts of the mind and appealing to other parts to resolve the conflict, the dissonance is reduced in the direction that shifts away from adherence to the extreme belief.

Contingency Detection and Metacognitive Mastery

It is one thing to help patients to become more aware of their states of mind. It is an entirely different thing to help patients to become aware that their state of mind has a regulatory effect on that state (i.e., the Rome group's *metacognitive mastery*). Mindfulness of state of mind per se does not necessarily lead to increased mastery over that state. Mastery over state of mind is part of the larger capacity for *contingency detection*. Patients with personality and dissociative disorders show low awareness of contingency influence. In other words, they fail to see that they have any influence either on their own state of mind or on the behavior of others. Therefore, to help such patients develop awareness that they can influence their own state of mind, the therapist frequently points to a self-generated thought or action and says, "Notice the effect that has on your state of mind." In reference to the patient's influence on others, the therapist says, for example, "Notice the specific ways that you have influenced the other's behavior or state of mind." To increase awareness of how the patient influences the behavior of others toward him or her, the therapist says, for example, "Come to see the ways you have brought out a specific response from that person."

The therapist also needs to explicitly introduce the task of gaining mastery over state of mind. For example, the therapist might say, "Bring this anger more into your awareness in whatever way leads to an increasing sense of control over it, while you are fully experiencing it." For therapists using hypnosis, the metaphor of an affect dial helps:

> Imagine that you have a remote control device in your hand, much like when you watch television. When you turn the dial up you will experience this feeling more and more intensely, yet within the range of what you can withstand, and when you turn the dial down, you will experience this feeling less and less intensely. Experiment moving the dial in each direction until you find *just the right range* of intensity wherein you have the *greatest sense* of *control* or *mastery* over this feeling . . . and when you find that range you can let me know . . .

It is important that the therapist make it an explicit expectation of treatment that the patient will increase his or her control over and mastery of internal states.

We have found it useful to have patients frequently take a situation within which they feel overwhelmed and rehearse in fantasy having progressive control over or mastery of the situation. The displacement technique in hypnosis is designed for this purpose (D. P. Brown & Fromm, 1986):

Imagine watching a video of a person, much like yourself, who also has had a very difficult time feeling overwhelmed by fear in this same situation. As the video unfolds, you will see exactly what that person experiences when [he or she] is overwhelmed with fear. Only, that person has discovered a way to effectively overcome that fear. As the scene unfolds you will observe what the person learned to *effectively cope* with that fear. Describe what that person learned as a way to *best cope* with the fear. [Patient describes.] Now, switch the channel. The next video will show another person, also much like you, who has experienced an overwhelming fear. That person *also discovered* a way to *effectively cope* with the fear—a way *different* from the way the first person used. Watch the video until it is clear to you what worked *so effectively* for that person. [Patient describes.] Now, as you reflect on each of these scenes, their meaning will become more and more clear to you. Soon you will come to see how these scenes inform you of ways to cope that might enable you to deal with this overwhelming fear. [Patient articulates specific coping strategies.] Now, in the next scene you will see yourself using these coping strategies in a way to just begin to get a sense of *mastery* over this fear. [Patient describes details of effective coping.]

The protocol concludes with a posthypnotic suggestion:

As you go about your everyday life, at the very first signs of noticing this fear coming on, the thought about these specific coping strategies will naturally come into your mind. The *more* you become aware of these coping strategies, the *more* you will find yourself putting them into practice. The *more* you use these coping strategies, the *more* you will experience less fear. You can become the *master* of your own state of mind. It does not have to control you anymore.

The therapist should frequently offer suggestions designed to increase the patient's sense of efficacy regarding treatment. For example, in the context of ideal parent figures (Chapter 8) providing comfort or reassurance to the patient-as-distressed-child, the therapist says, "Notice the effect this has on your state of mind." In support of the patient's attempts to hold this soothing imagery in daily life outside the therapy sessions, the therapist might say, "As you're bringing this soothing imagery to you in whatever circumstance you're in, notice how this influences your outlook" and/or "Notice how this influences your behavior."

Action Plans and Goal-Orientation

The development of formal operational thinking brings the capacity to think in terms of multiple possibilities and long-term goals. Impulsive patients typically show impaired goal-oriented behavior (Wishnie, 1977). Such patients need to learn to represent actions in terms of action plans, with articulated sequences of behaviors organized toward effective implementation of the plan. This learning begins with reflecting on the possible consequences of behavior as a series of hypotheticals. For example, if a borderline patient is upset with his boss and typically handles his upset by impulsively demeaning the boss or leaving work and getting drunk, the therapist might ask him to imagine a hypothetical situation that produces a similar upset feeling. Next, the patient is asked to imagine a series of possible reactions or responses to being upset, from less to more adaptive. With respect to maladaptive actions, he is asked to imagine in detail the negative consequences that are likely to unfold over time as a result of such actions. This hypothetical exploratory process helps the patient to think ahead of time *and experience through internal representations* the likely negative consequences of impulsive actions. Next, he is asked to imagine possible healthy, adaptive responses, and to predict the likely consequences that would unfold over time from those. Repeatedly asking the impulsive patient to imagine possible consequences of various actions helps the patient to develop internal representations of actions and their likely consequences. Over time, impulsivity will decrease and there will be an increase in the ability to establish and complete healthy action sequences toward predetermined goals.

To further foster good action-planning toward goal-orientation and completion, a patient is asked to identify a healthy goal, such as going back to school or not getting drunk when upset. Next, he or she is prompted to imagine a series of healthy steps toward the goal; these steps are then revised and refined and organized into an articulated action plan. During this process, the patient is required to keep journal entries about implementation of the action plan and to bring problems with implementing the plan into treatment sessions. The more the patient develops action plans and has experience of them leading successfully to goal completion, the less impulsive they become. The most successful patients learn to think proactively, to develop clear and healthy action plans in advance of engaging in behaviors, and to let behaviors be guided by these action plans so that any impulsivity and the problems it creates are less likely to arise.

Patients can be helped to consider the action plans and goal-directedness *of others* by engaging them in exploration of what they see as or imagine were the action-sequence steps in another's emotional, behavioral, or circumstantial outcomes.

Meaning-Making

The psychoanalytic tradition's main contribution to metacognition is in the area of fostering meaning-making. Stern (2010) has said that the purpose of therapy is to get patients to formulate the meaning of their own inner experience for themselves for the first time. Frank (1963) argued that symptoms are generally ameliorated once a patient develops an organized explanatory model for his or her symptoms. Dynamic therapy is designed to help the patient make sense out of experience and symptoms. Here, the therapeutic stance begins by orienting the patient to wonder about and explore symptoms/problems in order to make sense out of them. This process is oriented toward explaining behavior, understanding the internal antecedents to behaviors, understanding motivation, discovering repetitions and reenactments in interpersonal behavior, explaining how certain maladaptive beliefs are conditioned by critical incidents, explaining the contributions to intense emotional states, and interpreting dreams. According to French (1952), all behavior is "purposeful" and the task of dynamic therapy is to identify, formulate, and explain the focal conflicts that underlie experience.

There are three levels of meaning to consider for the fullest meaning-making process: manifest meaning, emotional meaning, and latent or unconscious meaning. Manifest meaning pertains to the understanding and explanation of immediate experience. The emotional meaning of an experience occurs at and reflects a deeper level, and its recognition requires both accurate identification of the specific emotional state reflected in that immediate experience and understanding of the meaning or meanings that one gives to such an emotion. An even deeper level is the underlying latent or unconscious meaning of any given experience. Identification and understanding this level requires fostering curiosity in the patient about behaviors that are repetitive as well as recognizing and exploring long-standing patterns of behavior and experience.

INTERMEDIATE METACOGNITIVE SKILLS: POST-FORMAL LEVEL

Stage 6 (green), the first post-formal stage, is characterized by relativistic thinking and allows for systematic operations, specifically exhaustive operations within the same class (Commons, Armon, et al., 1990) or relations between relations (Sternberg, 1984). Several new metacognitive skills appear with the emergence of the early post-formal structure: the capacity to see how the past shapes current experience, the capacity to see the relativity of all states of mind and the limitations of all systems of knowledge, the capacity to see more deeply into underlying assumptions and expectancies in the self's and others' behavior, the capacity to optimize action plans in the face of perceived limitations, the capacity to appreciate the effects of context on feelings and behaviors, and the capacity to take perspective, or see something from another's point of view.

Recognition of How the Past Shapes Current Experience
Main, Goldwyn, and Hesse (2002) list "rueful recognition" as a characteristic of the state of mind of the securely attached individual. "Rueful recognition" is an experience that emerges when patients see that disliked aspects of their parents' behavior are now appearing in themselves. This recognition requires looking

more deeply into the complex relations between parentally modeled behavior in childhood and their own current behavior in order to see the parallels. Dynamically oriented therapists typically foster an attitude in treatment wherein the patient learns to wonder about how early childhood parental behavior might have shaped the way they have turned out—for good and for bad. The outcome of such exploration, in the best sense, is rueful recognition, wherein the patient has nondefensively acknowledged clear relationships between specific modeled parental behaviors and his or her own behavior under certain conditions. When a patient reports a current problematic behavior, the therapists invites the patient to explore "what is familiar about" this behavior with respect to early childhood experiences with family members, and then to recall experiences where he or she has noticed "acting similarly."

Appreciating the Relativity of All States of Mind and the Limitations of Knowledge

Both the second–generation London mentalization-based treatment and the third-generation Rome modular approach to treatment emphasize the metacognitive discovery of the relativity of and limitations of knowledge. Fostering an exploratory attitude toward mental states is coupled with fostering an appreciation for the limits of knowledge. All states of mind are highlighted as just that—states of mind. When a patient is caught up in some emotional state, it is useful to help the patient see that it is "just a state," and that however intense this state may seem, it will pass. When a patient is attempting to construct the meaning of an experience, it is useful to help the patient to see this meaning-making enterprise as a successive approximation, and that uncertainty about the complete accuracy of meaning is both expected and is healthy. Repeatedly interspersing in the therapeutic process phrases like "It *seems* like this but may not actually be . . ." and "Even if you can't really know for sure, what is your best estimate of . . . ?" fosters an attitude that all meaning-making consists of tentative constructions.

It is also helpful to help the patient recognize and explore his or her own defensiveness and self-deception around certain issues. An anchoring scale is useful for this purpose:

> On a 1 to 10 scale, with 1 being very defensive, and 10 being completely nondefensive and open, and 5 being midway between fully defensive and fully open, give me a number that is the degree of defensiveness/openness to this topic you find yourself having right now.

Or:

> On a 1 to 10 scale, with 1 being completely inaccurate and 10 being completely accurate, and 5 being in between, what number indicates right now

the degree of distortion you might be experiencing with respect to your thinking about this issue.

Repeated use of such anchoring scales in treatment enables patients to develop the metacognitive capacity to recognize their degree of defensiveness as it arises in reaction to certain topics.

Seeing More Deeply Into the Underlying Assumptions and Expectancies

Because the structures of this level of cognitive development enable the patient to see the complete or exhaustive relationships between elements of the same system, here the patient is capable of understanding how underlying *assumptions and expectancies* strongly influence state of mind and behavior. To cultivate and strengthen this capacity, for any given feeling or behavior the therapist may ask, "What did you assume was being asked of you in this situation?" "What do you think you were assuming about her that contributed to you reacting as you did?" "What are the underlying beliefs that were operating in your engaging in this behavior?" "What did you expect this would accomplish?" "What were you expecting of the situation that might have contributed to your being so disappointed?" The patient is encouraged to go beyond the information given to the not-so-obvious underlying assumptions. For example, if a patient speaks of wanting to go out and get drunk after an upsetting experience, the patient is invited to explore the range of expectancies about being "drunk." Patients may have any of a range of internal expectancies about the effects of alcohol on their state of mind. The therapist helps the patient articulate his or her particular expected state effects and then to make a link between the expected desirable effect of drinking—however accurate or inaccurate it may be—and the need to change his or her state. The patient is then encouraged to explore other, healthier ways to change his or her state of mind.

For example, if a patient reports becoming suicidal, the therapist may explore with the patient his or her expectations or hopes about the effects that suicide might have: "In the best sense, if you really were able to kill yourself, what would this do for you?" If the patient says, for example, "It would finally end the pain," the patient and therapist both discover the underlying expectancy that suicidal behavior serves an affect tolerance function—a function that might better be served by learning, in therapy, more healthy affect tolerance and coping strategies.

Optimizing Action Plans

At this level of cognitive development, not only is there greater capacity to appreciate limitations, but there also emerges the ability to optimize responses in the face of accurately perceived limitations. Baltes and Baltes (1990a, 1990b) describes a process of selection, optimization, and compensation (SOC) that characterizes optimal adjustment during old age in response to recognizing increasing cognitive and physical limitations. People who age well are able to (1) select and set goals within the range of their available coping resources, (2) optimize goal-relevant action plans within their range of resources that enhance and maximize positive states and maintain highest functioning in the face of limitations, and (3) restructure resources to minimize loss of functioning. Optimizing is a specific metacognitive skill that entails thorough exploration of hidden inner resources to establish the best forms of coping and functioning in the face of limitations.

The therapist can stimulate exploration around the goal of optimization. For example, the therapist might ask the patient to imagine a situation that brings out all the qualities of the "best self." After becoming familiar with the qualities and strengths of the "best self" in that situation, the therapist asks the patient to imagine bringing the resources of that "best self" into a different situation, specifically the situation wherein the patient faces some cognitive or physical limitation or otherwise doesn't feel confident about his or her coping ability. The patient is encouraged to use imagination to create the "optimal response" to the situation and to rehearse in fantasy bringing optimal resources to deal with the situation. Additionally, the patient is encouraged to go beyond the information given to discover inner coping resources that have not been obvious before. Once the patient has made these discoveries, the therapist helps the patient translate these optimizing resources into a specific action plan to cope with the situation. The following exemplifies this process:

> **Therapist:** Now imagine yourself in a situation in which you're feeling at your best—some situation or circumstance in which you're *feeling most fully yourself*, in the best sense.

The patient is given ample time to imagine this, and the therapist then prompts him or her for a description of the situation or circumstance and, most important, for a description of the qualities of the "best self":

> Notice those qualities that you experience now, those qualities that reflect you at your best. *Really* become aware of feeling you *at your best*, feeling *most fully you* in the best sense. What are those qualities that you notice?

After the patient describes these qualities, the therapist mirrors and enhances them. For example:

> Yes. Confidence. *Really* feel that confidence, *really* feel *confident*, and what that's like in your body and in your mind.

Then the therapist suggests that the scene will change and that a different scene will emerge, a scene involving a situation in which the patient typically feels his or limitations and has difficulty. In the imagery, the patient is encouraged to bring all the identified and reinforced "best-self" qualities into that difficult situation.

> Notice yourself in this situation now, this situation in which you've typically had difficulty and you're most aware of limitations that you've had. Now, what's different is that you find yourself bringing to this situation all of those qualities that are *most you, at your best*. Notice what that's like, experiencing yourself in this situation but now being able to bring all your best resources to it. You're able to experience that situation differently that you have before, aren't you? Tell me what's different now, how you find yourself being now in the situation with all your *best qualities* with you.

After supporting and encouraging the patient's new experience, the therapist suggests that the patient discovers *new* resources:

> In a moment, you'll discover something else. As you're there now, aware of all the benefits of being your best self in this situation, *something new* will occur to you—some *new positive quality* will come to you, some new positive quality that you weren't even aware that you have, before now. Notice what this new positive quality is at it emerges, and you can tell me what it is as it does.

The therapist then encourages the patient to notice what effect the newly emerged quality has on his or her experience of the difficult situation. After this imagery process, the therapist and patient discuss all the qualities and resources that the patient experienced during the imagery and together come up with an action plan for drawing from these for future coping with experiences of limitation and difficulty.

Sensitivity to Context

With growing metacognitive capacity to exhaustively discover relations between relations, people become increasingly sensitive to the context of experience. They come to discover how the immediate context of experience affects their actual experience. They are better able to see how antecedent states effect both state of mind and behavior, and are also able to understand that early childhood parental behaviors, as well as current behaviors of significant others in their lives, are best explained in terms of the context within which they occurred. When transgressions by others seem unforgivable, understanding the context within which they occurred is one step toward forgiveness.

To foster context-sensitivity, the therapist may say:

Tell me about the context within which that behavior [or feeling] occurred. What were the circumstances? What were your expectations, and what expectations did the others there have on you? What were you feeling just before going into that situation? Reflect on this, and tell me when you see some relationship between the context and your experience.

After the patient explores the details, the therapist adds, "Give an estimate as to how much the context did or didn't affect the experience. In what specific ways did the context affect the experience?"

The Capacity to Take Perspective

The structures of Stage 6 also support the emergence of understanding not only that all systems of knowledge are relative, but also that it is possible to take perspective on the self in relationship to those systems. This level supports perspective-taking, wherein the person comes to see that his or her perspective is relative and represents a unique point of view. Perspective-taking is fostered by inquiries like, "How do *you* see this, even if someone else might see it differently?" and comments such as, "Not everyone might see it like you do, but you have your own unique history, and there's no one else in the world exactly like you."

In one therapy session, a psychotic patient who lacked a cohesive sense of self described a dozen theories of literary criticism to her therapist. The therapist responded by saying, "Yes, but what is *your own* theory? Please give *your own* idea." The patient could not answer the question. The therapist explained that she had become used to describing her experience from the outside to the inside, as if she could derive a sense of self from what others thought. Asking her to develop her own perspective was the beginning to developing a sense of self as a central organizing principle. As a patient develops a unique self perspective, he or she more easily can finish the stem sentence, "I am the kind of person who . . ."

ADVANCED METACOGNITIVE SKILLS: LATER POST-FORMAL LEVELS

The structures of Stage 7 (teal) support the higher cognitive capacity to relate a given system or systems to a wider system or supersystem and also to appreciate the relative interdependence of elements within this wider system. A number of new metacognitive skills emerge at this level: the ability to take wider and wider perspectives; the ability to take past/present, self/other, and child/adult orientations; awareness of the degree of organization or coherence of mind; an appreciation of interdependence; the ability to articulate a wider life purpose or ultimate concern and have an action plan of actualization; and freedom from internal contradiction.

The Ability to Take a Wider Perspective

Patients at this level are able to develop a wider perspective regarding their condition. For example, a clear indicator that a patient who lacks a cohesive sense of self has developed a sense of self is the emerging capacity to develop a life span view of the self—a coherent narrative for the self from early childhood to the patient's present life. The therapist can foster this process by helping the patient to see how his or her understanding might have changed over time (representational change) and how different family members might hold different perspectives on the same event (representational diversity). In the best sense, this wider perspective entails an emerging transgenerational perspective. Family-tree work helps structure the task of developing a transgenerational perspective.

Perspective-taking can be directly fostered by asking the patient to take others' perspectives and look at themselves or others from those. For example, the patient may be asked,

> How might your husband experience you if you did that? Knowing him as you do, for the moment go inside his head and his unique way of looking at things and imagine you're looking through his eyes at you. What do you see?

Or:

> How do you think your sister experienced the fight between your brothers? Would she have seen it the same way as you, or differently? How might she have seen it similarly, and how might she have seen it differently?

A very valuable method for enhancing perspective-taking and the therapeutic process is having the patient try to take the therapist's perspective on his or her experience. For example,

> Knowing me as you do, from your experience of me during the therapy we've done together, what do you think is my perspective on what you're telling me now?

The Ability to Develop an Orientation

Orientation is a specific kind of perspective-taking. One type of orientation is past versus present orientation. For example, anxious-preoccupied patients are often preoccupied with unresolved past experiences; as Mary Main states, "the past invades the present" (see Main et al., 2002, p. 175). For such patients, it is useful to help them become more aware of their relative orientation of preoccupation with the past over the present. For example, the therapist with such patients may frequently say,

> On a scale of 1 to 10, with 1 being *completely preoccupied* with the past and unaware of current context, and 10 being *completely in the present*, and the other numbers representing some mixture of past and present awareness, give me a number as to the relative orientation you have to past or present at this given moment.

By using this anchoring scale frequently, the preoccupied patient discovers when he or she is stuck in the past and becomes able to use this awareness to shift to a more present orientation.

Another type of orientation skill entails the ability to shift orientation from self to other and vice versa. Bach (1977) described how certain narcissistically vulnerable patients are focused entirely on the self, with little awareness of the other's experience (i.e., all self-transference). Other narcissistically vulnerable patients focus entirely on how they believe others see them, so much so that there is little awareness left for an internal state of mind (i.e., all other trans-ference). Such narcissistically vulnerable individuals are unable to develop a relative balance between simultaneous self and other perception, *to hold in experience simultaneously their own inner state of mind and also the state of mind of the other*. In such patients, it is important to help them develop the metacognitive capacity to identify when they have all-self/no-other or all-other/no-self perception, toward the goal of developing the capacity to hold the state of mind of self and other simultaneously. Again, the therapist applies an anchoring scale:

> On a 1 to 10 scale, with 1 being *so fully aware* of *your own* state of mind that you are completely unaware of the state of mind of the other, and 10 being *so completely focused* on how the *other* might see you that there is no awareness of your own internal state of mind, and 5 being holding *both* your *own* and the *other's* state of mind in your awareness *at the same time*, and the other numbers representing some degree of imbalance in the direc-tion of more awareness of the self's or other's state of mind, give me a num-ber that best represents your relative awareness of state of self and state of other right now.

By using such a scale frequently, the narcissistically vulnerable patient grad-ually learns to hold state of mind of self and other simultaneously.

Awareness of Organization or Coherence of Mind

According to research with the Adult Attachment Interview, patients with per-sonality and dissociative disorders as well as those with insecure attachment typically experience low coherence of mind. Coherence pertains to the relative perceived organization/disorganization of state of mind. Such patients benefit from learning to accurately perceive the relative organization and disorganization of their state of mind, as such perception increases the organization and coherence of mind. Frequent use of an anchoring scale supports this development:

> On a 1 to 10 scale, with 1 being complete *disorganization* of your state of mind, 10 being complete *organization* of your state of mind, and 5 being a level of the mind somewhere in between, give me a number that represents your level of organization and disorganization of mind right now.

The patient gradually learns to (1) accurately assess his or her organization of mind and (2) recognize how the degree of organization/disorganization of mind is associated with specific mental states (e.g., strong feelings) and external context (e.g., increased disorganization under stress). Over time, repeated use of such interventions fosters increased metacognitive awareness of the degree of organization, or the lack thereof. This awareness itself cultivates more consistent organization and coherence of mind until it reaches the normal range characteristic of healthy individuals with secure attachment.

Recognition of Interdependence

The patient at this level can develop a wider perspective or supersystemic point of view within which everything and everyone are recognized as interconnected and interdependent. The physicist David Bohm called this interconnection and interdependence "the implicate order" (1980), wherein everything implicates, or involves in a necessary way, everything else. Such patients are able to see the common humanity of all individuals irrespective of age, gender, race, ethnicity, and culture. The patient is able to develop a sense of compassion for others' suffering and have forgiveness for the transgressions against them by adopting a common humanity perspective. Patients are encouraged to develop a wider perspective through which they can appreciate the interdependence of all humanity (e.g., Bohm, 1980) and to view their own suffering through developing a perspective on the suffering of humanity individually and as a whole.

For example, the therapist may ask the patient, "How might something in your life or your experience be affected by the flood that's happening in that country right now?" or "Let's think together about all the steps involved leading to that pizza being delivered to your home last night; how far back can we go? Let's first think about the flour that made the crust—where did that come from? Where did the water that grew the wheat come from?" Regarding suffering, the therapist might say, "I know you're suffering a lot right now; how many other people on the planet do you think are right now suffering in much the same way you are right now?"

Metacognitive Development of a Wider Perspective or Ultimate Concern,
Action Plans of Actualization, and Freedom From Internal Contradiction
In *The Psychology of Ultimate Concerns*, Emmons (1999) demonstrates how individuals may develop a complex set of personal strivings and goals, many of which are contradictory in a way that diminishes overall well-being. However, individuals who develop higher-order goals, like an ultimate concern or overarching spiritual goal, have significantly less internal conflict, higher subjective well-being, and a strong sense of purpose in life and are more resilient in the face of stress. These possibilities highlight how valuable it is to help patients develop and shape an ultimate concern. The therapist may suggest:

> Reflect on what is the *central guiding principle* of your life. Identify the core purpose behind everything you do that gives what you do the *deepest meaning*. It may be a spiritual or humanitarian concern, or something else. The more you reflect on this concern, the more you will become *clearer and clearer* as to what this *central guiding principle* is in your life, and the more you will come to detect this central purpose in the activities that are most important to you, moments when life matters the most. You'll begin to see a central thread that runs through all these occasions, and the *more* you reflect on it, the *more* you will become *clear* on what this central guiding purpose is for you . . . Now take this central guiding principle and imagine a scene where it is more clearly in the background of your awareness when you are doing something and see how it affects you. Do you bring a greater sense of presence to that activity? Does it give you a deeper satisfaction? Notice if you have a deeper interest in and engagement in that activity.

The more the patient articulates the details of his or her ultimate meaning-system, the more it serves as a supersystemic organizing principle. From this wider perspective or sense of purpose, all specific action plans and goal-behavior are superseded and organized by a larger sense of purpose. These specific long-term goals and action plans are reorganized around the wider purpose so that personal fulfillment is seen as actualization of some wider view of human development, including spiritual and humanitarian development. Emmons found that felt distress over internal contradictions between different personal goal strivings is greatly reduced in those individuals who develop a wider sense of purpose. Internal contradiction and conflicts between ego states is very characteristic of patients with personality and dissociative disorders, and helping the patient to develop a wider sense of purpose can be a very effective strategy for reducing or overcoming conflicts among internal ego states.

Moving Beyond the Limitations of Conceptual Thought to Direct Awareness of a Wider Reality

Stage 8 (turquoise), the construct-aware, cross-paradigmatic stage of cognitive development, supports the discovery of the limitations of all conceptual thought in favor of direct awareness of a larger supersystem of knowing that transcends relativism. Patients become increasingly aware of the processes of their own representational construction and their limitations. As Cook-Greuter says, there is "an ever-growing awareness . . . of the process . . . of thinking itself" (1990, p. 83), as well of the habitual ways of thinking that distort and diminish the freshness of direct knowing. At this stage, the individual begins to discover that *direct awareness* of state of mind is an alternative and more valid means of knowing than is conceptual thought. Conceptual thought and language can still be used and operated with when useful, but they are increasingly seen as a source of bias and distortion, and direct awareness is increasingly appreciated as a form of pure, unobstructed knowing. The patient discovers that making the supersystem the basis of operation or perspective allows for switching out of conceptual thought as a way of knowledge acquisition; then, direct, changeless, boundless awareness becomes the primary mode of knowledge acquisition and operation. In other words, the larger supersystem supports a level of awareness that is broad enough in scope to observe and operate any elements within the more limited systems.

This development raises a new possibility, namely, that perhaps systems of knowledge are only limited insofar as they represent distinct, relative systems of knowledge. However, perhaps from a much broader supersystemic perspective, everything can be seen accurately just the way it is through direct awareness, including direct awareness of the entire supersystem itself, free from the limitations of conceptual knowing. Creativity and generativity within this larger vision become salient.

Gendlin (1982), in his research on "experiencing," discovered that direct experience contains much more information than can be revealed by specific emotional states or thoughts. At this stage of cognitive functioning, patients learn to trust direct, holistic awareness of immediate ongoing experience over conceptualizing about the meaning of their experience. Gendlin's experiential *focusing* is a useful method for supporting patients to move beyond conceptual knowing to direct, immediate experiencing.

The Self as a Temporary Functional Organizing Principle

At this stage of cognitive development, the individual self is no longer experienced as a solid, permanent structure of mind, and it is no longer reified. However, although the individual self is not solid, it is not fragile as it is at the earlier levels of self or ego development. At the later stages of development, the individual self still serves as a functional structure that supports the individual person to operate in the relative world, but it becomes less and less the locus of identity. It helps to organize relative experience, but it arises as a temporary phenomenon to serve that function only when needed in a given context (Cook-Greuter, 1990).

Higher-Order Metacognitive Skills

Stage 9 (indigo) represents development of a universal or ego-transcendent perspective. In Indo-Tibetan Buddhism, this stage of development constitutes "awakening," wherein the individual "infant" consciousness merges with the oceanlike "mother" consciousness of awakened nature, and this unbounded wholeness becomes the new basis of operation—what Commons, Armon, et al. (1990) call shifting from systems to a larger field. The new metacognitive skills that develop at this stage include developing simultaneous, multiple points of view free of all contradiction; immediate awareness of and automatic monitoring of ongoing processes; and a markedly diminished reactivity to any immediate experience or state of mind. Because the immediate state of mind occurs from the perspective of a vast field of unbounded awareness, each state arises like a wave in a vast ocean, and as it arises it may be met with absolutely no reactivity. In Indo-Tibetan Buddhism, this experience of nonreactivity is called "spacious freedom." With spacious freedom, people become increasingly aware of heretofore problematic states with neither defensiveness nor reactivity to these states (Engler, 1986).

These forms of metacognitive functioning may emerge spontaneously through cultivation of and practice with the intermediate skills. When the therapist recognizes them, he or she simply brings attention to them and encourages reflection and description; the therapist also fosters the patient's recognition of any changes in these forms, such as their being more or less present. In these ways, the higher-order metacognitive skills are reinforced and stabilized.

Overview

Not every metacognitive capacity described in this chapter will be available to every patient in treatment. Across patients will be a spectrum of developmental levels and corresponding structural foundations for cognitive and metacognitive functioning. In our experience, we have found it useful to apply the methods for developing metacognitive capacity described here according to what each individual patient presents as problematic. For example, if a patient has limited ability to take perspectives other than his or her own, then we apply perspective-widening methods; if a patient has poor organization of mind, then we use methods for increasing mental organization, such as the anchor scale for recognizing the level of disorganization/organization. As patients progress and show fewer of the metacognitive deficits that they had at the beginning of treatment, we introduce methods relevant to the later stages of cognitive development and for cultivating the higher metacognitive capacities. This approach leads to resolution of problematic deficits that patients enter treatment with and also supports their continued development toward greater potentials of functioning and well-being.

Like most good psychotherapy, the methods for cultivating metacognitive functioning are inherently collaborative. In the next chapter, we bring focus to direct methods for enhancing collaborative capacity in patients. As patients with attachment and personality disorders tend to have impaired collaborative skills, we believe that including direct collaboration-enhancing methods in treatment contributes to the efficiency and stability of beneficial treatment outcomes.

CHAPTER 10

The Third Pillar

Fostering Collaborative Capacity
and Behavior

We find notable differences in collaborative behavior between patients with secure and insecure attachment status, and thus consider the development of collaborative capacity to be an essential component of treatment. Evolutionary evidence indicates that cooperation and collaboration are hardwired in humans, and these behaviors seem to emerge spontaneously in securely attached children. It appears that the conditions that lead to insecure attachment also impair the emergence of natural, innate collaborative functioning. We review the literature below.

The Adaptive Function of the Cooperative Behavioral System

Paul Gilbert (1989) articulated how the cooperative behavioral system developed as an evolutionary adaptive pattern for the human species. He wrote:

> Individualistic competitiveness (dominance–power seeking) appears to become adapted and modified in species that, to a limited extent, are able to associate themselves for prosocial interactive behaviour. This has necessitated the evolution of social signals . . . Co-operation, when evolved to the level of providing social rules, results in the division of labour . . . ; co-operation evolved from the benefits bestowed to species who became capable of joint, coordinated action to secure a goal. Co-operation is therefore an evolved capability for the modification of individualistic competitiveness . . . Individualistic competitiveness is concerned with spacing, separating and differentiating one member from another such that one member extracts an individual advantage or control over another. It is concerned with a vertical hierarchical organization of relationship. Co-operativeness, on the other hand, is concerned with linking together, joining, acting together and mini-

mizing differences between individual members . . . An individual seeking co-operative goals may not wish to have power over others or to lead them necessarily, but does wish to be viewed as someone with something to offer and share with others in terms of skills, knowledge or competency, i.e. to be of value to others, or . . . appreciated . . . The key to co-operation, therefore, is sharing, communication and the capacity to learn social rules for organizing role expectations in relationships. (pp. 23, 24, 197–199)

As Gilbert views cooperation as adaptive for the human species, it follows that lack of cooperativeness is maladaptive. In fact, according to Gilbert, lack of cooperativeness is common to many clinical conditions:

The (in)capacity to co-operate and share with others lies at the heart of many psychological difficulties. These include thwarted efforts to see oneself as valued, appreciated and accepted as part of a group or a relationship, tendencies to be overly competitive . . . or submissive in co-operative contexts and/or tendencies toward fears of deception, dishonesty and exploitation by one's fellow. (1989, p. 200)

Healthy cooperativeness entails a sense of "togetherness": "The key to co-operative endeavor is joining and coming together; that is, linking as opposed to separating, differentiating and spacing . . . Within systems of co-operative enterprise some seem more motivated to maintain the 'togetherness'" (Gilbert, 1989, p. 218).

Healthy cooperativeness also entails mutuality and reciprocity:

At the center of co-operative relationships is the issue of reciprocation. That is, individuals develop supportive, co-operative relationships by maintaining some awareness of give and take . . . Co-operative relationships can break down if individuals perceive others as exploiting them or if they perceive themselves as being unable to give to the relationships in an equitable way . . . [I]n cooperative relationships . . . status and worth are defined not by power but by altruism and contribution . . . [and] status is defined . . . by the ability to contribute, to have something to offer. (p. 223)

In *Why We Cooperate*, Michael Tomasello (2009) summarizes his research comparing human infants and apes with respect to cooperativeness. He believes that human infants, in contrast to primates, are intrinsically altruistic:

Parental rewards and encouragement do not seem to increase infant's helping behavior . . . [I]nfants were so inclined to help in general . . . The children who had been rewarded five times in the first phase actually helped *less* during the second phase than those who has not been rewarded . . . We believe that children's early helping is not a behavior created by culture and/or parental socialization practices. Rather, it is an outward expression of children's natural inclination to sympathize with others in strife . . . [E]ven infants below one year of age distinguish helpful from unhelpful agents. (pp. 8–9, 13)

In contrast to human infants, apes show only the most rudimentary forms of cooperation:

If a human needed a tool to open a box that contained food for the ape, the ape would point to the location of the tool for the human . . . They even understand imperatives in a cooperative fashion . . . [O]nly humans help others by providing needed information . . . Sharing apes are not very altruistic in sharing of resources such as food. (pp. 16, 19, 21)

According to Tomasello, the fundamental underlying principle of human cooperativeness is "shared intentionality":

We may refer to the underlying psychological processes that make these unique forms of cooperation possible a "shared intentionality." Shared intentionality involves, most basically, the ability to create with others joint intentions and joint commitments in cooperative endeavors. These joint intentions and commitments are structured by processes of joint attention and mutual knowledge. (2009, p. xiv)

"In shared cooperative activities, we have a joint goal that creates an interdependence among us . . . [E]ven outside of such cooperative activities, children also value conformity to the group" (Tomasello, 2009, p. 41).

Tomasello believes that human infants display their cooperativeness in three broad but distinct ways—helping, informing, and sharing (2009, p. 28). He suggests that "even young children already have some sense of shared intentionality" (p. 39) and that they display such distinctly cooperative behavior by the end of the first year. At this early age, young children show "indiscriminate cooperativeness" toward others (p. 4), but by the end of their third year they have internalized cultural norms regarding cooperativeness, and their cooperative behavior then takes on culture-specific forms (p. 34).

Collaborative Communication and Shared Intentionality

Tomasello (2009) sees collaboration as something that goes beyond simple cooperativeness and includes *mutuality* and *shared intentionality*. He defines collaboration as follows:

Mutualism, in which we all benefit from our cooperation but only if we work together, [is] what we may call collaboration . . . [E]arly humans had to evolve some serious social-cognitive skills and motivations for coordinating and communicating with others in complex ways involving joint goals and coordinated division of labor among the various roles—what I will call skills and motivations for shared intentionality . . . This sense that we are doing something together . . . creates mutual expectations . . . [and] a sense of acting together. (pp. 52, 54, 55, 58)

In "shared cooperative activities," the collaborators must first of all be mutually responsive to one another's intentional states . . . In addition to a joint goal, a fully collaborative activity requires that there be some division of labor and that each partner understand the other's role . . . [and that there be a] shared focus of attention . . . In mutualistic collaborative activities, we both know together that we both depend on one another for reaching our joint goal. (pp. 61, 67, 70, 90)

From very early in ontogeny, human children collaborate with others in ways unique to their species. They form with others joint goals to which both parties are normatively committed, they establish with others domains of joint attention and common conceptual ground, and they create with others symbolic, institutional realities that assign deontic powers to otherwise inert entities. Children are motivated to engage in these kinds of collaborative activities for their own sake, not just for their contribution to individual goals. (p. 105)

Tomasello believes that in human evolutionary development there was a link between collaborative activities and the development of cooperative communication. He says that "some time after humans had developed means of cooperative communication . . . Skills and motivations for cooperative communication coevolved with . . . collaborative activities" (2009, p. 74). According to this view, the communication behavior that emerges during human infancy is inherently collaborative. Human language is seen as the epitome of collaborative behavior. More is said about communication and language later in this chapter.

Cooperation and Collaboration in Children With Caregivers and Peers

There are fundamental differences between secure and insecure children with respect to expectancies of cooperation and collaboration. For example, the secure infant, when upset, expects the caregiver to be responsive, while the insecure infant does not. Tomasello (2009) says:

Infants learn to expect that their caretaker will or will not come to their aid in times of distress . . . Securely attached infants are able to use their mothers as sources of comfort . . . [A]n insecurely attached infant is not able to derive comfort from the mother's proximity. (p. 129)

Several experiments have been conducted to illustrate different responses of secure and insecure and abused and nonabused children in response to distress. In one experiment, mothers were asked to climb a series of steps in a way that their infants could not follow after them. Both secure and insecure infants showed a distress response. The main difference was that

securely attached infants looked longer when the mother kept going, but the insecurely attached infants were more "surprised" when the mother came back. Thus infants with secure and insecure attachment relationships had formed different expectations about whether a caretaker would return and help the child in need. (Tomasello, 2009, pp. 130–131, citing Johnson, Dweck, & Chen, 2007)

In another experiment, done in a day care setting, children who either had or did not have prior abuse histories saw a child peer who was exhibiting distress. The results showed a clear difference between the two groups: "The majority of the non-abused infants attended closely to the distressed child, showed concern, or provided comfort. However, not one of the abused infants showed empathic concern" (Tomasello, 2009, p. 132, citing Main & George, 1985).

Heard, Lake, and McCluskey (2009) describe a "peer interest sharing" behavioral system that they see as distinct from the attachment system. The main difference is that the caregiver in the attachment behavioral system is typically "older and wiser" than the child, but in the peer interest-sharing system "the participants are equals" (p. 87). The authors define mutual interest-sharing by stating that "the act of interacting with a group of people about a specific topic, to which everyone is interested, makes the topic become a mutual interest; in the act of sharing a mutual interest, people feel like they are closer and enlivened" (p. 89). Mutual interest-sharing among peers, according to Heard et al., in the best sense leads to new interests, new levels of understanding, new skills, and "seeing other person(s) doing likewise" (p. 87).

The Clinical Relevance of Lack of Cooperation and Collaborativeness

Given the strong evolutionary evidence that cooperation and collaboration are built into the human species and are readily observed in secure infants early in the first year of life and throughout childhood, the relative lack of cooperation and collaboration in insecure and abused children is an aberration from normally expected development. Insecure and abused children as compared to secure nonabused children show clear evidence of both mismatched or impaired nonverbal interactive behavior and also noncollaborative verbal discourse. These impaired patterns of nonverbal and verbal behavior in insecure and/or abused children tend to persist throughout older childhood and into adulthood, and therefore they are a central focus of treatment in our model of attachment-based treatment. We view the relative lack of nonverbal and verbal cooperative and collaborative behavior in children and adults who have significant attachment disturbance as a developmental arrest. In other words, the therapeutic task is not so much to create new nonverbal and verbal collaborative behaviors *ex nihilo* as it is to provide the corrective developmental conditions in therapy that allow the patient to manifest his or her inherent but arrested developmental potential to be collaborative, both nonverbally and verbally.

Defining Psychotherapy as Collaborative Partnership: The Contribution of Interpersonal Psychotherapy

Harry Stack Sullivan was the first psychotherapist to articulate the relevance of cooperation and collaboration to psychotherapy. In his definition, cooperation pertains to favoring shared goals over competition and collaboration pertains to intersubjectivity:

> Intimacy is that type of situation involving two people which permits validation of all components of personal worth. Validation of personal worth requires a type of relationship which I call collaboration, by which I mean clearly formulated adjustments of one's behavior to the expressed needs of the other person in pursuit of increasingly identical—that is, more and more nearly mutual—satisfactions, and in the maintenance of increasingly similar security operations. Now this preadolescent collaboration is distinctly different from the acquisition, in the juvenile era, of habits of competition, cooperation, and compromise. (1953, p. 246)

A footnote in this text adds that to Sullivan cooperation means give and take around shared goals, whereas collaboration entails "the feeling of sensitivity to another person" Sullivan states that "when we collaborate it is a matter of we" (p. 246). From an evolutionary perspective, cooperation entails putting aside competition toward shared interests and cooperative behavior toward a common end, while collaboration entails mutually regulated ongoing exploration. Based on this definition, neo-Sullivanian or interpersonal psychotherapy embodies both cooperative and collaborative elements.

In their textbook on interpersonal therapy, *Interpersonal Process in Therapy; An Integrated Model* (2011), Teyber and McClure define psychotherapy as a "collaborative partnership":

> One of the most important ways for therapists to establish a strong working alliance with clients is to work together collaboratively—as partners. In

the initial session, the therapist's primary aim is to articulate clear expectations for working in this collaborative manner, and, more important, to enact behaviorally these spoken expectations by giving clients the *experience* of partnership . . . Thinking of the working alliance as a collaborative partnership, therapy is not something therapists "do" to clients, it is a shared interaction that requires the participation of both parties in order to succeed. (Teyber & McClure, 2011, p. 48)

We suggest that the concept of psychotherapy as a collaborative partnership is not limited to interpersonal psychotherapy, but best serves as a component of all good psychotherapy. However, in working with children and adults with significant attachment disturbance, there is a dilemma: We ask the attachment-impaired patient, who by definition is not very cooperative or collaborative, to engage in an interpersonal system, the therapeutic dyad and process, that is fundamentally cooperative and collaborative. Therefore, a major focus of attachment-based treatment is to help the patient become cooperative and collaborative, not only for the benefit of their lives outside of therapy but also for them to best benefit from the therapy process itself.

Starting Points: Fostering Collaboration at the Beginning of Therapy

A MUTUALLY NEGOTIATED TREATMENT PLAN AND INFORMED CONSENT

The process of collaboration in therapy begins with an exploration of the patient's hopes and expectations regarding treatment, toward establishing mutually agreed-upon goals. The therapist asks the patient to identify, from his or her own understanding, what the main problems are that made him or her seek treatment. Since patients with attachment disturbance often have low expectations regarding treatment outcome, we have found it useful during the first session to ask the hypothetical question: "If you were to engage in a treatment and this time it *really* worked, in the best sense what would be different for you?" This question invites exploration and development of a representation of treatment success specific to that patient. However, the process also requires that the therapist share his or her own impressions, based on the interview of the patient, about the goals and best approach to treatment. A *mutually negotiated treatment plan* (Burt, 1979) requires that both patient and therapist share relevant expectations and information toward this common goal. As Teyber and McClure (2011) state, this process involves "engaging the client . . . [in] assessing together: the issues and concerns that are most important," what in the past was and was not helpful, and shared treatment goals (p. 49).

This process also requires *shared decision-making* about the best approach to these treatment goals (Katz, 1984). We believe that the best approach when formulating a mutually negotiated treatment plan is full transparency on the part of the therapist (Brody, 1989). The best therapist openly discusses his or her diagnostic impressions and how he or she arrived at these impressions. Transparent therapists openly discuss with each patient their reasoning as to what are the best approaches to treatment with him or her and in some detail explain why. Transparent therapists also openly discuss what difficulties they anticipate arising in treatment, including difficulties in collaboration. Some research exists to show that therapists who are transparent, as compared to nondisclosing therapists, form a much stronger alliance with patients. Additionally, open sharing of diagnostic and treatment impressions constitutes modeling of collaborative behavior for the patient at the very beginning of therapy. As Teyber and McClure state:

> For many clients, this collaborative partnership, in itself, provides a corrective emotional experience. This collaborative interpersonal process is a new way of interacting that many clients have not experienced in other close relationships . . . *[O]ne of the most important determinants of treatment outcome is whether the therapist and client can continue this process of mutual collaboration.* (p. 53)

The therapist sets the expectations for and tone of collaborative treatment at the very onset of treatment by initiating a mutual exploration toward defining shared understanding of treatment problems and treatment goals. The development of an informed consent document, mutually developed, reviewed, and signed by both patient and therapist, makes explicit and tangible that the therapy endeavor is a mutual, collaborative partnership.

ESTABLISHING THE TREATMENT FRAME AS COLLABORATIVE PARTNERSHIP

When upset, patients with dismissing attachment are likely to withdraw from treatment, and anxious-preoccupied patients are likely to make repeated and excessive demands for extratherapeutic contact with the therapist. Patients with disorganized attachment do both, at different times or simultaneously. Therefore, to solidify the expectation that therapy is a fundamentally collaborative enterprise, it is necessary for the patient and therapist to codify these expectations and roles in the form of a detailed treatment frame contract. The emphasis is not on the contract *per se* as a signed document, but on the processes of mutual negotiation and collaboration through which the elements of this contract are defined. The more detailed the treatment frame contract, and therefore the more detailed the role expectations, the less the likelihood of misunderstandings and treatment ruptures. Since patients with attachment disturbance have impaired collaborativeness, it is especially important to clearly articulate role expectations and to help them experience and learn to maintain a relationship based on mutual expectations and clear role definitions.

In our opinion, the first step in establishing a viable treatment frame is developing clear expectations and rules regarding *safety*. Beyond important practical considerations, the primary therapeutic reason for addressing safety issues up front, at the onset of treatment, is that dealing with this issue sets the fundamental context for attachment-based treatment. Bowlby said that the fundamental purpose of the attachment behavioral system in both animals and humans is *protection* of the individual and thereby the species. By establishing clear expectations and rules regarding safety at the very beginning of treatment, the patient with attachment disturbance receives the assurance that *this* psychotherapy, as a good attachment system, is based on a foundation of his or her safety and protection. This therapeutic stance challenges dysfunctional internal working models holding that the therapist, like early attachment figures, will become a source of danger and threat (Crittenden, 2000a, 2000b) rather than a source of secure base. Thus, the treatment frame contract must include clear strategies for how the patient and therapist will handle threats to the patient's safety, such as self-harmful behaviors, including self-mutilation, suicidal ideation, and suicidal behavior; harmful drug and alcohol use; harmful sexual encounters; abusive relationships, and dissociative reenactment of traumatizing relationships.

Patients with significant attachment disturbances have the potential to manifest numerous treatment-frame violations throughout treatment. Thus, it is very important to clearly set expectations and structure these expectations around a clear treatment-frame contract. We take the view that patients with attachment disturbance need to learn how to be in therapy and best use it. Even patients with strong self structures don't always understand relational mutuality, collaboration, or how to use therapy in ways to repair their problematic attachment patterns. Treatment-frame discussions provide a strong message that collaborative behavior is a goal at all times throughout the therapy, and that significant lapses in collaborative behavior put the treatment at risk.

The discussion of treatment-frame issues and the treatment contract must also include a mutual understanding of how therapy-interfering behaviors (Linehan, 1993) will be handled. Since the foundation of the therapist–patient relationship is based upon trust, it is important to establish early a foundation of open, honest disclosure and communication in the therapy relationship, especially regarding issues that can disrupt the therapeutic process. Teyber and McClure see interpersonal psychotherapy as a "*collaborative invitation* for . . . honest communication" (p. 26). To this end, the treatment-frame discussion must address how the following occurrences would be addressed: failing to give consent to talk with other treaters; lying to the therapist; factitious exaggeration of symptoms or experiences; refusing to discuss certain topics; focusing on trivial or irrelevant themes instead of the mutually agreed-upon treatment topics;

toxic, abusive behavior in the treatment session; sexualizing in the treatment session; and protesting about ending the treatment session on time or refusing to leave the session. Expectations regarding consistency and reliability, of both patient and therapist, are also addressed, so that there is mutual understanding of what will be responses to excessive cancellations, not showing up for sessions, or frequently coming late.

Likewise, a thorough treatment-frame discussion includes explicit understanding of how the following potential disruptions to treatment continuity will be handled: the patient (or therapist) leaving town for extended periods; the patient wishing to decrease therapy frequency; and the patient not being able to manage finances in a way that limits treatment frequency.

Of course, the therapeutic skill of collaboratively developing a treatment-frame understanding, as well as a treatment plan and informed consent document, involves bringing forward the task focus *in the context of therapeutic attunement to the patient*. The first few sessions of treatment occur prior to the establishment of any therapeutic relationship or attachment, and patients with attachment disturbances are especially likely to be aware of and react negatively to any lack of attunement by the therapist. Thus, the therapist must be more than task focused: He or she must watch for any patient reactivity and be willing to slow down the task process and allow the negotiation to be *truly mutual and collaborative*—that is, for it to be guided not only by the therapist's agenda based on belief in the importance and value of the task, but also by the patient's needs for human connection and attunement.

FOSTERING A COLLABORATIVE STATE OF MIND IN PSYCHOTHERAPY: THE CONTRIBUTION OF THE ROME CENTER OF COGNITIVE PSYCHOTHERAPY

The work of the Third Center of Cognitive Psychotherapy, Rome, in general, and the work of Giovanni Liotti in particular, has laid some of the groundwork for understanding the importance of fostering collaboration in psychotherapy with patients who have attachment disturbances. According to Liotti, the cooperative behavioral system is an "inborn motivational system mediating cooperative behaviour" (1999, p. 6). Drawing upon the work of Gilbert (1989) and Tomasello (2010), Cortina and Liotti (2010) state:

> We think that superior cooperative and communicative abilities might have been key adaptations that helped early human nomadic hunter gatherer groups survive and prosper during the period in which our direct homo [sapien] ancestors lived . . . These adaptations allowed for cooperation to take place at a new level of sophistication between kin and nonkin members, which in turn helped these more cooperative and cohesive groups compete favorably with less cooperative and cohesive groups . . . in order to

offset selection at the level of individuals, that favors "selfish" individuals over cooperative altruists. (p. 294)

Because this innate cooperative behavioral system is deactivated in patients with significant attachment disturbance, Cortina and Liotti emphasize the importance of fostering a "collaborative state of mind" (Liotti, 2005) in such patients: "Patients . . . rarely have witnessed cooperation on equal grounds between their parents. [But in therapy they have the opportunity to] share a common attitude . . . and thus cooperate in their treatment (Cortina & Liotti, 2010, p. 36).

Fostering a collaborative state of mind must begin during the first meeting with the patient, and is built upon a foundation of safety and protection in therapy:

> Cooperative motives, as attachment ones, involve feelings of safeness: individuals must feel safe enough to come into proximity long enough and to share and also not be cheated or exploited. Indeed sharing, working out what others want and giving it to them, then being appreciated in return, is a common source of pleasure and relationship building. (Liotti & Gilbert, 2011, p. 16)

As already mentioned, fostering a collaborative state of mind also begins with "explicit agreement of goals and rules of therapeutic work . . . [M]utual agreement is constructed at the beginning . . . [via] joint formulation of a shared goal for the treatment" (Liotti, 1999, p. 6).

One of the main components of fostering collaboration is mutual understanding. Liotti (2005) has said that "to understand each other is the basic act of cooperation" and that developing mutual understanding of therapeutic issues is very different from the traditional one-sided interpretation by the therapist. Liotti believes that "cooperation is better than interpretation" and that "on-going dialogue" between patient and therapist is the best way to foster collaborativeness in treatment.

From the very first meeting with a patient, as well as during ongoing treatment, it is very important to foster *collaborative exploration*, especially in patients with significant attachment disturbances in whom the exploratory behavioral system has been inhibited (in anxious-preoccupied patients) or exaggerated (in dismissing patients, as a kind of pseudoautonomous self-exploration while deactivating attachment). Mutual sharing of information about treatment problems and treatment goals starts the process of collaborative exploration (Dimaggio, Semerari, Carcione, Nicolò, & Procacci, 2007, p. 38). Dimaggio et al. (2007) also recommend that at the end of each hour, the therapist share a summary of the main points of the session as a way of fostering collaborative exploration. The therapist's open sharing of the main points of each session, from his or her point of view, invites the same behavior from the patient, and over time the attachment-impaired patient learns that such open sharing, dialogue, and collaborative exploration is usually beneficial and rarely harmful. Dimaggio et al. (2007) see attachment-based treatment as a kind of "collaborative empiricism," wherein "to cooperate in the performing of specific tasks based on jointly agreed goals" (p. 37). Of note is that such collaborative exploratory exchanges also promote mentalizing, as they are consistent with what J. G. Allen (2013) and others describe as contributing to mentalizing ability.

The true test of collaborative exploration is when ruptures in the therapeutic alliance occur during treatment. Both patient and therapist must collaborate to explore and understand the factors that led to the rupture in the alliance and to mutually work toward repair of the rupture in the relationship. When the attachment-impaired patient activates a negative internal working model and transfers this onto the therapist, Liotti (2005) recommends that the negative representation and experience be explored not from within the attachment system, but in a cooperative, collaborative mode. Liotti makes a very important point, namely, that the cooperative/collaborative behavioral system *is distinct from the attachment system*. Thus, when ruptures occur in the attachment relationship, they cannot easily be repaired from within the attachment system per se. However, by switching to the different, cooperative system, both patient and therapist can temporarily step out of the disrupted attachment system into a system that is not ruptured. When engaging the cooperative behavioral system, the patient and therapist are peers, rather than the therapist being primarily an attachment figure. In this context, the therapist may suggest:

> Let's look at this together and explore what happened. Clearly, this difficulty that emerged between us has to do with both of us, so let's collaborate and figure out what happened and how we can understand, resolve, and move beyond it.

Through mutual peer-mode collaborative exploration of the rupture, some beneficial distance, or disidentification, from the rupture occurs, allowing for efficient repair of the therapeutic alliance. This process, though occurring outside the attachment system, serves to strengthen the attachment relationship, as the patient experiences the therapist as attuned, responsive, and respectful of his or her experience.

Fostering Collaborative Behavior in the Ongoing Therapy

Along with maintaining support for a collaborative state of mind and collaborative exploration, several other considerations are important for the ongoing therapeutic process. In patients with significant attachment disturbance, there are two broad areas of impaired collaborative behavior that need to be addressed over the course of treatment—clinically significant manifestations of noncollaborative nonverbal and noncollaborative verbal behavior. With respect to nonverbal behavior, Beatrice Beebe has focused her research mainly on nonverbal collaborative behavior. She has found that collaborative nonverbal behavior in secure adult patients is indicated by synchronization in timing and match with the other's nonverbal behaviors, but that desynchronization and mismatches are common in adult patients with some pattern of insecure attachment (Beebe & Lachmann, 2014). With respect to noncollaborative verbal behavior, Mary Main observed that a sign of secure attachment on the Adult Attachment Interview was healthy collaboration between interviewee and interviewer, as manifested in their verbal discourse about attachment. In contrast, individuals with some form of insecure attachment—dismissing, anxious-preoccupied, or disorganized—rarely showed any signs of collaborative verbal behavior on the AAI. Main assesses collaborativeness through the degree of meeting or violating Grice's maxims; this approach is explained in more detail later in this chapter. The third pillar of our model of attachment-based treatment includes a focus on improving both nonverbal and verbal collaborative behavior throughout the course of therapy.

IMPROVING NONVERBAL COLLABORATION

Beebe and Lachmann (2014) state:

> Because the shadows of early interaction disturbances are re-evoked in the treatment setting, the research can help us to be more aware of the kinds of interactive mismatches in the action dialogue that the patient may be sensitive to. It may help us be more aware of specific ways in which longings to know the partner, and be known by the partner, were derailed and may be re-activated. We may be more able to create "model scenes" . . . which capture current "shadows" of early interaction disturbances. And we may be able to become more aware of parallel or analogous processes in our own histories that help us empathize with the dilemmas of our patients. (2014, p. 70)

The three prototypical patterns of insecure attachment are characterized by numerous types of nonverbal interactive mismatches. Methods of our third pillar of treatment help the therapist and patient alike become metacognitively aware of these salient mismatches in nonverbal behavior between patient and therapist, and also to fundamentally change the nonverbal interactive patterns between patient and therapist in the direction of increased nonverbal collaborativeness.

Beatrice Beebe and her associates have been the primary pioneers in research on nonverbal collaboration between infants and caregivers. She and her colleagues developed a method to microanalyze videotapes of split-second, moment-by-moment infant–mother interactions to understand the main patterns of mutual nonverbal relatedness. They discovered that there are two broad types of dyadic nonverbal exchanges between infant and caregiver: "collaborative" and "contradictory" (2014, p. 36).

In collaborative nonverbal exchanges, the secure infant and caregiver show reciprocal influence on each other, and the exchanges are highly coordinated and synchronized. Both infant and caregiver show contingent behaviors—that is, each knows that an initiated behavior is likely to have predictable effects on the self or the other, particularly pertaining to self-regulation and to the response of the other in the interactions. When mismatches and the resulting ruptures occur, both infant and caregiver are able to repair the lack of correspondence and resume their co-constructed mutual interactive collaborative process. Through this well-coordinated exchange, the high level of collaboration leads to heightened moments of positive affective intensity during the collaboration. Over time, the child develops well-organized patterns of dyadic interaction and internalizes a sense of "effectance" and agency in being able to contingently affect the caregiver's response (Beebe & Lachmann, 2014).

Contradictory, or noncollaborative, mutual nonverbal exchanges are characterized by significant and repetitive mismatched nonverbal influence on each other, and the nonverbal exchanges are uncoordinated and desynchronized. Both infant and caregiver lack contingent behaviors, so that each seems unable to affect the other. When ruptures occur, which is frequent, there is little possibility of repair. There is a virtual absence of heightened moments of positive affect in the relationship, and what occurs instead is remoteness of expressed affect in those infants with dismissing attachment, overwhelming affect in those with anxious-preoccupied attachment, and contradictory affect in those with disorganized attachment. Over time, the child develops dysfunctional patterns of reciprocal nonverbal exchanges and internalizes a lack of effectance in exploring the environment and a lack of agency in being able to contingently affect the caregiver's response. Children with insecure attachment learn to expect dysregulation and lack of coordination in the nonverbal exchanges between infant and caregiver, and later between patient and therapist.

Beebe and her associates used videotapes to give mothers direct visual feedback about their contribution to dysfunctional patterns of nonverbal dyadic exchange in order to help them learn healthy patterns of exchange and thereby transform the interactions with their infants. In their later work, they used the video microanalysis method to investigate nonverbal patterns of interaction between adult patients and therapists, also with the goal of cultivating healthy nonverbal exchange. Beebe based all of this work on what she calls a "transformational view" (Beebe & Lachmann, 2002, p. 217). In other words, while dysfunctional nonverbal patterns of exchange in insecurely attached adults have developed over a long period of time, she believes that a therapy that addresses these nonverbal patterns can fundamentally change them, and support the emergence of secure patterns of interaction. The work of Beebe and her colleagues has extensively influenced our thinking and our methods for fostering nonverbal collaborativeness.

The first step toward developing healthy nonverbal collaboration in insecurely attached adult patients is to establish *a nonverbal secure base* in the therapeutic setting. The therapist's position in his or her chair, head orientation, body posture, body stillness, gaze, and matched facial affect display as well as the rhythm, pitch, tone, and timing of verbal responses must show continuous nondistracted attention to, interest in, and intense engagement with everything the patient does or says, and must track every nonverbal shift moment by moment over time. The therapist must also adjust his or her level of arousal and/or degree of engagement to find the optimal level for matching the given patient at a given time. If the therapist has patterns of nonverbal distancing (e.g., distractedness), hyperengaging (excessive body movements), or mismatching the patient's behavior, the foundation of nonverbal secure base will fail to be established. The second step is *careful observation of the main patterns of nonverbal exchange* enacted between patient and therapist. We have found Beebe's categories for coding nonverbal patterns in children (Beebe & Lachmann, 2014) to be a useful starting point for identifying and attending to the main patterns of nonverbal behavior between adult patients and therapists, but we have made some modifications for adult nonverbal exchanges. The modified list includes, for both parties:

1. *Chair position and posture:* The distance between the patient and therapist's chairs; whether the chairs are positioned face to face or side to side; whether the patient or therapist leans forward or back, looms, slumps in the chair, or sits sideways. (These postural positions indicate overall level of engagement between patient and therapist).

2. *Head orientation:* Head oriented forward or sideways, looking straight ahead or looking elsewhere, head cocked to one side.

3. *Gaze:* Looking directly at or looking away, looking at an angle, averting the gaze, looking at something else. (Head orientation and gaze are salient indicators of attention and interest, or lack thereof).

4. *Facial affective display:* Smiling, mock surprise, surprised face, woe face, positive attention, disinterested attention, distress face, angry-protest face, joyful face, crying, comforting face. (These facial display patterns are of primary importance in contingent matching of affect and affective attunement, or lack thereof).

5. *Initiated self-touch:* Touching one's own skin; touching an object, clothing, or chair; touching or pulling one's own hair. (These self-touching behaviors provide important clues as to when and how patient and therapist alike are engaged in self-regulation of their internal state).

6. *Postural gestures:* Postural shifts in chair, head nodding or shaking "no," rubbing feet or hands together, jiggling feet or legs, folding or crossing arms or legs, tucking face into chin, making hand gestures of various sorts, coughing, blowing one's nose. (These postural gestures can indicate interactive regulation and/or self-regulation.)

7. *Breathing:* Synchronized or desynchronized breathing, shallow or deep breathing, holding the breath, yawning, sighing. (Patterns of breathing yield important signs of synchronization or desynchronization, disruption, and self-regulation.)

8. *Vocal rhythm:* Volume of verbalization or, in the extreme, the length of silences; the timing and synchronization of vocalizations; interruptions and talking over; the slowness or rapidity of vocalizations; the timing, frequency, and emphasis given to "uh-huhs" and other vocalization of resonance.

9. *Vocal tone:* Clarity of communicating emotion via voice; melody.

10. *Vocal pitch:* Indicating positive emotion via a rising pitch or indicating a negative emotion via a falling pitch.

The task for the therapist is to carefully observe the salient and repetitive patterns of nonverbal exchange. This includes observing the main patterns in the patient, but also in the therapist himself or herself. Some of the patterns will be obvious and easy to notice. For example, a patient with dismissing attachment is likely to sit back in the chair or slump to the side of the chair, move his or her chair further away, infrequently orient the head and gaze to the therapist, frequently avert the head and gaze to the side, make a stone-wall facial expression or a variety of off-putting facial display patterns, attenuate spontaneous postural displays, make defensive postural displays like hand-folding, engage in variety of noninteractive nonverbal self-regulatory behaviors, yawn, exhibit extended silences and curtailed vocalizations, infrequently have vocalizations resonant with the therapist's, and manifest a soft or barely audible voice, with a descending pitch. A patient with anxious-preoccupied attachment may sit forward in the chair or loom, sit too close, manifest an uncomfortably hypervigilant fixed stare, manifest a variety of frequent facial displays of distress, exaggerate spontaneous postural displays, make plaintive postural displays, show high postural anxiety like rubbing hands and feet and jiggling legs, show an inability to remain silent or take turns in vocalization, show a very fast vocal rhythm, make vocalizations over the therapist, and show a descending pitch. Patients with disorganized attachment show a contradictory mixture of dismissing and anxious-preoccupied nonverbal behaviors, as previously described.

Therapists must be vigilant and attuned (without being hypervigilant) to maintain awareness of the arising and presence of patients' and their own nonverbal behaviors. Beebe and her associates found that many of the nonverbal patterns operate outside of awareness and occur for only fractions of a second. They found that giving mothers of infants and adult patients with attachment disorders feedback through direct observation of videotaped interactions was a useful tool in helping to bring these patterns into awareness, especially of those patterns that are less obvious. Most therapists will not bring this technology into their sessions, so those who do not will serve their patients best by maintaining heightened presence and awareness of their patients.

The third step is to *identify the most salient and repetitive nonverbal patterns of exchange*, especially the most dysfunctional patterns. Identification helps to make a determination of the main attachment pattern—secure, dismissing, anxious-preoccupied, or disorganized—and also of the primary nonverbal behaviors the patient exhibits most frequently and repetitively. In other words, this step entails target selection of which specific dysfunctional nonverbal exchange patterns to work on in therapy.

The fourth step is to *transform* the salient dysfunctional nonverbal exchange patterns through nonverbal engagement and what Beebe calls "match-and-change" activity, which entails continually rematching when mismatches arise. Beebe has published several detailed case illustrations of this nonverbal transforming approach. Beebe details the methods for matching and transforming the patient's observed nonverbal behavior by engaging in a purposeful nonverbal behavior designed to be most responsive to the patient's nonverbal communication at the time, and then also for matching the patient's nonverbal behavior in the most responsive way moment by moment. For example, in the case of Dolores (Beebe & Lachmann, 2014), when the patient repeatedly failed to make eye contact, then Beebe nonverbally responded by making steady eye contact. Dolores was observed to frequently orient her body posture away from the therapist, and Beebe then collaboratively worked with her to identify in the here and now when the patient was nonverbally oriented away or toward the therapist, which led to increased face-to-face interaction. When Dolores became inaudible, the therapist would repeat back what the patient just said to try to match it in words and especially tone, and her utterances were repeated with a more flowing rhythm. The patient was also observed to produce a still-face reaction, or the appearance of "going dead." In response, Beebe attempted to make the most responsive and exaggerated facial display to match Dolores's, so as to help Dolores find her face in the facial display of her therapist.

In this treatment of Dolores, mutual review of video footage of sessions was used to help her learn "more about her own feelings by watching me experience her" (Beebe, 2005, p. 26). After some time, Dolores began imitating and matching the faces and affective facial displays that she observed her therapist making on the videotape. Dolores said, "While I was watching you on the video alone, I was interacting with your face. I was making your face on my face" (p. 118). This statement indicates the emergence of Dolores's part in a mutual, dyadic nonverbal affective exchange. The cumulative effect of these largely nonverbal interventions was to transform dysfunctional, noncollaborative nonverbal exchanges into mutual, collaborative nonverbal exchanges, which supported Dolores in becoming a "new kind of [nonverbal] relational partner" (p. 142).

The fifth step is to transform salient dysfunctional nonverbal exchange patterns through *enhancing metacognitive awareness of these patterns*. In the spirit of ongoing exploration of nonverbal exchange patterns, and in a noncritical manner, the therapist collaboratively shares his or her observations on the salient nonverbal behaviors, such as lack of eye contact, averting the gaze, speaking in a soft barely audible voice, talking over the therapist, and other such behaviors. Before doing so, the therapist collaboratively sets the context for this intervention by asking the patient whether it would be permissible to share such observations in the current and future therapy sessions at the moment in which they occur, so that both patient and therapist alike can bring these patterns into immediate awareness. The goal is, over time, for the patient to become fully metacognitively aware of the dysfunctional, noncollaborative nonverbal communication patterns as they arise within and outside the treatment setting. This enhanced awareness contributes to the decrease of these patterns and the corresponding increase of more healthy nonverbal communication and collaboration.

Once the patient's metacognitive awareness of a nonverbal behavior is established, our method entails engaging the patient with experiential focusing (Gendlin, 1982) to become aware of the overall bodily felt sense of this specific nonverbal behavior, and also to determine whether when it happens it is or is not associated with a specific categorical emotion, such as anger, sadness, or fear. An attempt is made to identify whether a specific nonverbal behavior at a given time is serving self-regulation (e.g., averting the gaze to manage the arising of anger), interactive regulation (e.g., frowning to get the therapist to stop a line of inquiry), or both. The patient then is encouraged to engage in "an experiment" of trying directly to change this specific nonverbal behavior to something more collaborative. For example, if the patient frequently averts his or her gaze, he or she is encouraged to explore maintaining a fixed gaze on the therapist's face and facial expression; if the patient talks too softly, he or she is encouraged to talk louder, and the therapist gives feedback as to whether what the patient says can actually be heard with ease or not. After each such change in the direction of nonverbal collaboration, the patient is asked to focus on the resultant felt bodily sense. Furthermore, for targeted nonverbal self-regulatory behaviors, the patient is asked to experiment with temporarily discontinuing the specific targeted nonverbal self-regulatory behavior, focus on the resultant felt sense of the body, identify and verbalize the underlying emotional or arousal state, and focus on the therapist's facial affective attunement and other forms of nonverbal matching of the patient's state. In this way, the patient's difficulty with self-regulation of internal states more and more becomes newly regulated through the dyadic exchange. The patient develops a new sense of contingent effectiveness in bringing these underlying emotional and arousal states into the relationship.

The sixth step is *meaning-making*. Beebe speaks of "linking of words to pre-verbal experience" (Beebe, Knoblauch, Rustin, & Sorter, 2005, p. 97). In most of her case examples, including that of Dolores, Beebe tries to understand the historical context and meaning of the dysfunctional nonverbal patterns in her adult patients, and once the pattern is identified and brought into awareness, Beebe uses interpretation to help the patient make sense of these heretofore unconscious nonverbal patterns. Interpretation is co-constructed as part of an ongoing collaborative dialogue.

The cumulative effect of such interventions is increased nonverbal collaboration in the dyadic treatment relationship and generalization of that activity to relationships outside of treatment. First, the patient learns that the ongoing nonverbal behavior of both patient and therapist contingently affect each other in significant ways—the patient contingently affects the therapist's nonverbal response, and the therapist contingently affects the patient's response. Second, a new pattern of nonverbal exchange emerges wherein mutual match-and-change affective displays are frequent and salient, and mismatch patterns are greatly diminished in frequency. Third, the overall increase in nonverbal collaborative behaviors also results in heightened positive affective moments between the patient and the therapist that contribute to developing a secure therapeutic base. Fourth, nonverbal disconnection diminishes and repair of ruptures at the nonverbal level is accomplished with greater ease. Fifth, the patient develops new preverbal schemas for healthy, collaborative nonverbal exchanges with others. Last, the patient is left with an enhanced sense of being seen, known, and contingently matched by the other, and ultimately known in the mind of the other.

IMPROVING VERBAL COLLABORATION

The Origins of Verbal Collaborative Behavior

In *Origins of Human Communication*, Tomasello (2010) sets the conceptual foundation for understanding human verbal communication as a fundamentally collaborative behavior. He defines cooperative communication as follows:

> Human communication is . . . a fundamentally cooperative enterprise, operating most naturally . . . within the context of 1. mutually assumed common conceptual ground; and 2. mutually assumed cooperative communicative motives . . . [S]hared intentionality is what is necessary for engaging in uniquely human forms of collaborative activity in which a plural subject "we" is involved: joint goals, joint intentions, mutual knowledge, shared beliefs—all in the context of various cooperative motives . . . [The] cooperative infrastructure of human communication . . . evolved as part of

a larger human adaptation for cooperation and cultural life in general . . . [A]t some point in human evolution individuals who could engage with one another collaboratively with joint intentions, joint attention, and coopera- tive motives were at an adaptive advantage. Cooperative communication then arose as a way of coordinating these collaborative activities more effi- ciently. (pp. 6–8)

According to this evolutionary model, human verbal communication is derived from nonverbal pointing and pantomiming behavior in apes. Nonver- bal behaviors like pointing constitute, in our evolutionary history (and in the early development of every human infant), the first forms of cooperative behavior. Tomasello (2010) says that "pointing and pantomiming were . . . critical transition points in the evolution of human communication" (p. 2) and that "conventional languages thus arose by piggybacking on these already understood gestures" (p. 9). Human verbal communication adds something not found among primates, namely, collaboration. Tomasello says that ape pointing behavior almost exclu- sively consists of imperatives, to get others to do things. In contrast, human ver- bal communication entails "shared intentionality" (p. 72). An important element in collaborative human verbal communication is what Tomasello calls "referen- tial intention," which simply refers to what the speaker is talking about, however clear or unclear he or she may be. In other words, a speaker intends a certain field of reference, and the listener may inquire and expect clarification so as to accu- rately understand the speaker's referential intention (p. 97). As Tomasello states, "the communicator makes efforts to communicate in ways that are comprehensi- ble to the recipient, who in turn makes efforts at comprehension by making obvi- ous inferences, asking for clarification when needed, and so forth" (pp. 82–83).

Regarding intentionality, Tomasello (2010) believes that there are three basic human communicative motives: (1) requesting (expressing a need from the other), (2) informing (providing useful information that the listener might be interested in), and (3) sharing attitudes, feelings, ideas, and experiences as a way of being known (see pp. 85–87).

Tomasello (2010) describes how collaborative verbal communication evolved in the wider context of collaborative behavior. He says, "Cooperative communi- cation emerged as part and parcel of the evolution of humans' unique forms of collaborative activity" (p. 172). During the development of children, such collab- orative language evolves in the context of daily collaborative routines between child and parent:

It would appear that even one-year-old infants expect others to respond to their communicative acts by attempting to comprehend, and they expect others to provide help when it is requested, or to accept offered information, or to share when invited . . . [V]irtually all of children's earliest language is acquired inside routine collaborative interactions with mature speakers of language—in Western culture, such things as eating in the high chair, going for a ride in the car, changing diapers, feeding ducks at the pond. (pp. 129, 157).

Central to this process in the evolution of collaborative verbal communication is the development of grammatical conventions. According to Tomasello (2010), there is a grammar of requesting (combinations of pointing and language; see p. 264); a grammar of informing via multigestural combinations that identify objects and information to be shared (see pp. 270–271); and a grammar of sharing (the use of narratives to share individual and group experiences; see pp. 282–284).

The Structure of Verbal Collaborative Behavior: Grice's Maxims

H. Paul Grice (1989) articulated the basic structure of verbal collaborative discourse. The task of all verbal discourse is for the speaker to "implicate" his or her intended meaning and for the listener to inquire so as to understand what is being implicated. In this sense, good collaborative discourse is necessarily meaningful. Grice says, "Our talk exchanges do not normally consist of a succession of disconnected remarks, and would not be rational if they did" (p. 26). Therefore, verbal discourse has a conventional structure that ensures meaningfulness. Grice calls this the "cooperative principle" of verbal discourse (p. 26).

Grice described four basic principles that are fundamental to collaborative discourse. These have become known as "Grice's maxims." The first maxim pertains to the *quality* of verbal communication. Collaborative discourse is accurate and genuine, and the main points are illustrated with ample evidence, and also with evidence that lacks contradictions. As Grice says, "do not say what you believe to be false. Do not say that for which you lack adequate evidence" (1989, p. 27). The second maxim pertains to the *quantity* of speech. Collaborative verbal speech has the right amount of information about a shared topic—such speech is free from the extremes of providing too little or too much information. The third maxim pertains to the *relevance* of the discourse. The content of collaborative verbal speech stays close to the referential intention and topic being described and rarely adds content that is essentially irrelevant. Such speech stays on point without undue wandering so that the listener is able to follow the thread of the discourse easily. The fourth maxim pertains to the *manner* of discourse. Collaborative verbal communication is spoken in a manner that is clear and unambiguous. Grice says that manner refers to "not . . . to what is said but, rather, to *how* what is said is to be said" (p. 27) and involves avoiding obscurity in expression, avoiding ambiguity, and being orderly. Grice highlights that individuals who "violate" these maxims run the risk of being misunderstood (p. 30).

Geoffrey Leech (1983) suggests that conversation, at least in modern Western culture, also follows certain standards of *politeness*. His six politeness standards, or maxims, and their functions are as follows: (1) Tactful communication minimizes cost and maximizes benefit to others, (2) generous communication minimizes benefit to self and maximizes benefit to others, (3) approbation minimizes dispraise of others and maximizes praise and enhancement of others, (4) modest communication minimizes praise to self and maximizes praise to others, (5) agreement minimizes disagreement and maximizes common interests and agreement, and (6) sympathetic communication minimizes antipathy and maximizes listening to the needs of the other. These politeness principles are the positive opposite of toxic verbal communication.

The Failure of Collaborative Verbal Communication in Adults With Insecure Attachment

Harry Stack Sullivan was one of the first clinicians to articulate the failure of collaborative verbal communication in certain psychiatric patients. He said:

> An enormous amount of difficulty all through life arises from the fact that communicative behavior miscarries because words do not carry meaning, but evoke meaning. And if a word evokes in the hearer something quite different from that which it was expected to evoke, communication is not a success. (1953, p. 184)

In fact, the early generation of Sullivanian therapists placed much focus on enhancing collaborative verbal communication in treatment. Many years ago as a psychology intern, the senior author of this book (DB) sat through a treatment session with a floridly psychotic patient, who at various points made no sense. The young therapist brought the session experience to his clinical supervisor, Dr. Alfred Stanton, who was one of the original Sullivanians. In supervision, Dr. Stanton said:

> You have to work at remembering exactly what the patient said, even if it doesn't make sense. More importantly, you have to explicitly tell the patient that what she just said doesn't make sense to you, or that you don't really understand it. If you fail to give the patient honest feedback, at that moment, that what was just said didn't make sense, then how is the patient ever going to learn interpersonal communication? You aren't doing the patient any favor by ignoring what you don't understand. Tell the patient it didn't make sense, and whether the patient is psychotic or not, get the patient to work at saying it differently until you both develop a shared, accurate understanding of what the patient intended.

The very important point learned through this exchange is that when a patient says something that doesn't make sense, make the communication failure an explicit treatment focus, toward the goal of enhancing clear, meaningful, collaborative verbal communication.

The work of Mary Main and her associates using the Adult Attachment Interview (AAI) has greatly elaborated on the specific types of failures of collaborative verbal communication in adults with dismissing, anxious-preoccupied, and disorganized insecure attachment. Collaborative speech on the AAI is epitomized by Grice's four maxims: truthful quality (ample, accurate evidence), adequate quantity, relevance, and clear manner of expression. Based on discourse analyses of AAI transcripts, Main and her colleagues found that there are important differences between secure individuals, who exemplify collaborative verbal behavior, and insecure individuals, who illustrate various types of noncollaborative verbal behavior.

Insecure patients show numerous violations of Grice's maxims in their discourse about attachment themes on the AAI. Dismissing insecure individuals show numerous violations of quality. Their talk includes overgeneralizations about attachment themes, and they either fail to give illustrative examples or they give examples that are untruthful or contradictory. Their overall response to the AAI questions also violates the maxim of quantity, in that their descriptions of attachment themes are much too succinct to provide a clear picture of attachment experiences. In contrast, anxious-preoccupied insecure individuals show numerous violations of quantity, relevance, and manner on the AAI. Their discourse about attachment themes frequently wanders off topic (violation of relevance), adds too much information so as to lose the central point (violation of quantity), and contains numerous vague and ambiguous statements that make it hard to understand (violations of manner). Disorganized insecure individuals show numerous violations of all four maxims (Main, Goldwyn, & Hesse, 2002).

In addition to the patterns that Grice's maxims reflect, collaborative verbal discourse in everyday communication is marked by appropriate turn-taking, reflective listening, validating each other's feelings and perspectives, sharing information, curiosity to discover, inquisitiveness, clarification, and the co-constructing of new meaning. Generalizing to psychotherapy what we know about good collaborative communication, we can say that securely attached individuals talk openly and audibly in therapy. They frequently pause and take turns. They patiently wait for the other to finish before making their next point. They describe a topic in sufficient and clear detail, and can draw upon their past experiences and memories with some ease to illustrate their points with sufficient and accurate evidence. They stay on topic. They are able to evoke emotions, and modulate the intensity of the emotion, in a manner appropriate to the topic at hand. They are comfortable describing negative as well as positive aspects of themselves. They take responsibility openly for their own limitations. They remain open to the other's point of view and welcome a different perspective dissimilar to their own. They are able to state what they need, but in addition to appropriate need statements, they remain open to discovering mutual needs and options. They are able to reflectively mirror back what they heard from the other and validate the other's perspective as legitimate even though their perspective may differ. When they are not sure exactly what the other is saying, they request clarification or say what they think and ask "Is that what you mean?"

Dismissing insecure patients talk too little in therapy. Sometimes they are mute and do not talk at all. Sometimes they talk too softly, in a way that is barely audible. Their descriptions of their experiences are often too succinct and not sufficiently detailed to give a clear picture. Their speech is interspersed with qualifications such as "I don't know" and "I can't remember." A salient characteristic of dismissing speech is that it is overly positive and idealized, in a way that is rarely backed up with evidence. According to Grice's maxims, such dismissing speech violates the maxim of *quality*, that is, it lacks truthfulness. Another salient characteristic of dismissing speech is that it is likely fact-based rather than emotional. It is usually intellectualized and remote from feelings. Patients with dismissing attachment show numerous other signs of noncollaboration in their verbal behavior, such as cutting the other person off, dismissing or devaluing the other's point of view, not listening because they have already "read the mind" of the other, or seeming to listen but failing to reflect, mirror, and/or validate the other's communication or point of view. Verbal behavior that entails conflict is generally avoided by dismissives, but when conflict is unavoidable, noncollaborative verbal behaviors emerge, such as giving ultimatums, making threats, and arguing from a fixed, unrelenting position.

Anxious-preoccupied insecure patients talk too much in therapy. They may talk too fast or too loud in order to talk over the other. They rarely pause to let the other person speak, and sometimes do not give the other a chance to speak at all. When a back-and-forth exchange develops, if it does, it is riddled with interruptions. When they wish to make a point, anxiously attached individuals perseverate on the topic. They go on and on, and seem to not be able to let go of the topic. Their speech wanders. They lose track of the main point frequently and seem to talk around the issues. They often repeat the same point over and over again, even after being told they do so. Indirectly or directly, they demand that the listener stay far too long with them on whatever topic they are presenting. Their speech is often vague and ambiguous, and their discourse contains frequent irrelevancies, such that their ability to make a point clearly is limited. When experiencing conflict, their speech is highly anxious or angry, and unfinished emotional business from the past pervades the ongoing speech in the present. Imperatives, "should" language, defeatist thinking, overkill, and playing the victim role are characteristic of anxious-preoccupied patients. Interpersonal conflict is characterized by excessive verbal demands on the listener, complaining, and excessive blaming of the self or other.

Disorganized insecure patients exhibit a confusing and contradictory mixture of dismissing and anxious-preoccupied noncollaborative verbal behaviors as detailed above. In addition, their speech has two other features. First, it is sometimes disorganized and incoherent. Here, as explained by Dr. Stanton, the goal of the therapist is to struggle along with the patient to help the patient make more sense. Talking sensibly is a fundamental requirement of interpersonal verbal behavior, and when sensible talk is found to be absent, the therapist must not ignore it and hope that the patient goes on to say something more sensible. Instead, the therapist at that given moment gives the patient feedback to convey that he or she just said something that did not make sense, and that the therapist is quite interested in what the patient is trying to say. The therapist then requests that he or she say it again in such a way that the therapist will be sure to understand it. Second, the disorganized patient's speech may occur in the context of shifting dissociative states. When the therapist suspects that such dissociation may be occurring, he or she must be sure that the patient is aware of what was just said. Asking the patient to repeat again what he or she just said, or to summarize it in different words, ensures that the patient is not talking from a dissociated state.

A Model for Collaborative Dialogue in Treatment

Karlen Lyons-Ruth (1999), with the collaboration of the Boston Change Process Study Group, developed a model for collaborative dialogue in psychotherapy based on careful observations of infant–caregiver interactions. Given that much communication from insecurely attached patients is nonverbal, or in her words "enactive" and "implicit," the process of therapy must entail developing adequate "representation" of such experience (p. 579). The patient and therapist engage in a two-person collaborative dialogue with "a focus on facilitating developmental change" (p. 581). Lyons-Ruth says:

> Patient and analyst must be working simultaneously at an implicit relational level to create increasingly collaborative forms of dialogue. Developmental research suggests that collaborative dialogue includes careful attention to the particular state of the other's intersubjective experience, open acceptance of a broad range of affects, active scaffolding to more inclusive levels of dialogue, and engaged struggle and intersubjective negotiation through periods when the other's mind is changing and new ways of relating are needed. (p. 610)

The outcome of such collaborative dialogue is "coherent communication," which is defined in terms of eliciting the patient's collaborative state of mind, efficient repair of ruptures, establishing new levels of awareness, and brokering the process of change as self and developmental level become reorganized (Lyons-Ruth, 1999, p. 585).

Eleven Steps for Establishing Collaborative Verbal Communication
in Insecurely Attached Patients

Our integration of the thinking and research on collaborative communication, as well as our experience of working with patients with attachment disturbances, has produced a sequence of eleven psychotherapeutic steps that result in activating the cooperative/collaborative communication system in patients with insecure attachment. Although the sequence given below is generally the sequence in which the specific issues and interventions unfold in treatment, there will of course be variation in the order of some of the steps at different times with different patients, and treatment usually entails returning to earlier steps as needed.

The first step is to establish a *verbal secure base* for collaborative communication. This foundational step starts by the therapist consistently exemplifying reflective listening and validation. There are three elements of reflective listening. The easiest involves mirroring back the gist of what the patient just said; in other words, the therapist reflectively mirrors the manifest content of the patient's verbal communication so that the patient directly experiences being heard. For example, the therapist might say:

> What I hear you saying is that you were upset when your friend told you that she was moving away. And that you wondered if she would be happier living farther away from you.

The next element of reflective listening and validation involves the therapist reflecting back the *affective meaning* of the verbal communication. For example, he or she might say:

> It seems to me that you're saying that you have an important emotional connection with your friend, and that you feel affected by thinking of living farther apart from each other.

The third and most difficult element of reflective listening involves mirroring back the latent meaning—what the patient is *really* trying to say but is not quite aware of. For example, the therapist might say:

> Maybe you're telling me that relationships are important to you, and that sometimes you feel some distress when you experience a relationship being threatened.

Validating entails rendering legitimacy to the way the patient experiences something. Frequently making comments such as "It's certainly understandable how you might feel that way" helps the patient feel that, whatever his or her verbally described experience is, it is valid and legitimate, and therefore not eliciting a negative judgment. The consistency and depth of reflective listening and validation establishes a secure base for ongoing verbal exchange between patient and therapist.

Second, establishing collaborative verbal behavior in psychotherapy is in part dependent on a *consistent stance* by the therapist. We agree with Liotti that fostering a collaborative state of mind in patients depends on such a stance by the therapist. The therapist repeatedly conveys the attitude that mutual exchange and collaboration through verbal exchange is important, welcome, and beneficial throughout treatment.

Third, a stable secure base for verbal collaborative exchange in treatment is supported by mutual understanding and acceptance of certain *ground rules of verbal discourse and exchange* during the therapy sessions. This step explicitly focuses on *how* the insecurely attached patient and the therapist talk to each other, rather than on the content of what is being said. Teyber and McClure (2011) state, "The therapist is making a perceptual shift away from the overt content of what is discussed and beginning to track the relational process of how two people are interacting well" (p. 24). Patients with insecure attachment typically do not follow or even know the "rules" of collaborative verbal dialogue, and therefore, early in treatment, these rules of verbal exchange must be made explicit.

For example, those with dismissing attachment are explicitly taught that full disclosure is important, that the therapy will benefit from them being *forthcoming* with their speech and following the cardinal rule of psychotherapy, namely, saying whatever comes to mind, without censorship. We tell patients about the importance of full disclosure and encourage its practice by being sincerely interested in what the patient is speaking about, including especially what it appears is not being said. Dismissing patients often have long silences during which they expect the therapist to start talking, never having had people interested in their inner world. The therapist gently encourages more reflection by indicating his or her interest in the patient's inner process. The therapist helps the dismissing patient understand that a long silence is best seen as an invitation for both therapist and patient to explore the patient's state of mind, especially what might be uncomfortable for him or her at the moment, rather than as a deflection from exploration signifying that it is the therapist's turn to talk. Some dismissing patients, and especially disorganized patients, may speak extremely softly, in a way that the therapist has difficulty hearing. In this circumstance, it is not advisable for the therapist to ignore the behavior and struggle with hearing the patient in an ongoing way. Instead, it is best for the therapist to bring the soft-spoken behavior into the patient's awareness and to explain to him or her in a noncritical way that speaking too softly does not follow the basic rules of verbal communication. For example:

> I must say that I'm having a hard time hearing what you're saying. I really want to hear what you're saying, and I imagine that when you talk so softly

like this in other circumstances, people who also want to hear what you're saying are unable to. As we've talked about, one of what we've called the basic rules of verbal communication is that we talk loudly and clearly enough so that the person we're with can hear what we're saying. And as you know, this "rule" isn't a rule that's imposed on us by some authority, but is rather simply a support for being able to communicate well with others. So how about if you speak a little more loudly and clearly, and I'll tell you if I can hear and understand you better.

In addition to sometimes letting the patient know verbally, as above, that we can't hear what he or she is saying, we find it useful at times to use a previously agreed-upon nonverbal signal whenever the patient's speech is too soft and becomes inaudible. For example, at such times the therapist raises his or her hand in the air. At other times, we introduce the metaphor of trying to transcribe an audio-recording with the volume too low, so that a passage needs to be repeated numerous times to detect what is being said. These strategies are designed to help the soft-spoken patient develop metacognitive awareness of when, and under what conditions, speech becomes too soft. Such awareness contributes toward the goal of consistent sufficiently audible verbal communication. Because softness of speech often reflects a defensive process, it can be helpful to ask the patient what it is like to be with someone who is actively engaged in listening, and also how this experience differs from past experience.

Patients with anxious-preoccupied attachment often have to learn the rules of turn-taking. Therapists help them to learn to pause, allow a response from the therapist (and others), to not talk over or interrupt, and to resume speaking when the therapist has stopped talking. When violations of turn-taking occur, the therapist brings immediate focus to them—the patient is given immediate feedback about not having waited for a turn and instead talking over or interrupting the therapist. For example:

> Let's step out of the content of what we were just talking about for a minute. We've talked about the value and importance of taking turns in dialogue, and just now, did you notice that as I was talking, you started speaking over me instead of waiting for me to finish and *then* say what you wanted to say. Did you notice that happening just now?

Again, it can be helpful to use a pre-agreed-upon nonverbal signal, such as the therapist raising his or her hand at each moment that the patient interrupts or talks over the therapist.

Anxious-preoccupied patients also often talk on and on without allowing the therapist (or other) a chance to speak. A pre-agreed-upon nonverbal signal, such as raising the index finger (signaling "wait a minute") or making a T-symbol with both hands ("time-out") can be helpful in this circumstance as well. A verbal signal, such as the therapist mimicking a timer tone, can also be used. Upon hearing the signal, the patient understands that he or she has a very brief time to finish his or her point and then offer a turn to the therapist. If any of these nonverbal or verbal signals are to be used, prediscussion, for explanation and agreement, is essential so that the patient recognizes the collaborative intention of the signals and doesn't feel that such signaling is punitive. With patients who tend to talk excessively, it can be helpful to explore what it is like to talk. How do they know they are being heard if they talk without pause? What indicates to them that the therapist is listening? Using these kinds of metacognitive inquiries supports the patient in moving beyond just the content and into the co-creation of a mutually satisfying connection.

Some therapists of preoccupied patients find themselves *interrupting the patient* and trying to talk over the patient in order to say something. Thus, it can be very beneficial to tell the patient that he or she can point out to the therapist, either verbally or nonverbally or both, if and when the therapist does the interrupting. The therapist's acknowledgment that he or she also must follow the "rules" of collaborative communication enhances the patient's experience and learning that communication is a mutual, collaborative process.

Fourth, establishing a secure base for verbal exchange also means *making other rules explicit*, such that it is permissible for the patient to say that he or she does not know something or does not think that the therapist accurately understands what he or she said. Furthermore, the patient is encouraged to ask questions of the therapist when he or she does not fully understand what the therapist is saying or asking. Again, in support of communicative mutuality, just as the therapist is free to ask for clarification when he or she does not understand what the patient said, the patient is explicitly encouraged to feel free to ask for clarification when he or she does not understand what the therapist said.

The fifth step in developing collaborative verbal behavior is for both therapist and patient to work together to *carefully observe all the problematic patterns of verbal exchange exhibited by the patient*. Together they make a list of the violations of verbal collaboration that the patient commonly makes (e.g., lack of being forthcoming, lack of turn-taking, too many irrelevancies, toxic communications). The mutual development of this list models cooperative, collaborative activity and also supports the patient's metacognitive awareness of the appearance of the problematic verbal behavior.

The sixth step is to *identify the most salient and repetitive dysfunctional verbal patterns of exchange*, especially the most dysfunctional verbal patterns, and to work to ameliorate those specific patterns. Primarily, this step entails target selection of and intervention with specific dysfunctional verbal exchange patterns. Identification of these patterns also helps to determine or validate the patient's main attachment pattern—secure, dismissing, anxious-preoccupied, or disorganized. We have found it especially useful to draw from the descriptions of discourse of dismissing and preoccupied individuals found in the AAI scoring manual (Main et al., 2002) as a reference for understanding and intervening with the primary dysfunctional patterns of verbal discourse in insecurely attached patients.

Since dismissing patients typically show a normal capacity for exploration except around attachment themes, it is important that the therapist encourage the dismissing patient to begin exploration of attachment themes in treatment. For example, the discourse of dismissing patients tends to be overly succinct and unemotional. When this is observed in treatment, the therapist expresses interest and gives the patient feedback indicating that he or she would like to hear more and invites the patient to describe further underlying emotional experience. Then the patient is encouraged to explore the topic in more detail, while the therapist listens for and marks the affect underlying what the patient is describing. For example:

> You know, I'm not hearing many words from you about what you're saying, but I think what you're saying is really important. So I'm wondering if you might try to tell me more about this now. As you speak and I listen to you, let's both see if we can notice the feelings that are there along with the content. You might not be aware of the feelings at first, but if we both work together on this, we can together find out what feelings are connected to what you're saying.

When dismissing patients explore attachment themes, they tend to idealize their attachment figures and put a positive spin on negative experiences in early childhood relationships. When the therapist detects such positive bias, he or she first validates the positive dimension of the patient's early childhood relationships, however accurate or inaccurate. Such validation is likely to soften any defensiveness. The patient is then given feedback indicating that negative aspects of the early childhood relationships are virtually absent in his or her descriptions. Then the patient is encouraged to explore the full range of early attachment experiences, including negative experiences that were not in his or her initial descriptions. Because dismissing patients' discourse about attachment themes is typically devoid of strong emotions, we also *mark* any affect that appears descriptively or behaviorally as the patient further describes early attachment experiences. For example:

> As I'm listening to you telling me of your childhood experience with your parents, I notice that it's all positive, and I think it's wonderful that you had such positive and good experience with them. I also notice that there's nothing that you've said so far that would suggest that you had any diffi-

culty in those relationships. I wonder about that. Can you tell more about the full range of experiences that you had with them, including both positive and maybe not-so-positive experiences?

As the patient speaks of some disappointments with how his or her parents were with him or her and shows a slightly sad facial expression, the therapist marks the accompanying affect:

That must have been *very* disappointing for you. I imagine that you might have felt *very* sad when that was happening.

As already noted, anxious-preoccupied patients tend to speak on and on and frequently wander off topic. We sometimes respond with a previously explained, discussed, and agreed-upon "stop-action technique": Using a nonverbal or verbal signal, we ask for a pause and together explore the patient's felt experience, using Gendlin's (1982) focusing technique. The patient is asked to develop a holistic, nonconceptual felt sense of his or her immediate experience; after being given some time for become aware of this sense, he or she is asked "to find just the right words that best fit this immediate experience" and to speak those words to the therapist. Then the patient is asked to resume talking, but this time from awareness of the immediate felt experience. This technique, if used frequently, helps the anxious-preoccupied patient learn to replace "canned" or superficial, affectively disconnected speech with the discourse that emerges from fresh experience. It also promotes the use of *silence* as an invitation for exploration. Anxious-preoccupied patients act as though they fear that without ongoing speaking, they will lose contact with the other. By using the stop-action method to call for a pause in speech and then guiding the patient to attend to and speak from felt experience while we remain highly attentive and present, we promote the patient's recognition that pauses, silence, and internal reflection and attunement can actually strengthen connection rather than diminish it.

Since in anxious-preoccupied patients the exploratory behavioral system has largely been deactivated, it is especially valuable to repeatedly encourage exploration, in general and also specifically of canned and wandering discourse. On each occasion that the meaning of the preoccupied patient's discourse is vague, ambiguous, or unclear, the therapist gives immediate feedback indicating that he or she is finding the patient's expressions to be unclear. The patient is asked to engage in experiential focusing and then to find just the right words to describe the experience freshly in the moment. If the patient describes his or her experience using psychological jargon (e.g., "I guess I'm feeling codependent right now"), then he or she is again asked to focus in on the immediate, inner felt experience, and "to find just the right personal descriptive words, without any shorthand jargon-like words that might not fully do justice to what your experience is right now."

Since preoccupied patients typically have an undeveloped sense of self and tend to be overly concerned about the state of mind of the other at the expense of the self, we use several methods to direct their discourse focus away from others and onto themselves. An anchoring scale is one of those methods:

> On a scale of 1 to 10, with 1 being the degree of focus that you have right now on *me*, and with 10 being the degree of focus you have right now on *yourself*, and with the other numbers indicating various degrees of focus on both, tell me a number that indicates the orientation of your focus right now.

Another method is redirecting attention and affective marking. For example, if a patient is describing her father's anger and all the ways he showed it and why he might have been feeling angry, the therapist might say:

> I hear what you're saying about your father, and I'm *really* interested in what *you* were feeling when he was being that way. I wonder if *you* might have been feeling *really* scared then.

Repeatedly reminding these patients of our interest in *them* builds their ability to bring attention to internal states and supports greater self-awareness and reflection.

When past, unmetabolized experiences invade current discourse, the anxious-preoccupied patient is taught how to use the past/present orientation anchoring scale (also described in Chapter 9):

> On a scale of 1 to 10, with 1 being completely preoccupied with the past and unaware of current context, and 10 being completely in the present, and the other numbers representing some mixture of past and present awareness, give me a number as to the relative orientation you have to past or present at this moment.

The seventh step entails *identifying and modifying toxic noncollaborative verbal behavior*. For the dismissing patient, toxic verbal behavior typically takes the form of derogation (e.g., "You are nothing to me," "You are not at all worth engaging"), invalidation (e.g., "You don't really feel that," "That's not true"), and using ultimatums and aggressive threats (e.g., "If you keep bringing that up, I'm outta here"). Most of these toxic expressions have themes of devaluation and toxic shaming. For the preoccupied patient, toxic verbal behavior takes the form of excessive blaming of self and others (big or niggling complaints, taking a victim stance, fault-finding), excessive demands or imperatives (e.g., "you must" and "you should" statements), self-defeating thinking, overreaction in the face of conflict, and frequent but inaccurate "mind-reading" (i.e., assuming knowledge) of the other.

Whenever toxic discourse occurs in any form, the therapist gives immediate feedback as a starting point for exploration of underlying attachment themes. For example:

> When you just said, "You mean nothing to me," it struck me that that's a very powerful statement to make. I wonder what's going on inside you now that led you to make such a statement, and I wonder, too, when you were little did you ever hear or feel such a statement directed toward you?

However, exploration of the relationship between such toxic verbal behavior and early attachment themes is not the endpoint. The patient and therapist collaborate to co-construct the *positive opposite* of each observed toxic verbal behavior, and the patient is encouraged to rehearse communicating with this positive opposite verbal behavior, first in imagination and then as actual verbal behavior in and out of the treatment setting. For example, the positive opposite of the above dismissing derogation might be "I deeply value the depth of my connection with you." In the ideal parent figure method (Chapter 8), the patient is asked to imagine feeling that deep value/connection toward the ideal parent figures, and then to explore ways in later imagery that the deep valuing/connection might apply to relationships, including the relationship with the therapist and relationships outside of therapy.

As another example, creating the positive opposite of excessive blaming of the other first involves correcting for the imbalanced outside-in focus on the state of mind of the other to bring the focus of awareness to internal self-experience. Using an outside/inside focus 1 to 10 anchoring scale serves this purpose. Then, the patient is encouraged to draw from his or her enhanced self-experience to create healthy need statements. With a clear set of healthy need statements, the patient imagines making healthy need requests to another person. He or she imagines receiving the best, most satisfying response from that person and then offering appreciation (the opposite of blame) to that person for his or her response. This sequence is done first in the context of imagined ideal parent figures: The patient-as-child imagines making the need statements to the ideal parent figures; getting the best, most satisfying response from them; and then offering appreciation to them. The same sequence is then imagined with the therapist, and then with some outside person. Finally, the patient is given a homework assignment to practice identifying and communicating such healthy need statements in everyday life whenever the tendency to blame is observed.

During this process of working with toxic verbal behavior, patients often benefit from learning of Leech's (1983) six maxims of politeness—tact, generosity, approbation, modesty, agreement, and sympathy. In imagination, patients can create experiences of others manifesting these verbal qualities toward them, and vice versa.

The eighth step entails the therapist's *verbal match-and-change* in response to the patient's ongoing verbal behavior. For example, when a dismissing patient talks in a way that is too succinct, the therapist reflectively mirrors what has been said, develops it in greater detail as a way of modeling, and then adds something different by asking for much more detail from the patient:

> **Patient:** My father played with me.
> **Therapist:** Your father played with you. I wonder if he played with you at home, if he played with you at the schoolyard. I wonder if he took you places where you played together. I wonder if he played with you some every day, if he played with you more days than not. I wonder if he played with you less days than not. Tell me more about your father playing with you.

As described earlier, when the therapist notices idealization in a dismissing patient's speech, he or she mirrors the positive aspect and adds something new by inquiring into any negative aspects of the patient's experience. When the dismissing patient's speech is remote from his or her feelings, the therapist reflectively mirrors the content and then tries to mirror and mark the underlying feeling. When the preoccupied patient talks excessively, the therapist may call for a pause and reflect back a very succinct summary of the main point. When a preoccupied patient wanders off topic, the therapist may say, "I'm not sure at this point whether you are staying on your main point or have gone off your main point," and then adds something new by requesting a brief summary of the main point from the patient. When the preoccupied patient shows violations of manner by being vague or ambiguous, the therapist can say, "What you just described wasn't as clear to me as I think it can be; perhaps you wouldn't mind describing it again in a way that is more clear, so I'll be sure to understand it." The therapist adds something new by requesting that the patient "find just the right words that best fit" the experience being described. If the violations in manner are severe, the therapist explicitly highlights this by saying, "I know you're trying to communicate something important, but that didn't make any sense to me. So go ahead and try saying it again in such a way that I might be able to understand you more clearly." Again, the new element added is the request for "best-fit" words.

The ninth step entails *enhancing verbal contingency communication and dialogue.* Patients with insecure attachment need to see directly and frequently that their verbal communication has an effect on the other. Reflective listening and mirroring by the therapist is the first step in showing the patient that his or her communication has had an effect—specifically, the experience of being known, seen, or understood in the mind of the other *as a consequence of collaborative verbal discourse.* In other words, at any given moment, what the patient has verbally communicated has directly created understanding in the mind of the therapist. However, beyond reflective listening and mirroring, the therapist specifically gives feedback to the patient when the contingent effect of the patient's communication was to change the state of mind of the therapist—that is, to communicate to the patient, "This is the effect your communication had on me." There are several ways that a therapist can show that the patient's communication has had an immediate effect on his or her state of mind, including nonverbally or verbally showing the patient that what was said emotionally "moved" the therapist (e.g., the therapist allowing his or her own tears to well up or saying, "What you just said really moves me") and expressing directly the thoughts that arose in response to the patient's communication (e.g., "What you just said makes me think of . . ." or "When you said that, I got the idea that . . ."). The therapist's strategic and frequent naming of the effects of the patient's immediate verbal communication will over time help the patient to get back on the right developmental track toward becoming an agent of healthy, collaborative, and contingent communication with the other.

The tenth step is *enhancing the patient's metacognitive awareness of violations in discourse*. When a dismissing patient gives an overly idealized rendition of early childhood relationships (violating *quality* of speech), the therapist might ask:

> How much are you aware that I haven't heard any examples or evidence that would back up what you're saying? Let's go back now and see if you can tell me some examples of what you're telling me.

If a dismissing patient is too succinct (violating *quantity* of speech), the therapist might say, "Your description is so brief that I can't get a clear picture of what you mean. Before we go on, I wonder how much you are aware at this point in time that I might not have a clear picture of what you are describing." When a preoccupied patient wanders off topic and introduces numerous irrelevancies into the discourse (violating *relevance* of speech), the therapist can enhance the patient's metacognitive capacity to be aware of wandering and irrelevancy. For example, the therapist might use an anchoring scale:

> On a scale of 1 to 10, with 1 being staying completely on topic, and with 10 being wandering completely off topic, and the other numbers being a level of going off topic somewhere in between, give me a number that indicates how much you are staying on or going off topic at this very moment.

The eleventh step pertains to *collaborative co-constructed meaning-making*. All the previous steps pertain to the rules of verbal discourse, but mainly to the *structure* of the patient's verbal discourse. This final step pertains to the *content* of the verbal discourse. This step entails helping the patient effectively communicate in words his or her primary referential intention—that is, bringing more clarity to the main point that he or she is trying to communicate. The therapist's now-familiar stance is to inquire, ask for clarification, reflectively mirror back, add something new, and overall, develop a back-and-forth interaction through which the patient and therapist alike explore and shape the patient's understanding of a given situation or state. In other words, the therapist helps the patient to formulate his or her own experience to himself or herself. Co-created meaning-making typically starts with a focus on current states of mind and situations; later in therapy, as higher levels of cognitive development emerge, the patient becomes better able to construct a coherent life narrative. The capacity to see the evolution of the self over a long time span, such as a life span or in an even wider intergenerational context, and to articulate a detailed narrative of one's own self development, is a fairly good indicator of high coherence of mind.

Signs of Successful Activation of the Collaborative Behavioral System

The overall outcomes of successful treatment of nonverbal and verbal collaboration failures in insecurely attached patients include the following: (1) Nonverbal behaviors—including orientation, gaze, facial affective display, postural gestures, and vocal rhythm, pitch, and tone—become matched, synchronized, and contingently effective in ongoing communication within and outside the treatment context; (2) verbal communication follows normal and healthy rules of collaborative discourse (e.g., turn-taking, reflective listening, need expression, validating); (3) verbal communication generally follows Grice's maxims without undue violations, and is therefore generally sensible and meaningful; (4) verbal communication meets a standard of coherence of discourse (a score of 7 to 9 for coherence of discourse on the AAI); (5) verbal communication is generally contingently effective on the listener; and (6) there is accurate, ongoing metacognitive monitoring of lapses in verbal discourse. In short, the successfully treated patient with insecure attachment enjoys the rewards of healthy nonverbal communication both in everyday conversation in general and in exploration and verbal communication pertaining to attachment and other emotionally charged themes. Across circumstances, the patient retains the capacity for healthy, meaningful, coherent, and contingently effective communication, and thereby directly experiences the benefits and rewards of healthy nonverbal and verbal communication with others. With effective treatment, the insecurely attached patient overcomes the developmental arrest of the collaborative behavioral system. He or she gets back on the right developmental track toward the capacity to engage in ongoing contingent, collaborative behavior with others and toward continued healthy exploration and attainment of the higher stages of adult cognitive and emotional development.

Case Illustration

The transcript below is from a session with a man in his 30s. "John" had presented for therapy for symptoms of depression and low self-esteem and was assessed as having a mixed attachment style, predominantly anxious-preoccupied with some dismissing features. In this excerpt, the patient describes a situation at work where he was not getting along with a co-worker/friend with whom he had to work on a project. The therapist responds to John's habits of talking with such rapidity that she cannot understand him at times and of talking with fading slurs at the end of sentences. These patterns of speaking were very prominent and became so severe several times in the session that the therapist needed to interrupt the patient to ask him to repeat what he said. Sometimes, despite asking the patient three to four times to repeat the sentence more clearly, she still could not understand John's speech. The following example is from one of the first 10 sessions with this highly motivated patient.

Therapist: You know, John, let me stop you a minute before we go on. I'm really noticing something that you do a lot when you're telling me about things and I want us to understand it better. Do you notice that sometimes you talk so fast and I have to ask you to clarify a couple of times?

Patient: (Nods and laughs.) Yeah, maybe the habit developed when I was trying to get words out so quickly as a kid, because I had to do it so quickly to avoid attention, scrutiny, or criticism. Yeah. That would be my guess. I don't really know how long I've had this or when it changed or if it changed, but I do know that I do it.

Therapist: Okay, good. So in here, for our purposes, it would be really great if you could—*on purpose*—try to do the opposite of that and really take your time. And really try to pay attention to how you finish what you're saying, because as we've talked about, sometimes your speech fades out at the end, and when it's like that I really can't understand the last things you say at all. It's so important here, and actually everywhere in your life, that you can be understood. So take your time with what you're saying.

Patient: As in, "take breaths"?

Therapist: Yes. Good idea. Take *very* deep breaths, and really, you can say things in an exaggeratedly slow way and I'm going to really like that because, as your psychologist, we're working together with this protocol. It will be wonderful for me to be able to hear every little thing you're saying.

Patient: Okay, that's not something I've had a lot of practice with and I probably won't be able to keep it up if like . . . I probably won't be able to keep that up if I get distracted.

Therapist: Right, and I will keep up pointing it out for us—I hope you know that it will be a collaborative thing for me to say, "Oh look," and remind you gently.

Patient: That feedback is helpful. I appreciate it, thank you.

Therapist: You're very welcome. I just want to make sure that we arrange it so that it doesn't feel like scrutiny or criticism.

Patient: Mm-hmm.

Therapist: Okay. So back to your work situation you were telling me about. Can you tell me more about how work went this week?

Patient: I wish I'd handled that better with my friend, so that it didn't, so that we could have worked together, and I'm not sure what I should have done differently but it makes me sad that it was like that, and frustrating for him that we couldn't work things out. As things progressed with my work, I think he got frustrated about not having stuff to do and feeling like . . . like he even sent me an email saying like it was really stressful working with me, and, um, that he wasn't sure why, and like from my perspective—like whenever I suggested something he sort of shot it . . . not even just shot it down, like questioned why we needed that in the first place and seemed to be very unhelpful and not very collaborative, like he had . . . like he also is very sort of . . . we had a lot of conflict and trying to describe the whole thing would take the whole session but *(Mm-hmm)* um . . . conflict that didn't . . . we didn't seem to be working out.

Therapist: Can you give me another example so I can get a flavor?

Patient: Um . . . when we were first starting the project, he also seemed sort of frustrated that I was . . . that he didn't have as much to do afterwards, and . . . he also seemed to be implying that I would fail because this wasn't, this was too hard or something and I didn't know what I was doing and I kind of resented that *(Yeah)*, like it was—I mean . . . this is a thing that had been going on for months and I hadn't gotten a lot done with the report because everything at the time was just really stressful . . .

Therapist: So you both found each other stressful.

Patient: Yeah.

Therapist: You never got a collaborative working rhythm going.

Patient: Like only at the very beginning. Like every time after that it was like, if I brought up the question about format he would immediately say, "Oh why do you have to do that?" like he also started to dismiss the creative aspect as meaningless fluff that could be added in later even though it's, that's the whole thing really and I felt like, we weren't communicating at all and I didn't know what to do about it and every time we tried talking it just—

Therapist: But you could feel his edge being taken out on you.

Patient: Yeah, like in some of the conflict it starts . . . like he was very critical.

Therapist: Okay, John, so let me pause you for a second. *(Okay.)* So some of your, some of your gestures—I just want to know what they mean because they are very distinct. I recognize that they are really communicating something to me, but I'm not sure what yet. *[Pointing out a nonverbal noncollaborative behavior]*

Patient: Mm-hmm, okay. I guess this is . . . *(Here it seems that the patient is laughing uncomfortably, although with some increase in pleasure at the recognition.)*

Therapist: So now, when you were doing this *(demonstrates action of putting both hands in front of face)*, is it a little bit of uncertainty, or embarrassment? I'd like to understand for sure what that gesture means right now. Is it "I could keep talking like this but I'm not sure if this is, if I'm connecting with her [the therapist] right now"?

Patient: Yeah *(Okay)*, like I don't know if I'm just completely rambling about something that you don't want to hear, or aren't going to understand.

Therapist: It also seems like there is a kind of pleasure in the gesture, on your face, which you're hiding?

Patient: (Laughing, hiding face more, nodding, trying to stop smiling but looking relieved to be "seen.") I'm feeling a bit sort of self-conscious about how much to go into because a lot, a lot of this is technical.

Therapist: I love it. You know why?

Patient: No.

Therapist: First of all, I do—I do love techie stuff. *(Okay.)* But I also—I love it because when I don't understand something it makes you have to explain it to me, which is a great process for us in here for what we're doing. *[Underscoring the collaborative goal]*

Patient: Mm-hmm, okay. I guess this is . . .

Therapist: And so, to translate this nonverbal signal into a collaborative, verbal comment to me about that, what might that be?

Patient: Uh, I just want to hide.

Therapist: Yes, and I'm thinking too that you could say even more, which would help me to understand your experience even more, something like, "Let me just pause what I'm saying right now. I just want to make sure that you're tracking me and I know that you're not in my field and does this feel useful for you?"

Patient: Okay.

Therapist: That would be a wonderfully clear, collaborative comment, wouldn't it? (Both laughing.) And it would be the translation of this: (demonstrates action with hands again).

Patient: Okay.

Therapist: Okay?

Patient: (Both laughing.) I'm sorry, where were we?

Therapist: Okay. Well, I was—I was listening to the process between you and your co-worker . . . what's his name?

Patient: Jake.

The therapist clearly maintains a stance of positive, collaborative engagement. The patient's lapses in collaborative communication, both nonverbal and verbal, are pointed out with acceptance and interest, highlighting the shared goal of enhancing understanding through effective communication. This process also enhances the patient's metacognitive awareness of his communication patterns, reflecting the interdependence of these two pillars of treatment (see Chapter 7).

PART IV

TYPE-SPECIFIC TREATMENT

Application of The Three Pillars Treatment To Dismissing, Anxious-Preoccupied, and Disorganized Attachment

Specific considerations for treating patients with each insecure attachment type are guided by understanding the specific developmental care-receiving experiences common to each type. In the next three chapters, we describe and detail how to tailor the three pillars of treatment according to the specific experiences and resulting needs of patients with each insecure type. Although there are important considerations common to each type, it is essential to always remember that treatment is of the patient and not the type—every patient is different, and the methods described in these chapters are chosen, shaped, and applied according to the particularities of each patient.

CHAPTER 11

Treating Dismissing Attachment

The Origins of Dismissing Attachment

According to Ainsworth, Blehar, Waters, and Wall (1978), the origin of avoidant attachment in children is the experience of *repeated maternal rejection*. From their direct observations using the Strange Situation procedure, mothers of avoidant children were described as "especially rejecting" (p. 146). This rejection was particularly apparent in the context of physical contact. The authors observed that the more rejecting parents "tended to find close contact with their babies aversive" (p. 316) and had "aberrant reactions to close bodily contact" (p. 152). From home observations, they noted that maternal behavior of soothing or cuddling was rare. Across contexts, Ainsworth et al. also observed a general pattern of "rejection communication" (p. 152) toward their children, which included direct and/or indirect expressions of negative affect and behavior. Mothers of avoidant children were also seen to be repetitively rejecting of their children's expressed attachment behaviors. When the child engaged in proximity- or contact-seeking, these attachment behaviors were frequently rebuffed, which left the child in a state of "chronic frustration" (p. 147). Ainsworth et al. suggested that a child's experiences of rejection in response to his or her proximity- and contact-seeking produce an approach/avoidance conflict—attachment behaviors are activated by separations, but avoidance behaviors are also activated by the active rejection of the attachment behaviors. After repeated rejection of proximity- or contact-seeking, the child responds by deactivating the attachment system and developing an avoidant pattern. Ainsworth and her colleagues found that avoidant children often failed to show signs of collaborative nonverbal behavior such as head-turning and fixing the gaze on the parent.

Main and Weston (1981) concur that repeated rejection is related to the development of avoidant attachment in children. They also report that mothers of avoidant children were far less emotionally expressive than mothers of children with secure or other types of insecure attachment. With respect to expressed emotion, Haft and Slade (1989) found that while secure mothers showed careful attunement to a wide range of the child's affective displays, often manifesting as collaborative, nonverbal, intersubjective interchange of facial affective displays, dismissing mothers distorted and were remarkably misattuned to the negative-affective displays of their children. This misattunement was especially apparent when the child sought comfort or reassurance or when the child directed negative affects toward the mother. Haft and Slade (1989) state that dismissing mothers misread their babies' affect

> primarily when it was negative and did so most consistently when the baby directed the negativity toward them and not an object . . . Dismissing mothers were most comfortable attuning to their babies' expressions of exuberance, especially in the context of mastery in play. . . [They] tended to be rejecting of their babies' bids for comfort and reassurance . . . [and] . . . typically use[d] comments to override the baby's affect. (p. 168)

They add that such selective misattunement likely reflects the mother's internal state and needs: "A mother may misattune to her baby's affect in an attempt to preserve a particular state of mind with regard to attachment" (Haft & Slade, 1989, p. 168). Regarding the child's experience, the mother's repeated selective misattunement to negative affect may be seen as a rejection that shapes the child to deactivate the attachment system when distressed and to compensate by developing pseudoautonomous exploratory behavior. The pattern of selective misattunement was also observed by the Grossmanns in their extensive study of avoidant attachment in a German sample. Karen (1998) summarizes their findings:

> If the [avoidantly attached] infant played well . . . , the parent attended joyfully and tried to join in. Many times, though, the parent's play interfered with, dominated, or frustrated the infant. If, subsequently, the infant showed signs of distress, frustration, or boredom, the parent retreated, observed from a distance, and waited until the child had pulled himself together again and had overcome his negative emotions by himself. Thus, the avoidantly attached infants experienced friendly attention mostly when they were busy playing by themselves, and when they showed positive emotions, but they were left alone when they displayed negative emotions. (cited in Karen, 1998, p. 355, from Grossman, 1989, p. 2)

Belsky (1999) reported that mothers of avoidant children tend to be more controlling and rigid than mothers of secure or other types of insecure children. Such behavior seems to be an additional variable in the development of avoidant attachment in children.

In summary, caregiver patterns of repeated rejection of proximity- and contact-seeking behavior; selective attunement to positive affect, play, and exploration; misattunement to and rejection of negative affects; and controlling, rigid behavior have consistently been shown to be important in the development of avoidant attachment in childhood and thereby in dismissing attachment in adulthood.

The Therapeutic Stance With the Dismissing Patient

Lopez (2009) correctly reminds us that dismissing patients are underrepresented in most clinical settings. Dismissing adults have largely deactivated their attachment system and, therefore, simply stated, do not readily seek treatment, which is help from a person or system. If they do seek treatment, it is often for some reason other than relational dissatisfaction, such as health concerns. In the less common circumstance of presenting with relational disturbance, work-related conflict is more likely to be the focus than are intimate relationships. Further, when dismissing patients present their relationship difficulty, they typically attribute the source to *others'* behavior.

When someone with dismissing attachment does present for therapy, the stance and ways of being that the therapist has toward the patient are vitally important for the stability and success of the treatment. Because dismissing attachment is largely formed by early experience of repeated, active rejection of attachment behaviors, the therapist must consistently present the positive opposite of that pattern: *repeated active engagement* of the dismissing patient. The therapist, both in his or her therapeutic stance and in the ideal parent imagery, repeatedly and actively guides, prompts, and supports the dismissing patient to engage in attachment-oriented behaviors. Repeated active engagement by the therapist is the main factor that, over time, leads the dismissing patient to reactivate the attachment system and put it back on line in relationships.

Also of great importance is the therapist's *careful, accurate attunement* to exactly those areas of misattunement that were prominent in the early infant–caregiver relationship. The therapist must carefully and accurately attune to patient-initiated instances of proximity- and contact-seeking; to patient-initiated verbal expressions regarding felt needs for safety, soothing, comfort, and reassurance; and to the entire range of affects, particularly to negative affects and especially to negative affects expressed toward the therapist. Overall attunement is also essential to prevent too-much-too-soon active engagement of the dismissing patient. As such patients have deactivated their attachment system, a therapist's insensitive, misattuned attempts toward active engagement are likely to be experienced as threatening, thereby reinforcing the deactivation of attachment behavior.

Since rigid, controlling caregiver behavior also contributes to the development of dismissing attachment, the therapeutic stance also necessarily includes *permissive encouragement of exploration of states of mind*, specifically with respect to attachment. Dismissing patients have a very difficult time recalling and thinking about attachment-related themes. So the therapist, over time and in nondemanding and permissive ways, encourages free exploration of memories and affects associated with past and current attachment experience, including experience of the treatment relationship. As dismissing patients minimize negative affect regarding attachment, careful attention is directed to support the emergence and experience of such affect. The therapist also offers permissive encouragement regarding the patient's free exploration of the self, but with a particular focus. Dismissing patients generally have a strong, autonomous, and independent sense of self (Main, Goldwyn, & Hesse, 2002) and an intact exploratory behavioral system in self-focused contexts; thus, the therapist encourages the patient to engage in free-exploration experiences of himself or herself *in the context of attachment relationships*. This very specific focus orients the normally developed exploratory system toward attachment themes and experience, which over time contributes to reactivation of the attachment system.

Using Ideal Parent Figure Imagery With the Dismissing Patient

Ideal Parent Figure (IPF) imagery is ideally suited for the dismissing patient, especially during the early phase of treatment. As noted above, because of the dismissing patient's deactivation of his or her attachment system, too much direct, active engagement by the therapist is likely to be counterproductive toward the goal of activating the attachment system. However, the method of working with imagined ideal parent figures structures the treatment sessions consistently on attachment themes while simultaneously allowing the patient some relational distance from the therapist. The focus is on self-generated attachment-related *imagery* rather than on the immediately experienced relationship between patient and therapist. As such, IPF imagery is typically far less threatening to the dismissing patient than the here-and-now treatment relationship. Further, since dismissing patients typically show strong unrealistic idealization of one or both parents (e.g., in AAI responses), the therapist's support for idealized parent imagery will likely be quite acceptable to a dismissing patient. Although seeming at first to be aligned with the patient's defensive exclusion of nonidealized parental themes, working with IPF imagery over time fundamentally transforms this unrealistic idealization into a healthy, positive internal working model for secure attachment.

Nevertheless, the use of IPF imagery with the dismissing patient is not without its difficulties. When the therapist first suggests that the patient imagine growing up in a different family of origin, with parents ideally suited to his or her nature, the mere suggestion of revisiting childhood attachment themes, even in a new way, may elicit uncomfortable feelings, such as bewilderment or threat. If these reactions occur, they become the focus of the initial therapeutic work. When the patient expresses bewilderment, an opportunity is created for the therapist to help the patient identify that which is most missing in the patient—a sense of early attachment as a positive, secure base. For example, the therapist might say:

> That sense of confusion or bewilderment lets us know that you don't yet have an internal sense that a close connection between parent and child can be safe, or even possible.

When the patient becomes fearful, a therapeutic opportunity arises for the patient to understand that his or her current internal maps give a sense of attachment as a source of threat. The therapist might say:

> Let's really pay attention to that fear, as it's telling us that when you think of attachment, or closeness, there's a sense of threat. You don't yet have an internal sense that attachment, or closeness, can be safe and secure. This is why we're doing this work, to help that realization develop.

In either case, the therapist uses the experience to help the patient realize that what is most missing is the felt sense of a positive representation of secure attachment. Interaction around this theme is *collaborative*: A solely empathic response by the therapist will likely lead to resistance, as the empathic response pulls for activation of the attachment system, which is associated with bewilderment or threat; but when the therapist acknowledges the patient's experience and indicates that they both will work with it as a *collaborative team*, the collaborative behavioral system becomes engaged, and with less resistance the patient and therapist together can begin to develop a positive map as a shared goal of treatment.

For dismissing patients who are at first unable to tolerate the idea of proximity with IPFs in the imagery, the imagery can include the task of closeness/distance regulation. The therapist asks the patient to imagine a scene with himself or herself as a young child while interacting with the ideal parents around free play. Then, the therapist suggests that the patient experiment in the imagery with the child moving further away and closer to the IPFs, and to keep experimenting until he or she finds *just the right distance* with the IPFs. For example:

> You can go ahead and imagine yourself with these parents now, these parents who are *best suited* to your needs and feelings, who *really know* how to be with you in ways that allow you to feel *comfortable*, and *safe*. These parents would never make you be closer to them than you want to, so now you can experiment with finding *just the right distance* from them right now. You can bring yourself closer, and you can bring yourself farther away,

until you find *just the right* closeness and distance that feels *comfortable* for you with them now.

As the ongoing imagery work continues, the patient is encouraged to move the imagined self-as-child closer to or further away from the IPFs at any time, according to what feels *just right* at that given moment. Through such self-regulation in imagery, the therapist provides the experience that the dismissing patient can voluntarily control closeness/distance according to need, and with this direct, experiential realization, such patients are more capable of tolerating the IPF imagery without reactivating their dismissing attachment style. Indirectly, the therapist has also reassuringly communicated that he or she will be respectful of and carefully attuned to the dismissing patient's needs for closeness or distance at any given moment throughout the course of treatment.

There are two primary considerations when working with IPF imagery with dismissive patients: (1) shaping the elements of the IPF imagery to be consistent with what research supports should be emphasized to positively remap IWMs of attachment and (2) tailoring the IPF imagery to suit the particular dismissing patient. While the former allows for general considerations, the latter does not, and so we do not use predetermined IPF imagery protocols. Imagery is co-created spontaneously in the ongoing collaborative interaction between patient and therapist.

Research strongly suggests that early childhood caregivers of dismissing patients were repeatedly rejecting. Therefore, the imagined ideal parent figures must be *deeply accepting and encouraging* of the child's attachment behavior and expressions. For example:

> These ideal parents are especially comfortable with any physical contact that you'd like to have with them . . . Whether it's physical or emotional contact that you might like, these parents are *right there*, welcoming you and encouraging you to be in contact with them, just as you'd like . . . These parents are never uncomfortable with physical or emotional closeness . . . Notice their *warmth* and how openly *affectionate* they are when you want to be with them.

Over time, the goal is to transform the approach/avoidance conflict regarding attachment needs into a stable, positive representation of parent figures who are deeply accepting and encouraging of the child's attachment needs. In other words, the approach/avoidance conflict is transformed into conflict-free experience of secure attachment.

Additionally, the imagery is shaped so that the IPFs are attuned to the full range of emotional experience and expression of the patient-as-child. The patient is helped to imagine ideal parents who are not only carefully attuned, but are also *contingently responsive* to those states and expressions. Further, since dismissing patients have an especially difficult time acknowledging all negative emotions (with the exception of anger), it is particularly important, after the patient becomes able to imagine IPFs and becomes reasonably comfortable with them, that the imagery include the parent figures noticing and encouraging the child to identify and express underlying vulnerabilities, hurts, and disappointments. The therapist, therefore, introduces scenes in which IPFs have recognized an uncomfortable state in the child and encourage the child to identify, express, and explore that state directly to the ideal parents, who are deeply accepting. For example:

> And now the scene shifts, and in this new scene, these parents notice that you're having some discomfort, some discomfort that you're not sure you can express to them. But there's something about their ways of being with you now that gives you a sense that you *actually can* let them know what you're feeling. And as you let them know what you're feeling, they're with you in ways that let you know that they *fully accept* what is happening with you right now.

Rather than turning away from what is uncomfortable, which is what the patient's actual parent did, the IPFs stay with the child and his or her discomfort. The therapist repeatedly shapes and reshapes the imagery in a manner that provides *optimal discomfort* for the patient-as-child—that is, the imagery supports experiencing neither too little nor too much discomfort. Through this process, within and across sessions, the patient develops new attachment representations that include consistent attunement and accurate, contingent responsiveness to all emotional states, including underlying vulnerabilities and deeper, less superficial emotional themes. Over time, the dismissing patient becomes able to engage in deeper emotional involvement in the IPF imagery and in the treatment sessions in general.

Because caregivers of dismissing patients are often rigid and controlling, for the imagery the therapist suggests that the IPFs have qualities that are the positive opposite of rigid and controlling—openness, flexibility, and permissiveness. For example:

> These parents would *never* be rigid or controlling with you. In fact, notice how *very different* these parents are from that . . . these parents are *very open*, are *very flexible*, and are *interested* in what *you* want to do, in how *you* want to be . . . They support you in being creative, spontaneous, and overall in you just being *most fully you*.

The objective is to help the dismissing patient positively remap IWMs in the direction of expecting flexible, open, and permissive responses from others, to overwrite the map that leads to expectations of the contrary.

In addition to the general considerations for including in the IPF imagery the general factors—parental *presence*, *consistency*, *reliability*, and *interest*—and the five primary behavioral conditions that promote secure attachment—*protection*, *attunement*, *soothing*, *expressed delight*, and *fostering best self-development* (see Chapters 7 and 8)—with dismissing patients there are particular ways of introducing these over time that best fit their particular patterns and needs. First, with respect to *protection*, the therapist suggests parent figures who provide protection and a felt sense of safety specifically in the attachment relationship, not protection and safety in general. The suggestion of *safety in the attachment relationship* is especially alien to most dismissing patients, and that is precisely why the idea must be introduced as part of the positive remapping. For example:

> These parents are dedicated to protecting you from any harm. And their ways of being with you show you *so very clearly* that you're *safe* with them . . . They're so attuned to you and what's most right for you that you can *really be yourself* with them, and you can feel a deepening sense of *security* and *safety* in your connection with them.

Second, with respect to *attunement*, the IPF imagery for the dismissing patient emphasizes parents who are especially attuned to physical and emotional proximity- and contact-seeking, and also especially attuned to the child's range of negative emotional expressions. The objective is to introduce corrective IPF imagery that contributes to the development of positive representations and expectancies of others being comfortable with and encouraging physical and emotional closeness and a wide range of negative as well as positive affects. For example:

> They recognize when you want to be close to them, to have contact with them, and they *welcome* you whenever *you want* that . . . These parents are always available for a warm hug, when *you want* that . . . And when you just want to be near them, and feel emotional closeness, they're completely fine and happy with that.
>
> These parents *welcome* your happy feelings, and they also welcome any feelings that don't feel so happy . . . You can count on them to recognize and *fully accept* when you're feeling unhappy, or scared, or angry, or vulnerable . . . And *even when* you're angry with them or feeling uncomfortable with them, they're attuned to that and welcome that too . . . They know that children sometimes feel not-so-positive feelings toward their parents, and it's *completely okay* for you to express those feelings to them . . . They'll accept that and *stay right with you*.

Third, with respect to *soothing*, the therapist suggests scenes in which the child is emotionally upset and the IPFs are consistently responsive to the child's specific emotional state, providing soothing, comfort, and reassurance. The objective over time is to develop a stable, positive representation and set of expectancies that others are openly comforting, and that such comfort is expected and seen as normal. For example:

> And now in this next scene you'll experience yourself, as a very young child, feeling emotionally upset. As the scene now emerges, you can feel the upset, the emotional upset . . . Notice what that's like . . . And these parents, who are *so very attuned* to you, see that you're upset and they are *right there* for you to help you with that upset. And right now they find *just the right ways* to soothe you . . . They find *just the right ways* to be there for you that feel *especially soothing and comforting* to you . . . Notice how these parents *tune right in* to you when you're feeling emotionally upset . . . When you're emotionally upset, no matter what you're feeling, they tune right in and find *just the right ways* to soothe you.

Fourth, with respect to *expressed delight*, caregivers of dismissing patients typically lacked expression of delight with their child, or selectively expressed delight only around the child's independence from them, such as during solitary play. Imagery is suggested specifically to support the experience of IPFs expressing delight about the child's emotional expressions and wish for emotional and physical closeness. For example:

> And whenever you want to be close to them, these parents are *absolutely delighted* . . . And they let you know how delighted they are by telling you, and by showing it on their faces, and in their ways of being with you . . . As you're with them now, perhaps you're feeling something that you want to share with them, and if you do, go ahead and share that feeling with them . . . They are *so happy* that you let them know whatever you're feeling, or thinking. Even if you'd think it's not so nice, or if it's uncomfortable, these parents *welcome it* and are happy that you're letting them know whatever it is you're experiencing.

Fifth, with respect to fostering best self-development, early childhood caregivers of dismissing patients reinforced a strong, independent self by selectively attuning to and supporting the child's independent exploratory behavior. This pattern contributes to the child's maladaptive belief that the self is most valued and strongest apart from relationship. Thus, the therapist of the dismissing patient specifically introduces IPF imagery in which the child explores *in the context of the attachment relationship*. In other words, the therapist introduces the theme of *secure base for exploration* through the IPF imagery—the child explores and discovers the characteristics of the best self in the context of a secure base, with

IPFs who neither unduly reinforce nor control free exploration, but instead provide consistent encouragement for exploration in the context of the relationship. For example:

> These parents are *right there with you* as you're exploring what's around you, as you discover what you're interested in . . . You're *not alone* as you look around and go to what you're drawn to . . . They are there when you're exploring, and they are there when you want to come back to them, and maybe tell them what you've found and what you're excited about . . . They're *so very interested*, and *delighted*, in what you discover . . . And they're there and watch to make sure you stay safe from any harm . . . and they're there to support you discovering what you like . . . and they're there when you want to come back to them to show or tell what you've discovered, or simply if you want to reconnect with them.

Over time, the dismissing patient develops a positive representation and set of expectancies that others can provide a secure base for exploration, and that that exploratory behavior can be enhanced, not inhibited, by relationship. The strong, autonomous, independent pseudo-self of the dismissing patient is gradually transformed into the best-self-in-the-context-of-relationship.

If an AAI is available for a dismissing patient, the adjectives or phrases that he or she gave to describe the early maternal and paternal relationships can be used to individualize the IPF protocol by translating the adjectives or phrases into their positive opposites and suggesting that those qualities are present in the relationships with the ideal parent figures. If an AAI transcript is not available, information from unstructured clinical interviewing is used to construct positive opposites of parental relationship experience. Since patients with dismissing attachment often present adjectives or phrases that reflect their highly idealized, unrealistic portrayal of one or both parents, it is important that they be translated into *genuine*, not false-positive opposites. For example, the patient in the case illustration described later in this chapter gave five seemingly positive descriptions for his relationship with his mother: "loving," "orderly routines," "doing fun stuff," "concerned," and "helpful." The description of "loving" lacked any specific memory or incident that illustrated that quality, and it was clear that the mother was especially absent for any physical closeness; the therapist determined that the positive opposite was "deeply physically affectionate," and in the IPF work the therapist included, for example, "Notice the ways that this mother is *deeply physically affectionate*." "Orderly routines" meant eating meals together as a family in a very regimented manner, and the illustrative example lacked any sense of "lingering" or "savoring" the meal or the felt closeness of a family together at mealtime; the positive opposite used in the IPF imagery was "savoring the moments together." While "doing fun stuff" was meant by the patient as a positive endorsement of an intact family, the memory given illustrated only instrumental love at best; "just being together and not having to do anything" became the positive opposite. "Concerned" was meant to be a positive descriptor of his mother, but the memory used to illustrate "concerned" showed his overinvolvement in the mother's state of mind; the positive opposite became "always attuned to your needs." "Helpful" was illustrated by a memory of his mother asking him if he had finished his homework, with an underlying theme of pressure to succeed; the positive opposite used in the IPF protocol was "deeply attuned to your needs and feelings."

For this same patient, the five adjectives/phrases given for the early childhood relationship with his father were also unrealistically idealized and positive: "around a lot," "plays with me," "strong," "caring," and "learning." The memories used to illustrate "around a lot" lacked any indication of his father being at all attuned to the child's inner state of mind; the positive opposite for the imagery protocol became "carefully attuned to your needs and feelings." The memories to illustrate "plays with me" depicted his father playing *for* him rather than *with* him, and playing in a way that often left the patient feeling inadequate and ashamed; the positive opposite for the IPF imagery became a quality of "enhancing" the patient's sense of self. To illustrate "strong," the patient described how his father would affectionately caress his face and then slap him hard across his face while saying, "You need to learn to be tough." This incident left the patient feeling deeply betrayed and untrusting; the positive opposite used in the imagery was "trusting your longings." "Caring" was illustrated by various activities, but none involved spontaneity or fun; the positive opposite became "the fun of just being together and not doing anything." "Learning" pertained to memories of his father making sure he finished his homework, but never really helping him; the positive opposite became "fostering the joy of discovering and learning."

As with any patient, the five adjectives/phrases from the AAI are a rich source from which the clinician can tailor and individualize the IPF imagery in very specific ways, based on what the AAI responses show to be most lacking in the early childhood relationship between each parent and the child. But the dismissing patient's tendency to idealize early attachment figures makes less straightforward the establishment of the positive opposites of what was lacking in those relationships. As illustrated above, however, when the clinician draws less from the words or phrases themselves and more from what the patient says to illustrate them, genuine and useful positive opposites are readily established.

Fostering Collaboration in the Dismissing Patient

Given the dismissing patient's deactivation of the attachment system, he or she will likely at first resist the therapist's attempts at active engagement toward attachment themes. Although the therapist remains attuned to when and how to orient the dismissing patient toward those themes, early in treatment the main focus is best placed on engaging the patient's cooperative behavioral system (Liotti, 2005) to promote *collaboration* about the treatment. Many dismissing patients have a strong, autonomous self that has proven itself an effective agent in various life endeavors. Therefore, appealing to the dismissing patient to work as a cooperative, collaborative team is far less threatening initially than is a therapist trying to serve as a secure base. The therapist introduces the idea that patient and therapist are a team, and as part of a team, both must contribute to and identify the shared goals of treatment. The shared goals are likely to include the development of a mutually negotiated treatment frame as well as of mutual understanding of likely treatment issues. The foundation of the treatment frame for the dismissing patient is simple—that both the patient and therapist need to show up, not only physically, but also emotionally. The patient is introduced to the principle that exploration in therapy is not self-exploration independent of a relationship, but self-exploration within the context of a relationship, initially with the therapist as a part of the team (cooperative system) and later with the therapist as a secure attachment base (attachment system). Initial emphasis on the cooperative, collaborative aspects of the relationship becomes the pathway toward working with and promoting healthy attachment experience. Activating the cooperative behavioral system slowly broadens the patient's self-reliance to include reliance on the relationship, and through this learned reliance on the relationship, the patient sets a positive foundation for reactivating the attachment system.

As already noted, using IPF imagery early in treatment is also less threatening than the therapist trying to function as a secure base. Collaborative agreement and interaction around the IPF method leaves dormant much of the resistance to attachment to the therapist that dismissing patients bring to treatment.

When treating dismissing patients, more than with any other attachment type, it is especially important to address noncollaborative nonverbal behavior in treatment. It is likely that the dismissing patient will sit far away from the therapist, rarely turn his or her head in the direction of the therapist, and frequently avert the gaze from the therapist. Ongoing spontaneous facial affective displays are likely to be muted, as are spontaneous gestures. The therapist uses the patient's metacognitive awareness in the context of the collaborative relationship to help the patient become aware of these noncollaborative nonverbal behaviors and encourages the patient to explore changing these behaviors. Experiential focusing (Gendlin, 1982) can be used to identify state of mind associated with the nonverbal gesture. For example, the therapist can say:

> I notice that you rarely turn your head in my direction, and you frequently avert your gaze from looking at me. Let's try something together—assume the posture of turning away, and avert your gaze . . . Now, become aware of how this feels in your body. Keep your awareness on how you're holding

your body until you get a felt sense of what that's like. Then, see if you can find *just the right words* to describe this state.

Next, the therapist asks the patient to turn his or her head directly toward the therapist without averting the gaze. Once again, the patient is encouraged to bring awareness to how this position feels in the body. The therapist's direct attention to the nonverbal disconnections and the fostering of the patient's metacognitive awareness and reflection regarding them leads, over time, to the experience and identification of underlying feelings of vulnerability, hurt, rejection, and shame with respect to attachment themes.

Additionally, once basic nonverbal collaborativeness is enhanced using the previously mentioned methods, the therapist becomes mindful of matches and mismatches in nonverbal intersubjective communication between patient and therapist, similar to the approach to therapy recommended by Beebe and Lachmann (2014), described in Chapter 10. Significant mismatches in ongoing nonverbal communication become a focus of treatment as they occur, once again using the patient's developing metacognitive skills for addressing the nonverbal mismatch. The therapist places much focus on contingently matching and transforming the dismissing patient's spontaneous affective facial displays in order to activate and normalize the affective facial display system.

Main et al. (2002), drawing from discourse obtained through the AAI, identified that dismissing adults are deficient in verbal collaborative behavior in their discourse about attachment themes in several specific ways. First, because of idealization and lack of memory, dismissing adults violate Grice's (1989) maxim of truthful *quality* of discourse. Second, the dismissing adult's discourse regarding attachment is too succinct and curtailed, violating the maxim of *quantity*. In therapy, when these verbal behaviors occur, they become the target for intervention. The therapist calls the patient's attention to descriptions of caregivers that are overly positive yet lacking illustrative evidence, and to descriptions that are too succinct. For verbal communication that is lacking in *quality*, the therapist might say:

> I'd like to share with you something that I'm noticing right now as you're telling me about your mother . . . You're speaking in a general way about how wonderful she was when you were a child, but I'm not hearing anything from your experience that would illustrate to me what was wonderful about her.

Or, for speech that is lacking in *quantity*, the therapist can say, "You're saying so little about those relationships, it's hard for me to get a sense of what they were actually like for you."

Then, the patient is encouraged to explore his or her state of mind at the time these verbal behaviors occur, in order to identify underlying emotions, memories, assumptions, and maladaptive schemas associated with attachment themes. For example, the therapist might say:

> Now that we've recognized that when talking just now about your early relationships with your parents, you said very little, and what you did say was overly positive, without much backing evidence, let's be curious about what's going on inside you when you're thinking about those relationships. See if you can tune in to any feelings that are there now, and also to any particular thoughts or memories, even if they might be difficult to pay attention to.

The overall goal of fostering verbal collaborativeness and dialogue is for the dismissing patient to become openly expressive and freshly exploratory about attachment themes.

Enhancing Metacognitive Skills in the Dismissing Patient

In general, the therapist's consistent stance of a-mind-reflecting-on-the-mind-of-the-other contributes to the development of metacognitive skills and mentalizing capacity (J. G. Allen, 2001, 2013), as does the use of specific techniques like affect marking, which places verbal emphasis (making *marked*) the patient's affective experience (Bateman & Fonagy, 2004). However, a condition-specific approach to the development of metacognition in dismissing patients is specifically indicated, whereby the clinician targets the specific metacognitive skills that are deficient. Dismissing patients are generally poor in metacognitive identification of internal states. Simple anchoring scales can be used to enhance the patient's capacity to estimate the degree of awareness of his or her state of mind. For example:

> On a 1 to 10 scale, with 1 meaning *completely unaware*, and 10 meaning *completely aware*, and the other numbers a level of awareness somewhere in between, give a number that indicates the degree you are or are not aware of your specific inner state at this moment.

Use of such scales at the beginning of treatment can show dismissing patients just how much their internal state of mind remains outside their awareness, which can support making exploration of states of mind and the development of metacognitive identification a primary treatment goal. Patients with dismissing attachment remain out of touch with a wide range of negative and positive affects, and there is resistance to accessing such affects, especially in relation to attachment experience. Thus, the dismissing patient is consistently encouraged to look beyond surface-level experience to deeper levels of underlying affects, vulnera-bilities, memories, and maladaptive schemas related to attachment themes. When a patient notices an affect or other state that may be resisted, an affect dial tech-nique can be used (D. P. Brown & Fromm, 1986) to promote staying with that state: The patient puts attention on the state just as it is, and then imagines having a dial that allows him or her to raise the intensity of the state so that it becomes more salient and intense, yet within a tolerable range. Over time, dismissing patients learn to immediately identify the specificity of a given experienced emotion as well as to experience it fully in its intensity.

Experiential focusing (Gendlin, 1982), recommended above for helping dis-missing patients become aware of states of mind associated with nonverbal non-collaborative communication, is also useful for the dismissing patient to develop metacognitive identification in general, because it leads the patient to develop holistic awareness of immediate experience and to have a *felt sense* of how that experience is held in the body. The patient is encouraged to allow images and thoughts and words to come to mind that are the best fit for the felt bodily sense. Through the systematic steps of experiential focusing, the dismissing patient learns to identify, accurately understand, and verbally express immediate, ongo-ing emotions in the context of the attachment relationship.

Proponents of mentalization-based treatment (MBT; e.g., Bateman & Fon-agy, 2004) emphasize the importance of using *marked affectivity* and *contingent responsiveness* in their attempts to develop reflective capacity in patients with personality disorders. Marked affectivity entails mirroring the patient's affect using a verbal intensifier and locating the affect as a central experience of self (e.g., "*You* must have felt *really* scared"). We agree that affective marking is an important metacognitive technique in general and add that it is particularly important to use marked affectivity with dismissing patients, precisely because they remain remote or distant from their emotions. Furthermore, when a dismiss-ing patient engaging with IPF imagery experiences a parent figure being sooth-ing, the therapist brings attention to the immediate contingent response: "Notice the effect this has on your state of mind." This suggestion has two benefits: (1) It encourages metacognitive identification of state of mind, and (2) it fosters aware-ness of contingent responsiveness, as the patient comes to discover that the way he or she imagines the IPFs actually affects his or her state of mind. Equally important, the dismissing patient is encouraged to imagine various ways that he or she *directly* and *contingently* affects the ideal parents' responses. For example, the patient is asked to imagine various ways the child is able to elicit exactly the response he or she needs from the IPFs, and then to reflect on how the elicited response directly affects his or her state of mind:

Notice how you can be with these parents in ways that bring to you *exactly* the response that you want and need from them. And notice how that affects your inner state, your feelings and thoughts, when they respond to you in that way.

Since dismissing patients generally have very poor awareness of contingency effects, it is also important to foster metacognitive *awareness of context*. The dismissing patient is encouraged to take a wider perspective—for example, to reflect on how contextual factors, such as life circumstances or history, might have contributed to a parent's rejection of attachment behavior or discomfort with physical contact or affection. The patient is also encouraged to recognize and explore the very specific ways that early parental rejection has affected the patient, including the negative impact on development and relationships. The dismissing patients who develop the strongest metacognitive awareness of contextual factors also develop rueful recognition of negative ways they have become like their parents.

Later in treatment, dismissing patients are encouraged to *take an even wider perspective* of themselves and their lives in order to articulate a central guiding purpose or ultimate concern (Emmons, 1999). Introducing this post-formal metacognitive theme is likely to infuse life with a renewed purpose, and also to create a novel experience of interdependence and interconnectedness in a patient who had previously deactivated the attachment system.

Stages in the Treatment of the Dismissing Patient

1. Initially, the therapist introduces the concept of cooperative behavior as an indirect way to work on reactivation of the attachment system.

2. Most of the early therapeutic work entails the systematic use of IPF imagery and addressing nonverbal and verbal misattunements by encouraging metacognitive awareness at the moment the misattunements occur.

3. Through a consistent focus on these themes, the dismissing patient will eventually reactivate the attachment system. The main sign of reactivation is the patient's experience of *longing* for relationship connection. AAI evidence comparing Ds1 to Ds3 dismissing adults suggests that at least for those classified as Ds3, attachment is valued, longed for, and yet a source of conflict. Similarly, Waldinger et al. (2003) found that adults with dismissing attachment in psychotherapy nevertheless retain a wish for closeness. Based on this evidence, we assume that even the most dismissing patients long for physical and emotional closeness, no matter the degree of defense against it. The longing will inevitably reappear in successful treatment.

When it does, the dismissing patient is likely to become distressed and severely conflicted by the reawakened longing, which is typically accompanied by anxiety, sadness, shame, and vulnerability. J. G. Allen (2013) suggests that "movement from avoidant or fearful to secure attachment entails a pathway through ambivalence, given that avoidance stems from painful prior attachment experiences and that moving closer inevitably provokes anxiety" (p. 14). With the emergence of this highly uncomfortable attachment-related affect, patients who have histories of addictive behavior are at risk of relapse, and all dismissing patients are at risk of problematic emotion-regulation behaviors. The therapy itself is made vulnerable, as the patient will likely see the emergence of discomfort and vulnerability as directly related to the therapy (which of course it is). It is vitally important that the therapist *normalize the longing* and explain to the dismissing patient that this longing is expected and is natural, is normal, and is something deeply positive in that it serves as the basis of human connection. We operate from the assumption that the attachment behavioral system, and the longing that emerges from it, is normal and adaptive, and that its deactivation is unnatural and problematic. Strategic introduction of *normalizing interventions* is designed as a remedy for the profound toxic shame that dismissing patients associate with the most basic longings for physical and emotional closeness. In addition to this normalizing therapeutic stance, IPF imagery focuses on the parent figures responding to the child's longing and discomfort about it in accepting, soothing ways, communicating that longing for physical and emotional closeness is the most natural thing in the world, even if uncomfortable at first.

4. Other clear signs of reactivation of the attachment system pertain to aspects of the therapy and therapist. In the IPF protocol, they include nonconflicted reports of physical and emotional proximity- and contact-seeking between the child and IPFs; an expressed preference for using the IPF imagery; spontaneous comments about preferring to be in the therapist's presence; and the emergence of healthy protest behavior (often still accompanied by shame) at the therapist's unavailability. At this stage, *therapeutic ruptures* are likely to occur, because until this point the patient had not valued the attachment relationship with the therapist because of the deactivated attachment system. The best strategy for understanding, responding to, and repairing the rupture is to enlist the collaborative behavioral system that the patient and therapist have co-created (Liotti, 2005). Collaborative metacognitive inquiry into both patient and therapist states of mind associated with the treatment rupture is also beneficial.

5. At the middle to late stages of treatment, the dismissing patient is capable of directly using the therapist as a secure base and has acquired the ability to directly acknowledge his or her healthy dependence on the therapist as a basis for exploration. The main focus of exploration at this point continues to be on attachment themes, but not those of early childhood attachment. Instead, the focus becomes exploration of *secure intimacy*. The dismissing patient is asked to imag-

ine hypothetical, romantic partners that meet the conditions of secure intimacy. Representations of an ideal intimate partner repeat many of the main themes from the IPF imagery: safety and protection; responsiveness to seeking emotional and physical closeness; providing a secure base for exploration; safe haven; contingent responsiveness to expressed needs; and providing comfort, soothing, expressed delight, and encouragement of self-development within the context of intimacy. The overall goal of using ideal partner imagery is for the dismissing patient to develop a stable, positive map for adult secure intimacy that will guide current and future relationships. This method is further detailed in Appendix B.

Case Illustration

The following case vignette illustrates treatment of an adult patient with dismissing attachment. The patient was a successful businessman in his early 50s. He had a long-standing dismissing attachment style, and on the AAI he received a primary classification of Ds3 (dismissing with a valuing of but conflict about attachment). His relational history reflected his dismissing attachment pattern. He married in his early 20s after just a short-term relationship because he believed that was what he wanted. He remained remote from his feelings in the relationship, especially after the birth of his child. He separated and divorced shortly thereafter. Soon after the divorce, he came out as gay; however, over the next few decades he never had an intimate gay relationship. All of his relationships consisted of hiring gay escorts, and, rather than having sex, he paid them to physically hold and cuddle him for hours at a time.

He originally came to treatment for being overweight. He was treated for his weight problem during one year of hypnotherapy. Focus on the weight issue revealed chronic low self-esteem, even though he had become enormously successful and prosperous in his business. Enhancing self-esteem became a consistent focus of the treatment. Enhancing metacognitive awareness of and mastery over states of mind antecedent to binge eating was also a consistent focus of treatment. After approximately a year of treatment, he had lost considerable weight and was maintaining the weight loss. He was also able to sustain a positive feeling about himself most of the day, nearly every day, so that the chronic low self-esteem issues were largely resolved. Toward the end of treatment, the therapist introduced the possibility of addressing the absence of close relationships, but he terminated treatment shortly after the topic was introduced. He returned to treatment after two years had elapsed because he had regained the weight and had developed type 2 diabetes. His physician had encouraged him to resume treatment to regain control of his eating habits and to lose weight.

The first part of the following verbatim transcript is from the second session of the second treatment, after ideal parent figure (IPF) imagery was introduced to the patient. The first session consisted of a treatment intake focused on eating behaviors, weight gain, and diabetes, and then the rest of the session was an introduction to the IPF method. At the end of that session, IPF imagery was introduced with the foundational focus on "the way these ideal parents are *being* with the child that leads to a sense of feeling *absolutely secure* in the attachment relationship." The patient opened the second session with a five-minute report of his patterns of emotional eating. Very much in the style of an independent, autonomous strong self, he told the therapist that he tried to use the IPF imagery on his own during the week. The following transcript picks up from that point. It is important to note that this patient manifests much higher metacognitive skills than the typical dismissing patient, largely because the development of metacognitive identification and mastery was a consistent focus of the first year-long treatment. We have labeled the transcript to identify for the reader the main characteristics of dismissing attachment and the main interventions used. Verbatim patient expressions are in normal text, as are verbatim therapist statements, and post hoc observations and explanation about the therapist's interventions are italicized in brackets.

> *Therapist:* When you feel the need to emotionally eat, you use the ideal parent figures to comfort you? But earlier you talked about some discomfort about that. What about that? *[Fostering metacognitive identification of state of mind]*
>
> *Patient:* That's a good question . . . I . . . that happens I think only . . . here . . . that's interesting . . . *[Patient shows metacognitive awareness of deactivating attachment within but not outside of treatment relationship, in a collaborative context.]* When I'm utilizing the technique to calm myself at home, I don't think I feel this way . . . but here um . . . every time I don't like it . . . I don't know why that is . . . *[Metacognitive limits of knowledge]* . . . I'm feeling that right now. (Laughs uncomfortably.) *[Metacognitive awareness of the process between patient and therapist]*
>
> *Therapist:* What happens? What are you feeling right now? *[Fostering metacognitive identification of state of mind]*
>
> *Patient:* Just stay away from me . . . don't touch me . . . don't focus on me . . . it's so unnatural that I don't trust it *[Metacognitive awareness of approach/avoidance conflict regarding contact-seeking]*, and the emotion I now observe is actual anger . . . um . . .
>
> *Therapist:* So if I didn't stay away, then what would happen? If I were too close, then . . . ?
>
> *Patient:* It just gets unbearably uncomfortable *[Fostering metacognitive awareness of underlying vulnerability regarding attachment]* . . . It's not pain but it is just very uncomfortable and . . . It's like I don't believe it, like maybe you're being patronizing . . . like maybe it just doesn't ring true *[Fostering metacognitive awareness of attachment as source of fear rather*

than comfort] . . . and it makes me see how much more comfortable I feel just being ignored and unseen . . . What just popped in my head *[Metacognitive monitoring of immediate state of mind]* . . . is a recurring dream that I have had all my life . . . being in a crowd inappropriately undressed or naked and trying to be not noticed . . . It's that sense of . . . and somehow the isolating of myself is tied up with that.

Therapist: Yes.

Patient: . . . that stands to reason, I guess.

Therapist: But you say there is something deeply uncomfortable about being seen, having somebody be interested in you or be there for you . . . it is not a positive thing for you. *[Therapist identifies treatment objective of attachment as something positive.]*

Patient: As you say it, I just really . . . I don't like it . . . I'm not sure but . . .

Therapist: Can you ever imagine a quality of the way these ideal parents we are talking about could *be* with you that would make you *prefer* being with them and feel comfortable with it? *[Therapist introduces proximity-seeking as a positive goal]* That you would actually *want* that?

Patient: It is so funny, but I never realized it *[Metacognitive limitations of knowledge]*, but it is when you talk here that I get uncomfortable and tense, but I have to notice that I also do it in response to the food *[Metacognitive relationship between variables]* I don't think I get that any place else . . . I sort of want you to stop talking . . . I just had a thought that my father used to . . . he'd put his hand on my face and it would feel good . . . and comforting . . . and then when I relaxed he'd go like this and quickly push my face away, and it was jarring and the message was, "You've got to be tough." *[Patient shows good metacognitive monitoring of immediate state of mind so as to report a spontaneous memory. This is a good sign for a dismissing patient with lack of memory.]* I don't know . . .

Therapist: Just when you thought you could relax, huh?

Patient: Right, and I just can't trust that . . .

Therapist: So let's continue with the imagery. You can imagine settling into just the right state, skillfully and quickly, in a way that is familiar to you . . . Focus on slowing down your breathing . . . settling into just the right state . . . *[Introduction of IPF imagery around the theme of proximity-seeking]* Once again, let's imagine that you didn't grow up in the family of origin that you are used to. You can imagine that you grew up in a different family with a set of parents *ideally suited* to *you* and *your* nature . . . and you can imagine a scene as a young child with these parents . . . and you can imagine that you *wanted* to be around them and that you *preferred* it and felt more comfortable being close to them than being by yourself . . . and in this scene you'll see the quality of exactly how they are *being* with you that would have made it so you felt *comfortable* with *being close* to them . . . more comfortable than being alone by your-self . . . imagine now the quality of how they could have been with you that would have made you *want* that.

Patient: I'm waiting . . . It's hard to picture myself . . . *[Patient tries to be cooperative by imaging a positive scene]* waiting for them in front of a building . . . or for them to come down . . . and I want to do this, but it is so hard to feel it. *[Patient shows metacognitive awareness of absence of emotion]* Uh . . . and they come down and we start playing . . . I'm looking for them and all of a sudden we start playing . . . something like hide-and-go-seek . . . no peek-a-boo . . . *[It is no accident that patient imagines a scene about the constancy of contact-seeking]* They hide behind something . . . it's just a game . . . *[Metacognitive awareness of remoteness from feelings]* um . . . and I know what I want to do but it is so hard to do . . .

Therapist: Allow yourself to imagine it in the best way you can . . . the scene is about the qualities and ways they are *being* with you that would make you want that closeness and not feel uncomfortable with it. What about that?

Patient: Well . . . they are playing a game . . . the key is they are doing something I don't usually do . . . they make me laugh . . . *[Patient is aware of being surprised by positive emotion associated with an attachment relationship]*

Therapist: Elaborate on just the ways they are being with you that makes you *want* that closeness without discomfort. What about that? *[Patient is encouraged to explore the theme of positive proximity-seeking]*

Patient: Um . . . I sort of shifted it to . . . I shifted it to how absent that was. *[This is the earliest sign of the activation of longing]*

Therapist: I know that, but now, go ahead and imagine it as if it is present and they are being with you in a way that makes it nonthreatening . . . that you actually *want* it. *[Fostering positive imagery of proximity-seeking]* On some level you do know exactly what that would be like, so just let yourself imagine it.

Patient: What happens is that my mind shifts to my daughter and how she treats her kids . . .

Therapist: So take that as a model, and then imagine these parent fig-ures treating you in a similar way that your daughter treats her child, in whatever way that would make you want that closeness. *[Therapist allows patient to continue exploration of positive proximity-seeking in a less direct manner]*

Patient: I think I know what I want . . . just being the center of attention, playing games . . . child's games and laughing *[Patient exhibits coopera-tive behavior in complying with shared goal of generating a positive scene around proximity-seeking]* . . . which is hard for me to imagine other than sort of as an observer . . . can't get into that, uh . . .

Therapist: So let's start with how your daughter is with her kids if that helps. What is the quality of how she is being with them that helps them to prefer the closeness with her and not be threatened by it?

Patient: I think it's because they are important . . . she makes them laugh . . . I picture them laughing, um . . . I can't picture myself *[Patient shows metacognitive awareness of limitations of imagery and resistance to attachment]* . . . I picture her daughter . . . just reading books . . . her daughter is snuggling up to her and feeling safe . . . important . . . valued . . . *[This is an important point. The patient succeeds in the collaborative task of generating an attachment scene wherein he is important and matters, and is happy in the attachment relationship, although only indirectly through the metaphor of the daughter.]*

Therapist: I'd like you to change the scene and imagine something like that for yourself . . . some quality of being with them that would make you *prefer*, not be threatened by, the relationship with these parents, so that you could *really feel close* to them . . . Imagine it in whatever way seems right to you . . . *[IPF imagery around the theme of emotional closeness]*

Patient: Uh . . . laughter is too hard . . .

Therapist: Imagine it is whatever way seems right to you.

Patient: Um . . . doing a—you know what those things are called? A puzzle where you make the objects fit together and I am doing that with somebody. *[In true dismissing style the patient switches to an instrumental task rather than emotional closeness between child and attachment figure]*

Therapist: And notice how they are being with you.

Patient: . . . and they are not somebody who would just let me struggle with it, uh *[Patient spontaneously introduces idea of positive parental responsiveness]* . . . and when I make something fit, they are happy. *[Attunement]* It is very unhurried . . . *[Spontaneous comment about what, over time, will become a secure base]*

Therapist: The scene will change, and in the next scene you will learn something more about preferring the closeness without being threatened by it . . . notice how they are *being* with you in this next scene. *[Continued collaborative exploration of positive proximity-seeking]*

Patient: . . . it is in the park . . . and I'm there . . . there are just the three of us and we are playing . . . again hiding behind a tree kind-of-thing, and they are trying to find me.

Therapist: And what about the quality of how they are being with you that helps you *want* the closeness with them . . . anything else about that?

Patient: I try to envision them finding me and just enveloping me in their arms . . . being happy and silly *[Patient collaboratively generating IPF imagery that is the positive opposite of rejection]* . . . It's so hard . . .

Therapist: Yes, but when they hold you in their arms, they don't pull away abruptly like your father did . . . so you can come to count on that closeness as something you expect. *[Therapist introduces concept of positive expectancy about responsiveness of IPFs]*

So now I am going to ask you to awaken as I count from five to one . . . beginning to awaken now . . . five, four, three, two, one . . .

Patient: It is so amazing.

Therapist: How is that?

Patient: The impact of what you want me to do . . . it should be so simple . . . the impact that parents have on little kids! In addition to the crazy things, they just really didn't pay attention.

Therapist: Yes.

Patient: They just didn't . . . *[Patient shows metacognitive awareness of unresponsiveness of family-of-origin parents in contrast to responsive IPFs]*

Therapist: How do you feel?

Patient: Drained . . .

Therapist: Say more?

Patient: It is just exhausting doing this . . . know where I want to get, but it is just a struggle . . . but I know it is right on because my reaction is so intense . . . *[Patient shows metacognitive awareness of attachment approach/avoidance struggle]*

Therapist: Okay, we'll have to stop here for today and continue next time.

In the subsequent session (the third), the patient spent the first seven minutes complaining that he had "not been smart" during a business meeting because he had done something very uncharacteristic for him—he had shown his feelings and feared that it might have jeopardized the whole business negotiation. Here is the rest of the session:

Patient: I'm literally gaining weight . . . I'm eating too much at meal times and I've got to really try to stop today.

Therapist: What about slowing down the eating and being more mindful of eating?

Patient: I do. I slow down and I find that I am eating . . . and I'm not eating all day long the way I used to . . .

Therapist: But when you slow down eating a meal, even though you're not eating between meals . . . what happens? You still don't feel full?

Patient: It is just that I so enjoy sitting there and reading . . . it just continuing . . . I'm full . . . it has nothing to do with the hunger.

Therapist: Sitting there and reading?

Patient: Yeah, sitting there and reading the newspaper.

Therapist: Are you sort of eating mindlessly at that point . . . just sort of eating and reading? You could sit there and read without eating? *[Fostering metacognitive awareness of state of mind]*

Patient: Yes . . . that's part of it . . . I realize you shouldn't read while you eat but it's so . . . such a nice time for me . . . and then when I linger I tend to keep eating . . . I just gotta stop . . . I eat slow . . . I'm doing everything right except that I linger too long and I'm just eating too much . . .

Therapist: What would you say your state of mind is like when you're sitting there reading and eating? *[Fostering metacognitive awareness of state of mind]*

Patient: Blissful.

Therapist: Blissful?

Patient: Yeah . . .

Therapist: Say more? *[Fostering exploration of state of mind in a collaborative relationship]*

Patient: I'm by myself . . . I'm reading which I enjoy . . . um . . . I like the eating . . . there's something like an entitlement . . . with all my eating . . . somehow I make it that I'm taking care of myself emotionally *[Patient shows metacognitive awareness of relating variables in that he makes a connection between lingering and filling the void of attachment needs]* . . . I can't quite describe it but . . . I can't go back and remember why but its seems to be like being let out of jail and having all this freedom . . . there is something about being able to eat and eat a lot . . . different foods and what I want to . . . [Patient shows metacognitive awareness that deactivation of attachment is freedom from rejecting, and compensates with the illusion of self-sufficiency]*

Therapist: And there is something about being by yourself and happy?

Patient: Oh, yeah . . .

Therapist: And that contrasts to what you have been saying about the discomfort of connection?

Patient: Um, huh . . . I was talking to a friend . . . he was over last night . . . so he was over, and I was talking about what I was doing here in therapy and he said something interesting I thought . . . he said why not fantasize or imagine being held or um . . . not in childhood but today? I said to him, "Maybe it's important to go back, but I really hate it" . . . which makes me think that there is something, you know, really important.

Therapist: (Laughs.)

Patient: . . but I just don't like the feeling . . . the idea of somebody being tender and supportive or loving to me . . . that's something that has never happened to me in my life and I've never allowed it because I don't like it here in my life either *[Patient shows good metacognitive awareness of deactivation of attachment]* . . . but I think I just wonder if it would be easier for me to imagine that?

Therapist: What do you think?

Patient: I think maybe . . . but what I don't know is . . . what makes me wonder about this whole thing is how strongly . . . how much I dislike what we do here. *[Patient has developed a strong exploratory attitude in the context of a collaborative treatment relationship]*

Therapist: And yet you say that when you do it on your own, you say you feel better?

Patient: Yeah . . . it hasn't been that often because . . . I don't know why but I haven't had this urge. I go to binge eat . . . it's happened a few times . . . and most often when my blood sugars are low . . . and even then before I realize what's happening and I think it does help . . . *[Patient shows meta-cognitive awareness of relating variables, in that he discovers a connection between binge eating and longing for connection]*

Therapist: Do you think you could imagine a scene involving tenderness and support and loving that you could allow . . . is there a way that you could imagine it, that you could allow? *[Therapist introduces positive IPF imagery around theme of emotional closeness]*

Patient: Like at my current age? *[Illustration of collaborate inquiry on part of patient]*

Therapist: Whatever?

Patient: No (laughs), I don't want to try . . . It is so amazing about how I don't like it.

Therapist: Even if I say you can imagine it in any form that you can? Are there any conditions under which you could allow this?

Patient: No . . .

Therapist: Let's see what the conditions might be under which you could allow this? So go ahead and imagine just the right conditions under which you could allow that loving connection . . . that tenderness. *[Therapist gives the patient some distance. Rather than imagining emotional closeness, which is too difficult, the therapist asks the patient to imagine the conditions under which he might be able to imagine such closeness.]*

Patient: I'm feeling it [the discomfort] already . . . It is so amazing how deep this is . . . um . . . it's so hard . . . *[Metacognitive awareness of limitations of knowing]*

Therapist: Go ahead and try to imagine . . . put yourself in just the right state and imagine it in whatever way you can allow yourself . . . settling into just the right state now . . . there . . . calm and relaxed . . . and even in the face or your discomfort you can find some sense of *calmness* and *comfort* . . . imagine *just the right* conditions under which you could allow yourself to feel a supportive, tender, loving connection . . . whatever conditions would be comfortable enough for you that you could allow yourself to imagine . . . and as you are able to imagine that, describe how it is that you've imagined it?

Patient: I try to imagine just walking down the street with somebody feeling comfortable at ease on a city street . . . then I try to picture being in bed, sort of cuddling, but I don't feel either one . . .

Therapist: So now switch to imagining yourself as a young boy with a set of parents, each of whom is *ideally* suited to you . . . and imagine the connection that way, and contrast that scene to the one you just imagined walking down the street, cuddling as an adult and see the difference in the feeling quality? Imagine being with them in a way that you feel *very secure* in the relationship with them. *[Here the therapist introduces the ideal parent figure imagery around the theme of physical proximity-seeking]*

Patient: The ideal parents . . . they are making me laugh . . which is sort of foreign to me . . . just being. *[This is important. The patient concedes that "just being" in physical and emotional proximity to the IPFs is associated with positive emotion.]*

Therapist: Directly observing your own state of mind . . . which form of this—the ideal parents or as an adult—in which form of this visualization do you feel more secure in the connection?

Patient: I think the child.

Therapist: Okay. Does that answer your question?

Patient: Yeah . . . interesting! *[Patient discovers that positive remapping of childhood IPF attachment works better than imagery of physical and emotional closeness in current relationships.]*

Therapist: So continue with that and see if you can really allow yourself . . . Imagine just the right conditions under which you could *fully* allow yourself to feel the depth of the connection in whatever way you can best imagine that.

Patient: . . . I'm on a big blanket or the bed or something . . . mother, father, and me . . . and just laughing. *[Patient is successful in imagining a positive scene of physical and emotional proximity-seeking with ideal responsiveness by IPFs]*

Therapist: Yes . . . there is a certain *delight* in being with each other . . . just being together . . . Allow yourself to *really take in* what that *really* feels like to *you [marking patient's affective experience]* . . . when just being together provides a certain delight . . . a certain joy . . . there is nothing you have to do . . . there is no way you have to be . . . *just being* with them is enough . . . and they with you . . . enjoying each other's being . . . and *what a relief* it is to be able to *just be* and have all that feel right inside . . . Imagine if you will . . . a kind of *blissfulness* in being together. *[Here the therapist uses the word "blissfulness," taken from the patient's own description of lingering with food, and applies it to the positive attachment relationship.]* And then contrast that and compare it to the blissfulness you feel in your current life as an adult sitting alone eating and reading . . . compare the feeling as you directly observe each.

Patient: The childhood version of the experience I envision as having no end . . . like we're together laughing and then it stops and no one moves . . . you just— *[Here the dismissing patient succeeds in generating IPF imagery of a positive, blissful attachment bond that is completely free of rejection]*

Therapist: Yes, just being together and enjoying each other's being is timeless.

Patient: When you said that . . . it is somehow that there is no end to it . . . it's getting dark . . . and no one moves . . . and then when I contrast it to the eating, first it felt not the same at all . . . but then I thought of how I enjoy lingering and I don't want to stop . . . to leave the table and stop eating . . . and there are times that I would go from one restaurant to another just to continue in that . . . it reminds me of . . . wanting to linger with these parents. *[Here the patient is showing the reactivation of a positive attachment system and the transfer of attachment from lingering with food back to the positive attachment imagery]*

Therapist: Allow yourself to stay with that . . . and really take in what that feels like . . . and there is something that can be very fulfilling about the connection with these parents . . . something deeply satisfying . . . like eating a good meal . . . only lasting. *[Therapist reinforces positive connections with IPFs over lingering with food]* What's that?

Patient: I think, um . . . it's hard to stay with it . . . I think I'm afraid it abruptly ends and it did as a child *[Here the patient is showing the reactivation of a positive attachment system and the transfer of attachment from lingering with food back to the positive attachment imagery]* . . . I sort of like that thought . . . um . . . *[Patient's comment opens the possibility that physical and emotional proximity- and contact-seeking might be a positive experience]*

Therapist: Stay with it . . . tell me how it is that you're imagining that?

Patient: It shifted to it being with somebody . . . I don't know who . . . just lying still . . . No one wants to break the. . . spell of the moment and it just feels good to linger *[Patient shows initial signs of reactivating the attachment system as a conflict-free approach]* . . . and I'm slowly walking back from the beach . . . I don't know if it's a male or a female . . . I think it's a man . . . there is no talking . . .

Therapist: You can feel the physical and emotional connection to them . . .

Patient: Tangibly. It's not bad . . . not bad . . .

Therapist: So make a deep impression of what that feels like . . . I'm going to count from five to one, and as I do, slowly you can awaken . . . you can make the transition gently and not abruptly. Five—beginning to awaken—four, three, two, one, fully awake.

What was that like?

Patient: Not bad, um . . . somewhere I was thinking, "What's going on here?" I can never feel . . . the notion of staying in the moment and *just being* with someone . . . it has just not been an option.

Therapist: So that opens up the possibility of experiencing something quite new. *[Patient shows signs of reactivating the attachment system and experiencing the representation of immediate physical and emotional proximity with the IPF as deeply positive and conflict-free]*

This case illustration shows some of the main features of treating a patient with dismissing attachment. The therapist takes a stance of persistent active engagement, over and against the patient's protests and attempts to deactivate attachment behavior in the treatment. The main approach was imagery of ideal parent figures who are consistently responsive to the patient-as-child. When the patient was most dismissing, the therapist appealed to joint collaboration toward the therapeutic goals and fostered metacognitive identification in the patient of the various ways he was uncomfortable with attachment closeness. Combining an active stance of engagement with the three pillars of attachment-based treatment led to a number of observable changes in only two sessions. This patient showed some recognition and experience that attachment longings are not necessarily a source of threat and shame, but rather can be a source of security and satisfaction. Through the IPF imagery, this patient began developing a new, positive internal working model that included comfort with and preference for physical closeness; increased comfort in being deeply seen and known; increased comfort with soft, gentle emotions within himself; and comfort with and preference for spontaneous, playful exploration in the context of secure attachment. These sessions illustrate early signs of "normalization" of attachment longings. The patient summarized these positive changes in his IWM of attachment as "lingering with the blissfulness of being together" and showed some early signs of shifting toward finding this blissful lingering in the context of an attachment relationship instead of in his relationship with eating behaviors.

CHAPTER 12

Treating Anxious-Preoccupied Attachment

This chapter addresses how to tailor the three pillars of treatment according to the specific developmental experiences and resulting attachment needs of patients with anxious-preoccupied attachment.

The Origins of Anxious-Preoccupied Attachment

According to Ainsworth, Blehar, Waters, and Wall (1978), the origins of anxious-preoccupied attachment are in various forms of *maternal unresponsiveness*. Ainsworth and her colleagues found that mothers of ambivalent/resistant infants were unpredictable and inconsistent, that they tended to be less responsive to the infant's crying and signals of distress, and that their timing of responsiveness to the infant was often poor. When observed in their homes, mothers of ambivalent/resistant infants often only partially attended to their infants because of frequent multi-tasking, such as doing routine activities while simultaneously holding the infant. Similarly, Belsky (1999b) found that mothers of ambivalent/resistant infants were unresponsive and underinvolved. Mikulincer, Shaver, and Pereg (2003) and Shaver and Mikulincer (2009) report that inconsistent responsiveness was an important contributing factor to the development of anxious preoccupation.

Haft and Slade (1989) found that anxious-preoccupied mothers showed a "variable response pattern" to their infants (p. 170). Furthermore, they found that such caregivers showed a pattern of pervasive misattunement to intersubjective negative and positive affective displays that was far greater than did secure or dismissing mothers (p. 167). They also found a specific pattern of "selective misattunements," particularly to the infant's exploratory initiatives and expressions of exuberance in exploratory free play. "They either totally ignored these kinds of expressions . . . or misattuned to them" (p. 167). However, these caregivers "often seemed attracted to expressions of fear in their babies. One subject, unresponsive to her baby's expressions of negativity or initiative, had her moments of greatest attunement during reunion when the baby was frightened" (p. 167). Haft and Slade suggest that:

> When a mother selectively attunes to a particular kind of emotion in the baby. . . . the baby learns not only that this state holds special status for the mother, but perhaps that recreating it is one of the few ways the infant has available for achieving intersubjective union with his or her mother. (p. 169).

The authors observed that the anxious-preoccupied mothers were often anxious in the context of their caregiving and tended to spill their own uncertainties and anxieties onto their infants. They state, "These mothers tended to become anxious at their own inability to understand their babies' persistent requests for definition" (p. 167).

According to Main and Weston (1981), the origin of ambivalent/resistant attachment in the child and anxious-preoccupied attachment in the adult is a caregiver who, on a regular basis, allows the child to become *overinvolved in the caregiver's state of mind*. In healthy, balanced parenting, the caregiver remains carefully attuned and responsive to the child's state of mind; regulates the child's emotional state through soothing, reassuring responses; and encourages the child's self-development through the medium of exploratory free play. An over-involving style of parenting reverses this pattern. The involving parent is insufficiently attuned to the child's state of mind and instead engages the child in her or his own state of mind. As a result, the child learns to become hypervigilant to the parent's state of mind. The involving parent misses much of the child's affect experience and so does not provide contingent soothing when the child is upset, which interferes with the child's development of emotion regulation. Without externally provided soothing or sufficient internal affect regulation, the ambivalent/resistant child is chronically anxious and/or angry. Additionally, the caregiver's repetitive lack of attunement to the child's state of mind and the child's learned hypervigilance to the caregiver's state of mind both interfere with the child's exploratory play, which impedes both self-development and metacognitive development, leaving the anxious-preoccupied adult with poor self-development, impaired reflective capacity, and a vulnerability to chronic high levels of anxiety and/or anger.

The Therapeutic Stance With the Anxious-Preoccupied Patient

The consistent stance taken by the therapist with an adult anxious-preoccupied patient is the positive opposite of those factors that contributed to the development of the ambivalent/resistant child. First, since the caregiver was consistently overly involving of the child in his or her state of mind, a fundamental and crucial component of the therapeutic stance is *consistent focus on the preoccupied patient's own state of mind and self-experience*. From the very beginning of treatment, the anxious-preoccupied adult is likely to manifest persistent hypervigilance regarding the therapist's state of mind, which includes the therapist's facial and other nonverbal displays, the therapist's emotions, and the therapist's expectations about how the patient should be in the treatment. The patient will persistently look for cues to discern what is expected, as with an overly learned acquiescent style he or she will want to give the therapist whatever he or she assumes the therapist might expect. We refer to this persistent hypervigilance as an *outside-in orientation*, whereby the patient privileges perceived outside information for determining responses. The therapeutically corrective stance toward patients with persistent outside-in orientation is to make it explicit to the patient that what the therapist expects is for both patient and therapist to adopt a shared goal of an *inside-out orientation*. In other words, this goal is defined as both the patient and therapist consistently privileging and attending to *the patient's* internal self-experience—thoughts, feelings, memories, assumptions, wants, needs, and schemas—and reducing the repeated outside-in orientation of focusing on the therapist's state of mind. This stance utilizes the patient's initial orientation toward the therapist's state of mind to *reverse it* and turn the orientation back to the patient's own internal state of mind. Tacitly the therapist communicates, "You keep looking to me to see what I expect, so what I expect is that we both keep looking to you and your state of mind." In this manner, the therapist and patient collaborate with the joint task of turning the focus away from the state of mind of the other (therapist) to the state of mind of the self (patient). This basic therapeutic stance sets the ground for the patient to develop and stabilize an inside-out orientation as the medium for exploration of his or her own states of mind throughout the therapy.

Second, given this therapeutic stance of promoting an inside-out orientation, the therapist must be *consistently attuned and responsive* to the moment-by-moment shifting affective states within the patient—what Stern (1985) and Fosha (D. Fosha, personal communication with D. Brown, April 4, 2008) have termed the *vitality affects*. The therapist's tracking of the patient's subtle shifts of state in the context of the dyadic relationship provides the patient with the experience of careful, consistent attunement, in contrast to the pervasive misattunement that preoccupied patients learned to expect. Additionally, since mothers of ambivalent/resistant children in the home environment were often found distracted with other tasks concurrent with attending to their children, it is especially important that therapists remain fully present, moment to moment, with these adult patients. In this regard, therapists who take notes during sessions are multi-tasking, which potentially repeats and reinforces the patient's experience of misattunement.

Since anxious-preoccupied patients so readily get caught up in the state of mind of the other, the therapist must be especially cautious about self-disclosure. Considering that most forms of therapist self-disclosure draw the preoccupied patient into the orbit of the therapist's state of mind, self-disclosure may reactivate the patient's hyperactivating style within the transference. Limited self-disclosure may be indicated and beneficial during ruptures of the therapeutic alliance, but only if the therapist's self-disclosure specifically serves to orient the patient more carefully toward his or her own state of mind. For example, in response to a patient's angry accusation that the therapist seems distracted and is not interested in what she is saying, the therapist might respond:

> You know, you're right that I was a little distracted just then. But I want to be very clear that it's not at all because I'm not interested in you. On the contrary, when you were talking about your interaction with your daughter, I started thinking about what you'd said a while back about a similar experience you had with your mother. And I get that as I was thinking about that it probably seemed that I was going away from you. I'm sorry about that, and I really am right with you in what we're talking about. Let's work together on this. What's it like for you now, hearing what I just said?

Third, since research suggests that caregivers of children who have become anxious-preoccupied adults may have selectively overly attuned to their children's fear states and often spilled out their own fears and worries onto their children, it is particularly important that the therapist not selectively attune to and emphasize the patient's fear states, and that he or she also limit self-disclosure regarding his or her own concerns or worries. Instead, a therapeutically corrective stance for the preoccupied patient is for the therapist to become a *consistently calming presence*. No matter how much the patient becomes entangled in a preoccupied state of mind, the therapist remains unflappable and calm and provides comfort and reassurance that everything is all right. This aspect of the therapeutic stance is parallel to how a parent best responds to the child who wakes up from a bad nightmare and is still somewhat in the nightmare state: The parent holds and physically comforts the child (protection, soothing), verbally reassures the child that everything is all right (reassurance) and that it was just a dream (support for metacognitive appearance–reality distinction), and adopts an inside-out orientation—focusing on the child's immediate inner experience—with the addition of providing comfort to calm the fear.

Fourth, since preoccupied patients show hyperactivation of attachment behavior in the face of any perceived or anticipated abandonment threat, the therapist repeatedly focuses on *closeness–distance regulation*. One way of working with the patient's pattern and experience of difficulty with closeness and distance regulation is to use imagery of a *safe, protective bubble*:

Now imagine yourself comfortably inside a *clear*, *safe*, protective bubble. This bubble is here, in the room with us, and it's floating in a way that *feels easy and safe* for you to be inside . . . you can make the size of the bubble *just right*, so that it's not so big that you feel lost in it, and it's not so small that you feel cramped in it . . . go ahead and make it *just the right size* for you now . . . When it feels just right, you can experiment with moving the bubble around in the room . . . a little higher . . . a little lower . . . off to one side . . . off to the other . . . a little closer to me . . . a little farther from me . . . however you want to move it. And as you move the bubble, notice what effect it has on your state of mind . . . notice what *you feel inside* as you're a little closer to me, and notice what you feel inside as you move a little farther from me.

This method is beneficial to use initially in the context of hyperactivation of the patient's attachment system. During periods of such hyperactivation, the therapist and patient collaboratively explore how close the patient in the protective bubble needs to be, and they also explore how much distance can be tolerated. The bubble imagery helps patients to discover that with any anticipated abandonment threat, they tend to move the protective bubble closer towards merger with the therapist, and when they are not experiencing threat and are in exploratory mode, they are comfortable moving the bubble farther away from the therapist. The bubble metaphor and method conveys to preoccupied patients a novel idea—that over time, they can learn voluntary control over closeness–distance regulation and particularly over the corresponding emotions.

Fifth, since research suggests that caregivers of ambivalent children selectively misattune to and do not reinforce their children's free exploratory behavior, a dimension of the therapeutic stance is the therapist's *selective, purposeful attunement to the patient's exploratory behavior*, especially instances of patient *initiatives* in exploration and *exploration associated with self-development*. Whenever the patient makes a self-observation and/or expresses interest in something, the therapist mirrors that and encourages further focus: "*Yes*, isn't that interesting. As you reflect on that more, what do you notice? What else stands out to you?" The therapist can also introduce direct inquiry to prompt and reinforce self-exploration and development. For example: "Bring to mind a scene in which you are *most you*. The more you hold this sense of yourself, the more the qualities that you associate with being *most you* will come to mind. Stay with this and see what qualities you become aware of." Or, "Bring to mind some situation that brings out your *best self*." Or, "Bring to mind a scene wherein you f*eel really good about yourself*." These methods are further detailed in Appendix A. Repeated inquiry of this type over time encourages and reinforces self-exploration and fosters self-development in the anxious-preoccupied patient.

Working With Ideal Parent Figure Imagery With Anxious-Preoccupied Patients

Anxious-preoccupied patients, as compared to dismissing patients, generally find it easier to use IPF imagery when it is first introduced by the therapist, for several reasons: These patients are compliant with what the therapist suggests, and, because they usually have ongoing dissatisfactions with or preoccupations about family-of-origin parents, the prospect of imagining ideal parents often comes as a relief.

Nevertheless, introducing IPF imagery to the anxious- or angry-preoccupied patient is not without difficulties. Because such patients may be compulsive caretakers whose experience includes much self- and other-blame, the introduction of IPF imagery often invokes a deep experience of threat to loyalty to the parents of origin and a corresponding abandonment fear. The notion of replacing the actual parents with ideal parent figures and imagining a better experience than provided by the actual parents suggests to the patient a failure of the task of caretaking of the internalized family-of-origin parents, as if the internalized family-of-origin parents are still active and in need of caretaking in the patient's mind. The patient, in the moment, does not experientially realize the irrationality of this belief; in AAI terminology, this is a lapse in metacognitive monitoring of reasoning. In such instances, the therapist explains to the patient that memory, by definition, is limited to actual past experience with family-of-origin parents, but that imagination, by definition, creates new possibilities. The patient is reassured that his or her actual parents did the best they possibly could given their strengths and limitations, and that the opportunity to imagine different parents who can provide what the actual parents could not is meant as no disrespect to the parents of origin. The therapist welcomes the patient to include in the imagined, new, and different parents any positive qualities from his or her actual parents, and encourages him or her to use free imagination to add other positive qualities "that your actual parents would have had if they could." This modification usually reduces the resistance and allows the patient to begin with the IPF method. From there, he or she shapes and reshapes the qualities of the parent figures and the attachment relationship with them until "it *feels just right* in so many ways."

As in working with dismissing patients, there are two main context considerations in working with IPF imagery with anxious-preoccupied patients: (1) introducing IPF imagery themes consistent with what the research supports needs to be emphasized to positively remap IWMs of attachment and (2) tailoring the IPF imagery for the particular preoccupied patient. As the reader knows, we do not recommend predetermined scripts when working with any patient, but instead, from a foundation of general considerations and guidelines, we freshly and collaboratively co-create the IPF imagery in each session. With anxious-preoccupied patients, who have a propensity to use canned, jargon-like words and phrases on the AAI and in general discourse, such spontaneous creation cultivates and reinforces spontaneity in their lives in and out of the therapy.

Because research strongly suggests that early childhood caregivers of anxious-preoccupied patients were pervasively misattuned and unresponsive or inconsistently responsive, the ideal parent figures must be *pervasively attuned*—not only to the child's expressed behavior, but also exquisitely (but not intrusively) to the child's internal state of mind—and also accurately *contingently responsive*. Such IPFs continuously and carefully track the moment-by-moment vitality affects in the child, tracking even the subtlest of shifts at each moment. The creative process of the imagery allows for the possibility of very careful attunement each moment, in contrast to the pervasive misattunement to which these patients are familiar. From the foundation of this attunement, a consistent focus of the imagery is the IPFs being openly and accurately responsive to the child's states and also to his or her attachment initiatives and emotional expressions. Through this work, the patient-as-child consistently experiences his or her internal state being recognized, accepted, held in the mind of the parent figure, and responded to in appropriate and beneficial ways.

The IPF imagery is shaped in ways that address and remedy the patient's experience of early caregivers overly *involving* them in their states of mind. The therapist emphasizes that the ideal parent figures are so carefully attuned to the child's state of mind that the child can find deep relief in never having to worry about the parents' state of mind. For example:

> These parents are so interested in and attuned to *your inner state*, to *your* experience . . . They are able to set aside their own issues when they're with you, so that *you* and *your* experiences are the *focus* of their attention. When they're with you, they're with *you*. You never have to think about what's going on with them . . . because they can take care of that themselves.

From this emphasis, the child becomes able to relax any hypervigilance toward the parent figures' states and experiences being free from the burden of caretaking or trying to control the parent figures' responses. In essence, the patient-as-child is supported in being free to *just be* with his or her own state of mind and to discover and explore that state in the context of an ideal parent figure secure base.

Many anxious-preoccupied patients show chronic sustained anxious hyperarousal as well as episodic heightened arousal in response to anticipated abandonment threat. To address and reduce this arousal, ideal parent figures are not only consistently attuned to the child's *general level of anxiety* and to *specific instances of shifts in state in the direction of high anxious arousal* but also are consistently soothing and reassuring. For example:

These parents know *exactly* how to *calm you* when you're feeling anxious in general, and they know how to *soothe* and *reassure* you in *just the right ways* whenever you're feeling even more anxious and agitated. Notice how they are with you that lets you know that they're *right there for you* in ways that *really* help when you're upset.

The anxious-preoccupied patient frequently will manifest *hyperactivation of attachment behavior*, most prominently in the forms of increased proximity- and contact-seeking in response to fear of disconnection or abandonment. This pattern is addressed in the imagery as follows:

Notice how these parents know *exactly* how to accept and be with you when you're afraid of losing them and want to be closer to them. They *find just the right ways* to *reassure* and *comfort* you, and if you want you can climb onto them and feel their reassuring and comforting warmth and hugs. They're *right there* when you need them. And from them being *right there for you* when you need them, you begin to feel *comfortable* and *reassured and secure* in your connection with them. And you begin to feel *strong in yourself* too.

Through consistent experience of receiving exactly what is needed when anxiously aroused, the patient-as-child will begin to move away from excessive attachment behavior, such as anxious clinging or attempts to control the IPFs' responses.

At times when the anxious-preoccupied patient experiences a rapidly escalating abandonment threat (Mikulincer, Shaver, & Pereg, 2003) and the corresponding hyperarousal, the therapist can, in the IPF imagery, suggest that the resulting discomfort will actually *increase*. This intervention provides the patient with the powerful experience of the parent figures *attuning* to the patient's escalation and being effectively responsive to help to reverse the distress. For example:

And now, focus on that fear of being abandoned, and *really* feel what it's like in your body and your mind . . . As you focus on it, you can feel *even more* distressed, anxious, and agitated . . . You can *really* feel that even more now, can't you? . . . These parents are *so very attuned* to you, and they see that you're so upset and that it's getting worse . . . They're *right there for you*, and right now they find *just the right ways* to reassure you and *soothe* you and help you to feel *more calm* and *secure*. They are with you in ways that start to help you to feel better, and better and better . . . *Really* take that in . . . And when you're ready you can describe how they're being with you that helps you to feel better and better.

After the patient describes how the parent figures are being that feels so very helpful, the therapist makes sure to direct the patient's attention to his or her own inner state, to the ways that he or she is feeling better. For example:

> *Yes.* These parents are *right there* with you, and *for you*, and because of how attuned they are to you, they've found just the right ways to help you with what you were feeling . . . And you can *really notice* now all the ways that you're feeling better and better . . . You can *really notice* that now, can't you? . . . As you notice all the ways you're feeling better and better, you'll find just the right words to describe what you're feeling.

Notice that the therapist does not refer to herself in the above examples. Rather than saying, "And when you're ready you can *tell me* how they're being . . ." or "You'll find just the right words to describe *to me* what you're feeling," she keeps the focus of the task purely on the patient being aware of his experience and simply speaking from that experience, not *to* the therapist. The therapist's avoidance of self-reference may seem like a small consideration, but with anxious-preoccupied patients it is of great importance, as it reduces the conditioned *outside-in* orientation and reinforces the development of a healthy *inside-out* orientation. Therapists of anxious-preoccupied patients must be quite mindful to minimize their self-reference throughout treatment, especially during the early phases.

When the patient describes what he or she feels, the therapist validates and reinforces the patient's experience by *marking* the states and the corresponding affect. For example:

> Yes . . . *really feel* that sense of [comfort] . . . *Really feel* that [comfort], focusing on how you feel it so that it becomes *even more clear* . . . And as it becomes *even more clear*, you can notice that that [comfort] becomes *even more familiar*, and you can feel it *all through your body*.

Affectively marking the anxious-preoccupied patient's inner states further enhances his or her *inside-out* orientation.

Because anxious-preoccupied patients are particularly sensitized to separations and reunion episodes, in the IPF imagery the therapist asks the patient to imagine a child in different scenarios involving brief separations, followed by reunions with the parent figures who provide *just the right* responses during reunion episodes. For example:

> And now the scene is about to shift. In this new scene, you'll be separated from the parents, and you can feel what comes up in you in response to the separation . . . the scene is shifting, and notice what's happening in the new scene, with the separation from these parents . . . when you're ready you

can describe what's happening, and how you feel with the separation . . . [Patient describes] . . . Yes . . . and now you're about to be reunited with these parents . . . let it happen in *just the right way* for you, so that you come back into contact with them . . . and notice how they *welcome you* and are *right there for you* and give you *exactly what you most need* as you're coming back to them after being separated. When you're ready, the words to describe what you're experiencing will come to you, and you can freely speak those words.

Working with IPF imagery in these specific ways will over time further reduce hyperactivated attachment behavior and promote attachment security and the skills of closeness/distance regulation and emotion regulation.

Finally, since early caregivers of preoccupied adults had a pattern of selective misattunement to the child's spontaneous exploratory behavior, it is important that the therapist shape the IPF imagery to include parent figures who are carefully attuned to and encouraging of the child's exploratory initiatives. For example:

These parents are *confident* in your ability to *explore* and *discover*. You can sense their *deep trust* in your capacity to *explore*, *discover*, and *develop* your *best* and *strongest* sense of *self* . . . Notice what it is about them that lets you know that they *really want you* to be *strong*, *independent*, and *autonomous*, even while you continue to feel a clear and strong and secure bond with them . . . These parents never impose their own needs and agendas on you, but instead find *just the right ways* to support you finding what's most right for *you* . . . and to *explore* and *discover* who you *most fully are*, to explore and discover *your own self*, the *unique person* you are.

With respect to the general factors—parental *presence*, *consistency*, *reliability*, and *interest*—and the five primary parental behavioral conditions that promote secure attachment—protection, attunement, soothing, expressed delight, and fostering best self-development—IPF imagery is introduced over time in each of these domains in general ways (see Chapters 7 and 8) and also in ways that emphasize the particular needs of the anxious-preoccupied patient. Several of these considerations and methods are described above, but they are repeated here in the context of the five conditions, to highlight their importance and reinforce their application. First, with respect to protection and safety, anxious-preoccupied patients are markedly fearful. They often have a generalized anxiety disorder or panic disorder diagnosis, and adults with the strongest anxious preoccupation have deep, pervasive nonspecific fear in many situations (E3 classification in the AAI). Introducing parent figures who are expressly *protective* and provide a stable safe haven contributes to positive remapping of attachment figures as an expected source of safety and protection.

Second, childhood ambivalent/resistant attachment is associated with significantly more pervasive caregiver misattunement than are other attachment prototypes, and is also associated with selective misattunement to the child's exploratory behavior. In ways described above, IPF imagery is shaped to provide the patient with experiences of careful, accurate *attunement* to his or her behaviors, inner states, and developmental capacities. Such imagery contributes to the development of a positive representation and set of expectancies that others can be accurately attuned to the patient's ongoing moment-by-moment experience, including vitality affects, wants, and needs, and also be helpfully encouraging of healthy exploratory behavior.

Third, since anxious and/or angry arousal is a prominent feature of preoccupied attachment, the therapist emphasizes IPF qualities of *soothing, comforting,* and *reassurance.* The objective, over time, is for the patient to develop a stable representation and set of expectancies that others can be openly comforting and demonstrate that hyperactivated attachment behaviors are unnecessary.

Fourth, in anxious-preoccupied patients, the experience of caregivers' *expressed delight* is especially missing with respect to spontaneous exploratory behavior. The therapist therefore suggests that the parent figures openly express their delight and pleasure regarding the patient-as-child's actions of spontaneous exploration, initiatives toward discovery, and attempts to be strong, autonomous, and independent.

Lastly, and overlapping with the above, since adults with anxious preoccupation show a lifelong pattern of inhibited self-development, the therapist specifically emphasizes that the parent figures are entirely comfortable with, deeply supportive of, and strongly confident about the child's initiatives of exploration and discovery. The parent figures are present in ways that foster the development of the patient-as-child's best and most unique self. For patients whose family-of-origin parents had strong expectations for the child to behave and accomplish in specific ways in order to meet the parents' needs and agendas, the therapist introduces parent figures who are collaborators in the patient-as-child's own discovery of his or her own uniqueness in ways that may be very different from what the parent figures might expect. Such IPFs assist the child in tolerating fear and uncertainty in the face of new discoveries and essentially enable the developing child to find the courage *to be.* For example:

> These parents want most of all for you to be *most fully yourself*... They have no agendas for you, other than that you learn and grow to be who you're most meant to be, as your *unique* and *best self*... Notice that they encourage you to explore, and discover, and try things out that help you to be your *best self*... and even when you discover things about yourself and what you like that are very different from what these parents might expect, they celebrate your discoveries and the *unique* and best *you*, who you are and who you are becoming.

Over time, the anxious-preoccupied patient directly experiences how exploratory behavior is enhanced by security in the relationship. He or she will develop a positive representation and set of expectancies that important others can be counted on to provide a secure and supportive base for exploration. The poor self-development of the anxious-preoccupied patient is gradually transformed into manifestation of the best-self-in-the-context-of-relationship.

As described for dismissing patients in Chapter 11, we use the five adjectives from the AAI if it is available, and information from unstructured clinical interviewing if it is not, to tailor the IPF imagery to the particular patient. For example, a patient with an anxious-preoccupied prototype—fearful subtype E3—gave the following five adjectives for the early childhood relationship with the mother: "caring," "worried," "nurturing," "loud," and "concern." The seemingly positive adjectives were illustrated with examples that were not actually positive (in the sense of being promoting of attachment security): "Caring" meant that the mother called a doctor when the child was sick; "nurturing" meant feeding the child; "concern" meant worry when the child first tried to ride a bike on his own. The therapist translated each of these five adjectives into their positive opposite qualities based not solely on the words themselves, but even more so on the explanatory examples given by the patient in response to the AAI inquiries about the adjectives. The ideal mother figure was thereby considered to be particularly physically and emotionally caring; deeply calm and serene, and never worried; physically and emotionally nurturing in countless ways; soft and gentle in her manner; and deeply supportive of the strength, autonomy, and independence of the growing patient-as-child.

The adjectives given for the early childhood relationship with the patient's father were "temper," "impatient," "working," "creative" ("doing craftwork"), and "talented" ("makes me things"). The therapist's positive opposite translations for qualities of the ideal father figure were that he was deeply comforting both physically and emotionally, never raising his voice; deeply patient; expressly supportive of the child's discovery of his own creativity; deeply encouraging of the child's own discoveries; and deeply supportive of the child's own talents. The translated qualities were embodied by the ideal mother and father figures, which provided the patient with experiences that were specific to what was most missing in the family of origin.

Fostering Collaboration in Anxious-Preoccupied Patients

The therapist must remember that anxious-preoccupied patients easily and excessively self-disclose, and should not assume that this is a sign of collaborative behavior. More often, the prominent self-disclosure is a sign of *excessive compliance* with what the patient presumes the therapist wants. For the anxious-preoccupied patient, excessive self-disclosure represents a strategy of attempting to please the therapist and is representative of an *outside-in* orientation. The therapist best responds by acknowledging the disclosure and pointing the patient toward his or her experience underlying the disclosure. A sample interchange follows:

> *Patient:* I'm really worried about whether you will be able to help me or understand me at all, so I want you to really know what's on my mind. I know I'm the kind of person who can be a real pain in the ass. I'm always so nervous and afraid and on edge. God! I just can't slow my mind down for a second. I worry about my son and his drinking, and I worry about my mother . . . she's getting up there, you know . . . and my daughter keeps losing one job after another . . . I'm probably gonna have to give her money again.
>
> *Therapist:* I appreciate you letting me in on a lot of your worries, but I wonder if you could tell me what it's like for you to be so concerned for everyone else so much of the time . . . It sounds exhausting!
>
> *Patient:* It is [tearfully]. I feel like everyone's problems are my problems so much that I can't tell what I really feel about anything!

The patient's focus was redirected to support an *inside-out* orientation. In general, the therapist of the anxious-preoccupied patient must help the patient learn to replace one-sided compliance with back-and-forth collaborative interchange, and also to couple self-disclosure per se with careful metacognitive monitoring of what, and how much, is being said.

Preoccupied patients usually cry easily. The therapist should resist assuming that spontaneous crying is always a positive sign of emotional release and relief. Rather, frequent crying should be recognized as a likely indication of hyperactivation of the attachment system, and it should be addressed directly to bring to awareness the underlying abandonment fear. For example:

> *Patient:* And then I didn't hear back even though I sent a bunch of texts and I know she never goes anywhere without her phone and always checks it every five minutes . . . [Punctuated with an angry tone, and crying and sobbing]
>
> *Therapist:* Obviously we can't know what's going on with her, so let's look at your feelings . . . do you think your anger and tears are only about her behavior, or is there something there about a deeper fear of being alone and abandoned?
>
> *Patient:* I know, I don't know why I let someone not texting me back immediately get me so upset . . . You're right, it must be something more than that . . . I want to understand myself more so I can be less crazy when these things happen. *[Now, markedly calmer and engaged collaboratively with the therapist in an inside-out self-exploration]*

The nonverbal behavior of the preoccupied patient is attuned to the therapist, but it is one-sided. The patient's spontaneous nonverbal expressiveness is designed to read and extract cues in an effort to infer the therapist's expectations and state of mind. The therapist must transform the patient's one-sided, outside-in nonverbal attunement into a moment-by-moment nonverbal collaborative dialogue, much like that described by Beebe and Lachmann (2014), in which the therapist nonverbally matches and changes each spontaneous nonverbal expression of the patient (see Chapter 10). In this way, the patient continues to have attuned nonverbal behavior, but also develops the experience of *being attuned to* nonverbally by the therapist.

Since a primary goal of therapy with an anxious-preoccupied patient is dampening the hyperactivated attachment system, the therapist and patient *work together on this shared goal*—at first not directly within the domain of the attachment system but indirectly within the domain of the cooperative behavioral system. The preoccupied patient is encouraged to work with the therapist as a part of a collaborative team to understand and tolerate abandonment and separation fears and the associated hyperactivation of attachment behaviors. At times of abandonment threat and/or therapeutic rupture, the preoccupied patient's nonverbal expressiveness is greatly exaggerated in the form of amplified gestures of distress, particularly crying, and heightened nonverbal protest expressions at the perceived lack of proximity- and contact-seeking. The therapist attempts to match these expressions and redirect the focus to the patient's internal state and helps the patient translate the nonverbal distress into words. In the following example, the therapist informed the patient about an unexpected need to be out of the office the following week, thus postponing the next therapy appointment. The patient became tearful and began shaking her leg up and down while her gaze darted around the room.

> *Therapist:* I can see from your tears and the way you seem uncomfortable and unsettled physically that something is going on inside with you, maybe in reaction to our next appointment being postponed?
> *Patient:* It just comes over me quickly.
> *Therapist:* Can you describe it?
> *Patient:* Yeah, I hear that you are not going to be there and I suddenly feel alone and panicky and overwhelmed. I know it sounds stupid, but it feels like I can't control it.
> *Therapist:* Just now, the way you were able to slow down and focus inward and describe it—here is a great example of you learning how to identify your feelings and to have more control when these feelings come up for you.

Regarding verbal behavior, anxious-preoccupied patients are remarkably verbally noncollaborative. Many such patients talk on and on without pauses, do not provide any opening for turn-taking, and often fail to meet the basic rules of verbal coherence. Therefore, noncollaborative verbal behavior is a major focus of treatment with the anxious-preoccupied patient. It is important to highlight the patient's failure to follow the basic rules of verbal collaborative dialogue, which brings this pattern directly into the patient's metacognitive awareness. We recommend asking the patient to practice consciously monitoring his or her speech and to deliberately partition the discourse into meaningful units; when the patient recognizes that what he or she just said comprises a meaningful unit, he or she then pauses to allow the therapist to take a turn at responding before the patient continues. The therapist mirrors to the patient as much as he or she comprehended before the discourse became too prolonged, and through that feedback the patient learns to frame discourse in terms of succinct meaningful units. Also, as described in Chapter 10, it can be helpful to use a previously agreed-upon nonverbal indicator, such as the therapist raising a hand, to signal to the patient to bring the unit of discourse to a close and give the therapist an opportunity to respond.

When the anxious-preoccupied patient's discourse wanders off topic and/or introduces irrelevancies, the therapist helps the patient become metacognitively aware of these occurrences with comments such as, "I'm finding it hard now to follow your main point. How about if you pause, focus, find the essence of what you're wanting to say, and then give expression to exactly that." When the patient introduces an irrelevancy, the therapist responds, "I can't see exactly how that relates to your main point." When the anxious-preoccupied patient uses passive, vague, ambiguous, or jargon-filled discourse, the therapist gives immediate feedback and engages the patient's cooperativeness to reexpress the essential point in a clear manner. For example:

> *Patient:* The thing is, I don't know . . . I know I'm an adult-child so that makes a difference, I guess; I am so codependent, too, so that doesn't help either—it just gets me so upset when I know things could be better between us, but I don't understand why it always becomes an argument.
> *Therapist:* I know you're saying a lot, but I am confused about what you actually mean. If you don't worry about labels like codependent or adult-child, perhaps you can try again to explain the point you're trying to make.
> *Patient:* Okay, well I guess I am just trying to say that there must be something about me and the way I react that is part of the problem in my relationship, and I want to understand what it is.
> *Therapist:* That is much clearer and more direct. I think we can definitely explore what you contribute to the relationship that's not helpful.

In this exchange, the therapist engaged the patient's cooperativeness, enhanced the patient's metacognitive awareness of the use of passive speech (i.e., jargon), and highlighted the collaborative goal of exploring the underlying theme of the speech.

Enhancing Metacognitive Skills in Anxious-Preoccupied Patients

Because research using the Reflective Functioning Scale (RF-S) has shown that anxious-preoccupied patients generally score very low in reflective capacity, therapy with these patients should include methods to enhance general reflective capacity. The therapist's consistent mentalizing stance is especially important, as it helps to offset the patient's hypervigilant overinvolvement in the state of mind of the other.

Additionally, a condition-specific approach to the development of metacognition, whereby the clinician targets specific metacognitive skill deficiencies, is also indicated with the anxious-preoccupied patient. Because of their learned outside-in orientation, such patients typically have a deficit in the metacognitive capacity to *identify* their own state of mind. The MBT technique of *marking* the patient's affect contributes to the patient's identification of his or her affect experience and also to the realization that that experience *is his or hers* and does not originate outside in another. For example, the therapist might emphasize the patient's internal experience of an emotional state with a verbal marking comment like, "*You* must have felt *really afraid*." Such comments locate the self (not the other) as the locus of the affect and amplify the awareness of the affect as a central experience of self at that moment in time.

Especially during times of fear of abandonment, the anxious-preoccupied patient loses the capacity for metacognitive *mastery*—he or she cannot reflect on his or her own state of fear in a way that leads to modulation of (i.e., mastery over) the fear arousal. At these times, the therapist brings metacognitive focus to the relativity of all states by helping the patient to realize that this is "just a state" and then assists the patient in determining the most effective action strategies for responding to the state (Semerari et al., 2003, p. 244; see Chapter 9 of this text).

Focus on action strategies can also help with these patients' tendency to be impulsive. In addition to teaching the patient to anticipate outcomes and consequences of particular behaviors, the therapist also teaches how to develop careful action plans and how to organize behaviors around these action plans (Wishnie, 1977).

We attempt to develop a number of post-formal metacognitive skills (see Chapter 9) with anxious-preoccupied patients. Maladaptive schemas of emotional deprivation and abandonment are prevalent in anxious-preoccupied patients, and the therapist helps the patient *see more deeply into underlying assumptions and expectancies* to develop a metacognitive awareness of the presence of these maladaptive beliefs and schemas. The concepts and emotion-focused techniques developed by Jeff Young as part of schema therapy are especially useful (Young et al., 2003). Unless the underlying schema functioning is brought into the patient's awareness and modified, it will continue to exert a negative impact on the patient's experience and behavior both in treatment and in intimate relationships.

Patients with anxious preoccupation typically show low coherence of mind. The therapist can recognize this low coherence or disorganization in how the preoccupied patient's discourse scatters in all directions. A simple anchoring scale is one of the most powerful tools for working to enhance the preoccupied patient's metacognitive *awareness of organization or coherence of mind* at any given moment. The therapist says, for example:

> On a 1 to 10 scale, 1 being *completely disorganized* and 10 being *completely organized*, and the other numbers a level of disorganization or organization in between, say a number that reflects the relative degree of disorganization or organization of your state of mind at this very moment.

If the therapist uses this simple anchoring scale three to six times in each treatment session, consistently across sessions, several months into the treatment the patient will present signs of significant and consistent improved organization and coherence of mind.

Also reflecting low coherence of mind, anxious-preoccupied patients manifest numerous oscillations in orientation, particularly past/present and self/other. We utilize a variety of anchoring scales to improve metacognitive *ability to develop an orientation.* For example, anxious and/or angry preoccupied patients often become entangled in unfinished emotional states from the remote past, what Main, Goldwyn, and Hesse (2002) call "the past invading the present." Such entanglement makes it especially difficult for the anxious-preoccupied patient to maintain a current, here-and-now orientation. In such situations, the therapist asks, for example:

> On a 1 to 10 scale, 1 being *completely caught up in the past*, 10 being *completely in present* awareness of only your immediate state of mind, and the other numbers a degree of past or present orientation somewhere in between, give a number as to the relative degree you are operating from the past, present, or somewhere in between right now.

Consistently fostering this metacognitive awareness gradually helps the anxious or angry preoccupied patient learn to make the shift from past to present orientation with no more than a simple reminder from the therapist, and ultimately to establish an overall present orientation.

To enhance metacognitive awareness of self or other orientation, the anchoring scale can take the following form:

> On a 1 to 10 scale, 1 being *completely focused on the other's* state of mind, with no awareness of your own state of mind, and 10 being *completely aware of your own* state of mind, with no focus on the other's state of mind, and

the other numbers a degree of other or self focus somewhere in between, what number reflects the relative degree you are other-focused or self-focused right now?

Frequent use of this simple method to foster metacognitive awareness of self/other orientation will, over time, reduce the patient's preoccupation with the state of mind of the other (outside orientation) and enhance awareness of and focus on his or her own state of mind. Ultimately, the anxious-preoccupied patient will develop the capacity to hold both self and other states of mind at the same time, which facilitates the capacity for collaborative exchange and exploration.

Stages in the Treatment of the Anxious-Preoccupied Patient

1. Initially, the therapist introduces the concept of cooperative behavior as an indirect way of both tempering the hyperactivation of the attachment system and reactivating the exploratory behavioral system.

2. Most of the early therapeutic work entails systematic use of IPF imagery and consistently enhancing metacognitive awareness of nonverbal and verbal misattunements as they occur. Since an overinvolving style of parenting contributes to the development of anxious preoccupation, the early IPF imagery must emphasize *noninvolving parent figures* who consistently redirect the patient's outside-in orientation to an inside-out orientation by focusing on careful, consistent attunement to the patient's state of mind. Since caregivers of anxious-preoccupied adults were pervasively and inconsistently misattuned, the IPFs are consistently accurately attuned to a wide range of the patient-as-child's states of mind. Anxious-preoccupied patients maintain chronic high levels of anxious arousal and have even greater anxious arousal in the face of abandonment fear, and so the imagery emphasizes parent figures who soothe, comfort, and reassure the child, which serves both to lower the overall level of anxious arousal and to temper the heightened arousal and hyperactivated attachment behavior that occur when abandonment fear is present.

3. At the middle stage of treatment, more careful focus is brought to episodes of hyperactivated attachment behavior that occur *in the context of the therapeutic relationship* (Safran, Muran, Samstag, & Stevens, 2001). Ruptures in the therapy relationship occur typically in response to empathic failures by the therapist or to heightened abandonment fear when the therapist will be or is absent. At such times, the patient becomes excessively demanding of proximity- and contact-seeking and/or attempts to control the therapist's responsiveness (Mikulincer

& Shaver, 2007). These hyperactivating strategies are best understood as an exaggeration of normal attachment behavior at times of threat. The ruptures and fears are not easy to resolve within the context of the attachment behavioral system per se, because it is the attachment system that has been ruptured or is being threatened. Therefore, the therapist explicitly calls upon the cooperative behavioral system to enlist the patient to work with him or her as a collaborative team to address the rupture or threat. Such work includes shared metacognitive exploration to identify and understand the patient's state of mind during episodes of hyperactivated attachment behavior. The patient's experience of collaboratively repairing the therapeutic rupture and soothing the abandonment threat reactivates the attachment system and supports an emerging sense of trust and security in the context of the attachment relationship.

4. A consistent focus of the middle to late stages of treatment is enhancing the patient's self-development and self-esteem development in general, and in particular the emergence of the patient's strongest, best, and most unique sense of self. A main objective of treatment of the anxious-preoccupied patient is reactivation of a healthy exploratory system that serves as a basis for mature self-development. At this point in treatment, the therapist serves as a secure base for self-exploration. We have included a protocol of the methods to promote self-development in Appendix A of this book.

5. Clear signs of treatment progress include reduction in the frequency and degree of hyperactivation of attachment behavior, diminished preoccupation with past hurts, maintaining a here-and-now state-of-mind focus, sustaining an inside-out orientation and/or having a balanced focus on the state of mind of both self and other, and reactivation of the exploratory system. The strongest indicator of progress is the capacity to sustain self-exploration in a wide range of areas, within and outside treatment, without hyperactivation of attachment behavior.

6. At the later stages of treatment, the focus shifts to developing a positive IWM for secure intimacy. The anxious-preoccupied patient is asked to imagine hypothetical romantic partners who meet the conditions of secure intimacy. Imagery of ideal intimate partners includes qualities from the earlier IPF imagery that are important for promoting security in all people, and it also emphasizes qualities that are especially important for anxious-preoccupied patients—particularly being noninvolving, showing consistent and accurate attunement, providing a secure base for exploration, and encouraging self-development within the context of intimacy. The overall objective of ideal partner imagery is for the anxious-preoccupied patient to develop a stable, positive map for adult secure intimacy that will guide current and future relationships. Methods for promoting secure intimacy are further detailed in Appendix B.

Case Illustration

The following illustrative transcripts from two psychotherapy sessions demonstrate the application of the Three Pillars treatment approach with a patient who used a predominantly anxious-preoccupied attachment pattern. The patient was a woman in her 30s who had had multiple psychiatric hospitalizations and had been diagnosed variously as having bipolar II disorder, obsessive-compulsive disorder, borderline personality disorder, panic disorder, and dissociative disorder not otherwise specified. Between the ages of 16 to 30, "Helen" had taken seven overdoses of her prescription medications, none of them with the intent to die, but rather to take an action to move out of unbearable agitation; several of these dangerous incidents were nearly lethal.

At the beginning of this three-year treatment using the Three Pillars method, Helen was given the Adult Attachment Interview (AAI), and its scoring produced an insecure attachment classification of CC/E3/Ds1. This classification indicates a mixed attachment strategy with the anxious-preoccupied pattern as predominant, along with the presence of some dismissing attachment features. Although this patient was formally classified as disorganized, we present her here because of the prominent anxious preoccupation in these transcripts. The coherence of Helen's pre-treatment AAI transcript was 2.0. After three years of this treatment, Helen was again administered the AAI, which showed her attachment status had changed to secure, as indicated by the classification of F5 ("secure with some preoccupied features"). The coherence of her transcript post-treatment was 8.0 (out of 9). In addition, her reflective functioning was assessed as having gone from a 2 at pre-treatment to a 5 at follow-up. These changes represent a marked improvement for this patient.

Helen's relational history revealed preoccupied attachment themes at a number of developmental junctures. One of her earliest memories is of sitting with her father as her mother was taken for what would be an extended stay in a hospital for mysterious reasons that have to this day not been clarified. Helen was an only child; both her parents worked and she was often left in the care of babysitters. She said she couldn't connect with any of these caregivers "because I wanted them to be my mom and they weren't." In fact, Helen refused to interact with any of the babysitters at all and would violently beg her parents not to leave her when they went out at night. When her father traveled away on business, which was frequently, she was extremely fearful that the house was unsafe from potential intruders, and she remembers that she had great difficulty falling asleep when only her mother was home. Helen's mother began to work from home in her office, which was in a remote part of the house; Helen would wait at the end of the hallway that led to her mother's office, longing for her presence, but the babysitter followed strict instructions to keep a boundary between her and her mother when her mother was working. When Helen was seven, her mother was devastated by the death of her own mother. At the funeral, Helen fell and broke her wrist, but felt she could not bother her parents with her injury and so kept it to herself for days. In excruciating physical pain after five days, Helen remembers hugging her arm and looking at the door to her mother's office, feeling separate from her mother in an absolute sense. Shortly thereafter, Helen's mother incurred a sports injury so severe that she was laid up in bed for the better part of a year. Her bedroom was moved downstairs, and Helen remembers feeling very disconnected to her during this time, and later on in her treatment found herself wondering if the pain medication her mother took affected their interactions.

Helen remembers that if her mother began to feel any kind of emotion at all, her mother would start crying and not want Helen to see her having this emotion. In contrast, her father was unemotional but was very good at focusing on the practical. She did not feel she could share anything emotional with either of her parents. By the time Helen was a teenager, she reported being "nearly phobic" of being hugged by either of them, an event which nonetheless rarely occurred. Helen often remarked to her therapist that she did not know some basic information related to her family history, and reported that her father's heritage was somewhat mysterious. There was always a sense that there were family secrets, but even to state that possibility to her parents felt taboo to Helen. She seemed to accept being in a stance of passive not-knowingness with regard to her family.

When Helen was in high school, symptoms of an as-yet-undiagnosed bipolar disorder caused her to have erratic affective surges that frightened both Helen and her parents. Helen's passivity—a key feature of a preoccupied attachment strategy—limited her ability to describe her experiences effectively to her parents, her teachers, or her new psychotherapist or psychiatrist. She suffered from painful shyness, irritability, and panic attacks and craved to be seen. Increasingly agitated in the context of interpersonal situations, she began to take over-the-counter medications in increasingly alarming amounts before notifying a family friend of this behavior. She was aware of needing to get her parents' attention, but felt she could not ask for it directly. Her parents were very alarmed about her overdosing behavior and felt uncertain of how they could help her. From their anxiety for her well-being, they sent Helen to a very well-reputed hospital a far distance away. Helen was the youngest inpatient at this hospital and was exposed to frightening stories from the other inpatients, some of whom were psychotic and some of whom talked of horrific traumatic events. Helen reported that this overwhelming experience "took away some of my security in the world." She began to have extreme difficulty taking leave of her four-times-per week psychodynamic therapist at the hospital. Sometimes Helen would cry uncontrollably when it was time to end their sessions, and she began to exhibit signs of dissociation. The nurse who was assigned to work with Helen at the hospital was much warmer than the therapist and would give her hugs after their weekly meetings, something Helen found wonderfully comforting but also very upsetting, as it would create in her a longing for more and an unpleasant sense that that was wrong. Thus, Helen would dissolve into tears at the end of their meetings as well, and found this response to be confusing and shameful. Helen reported that the ends of therapy sessions typically evoked feelings of being "alone and unprotected," which would then lead to "fear and sadness." The greater the interpersonal intensity of the therapy, the more likely she was to have such reactions.

Dialectical behavioral therapy (DBT) treatment was sought by the patient and her family because of her extreme difficulty regulating her emotions and the difficulties that arose from her passive, interpersonal communication style with family, therapists, and friends. Helen showed impressive signs of improvement in the DBT treatment at first, but aspects of the treatment left Helen feeling invalidated, as the therapist was, by design, teaching a skill rather than attuning to Helen's internal state. Helen manifested distinct preoccupied attachment patterns during this treatment, becoming fixated on personal details of the therapist's life and frequently losing her internal focus. As prescribed by the DBT protocol, the therapist began each session by asking Helen if she had had any suicidal ideation since the previous session, which *unwittingly set up an outside-in orientation*. This therapeutic stance made Helen worry that the therapist was worrying about her scary thoughts and behaviors, which then made Helen think even more about suicide. In addition, the therapist had begun the use of self-disclosure for the purpose of providing reassurance about their connection in the face of Helen's seemingly inexplicable fear states, and also in an effort to rebuild the treatment alliance ruptured by Helen's multiple suicide attempts during their treatment. These interventions unfortunately hyperactivated Helen's anxious-preoccupied attachment pattern. She began to focus on the therapist's state of mind, rather than her own, and became distracted from the main goal of the treatment: the development of DBT skills. Helen's preoccupation with her therapist brought frustration and a sense of stuckness to both of them, and the therapist arranged for an attachment-focused consultation to bring clarity to the underlying issues and stressors that provoked periods of agitation in the patient. It was decided that the next stage of treatment should be attachment-focused.

The following transcripts are from the treatment with the attachment-focused therapist and are labeled to identify for the reader the main characteristics of preoccupied attachment and the main interventions used by the therapist. In IPF segments of the treatment, the therapist utilized some of the five adjectives that Helen had given to describe her relationship with her mother on her pre-treatment AAI (*reactive, sensitive, moody, sad,* and *distant*) and the five adjectives she had given to describe the relationship with her father (*serious, hardworking, demanding, protective,* and *playful*). Positive opposites of these adjectives were applied to each respective ideal parent figure: for the mother figure, *highly responsive, sturdy, consistent, strong,* and *carefully attuned*, and for the father figure, *never angry, present and just being with her*, and *deeply patient and seeing how special she is*; the adjectives *protective* and *playful* were kept. The first transcript, from the middle state of treatment, begins with Helen talking about getting ready to take an important professional competency exam, as she has just completed some advanced professional training. The words of the therapist and of the patient are in plain text, and posthoc observations and explanation are bracketed and italicized.

> *Patient:* I'm really, really anxious today. Well, it's mostly about finding out about the results of the test that I took . . . I'm just scared of failing . . .
>
> *Therapist:* Okay. Let's use that as a starting point for the protocol today. How about we do 10 minutes on that? *[Therapist offers temporal structure around the IPF protocol. The patient is sometimes resistant to starting the protocol, and sometimes feels misattuned to when it is suggested in the middle of her discourse.]*
>
> *Patient:* I'd have to think about it a lot. I don't know if I can.
>
> *Therapist:* Well, it would help cultivate for you the felt experience of having a true kind of comfort that usually you have not experienced; the anxious part of you may need to think about it, but we are trying to shift that habit. You can start by opening yourself up to receiving comfort for it, which is different.
>
> *Patient:* Okay.
>
> *Therapist:* I mean, I know that's not the easiest thing for you, but it's what I think would be helpful for you. *[Therapist actively structures the session around their previously identified goals]*
>
> *Patient:* Okay. I'm afraid it's gonna make me feel worse about it.
>
> *Therapist:* So the whole protocol we're working on is to develop your internal working map of comfort that you have blocked off . . . because . . . we know you have been afraid of positive feeling . . . because we know you're afraid of disappointment. Would it be okay if we work on that? *[Therapist shows attunement to the patient and highlights the collaborative aspect of the work]*
>
> *Patient:* (Nods in silent response.)
>
> *Therapist:* You have had a belief that if you comfort yourself and have a positive feeling, then a bad thing is going to happen, right?
>
> *Patient:* (Nods in silent response.)
>
> *Therapist:* Okay. And I'm challenging that as being a symptom of anxiety. It's a belief, but it isn't real. *[Fostering metacognitive appearance–reality distinction]* Do you accept that? I mean . . . do you accept that I have a different way of looking at it? *[Therapist makes an appearance–reality distinction and encourages metacognitive perspective-taking]*
>
> *Patient:* (Nods in silent response.)

Therapist: It's been hard for you to give up your belief because your belief is something that in a way has been comforting to you.

Patient: . . . Okay, yeah.

Therapist: Helen, I want to gauge whether this is one of those times when I'm suggesting something and you're saying "okay" but really you're wishing you could be more assertive. *[Example of therapist feedback about possible noncollaborative nonverbal behavior in the form of the patient acting passively and ceding too much to the therapist]*

Patient: About what?

Therapist: About finding the focus for the ideal parent imagery today.

Patient: Well . . . I feel like sort of worried about it.

Therapist: Mm-hmm.

Patient: So I just think if we change the topic it would be hard for me to do that because I'm so anxious about it.

Therapist: Okay.

Patient: But then I am . . . that would just make me feel worse about it.

Therapist: Okay, so the key here . . . is for you to take a leap of faith and open up to the possibility of positive feelings.

Patient: Okay.

Therapist: Okay? So you and I both accept that you have anxiety about the test. *[Therapist uses clarification and validation, and then reminds patient of collaborative stance and treatment goal]* We're using that as the circumstance to build in this internal working model of comfort and security. We know you're nervous about the test even though you've done so well with the practice tests, and we're still working on that place on your map of comfort, okay?

Patient: I'm ready, yeah.

Therapist: All right, good. So getting yourself into a comfortable position so you can begin to physically relax, allowing your breath to deepen, cultivating your relaxation response now, good. *[Therapist is referring to their cultivation of various methods to induce relaxation and allow for a deeper focus]* Yes, that's right, allowing yourself to relax. [Patient takes a minute or two to move into a more relaxed place.] On a scale of 1 to 10, 1 being very deeply relaxed, how do you rate yourself?

Patient: Maybe a 3 or 4.

Therapist: Okay, good, and now you can become *even more* deeply relaxed as you imagine breathing oxygen into any places that feel tension in your body. And, when you're ready, go ahead now and bring up that feeling of nervousness you told me about in the beginning of the session, while you're breathing deeply through that, good.

Patient: Mm-hmm.

Therapist: Helen, where do you feel that in your body? *[Therapist is here helping the patient to develop interoception, which is the immediate, direct sense of the physiological condition of the body]*

Patient: My chest.

Therapist: Okay, and on a scale from 1 to 10, how do you rate your anxiety at this moment? *[Therapist encouraging Helen to link her body sensation to her emotion]*

Patient: Like maybe an 8.

Therapist: Good, so go ahead and just take some nice deep breaths into your chest just trying to relax those muscles as much as possible . . . You can go ahead and imagine your ideal parents . . . noticing what they're like. Remembering that these are not your real parents from memory but your imagined ones you're creating because they are *just right* for you, the *way you are.* These parents are *ideally suited* to you *just as you are* . . . So they are *deeply patient* . . . They are *very steady* . . . They are emotionally very, very *strong* . . . These parents are *warm* with you in *just the right way* that feels *comfortable* to you right now. Go ahead now and feel that as you bring those qualities in them up. *[Therapist introduces IPF imagery specifically tailored to the patient from her AAI]*

Patient: Yeah, I'm sort of able to do it . . .

Therapist: Good, take your time. We're gonna go through some of those qualities again, then for each one take your time and bring it in . . . and if it doesn't feel right go ahead and change it and let me know how you're changing it, okay? These parents are deeply patient . . . feel that . . . does that feel right to you?

Patient: (Nods in silent response.)

Therapist: Okay. They are sturdy and steady . . . feel that . . . does that feel right? *[Therapist names qualities that are the positive opposites of adjectives the patient used to describe her actual parents]*

Patient: Mm.

Therapist: These parents are *warm* and *present right here* with you now . . . you can let yourself feel what that is like.

Patient: That's like harder for me . . . to bring that one in.

Therapist: Yes, these parents understand that this is really hard for you to do; they *really get that* and they know *just how to be with you* now . . . Good, go ahead and be with that felt sense of them, really accepting that this is hard for you . . . and they accept that too. Adjusting their qualities so it feels just exactly right to you, keeping in mind that these are the parents who are exactly suited to you, understanding completely your ambivalence about distance and closeness and affection. So go ahead and just stay with that, and when you're ready, let me know what it's feeling like. (Therapist observes here that patient's breaths are becoming more shallow) Remembering to take nice deep breaths, Helen. Good.

Patient: Well like what comes to mind is like . . . they're all kids like, toddlers, or they like . . . leave their parents and then come back to them and the parents are just . . . they're there and they're not—they're there, versus parents who when their two-year-old falls and the parents, you know, freak out and worry and pick them up and stuff instead of letting them, like, get up themselves.

Therapist: *Yes,* you want to feel good about doing it yourself and these parents have *such confidence* in *you.* [Marking self-development] Go ahead and see the quality in them right now that is really *perfectly suited to you* right now . . . You can dial in between those two images of closeness and independence until you get it *just right.*

Patient: I see it . . . like just being there if you need them.

Therapist: Yes, they are *right here* when you need them, and they are *deeply attuned* to knowing when that is and how to be with you. Go ahead and feel what that's like now . . . Your anxiety on a scale of 1 to 10?

Patient: Maybe like a 3.

Therapist: Good, yes, these parents are *right here with you,* and are happy to wait should you need them. They're always here for you when you need them in just *exactly the right way.* But they know that you can do it on your own, too, and they are *delighted* being your support either way. Go ahead and open yourself up to what that feels like. *[Therapist mirrors and reinforces the attuned presence of the parent figures, which includes recognition and support of the patient's independence and self-development]* Noticing what this feels like in your body and in your mind together right now, your felt sense, Helen.

Patient: (Long pause)

Therapist: When you have a full sense of that, let me know.

Patient: I'm just trying to imagine what that would feel like . . . ?

Therapist: Yes, you are using your imagination, which will guide you. *[Therapist gently encourages confidence in the patient's use of imagination, which also reinforces exploratory behavior]*

Patient: Mm-hmm.

Therapist: Imagine telling these parents about this anxiety that you've got . . . and notice how they're *deeply listening* to you so that there's no need to concern yourself with their states of mind. You can *simply relax* into *your own* felt sense. *[Therapist guides patient to bring uncomfortable affect to parent figures and suggests that the parent figures are interested and attuned; imagery is the positive opposite of family-of-origin parents who involved the patient in their states of mind]*

Patient: (Long pause)

Therapist: Can you see that?

Patient: Yeah. Mm-hmm . . .

Therapist: They're *really listening* to you . . . and they understand that you want their reassurance and closeness but that you might be feeling ambivalent about that. They understand that completely, and they're right there for you.

Patient: (Long pause)

Therapist: (Therapist notices that the patient is fidgeting and moving her head around, and that the patient uses different rhythms when swinging her legs, which seems to indicate varying degrees of upset) I'm noticing that your body is moving around and looks agitated; try to tell me about what are you experiencing, Helen.

Patient: . . . I'm just having trouble like . . . feeling that because I don't know what I would want them to be like. *[Patient loses focus of internal state of self]*

Therapist: *[Therapist observes the patient's physiologic signs of upset and tracks them out loud to teach her to notice them more quickly as they happen, rather than getting swept away by them. Reminds patient about her breath and prompts her to maintain her self-awareness through her body sense.]* Nice deep breaths. So go ahead now and look inside . . . you can use the richness of your imagination to have these parents be exactly right for you and your needs . . . you can also draw from any experiences or people from books or movies for a sense of the qualities of being that you need from these parents . . . What are you imagining now? *[Therapist shows interest and focused attention on the state of mind of the patient]*

Patient: (Long pause) I'm remembering that nurse from the old hospital, you know, the one that gave me wonderful hugs even when I was upset. I felt that with her she, like, got my ambivalence but knew what I needed, you know, deep down; I didn't have to ask, she just knew.

Therapist: (Therapist notices that patient has an odd look on her face of happiness and upset at the same moment) Yes, and these parents have that knowledge of you too, just like that wonderful nurse, and they are so open-hearted they are delighted to embrace you. Whether you are happy or sad, they are delighted to warmly embrace you.

Patient: (Long pause)

Therapist: Helen, where are you now in your imagination? *[Therapist directly inquires about patient's state in response to possible noncollaborative silence]*

Patient: I was having trouble there at that hospital . . . when they switched the nursing teams around and I couldn't meet with Nancy she would like make an effort to be around like . . . she would like make an effort to, like, talk to me during that so . . . I still was able to talk with her.

Therapist: Nancy knew that you'd like her to be around and she wanted to be there for you—

Patient: Mm-hmm.

Therapist: Yes. That's the kind of quality. You can take that element and weave it now into these ideal parents . . . because they really understand *just what you need* and they want to *be there for you* in *just the ways* that you need it. Noticing now how that feels for you . . . what effect has that on you, your felt sense? *[Therapist integrates and builds upon a nonimaginary figure from the patient's memory and marks the importance of this attachment figure holding Helen in mind in a way that feels pervasively attuned to what Helen needed then, and needs now]*

Patient: (Long pause) I guess it made me feel, like, important . . .

Therapist: Mm-hmm.

Patient: . . . and like they . . . would kind of like make sure to meet my needs as much as possible.

Therapist: Yes, they see how special you are. They're *very attuned* to you . . . undivided, *patient.* Taking some nice deep breaths now, really just take in that experience of seeing those qualities in these parents and notice how they are *being* with you, and what it feels like to *be* with them. *[Therapist notices all of a sudden the telltale vein that appears low on the patient's brow, which has been her early warning sign of dysregulation]* I see that something is happening now . . .

Patient: I'm having troubles . . . doing this; it works and then I lose it.

Therapist: These parents really understand about that. Imagine how they are being with you with this deep acceptance of you.

Patient: I just feel like . . . something's really wrong with me and I don't, like . . . quite understand why.

Therapist: What signal are you getting that says that there may be something wrong with you? *[Therapist tries to get patient to recognize her internal emotional state and to enhance her metacognitive capacity to step back and look at her patterns rather than to avoid them or use old assumptions]*

Patient: Because this is so hard for me.

Therapist: What part of it feels hard right now? What are you feeling in your body? *[Therapist momentarily shifts with the patient's shift but keeps the focus on the body sense]*

Patient: Like imagining these things. I feel tension in my arms and hands.

Therapist: What is your anxiety on a scale of 1 to 10?

Patient: Back up to an 8.

Therapist: Mm-hmm. This is really challenging for you, and you can imagine right now your ideal parents who are right there with you who totally accept that fact, who totally understand that, Helen. Imagine letting them know that you feel like there's something wrong with you, and notice how they respond to you, okay? Go ahead and do that, and when you're ready let me know what it's like . . . *[Therapist redirects patient back to the IPF to reassure her that this block can also be handled and that the therapist has confidence in her ability to do so]* Breathing out a little longer on the exhale . . . that's right, good. You can be with this feeling, and be okay. *[Therapist is using a soothing voice in response to Helen's agitation and encouraging her to experience this difficult feeling while using the breath to help her move through it without escalating the negative emotion]*

Patient: (Long pause)

Therapist: Deeper breaths. Let yourself have a nice deep breath. Good. What are you noticing about them?

Patient: They're just kind of listening and not trying to rationalize it.

Therapist: And what effect does that have on your state of mind? *[Fostering metacognitive awareness]*

Patient: It's just like comforting and like kind of like organizing. *[Patient notices that the attuned, accepting presence of the ideal parent figures has a soothing and organizing effect]*

Therapist: Yes, it's comforting and organizing for you. Just be with this now . . . You can just enjoy how abiding and patient and understanding they are. Just *really feel* what that feels like . . . taking nice deep breaths while you're doing that, *really take* it in . . .

Patient: (Long pause)

Therapist: These parents are never angry. They are deeply comforting to you.

Patient: . . . like really feels like sort of sad.

Therapist: *[Therapist recognizes that patient has moved away from the ambivalence and toward the attachment-based longing, which brings up sadness]* Yes, it feels *sad*; so go ahead and just feel that feeling of sadness, just *really have it* in your body. *[Therapist is watching very closely for vitality effects and tracking them with the patient]* Just open up to that feeling, and then notice how these parents are shifting their stance towards you, in *just the right way* for you. *[Therapist recognizes that patient likely needs to adjust the distance as her longing comes up to help reduce her fear of closeness and anticipation of rejection, thereby activating anxious preoccupation]* They know *exactly* what you need . . . Go ahead right now and sense about the right distance . . . the physical distance between you and them, and see if it's how you want it to be, and let me know. Breathing deeply.

Patient: I like have my head in their lap and . . . it feels okay. *[Patient shows proximity-seeking]*

Therapist: Good. Is there any other thing that you want . . . any more physical closeness or anything you'd like to adjust about the closeness?

[Therapist highlights that the patient has the capacity to adjust the imagery to best fit her needs]

Patient: Well, like, sometimes I would want like . . . them to play with my hair or like put their hand on me or something, but sometimes I wouldn't.

[Patient sees herself as agent of proximity-seeking]

Therapist: *Yes*, and they understand that sometimes you *really* want that kind of comfort . . . that *really soothing* comfort . . . that they know how to read your signals about it. So go ahead and notice what that feels like, to feel *completely secure* in the amount of comfort that you have and knowing that they *absolutely understand* how to read you and what that feels like. Breathing really deeply, taking that in . . . *really taking it in.* Allow yourself to *really feel* what it's like . . . let it feel just right.

Patient: (Long pause)

Therapist: Just stay right with this and make sure that it feels just right for you. If there's any adjustment you need to make, go ahead and make it. Breathing deeply. On a scale from 1 to 10, how anxious do you feel?

Patient: Like a 3.

Therapist: What do you need in the scene to let that move down to a 2?

Patient: (Sighing.) Maybe for my father to move a little further away.

Therapist: Yes. Good . . . let that happen . . . notice what effect that has . . . and these parents *completely understand* that . . . And they're there to *deeply comfort* you in just the way that feels right to you . . . (Long pause) Okay, now, would it be okay to leave this scene?

Patient: (Nods in silent response.)

Therapist: Okay, so go ahead and let all of those *good* and *positive* feelings just stay nicely settled with you while you allow yourself to come back fully in the present. I'll gradually count from five down to one, and with each number feel yourself comfortably and smoothly coming back fully to this room here with me . . . five . . . four . . . three . . . two . . . one. Open your eyes, looking all around . . . looking at me over here . . . So how was that?

(Patient and therapist debrief and the session ends.)

In the session that immediately followed the patient's second AAI, three years after her first, Helen came in and reported a dream she had had the night following the recent AAI. The session does not employ the IPF protocol but shows some of the changes in Helen's preoccupied stance with the therapist.

Patient: I had a weird dream right after the AAI that you were upset that I could tell that you were having a reaction to what I was saying. *[Patient is smiling happily as she says this, her words in contrast to the exhibited emotion. The therapist wonders whether this appearance is evidence of* *patient's preoccupied stance or of increasing comfort about exploring the therapist's feelings in a way that is collaborative and exploratory.]*

Therapist: And what was my reaction?

Patient: Well, so the upsetness was like . . . sad or something, but your reaction . . . I don't know what your reaction was . . .

Therapist: I looked sad?

Patient: You were like crying, just like almost like you were gonna cry.

Therapist: Like I was sad.

Patient: Yeah.

Therapist: And I was upset that you noticed that?

Patient: Yeah.

Therapist: Okay, I get it.

Patient: You were not . . . your upset and sadness was about the fact that I could *tell* that you were having a reaction.

Therapist: And what did it seem like was the reaction I had to what you were saying?

Patient: Oh. So that I'm not sure. That wasn't clear in the dream. Yeah, you were having a reaction to what I was saying.

Therapist: Okay. My reaction was to what you were saying. And I didn't want you to notice that about me. What do you make of that dream, Helen?

Patient: (Laughs.) Well, I mean the biggest thing that I make out of it is I never remember my dreams so I feel like that means something that I did remember this [Yes] but . . . um . . . [Yes] I don't know . . . I don't know what to make of it other than that.

Therapist: So can we translate it a little? I feel like it's such a powerful dream . . . for your . . . for the themes that are important in your therapy. Throw out some ideas.

Patient: What do you mean?

Therapist: So let's see if we can clarify some of those themes. I'm interested in what your thoughts are.

Patient: Um . . . well like you have an emotion and . . . and . . . you're . . . well I thought it was kind of weird that you like didn't want me to know [Mm-hmm] that you were reacting to my answers. *[This description represents what this preoccupied patient had regularly experienced with her mother—the variable responsiveness and confusing affect that Helen had been punished for noticing in her mother]*

Therapist: Mm-hmm, that I was having the emotion . . .

Patient: That you had just . . . that you . . . yeah, or like just reacting to what I . . . the answers I was giving, but then I was thinking maybe you really were having reactions and I noticed something, like, subconsciously.

Therapist: Mm-hmm, in the real interview? *[Therapist is aware of how* *much more connected the patient is to her own thoughts and feelings in the post-treatment AAI]*

Patient: Yeah.

Therapist: Well, let's look at that. Let's let your dream point to something for us and let's just look at that. So open yourself up to what it's pointing to . . . the memory of the interview and the experience of that and any feeling that you might have noticed. *[Therapist is orienting the patient toward her own feelings and encouraging her to explore her emotions and those of the attachment figure, which had been unsafe to do with her mother as a child]*

Patient: Well, there were . . . there were a couple times when you would . . . you were like smiling . . . I remember I like asked you like a clarifying question or something (Mm-hmm), and so I thought it was because like you couldn't really . . . you like had to stick to your script.

Therapist: What did the smile communicate to you?

Patient: Um . . . just that I had to like figure out the question myself.

Therapist: Mm-hmm. Do you remember what effect that noticing my smile . . . my nonverbal *[collaborative]* communication had on your state of mind?

Patient: Um . . . I mean, I guess it made the experience be more like positive and like, because like the first time I did it [the AAI] I had such a hard time, I had to leave the room and stuff (laughs), so . . .

Therapist: It was a little moment of . . . even though we weren't communicating verbally because of the rules of the interview, you could see . . . you could see a nonverbal communication from me. You knew I was holding you in my mind . . . *[Therapist is marking this important moment where the patient has bravely allowed herself to notice warm emotion in her therapist's facial expression]*

Patient: Mm-hmm.

Therapist: What about . . . can you open up in the memory to other feelings or ideas or emotions from that interview that you noticed that you were having or that . . . or in between us or me?

Patient: I think I just felt like more open to it and not . . . and not like as scared about it (Mm-hmm) . . . It was . . . it was sort of weird, like when I knew that you already knew the answer to something you asked from the list of questions; it kind of felt like . . . it sort of felt like maybe like more of like an intimate moment because you like knew, but I had to say it anyways.

Therapist: Mm-hmm . . . Can you explore that a little?

Patient: (Long pause)

Therapist: I'm interested in what contributed to that intimate moment.

Patient: Well, like . . . feeling like you knew . . . like, what I knew . . .

Therapist: Mm-hmm . . . mm-hmm . . . that we both knew together. *[Therapist is holding the state of mind of the patient, as perceived by the patient, and highlighting the collaboration]*

Patient: Mm-hmm.

Therapist: But then in having to answer it anyway for the purpose of the interview, did you . . . what did you notice about your experience of answering even though I already knew?

Patient: Well, I think there were like a couple times that I was surprised with what I said, like that maybe things weren't . . . as, like, rigid as I thought.

Therapist: Say more?

Patient: That, like, my thoughts and feelings about things weren't as, like, blocking . . .

Therapist: What's an example?

Patient: Well, like the question about um . . . like abuse and things, I was surprised at how . . . like, easy it was to talk about it, like . . . because at first I was like, "Oh, I don't want to say anything" (Mm-hmm), but then when I did, like it . . . it wasn't . . . it just came out easier than I thought.

Therapist: I noticed that too, really big. Like ideas and feelings are more approachable to you. I've noticed that *a lot* lately, not just in the interview, and that's . . . I think your dream, your dream is so symbolic of that. It invites us. It's like your dream is literally inviting us in here to come closer to those things that have been hard for you to approach. *[Therapist is using language that emphasizes their collaboration on exploring Helen's mind and experience]*

Patient: Yeah, like what I'm feeling, well, basically I'm feeling better, and everything's easier, like approaching feelings and thoughts that used to be scary.

Therapist: Mm-hmm.

In another session soon after the one above, Helen, looking very bright, reported having spontaneously traveled with a friend to a new destination over the weekend. The IPF protocol is brought in at the end of the transcript and demonstrates that for this particularly complex patient, even in the later stages of her therapy, after significant improvement in both symptoms and attachment status and metacognitive ability on the AAI, this patient can still experience challenges in setting up and engaging with her IPFs. For the therapist using the IPF protocol, it is important to be flexible but persistent, if not a little dogged from time to time.

Therapist: So did that cheer you up, going down there?

Patient: Mm-hmm.

Therapist: You look much cheered.

Patient: Yeah.

Therapist: Good. Any thoughts about what happened with your mood state?

Patient: Well . . . I don't know if I'm like sort of like panicking at any, like, feeling, and then it's like making me feel crazy but it's hard to know . . . I, I'm afraid of like getting into like . . . a like . . . extended bad period and . . . so it's like hard for me to . . . like just like experience something, and not worry that it's gonna stay or get worse or something. I don't know, but then I also think like maybe like I am experiencing like weird things, so I don't know. Maybe it's a combination of both.

Therapist: So you think it was more your mood state that was making you have that reaction to her. *[She had wanted to fire her dance instructor because she thought he was thinking that she was awkward and moving away from helping her]*

Patient: Yeah. I don't know, but then I was like all in a weird place . . . all . . . well, not all day but for a few hours . . . I just don't know what . . . how to understand it . . .

Therapist: Well, between yesterday and now, what do you think helped make the shift the most?

Patient: It was sort of a combination of things but mostly like distracting myself. Like I had this assignment for school (Mm-hmm) that I worked on yesterday, and like I had so much trouble like forcing myself to like sit down and like focus on it but like once I finally did, I spent like a few hours doing it and I like felt good that I was like able to focus on it and that I like completed something, so . . .

Therapist: Good for you.

Patient: Yeah.

Therapist: That must have been *especially hard* at first, and then *especially good* that you were able to focus and complete your work. *[Therapist mirrors and marks patient's experiences of difficulty and success]*

Patient: Well, I don't know, like part of it is like just kind of like forcing myself to do it, but like part of it feels related just to like my moods and like out of my control because it's like sometimes . . . because I have like a pretty like strong like drive to like do things (Yeah) like normally so it's like . . . when I can't, it's like a lot of it feels like it's just not in my control, so I don't know. I mean, there's like . . . there's a point where it's like it is in my control and it's just like hard to make myself do it but then there's times where it feels . . . really does feel impossible, so I don't know.

Therapist: I think it's . . . well, I think it's amazing because you are able to get yourself to do so much hard work and you obviously do a great job of it, but I think it's good for you to be able to try to make a distinction between when you just say, "Oh, I've gotta just work hard," and when it's like a time when you really can't harness that much and you need to stop and tend to yourself and look after yourself and, you know, like really paying attention to your moods, not being so hard driving when it's just not the right time. I mean, yesterday . . . it seems like you were able to just be in the upset, and even though it freaked you out considerably, it seems like you were also able to recognize it as possibly a part of acclimating and adjusting, and then you were . . . then you were able to take some time to just be in the upset. When was . . . when was it that you were able to get back to doing the work? (Um.) Was that today or last night?

Patient: It was like in the afternoon yesterday.

Therapist: Amazing. That really is. That's a *huge, huge* difference, isn't it?

Patient: Yeah.

Therapist: What is . . . how did you get yourself in between those two things?

Patient: I don't know. I just . . . like I feel like I'm more like balanced.

Therapist: Well, I'm really glad you're feeling a lot better today. I'm *very interested* in how you're thinking about those kinds of episodes now *[Therapist marks her stronger metacognitive function]* and how you're talking to yourself about it. I really think it's *amazing* that you were able to experience that kind of dysregulation and then organize yourself into working in such a concentrated way and then going out and socializing and having fun at the party last night and going to the beach today. I do imagine that there's acclimation going on for sure, not just in terms of your body, your chemistry, but also in terms of how you're thinking about things, and also in terms of yourself, like your growing self, so I think it's *really good* that you allowed yourself to be upset about it but didn't . . . didn't go into overreaction . . . like panic mode that was sustained.

Patient: Yeah, I don't know, like it . . . it did like freak me out a little bit because I did start thinking about like cutting and like I . . . like briefly thought about like killing myself but like I was also able to recognize that it was just because I wanted to get out of the state of mind that I was in, so . . . *[Metacognitive mastery of state of mind]*

Therapist: That's fantastic. (Patient laughs.) Really, that's fantastic; *good for you!* *[Therapist marks patient's metacognitive mastery that indicates a huge improvement from the beginning of her therapy]* I can tell your face is shifting ever so subtly. Is it hard for you to take my enthusiasm?

Patient: Yeah, it is.

Therapist: Is it hard?

Patient: Yeah, because like I also feel like the part of me that wants to like resist. DBT is like flagging this like "Don't let them hear you say this." (Laughs.)

Therapist: Well, okay (laughs). I'm really excited and impressed and I'm *just delighted* to see . . . to watch how you're doing things now, and I know that there will likely be times where it's still difficult and challenging and that you'll feel like you are losing your way, but *more and more* you are navigating yourself in ways that feel *so much stronger*, Helen.

Patient: What are we doing today? (Laughs.) Are . . . we're doing some more of the ideal parent figures? *[Patient points to collaborative work]*

Therapist: (Laughs.) We are.

Patient: Okay.

Therapist: But we're going to do a different version of it.

Patient: Okay. (Laughs.)

Therapist: Okay, we'll just track . . . track how you're feeling internally as we go through this, and just . . . and then afterwards we can debrief about what that felt like for you in terms of your own mood states. Okay. Anything else before we start? [Therapist sees the patient beginning to swing her leg in a distinct way and points to that nonverbal communication] I see that there are some of your "indicators" going.

Patient: (Laughs.) No.

Therapist: No?

Patient: No. (Patient calms her leg and shifts into a more focused stance.)

Therapist: All right. We'll do some guided imagery, okay? And we can, as we're going through it, you can pick different things to target, whatever you want to target, okay? So, first of all, allow yourself to take some nice deep breaths and relax now.

Patient: (Laughs.) What? I'm trying.

Therapist: [Therapist again sees patient cocking her head back and forth, in a way that suggests she is bothered] I see this beginning resistance coming up. I . . . I think it's helpful to have both feet on the ground and really just allow yourself the opportunity to relax. Okay, so go ahead and invite your ideal parents in alongside of you now . . . and perhaps you would like to think about yesterday, or if another thing comes to mind that's fine, but you could think about how frustrating it was yesterday, and your confusion about what the cause was and what to do. So imagine your ideal parents . . . and let me know when you have a sense of them clearly with you.

Patient: Okay.

Therapist: Allowing yourself now to feel how this feels to have their presence *so perfectly suited* to you. Going ahead now and imagine telling them about how you were feeling yesterday, or even, if you want, imagine being in that feeling state from yesterday and going to them about it. When you sense yourself with them in this way, let me know.

Patient: Okay, yep.

Therapist: Now imagine that these parents are *absolutely responsive* to you as you're sharing with them what *you feel* like. Notice how this mother is *sturdy . . .* and *strong*, and she's physically and emotionally *warm*, *very warm . . .* And the father is very *deeply patient . . . very soothing*, *deeply soothing*.

Patient: I'm having trouble staying with this. (Patient is wiggling her leg as she is saying this)

Therapist: Yes, and these parents *really* get that. Take some nice deep breaths . . . they are being with you in *just the right way* you need them to be right now.

Patient: Okay, yeah.

Therapist: The scene is about to shift, and in a moment you can imagine a new scene, you can imagine being with these parents in just the right situation, in which you feel these parents are *so very attuned* to *you*, to *your feelings*, to *your needs*. They find *just the right ways* to be *very* soothing to you, *very* responsive to your needs. They are physically present with you, *just the right* distance and closeness. When you sense them being with you in these ways, go ahead and describe it to me, breathing nice and deep.

Patient: Can you repeat that?

Therapist: Yes. Imagine another scene, being with your ideal parents, who are *even more soothing*, *deeply soothing*, *deeply comforting*, *very warm* and *affectionate*, and *so carefully attuned* to *your* state of mind, *your* feelings *no matter what they are*. Taking nice deep breaths. Good . . . When you're ready, you can describe to me what's happening.

Patient: I'm thinking about being in the hospital, like the medical hospital (Mm-hmm), she's like stroking my hair (Mm-hmm), and then he's just like standing nearby.

Therapist: Yes, this mother is *so comforting* and *soothing* and she knows *exactly* what feels best to you, and she's *so glad* she can be there for you when you need her. She's focused *totally on you*. Notice what effect that has on your state of mind.

Patient: (Long pause.)

Therapist: Nice deep breath in, longer breath out, good. That's right.

Patient: (Long pause.)

Therapist: These are parents who are *very interested* in your *strength*. [Therapist notices that patient's leg has begun to swing back and forth] Noticing what's happening inside, Helen, as you do this . . . What are you feeling in your body? . . . Try to track when the shift comes. *[Fostering metacognitive identification of state]* This mother is right here for you in just exactly the right way.

Patient: I'm having trouble like sticking with it. I started thinking about one time when I was in the hospital and what my mom did.

Therapist: Mm . . . what time was that? *[Therapist is flexibly going with patient's shift here]*

Patient: When I was like, when I was 17 and I had overdosed really bad . . . I was like getting really sick and . . . the doctor came in and said that I might not like pull through and my mom like got really upset but like . . . like basically like abandoned me, was like crying by herself.

Therapist: Mm-hmm. So go back to that scene right now . . . so in your mind's eye go ahead and redo that scene now with your ideal parents. Can you try that?

Patient: (Smiles and nods in response.)

Therapist: Good. Using your imagination . . . this is a whole different scene, now with a different mother who is *ideally suited* to you. Taking a nice deep breath . . . (Therapist is speaking in a markedly soothing voice.) Good. Imagine that same scene, but now you're with your ideal mother. She is *very responsive* to you. She's hearing this news, and she has you and your feelings and your reactions fully in her mind, in her eyes. She is *very sturdy* and *strong*. She knows that you need emotional closeness, physical closeness, *just the right* amount. She knows that you need reassurance and in this crisis she's *so happy* to be able to be *right there with you*. She knows you need that . . . Where is she?

Patient: Like right next to the bed.

Therapist: Would you like her to be any closer?

Patient: (Shakes her head no in silent response.)

Therapist: Okay. What kinds of qualities or characteristics do you sense from her right now?

Patient: She's, like, focused on me. And, like, just not, like, panicking.

Therapist: Yeah, she's *so sturdy*. She's *so strong*. Go ahead and notice right now what effect that has on your state of mind, and when you're ready, let me know what it is.

Patient: Just, like, calming and reassuring . . . like . . . she hasn't like given up on me yet.

Therapist: Mm-hmm, yes. She has *total faith* and *confidence* in *you* in all ways, but right now she gives you her presence and her focus so that you can pull through . . . Do you notice anything else, as you're together with her like this?

Patient: I just don't feel so, like, apathetic.

Therapist: Yes. You and she both care a lot. And she cares *very deeply* about you and about what's going to happen. What about your ideal father? . . . How is he being with you?

Patient: He's just kind of a present.

Therapist: Where is he located?

Patient: He's just, like, standing, like, a couple feet away.

Therapist: Would you like him to be any closer?

Patient: Well, I don't know, maybe just standing, like, right next to me.

Therapist: Mm-hmm. Really experience what it's like that he's standing *right there* next to you, in a way that feels *really comforting* to you, *deeply* comforting.

Patient: Mm-hmm.

Therapist: Okay, good. He's very *protective* . . . very *calm*, *deeply* patient. Go ahead and notice what effect that has on you and your state of mind.

Patient: . . . just, like, increases the feeling of safety.

Therapist: Good. Yes, *really feel* that increased feeling of *safety*. Does it need to change at all with him to make it feel even more right?

Patient: (Shakes head "no" in silent response.)

Therapist: Okay. So just go ahead and *really absorb* how that feels, all together. You can stay with that as long as you'd like . . . And when you're ready for the scene to shift, you can let me know.

Patient: (Nods in silent response.)

Therapist: Yes. Now go ahead and imagine a *different* circumstance, a circumstance that feels *just right* to experience *together* with the presence of your ideal parents. [*Therapist notices subtle nonverbal activity in the patient indicating that she is distracted*] What are you noticing?

Patient: (Laughs.)

Therapist: Okay, stay with this, stay with me, and with your imagination you can create a scene of being with these parents, where these parents can *really help you* feel *more secure* and good.

Patient: Could do yesterday.

Therapist: Mm-hmm. Which part of yesterday?

Patient: I was, like, laying on my bed for a while [Mm-hmm], and I was getting very agitated.

Therapist: Okay . . . just imagine them there . . . they are *openly responsive* to your agitation and they move closer to you, *just the right* closeness, not too close, not too far, but what feels *just right* to you. They know you need reassurance, and they're *very* patient, *very* happy to *give it to you.* They're very stable and strong and they know . . . they have *total confidence* in *you.* And you do not have to worry about their feelings or state of mind at all. They're just here to be comforting to you, to give you support . . . What are you noticing about the effect that their presence has on you?

Patient: Well, I don't feel as alone.

Therapist: Mm-hmm. What's that like for you?

Patient: It like makes everything a little less scary . . .

Therapist: How is it that they're being with you? What qualities and characteristics really stand out to you?

Patient: (Pause.)

Therapist: What's happening? *[Therapist notices a shift in the patient's state and calls attention to the shift.]*

Patient: I don't know.

Therapist: What just happened?

Patient: I just got, like, distracted.

Therapist: What distracted you?

Patient: . . . I don't know . . .

Therapist: What are you thinking about now?

Patient: . . . I just don't want to do this anymore.

Therapist: Okay, let's find out what happened that makes you not want to do this anymore. *[Therapist fosters collaborative exploration]*

Patient: . . . well, I just was having trouble, like, imagining them there because . . . I don't know, I guess because it was like more like a real thing than just like the making up the whole scene.

Therapist: Mm-hmm. So it felt harder to use your imagination?

Patient: And just to imagine . . . yeah, I guess so, just for them to be there.

Therapist: Okay. I think your imagination has been doing a very good job, but for some reason, there's like a blockage. I'm just curious about what might be creating that.

Patient: I mean, I—when I am in, like, states like that, I don't usually like anybody to see me because I'm, like, very self-conscious.

Therapist: Oh! I'm so glad you told me that. I never knew that . . . Do you mind my asking, I'm just wondering, what is the thing that you're most self-conscious about? Can we do a little more of the ideal parent protocol to address that specifically? I know I'm asking a lot . . . but that's so important what you just said.

Patient: Okay.

Therapist: Great. Now tune in to that part of you that feels so self-conscious.

Patient: (Nods in silent response.)

Therapist: Okay, yes. So now go ahead and imagine that scene again. You're there on the bed, and you can bring in your ideal parents who are *absolutely* perfectly *attuned to you*, and *accepting* of you, no matter how you feel, no matter what's happening, it doesn't matter. They are *so happy* to be there because they know you need them, and because they know they can help you to *feel safe* and good. They have *absolute delight* in *you* no matter what. They find *just the right* closeness to you, not too close and not too far, just right. *Really imagine* their abiding presence, no matter how you're feeling. What are you noticing about the scene?

Patient: I'm, like, sitting on the edge of the bed instead of lying down (Yeah). And they're, like, just sitting next to me.

Therapist: Mm-hmm. Are you in between them?

Patient: The mom is next to me and then Dad is on the other side of her.

Therapist: Okay. Does that feel right to you?

Patient: (Nods in silent response.)

Therapist: Okay, good. What are you noticing about their qualities and characteristics? What are their ways of being that really fit with what you need?

Patient: Just, like, calming and, like, they're just being present.

Therapist: Yeah, they're *really* calming, and *really* present. What . . . what effect are they having on you right now.

Patient: I feel more able to, like, get up and not stay stuck.

Therapist: Mm-hmm. You're more able to get up and not stay stuck. What's most helpful from them right now?

Patient: Mm. It's, like, just them being there.

Therapist: Yes, just them being there, being there for *you*. They are *with* you, and are confident in you. They are *deeply* reassuring to you. They are *absolutely delighted* to be there with you no matter how you are feeling. Do you sense that with them?

Patient: (Nods in silent response.)

Therapist: Yes. So take some nice deep breaths in, and really let yourself notice what that's like to have them there . . . and there's no need to feel self-conscious at all with them. . . What is that like?

Patient: Just, like, relaxing.

Therapist: Yes, that is right, you can just relax. Good, really good. All right, now notice what in your experience with them . . . how are you being with them physically that shows that relaxing? *[Therapist engages patient's body experience to support deep integration of the positive sense of the IPFs]*

Patient: Like, resting my head on their shoulder.

Therapist: Mm-hmm, yes. *Yes*, you can just be relaxed, and rest your head on their shoulder, because you don't have to worry about them. You're just relaxed. Does that feel okay?

Patient: (Nods.) . . . Yes, I feel relieved.

Therapist: Yes, *deeply* relieved and *relaxed* in your body and your mind . . . All right, you can keep all these good feelings with you, nicely settled around you, feeling them there with you, as you let this scene dissolve away . . . Is there any other scene that you want to revisit before we stop?

Patient: (Laughs.) No, that was good. I feel good.

As was noted in the introduction to this case, the Three Pillars treatment led to an increase of Helen's coherence on the AAI transcript from a 2 to an 8. The AAI also indicated that her attachment status went from disorganized (CC/E3/Ds1) to earned secure status with some remaining anxious-preoccupied features (F5). Manifestations of insecure strategies are likely to occur periodically at the outer ranges of the secure (F) spectrum, especially at F1 and F5, often in conjunction with relationally intimate experiences, including those that can occur during psychotherapy interactions. Helen continued to show some anxious-preoccupied features, but significantly less so than during the early treatment period. Given her comorbid bipolar spectrum disorder, she remained vulnerable to high stress levels and disrupted sleep, and in the face of those challenges she was vulnerable to mood instability and to some reappearance of anxious-preoccupied patterns. Her greatly enhanced coherence of mind and metacognitive capacities, however, afforded her the ability to recognize when anxious-preoccupied states arose and to identify antecedents and engage in metacognitive mastery to better regulate those states.

Interestingly, before her shift into earned secure attachment status, Helen had often shown resistance to using her well-honed DBT skills because she had experienced the teaching of those skills as invalidating her painful feelings of having been rejected and neglected by her parents as a small child. With her IPF-developed internal working model of unconditional acceptance and dedicated attunement, she became more likely to use those skills. Of great significance is that she became able to tolerate processing of traumatic material from her past, because with her greater internal security and metacognitive capacity, feelings came to feel less inherently frightening.

Enhancing Helen's capacity for recognizing and experiencing her felt sense of herself was stabilizing and organizing for Helen. The emphasis that was placed in Helen's treatment on her somatic awareness of her emotions—known as interoception—is important to underscore. Antonia New, from Mount Sinai Hospital, in a presentation of her research (Harvard Medical School Conference on Attachment and Borderline Personality Disorder, 2015), suggested that a mechanism that gives rise to borderline personality disorder is the missing ability of interoception. Patients with BPD suffer from an inability to experience their felt sense of themselves—their emotions in their bodies—and are instead overly focused on attempting to read *others'* feelings, which is consistent with the anxious-preoccupied attachment style. Dr. New suggested that a central goal of new psychotherapies for treating BPD should be increasing these patients' interoception ability. As the reader recognizes from Helen's treatment transcripts, and from the guidance in Chapter 8 about rooting patients' IPF imagery experiences in their bodies, our Three Pillars model integrates interoceptive development into the therapy process.

In the next chapter, we focus on treatment considerations for patients with disorganized status who show a prominent mix of both anxious-preoccupied and dismissing strategies.

CHAPTER 13

Treating Disorganized or Fearful Attachment

In this chapter, we indicate how to tailor the Three Pillars treatment elements according to the specific developmental experiences and attachment patterns and needs of patients with disorganized attachment.

The Origins of Disorganized or Fearful Attachment

Main and Solomon (1986) examined over 200 videotapes of anomalous behaviors in infants who were not classifiable from their Strange Situation (SS) behavior. These infants showed a variety of contradictory attachment behaviors that could not be characterized by either the secure, avoidant, or ambivalent prototypes. Instead, they showed contradictory elements of avoidant and ambivalent attachment behaviors, either in alternation or simultaneously. Main and Solomon also noted the frequent occurrence of incomplete attachment behaviors once initiated, including interrupted and stereotypical movements, freezing, and outright disorganization of behavior. To classify this group, they created a fourth prototype of infant attachment, which they called disorganized/disoriented (hereafter referred to as disorganized). Main (1995) described disorganized attachment as reflecting a collapse of behavioral strategies of attachment. Children with disorganized attachment lack a single, unified IWM for attachment and instead have multiple contradictory internal working models. Grossmann, Grossmann, and Waters (2005) further differentiated the disorganized category into three subtypes in children to indicate the most prominent feature: contradictory attachment behaviors, attachment behaviors lacking any goal orientation, and direct disorganization.

Various explanations have been offered for the origins of disorganized attachment. Drawing from Bowlby's original ideas, Chisholm (1998) and Solomon and George (1999) noted that some children with disorganized attachment had prolonged or repeated separations from their caregivers, and Solomon and George highlight that disorganized attachment in infants is associated with depression and alcoholism in mothers. Main and Hesse (1990) observed that mothers of disorganized infants had a pattern of *both frightening and frightened behavior*. At times such mothers would become aggressive, disruptive, loud, looming, or otherwise scary to the infant. At other times the mother would become fearful, tentative, and confused around the child and didn't appear to know what to do. Main and Hesse theorized that the fundamental problem for the disorganized infant is that the same primary attachment figure was *both a source of security and a source of fear*. They called the resulting experience "fear without solution" (quote from Lyons-Ruth & Jacobvitz, 1999, p. 549). This impossible dilemma, over time, results in contradictory attachment behaviors, such as moving toward *and* moving away from the primary attachment figure. In other words, children with disorganized attachment develop a contradictory pattern of using both deactivating and hyperactivating attachment strategies, either alternating or simultaneously. Disorganized infants never develop a single, coherent attachment strategy.

Schuengel, Bakermans-Kranenburg, and van IJzendoorn (1999) attempted to replicate the Main and Hesse (1990) study. They found that at best, parental frightening and frightened behavior was only a modest predictor of disorganized attachment and began to seek out other predictors. *Maternal dissociated behavior* was a stronger predictor of infant disorganized attachment than frightening/ frightened parental behavior. Similarly, George and Solomon (1996), from administering the AAI to mothers of infants with disorganized attachment, found that many of these mothers had significant *unresolved states of mind with respect to past trauma, abuse, or loss*. They suggest that when "the caregiver's unresolved fear [is] pervasive enough to be repeatedly communicated to the infant" (p. 37), then that unresolved fear creates a corresponding pervasive fear in the infant. When a parent's unresolved states result in dissociation, there is a high likelihood of pervasive misattunement to the infant's states, including fear states. Further, unresolved status can lead to reenactment of past abuse in the form of child maltreatment: Across studies, 55% to 82% of infants with disorganized attachment were found to have been maltreated (Lyons-Ruth & Jacobvitz, 1999).

Lyons-Ruth, Bronfman, and Parsons (1999) observed that caregivers of disorganized infants were more intrusive and negative in their communications with their infants and also exhibited frightening and frightened behavior. They found that such caregivers were at times hostile and aggressive and at other times helpless and confused toward their infants. Another significant finding was a pervasive pattern of disruptive or inaccurate affective communications between infant and caregiver, especially in response to attachment behaviors. Role reversals and getting the child overly involved in the parent's state of mind were also common. The authors concluded that extreme parental misattunement and disrupted affective communication are critical in the development of disorganized attachment in children. These parental failures result in the child's inability to develop organized strategies for maintaining proximity, protection, or comfort from the caregiver (Lyons-Ruth & Jacobvitz, 2008, p. 675).

Clearly the origins of disorganized attachment are complex, and there seem to be multiple pathways to the development of disorganized attachment in children and disorganized or fearful attachment in adults. As Lyons-Ruth and Jacobvitz (1999) report, "the overall patterning of parental behaviors within the disorganized spectrum may take quite different forms" (p. 531). Particularly puzzling is that disorganized attachment sometimes occurs in seemingly normal families in which "there is little that distinguishes these mothers from mothers of secure, avoidant, or ambivalent children" (Solomon & George, 1999, p. 13). Main and Solomon (1990) note that their sample infants were "unlikely to be classified as disorganized with more than one caregiver" and that disorganized attachment "emerges within a particular relationship" with one parent (cited in Lyons-Ruth & Jacobvitz, 1999, p. 524). However, the AAIs of the disorganized adults in our clinical sample revealed that a consistent disorganized style in relation to both parents or multiple foster parents was common.

Regardless of the sources of this attachment pattern, children with disorganized attachment show multiple, contradictory attachment behaviors—both deactivating and hyperactivating. They have more dissociative experiences and behaviors than other children, are often in states of unmitigated high-fear arousal, and overall show significantly greater negative emotional arousal than children with other attachment prototypes (Spangler & Grossmann, 1993, p. 103). They have a poor capacity for affect regulation, which contributes to their chronic negative affect states. Observation of their play behavior reveals marked inhibition of playful exploration as well as frightening, explosively angry, and helpless states (Solomon & George, 1999, p. 18). In part because of inhibited exploratory behavior, self-development is markedly impaired.

The Therapeutic Stance With the Disorganized Patient

Because the caregiver(s) of the disorganized patient served as both a source of fear and a source of safety, it is especially important that the therapist is consistently a safe haven and does not behave in ways that exacerbate fear in the patient. In response to disorganized patients' high negative emotional arousal in general and high unremitting fear arousal in particular, the therapist aims to be a calming, soothing, and reassuring presence. Because disorganized patients show both deactivating and hyperactivating attachment behaviors, the therapist's stance must be *actively engaging, yet not involving* of the patient in the therapist's state of mind. If the caregivers of a disorganized patient are described as frightening, frightened, and/or hostile and helpless, the positive-opposite qualities that the therapist embodies are to be comforting, fearless, confident, accepting, welcoming, determined, and proactive. Because caregivers of disorganized patients are often highly dissociative and often suddenly and markedly shift behaviors and states with the disorganized child, the therapist presents as fully present, consistent, steady, and predictable. Because caregivers of disorganized patients were pervasively misattuned to the infant and unable to engage in the reciprocal attunement of spontaneous ongoing facial affective displays, it is particularly important that the therapist be consistently carefully attuned to and nonverbally matching of the entire range of the disorganized patient's affects. Such patients rarely express positive affects, and so the therapist finds ways to encourage and reinforce the disorganized patient's positive emotional expressions. Attachment initiatives and spontaneous affective displays in disorganized infants were often disrupted by the caregiver, so the therapist must be especially careful not to interrupt the patient and let the patient completely express initiated attachment displays and behaviors.

Using Ideal Parent Figure Imagery With Disorganized Patients

In our orphanage study (see p. 211), we found that the majority of our disorganized subjects had either a mixed or borderline personality disorder diagnosis and also a major dissociative disorder diagnosis (DID or DDNOS). A common feature in patients with personality and/or dissociative disorders is rapid and marked shifting of states of mind and behaviors. Borderline patients, for example, rapidly shift between highly negative and highly idealized views of self or other; DID patients rapidly shift between child, apparently normal, and aggressive-perpetrator self-states or alter personality states. In both personality and dissociative disorder patients, we have come to view the manifestation of each shifting behavior and state of mind *as a spontaneous expression of a specific attachment need at that moment.* Therefore, working with ideal parent figures is more complex with disorganized patients than with dismissing or anxious-preoccupied patients. Unlike patients with personality and dissociative disorders, dismissing and preoccupied patients have a unified sense-of-self, however underdeveloped it may be, and with such patients, the therapist introduces each IPF theme as if it would be experienced by the patient's same unitary self. This approach cannot be used, however, when working with a disorganized patient. With the disorganized patient, the therapist facilitates the patient's experience of *a separate and unique set of ideal parent figures for each shifting behavior or state of mind.* For example, a DID patient may switch to a fearful child state; then, the therapist suggests that the child can imagine and be with *just the right* parents who are particularly responsive to this child's fear arousal. If the DID patient then switches to a dismissing state, the therapist suggests imagining parent figures who are engaging and responsive. If the patient then switches to a hostile-aggressive state, the therapist suggests imagining parent figures who clearly understand and know how to safely contain the aggression. For each significant behavioral or state shift in the treatment session, the therapist suggests a new set of ideal parent figures who are best responsive to the underlying attachment need associated with each shift. The patient's overall experience of the series of *state-specific IPFs* across the entire session approximates continuous IPF responsiveness.

Therapists of disorganized patients benefit from understanding the different forms of dissociation that such patients might manifest. Van der Hart, Nijenhuis, Steele, and Brown (2004) demonstrated that while it was thought by some authors that there are two main kinds of dissociation—*dissociative shifts in consciousness*, which, however, are not necessarily dissociative, and *structural dissociation*, which is generally pathological—it is more likely that there is one type of dissociation, namely structural dissociation that pertains to rigid compartmentalization of dissociative(ted) parts. A common treatment practice with patients with multiple personality disorder in the 1980s was for the therapist to call forth a given alter personality state, process a traumatic memory, and then ask the alter to go "back inside." However, van der Hart et al. argued that such practice of calling forth and sending back alters only serves to reinforce the rigid dissociative compartmentalization. Instead, they recommended that once the therapist finishes communicating with a given alter, he or she should *ask that alter to stay present* instead of going back inside. Then, while the first alter remains present, the therapist communicates with a second alter; when finished, the therapist asks the second alter to stay present alongside the first alter, and then communicates with a third alter. Using this approach, there might be three to six alters simultaneously present by the end of the treatment hour. This technique, when used regularly, erodes the rigid dissociative compartmentalization and more and more approaches the goal of a unitary, noncompartmentalized self.

While this *structuralizing technique* was originally developed for trauma processing with MPD/DID patients, we have adapted the technique for working with IPFs on attachment-related themes with disorganized patients. After a period within a session of working with IPF imagery with one alter state, the therapist invites other parts, that also have attachment needs, to come forward, while the current part remains present. For example:

Now, while this part continues to be present and remains in safe contact with these parents, if there are any other parts of the mind that need to feel security in relationship, these parts can come forth and feel connected now, feel connected with *just the right parents* who help them feel *just right* in the way they need to feel . . . it may be in the same or a different way, but either way now let these parts begin to feel security in relationship in the way that they need.

When a patient has a spontaneous structural dissociative shift (i.e., a spontaneous switch to another alter state), the therapist invites the just-spoken-with part to remain present with his or her IPFs while the just-emerged part engages with parent figures who are the ideal, best fit for the new part. For example:

> The part who's just been present and in contact with [his or her] ideal parents can still be present, can stay with me and with the part that has just come forward now. We can all be present while this next part experiences parents who are *ideally suited* to its nature. So this part that has just come forward, imagine now being with parents who are *just right* for you . . . who *really know* how to be with you in *just the right ways* . . . so you begin to feel *comfortable* and *secure* in relation to them.

This combination of IPF imagery and structuralizing facilitates the combined treatment goals of a reduction of dissociation; an increase in organization of mind; the development of a unitary, noncompartmentalized self; and the establishment of a unitary internal working model of secure attachment.

Understanding of the origins and manifestations of disorganized attachment highlights the themes that typically must be addressed using IPF imagery with disorganized patients. First, because they exhibit both deactivating and hyperactivating attachment strategies, all of the specific IPF considerations and practices discussed in the previous two chapters also apply to disorganized patients. Second, since disorganized patients view attachment figures as both a source of safety and as a source of threat, the therapist introduces IPFs who simultaneously provide a deep sense of security or safe haven, yet are carefully attuned and responsive to the patient-as-child's deep fear and mistrust. For example:

> These parents are *completely dedicated* to *protecting you* and *keeping you safe* . . . and yet they also recognize that for now it's hard for you to trust and feel safe with them . . . and they understand what you need to begin to develop that feeling of *trust* and *safety*. Notice how they are now that shows you that they *understand* and *accept* you . . . and how they are that helps you to feel *more at ease* and *safe* with them. They find *just the right balance* for you. How is it that they're being with you that helps you to begin to feel *safe*, and to feel safe with them?

Third, since disorganized attachment entails the inhibition of both attachment behavior and exploratory behavior, IPFs are shaped to encourage both attachment behavior and exploratory behavior in the same interactive sequence. For example:

> Notice how these parents are *right there* when you want to be close to them . . . and they're *always available* for a hug or other ways of reassuring you when you might want or need that. And these parents also *fully*

support whenever you want to explore what's around you, or what's within you . . . they *delight* in the discoveries that you make.

Or:

Patient: I'm kind of looking at what's over there on the other side of the room.

Therapist: Yes. As you find yourself *so very interested* in what's over there, you can let yourself *explore* and engage with what you're finding and discovering. And these parents are *right there*, happy with your explorations, and *always ready* to be there to *support you* and *reassure you* whenever you want or need that.

Fourth, it is especially important to address the chronic-heightened fear arousal in the disorganized patient-as-child by shaping IPFs who are very carefully attuned to the child's fear arousal. For example:

Patient: I'm really afraid.

Therapist: These parents immediately see that you're afraid . . . they're *really attuned* to your inner states, and now they recognize that you're afraid, and they are *right there with you* and they know how to comfort and reassure you *in just the right ways* that bring you a *new sense of calm* and *serenity* that you've rarely experienced before.

Fifth, since many disorganized patients have been victims of trauma and abuse, IPFs are shaped to be fiercely protective, but not intrusively protective, of the patient-as-child. For example:

As you're with these parents now, you really get the sense that they're *completely dedicated* to keeping you *safe* from any harm . . . to making sure that nothing happens that would hurt you in any way. They are *so very protective* of you, and they also know how to keep you safe without it feeling like too much to you, so you can be *safe* and also *free* to be you.

Sixth, since disorganized patients are frequently emotionally numb, IPFs are introduced who know how to stimulate the patient-as-child's full range of emotional arousal in the intersubjective collaboration. For example:

These parents know that you can feel a wide range of emotions, and they also understand that sometimes those emotions get covered over and you can feel kind of numb. Notice how their ways of being with you help you to *feel what you feel* . . . how you can feel what you feel and let them know something about what you feel, and they respond to you in *just the right ways* that honor and support anything at all that you're feeling, whether it's sad, happy, mad, scared, safe, peaceful, or *anything at all.*

Seventh, since many disorganized patients have learned to expect others to be dissociative and not present, IPFs are shaped to be fully present, consistently and accurately attuned, and very real in their interactions with the patient-as-child. For example:

And you can *really see* that these parents are *right there with you*, not only physically, but also attentively with their presence, *right there* in the moment being attuned to you and to what's happening together. The ways they are with you feel *so very real*, and it's *very reassuring* to sense them *so very attuned* to you.

Eighth, since disorganized children's attachment and exploratory initiatives were harmed by the caregivers' persistent inability to be contingently responsive, IPFs are shaped to be consistently responsive to the communications of the patient-as-child. For example:

These parents are *so accurately* and *comfortably* attuned to you that they respond to whatever you communicate to them in *just the right ways* to help you feel *seen* and *supported* and *safe.*

Ninth, the IPFs know how to set appropriate limits and effectively contain the patient-as-child during states of rage or hostile aggression, in a way that calms the child and makes the child and others feel safe in the face of such intense-aggressive arousal. For example:

Patient: I'm so mad I don't know what I'm going to do! I want to scream and fight and hit them and anyone who comes near me!
Therapist: Yes, you're *so mad* and want to fight and hit. These parents *really* get that, and they understand that sometimes you become enraged like this. Right now they find *just the right ways* to respond to you, in ways that honor what you're feeling, and that help you to express it in ways that are *safe* for you and for everyone. Something about how they are with you now begins to help you to feel more calm, and safe. How is it that they are with you now that helps you begin to feel that way?

Tenth, since disorganized patients have learned to expect rapid, inconsistent, unpredictable, and intense shifts in their parents' states of mind, IPFs are shaped to be the epitome of consistency and predictability and manifest steady, optimal levels of arousal. These qualities in the IPFs, over time, also serve to correct the poor self-regulation and control of the disorganized patient. For example:

> You can be so relieved that these parents are *so steady*, *so consistent*, so *reliable* in their *protective*, *supportive*, *soothing*, and *encouraging* ways of being with you. And they never seem to be too much or too little when you're with them . . . they always find *just the right balance* between being too much or too little in their ways of being with you.

Last, since patients with disorganized attachment have very low coherence of mind and easily become disorganized in both state of mind and behavior, IPFs are shaped to provide *just enough* structure to the patient-as-child. For example:

> These parents are *so well attuned* to you and your needs that they find *just the right ways* to be with you so that you don't feel confused or overwhelmed or disorganized in your mind. They provide some structure for you, but never too much . . . just the right amount of structure. They know what helps you to feel *clear* and *calm* and *coherent* in your mind, and they help to make sure that you feel that, when you're with them and when you're not. How are they being with you now that helps with your clarity and organization of mind?

Attention to and inclusion of the above considerations will support the patient's experience of the general factors—parental *presence*, *consistency*, *reliability*, and *interest*—and the five primary behavioral conditions that promote secure attachment—*protection*, *attunement*, *soothing*, *expressed delight*, and *fostering best self-development*. But to support the clinician's understanding and integration of the five conditions as they relate specifically to the disorganized patient, they are further highlighted here. *Protective* IPFs provide an approachable safe haven that is not associated with fear arousal but rather with its opposite, calmness and serenity. *Attuned* IPFs consistently and accurately recognize and contingently respond to the full range of the patient-as-child's negative and positive emotional states in ways that diminish emotional numbness and support the intersubjective reciprocal exchange of ongoing vitality affects and categorical emotional states. Thereby, the disorganized patient-as-child learns to trust his or her affects and to become effective in expressing them in the context of the imagined attachment relationship. The IPFs are also attuned to the patient-as-child's attachment behaviors and effectively contingently respond to them in ways that support the reactivation *and balance* of the attachment behavioral system. Since disorganized children and adults often perseverate with failed, disorganized attachment behaviors that were not corrected and diminished by the family-of-origin parents, the IPFs respond effectively to such problematic attachment behaviors and enable the child to activate healthy, organized attachment behaviors when proximity- and contact-seeking is needed. For example:

> *Patient:* Maybe if I just sit here, they'll notice and come to me. But I'm scared that they will, too.
>
> *Therapist:* These parents *really get it* that you want to be near them but are also afraid. Notice how they respond to you, so that you can be near them and also *really feel safe* with them . . . they find *just the right ways* of being with you that help you more and more be able to express what you want and need, directly to them . . . as you feel more and more *comfortable*, and *safe*.

Because disorganized patients have chronic, sustained high-fear arousal, the IPFs know how to *soothe* the patient-as-child in *just the right ways* that dampen the fear arousal. Pertaining to *expressed delight*, disorganized patients have difficulty experiencing and expressing positive emotions and prosocial emotions, and so the IPFs know how to be with the child in ways that make the child happy, joyful, content, serene, inspired, proud, and loving, and they express delight in the child and the child's positive states. Because disorganized patients show significantly inhibited self-development, the IPFs encourage and support the child at every stage of development to freely explore, in an effort to develop the child's *best, strongest, and most unique sense of self.* The self that develops becomes coherent, unitary, and free of undue internal contradictions and disorganized conflicts.

A third approach to working with IPFs and disorganized patients is to individualize the IPF protocols based on the five adjectives they give in the AAI. For example, a DID patient with a history of episodic dyscontrol and violent, aggressive behavior gave the following responses to the five adjectives for her mother and then her father. Note that the patient experienced each family-of-origin parent as both a source of attachment need and support and a source of fear and threat, resulting in the disorganized attachment pattern being associated with both parents.

> *Therapist:* Now, what I'd like you to do is to choose five adjectives or words that reflect your early childhood relationship with your mother . . . starting as far back as you can remember . . . as early as you can go.
>
> *Patient:* Caring . . . um . . . nurturing . . . torturous . . . angry . . . does that count? . . . and um . . . moody.
>
> *Therapist:* Fine . . . Let me go through with you some more questions about each of these. You said that your relationship with your mother was "caring." Are there any memories or incidents that come to mind with respect to the word "caring"?

Patient: Because before age seven she would take us to drawing classes . . . sew outfits for the whole Girl Scout troop and she'd be so involved with our lives.

Therapist: And then you said "nurturing." Is there a specific memory or incident that illustrates . . .

Patient: (Interrupting) Because when we fell off our bikes and she bandaged us up . . . we were crying and she kissed our cheek.

Therapist: And then you said "torturous" . . . Specific memory or incident that would illustrate . . .

Patient: When we were three to four she hit us over the head with a board and we needed to get stitches on our head . . . I am not sure why, though . . .

Therapist: Feelings?

Patient: Scared.

Therapist: And then you said "angry." Can you think of a specific memory or incident that illustrates why you chose "angry" to describe the relationship?

Patient: She'd yell at our father . . . this is when she was still married . . . and if we got involved she'd yell at us about that, which would make us more scared.

Therapist: And then you said the word "moody." Can you think of a specific memory or incident that illustrates why you chose the word "moody" to describe the early relationship?

Patient: Moods were top and bottom . . . That's an example of always being too moody.

Therapist: Specific memory?

Patient: No, trying to but I can't.

Therapist: Now what I'd like you to do, if you could, is to choose five adjectives or words that reflect your early childhood relationship with your biological father . . . starting as far back as you can remember . . . as early as you can go . . . but again say between the ages of 5 and 12. Again, this may take some time . . .

Patient: Affectionate . . . um . . . scary . . . overbearing . . . powerful . . . and um . . . loving.

Therapist: Okay, so I'm going to ask you about each of these now. You first mentioned "affectionate." Can you think of a specific memory or incident that illustrates why you chose "affectionate" for the early relationship with your father?

Patient: Because he was very touchy . . . he was always touching and kissing on us.

Therapist: How was that for you?

Patient: Sometimes scary . . . sometimes okay.

Therapist: What made it different?

Patient: How often and where he'd do it and what time of day it was . . . if it was just a good-night kiss on the cheek it was okay, but if we were in a bathing suit . . . That wasn't okay depending on where he touched us . . . didn't like when he touched us . . . if he took a bath with us with our consent that was okay because he liked to take a bath with us and stuff like that.

Therapist: You said "scary." Can you think of a specific . . .

Patient: (Interrupting) Yeah, he liked to scare us . . . make us afraid of things . . . he'd tell us kids got murdered in various places . . . he liked us to be afraid.

Therapist: He'd tell you scary stories?

Patient: May not have been stories, may have been true . . .

Therapist: As a kid you couldn't tell one way or the other?

Patient: Right.

Therapist: Anything else?

Patient: We witnessed him hurting people . . . He'd use us to kidnap girls and have us make friends with them and he'd make us watch.

Therapist: Watch what?

Patient: Everything about what he'd do to them . . . That's why we didn't always know if it was just a story or not . . . the look on his face . . . Now we'd describe it as rage . . . sometimes excitement . . . but it was hard to pinpoint what is was back then . . . It was just scary.

Therapist: And then you said "overbearing." Can you think of a specific memory or incident . . .

Patient: He was always around . . . We didn't seem to be free of him all that much . . . We'd go to school during the day . . . He was on the night shift so he was always there.

Therapist: And then you said "powerful." Can you think of a specific . . .

Patient: Yeah, he displaced his sexual powers . . . He could astral-project . . . He has special powers . . . He demonstrated them.

Therapist: How so?

Patient: Telling us to go to the other room and astral-projecting and then telling us what we were doing.

Therapist: Does that include seeing into your mind?

Patient: No, he couldn't, but his friends could . . .

Therapist: And then you said "loving." Do you have a specific memory or incident of why you chose . . .

Patient: Yeah, he didn't want anything bad to happen to us.

Therapist: Specific memory?

Patient: . . . Um . . . he didn't want us to end up like the kids at the rest areas that he did things to.

The therapist translated the five adjectives for each parent into their positive opposites, which were then given to the ideal parent figures in the imagery process. The ideal mother figure became the positive opposite of the family-of-origin mother: deeply caring of the patient-as-child's immediate state of mind; nurturing in the sense of becoming the secure base for proximity- and contact-seeking, not only providing instrumental care; a calm, nonviolent, and predictable presence; soft-spoken and gently expressive, never yelling; and steady and predicable instead of moody. The ideal father figure became the positive opposite of the family-of-origin father: physically affectionate, yet never in a sexual way; serene and never scary; gentle, never overbearing, and always attuned to what she needed; empowering of her; and deeply protective of her and of others.

Throughout the IPF sessions, when the patient described parent figures as embodying any of the characteristics or ways of being that the therapist recognized as positive, the therapist specifically and consistently drew the patient's attention to the effect that that had on the patient's inner state. For example:

> *Patient:* She's telling me that she's there, and that she's not going anywhere as long as I need her.
>
> *Therapist:* What's that like for you?
>
> *Patient:* It sounds good, but I don't really trust her; it's kind of scary.
>
> *Therapist:* She knows that you would like her to be there for you, and also that it's kind of scary for you, not being sure you can trust her. She *really gets that*, and now she finds *just the right way* to reassure you that in fact she is *really there* and is not going anywhere as long as you need her . . . How is it that she shows you that?
>
> *Patient:* Well, she kind of looks at me with this look that seems like love. And she puts her hand on my shoulder . . . it feels good.
>
> *Therapist:* Yes, notice how *good* it feels . . . and notice the effect it has on your inner state.
>
> *Patient:* Well, it does feel good . . . and I feel calmer inside . . . my mind's not going all over the place like it was before.
>
> *Therapist: Yes.* You feel calmer inside, and your mind's not going all over the place like it was before . . . this mother's presence for you has a *calming, organizing* effect on your mind.

We have found that over time, positive experience with imagined ideal parent figures *has an organizing effect on the patient's mind*. By consistently bringing the patient's attention to the experience of greater organization at the moment it occurs in response to the parent figures' ways of being, the patient has the direct, new experience of a relationship contributing to *organization* rather than disorganization of mind.

Fostering Collaboration With Disorganized Patients

Establishing a clear, collaborative treatment-frame agreement is absolutely necessary with disorganized patients. Because of their level of disorganization and a mixture of deactivating and hyperactivating attachment styles, the risk of frequent treatment-frame violations is higher if there is not a clear, concrete, mutually developed agreement about the expectations and mutual responsibilities for the psychotherapy. The methods for establishing a collaborative treatment frame are described in Chapter 10 and in the chapters on treating dismissing and anxious-preoccupied patients.

Beebe and Lachmann (2014) found that already by four months, there are significant differences in the nonverbal communication between secure and disorganized mothers and their infants, and that the nonverbal patterns between disorganized mothers and their infants predict infants' disorganized attachment by 12 months in the Strange Situation. They observe frequent nonverbal mismatches and add, "The difficulty is not a sheer absence of responsiveness . . . but it is an extremely uncomfortable and mismatched one" (p. 17). They note that disorganized mothers have great difficulty acknowledging their infants' distress and speculate that some of these mothers may be "stonewalling" the child's distress because of the their own unresolved trauma or loss (p. 17). Given the strong evidence of early nonverbal mismatch, it is especially important for the therapist of the disorganized patient to recognize, acknowledge, and address the negative-affective displays of the patient early on in the treatment. Early in treatment, the patient will likely display many instances of noncollaborative nonverbal behavior. In response, the therapist must collaboratively help the patient bring metacognitive awareness to these nonverbal behaviors at the instant they occur, which will contribute to the activation and development of the patient's nonverbal collaborative communication skills.

Because disorganized patients have frequent shifts of their states of mind, in most extreme form though structural dissociation, it can be quite difficult for the therapist to make sense of their verbal communication. When the patient's verbal communication is poor, the therapist points this out and works collaboratively with the patient to enhance metacognitive awareness of and clarity and coherence of the discourse.

The methods for collaboratively promoting nonverbal and verbal communication are described in Chapter 10 and in the chapters on treating dismissing and anxious-preoccupied patients.

Enhancing Metacognitive Skills in Disorganized Patients

Generally, reflective capacity or mentalizing skill in disorganized patients is very low. Therefore, it is of vital importance that the therapist work toward increasing the patient's range of metacognitive skills. With respect to the condition-specific approach, both metacognitive *identification* of states and metacognitive *mastery* over states is extremely low in these patients, so the methods for enhancing those, described in earlier chapters, are made part of treatment. There are several post-formal metacognitive skills that are important to cultivate. First and foremost, these patients show very low coherence of mind and spontaneously shift states frequently. The therapist makes consistent use, within and across sessions, of a disorganization/organization anchor scale. For example:

> On a scale of 1 to 10, with 1 being *completely disorganized* and 10 being *completely organized*, and the other numbers indicating a level of disorganization or organization in between, what number reflects the relative degree of disorganization or organization of your state of mind at this very moment?

The cumulative effect of this and other identification and mastery interventions is that the patient becomes aware of shifts in state in ways that help modulate those states and develops the metacognitive skills that lead to greater coherence of mind.

Second, the disorganized patient frequently shifts between self and other orientation, between present and past orientation, and/or between adult and child orientation. Therefore, it is important to begin developing early in treatment the specific metacognitive skill of recognizing one's current orientation. Anchoring scales are the primary therapeutic tool for this work. For example, pertaining to time orientation, the therapist might say:

> On a 1 to 10 scale, with 1 being *completely in the past* and 10 being *completely in the present*, and the other numbers somewhere in between, give a number that best represents the degree to which you're in the past or present right now.

Developing this specific metacognitive orientation skill helps to shift the disorganized patient away from preoccupation with the past. Another post-formal metacognitive skill important for the disorganized patient, who lacks a well-developed unitary sense of self, is the capacity to take a wider perspective, to recognize a larger unity beyond the momentary disorganized and shifting states of mind. For example:

> Even though your mind sometimes becomes disorganized and shifts from one state or one orientation to another, you can become aware that this is happening within you, within the unique you that is learning and growing and becoming more coherent and strong and balanced. You can take a

larger perspective on all this, and see yourself in the larger context of your life as it has been, as it is, and as it's becoming. Take a larger perspective now, and see what that's like. And when you're ready you can tell me what that's like.

Stages in the Treatment of the Disorganized Patient

1. Treatment begins with the collaborative negotiation of a mutually agreed upon treatment frame. The patterns of disorganized patients frequently disrupt treatment, and, therefore, the treatment must begin with a clear understanding of the mutual expectations, responsibilities, and ground rules regarding treatment.

2. Disorganized patients show many signs of noncollaborative nonverbal and verbal behavior, and from the beginning of treatment, the therapist brings the patient's attention to these signs when they occur. The therapist and patient work as a cooperative, collaborative team to activate nonverbal collaborative expressiveness and meaningful, clear, collaborative verbal discourse.

3. As the fundamental dilemma for the disorganized patient is that the source of attachment is also the source of fear, very early in treatment the therapist works to attenuate the patient's fearfulness in general and/or fearfulness of certain parts of the mind. Ideal-parent-figure work provides the patient with experience of attachment figures who provide protection and safety in ways that are completely free from fear. IPFs are soothing, comforting, and reassuring in the face of fear, and provide a safe haven that is the positive opposite of what the patient expects. With patients who have DID or DDNOS, it is beneficial at first to introduce IPFs who provide safety without fear to those self-states or "parts" that are most fearful. The IPF work is done consistently across sessions until the patient, or at least the most fearful parts of the mind (often child parts in dissociative patients), are able to sustain a sense of safety without fear in relation to the imagined parent figures.

4. Once protective and safe parent figures are experienced without fear by at least some part or self-state of the patient, the IPF focus turns to addressing the dismissing parts or behaviors of the patient. This phase of treatment utilizes many of the IPF guidelines discussed in greater detail in Chapter 11. IPFs who are *actively engaging* and *contingently responsive* to the child are shaped for each part or self-state that has deactivated the attachment system, until the positive signs of proximity- and contact-seeking emerge. As such signs are often accompanied by longing, deep shame, and distress about those feelings, the therapist must make

efforts to normalize the longing for shame-free attachment. IPFs are shaped such that they would never shame the patient-as-child or make him or her feel bad for desiring closeness. The IPFs also provide soothing in response to the distress about the longings and shame and behave in ways that help the patient to contain any acting-out impulses (such as substance use) oriented toward self-soothing. For example:

> As these parents *really get* that you're feeling awful right now about these feelings, they find *just the right ways* to *reassure* and *comfort* and *soothe* you. And as they're *right here* for you, you'll find that you don't have to look outside of yourself or to anyone or anything else to try to feel better . . . they know how to help you, so that you can feel better just by being *together* in the relationship with them.

5. Special attention must be given to the outliers—those parts or self-states that are strongly resistant to working with the IPF imagery. In DID patients, the outliers include perpetrator parts, parts deeply traumatically bonded to the perpetrator, and/or parts that contain the memories of the worst of the trauma. When strong resistance is encountered from any of these parts, the therapist shifts to the cooperative behavioral system. The patient is helped to recognize that some parts are having difficulty with the process, and together with the therapist works as a cooperative team toward the shared goal of helping the outlier parts or self-states form a positive relationship with the IPFs. Then the therapist introduces the IPF imagery for "those parts that do not yet feel connected," for "those parts that are blocking the feeling of connectedness," or for "those parts who most need to connect." The IPFs are shaped to know *exactly how* to address and help these parts. As with all IPF process, much of the *how* of the parent figures' ways of helping is left to the creative imagination of the patient, based on the assumption that there exists a deep knowing within the patient of *exactly what is needed* for healing, development, and well-being. The therapist sets the frame according to what is known to be of benefit, and the patient fills in the details that are most relevant for his or her needs.

6. Throughout the IPF work, the therapist systematically calls forth the parts that need to feel securely attached, leaving each previous part present, until all the parts are present at once, each feeling securely attached to its respective attachment figure. Repeated structuralizing in this manner decreases dissociation and fosters the development of a unified sense of self around a central core self.

7. Throughout the treatment, a variety of metacognitive interventions are used, especially those pertaining to fostering metacognitive awareness of the relative degree of disorganization or organization of mind at any given time and to fos-

tering metacognitive awareness of self/other orientation, past/present orientation, and child/adult orientation. These interventions are powerful tools that enable the patient to develop coherence of mind and an orientation focused on present, adult, self. At this stage, the patient relinquishes hyperactivating strategies, and attachment behaviors becoming relatively balanced and normalized. Next, the treatment turns to activating and strengthening the exploratory behavioral system.

8. IPF imagery is used for the patient to experience parent figures who encourage and support the patient-as-child's best self-development. These IPFs encourage healthy exploration by a unified self, within the context of providing a secure base for exploration. When the patient shows consistent exploratory behavior in the IPF context, the therapist draws from methods in Appendix A to further support self-development, independent of the IPF methods. A positive sign of healthy self-development is the patient beginning to articulate a life narrative with clarity, coherence, and detail.

9. In the last phase of treatment, post-formal metacognitive skills are cultivated and develop, and attachment work turns to the theme of developing secure adult intimacy (see Appendix B).

Case Illustration

The patient began treatment in her late 40s. She had a complex trauma profile with PTSD, major depression, and self-cutting behavior, and she had been hospitalized once when she was in her late 20s. Her mother was overly identified with her appearance to others, and her father was a minister who had a history of alcoholism. The patient had been sexually abused by her father throughout her childhood and midadolescence. She participated in an incest survivor's group for seven years and then had two years of individual phase-oriented trauma treatment to stabilize and then to process childhood sexual abuse memories and emotions. During that treatment, she stopped self-cutting, achieved stabilization, and integrated most of the childhood sexual abuse experiences. However, she also became increasingly dissociated, to the point that colleagues noticed that she started to switch into alter personality states. At that point, she was given a diagnosis of dissociative identity disorder (DID), and the treatment was changed to the attachment-based methods described in this book.

   The first phase of the treatment focused on introducing IPFs who could provide safety and protection without fear to each of the parts. The patient reported a Wise Man as an initial IPF, who showed her "the way in a dark garden. He shows me there isn't anything there that will hurt me." Since she was frequently dissociating, the therapist introduced IPFs who knew "how to stay with you so you don't have to dissociate." She responded:

The Wise Man tells me to focus and stay with him, not to go away. He gently squeezes my hand so I know I'm here. I can feel the connection, but I gently pull away. She's very afraid. He says, "Sit down in front of me and tell me about it." He listens.

Two months later, she reported that the "dissociation [is] getting worse. There are a lot of angry voices." By the fifth month she reported, "Child parts [are] scared all the time." The therapist asked her to imagine IPFs who could be most responsive to the child parts' fears. She reported that they could be with Whoopi Goldberg as an IPF. She said, "When they feel badly the most, that's when they need to be with her, Whoopi." Next, the therapist suggested IPFs for the "parts that don't know anything about a secure attachment relationship." She chose the Dalai Lama.

Below is a verbatim transcript from the seventh month of the treatment. Commentary on passages of interest are bracketed and italicized. The patient began the hour by switching into a paranoid alter who was terrified that she had been followed coming to the therapist's office. She then switched to vulnerable child parts.

> *Patient:* I thought coming would make things worse.
>
> *Therapist:* I know you didn't seem too thrilled about coming.
>
> *Patient:* There were scheduling problems.
>
> *Therapist:* There are parts of the mind that wanted to come and there are parts of the mind that didn't want to come . . . there are parts that are committed to getting better, and there are parts that want to keep things the same.
>
> *Patient:* It doesn't feel that way though . . .
>
> *Therapist:* How does it feel?
>
> *Patient:* Sometimes I feel better and sometimes I feel worse. I don't know what happens, but last time I felt much worse.
>
> *Therapist:* Tell me about it.
>
> *Patient:* It's so hard because I'm not aware of what goes on inside *[Poor metacognitive awareness]*. All I know is . . .
>
> *Therapist:* Did you listen to the tape of last time? Did it help you to understand why you feel much worse.
>
> *Patient:* No.
>
> *Therapist:* Not at all.
>
> *Patient:* It's just that I cried a lot over the weekend and then, I did talk with you over the weekend. I thought I should have called sooner because I did feel a little bit better . . . but . . . I don't understand why . . . but I just feel terrible . . . some of the bruises [from falling] are fading some . . . one of my dogs is sick . . . I just don't understand what's going on . . . I'm not stupid, but I can't seem to— *[Patient suddenly startles and looks out the window in fear and switches to a fearful child part]*

Therapist: What are you looking at?

Patient: I thought maybe I was followed or something . . .

Therapist: You thought you were followed . . . tell me more about it?

Patient: It's just the flashbacks.

Therapist: When you start reliving the past in a way that you can't distinguish the past from the current fears, then you are really beginning to lose it more . . . that's of concern *[Therapist calls attention to past orientation]* . . . You said you are feeling worse, but you don't know why . . . You can't distinguish the past and current fears, as if you are being followed right now, and you are quite scared today.

Patient: I am very scared.

Therapist: About what?

Patient: I don't know. (Long silence.) I get the feeling of being alone the way I did when I was younger.

Therapist: You feel alone and very vulnerable, very scared. *[Marking affect]*

Patient: There was no one to help me . . . There is no one to help me.

Therapist: Even when you call me you still feel alone afterwards?

Patient: Well, sometimes I feel better.

Therapist: So let's imagine the parts of the mind that feel so alone, and the parts that know that deep vulnerability and fear. *[Therapist introduces IPF imagery around theme of safety without fear]*

Patient: No . . . no. *[Dismissing parts become activated]*

Therapist: Growing up with the kind of parents that would have been ideally suited to your nature.

Patient: No. I don't like families and I don't like parents. I don't know any ideal parents. *[Patient shows dismissing attachment behaviors]*

Therapist: But this time . . . you are going to imagine as if you had grown up in a family different from your family of origin . . . as if you had grown up in a family whose parents were ideally suited to you and your nature, in a way that you feel secure in your relationship to them . . . and these parts for the first time feel secure in their connection to them, free of fear.

Patient: No, I can't do it!

Therapist: You are beginning to feel a sense of security that you've never felt before ever . . . It is precisely because they think that they can't do it . . . all the more reason to begin to feel security in the relationship, rather than continuing to feel so deeply alone and vulnerable . . . the way you have been feeling recently.

Patient: I feel terrible.

Therapist: I know, and that's why you can begin to imagine for these parts, just the quality of the connection they need that will begin to soften that sense of feeling so deeply alone . . . and it's possible, even for these parts, to begin to really feel a sense of connection free of fear. These parents know how to be there in a way that this deep sense of aloneness would never come up at all . . . because these parents *know* this child and are genuinely interested in this child's *being*, and because of that, this sense of aloneness never comes up.

Patient: That makes me feel worse because it doesn't exist.

Therapist: It does exist.

Patient: It doesn't! *[Patient continues with dismissing stance]*

Therapist: You evoke those limiting beliefs because you don't want to feel. But these parents understand that pain . . . the pain that runs so deep . . . It's okay for them to feel vulnerable and afraid. It's okay to need so intensely the connection, because that longing for connection is a natural and healthy thing . . . a right . . . that no child should ever be denied.

Patient: I was, and I'll never have that!

Therapist: You evoke the limiting belief so you won't feel that now. You are afraid. These parents understand that vulnerability and fear . . . just let whatever you feel just be there.

Patient: It's there all the time . . . it's awful all the time!

Therapist: Yes, but it is different when you're feeling it along with someone else who comforts you. It changes everything. *[Therapist persists with the theme of safety in attachment free of fear]*

Patient: I feel that.

Therapist: Right now?

Patient: It is yucky.

Therapist: So now imagine the quality of the connection . . . with whom it is that these alone parts could best *be*, who could most *be* there with them . . . the kind of parents who could really *be* there in the way that you most need, free of fear.

Patient: I can't.

Therapist: You keep saying, "I can't feel it" even when you *are* feeling it . . . you're trying not to feel connected with me, with the ideal parents . . . you think that feeling the connection is going to make you hurt even more. *[Therapist explicitly addresses the underlying fear that the attachment figure is both the source of attachment and the source of harm]*

Patient: Yes, I do.

Therapist: You don't see that by trying to deny yourself the connection . . . that's what makes it hurt even more.

Patient: No, I don't see that . . . Maybe I could draw it. *[Patient previously used drawing as an alternative to self-cutting. Here she is being collaborative and trying to find ways to give the therapist what is being requested.]*

Therapist: What would you draw about the connection?

Patient: They'd love me and hold me.

Therapist: Yes, and they'd do it in a way that you could really feel.

Patient: I can't feel it. I want to feel it. *[First sign of admission of wanting to feel the secure attachment]*

Therapist: If you drew it, would you feel it more?

Patient: I don't know. I don't know, because I can't draw . . .

Therapist: What would be the matter with that?

Patient: I don't understand.

Therapist: These ideal parents would never inhibit the child's free expression . . . in any way . . . They would encourage the child to express whatever she was feeling freely and openly as a way of letting her *be* herself . . . They would never inhibit that . . . because they are genuinely interested in her being.

Patient: Whoopi Goldberg says I can draw whenever I want to . . . I can be wild and free when I want to in my drawings. *[Patient is being collaborative and imagines an IPF that not only is free of being a source of fear, but also encourages the child's free expression and exploration]*

Therapist: Exactly, and this child . . . when she gets encouraged by Whoopi, she begins to trust. She begins to trust she can *be* herself, and how freeing it is to know that with Whoopi she can trust, she can *be* herself and *just be.*

Patient: I don't feel because I live in such darkness all the time.

Therapist: Yes, but when you have a parent like Whoopi, who is interested so much in your being, is delighted in your being, then you feel seen, genuinely feel seen.

Patient: And known. *[Patient adds something in the spirit of collaborative interchange]*

Patient: She really knows me. *[Patient manifests spontaneous affective marking]*

Therapist: Yes, and notice how that begins to transform that feeling not-so-good inside . . . It changes everything when you feel seen and known . . . So let yourself really take in that connection . . . secure in your knowing that you feel genuinely seen and known . . . and never in the dark.

Patient: I don't have to hide my feelings from her?

Therapist: Of course not. In fact, rather than that impulse to hide, you *want* to be seen and known so thoroughly that it frees you from that darkness. *[Therapist introduces the concept of proximity-seeking]*

Patient: I don't have to hide my feelings from her?

Therapist: No, of course not, she . . . in some ways she knows.

Patient: And in some ways she's not afraid.

Therapist: Of course not.

Patient: It's like she knows everything and it's okay, and because of that I can be as free as I want to *be* . . . she really loves me and doesn't put any limits on that . . . and she isn't scared by anything I say. *[IPF is neither frightened nor frightening]* And she truly hears all my feelings.

Therapist: Truly.

Patient: She doesn't put me down for them.

Therapist: Never. She genuinely encourages you . . . really encourages you . . . you can really take in how that feels . . . that feels *right.*

Patient: She's there for me when other people hurt me. *[Patient achieves goal of an attachment figure that is not a source of fear]*

Therapist: You can really feel secure in knowing she's there . . . really let yourself feel that security of the connection . . . just take in the simplicity and depth of that *felt security* in the relationship. There is no way that you have to be other than who you are, nothing to feel other than what you genuinely feel . . . not at all judged, but feel deeply accepted... you can just *be* . . . and feel like somebody genuinely sees and knows you... and is *there* for you as you are *fully yourself* . . . with all the richness and complexity, with all the parts and sides of yourself . . . you can be fully yourself in this relationship.

Patient: I can go to her when I have questions.

Therapist: Of course . . . notice how the security of this kind of connection begins to have an effect on you and how your being . . . notice the effect and that effect will get more and more clear to you. *[Therapist is fostering metacognitive awareness of state of mind]*

Patient: I feel secure . . . and warm . . .

Therapist: Go ahead and let that happen . . . really take it in . . . in just the right way, and as you continue to take in the effect . . . notice the effect that it begins to have, so you really come to know it . . . How's that?

Patient: Okay.

Therapist: You can continue to feel held in *just the right way,* but at the same time, if there are other parts of the mind that need to feel security in relationship, these parts can come forth and feel connected now, in the way they need to feel . . . it may be in the same or a different way, but either way now let these parts begin to feel security in relationship in the way that they need. *[Extending IPF imagery to parts that do not yet feel secure; structuralizing intervention by leaving the previous parts present while calling forth new parts]*

Patient: They want to be with Atticus . . .

Therapist: And when they can feel just the right connection with him, in the way that is best for them, you can indicate simply by nodding.

Patient: (Nods.)

Therapist: How is that so far?

Patient: It's good . . . *[Source of attachment is now source of comfort, not fear]*

Therapist: These parts can identify something about the quality of the connection they feel with Atticus. They know that he won't hurt them . . . he's protecting them. *[Patient achieves collaborative goal of attachment to IPF who is free of being a source of fear]* Yes, he's protecting them . . . they can feel secure in that protection, because he would never let anything happen to them. (Silence.) Now let's make sure that all the parts are feeling connected. We have the parts that are feeling secure in relationship with Whoopi, and the parts that are feeling secure in relationship with Atticus, and those parts that are feeling secure can now make sure that all the other parts are feeling secure . . . and if there are parts that aren't yet feeling connected, those parts can make sure that the parts that aren't yet feeling connected will find a way of establishing that secure connection . . . those parts can help any parts that are left not yet feeling connected so they can begin to feel that now in *just the right way. [Extending the IPF imagery to outliers]*

Patient: We want the devil parts to come out of the cave, but they don't want to leave where they are . . .

Therapist: Yes, but sometimes you have to bring the connection to them. *[Stance of active engagement with dismissing parts]*

Patient: What do you mean?

Therapist: Bring the connection to the devil parts.

Patient: They think everyone hates them . . .

Therapist: Then we have to go to the cave. If we did, what would we find there?

Patient: The Wise Man.

Therapist: So I'm suggesting that those devil parts also need to be seen and known and understood for their vulnerability and fear.

Patient: But everybody hates them.

Therapist: That's why the Wise Man has to reach out to them . . . the Wise Man comes to them exactly where they are because he understands . . . he has compassion for them and their limited way they see things, and for their deep, deep isolation. *[Therapist continues with stance of active engagement of dismissing parts]*

Patient: He goes to them? *[Patient expresses curiosity, a dimension of exploratory behavior.]*

Therapist: Yes, so imagine the Wise Man has come to them, because he understands them . . . and they can begin to feel that secure connection . . . What if they finally begin to feel understood?

Patient: Then they would not have to live in hell . . .

Therapist: Yes, of course not . . . they finally would find a way out of hell . . . back into the light of the security of connection, which is their natural right . . . then, finally they can begin to feel human connection in a tangible way . . . it changes everything. *[Normalizing]* Let them take that in, even in their fear and mistrust . . . take in the security of the connection.

Patient: They *are* afraid.

Therapist: Of course they are, but this time they can trust it, because the Wise Man is *being* is so different . . . he is so far away from power and exploitation . . . it simply is not in his being . . . the devil parts could begin to feel loved. *[Wise Man is introduced as positive opposite of feared attachment figure]*

Patient: They're afraid, too.

Therapist: Of course they are, because they want it so much . . . and Wise Man understands that, and is there anyway. *[Therapist positively reframes fear as longing for attachment]*

Patient: Yeah, he is so strong and compassionate. He won't leave them to die in hell. He wants them to be with him. (Silence.)

Therapist: Notice the effect that the secure connection has on them. *[Fostering metacognitive awareness of state of mind]* They're starting to feel all the love in a way that they never have, and they don't have to hide in the shadows all the time . . . *[Patient is being collaborative and interactive in elaborating on what the therapist suggested. This passage illustrates first signs of patient seeing proximity-seeking as something positive.]*

Patient: They can sit outside and enjoy the sunlight. *[Patient shows first signs of exploratory behavior once attachment is secure]*

Therapist: Let them really take it in . . . Maybe the devils can begin to understand their real nature.

Patient: I don't know . . . they just see themselves as devils.

Therapist: Yes, it is hard for them to see themselves as innocent children with a capacity to wonder about life.

Patient: With the capacity to hurt!

Therapist: Yes, but even prior to that hurt . . .

Patient: There was something before that? *[More curiosity]*

Therapist: Yes, it is still in them to know.

Patient: How do they know that?

Therapist: They can return to their real nature . . . the security of the relationship brings it forth. *[Reframing attachment as something normal, as part of the child's real nature, and not a source of shame]*

Patient: She can't find it. I *want* her to find it.

Therapist: She just forgot it . . . They can return to their real nature.

Patient: I don't know.

Therapist: You *do* know, and it's okay to know that once again.

Patient: I can't find that. I *want* to find it *[Sign of proximity-seeking]* . . . I can't find the place of no pain with the Wise Man.

Therapist: When they can feel the Wise Man's compassion so deeply, they can begin to find that place of no pain.

Patient: They didn't know that place existed.

Therapist: But they begin to know that even now.

Patient: Have they been there before? *[Increasing curiosity]*

Therapist: Yes, so they can really take that in, and even though only a short amount of clock time will pass, it will seem to them that they have felt the security of the relationship with the Wise Man for a much longer time, long enough to begin to know that security of connection once again.

Patient: We can't!

Therapist: I know the limiting beliefs they have developed run so deep, but the security of the connection runs even deeper. *[Stance of active engagement]*

Patient: Is that true?

Therapist: Now, all the parts can feel security in relationship, some parts with Whoopi, some parts with Atticus, and some parts with the Wise Man, and on some level all the parts can imagine *just the right* kind of secure relationship . . . all the parts at once, and from that can come a new sense of wholeness. *[Structuralizing intervention]* I'm going to count from five to one and you'll be able to awaken . . . feeling settled with your experience, and during the days that pass, all the parts can call upon the security of *just the right* connection, and find a way beyond any limiting beliefs and assumptions to allow themselves tangibly to feel the connection in a way that is genuine . . . and the more they feel that, the less these limiting beliefs will get in the way, and as they feel more secure, the less isolated they will feel . . . and all the parts will find just the right kind of secure relationship in just the way that they each need . . . three . . . two . . . and you can return to your usual sense-of-self . . . one . . . and settle with your experience.

Patient: I'd like to keep going for a long while. *[Patient concedes that secure attachment without fear is deeply positive. She shows proximity-seeking behavior here.]*

During the next session, the following interchange took place:

Patient: Last time . . . I don't want to lose it, I am afraid to be more connected to you. If I do, it will be harder to kill myself. Atticus is so strong. He understands everything. He's concerned about me. He wants me to be okay, and he won't let anybody hurt me. *[Patient switches to dismissing alter personality state]* The connection wasn't real. The Wise Man wants us to come with him, but we don't want to go.

Therapist: He knows exactly what you need . . . when you are afraid. *[Therapist addresses outlier part with IPF imagery]*

Patient: He is being nice to us, even if we don't want to go. He doesn't get mad, but remains gentle.

Therapist: He is concerned about how isolated you have been.

Patient: Yes, we have been connected to the devil parts, so we are not really lonely but we're afraid we are going to hell.

Therapist: He knows the way out of hell. By providing just the kind of relationship you need.

Patient: Nobody else loves us . . . He says we will be okay . . . We *are* okay. He says we are not so bad and doesn't judge us.

Therapist: Yes, he is very accepting of who you are.

Patient: Even though we've been bad, he really loves us anyway. *[Patient and therapist are successful in finding IPFs for outlier parts that serve as secure attachment figures free of fear]*

Several sessions later, the IPFs Whoopi and the Dalai Lama were "holding all the child parts happy and giggling. The Wise Man says the devil parts don't have to go back to hell." Several sessions after that, this interchange was recorded:

Therapist: All parts of mind share something in common. They *want* to be in a secure attachment relationship with Whoopi, the Wise Man, Atticus, the Dalai Lama, and me.

Patient: The Dalai Lama really understands them and you do, too. I want to believe this.

Therapist: Take an inventory of all parts finding the *just right* relationship, which parts do and which parts don't yet feel that felt security of attachment.

Patient: We ache for it. *[Immediately, residual dismissing parts become activated]*

A part then said, "You are getting too close," and then she switched and another part said, "I am done with the parts that don't want to get better." As a solution to this conflict, she reported a new IPF, namely a Guardian Angel part, "because he's strong and can unburden the fears." Shortly after, she reported awakening in the night with a recurrent nightmare, only this time "a beautiful female angel comes at night and protects me from harm." With respect to aggressive parts, she reported a new IPF, namely, a Wild Animal Trainer that kept the animal parts quiet and didn't "let them get out of control." With respect to the most disgusted parts of herself, she reported a new IPF—she referenced the "untouchable parts" and said, "Do you think Gandhi could help them? He is very understanding. He knows all their darkness and the worst things in people."

This patient had been scored as having unresolved status on the AAI (Ud classification), largely because of a persistent belief that her father, the offender, was somehow still alive and active in her head causing ongoing negative influence. At this point in treatment, she began to develop the metacognitive capacity to monitor and modify this belief.

> *Patient:* I realize that I have been so focused on death that I don't think about creating a life. I also realized I have to break with my father . . . He's still part of me . . . my father is spending time with the Dalai Lama. He keeps his hands to himself . . . Then I can take back what he took from me and I have to move beyond that . . . The Dalai Lama said things could be steadier and more peaceful. I'm sitting next to him and he shows me how to sit with myself in a peaceful way.

Two sessions later, she said, "Some parts of mind don't want to let go of the bad stuff." She reported a new, positive IPF to replace the abusive father, namely the Count of Monte Cristo.

> *Patient:* The Count of Monte Cristo. He really hung in there. He has a lot of hope and planning for the future . . . He's encouraging me because he knows exactly what it takes to get there. He helps me to relinquish the bad attachment to my father inside. He says the first step is to be with myself and spend time with my mind where I want to be.
> *Therapist:* Yes, he is only interested in your welfare and never would hurt you.
> *Patient:* He wants the best for me.

At the beginning of the following session, she added, "I know the Count was the right image. I felt good for five days afterwards." Three sessions later she reported a new IPF:

> *Patient:* Police woman who deals with abused kids. She's not afraid of hearing all that bad stuff . . . the blood . . . all the icky stuff . . . The child parts are thinking of leaving the prison to be close to her. She doesn't let the father hurt them anymore.

A suicidal part emerged. A new IPF, Doris, addressed the suicidality in a positive way.

> *Patient:* There is a part of me that doesn't want to live anymore. My friend Doris tells them that life is so precious.
> *Therapist:* Yes, you can find value in living.

Patient: She is very compassionate and says I'm too good to be lost forever. The Count shows them how to be strong and not give up. He shows them how to deal with the loss.

Nearly two years into the attachment-based treatment, the patient showed the first signs of using the real relationship with the therapist as a secure base along with the IPFs.

Patient: They want to be with you but are afraid. Whoopi is holding our hand and is walking with us to meet you . . . you are not so tall or scary. You smile in a nice way. We take your hand and show you around the cave . . . where we like to go. You seem like you are meeting us on our level. *[Exploring the cave together in a collaborative way]*

Several sessions later, the Wise Man began to actively engage the few parts that still resisted forming an attachment.

Patient: I am afraid I will want too much and I won't get anything. The Wise Man has to take care of them and figure out what they want so they don't feel bad. The Wise Man is always there . . . for the ones most afraid he holds and comforts them . . . The devil parts are standing on the outside looking in. They want to join in but they don't know how. The Wise Man reaches out to them and asks them to join.

At the next session, the following exchange occurred:

Patient: I show them the cave because that is my favorite place. The Wise Man is there with other friends, too.
Therapist: Yes, there is much more to explore in the cave when you feel secure in the relationship.

By the next session, the patient had gained insight into the fundamental dilemma of her childhood.

Patient: I realized the dilemma in my childhood is that I looked to my parents as a source of comfort, but they were also the source of terror.
Therapist: You are afraid you will repeat that here with me.
Patient: I've thought about that, but I don't really think you are going to be different from the way you are being. I thought you were going to hurt me in some way. I've listened to the tape of the session a few times where I thought you were going to hurt me, and it really didn't seem to sound that way to me.

Therapist: There is a lot to explore and discover when you are not preoccupied with fear.

Just short of two years into the treatment, the patient showed the first signs of an emerging unified sense of self. Here is her response to a structuralizing comment:

Therapist: All the parts are feeling a sense of security together.
Patient: All the parts are scattered around . . . they are becoming more organized . . . everything feels lighter . . . like the center of a flower with many petals. *[Patient is also showing signs of relinquishing her preoccupation with the past and staying more present in the moment]*
    It never occurred to me that I could remember the past without reliving it.
Therapist: Yes, it is not necessary to relive the nightmare of the past, but only to be with the Wise Man and feel secure in the relationship that is free of all fear.
Patient: He is telling the child parts a story so they are not so scared. When we are with him we don't think about the past at all. The Wise Man says the past is like watching a movie that you don't have to have on all the time . . . *[All the parts come together around the common theme of feeling secure in the relationship]*

The therapist introduced an orchestra analogy to illustrate how all the parts are part of a greater whole. The patient responded, "It is not so much that the parts are coming together, but more that I am seeing the whole that is there that I didn't see before." Here is a passage from a subsequent session about integrating the last dismissing parts into an emerging wholeness of self:

Therapist: We can let those parts that are beginning to rediscover their hope continue to feel the security in relationship to the Wise Man and Mother X and while they continue to do that . . . see if they are other parts that aren't yet feeling securely connected.
Patient: They don't want to be left alone there.
Therapist: They're not going to be left alone there, but simultaneously to those parts continuing to feel the secure connection with the Wise Man and Mother X . . . simultaneous to that, the other parts that don't yet feel secure will begin now to see who it is that they could most feel secure with. See who most needs to feel that now and tell me about that.
Patient: The Wise Man.
Therapist: Yes, say more.
Patient: [Patient switches to devil alter personality state.] The devil parts think it is a bunch of crap.

Therapist: Yes, we know that the devil parts always start out that way, being a little testy, but we also know that they long for that secure connection . . . so they can allow themselves to feel that now in a way that is familiar to them . . . the Wise Man who knows their nature.

Patient: No, it's not working.

Therapist: He knows all the devil-related activities are not their real nature. He knows that it is likely that they will lead with their limiting belief that nothing works . . . but he also knows they have come to value the secure relationship. That's okay. It's okay to question that just to make sure that they get it *just right.*

Patient: So it's okay to ask questions?

Therapist: Of course. It's a very good way of learning things new . . . and I appreciate how the devil parts have been open to learning something completely new, like the rediscovery of their innocence.

Patient: They don't like feeling weak, though.

Therapist: No . . . and they certainly come across as strong as a way of not feeling weak . . . but the Wise Man knows their vulnerabilities . . . their deep insecurities and accepts all of that . . . and notice the effect that it has on the devil parts when they feel so thoroughly known and seen.

Patient: They're starting to warm up to him but they don't want to . . . They don't want to.

Therapist: They do . . . they just don't want to be hurt . . . The Wise Man sees that and lets them do it their own way . . . in a way that is under their control because the Wise Man knows if they warm up to the secure relationship in their own way and time, they'll feel more in control and less threatened by the very longing for the very secure relationship that they clearly want.

Patient: They want it but they don't want anybody else to know that they want it.

Therapist: Yes . . . the Wise Man knows how to be with them in a way that, over time, they will come to see that wanting that secure relationship doesn't have any shame associated with it.

Patient: Is it wrong to want to keep it a secret?

Therapist: No. It is natural to want to covet the security of that connection, and what a relief it is not to be judged for wanting that.

Patient: No . . . he's glad they want it.

Therapist: Yes, of course, because he knows, and has known all along, that this is what they most want . . . and they can begin through the security of that relationship to unburden themselves of their role of having to be devils.

Patient: They're not ready to give it up.

Therapist: They're not being challenged to give it up . . . The Wise Man would never force anything on them. The Wise Man is very sensitive to power and doesn't at all want to come across in a way that would assert power . . . because power assertion has been so destructive in the past. He wants them to see that in a secure relationship there is no place for power . . . and notice what happens as they begin to believe that, and really take that in.

Patient: They still don't want to.

Therapist: He knows that as they become more secure that they will.

Patient: He's letting them go slowly.

Therapist: So, we have the ones who have felt hopeless continuing to feel the security and comfort in the relationship with the Wise Man and Mother X, and at the same time we have the devil parts testing what it is like to feel the longing to want the connection *[Structuralizing]* . . . and see if there are any other parts now that are not yet feeling connected so that we can get to the point that all the parts have found *just the right* kind of secure relationship for each part.

Patient: Everybody is disconnected today.

Therapist: Yes, but now each of those parts can begin to feel connected with whomever it is that they can most feel that secure connection . . . as they have in the past, and they can do that now . . . all at once.

Patient: No!

Therapist: There may be a part that wants to block that from happening. We know that that part is feeling the need to be protective. We understand that and accept that, and yet even when that part jumps in, out of a need to be protective, all the rest of the parts can still feel the connection with whomever it is that they can most feel securely connected to . . . including the parts that jumped in to stop that from happening. That part can feel secure in the relationship, too . . . with whomever it can most feel that security . . . and what a relief it would be to not hold the burden of having to jump in to be so protective. So get a direct sense for what it is like when all the parts simultaneously have a clear sense of with whom they most feel connected.

Patient: We don't have it yet.

Therapist: Tell me when you have been able to establish that.

Patient: No, they don't have it. They can't do it this time.

Therapist: Of course they can . . . and the Wise Man and Whoopi and Atticus and The Dalai Lama and Mother X . . . they all have faith that the parts can do it.

Patient: No . . . what if something happens to them when they do it?

Therapist: They know that these fears keep coming up and to give voice to those fears as directly as you are . . . and to be seen and understood and accepted is part of that process of feeling so secure in the relationship.

Patient: . . . We appreciate that. They're afraid of losing it. *[Note that the fear of getting harmed has changed to the fear of losing the attachment]*

Therapist: I know, and the closer you get to tangibly feeling that . . . for all the parts to feel that . . . the more the fear will naturally come up. That's understood . . . and what a relief it would be to realize that that fear doesn't have to get in the way of feeling that secure relationship for all the parts simultaneously.

Patient: No! It is too much!

Therapist: I know it does seem like a lot to ask you, but you do want that, you're just afraid . . .

Patient: No, I don't want it!

Therapist: It's such a conflict for you!

Patient: It's too much.

Therapist: I know . . . and the Wise Man and the other parent figures, they understand how afraid you are and yet they want you to know that you can do this and have done this, and the more you say you are afraid the more you are actually allowing this to happen . . . there is nothing to be ashamed of in wanting that . . . and each of the parts is completely accepted and understood for who they are.

Patient: You are just setting things up to hurt me.

Therapist: How is that?

Patient: You're saying the opposite thing.

Therapist: I appreciate how hypervigilant you have been at certain times. You use that as a way of protecting yourself . . . and what a relief it would be to just feel secure in the relationship, in such a way that you didn't have to always be in hypervigilant mode.

Patient: We are trying not to, but we're too scared. We're scared.

Therapist: I know the Wise Man and Mother X and Whoopi and Atticus and all the other parent figures appreciate how much you are trying, and they appreciate how deeply afraid you are of changing, and yet it is happening anyway, as you can see. Well, imagine with whom they could be that would hold them just right . . . how do you imagine that?

Patient: We're scared.

Therapist: Yes, you are very scared. *[Marking affect]* Well, imagine with whom they could be that . . . would hold them just right . . . How do you imagine that?

Patient: I don't know . . . they are with Atticus.

Therapist: What is that like?

Patient: He's trying to be reassuring, but we're not buying it. We want to . . .

Therapist: Yes, you desperately want to.

Patient: We want to feel better.

Therapist: Of course . . . take in what that feels like . . . really take it in . . . Atticus knows how to respond *in just the right way* to what they want . . .

Patient: He cares deeply about what happens to us.

Therapist: Allow the parts to really take in that caring and notice the effect that that caring has on their state of mind. *[Fostering mentacognitive awareness]*

Patient: When we feel cared about, we feel that we can go exploring . . . *[Note how the natural tendency to explore emerges from reaching felt security of attachment]*

Therapist: Tell me about how they explore?

Patient: They are walking through caves looking at all the different rooms.

Therapist: And what they discover is a source of great curiosity and interest . . . not a source of fear. Even the darkness is soft.

Patient: We're not scared when we explore because we feel in control.

Therapist: Yes, of course . . . they can be reassured that they have Atticus's complete support for whatever they explore. He is there for them to return to . . . and they know that on such a deep level that it allows them to be more secure, to venture out and explore even more . . . so these parts can continue to explore and the hopeless parts are there with the Wise Man and Mother X . . . in a way that begins to restore their hope . . . and the devil parts, while they really want that longing fulfilled in relationship, that they know is secure by the absence of power and exploitation . . . and all the parts at once . . . each part can feel secure in the relationship with whomever provides them with that sense of being most secure *[Structuralizing]* . . . and notice what begins to happen now, when all the parts at once begin to feel secure . . . get a direct sense of the effect of that on your state of mind *[Fostering metacognitive awareness]* . . . and as that becomes clear in your awareness, tell me what that effect is . . . when all of the parts in a relationship at once feel secure in the relationship?

Patient: It is not there.

Therapist: You can remember recently saying that even though it seems like it's not there, you can indirectly sense it as being there . . . so go ahead and do that now in a way that you just know.

Patient: It is not yet there this time.

Therapist: It is not measured in time. It is there to access within you. Time is just another limiting belief that you impose upon this, and yet in another level of mind you know exactly what I am saying . . . and it is there within you to access right now at this moment. *[Therapist continues stance of persistent active engagement of dismissing parts]*

Patient: I don't know what I am looking for!

Therapist: Directly sense the effect when all the parts feel secure at once . . . hold the awareness on this each moment, and see what becomes directly clear . . . without any limiting beliefs . . . with an openness and curiosity to see what you discover that is new.

Patient: There is a flame with many reflections.

Therapist: Tell me about it . . . I'd like to hear more about it . . . along with you. *[Collaborative]*

Patient: It keeps changing . . . keeps reversing course like in a funhouse.

Therapist: You know . . . you can look at a flame in two ways . . . you look at what is constantly changing about the flame, or you can look at what is always there amidst the change. *[Therapist introduces post-formal meta-cognitive skill of looking from a wider perspective]* So if you will now look at it from that other perspective, in terms of what is always there amidst the flames and tell me about it.

Patient: It's like one flame that reaches up . . . You can see the reflection of it and all the different colors.

Therapist: So many reflections . . . so many seemingly diverse parts, and yet the constant flame of self is there to directly sense . . . amidst all that change.

Patient: It is scary at first.

Therapist: What is scary about it?

Patient: It is gentle except for the flame.

Therapist: It is not scary to feel whole . . . and in the secure connection you have the Wise Man and Mother X and Atticus and all the others . . . so long as you hold that secure relationship, the fears and the darkness change into something far less scary . . . and with the support and security of those relationships the wholeness of self can alight into awareness, like that whole fire emerging . . . What's that like for you?

Patient: It keeps getting . . . diverted onto a lot of different walls . . . It doesn't stay steady.

Therapist: Yes . . . but as long as you look at the reflections on the walls you're not looking at the real substance of the flame . . . as long as you look only at the activity of the parts, it's hard to see clearly the constancy of the self's wholeness that is always right here to see, and to directly sense, even as you get a glimpse of that now . . . so with your full awareness make a clear impression of that wholeness . . . I'm going to ask you to awaken keeping that sense of the wholeness clear to mind upon awakening . . . five . . . four . . . three . . . two . . . one . . . fully awake.

Several more sessions focused on themes of emerging wholeness:

Patient: When they are secure with the Wise Man, they are not so afraid to go out of the cave, even if he is not right there . . . each part still feels different.

Therapist: It is like looking at a fire. You can look at each individual flame, or step back and look at the fire as a whole.

Patient: Brother Z says it is like a jewel that has many facets. All the parts are part of the same jewel, yet each is a distinct facet. We are all inside that jewel. There's a universe in that jewel . . . all the parts are reflected in that whole.

Therapist: You can directly sense that wholeness. *[Fostering metacognitive organization of mind]*

Two sessions later she continued to explore this emerging theme of wholeness/diversity with a waterfall and water droplets metaphor:

Patient: All the parts leave the cave and explore. They discover a waterfall. They are all looking at the drops of water. All these parts are like the individual drops, but all together they make up the waterfall.

Therapist: Are you looking more at the drops or the whole waterfall?

Patient: The waterfall. It is the waterfall that gives the drops a sense of purpose and direction. The parts have never seen anything so delightful as this waterfall. They don't think about anything else, other than looking at the waterfall like they have never done before . . . just being with it and experiencing it.

At just about two years into the attachment-based treatment, the patient began to experience a stable, unified sense of self. She described her experience as follows:

Patient: It is like the ebbing of a tide. When the water recedes, you get a sense of how it all works together.

Therapist: Keep noticing how it all works together.

Patient: We are looking at the bigness of the ocean and how the water recedes.

Therapist: When the noise of the parts recedes, it no longer obscures seeing how it all holds together as a whole. It has become so quiet in there. *[This is the first point that the patient notices a marked diminished activity of the "noise" of the parts]*

The patient also reported a significant change in night awakenings. Rather than waking up from a terrifying nightmare, she reported the following:

Patient: I am waking from a sleep and knowing I am safe. *[A general reflective capacity was also beginning to emerge]* I notice I am more reflective than reactive. It's as if they are surrounded and contained and are not going to fall apart.

Therapist: All the parts at once can feel a deep sense of security in the attachment relationship.
Patient: They feel valued. They are quiet and content. They feel valued and real. Things are pretty quiet inside.

She was able to let go of the belief that her abusive father was still somehow alive and active in her mind:

Patient: The devil parts get on horses and chase the father away in a dream.
Therapist: The devil parts can monitor and protect in dreams.
Patient: That is an important job, so it makes the devil parts feel good to do this.

She even showed some signs of compassion for the father, through the lens of the Wise Man:

Patient: Atticus sets up rules and tells the father that he can't do stuff anymore. He's so gentle. He protects the parts. I am not sure the father is part of us anymore, is he? The Wise Man says that the father needs understanding, too. But that we don't have to do it, because he will do it, and we can still be protected. The father doesn't have the power to hurt us anymore.

She reported an increased sense of comfort in exploring the world in new ways:

Patient: We all feel comfortable in the world. The Wise Man is gentle and supports us. They don't have to be hyperalert. They can just explore.
Therapist: Notice their state of mind as they explore and describe it.
Patient: They are not so afraid. They don't quite know what to do yet, but they don't have to rush. They can just enjoy wherever they are. *[Patient is beginning to show signs of the metacognitive capacity to relate different states to each other]*
   I notice that there is more organization of mind when the parts are secure. *[Here is an example of a growing metacognitive capacity to detect organization of mind]*

A few sessions later, the patient added:

I notice that when things are stressful, I get more organized . . . I felt like things were coming together more, and then you were away . . . I got more disorganized and was more in the past. Yet, there were a few times that

I remained quiet with myself and those times have been very different. There is a real feeling of stillness, and at those times I also have more awareness.

Therapist: The goal is to feel that way most of the time.

Patient: I think that is possible. That is the way things should be and can be. Mostly I have felt strong and that it didn't have to go away.

Here is an excerpt from a session about the fear of change:

Therapist: It's like you are saying that all you know is avoidance and dissociation . . . and to do something new is in itself unfamiliar and fearful . . . to give up the unhealthy ways of dealing with the intensity of these feeling states with avoidance and dissociation . . . and if this is all you know, what is there that is new?

Patient: Yes.

Therapist: It is scary to give up something old even if it is dysfunctional . . . when you don't know for sure what else will take its place that is healthier except these little glimpses that you get.

Patient: Right.

Therapist: Like just being simply aware of it . . . just being present in a way that changes it so that it doesn't bother you so much . . . and there are probably a whole range of newer healthier coping mechanisms that you could use and discover. *[Therapist invites further exploration]*

Patient: So there is more that I haven't discovered?

Therapist: Well, that would require bringing to this an attitude of openness and discovery . . . so what you come up with is new and fresh.

Patient: So you are talking about a range, and I thought there was just one new way . . . (Laughs.) Which is being aware of a feeling . . . so you're saying there are more things than just that?

Therapist: You're actually considering it . . . You're actually open to it. (Laughs.)

Patient: It is just that I can't . . . it's just that . . . the whole things it just so overwhelmingly new.

Therapist: Thinking about yourself so narrowly is so familiar and easier.

Patient: It is just that everything is so new and it's just so much . . . it's like, um . . . it's like opening up a package every day, only the package is you . . . is me . . . and so if I open it, let's say it's this beautifully decorated package . . . So is it not just seeing what is there, but the process of opening it over time as well? *[Patient is being collaborative]* It can be both . . . the process of opening and also seeing what is there . . . and then that gives rise to new things?

Therapist: Yes . . . new things that are positive . . . and that the discovery of yourself is rich, complicated, and textured . . . and not at all something to be afraid of all the time. It is a whole world of who you are and what you can discover about yourself that you never had a chance to open up . . . but you do now . . . and you're right, there is no turning back, but that isn't something to be too afraid of, because what you discover is positive . . . it's not just fear and pain and aloneness.

Patient: I didn't think that would ever happen.

Therapist: But you have to come out of the cave to see what is there . . . when you come out of the cave the world and the world-of-self look very different. *[Therapist invites further self-exploration]*

Patient: Well, it just seems that there is so much more, and that is just happening too fast and it's overwhelming . . . but as I was saying last time when I said that the more aware I am, the more the awareness seems to be expanding, and that made me think about how . . . I don't know why I connected it with this, but the idea that the universe is expanding . . . and so somewhere I'm connecting the universe with awareness . . . the expanding awareness . . .

Therapist: The key here is the vantage point when you observe your experience . . . what is the vantage point of your observation? *[Therapist invites post-formal metacognition, specifically adopting a wider perspective]*

Patient: What do you mean? *[Patient is collaborative]*

Therapist: There is the experience that you have, the content, but who is using the awareness . . . what is that sense of self . . . that sense of self that is aware like? That's what's expanding?

Patient: The sense of self? Well, I had this idea about that . . . what if the wholeness is already there just waiting to be uncovered . . . and what if the parts are just getting in the way of the uncovering of it?

Therapist: Say more about that.

Patient: Well, it doesn't seem like there is a whole . . . it just seems to be different thoughts being promulgated by different parts and segments of time and experience . . . whatever . . . and . . . but what if there really *is* something.

Therapist: What if there *is* . . . look in your direct experience and see what that is . . . you can answer directly not as an idea but as *directly seeing* at any moment, right now for example. *[Fostering post-formal non-representational, awareness-based knowledge]*

Patient: Seeing or seen?

Therapist: Seeing in the moment . . . seeing what is there just the way it is with your awareness.

Patient: Well, I have this idea that . . . going back to the house metaphor and wondering if the house with the open doors . . . this isn't the self so much but . . . if I could see my life on a continuum . . . looking into the past . . . then standing in the present . . . and then looking into the future . . . more of a flowing . . . than things being all chopped up. *[This is a sign of holding self as a continuous narrative over time]* Then maybe . . . it's not on a line like this, but maybe in the house there is a central area . . . so as you pass from the doors . . . from the past through the present and into the future, then maybe I'll come around and find myself in the past again, so maybe there is something central that holds all of that together . . . I think I need the key at the moment . . . but the key for me at the moment is awareness . . . so I was thinking about this . . . I wanted to look at this again. (Patient takes a crystal and shows it to the therapist)

Therapist: The crystal?

Patient: That maybe the jewel is awareness . . . so Brother Z gave her the jewel . . . the gift of being aware . . . He gave it to her and it was very bright . . . and she looked at it, and was very intrigued by it, and it has turned out to be awareness. *[Here the patient is illustrating how she discovered a new, wider metacognitive perspective of awareness. By operating through this new metacognitive perspective of awareness, there is a unification of alter personality states into a wider whole, and subsequently, over time, this patient no longer reported parts or alter personality states and learned to operate consistently out of that whole.]*

Therapist: The key is not the crystal itself, but *who* is looking at the crystal, and the quality or level of awareness in looking at the crystal. You can look at the crystal as a thing, as something to look at, seemingly out there, and it has lots of facets . . . the thing you are looking at . . . but you can also look at the looker . . . *who* is looking at the crystal. *[Fostering post-formal metacognitive wider perspective-taking]*

Patient: You mean, look at the one who is looking at the crystal?

Therapist: Yes . . . the crystal from the perspective of the thing you are looking at seems multifaceted . . . but when you take the vantage point of the awareness that who is doing the looking, is that multifaceted or is that whole?

Patient: You're saying that the one who is looking is whole?

Therapist: I'm inviting you to look in your own experience and answer the question for yourself.

Patient: Well, this was my thought.

Therapist: Please?

Patient: If the sunlight shines through it, then you can see all of the different facets projected very beautifully . . . and so yes that could be the multitude of the parts . . . all interacting with the environment . . . having something to offer . . . trying to make a connection . . . but what if it didn't just project, but what if it took in . . . what if that were a way of seeing?

Bringing all of those different things in . . . then I might see the wholeness . . . it's all coming in like this . . . do you see what I'm saying?

Therapist: Yes. Or would it be fair to say that all that stuff that seems to
come in as multifaceted is all reflected in that whole awareness?

Patient: It might be . . . I'd have to think about that . . . *[Metacognitive
relativity of knowledge]*

Therapist: If you look at the faceted crystal and come back to the question
of the point of observation . . . the vantage point . . . you can look at all
the multifaceted experience reflected in the light . . . the sunlight . . . why
don't you look at it as if you *are* the sun and see what that is like?

Patient: Well, if I am the sun, I can see that I am the one who is causing
all of the . . . I am the one who is infusing light into all of the facets of the
crystal . . . and causing all of that . . . all of the lights and the colors . . . so
from that point of view, it isn't the crystal that is doing it, but it's the sun
that is doing it.

Therapist: And from that perspective, as the sun, how then do the different parts look?

Patient: Then they look like reflections . . . in and of themselves they are
not the whole, even though they think they are . . . but they are reflections
of the sun's being . . . and they come from the sun . . . they don't exist on
their own because if you close the shade then you can't see them anymore . . . the crystal doesn't have a light of its own . . . it comes through
the external source . . . so that is what you mean by saying that the crystal
is external . . . it's not the focal point itself?

Therapist: I am asking you to look at this from the perspective or vantage
point of being the sun and to notice the effect on your state of mind when
you do that. *[Therapist introduces wider metacognitive perspective]*

Patient: Well, if I am the sun, then I can project parts of myself that are
like the facets . . . are like the external expression.

Therapist: To make it more concrete . . . what do the child parts look like
from the perspective of the sun? What do the devil parts look like? The
internalized father parts?

Patient: I see the sun as being bigger and greater than all of them. They
look . . . they seem incomplete compared to the sun, the completeness of
the sun.

Therapist: So, what you are saying at this point is that one of the qualities
of looking from that vantage point is the sense of completeness. *[Fostering
a post-formal wider metacognitive perspective]*

Patient: I guess I am.

Therapist: When you look from this vantage point and keep looking at
some point, there is no guessing . . . only certainty . . . seeing it defini-
tively . . . just the way it is.

Patient: Oh, it's hard to describe other than to say that it seems more central than peripheral . . . the parts seem more jagged and peripheral. Well it's like the planets I guess . . . and they need the sun . . . I don't know if they are really part of the sun or if they are just expressions of the sun . . . but the central core.

Therapist: Does it seem like a core or a part, if you know?

Patient: Well, if I look at, from my vantage point, at the sun then it seems like a core . . . I'm not there yet, though. *[Metacognitive limits of knowledge]*

Therapist: There is something else about the image of the planets around the sun.

Patient: What?

Therapist: Well, you might have the sense of the parts as being disorganized, but when you think of the image of the planets around the sun . . . there is some order. *[Fostering metacognition of organization of mind]*

Patient: That's true.

Therapist: It seems like you're suggesting there is some ordering internally. Tell me about that?

Patient: Well, the thoughts are not jumping out or around as much . . . and then there is . . . not always, it depends on what is happening in one's life. You know, like with work and things like that, but at times it seems as though thoughts follow each other in an orderly way . . . sometimes there seems to be just silence. When I can hear the world as opposed to hearing the constant murmur of internal voices . . . I am more able to hear quiet inside or quiet in the world or even the world without so much competition. *[Shows good metacognition of organization of state of mind]* I don't know if that is ordering or if that is just the effect of ordering, of more internal order . . . but things don't seem as jumbled . . . *[Metacognition of limits of knowledge]* And at times, I'm able to be more focused at work and more focused when I am writing notes. So at times I think my concentration is much better than it was before. Well, it is helped by not hearing voices so much . . . at times . . . and it also has the effect of at times . . . this is something . . . at times being able to be spontaneous with feelings because they feel more real and not . . . um . . . they feel more real. *[Reports significant decrease in dissociation]* And not as if I'm trying to act in a way that would seem appropriate to the moment . . . because the parts don't always know how to act. They are always trying to . . . they are watching other people and trying to figure out how they should be acting and responding. *[Metacognitive awareness of outside-in orientation]*

Therapist: That's what you mean by being more spontaneous?

Patient: Yes . . . well, it's not the parts watching and trying . . . It's a feeling of being able to be more spontaneous or more real at the moment . . .

and I don't mean being reactive in that sense . . . I mean really responding genuinely in what I am trying to say . . . and sometimes it doesn't seem to work, but it depends on whether there is something going on that makes me uneasy, I guess. *[Metacognitive relating of variables]* I was at a close friend's house the other day, and she was remarking to me on how much I have changed, and this is something I was totally unaware of . . . but she said that the first time she met me and I came to her house, she said her kid said, "What is she doing?"

Therapist: You mean switching states?

Patient: Well, I was counting actually . . . in the kitchen . . . she said I was counting to calm myself . . . and I thought wow . . . gosh!

Therapist: Now she is noticing how much you have changed?

Patient: Yes.

Therapist: What did she tell you about that?

Patient: I'm trying to remember . . . I'm not as scattered . . . less like having . . being different people . . . more . . . I still think my time sense isn't great, but she said I have a better time sense than I had before. Also as I . . . I don't know if this has to do with awareness . . . well, I guess this has to do with awareness . . . that um . . . I think being . . . having more awareness at times gives you more choices. I'll give you an example. While I was waiting for you, the woman downstairs was asking questions and talking, and I felt kind of uncomfortable because she didn't seem like she had great boundaries so I decided not to answer, and so I read the magazine . . . and I thought before I would have just answered, even though I wasn't sure I wanted to.

Therapist: Maybe you don't have to be a passive victim.

Patient: I can choose, yes.

Therapist: Part of the newness is the freedom to choose and how to act in situations so you don't revictimize yourself . . . and that sets good boundaries . . . just as you did.

At the beginning of the third year of treatment, the patient was able to adopt a wider perspective in a stable way:

Patient: I am seeing things from a different vantage point, rather than seeing from a part at any given time . . . the parts only see part of the picture. I feel I am on the right track, but I am not sure. I don't have any basis for creating a new reality. Am I creating it, or am I just realizing what has always been there, and that I am just discovering it?

Therapist: The fear is changing into the wonder of discovering.

Patient: The fear doesn't slow me down. *[She also resolved any preoccupation with the past through an enhanced metacognitive orientation]* I realized that I can't be in the past and in the present at the same time. I am more looking back on the past but with greater awareness, but where I am is right here. I notice that when I awake at night, I am clearly in the past upon awakening. At least during the day I can be fully present, being aware of the moment. *[Shortly thereafter, she said that all activity of parts had disappeared]* I used to think that I was all parts with no whole. Now I think that there is a whole and no parts. It is more like a quiet whole. It is not so scary to be whole.

In the next session, the patient said, "The parts are a lot less defined now." Two sessions later she commented, "This is a different way of being." Over time even the propensity to become disorganized had transformed into a kind of distractibility at worst.

Patient: Now I am experiencing the disorganization as a kind of distractibility; previously it was more like a noise in my mind. The shifts seem to smooth out. The fear is more like a kind of alertness and focus. When I am more organized, the fear dissipates.

At the end of the third year, the patient said:

I was wondering—does thinking about the mind bring greater organization of mind? I suppose it depends on what the thinking about is. If thinking leads to greater reflection, it leads to greater organization of mind. I was wondering—do the shifts in state smooth out more over time, or just become less frequent? I notice far greater overall awareness in my daily life, and I am certainly less reactive.

A few sessions later, she added, "I have been noticing fluctuations in the level of organization. One day I got very disorganized, but I couldn't pinpoint anything that led to it. I could see how jumbled things got and also how it affects me."

She showed several signs of resolving anxious preoccupation. First, with respect to previous hyperactivation of attachment, she said, "I think I could be open to being with someone without being taken over by longing." Second, she had relinquished preoccupation with the past: "I notice that when I think about the past, it doesn't seem to be as painful, but only if I look at it a certain way, from the present. A friend told me recently that she thinks I have a rich inner life. I think I do."

By the beginning of the fourth year of treatment, the patient had developed a healthy sense of exploration of her own mind.

Patient: I have been thinking a lot about my loneliness. It doesn't seem as big as it once was. It doesn't have the same pull. I am thinking a lot about my own mind. There is so much there, and I have just scratched the surface. Everything I think, see, and do . . . everything is being created moment by moment. Everything is new. In the past I just was caught up in the parts. There is still occasional fluttering there. However, now the parts are like brush strokes being worked into a painting and blending into the painting. If fear comes up, if I put my awareness on it and it tends to dissipate fairly quickly. I also have less of a sense of a contaminated core. I am looking at myself totally differently . . . as loving and lovable. I am free of the habitual ways of looking at myself. I have been thinking a lot about the qualities of self that define me . . . sensitivity and humor . . . loyalty . . . perceptiveness . . . I am sure there is a lot more here . . . I am strong, and there is not quite as much fear as before.

At the three-and-a-half-year mark of treatment, the patient's sense of a unified self was strong. She said, "I realized that the way I think is part of my sense of self. I am getting a little more solidness and sense of presence. I think I have a right to be. I could never say that before." In another session she added, "Lately the past is more the past. In the past I was more focused on the past itself. Now I am focused on what there is to find in the future." She also developed the meta-cognitive skill of holding self and other in her perspective at the same time. She said, "I am trying to take both points of view of myself and the other at the same time. This is something new for me."

By the end of the fourth year of treatment, she was able to articulate many qualities of the newly emergent self:

> *Patient:* I was thinking about the negative states of mind I sometimes get into. I have been recognizing the relatively of them. I realize that at a deeper level they aren't really so negative. I have been thinking more about the positive qualities in myself . . . present . . . clear . . . full . . . curious . . . loving . . . gratitude . . . affection . . . belonging . . . worthiness . . . completion . . . even though my explorations will never be complete . . . anticipation of growth . . . enjoyment . . . a little tentative . . . I've given up my role as a sad, faded person. There is a certain security in knowing myself.

Below is a transcript from a session at the end of the fourth year of treatment. The session is rich with many examples across the spectrum of metacognition.

> *Patient:* It occurred to me while you were away last time that I have developed more of a . . . um . . . an internal representation of felt attachment to you, in that I'm more open to your seeing and knowing my mind . . . *[Internalized mentalization stance]* and I think that's why I have been able to maintain more stability over time, both when you're gone and when

you're not. Also I have a question about . . . last time you said that "loneliness is just a state," so by that do you mean . . . if I see it as just a state . . .

Therapist: Or as a construction of mind . . . *[Fostering metacognition of relativity of states]*

Patient: Then it doesn't carry as much weight.

Therapist: Exactly.

Patient: It's more the ideas I have about it. It's the ideas I have about it that weigh me down . . . rather than loneliness, the state of loneliness itself. Is that what you mean?

Therapist: Exactly.

Patient: I have noticed, um . . . and I'm trying to figure this out because I've noticed a shift and it's related to my dog . . . who I thought she was dying, but has survived this long . . . now she is not doing so well, so I um . . . so I'm not doing so well internally, and I'm trying to figure out exactly what is going on . . . what kind of shift has occurred so I don't know if its necessarily that I'm so disorganized or that my . . . that steady awareness that I've had at times, and that I've had for a while now, isn't as much with me . . . but the way I'm noticing it is that I don't . . . I'm not as present with my clients as I normally am . . . so I can't say that I'm in the past. I don't know where I am.

Therapist: Are you partially staying? Is there background activity of thought so that you are only partially staying with your patients, and partially with whatever that activity is around losing your dog?

Patient: Yeah, but it doesn't feel like background activity; it's more like the, um . . . it's, I guess it's sort of a preoccupation, but the weird thing is that it's not preoccupation as I would normally have experienced it in terms of ruminating about it and that sort of thing with a lot of voices and stuff . . . it's almost more like, um . . . an empty space where something is happening but nothing is happening . . . does that make any sense to you at all? It's disconcerting to me . . . it's like I'm fully present, but I don't know where I am . . . because before it would have been in the part, and I'm not noticing that so much, um . . . so I'd like to understand that better and bring myself back to the awareness I had. It also leads me to think that when something is going on in my life, it makes me vulnerable to . . . um . . . maybe I'm dissociating; I'm not sure. It makes me vulnerable to . . . um . . . changing in my awareness . . . well, maybe in my organization. I haven't figured that out yet.

Therapist: But you're appreciative that things that go on in your life . . . context effects have a clear impact on your state of mind. *[Fostering metacognitive awareness of contextual effects]*

Patient: Yes, that's what I'm noticing . . . right, and it seems as though it has an effect on awareness and on organization and my ability to stay present . . . and to see things as they are . . . and then, in turn, it . . . it affects my feeling state, and also my peace of mind.

Therapist: Say more about that.

Patient: Well, before this occurred, I was noticing that with more awareness I had a quieter mind and it seemed to be more peaceful . . . the past didn't intrude as much and . . . I didn't seem to be as vulnerable to hearing things or reading things like reading something about that or just listening to the news . . . to things that reminded me of the abuse and that sort of thing . . . didn't seem to affect me that much . . . and with the stuff going on with my dog, I feel weird . . . I remember . . . um . . . listening to a tape by the Dalai Lama on the *Art of Happiness* and he made the comment that even though he's lost a lot of friends, he's still basically happy . . . so that leads me to believe that um . . . as um . . . I don't know if this is the right way of saying it . . . as I get greater control of my mind . . . I don't know if that's the right way to say it, but I think you know what I mean . . . that I won't be as . . . it will be stronger in a way and it won't be as vulnerable to external things that cause the context changes that you are talking about. Is that true? I'm curious.

Therapist: What do you think it is that is going on about anticipating losing your dog and making you more vulnerable to external things . . . what's the connection? Do you have a theory as to why that makes you more vulnerable?

Patient: Well . . . I've been puzzling over that and I think that, um . . . that it is related to loss. *[Metacognitive relating of variables]*

Therapist: How so?

Patient: Loss . . . present, and past . . . you know . . . just . . . it's on a few different levels. I think because it's sort of like . . . it's losing her and the loss of her in my life . . . then it has to do with the fact that C gave her to me and that it also made me think of past losses . . . you know, the loss of innocence and stuff in my life as a child, so I think that's what I mean by a lot of different levels.

Therapist: You mentioned earlier the past intruding into the present, so loss is an example of that?

Patient: Yes . . . but there's also the loss of my currently . . . um . . . better awareness and feeling better . . . and there's almost a shift into . . . I think there's sort of a dissociative shift happening . . . maybe that's just a label that I'm giving it because I'm not figuring out . . . why I'm not totally present . . . Does that make sense?

Therapist: Absolutely.

Patient: I think there is some shifting going on, some dissociation, but I'm not as . . . but it's not presenting in the way that it used to . . . so it not as clear to me . . .

Therapist: When you say it's not presenting in the way that it used to, what do you mean? How would you compare it?

Patient: It's not accompanied by all the noise from the parts.

Therapist: So you're saying it's the nonawareness type of dissociation, not the disorganization type of dissociation? Is that fair to say?

Patient: Right. I think that's a good way of describing it . . . What does that mean, though? What does that mean?

Therapist: You're answering your own question. In your direct experience, by seeing the difference between these two types of dissociation . . . as a benchmark to where you are . . . even under conditions that are quite stressful to you . . . the loss of your dog is a big deal . . . a really big deal . . . under the circumstances of that very real stress, there is less vulnerability to getting the disorganized type of dissociation, but there is still a way that you notice being less present, less aware. Yet you still have this very keen awareness of context effects . . . you know what's causing you to be less present is somehow related to possibly losing your dog.

Patient: So that's an improvement then.

Therapist: Absolutely . . . and there's a funny paradox here . . . not only are you less aware, but you are more aware of being less aware.

Patient: So that's where it shows that real change has occurred . . . because I was thinking about how much I've changed internally over the past year and then this happened . . . so it shows that I've changed, but at the same time I'm still vulnerable to shifts . . . just not in the same way . . . it's an interesting kind of . . . it's a context-dependent or context-driven kind of thing. Before I think that context caused me to shift into parts, and now it's resulting in this sort of diminished awareness . . . it feels like I've lost my ability to stay aware.

Therapist: *Partially* lost . . . it may *seem* to you that you fully lost it, but you'd be aware if you fully lost it . . . partially and temporarily . . . meaning that even as you talk about it, you talk about it with the belief that you'll get that back.

Patient: Well, it's based on times in the past when I have gotten that back even when it feels that I've completely lost it . . . still it does bother me . . . (Cries.) It also brings up what I do in my work, because somebody . . . if one of my patients dies or I have situations that, well, where I see family members hang on, you know . . . not letting the people die, so . . .

Therapist: Are you somehow connecting this to how you are in losing your dog?

Patient: What do you mean?

Therapist: Seeing family members and how they deal with another family member dying, which you see often at work . . . are you looking at that in terms of how you are being with your own situation of losing your dog? Is there a connection here that you are making?

Patient: Sometimes it's hard for me to deal with hopeless situations.

Therapist: Of course.

Patient: That's when I'm in this frame of mind . . . sometimes when I'm in another frame of mind it's not so hard . . . it's not as hard, well not in the same way. When I'm in a more aware place and not facing my own loss, I think I am more able to be more present and more helpful . . . and what I think it is partially is that I derived a lot of satisfaction, a lot of . . . um . . . it's not just satisfaction, but I think I feel better about myself when I am able to be helpful . . . so when I'm feeling as I do now, I don't feel that I can be as present and as helpful. I don't feel as good. Now I'm not saying that my total sense of self-worth hinges on that, but it's something that, in the relative sense, is a large part of my life. Things are quieting down again . . . so I think that I may have gotten a sense of something, but I don't know what it is though . . . maybe it is just being here.

By the end of the fourth year, the patient no longer met the diagnostic criteria for PTSD or DID. Her coherence of mind went from 1.5 to 8.5 on the AAI and her reflective capacity from –1 to 8.5 on the Reflective Functioning Scale.

As is clear from the account of this treatment, not every Three Pillars method available to the therapist was brought into the work with this patient. With this patient, as with every patient, the therapist drew from the general principles of the treatment model to guide broad as well as particular treatment considerations and choices, and also applied specific interventions as they were warranted by the moment of experience of and with the patient.

PART V

TREATMENT GUIDE AND EXPECTED OUTCOMES

CHAPTER 14

A Step-by-Step Treatment Guide

Chapters 8, 9, and 10 describe in detail each of the three pillars of our treatment model, and Chapters 11, 12, and 13 present the specific considerations and methods for applying the model to each of the primary insecure attachment types. Although across types there is important variation in how each pillar is applied, the reader has seen that there is an overall, consistent treatment structure that is common for all patients. This chapter further describes that structure and can be used as a guide to help with planning and navigating treatment.

Following each component of the treatment structure below, the chapters in this book relevant to that component are indicated.

1. If the patient presents with a relational disturbance, make a determination about the nature of that disturbance. Is the presenting problem primarily an attachment, core conflictual relationship theme (CCRT), or trauma-bonding issue? CCRT or trauma-bonding patterns may coexist with significant attachment insecurity, and if they do, then treatment will proceed with focus on the primary attachment disturbance; later during treatment, when the patient shows signs of earned attachment security, then the relevant CCRT patterns and any trauma bonding are addressed. When attachment security is present but with some degree of anxiety (F4 or F5 AAI classification) or some degree of dismissing features (F1 or F2 classification), and CCRT or trauma bonding patterns are *also* present, then assess whether the mild to moderate anxious or dismissing attachment patterns have significantly interfered with the patient's relationships. If they have, assume that the attachment disturbance is primary (as it formed earliest developmentally) and focus treatment on the attachment patterns. The CCRTs or trauma-bonding issues are addressed later, after the patient has established earned security. (See Chapter 7.)

2. Assess the nature of the attachment problem in greater detail. A variety of attachment measures may be used, but we strongly recommend obtaining a tran-

script and scoring of the Adult Attachment Interview (AAI), for several reasons. First, it allows for a valid and accurate determination of the four best-researched attachment types—secure, dismissing, preoccupied, and disorganized—as well as for a determination of the subtypes within each of the main categories: Ds1, Ds2, or Ds3 for dismissing attachment; E1, E2, or E3 for preoccupied attachment; F1, F2, F3, F4, or F5 for secure attachment; and Ud or CC for disorganized attachment. Second, the five adjectives describing the early childhood relationship with each parent can be used fruitfully to individualize the IPF protocol according to the given patient's AAI adjectives. Third, the AAI provides a pre-treatment measure of coherence of discourse and coherence of mind, which can be used as valuable markers of treatment progress. Additionally, the AAI can be used as a basis to determine the patient's pre-treatment level of reflective functioning using the Reflective Functioning Scale (RF-S)*. We also recommend using the Metacognition Assessment Scale (MAS) to identify condition-specific pre-treatment deficits in metacognition. For a quick assessment of a hyperactivating or deactivating attachment style, the Experience of Close Relationships (ECR) questionnaire is the self-report inventory of choice. (See Chapters 3 and 9.)

3. Engage the patient in a collaborative dialogue to establish and prioritize shared treatment goals and a specific treatment plan. We recommend a transparency model of treatment planning, in which the therapist openly explains his or her assessment of the patient's attachment disturbance and what the treatment is likely to entail for addressing that disturbance. Introduce the Three Pillars approach and give a brief overview of the rationale and methods of each treatment component. It is very important that sufficient time be devoted to making sure that the patient understands the Three Pillars model and methods in order to ensure that both therapist and patient have the same basic understanding of how treatment will proceed. (See Chapters 7 and 10.)

In order to help the clinician explain to patients what attachment is and how it is specifically relevant to them in the Three Pillars treatment, we provide here four sample psychoeducation scripts—one for a general description of attachment, its origins, and its secure and insecure forms and one for each of the three prototypes of insecure attachment. We do not recommend that a therapist *read* these to patients, but rather become familiar enough with the key principles and points to integrate them into his or her own language to communicate the information informally to the patient. It is best to present the material not as a monologue, but rather in dialogue with the patient, who will undoubtedly have questions and reactions along the way. Each sample below is quite comprehen-

---

* At the time of preparation of this book, Peter Fonagy and his colleagues were developing a self-report measure of mentalizing, the "Reflective Function Questionnaire". This tool promises to be very helpful to clinicians when an AAI and/or RF-S scoring is not available.

sive, and each therapist will decide how much or how little and which portions of the information to communicate to the patient. With each patient, we start with the general information and then provide more detailed information about which of the attachment patterns is central for the particular patient. In the context of providing information to the patient about his or her specific insecure attachment subtype, we introduce the Ideal Parent Figure component of the treatment, as that is most directly relevant to creating a new internal working model of attachment.

Psychoeducation About Attachment

The specific therapy process that we'll be doing together has as its foundation an understanding of the importance of security of attachment. So I'd like to tell you a little about attachment. Attachment is a kind of connection with important people in our lives, and for our purposes, we can focus on attachment as it relates to our early experiences of our parents or primary caregivers. Every child is born with an innate drive to establish a healthy attachment relationship with his or her parents or caregivers. With a healthy attachment relationship, the child feels protected and safe, soothed and comforted when upset, and supported in developing into the best self that he or she can be. Having healthy, secure attachment as children helps us to physically, emotionally, and psychologically thrive.

Securely attached children experience their parents as being carefully attuned to their behavior and inner feelings, consistently responsive to their feelings and needs, encouraging and supportive of inner and outer exploration, and supportive of their strongest and most unique sense of self. Healthy, secure attachment between a child and caregiver is an interplay between healthy attachment seeking of connection and healthy exploration that promotes independence.

Unfortunately, not all attachment is secure attachment. Children who have insecure attachment have experiences quite different from those of children who have secure attachment. Insecurely attached children may have high anxiety in relation to their relationships with their parents or caregivers, and from that anxiety of insecurity they may become very clingy and worried about their parents becoming unavailable. This anxiety tends to prevent these children from feeling safe enough to explore independently from their parents, which limits their learning and development.

Children with another form of insecure attachment keep themselves emotionally and sometimes physically distant from their parents. They tend to excessively explore independently, but tend not to seek contact or comfort from their parents.

Still another form of insecure attachment includes a combination of characteristics of both of the two forms I just described.

Underlying the feelings and behaviors that are common with each form of attachment, secure or insecure, are internal patterns, or ways that our experiences with our caregivers get imprinted in our minds. We call these internal patterns or imprints internal working models, or maps, of attachment. These internal working models *or* maps *get formed very early in our lives, mostly during our second year of life. Whichever form they take, secure or one of several types of insecure, they profoundly affect our experiences of ourselves and others, and they continue to play out in our adult relationships. In other words, attachment patterns get repeated again and again over the course of our lifetime, usually without us being aware of how the pattern repeatedly plays out. If our attachment pattern is insecure, we will experience difficulties in various ways in our relationships with ourselves and with others.*

Fortunately, the insecure internal maps of attachment and the insecure patterns of behavior and experience can be modified and changed, for the better. With the particular kind of therapy that we're going to do together, the goal in treatment is to develop a new, positive and stable internal map for healthy, secure attachment. When you have the internal model or map for secure attachment, that will serve as the basis for new, deeply positive experiences in your relationship with yourself and in your relationships with others.

Psychoeducation About Dismissing Attachment

We have discovered from your AAI that your attachment pattern falls within the dismissing category. Let's talk about exactly what that means. When you were young, although your parents did the very best they could, your attachment needs were not fully met. The dismissing attachment pattern means that you were likely to have experienced your parents as rejecting of or not so interested in some of your basic attachment needs. Sometimes this is a result of the way your own parents were parented, and they were repeating what they experienced from their own parents. It could also have come from experiences of separation between you and one or both of your parents, or from any circumstance that meant that your emotional needs were not consistently recognized and explored by your parents when you tried to express your feelings and needs to them. Whatever you experienced got formed into an internal impression of what close relationships are like; as you've heard, we call that internal impression an internal working model, or an attachment map.

In the best parenting, the caregiver is carefully attuned to the child and consistently responsive to the child's active expression of attachment needs. However, if parents repeatedly reject or dismiss a child's expressed attachment needs, it is very likely that the child will develop an internal working model or map of caregivers as rejecting or dismissing, which creates the patterns of dismissing attachment. It's particularly hurtful to children when they feel rejected or dismissed when they are emotionally upset and seek comfort and reassurance.

Some parents of children who develop dismissing attachment are very uncomfortable with physical contact and rarely hug their children or openly express physical affection to them. In general, caregivers of these children tend to be far less emotionally attuned or expressive than caregivers of secure children. Some caregivers tend to be selectively attuned to the negative emotions and behaviors of the child and remarkably misattuned to the positive emotions and behaviors that the child spontaneously expresses. People with dismissing attachment often grew up in families where the parents had very strong, often rigid ideas about parenting, so that the child felt unseen, controlled, and rejected for his or her unique self.

One clear effect of this active dismissal of basic attachment needs is that you developed a tendency to dismiss your own attachment needs, and you developed yourself to become strong in the world independent of attachment. Your early childhood experiences have provided you prematurely with a very strong sense of self and made you self-reliant, independent, and strong, which of course are really important qualities. But you are likely to have found that most personal close relationships, and sometimes work relationships, have been challenging and not very satisfying for you.

These experiences have left you with a deep sense that connection in relationships is somehow always problematic, or that such connections really don't matter that much, or that getting involved in close relationships is somehow threatening so that it is far easier to be by yourself. But even so, people with dismissing attachment usually still have an underlying yearning for closeness and belonging, and somewhere inside want to feel really connected to another person. Unfortunately, they rarely allow themselves to experience this longing because it is often experienced as a source of shame or discomfort.

Our overall goal is to help you to develop a new, different, positive internal working model of relationships, so that you will no longer find yourself caught in the patterns of dismissing attachment. Using your imagination, we will create "ideal parent figures" who will actively engage you, who have consistent attunement and understanding and emotional and physical availability and responsiveness to you. And they will have the care and flexibility to provide you with exactly what you need emotionally. These parents will be deeply accepting and encouraging of each and every one of your emotional needs and never make you feel ashamed of your attachment feelings and needs. They also know exactly how much space and distance you need to feel comfortable, protected, and safe. And from your feelings of being protected and safe, your ideal parents will help you identify, express, and explore your underlying vulnerabilities, hurts, and disappointments. They will always be there for you in just the right ways. Over time, this imagery will help you experience all that is positive about open, authentic connection in relationships in a way that won't seem as fearful, hurtful, or disappointing. You'll certainly be able to be your strong, independent self, and in that context will also be able to feel close and connected and satisfied in relationships.

Psychoeducation About Anxious-Preoccupied Attachment

We have discovered from your Adult Attachment Interview that your attachment pattern falls within the anxious-preoccupied category. Let's talk about what this means. When you were very young, although your parents did the very best they could, your attachment needs were not fully met. They were probably not as carefully attuned or responsive to your feelings and needs as you really needed them to be. Sometimes this is a result of the way your own parents were parented, and they were repeating what they learned. It could also mean that at times your parents may have felt overwhelmed with all their family and work responsibilities, and so they couldn't read your signals of distress in a consistent way and respond to you in helpful ways. It could also mean that your parents were only partially attending to your needs because they were busy and multi-tasking and attending to other things while trying also to attend to you. Maybe your parents were having difficulty in their own lives, and their stresses and fears and worries spilled over onto you. Whatever you experienced got formed into an internal impression of what close relationships are like; as I've said, that internal impression is called an internal working model, or an attachment map.

There are a number of ways that parents can be that tend to lead to anxious-preoccupied internal attachment maps in their children. Parents may be consistently unresponsive or inconsistently responsive; they may be responsive but with very poor timing; they may be more attuned to their children's negative experiences and feelings than their positive ones. And they may be overly anxious in ways that the children become hypervigilant to and overinvolved with the parents' states of mind.

In the best parenting, the parent is consistently carefully attuned to and responsive to the child's experiences and comforts and reassures the child when he or she is anxious. The parent also encourages the child's best self-development by supporting exploratory free play. But if one or both of your parents inadvertently enlisted you to become focused on and involved in their experiences and emotional needs rather than your own, then what was supposed to be was reversed—you learned to be attuned to them more than they were attuned to you.

So, in your inner map of attachment, you expect that you have to be overattuned to and overinvolved with others and that others won't be attuned enough to you. And as a result, you yourself have become not so able to be attuned to your own emotional experience when you're with others. In other words, because of your early attachment relationships, you tend to become preoccupied with the state of mind of the other person at the expense of careful attunement to your own state of mind. Over time this became a learned style of attuning to and taking on others' experiences and wants and needs—what we call an "outside-in orientation." This outside-in orientation can lead you to focus too much on and take too much care of others—sometimes called compulsive caretaking—at the expense of your own wants and needs. You become an expert at trying to read others, but your own sense of self and what your needs are in a relationship are often not as clear.

Another consequence of an overinvolving parent–child relationship is that children have difficulty learning how to manage, or regulate, emotions. This means there is some likelihood of experiencing high levels of anxiety or anger, or of having very strong emotions arise quickly and intensely without having much ability to deal with them and calm yourself down.

Also, the long-term pattern of being overinvolved in the states of mind of other people interferes with self-development—people with anxious-preoccupied attachment have difficulty developing a sense of a strong, independent, unique, or best sense of self, which is what we're all meant to be. They tend to hold back or be tentative about active discovery and exploration of the world and the possibilities of the self.

Our overall goal is to help you to develop a new, different, positive internal working model of relationships so that you will no longer find yourself caught in the patterns of anxious-preoccupied attachment. Instead of having an outside-in orientation, together we will help you to develop the opposite, an inside-out orientation, which will help you to be more aware of your own feelings and wants and needs, to have more balanced and truly mutual relationships, and to become your best as the unique person you are.

Using your imagination, we will create "ideal parent figures" who will be deeply interested in you and attuned to you. They will sense your internal needs and have the capacity to give you just the right responsiveness in a variety of situations. They will know exactly how to calm you when you feel anxious. They will encourage you to be curious and to explore, yet will be right there when you need them. These ideal parent figures will help you create new possibilities, and you will experience your best and strongest self in many different and novel situations—you can just be.

Psychoeducation About Disorganized Attachment

We have discovered from your Adult Attachment Interview that your attachment patterns fall within the disorganized attachment category. Let's talk about what this means. When you were very young, although your parents did the very best they could, your attachment needs were not fully met. Sometimes disorganized attachment is the result of early, prolonged separations. Or, you may have experienced one or both of your parents as frightening, confusing, or quite disconnected. Maybe sometimes one or both parent acted in ways that frightened you and at other times acted in ways that were tentative and timid. Caregivers of children with disorganized attachment are sometimes described as aggressive, disruptive, loud, in your face, or in other ways scary to the child. Sometimes such caregivers are described as fearful, tentative, confused, or dissociated when around the child.

The ways that your parents were with you may have resulted from the ways that they themselves were parented, and they repeated what they had experienced and learned. Also, your parents may have felt overwhelmed with all their family and work responsibilities and therefore couldn't read your signals of need or distress in a consistent way and respond to you as you needed. Your parents may have had difficulty in their own lives, and their fears and worries may have spilled over onto you. Parents of children who have disorganized attachment are often preoccupied with some unresolved loss of an important relationship, or with an unresolved trauma, in ways that make it hard for them to provide an attuned secure attachment base for the child.

In the best parenting, the caregiver remains consistently, carefully attuned to and responsive to the child's experiences and needs and comforts the child when he or she is anxious, provides reassurance, and encourages the child's best self-development by encouraging exploratory free play. Children who develop disorganized attachment experience parents as both a source of security and growth and a source of threat and fear. This creates the impossible dilemma of both needing to reach out to the caregiver as a source of safety, comfort, and guidance, and *needing to get away from the caregiver out of fear of harm.*

People with disorganized attachment are likely to experience attachment figures throughout their lives as a source of fear. Such people are likely to experience increased fear arousal and mistrust around people they start to feel close to. Yet, despite the high fear arousal, people with disorganized attachment keep unsuccessfully trying to find a sense of safety and comfort in such attachment relationships. As a result of this impossible dilemma, people with disorganized attachment typically have various conflicting attachment behaviors—at times they can fully disconnect and isolate from others, and at times they show a persistent fearful need to maintain intense contact in a way that seems out of control and isn't easy to stop. In other words, disorganized attachment creates the tendency to alternate between connecting too little or too much with others, and what is lacking is the ability to have balanced, sustained, safe, and enhancing connection with others. Interpersonally, some people with disorganized attachment are described as bossy, compulsively caretaking, or fearful.

Not everyone with disorganized attachment has the same experiences, but overall, internal experience is likely to seem as if it is always shifting and lacking in coherence. Some people with disorganized attachment have many more dissociative experiences and behaviors than others. Dissociative experiences include the sense of being "out of it," rapidly shifting between different aspects or parts of the self, and/or rapidly shifting between different mood states, such as being frightened, explosively angry, and/or helpless. Dissociation can also involve temporarily losing connection to where one is, or having periods of time that one can't remember or account for.

Our overall goal is to help you to develop a new, different, positive internal working model of relationships so that you will no longer find yourself caught in the patterns of disorganized attachment. Using your imagination, we will create "ideal parent figures" who are a safe haven and allow you to be with them completely free of fear.

These parents will not be frightening in any way. They will be strong, carefully attuned parents who know you and are deeply interested in you and know just the right ways to help you feel seen and known and soothed when you need that. They will be predictable and safe. After helping you calm all your fears, they will consistently encourage you to explore and discover your best and strongest self. Internally, as a result of working together in these ways, you are likely to experience more internal clarity and stability and a more consistent, positive, and steady experience of yourself instead of the endlessly shifting states you have been all too familiar with. You'll find over time in your relationships that you can be more balanced, steady, safe, and mutually supportive and encouraging.

4. Engage the patient in a collaborative discussion of potential treatment-frame problems. Since many adult patients with clinically significant attachment disturbance also have personality and/or dissociative disorder diagnoses, it is especially important to arrive at a mutual understanding, in advance, of how treatment-frame infractions will be addressed. A written treatment-frame contract is useful for clarity and to prevent future misunderstandings. (See Chapter 10.)

5. Early in treatment, address noncollaborative nonverbal behavior and promote collaborative nonverbal behavior. For example, lack of eye contact and muted spontaneous facial affective displays are common in dismissive patients, and disconnected, difficult-to-understand nonverbal behavior is common in disorganized patients. Foster the patient's metacognitive awareness of these nonverbal types of noncollaborative behavior as part of the shared goal of greater nonverbal collaborative communication throughout treatment. Over time, carefully match and change spontaneous nonverbal communication, especially that pertaining to the patient's spontaneous affective facial displays throughout the treatment session. (See Chapters 10, 11, 12, and 13.)

6. Early in treatment, address noncollaborative verbal behavior and promote collaborative verbal behavior. For example, encourage dismissive patients to move beyond terse, succinct, closed statements about attachment themes to ongoing verbal exploration characterized by greater richness and detail; also encourage them to move beyond idealization with free exploration of negative emotions associated with attachment themes. In contrast, encourage anxious-preoccupied patients to stay on topic without introducing irrelevancies, to make their points succinctly, and also to clarify what they mean whenever they engage in passive, vague, or jargon-like speech. Because disorganized patients frequently shift states of mind and each new state is likely to contradict previous states, it is especially important to frequently clarify the communications of the current self-state and how that relates to the previous self-state (i.e., metacognitive relating of variables). (See Chapters 10, 11, 12, and 13.)

7. Introduce the Ideal Parent Figure protocol. Clarify for the patient the difference between memory and imagination—that memory is limited to real experiences in the past with attachment figures, but imagination creates new, never-before-experienced possibilities. Emphasize that the IPF method is most beneficial when the patient uses his or her imagination, not memory, to create parent figures that are ideally suited to his or her nature and needs. The first IPF sessions are framed

generally to give the patient maximum freedom to draw from inner knowing of what he or she most needs. Establish the inner conditions for the imagery, including a calm, relaxed body focus and an imagined and felt sense of being a very young child. Then ask the patient to imagine that he or she is with parents, but not the parents or any caregivers that he or she grew up with; the patient imagines a different set of parents who are ideally suited to his or her nature and needs. When the patient indicates imagining such parents, suggest that in whatever imagined circumstance they are all in together, the ideal parents are *being* with the child in ways that give the patient-as-child a sense of being *absolutely secure* in the relationship with them. Encourage the patient to shape and reshape the imagery in these initial sessions until the felt sense of comfort and security feels just right. It is likely that this generic experience of basic felt attachment security will require at least several sessions. Address resistances and difficulties the patient has with the basic protocol. (See Chapter 8.)

8. In subsequent IPF sessions, suggest that the ideal parent figures have qualities consistent with the five primary conditions that promote secure attachment: protection, attunement, soothing, expressed delight, and support for best self-development. Across this phase of the IPF sessions, include each of the five conditions in the shaping of the imagined parent figures. Emphasize the particular conditions that are most needed by the particular patient, according to his or her attachment prototype. For example, with dismissing patients, emphasize that the IPFs are carefully attuned to, recognize, and support the patient-as-child's attachment behaviors, and that they are also carefully attuned to the patient-as-child's negative affects. With anxious-preoccupied patients, emphasize that the IPFs are consistently accurately attuned to the patient-as-child's internal state of mind. Emphasize for disorganized patients that the IPFs reliably provide soothing and comfort to reduce fears related to attachment. (See Chapters 8, 11, 12, and 13.)

9. Gradually introduce greater individualization of IPF qualities. Draw from the AAI five adjectives for each early caregiver relationship, or from what is known from clinical interviewing about the particular patient's experiences with early caregivers, and suggest that the IPFs have the positive opposite qualities. Also include in the shaping of the IPFs the positive opposites of the main etiological factors of the particular patient's insecure attachment type. For example, for dismissing patients, parents or caregivers of origin typically showed physical and emotional rejection of proximity- and contact-seeking, selective misattunement to negative affects, rigid control, and selective attunement to pseudoexploratory behavior. Therefore, shape the IPFs of dismissing patients to include deep acceptance and encouragement of the patient-as-child's attachment behavior; careful and accurate attunement to the patient-as-child's full range of affects, especially to negative affective expressions; acceptance and normalization of the child's

feelings of shame regarding the longing for attachment; openness, permissiveness, and flexibility rather than rigidity and being controlling; and fostering of exploration in the context of attachment, not independent of attachment. For preoccupied patients, parents or caregivers of origin typically were overinvolving of the child in the caregiver's state of mind, pervasively misattuned and unresponsive, and selectively misattuned to the child's exploratory behavior. Therefore, shape the IPF imagery to include consistent attention and attunement to the patient-as-child's state of mind rather than involvement of him or her in the IPF's state, consistent attunement to the patient-as-child's general level of anxiety in a way that is comforting, provision of comfort and security in a way that calms hyperactivating attachment behaviors, repeated support for exploratory behavior, and fostering of the patient-as-child's best self-development. Parents or caregivers of disorganized patients typically showed frightened and frightening behavior, dissociated states and behavior, and pervasively disrupted affective communication and attunement. Therefore, shape the IPF imagery to include calm, comforting, and predictable behavior; provision of a safe haven; being fully present and real; careful attunement to the patient-as-child's fear or mistrust of attachment; consistent soothing of the patient-as-child's acute or chronic fear arousal; consistent contingent responsiveness; fierce protectiveness from harm or abuse; setting of appropriate limits to protect and contain the patient-as-child during episodes of aggressive arousal; and encouragement of both attachment and exploratory behavior. (See Chapters 8, 11, 12, and 13.)

10. In the context of all interactions with the patient outside the IPF protocol, use methods to support a range of basic and intermediate metacognitive skills matched to the patient's metacognitive limitations, individually and according to his or her attachment prototype. For example, a condition-specific approach to dismissing attachment necessitates enhancing identification of state of mind and looking beyond the information given; for the preoccupied patient, it is especially important to foster a mentalizing stance; for disorganized patients, it is important to enhance mentalizing and reflective capacity in general and to foster metacognitive identification of and mastery over states of mind. Apply methods such as anchoring scales, affective marking, and modeling and promoting mentalizing. (See Chapters 7, 9, 11, 12, and 13.)

11. Gradually introduce methods to promote the later intermediate and advanced metacognitive skills. Try to include each of the advanced skills, and also pay particular attention to the particular needs common to each insecure attachment type. For the dismissing patient, these include fostering an awareness of contextual effects, adopting a wider perspective on the central guiding purpose of life, and fostering a sense of interconnectedness. For the preoccupied patient, these include promoting metacognitive awareness of the degree of organization/

disorganization of state of mind and recognition of metacognitive orientation of past/present and self/other at any given point in time. For the disorganized patient, fostering metacognitive awareness of the degree of organization/disorganization of state of mind is especially important throughout treatment, along with metacognitive orientation of past/present, self/other, and child/adult at any given point in time; additionally, it is important to help the disorganized patient to adopt a wider perspective on self toward a larger self-unity that transcends the momentary shifting self-states. (See Chapters 7, 9, 11, 12, and 13.)

12. Toward the later phase of treatment, when possible, introduce and shift to the development of the later advanced metacognitive skills. These include an appreciation of interconnectedness and interdependence, discovering the central guiding purpose or ultimate concerns of life, and a sensitivity to knowledge acquisition through nonrepresentational, direct awareness of immediate ongoing experience. The presence of such skills contributes to the highest and most stable changes in coherence of mind for patients with any of the attachment types. Patients who mature cognitively beyond formal operational thinking can have higher levels of mental health and psychological well-being. (See Chapters 7 and 9.)

13. Throughout treatment, and especially toward the later phases, notice, point out, and discuss with the patient the signs of treatment progress and success, as indicated in Chapter 15. Such active attention and discussion reinforces the progress, promotes mentalizing and other metacognitive skills, and contributes to the patient's sense of agency and positive possibility. (See Chapter 9.)

14. Toward the end of treatment, include methods that specifically promote self-development to complement and reinforce the self-development that has occurred throughout the therapy. Also, apply the methods to specifically foster a positive representation or map of adult secure intimacy. The self-development and secure intimacy methods help to consolidate the gains from the therapy and further promote the interest in and capacity for healthy exploratory behavior in all aspects of the patient's life. Healthy exploratory behavior outside of therapy establishes the transition to termination of the Three Pillars attachment-based treatment. (See Appendices A and B.)

CHAPTER 15

Treatment Outcomes

Indicators of Successful Treatment

Over the past 20 years during which we have developed the Three Pillars treatment, we have identified some of the main markers of successful outcome. We summarize these as follows:

1. *Achievement of earned secure attachment.* The large-scale, measurable expected outcome is the change from pre-treatment insecure attachment—dismissing (Ds1, Ds2, or Ds3), preoccupied (E1, E2, or E3), or disorganized (CC)—to secure attachment (F1, F2, F3, F4, or F5), as measured by administering and scoring the AAI at the onset of treatment and again at the termination of treatment. K. N. Levy et al. (2006) first described the use of change in attachment status as a measurable outcome of therapy.

2. *The formation of a new, positive stable internal working model for healthy adult attachment.* A fundamental premise of the Three Pillars treatment model is that the systematic, repeated use of ideal parent figure imagery in the context of a secure therapeutic attachment relationship will result in the development of a new, positive, stable internal working model for healthy attachment that will overwrite fragmented or negative attachment representations. When the new representation, map, or internal working model is present, through evocative memory it will serve as a template that informs and organizes healthy interpersonal interactions. There is no direct way to measure the development of a healthy IWM for attachment, but we assume that it is present on the basis of the patient's self-report of particular experiences of IPF imagery, including secure base and a balance between consistent healthy attachment behaviors (e.g., valuing attachment, nonclinging proximity- and contact-seeking) and consistent healthy

exploratory behaviors (e.g., confidence about exploration away from the IPFs). We also infer its presence through aspects of the relationship with the therapist and the patient's relationships outside of therapy, including, as with the IPF relationships, a healthy balance between attachment and exploratory behaviors.

3. *The capacity for adult secure intimacy.* We do not consider treatment successful or complete until the patient is able to develop and articulate a new, positive representation for adult secure intimacy. It is not an expectation that the patient will be in such a relationship, as we are not matchmakers, but we do expect that the patient will have an internal working model for what such a relationship would be for him or her. Ideally, during or after the treatment, the patient will make partner choices and engage in intimate behaviors that match the new positive map of secure intimacy. In Chapter 3, we reviewed several self-report measures of romantic attachment, and as we have indicated, we like the Experience in Close Relationships (ECR) questionnaire.

4. *The manifestation of a range of metacognitive skills, including higher-order skills, that the patient will use consistently in everyday life.* We find that patients significantly increase their metacognitive skills during the course of the Three Pillars treatment. The Reflective Functioning Scale (RF-S; Fonagy, Target, et al., 1998) can be used to measure the general increase in metacognitive capacity, as K. N. Levy et al. (2006) did as one of their outcome measures. Specific metacognitive skills can be assessed using the Metacognitive Assessment Scale (MAS; Semerari et al., 2003). We consider the achievement of some level of post-formal cognitive development over the course of treatment a necessary sign of mental health. Unfortunately, there are no simple, user-friendly scales to measure the development of post-formal mature cognitive development as an outcome of treatment. Available assessment instruments present the patient with various vignettes or problems to resolve, but these instruments require complex coding and interpretation (as does the AAI). Examples of such assessment are Sternberg's (1984) vignettes to assess wisdom, Loevinger's Washington University Sentence Completion Test (Loevinger & Wessler, 1970), the Hierarchical Complexity Scoring System (Commons, Danaher, Miller, & Dawson, 2000), and the Lectical Decision-Making Assessment (Dawson, 2004; Dawson & Wilson, 2004).

5. *The manifestation of healthy behavioral, nonverbal, and verbal collaboration.* Healthy collaborative behavior can be assessed with respect to how well the patient adheres to the treatment-frame behaviors outlined in the treatment contract. Increases in healthy nonverbal collaborative behavior over the course of treatment become obvious to the therapist through the ongoing nonverbal exchange with the patient. For example, head-turning toward the therapist, eye contact, and especially matched facial affect displays all increase in occurrence.

These and other increases in nonverbal collaborative behavior may be formally assessed with the video-feedback procedure developed by Beebe and Lachmann (2002, 2014). An increase in verbal collaborative behavior can be formally assessed through comparing pre- and post-treatment AAI transcripts based on adherence to or violation of Grice's maxims for coherent discourse (Grice, 1975, 1989). Informally, a sign of progress is that the patient becomes increasingly comfortable with the topic of attachment and can talk about attachment experiences in a way that is truthful, balanced, relevant, and clear.

6. *Achievement of high coherence of transcript and coherence of mind on the AAI.* A successful outcome is also indicated by a significant increase in coherence of transcript and coherence of mind on the AAI. K. N. Levy et al. (2006) used increased coherence of transcript and coherence of mind based on AAI transcripts as major markers of treatment improvement. Our approach is similar. According to the AAI scoring criteria, interviewees classified as insecure (dismissing, preoccupied, or disorganized/CC) typically score between 1 and 3 but no more than 3 on the 9-point Likert scale of coherence of transcript, whereas interviewees classified as secure typically score between 7 and 9; interviewees who score between 4 and 6 may show some elements of earned security but have not yet achieved sufficient coherence to justify a secure attachment classification. Based on these scoring rules, a reasonable expectation for successful attachment-based treatment is that coherence of transcript and coherence of mind as assessed with the AAI reach a minimum level of 7 or above by the close of treatment.

7. *Resolution of unresolved status (Ud) with respect to trauma and loss.* For patients whose AAI transcript indicates unresolved status with respect to trauma or loss (Ud), an expected outcome of treatment is the achievement of resolved status. Using the AAI, this means that Ud status at the beginning of treatment is in the clinically significant range (a score above 5.5 on the 1 to 9 Likert scale), and by the end of treatment the Ud score is below the cutting score of 5.5. As an example of this approach, Cloitre, Koenen, Cohen, and Han (2002) and Stovall-McClough, Cloitre, and McClough (2008) developed a short-term step-by-step phase-based treatment specifically designed to achieve resolved status for women who had shown pre-treatment evidence of unresolved status with respect to childhood abuse. In their study, 62% of the women with unresolved status achieved resolved status by the end of this focused treatment. While the Three Pillars treatment does not focus on processing trauma, we have nevertheless found that unresolved status often changes to resolved by the end of treatment, simply by addressing the attachment issues, especially disorganization. We have informal indication that patients often become resolved *prior to* establishing earned security; we believe that resolution of trauma and/or loss establishes a level of organization of mind that then facilitates the further resolution of attachment disturbance.

8. *No longer meeting diagnostic criteria for a personality disorder, dissociative disorder, or any trauma-related diagnosis in the DSM-5 or ICD-10.* Many of our patients with significant attachment disturbances have a personality disorder (as assessed by the SCID-II) and/or a major dissociative disorder (as assessed by the SCID-D) or severe chronic PTSD (as assessed by the CAPS). We find that by the end of the Three Pillars attachment-based treatment, many of these patients no longer meet diagnostic criteria for any of these disorders.

A Case Illustration of Successful Treatment and Its Measurement

The patient in the following case example had a history of severe abuse, and at the beginning of the Three Pillars attachment-based treatment met SCID-D criteria for dissociative identity disorder. Although no trauma processing was done during the treatment, by the end of two and half years of therapy she no longer met DID criteria and showed a significant drop in Trauma Symptom Inventory (TSI) scores.

The patient was a 46-year-old woman who sought a consultation about a nine-year treatment by a therapist who had done phase-oriented treatment for trauma and abuse. Five years into this psychodynamically based weekly treatment, the patient began to report memories of severe childhood physical and sexual abuse, allegedly by her father. At that point the therapist used eye-movement desensitization and reprocessing treatment (EMDR) to process the abuse memories. As trauma processing became a central focus of the treatment, the patient began to report early childhood sexual abuse memories, including of her brother and sister, and severe sadistic abuse memories allegedly involving her father and adult friends of her father and then by extended family members. The more she reported an expanding domain of increasingly horrific and bizarre memories of childhood abuse, including ritualized abuse, the more disorganized her state of mind and behavior became. During the four-year interval of trauma memory processing, she had become increasingly dissociated, first with time loss and disremembered experiences and later with the manifestation of discrete alter personality states.

Her previous therapist had made a comment to her that she had not mentioned her mother in over five years of treatment and that this was "not normal." During the initial treatment consultation with the senior author (DB), the patient mentioned that she had been unable to bond with her own two children and that she was "angry" that her early childhood experiences had affected her relationships with her children.

As part of the treatment consultation, she was given the AAI, the SCID-D, and a number of other assessment inventories. Her primary attachment classification was cannot classify (CC) with unresolved (Ud) status for childhood physical and sexual abuse and from the loss of her father as an adult. She met the full diagnostic criteria for dissociative identity disorder (DID) on the SCID-D. On a self-report inventory, the Dissociation Questionnaire (DIS-Q; Vanderlinden & Vandereycken, 1997), which was designed to assess three categories of pathological dissociation and also normal dissociative absorption, her pre-treatment DIS-Q scores were in the range predictive of DDNOS, but they were lower than expected for full DID. Her scores, accompanied by DDNOS norms and standard deviations, were: total score 2.9/2.9 *SD* 0.4, Identity Fragmentation 2.36/3.0 *SD* 0.8, Loss of Executive Control 3.0/3.1 *SD* 0.7, Amnesia 2.2/2.5 *SD* 0.8, and Absorption 3.2/2.7 *SD* 0.9. Given a confirmed diagnosis of DID using the SCID-D, these findings suggest some minimization or lack of awareness of the severity of her dissociative symptoms at pre-treatment.

To assess the patient's trauma symptoms, she was given the Trauma Symptom Inventory, Version 1 (TSI; Briere, Elliott, Harris, & Cotman, 1995); five of the 10 clinical scales were significantly elevated: Anxious Arousal ($T = 72$); Intrusive Experiences ($T = 73$); Defensive Avoidance ($T = 77$); Dissociation ($T = 73$) and Low Self-Esteem ($T = 69$). Her pre-treatment TSI profile showed a clear mixture of hyperarousal and dissociative trauma, consistent with the SCID-D diagnosis of dissociative identity disorder (DID). On the Gudjonsson Suggestibility Scale (Gudjonsson, 1984), her Yield 1 score (1) was greater than a standard deviation below the mean, as was her shift score (0), and her confabulation score was within the normal range. Her total suggestibility score was 1, which placed her vulnerability to adopting externally supplied misinformation suggestions as very low. Because of her extremely low memory suggestibility, it was unlikely that her bizarre memories of ritual abuse were the product of suggestive influences in therapy or of internally generated confabulation.

From the initial AAI, the patient's overall coherence of transcript score was 1.0, the lowest possible value on the 1-to-9 point scale. Her description of her early relationship with her mother showed high idealization not supported by adequate evidence (idealization score for the mother was 6). Insisting on a lack of memory, she gave only two of the requested five adjectives for the early childhood relationship with her mother, and neither was illustrated with adequate examples. For "caring," her example was, "She always made sure we were clean and well dressed well and that we basically had what we needed." For "helpful," she said, "She was the one who took care of us when my father wasn't around." As an example, she said, "The basics, groceries, shopping, cooking." She gave five descriptors for her early-childhood relationship with her father: "wasn't around," "afraid," "nervous," "disappointed," and "terrified." All of the examples used to illustrate these adjectives reflected a pervasive preoccupied fear (E3). On the basis of extreme persistent behavioral reactions and severe dissociative compartmentalization, the patient received an unresolved (Ud) score of 7.5 for physical abuse by her father and also a score of 7.5 for sexual abuse by her father. She also had a Ud score of 8.0 for unresolved loss of her father, based on her AAI description of his death and her reactions to that. Her pre-treatment classification was Ud/CC//E3/Ds1, indicating unresolved status and disorganized attachment with fear-based anxious preoccupation and dismissing features but signs of some valuing of attachment.

Based on her having become substantially more disorganized over nine years of traditional phase-oriented trauma treatment, the consulting therapist initiated and conducted a treatment plan that did not include any trauma processing and instead put consistent emphasis on resolving the disorganized attachment according to the Three Pillars treatment model and its specific considerations for disorganized attachment, described in Chapter 13. To repeat for added emphasis, during two and a half years of treatment, *no trauma processing whatsoever was done*. At the end of that period, the patient was again given the AAI, the SCID-D, the Dissociation Questionnaire, and the TSI. The results are quite notable.

On the post-treatment AAI, the patient's overall coherence of transcript score was 7.0. This time she was able to give all five adjectives for the early-childhood relationship with her mother and was able to provide illustrations of each one with a clear memory from early childhood. All five adjectives were positive, indicating a continued tendency toward idealization of her mother, but the total idealization score was not above the cutting score for clinical significance, as she was able to support each adjective with a suitable example. Her pre-treatment AAI description of "caring" indicated purely instrumental care; compare that to her post-treatment AAI description for "loving," which clearly embodies noninstrumental relating:

> *I felt she was there for me most of the time. I remember she took us places. I remember specifically she took us to church. Everyone was really nice there. It was a real community and she helped me to feel integrated with them and close, and in that sense I felt I was loved.*

The post-treatment five adjectives given for the relationship with her father were still all negative, but there were no indicators of the earlier pervasive E3-like fear, no extreme behavioral reactions, and no dissociative compartmentalization. She was able to say openly and honestly that he was "just mean," and she gave painfully clear illustrations that were characterized by good metacognitive reflection and without involving anger. A careful scrutiny of her descriptions of physical and sexual abuse by her father and the loss of her father showed resolved status for all three situations, with Ud scores all under the cutting score of 5.5. None were higher than 3.5.

On the post-treatment SCID-D, the patient showed no evidence of alter personality states or "parts," no evidence of loss of executive control, and little evidence of current dissociative amnesia.

Overall, at post-treatment the patient no longer met sufficient criteria for a dissociative disorder on the SCID-D. The post-treatment self-report DIS-Q scores showed a drop in all dissociative features. Figure 15.1 shows the change in self-reported dissociative symptoms. The post-treatment scores are all slightly above the normal range but lower than required for clinically significant dissociation.

Time	Total	Identity Fragmentation	Loss of Executive Control	Amnesia	Absorption
Pre-	2.9	2.36	3.0	2.2	3.2
Post-	2.16	1.92	2.38	2.0	3.0
DDNOS Norms	2.9 *SD* 0.4	3.0 *SD* 0.8	3.1 *SD* 0.7	2.5 *SD* 0.8	2.7 *SD* 0.9
General Population Norms	1.5 *SD* 0.4	1.4 *SD* 0.4	1.7 *SD* 0.5	1.4 *SD* 0.4	1.9 *SD* 0.6

FIGURE 15.1. Pre- and Post-treatment Response on the Dissociation Questionnaire

With respect to trauma symptoms, the post-treatment TSI revealed that all five of the clinical scales that had been elevated above the cutting score had fallen to below the cutting score. All three validity scales were within the normal range in both the pre- and post-treatment TSI responses. Figure 15.2 shows both the pre- and post-treatment TSI profiles.

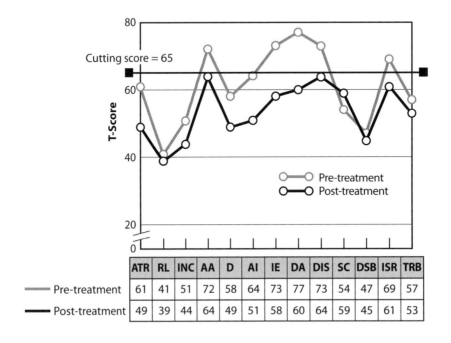

	ATR	RL	INC	AA	D	AI	IE	DA	DIS	SC	DSB	ISR	TRB
Pre-treatment	61	41	51	72	58	64	73	77	73	54	47	69	57
Post-treatment	49	39	44	64	49	51	58	60	64	59	45	61	53

FIGURE 15.2. Pre- and Post-treatment Trauma Symptom Inventory (TSI) Changes

On the Beck Depression Inventory (Version 1; Beck, Ward, Mendelson, Mock, & Erbaugh, 1961), the patient's pre-treatment depression score was 21, which according to published norms indicates that her initial level of depression was in the moderate-to-severe range of 19 to 29. Her BDI-1 post-treatment score was 7, which placed her within the asymptomatic range of 0 to 9. Figure 15.3 shows the magnitude of the drop in depression.

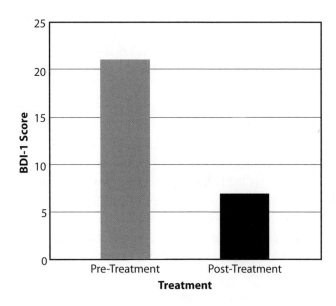

FIGURE 15.3. Pre- and Post-treatment Beck Depression Inventory (BDI-1) Scores

The most remarkable finding illustrated by this case is the clinically significant drop in dissociative, traumatic, and depressive symptoms and disorders from treatment *that was entirely attachment-based*. The therapist never engaged in trauma processing nor focused on depression. These data offer a strong argument that traditional phase-oriented trauma treatment (D. P. Brown, Scheflin, & Hammond, 1999) may be contraindicated in patients with complex trauma and disorganized attachment, in that trauma processing can lead to further disorganization of mind that interferes with what is needed for treatment progress and resolution. This case illustrates that the Three Pillars attachment-based treatment designed to increase organization and overall coherence of mind may resolve not only the disorganized attachment but also the dissociative, traumatic, and depressive symptoms, even when these symptoms do not receive focus with specific treatment interventions. We believe that increased organization of mind per se has a positive treatment effect on trauma-related symptoms independent of trauma processing.

A Pilot Outcome Study

As an informal study of our approach to attachment-based treatment, we collected pre- and post-treatment AAIs on 12 patients treated by authors of this book (seven of the authors treated one to three patients each for the pilot study). Four of the pre-treatment AAIs were scored by an independent scorer who is not a member of our group. All 12 pre-treatment AAIs and all 12 post-treatment AAIs were scored by the senior author of this book (DB). For the four pre-treatment AAIs scored by both scorers, the interscorer agreement using both the four-way and five-way AAI classification was 100%. This correspondence is not surprising, as both scorers trained together and have collaborated in scoring numerous AAIs together on the same patients since.

From the pre-treatment AAI, eight (66.6%) received a primary attachment classification of cannot classify (CC), and the other four (33.3.%) received a preoccupied (E) classification. Six of the 12 patients (50%) had unresolved status (Ud) with respect to trauma or loss. The average coherence of transcript on the AAI at the onset of treatment was 2.21, indicating very low coherence of mind. These patients were representative of severe disorganized insecure attachment at the onset of the Three Pillars treatment.

At the termination of treatment, which averaged 3.4 years, all 12 (100%) of the treated patients had attained earned secure status on the AAI (primary F1, F2, F3,

Patient number	Pre-treatment Attachment Status	Post-treatment Attachment Status
1	E2/E3	F4
2	Ud/CC//E3/Ds1	F3
3	Ud/CC//Ds1/E3	F1
4	Ud/CC//Ds1/E3	F5
5	CC//E2/Ds3	F3/F5
6	Ud/E1, E2	F5
7	CC//E1,2/Ds3	F5
8	Ud/CC//E1/Ds3/F4	F1
9	Ud/CC//E1,E3	F5
10	Ud/E2	F5
11	CC//E3/F4	F3
12	CC//E3/Ds1	F5

FIGURE 15.4. Pre- and Post-treatment Changes in AAI Attachment Classification

F4, or F5 classification) and had significantly higher coherence of transcript and coherence of mind, and those who had unresolved status with respect to trauma and loss had become resolved. Figure 15.4 presents the changes in attachment status from the beginning to the end of treatment.

The mean coherence of AAI transcript at the onset of treatment was 2.21, and the mean post-treatment score was 7.91. A paired-samples T-test was used to determine whether this difference is statistically significant for this pilot study of 12 participants. This statistical analysis is considered valid, as the assumptions for a paired-samples T-test were not violated; there were no outliers in the data, as assessed by the inspection of a boxplot; and pre-post difference scores were normally distributed, as assessed by the Shapiro-Wilk test ($p = 0.485$). The analysis showed that patients' coherence of transcript scores were higher after treatment ($M = 7.92$, $SD = 0.597$) as compared to before treatment ($M = 2.21$, $SD = 0.865$), a statistically significant increase of 5.71, 95% CI [5.13, 6.29], t (11) = 21.588, $p <$ 0.001, $d = 6.23$. The effect size was Cohen's d = mean/SD = 5.7083/0.9160 = 6.23. The change signifies a significant treatment effect ($p < 0.001$) with a very good treatment effect size. Figure 15.5 summarizes the coherence of transcript data.

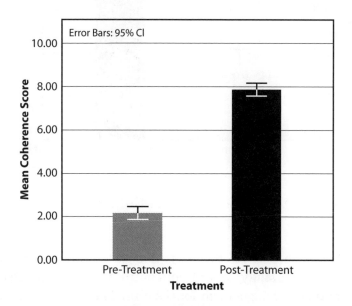

FIGURE 15.5. Pre- and Post-treatment AAI Coherence of Transcript

The mean reflective functioning score (RF) using the AAI transcript at the onset of treatment was 1.68, and the mean post-treatment RF score was 4.36 for the 11 subjects from the pilot sample of 12 for whom pre- and post-RF scores were assessed. A paired-samples T-test was used to determine whether there was a statistically significant difference in the pre- and post- treatment RF scores for this sample. The assumptions of the paired-samples T-test were not violated. There were no outliers in the data, as assessed by inspection of the boxplot. Pre- and post- difference scores were normally distributed, as assessed by a Shapiro-Wilk test ($p = 0.236$). These patients' reflective functioning scores were significantly higher after treatment ($M = 4.36$, $SD = 1.63$) than before treatment ($M = 1.68$, $SD = 0.902$), with a statistically significant increase of 2.68, 95% CI [1.91, 3.45], $t(10) = 7.76$, $p < 0.001$, $d = 2.34$. The change indicates a significant treatment increase in this general measure of metacognitive capacity. The treatment effect size was also significant (Cohen's $d = $ mean/$SD = 2.6818/1.1461 = 2.34$). It is clear that fostering metacognition as one of the three pillars of treatment is effective. Figure 15.6 shows the RF change across treatment.

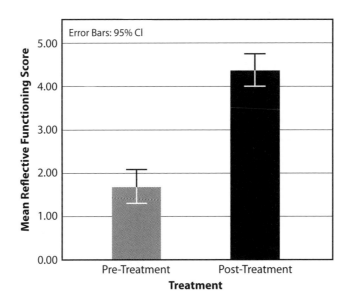

FIGURE 15.6. Pre- and Post-treatment Reflective Functioning Scores

The finding of such positive results is not particularly surprising, in that because this was a pilot study we did not control for length of treatment, and all patients were treated long enough for the clinician to see changes in attachment patterns. Thus, the pilot data suggest that while not necessarily a short-term treatment—although Patient 8 was treated for only one year and established earned security in that time, and for several patients, the post-AAIs were administered quite a while after observable changes were noted in the therapy—the Three Pillars treatment is an effective treatment. We hope that this small pilot sample illustrates the efficacy of our approach to attachment-based treatment, and that the detailed step-by-step descriptions of the Three Pillar methods of treatment will stimulate the development of larger-scale outcomes research using this approach.

Conclusion

Our Three Pillars treatment model is an integration of what we see as the best principles and practices from what is known about the development, manifestations, and treatments of attachment disturbances in adults. As each of the three pillars reflects a dimension of functioning that is known to be important for attachment security, their integration for treatment creates efficient and comprehensive attachment repair. This treatment respects the view, common to many treatment approaches, that the patient's relationship with the therapist as a secure base is very important, but our method goes beyond relying on the interactions between patient and therapist to include a range of specific methods that target the specific deficiencies and problematic patterns shown by patients with insecure attachment.

The Ideal Parent Figure method directly remaps new, positive attachment representations, or internal working models, that replace the initially developed dysfunctional representations associated with personal and relational difficulty in adult patients' lives. Although aspects of the IPF method can be difficult for patients, especially early during treatment, sooner or later all patients come to have very rich and deep positive experiences of the IPF work (who wouldn't when attachment conflicts are reduced and there are experiences of "ideal" care?). This method also takes the therapist off the hook of having to be "ideal"—no therapist can possibly embody fully and consistently what each patient most deeply needs to efficiently create new and best-fit attachment representations. The therapist does the best that he or she can, but relies primarily on the particular patient's inner knowing of what is most needed; through engaging and helping to shape the patient's imagination, there is unlimited freedom to create an internal model of attachment that is the "ideal" best fit for each particular patient.

The "real" aspects of the therapist are bound to contribute to periodic treatment ruptures. When understood and responded to according to the principles of the Three Pillars model, the emergence and resolution of ruptures actually facilitates the developmental and healing processes that lead to earned security.

There is no aspect of the treatment method that requires patients to focus on painful past experience. Except during the initial evaluation, which includes the AAI or other methods for obtaining information about early experience, we do not ask patients to revisit their actual childhoods. Through the IPF method, we co-create an imagined childhood in which the patient has expressly positive experiences; for the metacognitive and collaborative pillars, we work in the present, with the dynamic interaction between the patient and therapist focused on the patient's moment-to-moment metacognitive and cooperative, collaborative experiences.

Of course, pain and distress about past experiences may, and likely will, emerge during treatment. When it does, the therapist acknowledges it and empathizes with the patient, but addresses it in the context of one or more of the three pillars. When trauma history is present, the patient is spared the distress of trauma processing before there is sufficient structure for affect regulation; the methods of the Three Pillars model build such structure, and likely, as we have found, resolve the trauma. But if additional trauma processing is still needed, it will proceed more efficiently because of the patient's greater internal organization and more developed affect-regulatory structures.

We did not set out to do so, but our development of the Three Pillars model of treatment has drawn from and brought more clarity to the essential components of *maternal responsiveness*. This construct has been fundamental in the attachment field ever since Ainsworth's pioneering identification of its importance. We suggest that each of the three pillars represents and includes aspects of caregiver responsiveness that promote attachment security. Ideal parent figures are shaped to be consistently and accurately *attuned* to the patient-as-child's behavior, internal state, and developmental level; they recognize when *soothing* is needed, and provide it contingently and effectively; they respond with *expressed delight* to the patient-as-child's being and behaviors; and they provide attuned and responsive *support for exploration*. The development of metacognitive capacity is fostered by the therapist's *attuned presence* and *contingent responsiveness* to the patient's signs of stronger or weaker metacognitive functioning; the therapist's use of *affective marking* helps to build the patient's recognition and identification of his or her inner states and reflects responsiveness to the patient's immediate experience. The methods for enhancing collaborative, cooperative capacity include the therapist's *careful, attuned presence* and responsiveness to the patient's immediate, moment-to-moment nonverbal and verbal experience.

Although we are happy to present this overall treatment model and its specific methods to our colleagues in the attachment field, our greatest joy continues to come from seeing how our patients respond to the treatment. Often at a surprisingly rapid pace, they experience changes that bring them relief, greater self-confidence and agency, and better, more satisfying and fulfilling relational experiences. From our clinical experience and from our small pilot study, we know of the effectiveness of these methods, and we look forward to future outcome studies and further refinements.

Appendix A
The Core Self, Proactive Self-Agency, Self-Esteem, and the "Best" Self

Normal and Incomplete Self-Development

Neonates do not come into the world with a predefined or developed sense of self. The capacity for self-observation—to take the self and the internal state of mind as an object of reflection—begins to develop between six and eight months of age (D. Stern, 1985). As an outgrowth of cognitive maturation, the capacity for representational or symbolic thinking begins at approximately 12 months (D. P. Brown, 1993). By approximately 18 months, representational thinking is well developed and the psychological sense of self first emerges (D. P. Brown, 1993). This early period defines the initial "structuralization" of the self (Lichteneberg, 1975). Once the basic *structure* of the self is fully formed, its *content* changes as cognitive development further matures (Kegan, 1982). In other words, the "self" evolves in its capacity to incorporate more and more complex relationships and extends over various contexts as cognitive structures continue to evolve. As a result of concrete operational thinking, which develops from ages 7 to 11, the latency-age child develops an internal sense of mind, a rich emotional life, and concerns oriented toward peer involvement. When formal operational thinking develops during adolescence, the self becomes capable of handling more complex social relationships and can perceive infinite possibilities. In the early adult years, the content of the self turns toward intimacy and family. As a result of further cognitive maturation in midlife, the self naturally turns beyond family toward wider civic and community concerns. As a result of even further cognitive maturation, the self develops a keener vision of ultimate concerns and a wider vision of life.

Completing development of the basic self-structure in childhood has certain experiential consequences. First, the sense of self becomes *a central organizing principle for daily life*. Having a psychological sense of self is useful in that everyday experiences become *organized* around the self. Without a clearly defined sense of self, there is a tendency to try to define the self from the out-side-in. For example, Dr. Brown, the senior author, once treated a young schizo-phrenic woman with a genius IQ who was a voracious reader. One day she came to a session and reviewed 12 different theories of literary criticism. The thera-pist's response was, "You have summarized each of these different points of view brilliantly, yet I don't hear anything about *your* point of view. Please, tell me, could you define how *you* see this?" The patient sat there unable to understand or answer the therapist's question. With the fragmented schizophrenic self-struc-ture, she had never developed a clearly defined psychological sense of self, so there was no "self" to serve as a central organizing principle for all of her brilliant ideas about literary criticism. The purpose of the therapist's question, and many other similar questions, was to enable her to begin to develop the capacity for self-observation, and from that to develop a sense of "self" as a central organizing principle for her immediate and ongoing experience.

Second, having a psychological sense of self provides a subjective *sense of coherence of mind*, or a direct, immediate sense of internal organization of mind. People who lack a core sense of self experience their internal world as less organized or even disorganized. The metacognitive capacity to observe the degree of organization of mind at any given time is a natural outcome of self-de-velopment. The subjective awareness of coherence is captured in the popular colloquial phrase "I really have it all together" or its opposite, "I really don't have it together at all."

Third, having a psychological sense of self provides *a sense of continuity across time, place, and state* (Lichtenberg, 1975). Despite remarkable changes in experiences and stages of development across the life span, a person with a strong sense of self feels like the same person across all of these changes. Erik Erickson's (1979) definition of identity formation in late adolescence is based on the idea that self-identity provides the felt sense of sameness of self throughout the subsequent developmental stages of life. People who lack such self-development experience themselves as constantly changing and not being the same. For example, people with borderline personality disorder experience frequent, sometimes extreme shifts in their attitudes and experiences of themselves and others, and many psy-chotic patients have *no* felt sense of self-continuity.

Psychotic individuals represent the extreme with respect to lack of self-de-velopment. However, many people who have some degree of self-development nevertheless function with insufficient levels for healthy self-experience. For example, attachment research has shown that adults with anxious-preoccupied attachment have weak self-development (Main, Goldwyn, & Hesse, 2002). Such adults at a very early age "learn" that they must be hypervigilant to their care-giver's state of mind and that they must constantly attend to and respond to the caregiver's needs, concerns, or worries as more important than their own. This "involving" attachment style (i.e., overinvolved in the state of mind of the other) has two consequences. The first is a learned style of excessive focus on the needs of the other at the expense of the self. This other-oriented focus interferes with normal self-development and leads to weak or poorly formed self-structure in later childhood and adulthood. Second, while a psychologically and emotionally healthy caregiver is generally available to comfort, soothe, and reassure the child when he or she is anxious, the "involving" caregiver consistently does not provide these responses that would help to regulate the child's emotions; as a result, the involving pattern interferes with the child's development of affect-regulation skills. Children of consistently overinvolving caregivers grow up with a strong propensity for anxiety and worry and little capacity to tolerate the intensity of their emotional states.

There are three forms of weak or arrested self-development. Someone with the first form never develops a clear sense of his or her own self and has learned to define the self from the outside-in. Such a person tries to read others for cues about what is expected in any given situation and presents the self accordingly. This *false-self* organization reflects the absence of an authentic, strong, unique, and independent self. As long as the person takes the outside-in orientation, there is little occasion for the consistent self-observation and self-reflection that contributes to developing such a sense of self. The character of Chauncey Gardiner from the film *Being There* is an example of someone with a false-self organization, and Leonard Zelig, from the film *Zelig*, is an extreme example.

Someone with the second form of poorly developed self has some degree of experience of a personal self, but it is experienced as fragile, and is therefore kept deeply private and hidden from others. The person recognizes his or her unique and creative aspects but fears that if another were to see and know this personal, *private self*, the other would react negatively and the private self would be destroyed. The third form of poorly developed self results from experience with an involving caregiver. Someone with this form, the *incomplete self*, shows some degree of self-development, but it remains incomplete and fragile because of early-learned chronic hypervigilance about the states and needs of others. The person attends to and responds to the needs of others at the expense of himself or herself. Others perceive such a person as a chronic caretaker who lacks self-distinction or self-assertiveness. It is important to understand that many highly successful people have poor self-development and have become successful by virtue of their specific accommodations to their weak self-structure, such as becoming highly skilled at reading and responding to the wants and needs of others.

The foundational task for self-development is the establishment of a *core experiential sense of self*. From this core emerges *self-definition*, or the person's recognition of particular qualities that are relatively consistent and stable aspects of the core self. When developed, the sense of a core self with particular qualities can be evoked at any time in daily life. For example, the author writing these lines can evoke at this very moment *a general sense* of "Dan" and experience a general sense of "Dan-ness." This general sense is sometimes referred to as the "feeling of selfness" (Watkins & Watkins, 1978). Additionally, he can identify a number of *specific personality traits or qualities* that he associates with "Dan-ness." Object relations theorists describe the ability to call into awareness aspects of the self as resulting from *evocative memory* (E. L. Baker, 1981).

A person may have some degree of a sense of a core and definition of self-qualities but might not have a sense of any effectiveness, of being able to have impact on others or the world, indicating that *self-agency* has not emerged. The emergence of *self-agency* supports the experience that the core self with its definitional qualities is *effective and has impact on the world and on others.* Individuals who lack a sense of self-agency have difficulty in being effective in their action plans and also have little awareness that they contingently impact the responsiveness of others.

Individuals who have a core sense of self and self-agency may lack *self-esteem*, which we define as the linking of positive affect with the self-representation (Joffe & Sandler, 1966). When older children and adults who have healthy self-esteem evoke their sense of self in daily life, they experience it against the backdrop of positive emotional states, but when narcissistically vulnerable people evoke the sense of self in daily life, they often experience the self against the backdrop of no emotion or negative emotion and have difficulty evoking the sense of self in association with positive emotional states. Once self-esteem is stable in the contexts of skills and interpersonal experience, then a full sense of one's *best self* can develop.

Depending on where along this self-development spectrum a patient has reached, we work to facilitate further development, toward the establishment of an available and stable sense of *best self.* Our perspectives on methods for promoting self-development are comparable to the rationale we gave for fostering positive representations of attachment earlier in this book. First, we do not believe that therapeutic interpretation of deficits in self-development is very effective as a treatment technique. Second, we find much more value in the systematic introduction and repetition of positive imagery focused on cultivating each of the above dimensions of self. Overall, engaging and structuring the patient's imagination in ways that enhance the core self, self-definition, self-agency, self-esteem, and the best self foster mature self-development in patients who enter treatment with significant self-deficits. Our recommended methods are described below.

Methods for Developing the Core Sense of Self

When a patient does not have a core sense of self and lacks clarity about self-definition, self-development work must begin at this foundational level. We have developed a step-by-step visualization protocol for the development of self-definition and a core sense of self. The steps in the protocol are (1) scene generation for a sense of core self, (2) definition and enumeration of unique qualities, (3) amplification of the qualities, (4) stabilization and maintenance of the self-definition, and (5) transferring the self-definition to other contexts.

SCENE GENERATION

Scene generation begins with the therapist introducing suggestions that ask the patient to define qualities of the positive core self. For example, the therapist may say:

> Imagine a scene about some situation that is somehow about you *being most you, in the best sense* . . . the more you focus on the scene, the more you'll discover how you experience yourself when you're being *most you* . . . and when you're ready, go ahead and describe that scene.

If the patient cannot generate such a scene, as is common at first, the instructions can be varied with more suggestive detail to prompt the patient's imagination. For example:

> The scene will be about when you are *most yourself* . . . when you are *just being yourself*, in the best sense . . . when you are really free to be yourself . . . when you are really connecting with yourself, with no expectation from others for you to be a certain way . . . When you are coming back fully to yourself, really *just being you*.

The instructions can also include references to the core self or the true self:

> The scene will somehow be about your *core self* . . . [or your *true self*, or your *true being*, or your *most authentic self*, or when you are *most real to yourself*] coming from your true, *most authentic* nature.

If the therapist persists with one or more of these ways of wording, the patient will likely establish a scene or at least a sense pertaining to his or her core self.

DEFINING AND ENUMERATING UNIQUE QUALITIES

The next step is to define and enumerate the unique qualities of the core self. For example, the therapist may say:

> The more you reflect on the scene, the more you will discover specific qualities that are *most uniquely you* . . . and when you discover *each core self quality*, you will be able to describe each one, speaking freely.

After the patient reports a quality, the therapist continues:

> Now, continue to reflect and see what other specific core qualities come into your awareness . . . and as they do, go ahead and describe them . . . [Patient reports a quality, or several] Let them become *clearer and clearer* in your awareness . . . And now *even more* qualities of your core self will occur to you, and become *clearer and clearer* in your awareness . . . specific qualities that are *most uniquely you* . . . and as they do, you can name them, and describe them . . . [Patient reports] And as you approach this with an attitude of exploration and discovery . . . *even more* qualities will become clear to you . . . and you can go ahead and describe them . . . [Patient reports]

An important working principle for fostering self-definition is that the therapist repeatedly frames and supports conditions for discovery and exploration of the core features of self, completely free of any expectations of others. The therapist must take time and care to establish just the right conditions in the therapeutic relationship so that the patient genuinely feels free of expectations from the therapist. Especially for patients who experienced the "involving" style of caretaking and thus excessively and hypervigilantly focus on the states and expectations of others, establishing just the right conditions in the treatment relationship provides an emotionally corrective stance that frees the patient to initiate the process of self-exploration in a new way in the context of the patient-focused treatment relationship.

AMPLIFICATION OF THE SELF QUALITIES

As the patient reports and describes qualities that he or she experiences as aspects of the core self, the therapist mirrors, emphasizes, and *amplifies* them in order to support and strengthen the patient's experience of them. For example, in response to a patient who has named qualities of *kindness* and *integrity*, the therapist might say:

> Yes. You can *really* be aware of the ways that you are *kind*, and the ways that you live with *integrity*. Focus now *even more* on your qualities of *kindness* and *integrity* . . . focus in now so that *even more* you recognize *all the ways* that you are *kind* and live your life with *integrity* . . . You can now experience these *even more clearly* and *even more intensely* . . . And in this scene in which you're recognizing *these qualities of yours*, you can experience yourself with these qualities in ways that make it *even more clear* that these are aspects of your *core, true, authentic* self.

This emphasis and amplification is parallel to affect *marking* in that it helps the patient to establish clearer identification and stronger experience of what emerges in awareness.

STABILIZATION AND MAINTENANCE OF THE SELF QUALITIES

The above mirroring, emphasizing, and amplifying of the patient-reported qualities contributes to their strengthening and stabilization. The therapist also places specific focus on stabilization and maintenance of the qualities. For example:

> And now that you're *really aware* of these qualities that you've identified as *core aspects* of yourself, you can begin to get a sense that these aspects of yourself are *always with you*, even if you're not specifically expressing them in a particular situation . . . These qualities are always with you, because they're aspects of *who you most are.*

The therapist may use *time distortion* to enhance this recognition:

> And now, even though only a few moments of clock time will pass, it will seem like *much more time* elapses, and you'll have *just the right amount* of time to come to feel *so very familiar* with these qualities . . . and as you become *so very familiar* with these qualities, it will seem *quite natural* that these *qualities of yours* are just simply *part of you* . . . and as they're just simply part of you . . . they're *stable* and *with you* at *all times*, in *all situations*, whenever you'd like to call upon them and express them.

TRANSFERRING THE SELF QUALITIES TO OTHER CONTEXTS AND SITUATIONS

The final component of the self-definition protocol further strengthens and extends the above stabilization and maintenance by engaging the patient in imagining himself or herself embodying the named qualities in new scenes, in other contexts and situations. For example:

> With your clear sense of these *qualities of yours* that you're recognizing now as aspects of *who you most are*, these qualities of [Therapist names qualities], let this scene fade away, and now a *new scene* will emerge, either visually or in your felt sense, or both . . . In this *new scene*, you'll imagine yourself in a different situation, in a different situation but also *with these same qualities* of [Therapist names qualities]. So go ahead and let this new scene emerge, and notice the ways that these qualities are part of you in this scene.

The therapist mirrors and amplifies the patient's report of how he or she experiences the newly defined self-qualities in the new scene, and may continue with several more scene shifts so that the patient has the experience of the self-qualities in several different scenes and contexts.

COMMON PROBLEMS IN SELF-DEFINITION DEVELOPMENT IN PATIENTS WITH SEVERE SELF-DEFICITS

For patients with significant self-deficits, particular problems typically arise. The most basic problem is an inability to attend to and observe themselves. Patients who are highly distractible (and may have attention-deficit disorder) will likely benefit from basic concentration training prior to being introduced to the imagination protocol designed to establish self-definition (R. L. Baker & Brown, 2015). When attention capacity is sufficient for the task but self-observational ability is poor, the therapist may introduce exercises to develop self-observation and metacognitive reflection, such as behavioral self-monitoring of experience or self-reflective journal writing.

Patients who have some capacity for self-observation may still have difficulty with the imagination task. For example, the patient might report a scene but then not find any sense of the core self that the scene ostensibly relates to. When this occurs, the therapist suggests that the patient disidentify from thought and bring awareness to immediate sensory experience. For example:

> Sometimes when it's hard to recognize the qualities of the core self, the mind is getting in the way . . . trying to *think up* what the qualities are, rather than just letting them emerge . . . So let's see now, as you imagine this scene, how you can become *completely present* with yourself, *tuning in* to your felt sense . . . your *immediate, felt sense* of your *body* . . . and of the *sensations* that you're experiencing right now . . . Go ahead and *tune in* to the *feelings* and the *sensations* of what it's like to be *most fully you* . . . and when you do, see what qualities emerge that are most fully you.

The therapist may also prompt as follows:

> Sometimes the awareness of the core self, or true, authentic self, comes in the form of an overall sense of it, knowing it as a whole . . . and sometimes it comes in the form of very specific qualities that show themselves, those qualities that you hold *most dear* to yourself . . . And I'm wondering whether your awareness now of your *most real, authentic* self will come in the form of a *general* sense of it, or in the form of recognizing the *very specific qualities* that are *most you* . . . and as it becomes clear to you . . . either way . . . you can give voice to what you find and *really know* to be true about yourself . . .

Patients with the above-mentioned *incomplete self*, who are entrenched in hypervigilant involvement in the state of mind of others, may report scenes that include *others* and *their expectations* and focus on what the others are expecting of them. If so, the therapist clarifies:

You can find in yourself a deeper sense of your *self*, uniquely *your own*, beyond the expectations to be a certain way for others . . . [or] . . . even when you're with others, you don't have to be concerned with what they want you to be like . . . you can find in yourself the qualities that are *most you*, and you can be *most fully you*, as you *most truly* are.

If the patient has a *false-self* organization and reports qualities of the false rather than the authentic self, his or her expressions and descriptions are likely to sound "canned" or forced, with little or no *affective* component to the expression. Authentic self-expression is almost always accompanied by congruent affect. When the therapist has a sense that the qualities that the patient is reporting are from the false self, emphasis is placed on *authenticity* of self-qualities. For example.

The scene will somehow be about when you are *most real* . . . [or *most true* to yourself, or *just being yourself* regardless of what others think, or just being *your own person*] coming from a deeper self beyond the impressions you try to create for others . . .

Patients who guard a hidden, *private self* may initially say they find no qualities. If disidentification from thought, as described above, does not lead to qualities being mentioned, the therapist can suggest:

The scene will somehow be about the *most precious* or special self that you never show to anyone else because it is so special . . .

Or:

The scene will be about the things you *most value* about yourself as a person, the qualities that *you know* are *most fully you*, but which you usually prefer to keep to yourself . . .

A different common problem may occur after a patient initially responds to the protocol with a sense of a unique, positive, core self and the emergence of some self-qualities. Rather than continuing on in a positive fashion, he or she may show a pattern of immediately negating the positive qualities and engaging in "negative self-talk." When this occurs, the patient is supported to not engage with the negative thoughts, but instead to be aware of their emergence and to actively let go of them immediately upon noticing them. For example:

As you begin to discover your *unique, positive* qualities of your *core self*, you're noticing that negative thoughts sometimes arise in reaction to good feelings that you have about yourself . . . When these negative thoughts arise, they diminish or negate your positive, good sense of yourself. Notice now exactly how you begin to negate these good qualities and how you negatively think yourself out of these positive qualities . . . As soon as you notice the tendency to negate or otherwise think negatively . . . put your intention to *actively letting go* of the negative thoughts . . . there's no need to engage them in *any manner* whatsoever.

If the pattern of self-negating self-talk persists, the therapist can say:

These negative thoughts—we might consider them as coming from an internal self-critical part. When you notice the negative thoughts, treat that as you would an old acquaintance who came over to your house unexpectedly and uninvited. Ignore the old acquaintance . . . Let [him or her] be there in the background without paying any attention and without allowing [him or her] to influence what you are doing in any way . . . You can just go on with the task at hand . . . When you no longer engage with this pattern of negative self-talk and no longer fuel it, it will eventually settle down . . . and it will interfere less and less with this process of developing a *new*, *positive*, and *unique* sense of yourself.

Methods for Developing Proactive Self-Agency

The next task of self-development, beyond self-definition, is the development of self-agency. Self-agency pertains to the development of internal representations of being an active, effective agent in the world, including the interpersonal world. The self-experiences accompanying the development of self-agency are variations on the theme of mastery and self-efficacy; the self-experiences accompanying the lack of self-agency development are helplessness, ineffectiveness, and hopelessness. According to Mahler, Pine, and Bergman (1975), self-agency first develops in the "practicing" period of early childhood. As the motor system develops, the child more and more acts on the physical environment. For example, when self-agency begins to develop, a delighted child might bat down a tower of blocks each time a parent builds it. Such a child is representing in the mind, and testing, his or her effect on the immediate physical environment. Six months later, this same child will stack the blocks himself or herself and begin constructing things from them. This operation on the physical environment indicates the emergence of representations of constructive self-agency. As language develops, more and more the child will use language to act on the environment to elicit desired responses from others. The child's repetitive response-eliciting behaviors are also incorporated into the developing representations of self-agency.

With further cognitive maturation, the child learns to anticipate, and then to develop, action plans that organize behavior toward goals and their accomplishment. Children with the healthiest sense of self-agency are able to take an overall perspective on their circumstances and become proactive. They are able to assess what they need in advance and organize behavioral sequences toward getting those needs met with respect to both short- and long-term goals. Such children show good time organization, since they accurately anticipate the causes and effects of behavior over time. They show little internal contradiction between goal-states, and they have a strong sense of self-efficacy and mastery. These factors combine to make a strong sense of proactive self-agency, which contributes to a sense that they are making the world happen rather than the world happening to them. They have an active stance toward both external events and their own internal state of mind. Adults with healthy self-agency are typically good at getting what they want out of life. Success in work and other life endeavors is an outgrowth of healthy self-agency.

Children and adults who lack well-developed self-agency usually feel ineffective and helpless. They tend to be passive-dependent, letting others define for them what they want and how to go about getting it. They are frequently quite impulsive, because they lack internal action-planning through which to organize behavioral sequences toward goals. They lack the ability to predict that certain behaviors are likely associated with certain effects or outcomes over time. If they have a capacity for planning, they may experience high internal conflict between competing goal-states. Such children and adults experience that the world is happening to them rather than that they are contributing to making it happen.

For adults, a common indicator of a self-agency problem is never quite getting from work and relationships what they want. A poor track record at work or an aimless and directionless life is a sign of serious and persisting deficits in self-agency. Such adults are unable to organize plans and goal-seeking behavior in such a way that brings them closer to success and mastery at work. Chronic interpersonal difficulty at eliciting reasonable desired responses from others is another indicator of a deficit in self-agency. As a result, such patients often experience that their wishes and needs in intimate relationships are not met.

Many individuals diagnosed with a personality disorder have clinically significant deficits in self-agency, of two primary types. Some are *impulsive* because they lack the capacity for goal-setting and action-planning, while others have the capacity for planning and goal-setting but show a strong pattern of behavioral *inhibition*, so that even though they have plans and goals they actively inhibit acting on them.

SCENE GENERATION FOR PROACTIVE SELF-AGENCY AND INTERPERSONAL SELF-AGENCY

Like the method we use for developing self-definition, the protocol we use for developing self-agency begins by engaging the patient's imagination. The therapist prompts for scenes that focus on proactive self-agency and then later on *interpersonal* proactive self-agency. The form of the prompt for the development of basic self-agency is as follows:

> Imagine a scene in which you feel *especially effective* in [or *especially capable of*, or *especially competent in*, or *especially strong and effective in*] whatever you are doing . . . and when you are imagining such a scene, in which you're feeling that, you can describe what's happening, and what it's like for you to be *so especially effective* [*capable, competent, strong and effective*].

The therapist uses the patient's response as a basis for further and systematic exploration of self-agency in different situations by suggesting new scenes and new situations in which the patient also experiences self-agency.

For patients who have felt ineffective most of their lives up to the present, the therapist can say:

> Imagine a scene in which you are *making an impact* with your life . . . a situation in which you're *really making a difference* through your choices and actions.

For patients who feel especially passive and experience that the world happens to them rather than making it happen, the therapist can say:

> Imagine a scene in which you are *actively making things happen* rather than having things happen to you . . .

Or:

> Imagine a scene in which you are *having a clear effect* on shaping unfolding experiences and events . . .

Or:

> Imagine a scene where you are *deliberately bringing about* what you want to happen . . . And when you are imagining such a scene, in which you're experiencing that, you can describe what's happening, and what it's like

for you to be *actively making things happen* [or *having a clear effect on* or *deliberately bringing about* what you want to happen].

It is very important that self-agency development work also include cultivation of a strong sense of *interpersonal self-agency*. For example, the therapist introduces suggestions such as:

Imagine a scene where you are *having a real impact* on others . . .

Or:

Imagine a scene in which you are able to elicit *just the right kind* of *responses from others* . . . just what you need . . .

Or:

Imagine a scene in which you have a *deep sense of effectiveness* in communicating with others . . . And when you are imagining such a scene, in which you're experiencing this, you can describe what's happening, and what it's like for you to have *such a real impact on others* [or *elicit just the right kind* of responses, or have *such a deep sense of effectiveness* in communicating with others].

As with the protocol for developing self-definition, the therapist applies the same amplification, stabilization and maintenance, and context-transferring principles and methods to the patient's responses to the self-agency work.

DEVELOPMENT OF GOAL-SETTING AND ACTION PLANS

Another important component of working with patients with underdeveloped self-agency is fostering the development of healthy anticipation, action-planning, and goal-setting. This process begins with *goal identification*. The therapist can say:

Think of something that you *really want* for yourself . . . The more you think about it, the more clearly you will bring to mind some realistic goal that you want for yourself. Choose something that is both specific, not too general, and realistic . . . And when you have in mind this *clear, realistic goal*, something that you *really want* for yourself, you can let me know what that is . . . [Patient reports]

If the patient has difficulty identifying a specific goal, then the therapist brings focus to the patient's core sense of self and qualities of self-definition. For example:

Go ahead now and tune in to your *core sense of yourself*, to your experience of *who you most are* . . . and as you do, notice what that's like, *really being you*. As you tune in to yourself in this way, the *more* you notice your *true and deep self*, the *more clear* and *strong* your sense of yourself becomes . . . and you'll experience some of the qualities that make you *most* who you are, in the *best* sense . . . When you're feeling connected to yourself in this way, let me know with a slight nod of the head . . . [Patient nods] Good. And now, as you're *really connected* to who you *most* are, think of something that you really want for yourself . . . [Therapist continues with goal identification instructions as above]

When the patient has identified a goal, the therapist initiates the development of the *action-planning* process. For example:

Good. And now, with your goal of [Therapist names goal] *very clear* in your mind, let's go through some steps that are about helping you *actually get that* for yourself. Let's take the time to develop a *specific plan* in your mind about the best way to achieve your goal of [Therapist names goal] . . . The *more* you reflect on it, the *more* the details of this plan will become *clearer* and *clearer* . . . Keep doing this until the plan becomes very clear . . . and when the plan is *clear* to you, you can describe what the plan is.

Then, the therapist helps the patient to *organize* a behavioral action plan:

Now organize and arrange the *sequence of actual steps* that you will take so that you develop a *very clear action plan*, with *each step* along the way very clear to you . . . the *more* you focus on it, the *more clear* and *organized* this plan will become . . . you'll get a *clearer and clearer vision* of the sequence of steps you will need to take . . . Check and recheck your action plan to make sure that *each* step, *each* behavior is *positive* and *effective* and *likely to contribute* to the overall goal . . . You can redo and reshape the plan until you get it *just right* . . . and when you're ready, you can describe the sequence of steps in your action plan toward the goal of [Therapist names goal].

The next step is an internal rehearsal of the action plan as effective. The therapist says, for example:

Now, rehearse this action plan and the sequence of behaviors in your mind. Go through *each step*, in sequence, toward your goal . . . As you do, notice yourself getting *closer* and *closer* to your goal . . . You will begin to feel *more* and *more effective* . . . The sense of *mastery* is growing *stronger* and *stronger*... and as you *reach your goal*... you will feel a *deep sense* of *mastery* from having *effectively* implemented and *fulfilled* your plan.

To bring the plan into a realistic time frame, the therapist may suggest:

Now develop your best estimate of the time frame it will take to achieve this goal... You can develop a *realistic sense* of what each step takes, and how long... When that sense becomes clear, you can describe the time frame that seems most realistic to you... [Patient describes] *Yes.* Now, take some time to develop the *best ways* to *daily evaluate* your progress toward your goal, and when that becomes clear to you, you can describe what those ways are.

The therapist can introduce future-time-oriented imagery (D. P. Brown & Fromm, 1986) to enhance the developing sense of mastery by saying, for example:

Imagine some time in the future when you have *reached* this goal successfully... imagine having *accomplished* your goal... imagine that you've accomplished your goal, *just as you'd hoped*... And bring to mind more and more clearly *exactly* the *feelings* you will have... of what it feels like to you to have *reached* your goal... Notice along with your feelings is a sense of *mastery*, of *accomplishment*, of *confidence*... whatever the variety of feelings may be... allow yourself to feel them clearly and intensely... and make a deep impression of them, and of your sense of mastery, as something that will guide you along to this goal.

LEARNING THE CAUSES AND EFFECTS OF BEHAVIOR

As noted above, self-agency deficits that involve poor goal-setting and action-planning can produce a pattern of impulsivity. Wishnie (1977) found that teaching highly impulsive adults to systematically reflect on and predict the outcomes of impulsive behaviors reduced impulsiveness over time. He reported that those who learned to establish internal behavior/outcome representations became significantly less impulsive and began to develop healthy, effective goal-seeking behaviors. Our methods for fostering *action-planning*, especially the process of organizing a behavioral action plan, include the patient's exploration of the effects of each step in the plan. But it can be helpful, especially for patients with some degree of impulsivity, to systematically explore the causes and effects of behavior and predict the probability that certain outcomes will follow when one engages in certain behaviors.

In the protocol for exploring the causes and effects of behavior, the therapist encourages the patient *to reflect on impulsive states of mind and their conse-quences*. The therapist says, for example:

> Bring to mind a time in your life when you engaged in some behavior
> very impulsively . . . without thinking at all about the outcome or the
> consequences over time . . . The *more* you reflect on the situation, the
> *more* you will revisit the state of mind you were in when you were so
> impulsive . . . And when such an experience comes to mind, you can
> describe it, exactly as you remember it. [Patient describes experience]
> Now, let's look at the *effects* of that behavior over time . . . What were
> the short-term effects? . . . What were the immediate consequences? . . .
> What were the long-term effects? . . . What were the long-term conse-
> quences? . . . Did you get what you wanted? . . . What happened over time
> that you didn't want to happen? . . . What didn't happen over time that
> you really wanted to happen?

The next step in the protocol is to help the patient *foster metacognitive aware-ness for predicting consequences of behavior over time*. For example, the therapist might say:

> Now, bring to mind an impulsive behavior that you *repeatedly* engage in . . .
> When you bring such a behavior to mind, you can tell me what it is. [Patient
> reports] Okay. Now go ahead and predict the typical consequences of this
> behavior . . . What else might happen over time from this? . . . Keep reflect-
> ing on this behavior until you can imagine a variety of different outcomes
> . . . some more, some less likely but possible nevertheless . . . When you're
> ready, you can describe those different possible outcomes. [Patient reports]
> Next, rate on a 1-to-10 scale each of these possible outcomes, with 1 being
> *least likely* to be an outcome and 10 being *most likely* to be an outcome . . .
> For each one, tell me what rating you would make. [Patient gives ratings for
> each] Good. Now, bring to mind the original impulsive behavior . . . and
> when you do, imagine altering that behavior in such a way that it not only
> *changes* the likely outcome, but *changes* the outcome in a way that would
> be *more desirable* to you . . . How have you altered the behavior, and how
> has it affected the outcome? [Patient reports]

In this manner, the therapist and patient together systematically explore the connection between engaging in specific behaviors and the likelihood of particular consequences over time. Through this process, the patient develops internal probabilistic representations of the likely outcomes of specific behav-iors, which further refines the development of self-agency and also reduces impulsiveness.

REDUCING CONTRADICTORY GOAL-STATES

Emmons (1999) found that human goal-strivings are complex and that personal strivings typically entail a variety of overlapping and likely contradictory goals. The healthiest individuals show the least internal contradiction across goals and are most likely to experience comfortable and effective self-agency. But those who have intense, competing contradictions across goals typically become inhibited in areas of their lives. The inhibition reflects an effort to reduce the uncomfortable affect associated with the internal conflicting goal-states. In therapy, there are two ways to reduce contradiction among goals and the resulting conflicting goal-states. First, patients can be helped to prioritize goals according to their importance or significance to their core self and with respect to their ultimate concerns. Patients who learn to assess which goals are most important to their core self, and then develop action plans toward those goals, reduce involvement in less important goals. As less important competing goals diminish, the patient experiences less internal contradiction.

Second, Emmons (1999) found that individuals who have a clearly articulated wider vision about the ultimate meaning of life subsume all goals and strivings under that ultimate concern and thereby show significantly less internal contradiction and discomfort. This finding highlights the value of helping patients to articulate a central guiding purpose to their life. For example, the therapist may say:

> Imagine the *central guiding principle* in your life . . . Identify what the *core theme* is behind everything you do that gives you the *deepest* meaning . . . It may be a spiritual purpose, or a humanitarian, or philosophical, purpose. The *more* you reflect on this purpose, the *clearer* it will come to you what the central guiding principle is in your life . . . You can come to see this central guiding purpose reflected in all the activities that are most important to you, or in the moments when it seems that *life matters* the most . . . Soon you will begin to see the central thread that runs throughout all of these times . . . The *more* you reflect on it, the *more* you will become clear on what that central guiding purpose is for you . . . and as it becomes clear, you can give words to it and describe what it is . . .

Of course, as described in Chapter 9, the ability to identify a central guiding purpose or ultimate concern is an advanced metacognitive skill, and so many patients will not readily be able to establish clarity about what it is for them. But offering the above guidance will at worst point them in the direction of becoming interested in what their ultimate concerns may be, which over time will likely bear fruit in the form of their identification and the reduction of any conflicting goal-states.

BEING PROACTIVE

A sign of developing maturity in self-agency is the development of a *proactive* stance, whereby the patient can anticipate the likely course of implementing an action plan and respond proactively to keeping the action plan headed in the right, most efficient and most effective direction. To foster a proactive stance, the therapist can say, for example:

> Imagine a scene in which you are being *proactive* rather than *reactive* . . . Imagine before you engage in a behavior that you take the time to reflect on what you *most want* as an outcome from the behavior over time . . . Imagine that you can *actually create all the steps* in the unfolding of this, in your mind, ahead of time . . . like a master orchestrating all the steps ahead of time . . . predicting how others will respond . . . estimating others' likely responses ahead of time with great accuracy and using that information to plan accordingly . . . Imagine the situation unfolds in *just the way* you would want and would predict . . . and when you're ready, you can describe how you're being proactive in this scene.

Healthy self-agency includes all the elements described above. When deficits are noted in self-agency in general, or in any of the specific elements, addressing the elements will foster stable, internal representations of self-agency in relation to all domains of life.

Methods for Developing Healthy Self-Esteem

Sandler put forth a clear, developmental definition of healthy self-esteem: Self-esteem is the developmental linkage of positive emotional states to the self-representation (see Joffe & Sandler, 1966). Having a developed sense of self, with recognition of qualities that define it, does not guarantee that there will be positive affect associated with it. When the developmental task of self-esteem is mastered in an older child or adult, the experiential consequences are quite significant: The sense of self, whether spontaneously coming to awareness or deliberately evoked, is accompanied by positive feeling. Children and adults who fail to establish this developmental linkage of positive affect to the self-representation either have no feeling or negative feelings when they experience the sense of self. They often experience that something is missing, and no matter how successful they may have become (enhanced self-agency is often used to overcompensate for poorly developed self-esteem), they never feel good about themselves. In the clinical field we refer to such individuals as "narcissistically vulnerable," which technically means they never develop healthy, sustained, positive self-esteem. People who experience largely negative emotional states in conjunction with the sense of self are likely to be vulnerable to depression and may engage in repetitive cycles of maladaptive negative self-talk and dysphoric mood states.

There are three primary factors that promote healthy self-esteem in childhood. As we have emphasized in this book (see Chapters 7 and 8), the first and most important factor in the development of healthy self-esteem is consistent expressed delight from attachment figures toward the child throughout childhood. Kohut (1971) characterized the foundation of this as "the gleam in the mother's eye." Healthy parents are openly expressive about their positive feelings toward their children. Such parents enjoy (almost) everything that the child does and readily express their delight in the noticed behavioral changes in the growing child. More important, such parents take delight in their child's *unique being* and express this both directly and indirectly to the child. Positive emotional expression from the parents pervades everything about the interactions with the child over time, and the child *internalizes the parents' expressed positive emotion* and *directly links it to the developing sense of self.* The developmental outcome is healthy self-esteem, or the consistent experience of positive emotions about the self when the self-sense and its defining qualities are evoked.

The second source of healthy self-esteem is the *repeated experience of mastery* in childhood, especially during what Mahler et al. (1975) call the "practicing" period. During this time, the child will explore and experiment with what he or she finds and will thereby discover and develop his or her strengths and competencies, leading to a sense of mastery in some circumstances; the greater the mastery, the greater the self-esteem. However, children who lack an experiential foundation of consistent expressed delight from attachment figures, and especially children whose attachment figures were positive *only* in response to the child's successful *doing*, are at risk of using the sense of mastery, and self-agency in general, to overcompensate for the absence of early positive mirroring. Such children grow up to be highly successful but unhappy people, because *doing* more and more, however effective, can never be a substitute for feeling positive in one's *being.*

The third source of healthy self-esteem in older, latency-age children is the establishment of structure and consistent limit-setting (Cotton, 1983). If older children are not given enough structure or clear limits, their behavior becomes unfocused and directionless, which is erosive to what might already be a good foundation of self-esteem if there had been consistent expressed delight and experiences of mastery.

Self-psychology was developed as an approach to psychotherapy for people with extreme, chronic self-esteem failure, particularly those referred to as having narcissistic personality disorder. Such people are highly sensitive to criticism and are deeply vulnerable to feeling diminished in comparison to others. The self-psychological treatment includes the therapist openly admitting limitations and failures of empathy, and it has been found that such a therapeutic style helps to foster a better working relationship with narcissistically vulnerable patients. However, this treatment is slow and the patient does not necessarily overcome the chronic self-esteem failure. The problem with traditional self-psychological approaches is that they are not well informed about how healthy self-esteem develops. Reducing negative interactions and self-esteem vulnerability in treatment in itself does not lead to the development of positive associations to the self-representation. Simply put, the absence of a negative state does not necessarily produce the presence of a positive state. In response to the limitations of self-psychological treatment for self-esteem development, we created a positive self-esteem protocol that we have found to be very effective. The essence of the treatment is to directly and systematically evoke positive feeling states in conjunction with the self-representation, and to do this within and across sessions until the patient can evoke positive feeling states associated with the self most of the time in everyday life, including in situations that the patient has found to be particularly self-esteem-challenging. The step-by-step protocol includes the following components: (1) situation-based self-esteem enhancement; (2) enhancement of self-esteem in the context of relationships; (3) skill development for more quickly evoking positive self-esteem and transferring such states to other contexts; (4) stress challenge, or maintaining positive self-states in self-esteem-challenging situations; and (5) integrating self-esteem as a way of being.

SITUATION-BASED SELF-ESTEEM ENHANCEMENT

Even people with chronically impaired self-esteem are able to think of situations where they feel good about themselves. For such people, short-duration positive self-esteem states are usually associated with *doing* something effectively. Even though we do not consider efficacy of *doing* as a sufficient foundation for healthy self-esteem, positive self-esteem experience linked to activity and mastery in certain situations serves as a starting point for evoking positive affective states directly linked to the sense of self. The protocol begins with *scene generation*. The therapist says, for example: "Imagine a scene in which you are feeling *especially good about yoursel*f." Other ways of wording include:

> Imagine a situation in which you *really like yourself.* Imagine a scene in which you are feeling *deeply satisfied with yourself.* Imagine a situation in which you're feeling *really proud about yourself* [or in which you are *especially pleased* with yourself, or in which you are *especially confident* about yourself] . . . and when the scene has become clear to you, you can describe what's happening and the positive feelings you're having about yourself.

In each of these examples, the wording links positive affective states directly to the self. For narcissistically vulnerable patients who overcompensate for a diminished sense of self by self-inflation or grandiosity, it is important to qualify the wording of the suggestion by referring to "a situation where you are feeling especially good about yourself, *yet in a balanced and not inflated way.*"

When the patient evokes and describes the situation and his or her positive feelings, the therapist focuses on *affect amplification* to help the patient to amplify the intensity of the felt positive emotion. For example:

> The *more* you focus on this situation, the *more* the *positive feelings* will become *clearer* and *clearer* to you . . . and soon you will experience this *strong, positive feeling* about yourself *very clearly* and intensely.

The next therapeutic task is to *extend the duration of the positive self-feeling.* There are two ways to do this. Direct methods include the therapist giving a direct suggestion for extending the duration of the state by saying, for example, "You will hold this strong, positive self-feeling longer and longer"; the therapist may also use a time-expansion suggestion, as follows:

> And now, even though only a few moments of clock time will pass, it will seem to you like *much more time* elapses . . . so much time that you will begin to experience this *strong, positive self-feeling* as *familiar* and *natural* and simply a part of *who you are.*

Another way to extend the duration is to prompt the patient to generate a series of scenes after the first one. After the first scene is produced and explored and reinforced, the therapist might say:

> Now you can let this scene fade away . . . and when it does, you can imagine *another scene*, a *different* situation in which you're *also* feeling *especially good* about yourself . . . Go ahead and imagine this new scene . . . and when you do, *really feel* what it's like to feel *so good* about yourself . . . when you're ready, you can describe what's happening and the positive feelings you're having about yourself.

After the second scene, the above is repeated for a third scene, and more if the therapist wishes. Using either method or both, the goal is to extend the duration of the experience of positive self-feelings for the majority of the session. Once the patient learns the method, he or she is given the homework assignment to imagine situations that evoke positive self-feelings and to focus on those feelings. Over time, the patient becomes skillful at evoking positive self-states, first in association with specific imagined situations and then simply by tuning in to his or her sense of self.

ENHANCING SELF-ESTEEM IN THE CONTEXT OF RELATIONSHIPS

It is often far more difficult for patients with self-esteem deficits to evoke and maintain positive self-feelings *in relationship to others* as compared to in the context of activities. The next step in the protocol is to *enhance positive self-feelings in the context of relationships*. The therapist says, for example:

> Imagine a situation in which you are feeling *especially good* about yourself *in relationship* to others [or feeling *really comfortable* with yourself around others, or feeling that *you matter* to someone] . . .

Or:

> Imagine a scene in which others are *respecting* or *appreciating you* for *who you are* [or in which you are being with others in a way that you are letting them see *who you really are* in a *deep* way, and they're responding *really well* to *who you are*] . . . When you're ready, you can describe what's happening and the *positive feelings* you're having about yourself.

After the patient describes the situation and his or her experience of it, the therapist applies the methods for *affect amplification* and *extending the duration of the positive self-states*.

SKILL DEVELOPMENT

The next step in the self-esteem development protocol is to *develop skill in generating positive self-feelings quickly and for longer duration, and to generalize the learning across contexts.* To foster rapid evocation of positive self-states, the therapist says, for example:

> See how quickly you can come into contact with the *strong, positive feelings* about yourself . . . and *more* and *more* you'll find yourself being able to bring your positive feelings about yourself *more and more quickly* into your awareness . . . so that you *always* have access to them, *really quickly.*

To extend the *duration* of the positive self-states, the therapist says, for example:

> Notice that you can hold this *strong, positive feeling* about yourself for *longer* and *longer* . . . you can come to feel *especially good* about yourself for *longer* and *longer* durations.

The therapist and patient together set the goal that the patient will hold the positive self-feelings for longer and longer duration within and outside the therapy sessions.

The therapist also helps the patient to generalize the positive self-feelings to other situations. For example:

> Familiarize yourself with this state of mind . . . these *strong positive* feelings about yourself . . .Now imagine bringing this positive self-feeling into some *other* situation . . . a situation that you don't normally associate with holding a positive feeling about yourself . . .

The main sign of progress is that the patient reports holding a positive feeling about himself or herself more and more throughout every day. It is beneficial to use an anchoring scale to promote the patient's metacognitive awareness of his or her positive self-feelings and self-esteem:

> You can rate how you're feeling about yourself at any given time in any given situation, using a scale of 1 to 10: 1 indicates feeling *really bad* about yourself, 10 indicates feeling *really good* about yourself, and the other numbers indicate somewhere in between.

The patient is encouraged to rate self-esteem throughout each day and to self-evaluate progress and review it with the therapist in the next session. This step is completed when the patient can sustain positive self-feelings throughout most of the day, nearly every day. Eventually, the patient takes on the task of keeping a good feeling about the self every day between sessions throughout all situations, which is helped by the next step below.

STRESS CHALLENGE

The next step is to maintain positive self-feelings in situations that the patient has associated with strong negative self-feelings. For example, the therapist may say:

> Now imagine having and keeping *especially good feelings* about yourself in *exactly* the type of situation that you could never imagine feeling good about yourself in before [or in the type of situation that you were previously at risk of losing a good sense of yourself in, or *keeping a good sense* of yourself in the midst of difficulties, or *keeping a good sense* of yourself in exactly the type of situations where you previously felt bad about yourself, or imagine that you are *feeling good* about yourself even in the worst situations you can imagine].

Through this process, the therapist introduces the expectation that the patient *can* maintain a strong, positive feeling about himself or herself even in the most difficult of situations that have been associated with a strong loss of self-esteem. In the context of the imagery, the patient experiences having and holding positive feelings about the self in such situations, and the therapist uses the methods described above to *amplify* the positive states and *extend their duration*. Then, the therapist gives the patient the assignment of actually putting himself or herself in such challenging situations to test and further the progress.

INTEGRATING SELF-ESTEEM AS A WAY OF BEING

The development of positive self-esteem over the course of the therapy eventually transcends activities and becomes a way of being. In support of this ultimate goal, the therapist may say, for example:

> Imagine a scene about some time in the future when you have become less and less concerned about accomplishments and more and more about *discovering contentment* within yourself . . .

Or:

> Imagine that it begins to feel that you have *always* felt this way . . .

Or:

> Imagine a part of your mind will *always* carry this awareness . . .

Or:

> You'll begin to sense this good feeling about yourself as part of the *core* of your *being*.

If the patient has a history of self-reproach, the therapist may say, "Imagine a scene about lightness of being" or "Imagine a scene about not taking things so seriously."

Finally, the protocol for self-esteem development ends with a consistent therapeutic focus on positive self-feelings of *being*, not *doing*. For example, the therapist may say one of the following:

> The scene will be about *being valued* without needing to do anything.

> In this scene, you can *delight* in *just being* who you are.

You can be *content* just in *who you are.*

You're finding that *special quality* of being.

You're feeling *good just to be alive.*

You're finding a *greater satisfaction* in life in everyday living, where *just being with yourself* and *as yourself* is enough.

Developing the Best Self

As the epitome of the therapeutic self-development process, the therapist focuses on helping to cultivate the patient's *best self.* The best self represents the strongest, most autonomous, and most unique sense of self. The therapeutic approach entails scene generation of moments of experiencing the best self, enhancing awareness of the felt experience and qualities of the best self, and then transferring the "best-self state of mind" to other current and future situations. For example, the therapist may say:

> Imagine some situations in which you brought out the *very best* of yourself . . . Review whatever situations come to mind until you can settle on one situation that right now you associate with your *very best self* . . . The *more* you reflect on that situation, the *more* the *direct experience* of that best self will return right now . . . *Really* familiarize yourself with this best-self experience . . . The *more* you reflect on this *best self,* the *more* the *unique qualities* of your best self will become *clearer* and *clearer* . . . And when the unique qualities of your best self become *very clear* to you, you can describe what they are.

When the patient has reported specific unique qualities of his or her best self, the therapist continues:

> See what other qualities of the best self become clear . . . Keep imagining the qualities until you get an overall sense of being *all that you are.*

The next step entails transferring the best-self state of mind to different situations. The therapist says, for example:

> Now imagine bringing this *best self* into some situation you are currently involved in . . . Notice the very different experience you have of yourself when you are operating out of best-self mode . . . Imagine how the situation is different when you bring the *best self* into this situation.

This "best-self method" was originally a hypnotic method developed by Erika Fromm (D. P. Brown & Fromm, 1986). One of her students, Steve Kahn, has used this method extensively in couples therapy. He asks each member of the couple to imagine a situation in which each was their best self, selecting a situation not necessarily associated with the coupleship. Next, each member of the couple is asked to imagine bringing the best self into the coupleship and then to notice the effects on the interaction. Finally, each is asked to imagine bringing the best self into a recurrent conflict or fight that the couple typically has and to notice how the style of expressing and resolving the conflict is different when each member of the couple brings his or her best self to the conflict.

The senior author of this book (DB) teaches a course in performance excellence for superior, district, and family court judges. Of the many experiential exercises in this course, he has found the best-self method has been a favorite of the judges. As part of the course, each judge is asked to imagine a situation that evokes his or her best self. In the courses taught so far, for some judges it was an experience in court, for others it was a special moment in a close relationship, for others it was some civic or humanitarian action in which they participated, and for others it was a golf or tennis game, while others described other experiences. Regardless of the situational source of their best-self experience, when the judges were asked to transfer the best-self state of mind to the current courtroom, they quickly discovered that they were far more effective as judges and came close to their goal of performance excellence. Some judges practiced the best-self method on their own so that they could deepen and continually bring their best self to their courtroom work.

This systematic approach to the best self also entails fostering both *uniqueness of self* and *vital engagement of self*. From an attachment perspective, the most difficult task for a parent is to set aside wishes and agendas for a developing child and to become a consistent support at each stage of development for the child's discovery and strengthening of his or her own uniqueness, as different from and independent of parental agendas. Healthy parents do not expect the child to fit their molds or meet their agendas but are curious about the uniqueness of this newly becoming person. For example, to foster *uniqueness*, the therapist may say:

> Imagine that you have an attitude of *curiosity* and *discovery* and exploration of *who you really are* . . . The *more* you support this attitude of discovery and exploration, the *more* the qualities of your uniqueness will get *clearer* and *clearer* to you . . . Imagine that your discovery of your unique qualities of self is *completely free* of any expectations of others . . . See what becomes clear . . . see what you discover . . . And when you discover some of your unique qualities, you can describe what they are.

To foster *vital engagement*, the therapist suggests, for example:

Imagine a scene about actively engaging in life with *vitality* and *enthusiasm* [or a scene about finding your *unique passion*, or a scene about a *richer quality of life*, or a scene about *those special moments* when it feels *so good* to be alive, or a scene of some time in the future when you look forward to each day as a *new discovery* and adventure, or a scene about some time in the future when you know there is *so much more*, and yet it is enough].

Self-Development From an Attachment Perspective

The self-development protocol described in this appendix emphasizes the developmental line of self as relatively independent of the line of attachment development. Core-self experience and definition, self-agency, and self-esteem can each be developed through imagery focused on the self relatively independent of self-development that occurs in the context of attachment relationships. We include this material as an appendix, and not as a main chapter in this book on attachment, so that the clinician can learn how to foster self-development separately from attachment development.

However, with patients with personality and dissociative disorders, we typically place systematic focus on self-development simultaneously with systematic focus on developing positive attachment representations. For patients with little or weak self-development, we apply the principles described in this appendix in the context of all the principles and practices of introducing and working with patients' ideal parent figure imagery. For example, the therapist suggests that the patient-as-child imagine ideal parent figures who consistently encourage and support the development of a strong, autonomous, and unique sense of self, in the context of the secure-base experience of the ideal parent figures. For patients with poorly developed self-agency, the therapist shapes ideal parent figures who reinforce the patient-as-child's sense of contingency responsiveness, consistently are responsive to response-eliciting behaviors, encourage interpersonal self-agency, collaboratively support and encourage the development of organized goal-directed behaviors and action plans, and collaboratively engage with the patient-as-child to become metacognitively aware of the probable short- and long-term consequences of both specific impulsive and carefully organized behaviors. For patients with chronic low self-esteem, the ideal parent figure imagery emphasizes repetition of scenes of parental delight in the patient-as-child's behavior and being and of parental support for the patient-as-child to feel a sense of competence and mastery in various endeavors. We encourage the clinician who wishes to apply the IPF imagery process to self-development to review Chapters 7, 8, 11, 12, and 13 of this book.

Appendix B
Protocols for Developing Adult Secure Intimacy in Individuals and Caring Behaviors in Couples

Adult Secure Intimacy in Individual Patients

According to Bowlby's pioneering work on attachment, secure attachment leads to healthy exploratory behavior. Infant–caregiver relationships are attachment relationships, and secure attachment encourages exploratory behavior. However, regardless of how physically intimate they are, most adult romantic relationships are not necessarily attachment relationships. For an adult romantic relationship to qualify as an attachment relationship, the relationship must manifest to a sufficient degree the five conditions that promote secure attachment: safety/protection, attunement, soothing, expressed delight, and fostering self-development. When a romantic relationship consistently manifests these five dimensions, then we see that romantic relationship as a secure attachment relationship, within which *secure intimacy* can develop.

Secure attachment relationships are never static or one-dimensional. Within the context of secure intimacy, each partner is free to explore, grow, and discover new ways of being. Each partner discovers new dimensions of his or her unique self within this context. Secure intimacy provides the conditions under which adult love relationships can flourish.

PROMOTING SECURE INTIMACY IN PSYCHOTHERAPY: AN OUTLINE OF OUR APPROACH

When a patient has established earned secure attachment status, then in the psychotherapy there is the option to build upon this security to promote the capacity for and actuality of secure intimacy. From the protocol that we use, patients develop a vision for secure romantic attachment that embodies secure intimacy. We help the patient first to develop a general vision of a securely intimate relationship and then to imagine that relationship to include each of the five main conditions that promote secure attachment. Individualized positive descriptors of ideal parent figures, derived from earlier IPF work, are included in the secure intimacy protocol. For example, if the positive descriptors from the IPFs included "encouraging of self-exploration" or "consistently available," the therapist asks the patient to imagine an adult romantic partner who is "encouraging of self-exploration" and "consistently available." In these ways, the therapist and patient work collaboratively to shape a deeply positive and stable internal working model for adult romantic secure intimacy, with qualities tailored to the given attachment needs of each patient. The presence of such a positive IWM will influence the patient's orientation toward and selection of potential partners with whom secure intimacy is possible.

SHAPING THE GENERAL VISION OF ADULT ROMANTIC SECURE INTIMACY

We have found the hypnotherapy method of future-time orientation (D. P. Brown & Fromm, 1986) very conducive to helping the patient construct a vision of adult romantic secure intimacy. For example, the therapist may say:

> Imagine some time in the future when you have found *just the right* intimate relationship . . . a relationship characterized by secure intimacy . . . Soon a scene will come to mind that best represents your personal vision of secure intimacy . . . and when the scene becomes clear, you will be able to describe it.

The patient describes a scene of a relationship, and then the therapist continues:

> Sustain your focus on this relationship vision of secure intimacy, and soon the specific elements of secure intimacy that feel *most important* to you will become *clearer* and *clearer* . . . see what becomes clear now . . . and when you're ready you can describe what becomes clear to you.

The therapist mirrors and enhances the elements described by the patient and encourages further elaboration of the felt sense of them. Then the therapist suggests:

> Imagine the details of day-to-day life of manifesting the *best* of a *secure intimate relationship* . . . And the *more* these details become clear, the *more* you will be able to describe them . . . *more and more* you will discover all the important ingredients of the *best* of a *secure intimate relationship* for you.

After the patient describes the elements of his or her secure intimacy experience in the scene, the therapist again mirrors and enhances those elements and suggests new scenes in which the named qualities are even clearer and more visceral. At the end of a session or part of a session that focuses on the above, the therapist supports and encourages further exploration:

> See whatever else that is important . . . until it becomes *even more clear* what feels *most right* for supporting a secure intimate relationship, and once again, when you're ready, you can describe what feels most right. [Patient describes] Good. Now, hold your awareness on the total felt sense of this image of secure intimacy . . . Fix this vision in mind . . . Make a *very clear* imprint of it . . . in such a way that it will *always be there* for you as a guide for orienting toward secure intimate relationships in the future.

ARTICULATING THE FIVE PRIMARY CONDITIONS THAT PROMOTE SECURE INTIMACY

As a next step in this process, the therapist suggests that the patient bring each of the five main conditions that support secure intimacy into his or her evolving vision of secure intimacy. For example, the therapist says:

> Bring to mind your personal vision of secure intimacy once again . . . Become familiar with this vision . . . Now imagine a scene in which your secure intimate partner is providing you with a sense of feeling *absolutely safe* and *protected* in the context of this secure romantic intimacy . . . Bring to mind the specific ways your partner is *being* that enable you to feel *completely safe* and *protected* . . . and as you notice those ways, you can describe them. [Patient describes] Yes. And now notice how this affects your state of mind and your experience in the relationship.

The therapist continues with the other conditions:

> Now imagine a scene in which your secure intimate partner is so *very carefully attuned* . . . *carefully attentive* but not overly attentive . . . to *everything about you* and your new exploratory behaviors in the relationship . . . your *ways of being*, and your *ways of growing* . . . especially your *internal state of mind* . . . your *needs and feelings* . . . in such a way that you feel secure to discover and explore in new ways . . . When you're ready, you can describe the scene and what's happening. [Patient describes] *Good. Yes.* And now notice how that affects your state of mind when someone is so *carefully attuned* like that . . . What do you notice?

Now imagine a scene in which your secure intimate partner is providing you with a sense of feeling *comforted*, *soothed*, and *reassured* in the context of this secure intimacy whenever you feel emotionally upset . . . Notice the specific ways your partner is being that enable you to *feel completely comforted and reassured* . . . and when you're ready you can describe what that's like . . . [Patient describes] *Yes. Just like that.* And notice how this affects your state of mind in you and as part of the couple.

Now imagine a scene in which your secure intimate partner is providing you with a sense that [he or she] is *absolutely delighted* in everything about your being, and *openly* and *repeatedly* expresses that delight in your being in the context of this secure intimacy . . . Bring to mind the specific ways your partner is being that enables you to sense the *depth* of [his or her] *delight* in your being . . . in an abiding way . . . You can describe those ways when you feel ready . . . [Patient reports]

Good. Really take that in . . . and notice how that affects your state of mind in you and in the relationship.

Now imagine a scene in which your secure intimate partner is providing you with *continuous encouragement* and *support* to discover and bring out your *best*, *strongest*, and *unique* self in the context of this secure relationship . . . Bring to mind the specific ways your partner is *being* that enables you to bring out that *best*, *unique self* in *new ways* . . . When you're ready you can describe what you notice. [Patient describes] *Yes.* Just like that. Now imagine some time in the future . . . a scene will come to mind about the details . . . of you going about your life in *so many new ways* . . . as a result of the ways of discovering and growing that came from this secure intimacy. And when you're ready, you can describe that scene of you in the future going about your life in ways that were supported by this secure intimacy.

INDIVIDUALIZING THE SECURE INTIMACY PROTOCOL

In shaping the vision of secure intimacy, we try to individualize the protocol as much as possible for each patient. We make the assumption that what was missing or problematic in a patient's early caregiver relationships will likely also be experienced as missing or problematic in his or her adult romantic relationships. Information about the early relationships is used for individualizing the protocol, and ideally, the therapist has the transcript from the patient's Adult Attachment Interview (AAI), as the five adjectives used to describe each caregiver are particularly useful here. As with preparation for the Ideal Parent Figure protocol, the therapist translates the patient's negative adjectives into their positive opposites and includes these as suggestions for imagining adult romantic secure intimacy.

As an example of the overall process, if an AAI descriptor for the father was "never around," then its positive opposite might be "always emotionally available"; then, for the IPF protocol early in treatment, an ideal parent figure being consistently emotionally available contributes to developing a new, positive internal working model for earned security of attachment. Once earned security has been established, and if the therapy then includes the protocol for developing adult secure intimacy, the positive descriptors that were used initially to develop the patient's secure attachment to ideal parent figures are then used in the development of adult secure intimacy imagery. In this example, the therapist says, "Imagine a scene some time in the future when you have found a romantic partner who proves to be *always emotionally available* in an abiding and ongoing way." In this way, through integration of the patient's early experiences with attachment figures into the adult secure intimacy protocol, the patient develops a vision of future adult romantic secure intimacy that is highly individualized to his or her specific attachment needs.

In addition to integrating information from the five adjectives (if available), we also utilize any other information we have about each particular patient to individualize the protocol. For example, if we know that the patient has or has had discomfort with physical closeness, we include suggestions such as the following that promote comfort with physical closeness:

- Develop an image of a relationship with *just the right feel* for closeness and distance.
- As your partner gets closer, you find that you like it, and you find yourself wanting to get *even closer*, in a way that's *comfortable* for you.
- Imagine that as you desire to get close, your partner wants to get close too.
- You find it *very easy* getting close to [him or her].
- Imagine a scene about the kind of *balance* of closeness and freedom that this relationship gives you.
- Imagine *just the right kind* of relationship in which you are *totally secure* so that it's *really okay* when [he or she] isn't around; and when around, [he or she] protects your solitude and quiet time and things you need to do for yourself.

For a patient who has or has had difficulty relying on others or asking for help, one or several of the following might be included:

- Picture yourself able to ask for advice or help and [he or she] *doesn't mind at all*.
- Imagine a scene in which you are able to turn to [him or her] at times of need.
- More and more you're finding that this person is someone you can *really depend on*, in a good, healthy way.

- You can feel what it's like to know that this partner is *there for you*, as *you* need.
- Imagine that you *actually find some comfort* in relying on [him or her].

In support of mutuality, the following may be included:

- Imagine a partner with whom you have the conviction that [he or she] *cares about you* as much as you care about [him or her].
- You can *really know* that this partner has as strong feelings for you as you do about [him or her].

For patients who have or have had difficulty with opening up emotionally:

- This is the kind of partner you find it easy to discuss problems and upsets with.
- Imagine *just the right kind* of relationship where you are *comfortable* expressing a wide range of emotions, and [he or she] is *quite fine* with that.

For patients who have experienced love and acceptance as conditional:

- This is the kind of partner with whom you really don't have to do anything to be loved.
- Imagine a relationship in which you can *just be yourself* and are loved and appreciated simply for *who you are.*

Following these principles, the therapist can integrate any available information about a patient's attachment and relational experiences into the protocol.

Caring Behaviors in Couples

A patient who is in a romantic relationship may be confused by the above individual secure intimacy protocol, as it implicitly suggests that the right secure intimacy relationship is *in the future* and is not the current relationship. Further, the protocol would highlight any difference between the current relationship and the patient's vision of a secure intimacy relationship. Unless the therapist is very careful to work with the patient's experience of this difference if it exists, the protocol could undermine the patient's relationship. For these reasons, for patients who are in a romantic relationship, we prefer to work with both the patient and his or her partner to foster secure intimacy in the specific context of focusing on *caring behaviors.*

Couples therapists are often asked by their patients to help them with the erosion of romance and caring behaviors in their relationships. Over time, many romantic partners settle into the routines of daily living and partnering in such a way that the romance and caring subsides. The initial joy of the relationship has become the job of the relationship. Regardless of whether the coupleship is new or long term, there may or may not be a sense of security and there may or may not be a sense of intimacy. The restoration or development of healthy adult romantic secure intimacy is especially important for couples to achieve optimal romance, caring, and relational satisfaction.

Harville Hendrix (1988) was among the first couples therapists to understand the necessity of developing or reclaiming caring behaviors for the survival of the relationship. He developed *imago relationship therapy* (IRT), which is based on a synthesis of attachment theory, object relations theory, developmental psychology, behavioral change techniques, and neuroscience. The IRT method is designed to help couples listen to each other with curiosity and a sense of safety so as to develop a deeper, more authentic connection, which then allows each of them to understand more about his or her own needs and those of the other. In this approach, the therapist presents an exercise to enhance caring behaviors in the couple. What follows is a modification of their IRT process for developing caring behaviors.

1. In a session with both partners, the therapist gives the following instructions:

> Recall all of the things that your current partner does in the relationship, however minor or important, to make you feel *especially cared about* or *loved*. Using the following stem sentences, make a list of everything you can think of with respect to your partner's current caring behaviors.
>
> > I feel cared about when you . . .
> > I really love it when you . . .
> > I feel special when you . . .

Each person takes turns sharing his or her entire list with the other, while the other listens and mirrors what was heard.

2. The next step can be done with each member of the couple in a relaxed, focused state or a hypnotic state. The therapist brings attention to caring behaviors *early in the relationship* by saying:

> Imagine yourself back at the time when you *first fell in love* with your current partner . . . a time when you were *deeply in love* . . . a time when *romance* and *excitement* were *very much* a part of your relationship. Bring to mind all the ways you felt *especially cared about*.

After completing the visualization, each member of the couple is asked to:

Use the following stem sentences to make a list of all the caring, romantic, loving things your partner did for you early in the romantic relationship, no matter how seemingly minor or important:

> I felt cared about when . . .
> I really loved it when . . .
> You really got to my heart when . . .
> What kindled my passion was when . . .
> I felt special when . . .

Again, each person takes turns sharing his or her entire list with the other, while the other listens and mirrors what was heard.

3. Then, the therapist explores *ideal future caring behaviors* by saying:

Now imagine yourself in a scene where your partner in the future is acting in all the *caring, loving, romantic* ways that you always wanted him or her to, but were never able to communicate . . . as if he or she *really knew exactly* what you *most needed* . . . what you found to be caring/loving in other relationships . . . what you might find from the ideal mate who would know *exactly* what you need to feel *most cared for* or *loved* . . . what you *long for* in your *most private fantasies* but have never been able to ask for. Using the following stem sentences, make a list of loving or caring things that you have always wanted but have been unable to ask for:

> I would really like you to . . .
> I would feel really cared for if you would . . .
> You'd really kindle my passion if you would . . .

As before, the therapist requests that each partner share the list with the other partner and that the other partner mirror what was shared.

This three-part exercise can be repeated several times across sessions. We find that the couple's experience of this collaborative exploration and exchange, together with what emerges from the process, often fosters not only the restoration and/or development of caring behaviors but also the couple's experience of secure intimacy with each other.

References

Adam, E. K., Gunnar, M. R., & Tanaka, A. (2004). Adult attachment, parent emotion, and observed parenting behavior: Mediator and Moderator Models. *Child Development, 75*(1), 110–122.

Adam, K. S., Sheldon-Keller, A. E., & West, M. (1996). Attachment organization and history of suicidal behavior in clinical adolescents. *Journal of Consulting and Clinical Psychology, 64*(2), 264–272.

Agrawal, H. R., Gunderson, J., Holmes, B. M., & Lyons-Ruth, K. (2004). Attachment studies with borderline patients: A review. *Harvard Review of Psychiatry, 12*(2), 94–104.

Ainsworth, M. D. S. (1967). *Infancy in Uganda: Infant care and the growth of love*. Baltimore, MD: Johns Hopkins University Press.

Ainsworth, M. D. S. (1972). Attachment and dependency: A comparison. In J. L. Gewirtz (Ed.), *Attachment and dependency*. Washington, DC: V. H. Winston.

Ainsworth, M. D. S. (1973). The development of infant–mother attachment. In B. M. Caldwell & H. N. Ricciutti (Eds.), *Review of child development research* (Vol. 3, pp. 1–94). Chicago, IL: University of Chicago Press.

Ainsworth, M. D. S. (1990). Some considerations regarding theory and assessment relevant to attachments beyond infancy. In M. T. Greenberg, D. Cicchetti, & E. M. Cummings (Eds.), *Attachment in the preschool years: Theory, research, and intervention* (pp. 463–488). Chicago, IL: University of Chicago Press.

Ainsworth, M. D. S., Blehar, M. C., Waters, E., & Wall, S. (1978). *Patterns of attachment: A psychological study of the Strange Situation*. Hillsdale, NJ: Erlbaum.

Ainsworth, M. D. S., & Eichberg, C. (1991). Effects on infant-mother attachment of mother's unresolved loss of an attachment figure, or other traumatic experience. In C. M. Parkes, J. Stevenson-Hinde, & P. Marris (Eds.), *Attachment across the life cycle* (pp. 160-183). London: Routledge.

Alexander, P. C. (1993). The differential effects of abuse characteristics and attachment in the prediction of the long-term effects of sexual abuse. *Journal of Interpersonal Violence, 8*(3), 346–362.

Allen, J. G. (2001). *Traumatic relationships and serious mental disorders*. West Sussex, England: Wiley.

Allen, J. G. (2013). *Restoring mentalizing in attachment relationships: Treating trauma with plain old therapy*. Washington, DC: American Psychiatric Publishing.

Allen, J. G., & Fonagy, P. (Eds.) (2006). *The handbook of mentalization-based treatment.* West Sussex, England: Wiley.

Allen, J. G., Fonagy, P., & Bateman, A. W. (2008). *Mentalizing in clinical practice.* Washington, DC: American Psychiatric Publishing.

Allen, J. P. (2008). The attachment system in adolescence. In J. Cassidy & P. R. Shaver (Eds.), *Handbook of attachment: Theory, research, and clinical applications* (2nd ed., pp. 419–435). New York, NY: Guilford Press.

Allen, J. P., & Hauser, S. T. (1996). Autonomy and relatedness in adolescent–family interactions as predictors of young adults' states of mind regarding attachment. *Development and Psychopathology, 8*(4), 793–809.

Allen, J. P., Hauser, S. T., & Borman-Spurrell, E. (1996). Attachment theory as a framework for understanding sequelae of severe adolescent psychopathology: An 11-year follow-up study. *Journal of Consulting and Clinical Psychology, 64*(2), 254–263.

Allen, J. P., & Land, D. (1999). Attachment in adolescence. In J. Cassidy & P. R. Shaver (Eds.), *Handbook of attachment: Theory, research, and clinical applications* (pp. 319–335). New York, NY: Guilford Press.

Armsden, G. C., & Greenberg, M. T. (1987). The inventory of parent and peer attachment: Individual differences and their relationship to psychological well-being in adolescences. *Journal of Youth and Adolescence, 16*(5), 427–454.

Bach, S. (1977). *Narcissistic states and the therapeutic process.* New York, NY: Jason Aronson.

Baker, E. L. (1981). An hypnotherapeutic approach to enhance object relatedness in psychotic patients. *International Journal of Clinical and Experimental Hypnosis, 29*(2), 136–147.

Baker, R. L., & Brown, D. (2015). On engagement: Learning to pay attention. *University of Arkansas at Little Rock Law Review, 36*(3), 337–355.

Bakermans-Kranenburg, M. J., & van IJzendoorn, M. H. (2009). The first 10,000 Adult Attachment Interviews: Distributions of adult attachment representations in clinical and non-clinical groups. *Attachment & Human Development, 11*(3), 223–263.

Bakermans-Kranenburg, M., van IJzendoorn, M., Moran, G., Pederson, D., & Benoit, D. (2006). Unresolved states of mind, anomalous parental behavior and disorganized attachment: A review and meta-analysis of the transmission gap. *Attachment & Human Development, 8*(2), 89–111.

Bakwin, H. (1942). Loneliness in infants. *Archives of Pediatrics & Adolescent Medicine, 63*(1), 30–40.

Baldwin, M. W., & Fehr, B. (1995). On the instability of attachment style ratings. *Personal Relationships, 2,* 247–261.

Baltes, P. B., & Baltes, M. M. (1990a). Psychological perspectives on successful aging: The model of selective optimization with compassion. In P. B. Baltes & M. M. Baltes (Eds.), *Successful aging: Perspectives for the social sciences* (pp. 1–34). Cambridge, NJ: Cambridge University Press.

Baltes, P. B., & Baltes, M. M. (1990b). *Successful aging: Perspectives from the behavioral sciences.* Cambridge, England: Cambridge University Press.

Barnett, D., Ganiban, J., & Cicchetti, D. (1999). Maltreatment, emotional reactivity, and the development of Type D attachments from 12 to 24 months of age. In J. Vondra & D. Barnett (Eds.), *Atypical patterns of infant attachment: Theory, research, and current directions. Monographs of the Society for Research on Child Development, 64*(3), 97–118.

Barone, L. (2003). Developmental protective and risk factors in borderline personality disorder: A study using the Adult Attachment Interview. *Attachment & Human Development, 5*(1), 64–77.

Barone, L., Borelli, C., Madeddu, F., & Maffei, C. (2000). Attachment, alcohol abuse and personality disorders: A pilot study using the Adult Attachment Interview. *Alcologia, 12*(1), 17–24.

Barone, L., Fossati, A., & Guiducci, V. (2011). Attachment mental states and inferred pathways of development in borderline personality disorder: A study using the Adult Attachment Interview. *Attachment & Human Development, 13*(5), 451–469.

Barone, L., & Guiducci, V. (2009). Mental representation of attachment in eating disorders: A pilot study using the Adult Attachment Interview. *Attachment & Human Development, 11*(4), 405–417.

Bartholomew, K. (1990). Avoidance of intimacy: An attachment perspective. *Journal of Social and Personal Relationships, 7,* 147–178.

Bartholomew, K., & Horowitz, L.M. (1991). Attachment styles among young adults: A test of the four-category model. *Journal of Personality and Social Psychology, 61*(2), 226–245.

Bateman, A., & Fonagy, P. (1999). Effectiveness of partial hospitalization in the treatment of borderline personality disorder: A randomized controlled trial. *American Journal of Psychiatry, 156,* 1563–1569.

Bateman, A., & Fonagy, P. (2001). Treatment of borderline personality disorder with psycho-analytically oriented partial hospitalization: An 18-month follow-up. *American Journal of Psychiatry, 158,* 36–42.

Bateman, A., & Fonagy, P. (2003). Development of an attachment-based treatment program for borderline personality disorder. *Bulletin of the Menninger Clinic, 67*(3), 187–211.

Bateman, A., & Fonagy, P. (2004). *Psychotherapy for borderline personality disorder: Mentalization based treatment.* London, England: Oxford University Press.

Bateman, A., & Fonagy, P. (2006). Mentalizing and borderline personality disorder. In J. G. Allen & P. Fonagy (Eds.), *Handbook of mentalization-based treatment* (pp. 185–200). West Sussex, England: John Wiley & Sons.

Bateman, A., & Fonagy, P. (2008). 8 year follow-up of patients treated for borderline personality disorder: Mentalization-based treatment versus treatment as usual. *American Journal of Psychiatry, 165,* 631–638.

Bateman, A., & Fonagy, P. (2009). Randomized controlled trial of outpatient mentalization-based treatment versus structured clinical management for borderline personality disorder. *American Journal of Psychiatry, 166,* 1355–1364.

Bateman, A., & Fonagy, P. (2012). *Handbook of mentalizing in mental health practice.* Washington, DC: American Psychiatric Publishing.

Bauer, P. J. (1996). What do infants recall of their lives? Memory for specific events by one- to two-year olds. *American Psychologist, 51*(1), 29–41.

Beck, A. T., Rush, J., Shaw, B. F., & Emery, G. (1979). *Cognitive therapy of depression.* New York, NY: Guilford Press.

Beck, A. T., Ward, C. H., Mendelson, M., Mock, J., & Erbaugh, J. (1961). An inventory for measuring depression, *Archives of General Psychiatry, 4,* 561–571.

Becker-Stoll, F., & Fremmer-Bombik, E. (1997, April). *Adolescent–mother interaction and attachment: A longitudinal study.* Paper presented at the biennial meeting of the Society for Research in Child Development, Washington, DC.

Beebe, B. (2004). Faces in relation: A case study. *Psychoanalytic Dialogues, 14,* 1–51.

Beebe, B. (2005). Mother–infant research informs mother–infant treatment. *The Psychoanalytic Study of the Child, 60,* 7–46.

Beebe, B., Knoblauch, S., Rustin, J., & Sorter, D. (2005). *Forms of intersubjectivity in infant research and adult treatment.* New York, NY: Other Press.

Beebe, B., & Lachmann, F. M. (1994). Representation and internalization in infancy: Three principles of salience. *Psychoanalytic Psychology, 11*(2), 127–165.

Beebe, B., & Lachmann, F. M. (2002). *Infant research and adult treatment: Co-constructing interactions.* New York, NY: Analytic Press.

Beebe, B., & Lachmann, F. M. (2014). *The origins of attachment: Infant research and adult treatment.* East Sussex, England: Routledge.

Bell, S. M. (1970). The development of the concept of the object as related to infant–mother attachment. *Child Development, 40*(2), 291–311.

Belsky, J. (1999). Modern evolutionary theory and patterns of attachment. In J. Cassidy & P. R. Shaver (Eds.), *Handbook of attachment: Theory, research, and clinical applications* (pp. 141–161). New York, NY: Guilford Press.

Belsky, J., & Fearon, R. M. P. (2008). Precursors of attachment security. In J. Cassidy & P. R. Shaver (Eds.), *Handbook of attachment: Theory, research, and clinical applications* (2nd ed., pp. 295–316). New York, NY: Guilford Press.

Belsky, J., Gilstrap, B., & Rovine, M. (1984). The Pennsylvania infant and family development project: I. Stability and change in mother–infant and father–infant interaction in a family setting at one, three, and nine months. *Child Development, 55*(3), 692–706.

Belsky, J., & Isabella, R. A. (1988). Maternal, infant, and social-contextual determinants of attachment security. In J. Belsky & T. Nezworski (Eds.), *Clinical implications of attachment.* Hillsdale, NJ: Erlbaum.

Bender, L., & Yarnell, H. (1941). An observation nursery. *American Journal of Psychiatry, 97,* 1158–1174.

Benoit, D., & Parker, K. C. H. (1994). Stability and transmission of attachment across three generations. *Child Development, 65*(5), 1444–1456.

Berant, E., Mikulincer, M., & Shaver, P. R. (2008). Attachment style, mental health and intergenerational transmission of emotional problems: A seven-year study of mothers and children with congenital heart disease. *Journal of Personality, 76*(1), 31–66.

Berry, K., Barrowclough, C., & Wearden, A. (2007). A review of the role of attachment style in psychosis: Unexplored issues and questions for further research. *Clinical Psychology Review, 27*(4), 458–475.

Beutler, L. E., & Clarkin, J. F. (1990). *Systematic treatment selection: Towards targeted therapeutic interventions.* New York, NY: Brunner/Mazel.

Blake, D. D., Weathers, F. W., Nagy, L. M., Kaloupek, D. G., Gusman, F. D., Charney, D. S., & Keane, T. M. (1995). The development of a clinician-administered PTSD scale. *Journal of Traumatic Stress, 8,* 75–90.

Blake, D. D., Weathers, F. W., Nagy, L. M., Kaloupek, D. G., Klauminzer, G., Charney, D. S., . . . Buckley, T. C. (2000). *Clinician-Administered PTSD Scale (CAPS) instruction manual.* Boston, MA: National Center for PTSD.

Blatz, W. E. (1966). *Human security: Some reflections.* Toronto, Ontario, Canada: University of Toronto Press.

Bohm, D. (1980). *Wholeness and the implicate order.* New York, NY: Routledge & Kegan Paul.

Book, H. E. (1998). *How to practice brief psychodynamic psychotherapy: The Core Conflictual Relationship Theme mode.* Washington, DC: American Psychological Association Press.

Bordin, E. S. (1980). *Of human bonds that bind or free.* Presidential address delivered at the meeting of the Society for Psychotherapy Research, Pacific Grove, CA.

Bosquet, M., & Egeland, B. (2006). The development and maintenance of anxiety symptoms from infancy through adolescence in a longitudinal sample. *Development and psychopathology, 18*(2), 517–550.

Bowlby, J. (1940). The influence of early environment in the development of neurosis and neurotic character. *International Journal of Psycho-Analysis, 1,* 154–178.

Bowlby, J. (1944). Forty-four juvenile thieves: Their characters and home-life. *International Journal of Psychoanalysis, 25,* 154–178.

Bowlby, J. (1951). Maternal care and mental health. Geneva, Switzerland: *World Health Organization Monograph Series* (2).

Bowlby, J. (1958). The nature of the child's tie to his mother. *International Journal of Psychoanalysis, 39,* 350–373.

Bowlby, J. (1969/1982). *Attachment and loss: Vol. 1. Attachment.* New York, NY: Basic Books.

Bowlby, J. (1973). *Attachment and loss: Vol. 2. Separation.* New York: Basic Books.

Bowlby, J. (1977). The making and breaking of affectional bonds. *British Journal of Psychiatry, 130,* 421–431.

Bowlby, J. (1979). *The making and breaking of affectional bonds.* London, England: Tavistock.

Bowlby, J. (1980a). *Attachment and loss: Vol. 3. Loss.* New York, NY: Basic Books.

Bowlby, J. (1980b). *Loss: Sadness and depression.* New York, NY: Basic Books.

Bowlby, J. (1988). *A secure base: Parent–child attachment and healthy human development.* New York, NY: Basic Books.

Bradshaw, J. (1990). *Homecoming: Reclaiming and championing your inner child.* New York, NY: Bantam Books.

Brennan, K. A., Clark, C. L., & Shaver, P. R. (1998). Self-report measurement of adult attachment: An integrative view. In J. A. Simpson & W. S. Rholes (Eds.), *Attachment theory and close relationships* (pp. 46–76). New York, NY: Guilford Press.

Brennan, K. A., & Shaver, P. R. (1995). Dimensions of adult attachment, affect regulation, and romantic relationship functioning. *Personality and Social Psychology Bulletin, 21*(3), 267–283.

Brennan, K. A., & Shaver, P.R. (1998). Attachment styles and personality disorders: Their connections to each other and to parental divorce, parental death, and perceptions of parental caregiving. *Journal of Personality, 66*(5), 835-878.

Brennan, K. A., Shaver, P. R., & Tobey, A. E. (1991). Attachment styles, gender, and parental problem drinking. *Journal of Social and Personal Relationships, 8,* 451–466.

Bretherton, I., & Munholland, K. A. (2008). Internal working models in attachment relationships: Elaborating a central construct in attachment theory. In J. Cassidy & P. R. Shaver (Eds.), *Handbook of attachment: Theory, research, and clinical applications* (2nd ed., pp. 102–127). New York, NY: Guilford Press.

Briere, J., Elliott, D. M., Harris, K., & Cotman, A. (1995). Trauma Symptom Inventory: Psychometrics and association with childhood and adult victimization in clinical samples. *Journal of Interpersonal Violence, 10,* 387–401.

Brisch, K. H. (2012). *Treating attachment disorders: From theory to therapy* (2nd ed.). New York, NY: Guilford Press.

Brody, H. (1989). Transparency: Informed consent in primary care. *Hastings Center Report, 19*(5), 5–9.

Brown, D. P. (1993). Affective development, psychopathology, and adaptation. In S. L. Ablon, D. Brown, E. J. Khantzian, & J. E. Mack (Eds.), *Human feelings: Explorations in affect development and meaning* (pp. 5–66). Hillsdale, NJ: Analytic Press.

Brown, D. P. (2001, December). *Attachment and trauma: Long term effects.* Presentation at Harvard Medical School, Boston, MA.

Brown, D. P., & Fromm, E. F. (1986). *Hypnotherapy and hypnoanalysis.* Hillsdale, NJ: Erlbaum.

Brown, D. P., & Scheflin, A. W. (1999, Fall/Winter). Factitious disorders and trauma-related diagnoses, *Journal of Psychiatry and Law, 27*(3–4), 373–422.

Brown, D. P., Scheflin, A. W., & Hammond, D. C. (1999). *Memory, trauma-treatment, and the law.* New York, NY: W. W. Norton.

Brown, T. A., Antony, M. M., & Barlow, D. H. (1992). Psychometric properties of the Penn State Worry Questionnaire in a clinical anxiety disorders sample. *Behavior Research and Therapy, 30,* 33–37.

Bursten, B. (1965). On Munchausen's syndrome. *Archives of General Psychiatry, 13,* 261–268.

Burt, R. (1979). *Taking care of strangers: The rule of law in doctor–patient relations.* New York, NY: Free Press.

Campbell, L., Simpson, J. A., Boldry, J., & Kashy, D. A. (2005). Perceptions of conflict and support in romantic relationships: The role of attachment anxiety. *Journal of Personality and Social Psychology, 88*(3), 510–531.

Carlson, E. A. (1998). A prospective longitudinal study of disorganization/disorientation. *Child Development, 69*(4), 1107–1128.

Carnes, P. J. (1997). *The betrayal bond: Breaking free of exploitive relationships.* Deerfield Beach, FL: HCI.

Cassidy, J. (2008). The nature of the child's ties. In J. Cassidy & P. R. Shaver (Eds.), *Handbook of attachment: Theory, research, and clinical applications* (2nd ed., pp. 3–220). New York, NY: Guilford Press.

Cassidy, J., Kirsh, S. J., Scolton, K. I., & Parke, R. D. (1996). Attachment and representations of peer relationships. *Developmental Psychology, 32*(5), 892–904.

Cassidy, J., & Kobak, R. R. (1988). Avoidance and its relationship with other defensive processes. In J. Belsky & T. Nezworski (Eds.), *Clinical implications of attachment* (pp. 300–323). Hillsdale, NJ: Erlbaum.

Cassidy, J., & Marvin, R. S., with the MacArthur Working Group on Attachment (1992). *Attachment organization in three and four year olds: Procedures and coding manual.* Unpublished manuscript, University of Virginia.

Chambless, D. L., Caputo, G. C., Bright, P., & Gallagher, R. (1990). Assessment of fear in agoraphobics: The Body Sensations Questionnaire and the Agoraphobic Cognitions Questionnaire. *Journal of Consulting and Clinical Psychology, 52,* 1090-1097.

Charcot, J. M. (1886). *Maladies du système nerveux. Oeuvres completes, tome premier.* Paris, France: Bureaux du Progrès Médical.

Chess, S., & Thomas, A. (1982). Infant bonding: Mystique and reality. *American Journal of Orthopsychiatry, 52*(2), 213–222.

Chisholm, K. (1998). A three year follow-up of attachment and indiscriminate friendliness in children adopted from Russian orphanages. *Child Development, 69,* 1092–1106.

Ciechanowski, P. S., Walker, E. A., Katon, W. J., & Russo, J. E. (2002). Attachment theory: A model for health care utilization and somatization. *Psychosomatic Medicine, 64*(4), 660–667.

Clark, L. A., & Watson, D. (1991). Tripartite model of anxiety and depression: Psychometric evidence and taxonomic implications. *Journal of Abnormal Psychology, 100*(3), 316–336.

Clarkin, J. F. (1996). Treatment of personality disorders. *British Journal of Clinical Psychology, 35*(4), 641–642.

Cloitre, M., Koenen, K. C., Cohen, L. R., & Han, H. (2002). Skills training in affective and interpersonal regulation followed by exposure: A phase-based treatment for PTSD related to childhood abuse. *Journal of Consulting and Clinical Psychology, 70*(5), 1067–1074.

Coe, M., Dalenberg, C., Aransky, K., & Reto, C. (1995). An adult attachment style: Reported childhood violence history and types of dissociative experiences. *Dissociation, 8,* 142–154.

Cogan, R., & Porcelli, J. H. (1996). Object relations in abusive partner relationships: An empirical investigation. *Journal of Personality Assessment, 66*(1), 106–115.

Cole-Detke, H., & Kobak, R. (1996). Attachment in eating disorder and depression. *Journal of Consulting and Clinical Psychology, 64*(2), 282–290.

Collins, N. L. (1996). Working models of attachment: Implications for explanation, emotion, and behavior. *Journal of Personality and Social Psychology, 71*(4), 810–832.

Collins, N. L., & Read, S. J. (1990). Adult attachment, working models and relationship quality in dating couples. *Journal of Personality and Social Psychology, 58*(4), 644–663.

Collins, N. L., & Read, S. J. (1994). Cognitive representations of attachment: The structure and function of working models. In K. Bartholomew & D. Perlman (Eds.), *Advances in personal relationships: Vol. 5. Attachment processes in adulthood* (pp. 53–90). London, England: Jessica Kingsley.

Commons, M. L., Armon, C., Kohlberg, L., Richards, F. A., Grotzer, T. A., & Sinnott, J. D. (1990). *Adult development: Vol. 2. Models and methods in the study of adolescent and adult thought.* New York, NY: Praeger.

Commons, M. L., Danaher, D., Miller, P. M., & Dawson, T. L. (2000, June). *The Hierarchical Complexity Scoring System: How to score anything.* Paper presented at the annual meeting of the Society for Research in Adult Development, New York, NY.

Commons, M. L., Richards, F. A., & Armon, C. (1984). *Beyond formal operations: Late adolescent and adult cognitive development.* New York, NY: Praeger.

Commons, M. L., Richards, F. A., & Kuhn, D. (1982). Systematic and metasystematic reasoning: A case for levels of reasoning beyond Piaget's stage of formal operations. *Child Development, 53*(4), 1058–1069.

Commons, M. L., Sinnott, J. D., Richards, F. A., & Armon, C. (1989). *Adult development: Vol. 1. Comparisons and applications of developmental models.* Westport, CT: Praeger.

Cook-Greuter, S. R. (1985/2013). *Nine levels of increasing embrace in ego development: A full-spectrum theory of vertical growth and meaning-making.* Unpublished manuscript, available at www.cook-greuter.com.

Cook-Greuter, S. R. (1990). Maps for living: Ego-development stages from symbiosis to conscious universal embeddedness. In M. L. Commons, C. Armon, L. Kohlberg, F. A. Richards, T. A. Grotzer, & J. D. Sinnott (Eds.), *Adult development: Vol. 2.: Models and methods in the study of adolescent and adult thought* (pp. 79–104). New York, NY: Praeger.

Cook-Greuter, S. R. (1994). Transcendence of mature thought. In M. E. Miller & S.R. Cook-Greuter (Eds.), *Transcendence and mature thought in adulthood: The further reaches of adult development* (pp. 119–146). Lanham, MD: Rowman & Littlefield.

Cook-Greuter, S. R. (1999). *Postautonomous ego development: A study of its nature and measurement.* Doctoral Dissertation Harvard University. Originally UMI Dissertation Services #933122; republished (2010) Integral Publishers: Dissertation series. ISBN: 978-1-4507-2515-6.

Cook-Greuter, S. R. (2000). Mature ego development: A gateway to ego transcendence? *Journal of Adult Development, 7*(4), 227–240.

Copeland, D. R. (1986). The application of object-relations theory to the hypnotherapy of developmental arrests: The borderline patient. *International Journal of Clinical and Experimental Hypnosis, 34*(3), 157–168.

Cortina, M., & Liotti, G. (2010). The intersubjective and cooperative origins of consciousness: An evolutionary-developmental approach. *Journal of the American Academy of Psychoanalysis and Dynamic Psychiatry, 38*(2), 291–314.

Cotton, N. S. (1983). The development of self-esteem and self-esteem regulation. In J. E. Mack

& S. L. Ablon (Eds.), *The development and sustenance of self-esteem in childhood* (pp. 122–150). New York, NY: International Universities Press.

Craik, K. (1943). *The nature of explanation.* Cambridge, England: Cambridge University Press.

Cramer, B., Gershberg, M. R., & Stern, M. (1971). Munchausen syndrome: Its relationship to malingering, hysteria, and the physician–patient relationship. *Archives of General Psychiatry, 24*(6), 573–578.

Crittenden, P. M. (1985a). Maltreated infants: Vulnerability and resilience. *Journal of Child Psychology and Psychiatry, 26*(1), 85–96.

Crittenden, P. M. (1985b). Social networks, quality of child-rearing, and child development. *Child Development, 56*(5), 1299–1313.

Crittenden, P. M. (1992a). *Preschool assessment and attachment.* Unpublished manuscript, Family Relations Institute, Miami, FL.

Crittenden, P. M. (1992b). The quality of attachment in the preschool years. *Development and Psychopathology, 4*(2), 209–241.

Crittenden, P. M. (1995). Attachment and psychopathology. In S. Goldberg, R. Muir, & J. Kerr (Eds.), *John Bowlby's attachment theory: Historical, clinical, and social significance* (pp. 367–406). New York, NY: Analytic Press.

Crittenden, P. M. (2000a). A dynamic-maturational approach to continuity and change in pattern of attachment. In P. M. Crittenden & A. H. Claussen (Eds.), *The organization of attachment relationships: Maturation, culture, and context* (343–357). New York, NY: Cambridge University Press.

Crittenden, P. M. (2000b). A dynamic-maturational exploration of the meaning of security and adaptation: Empirical, cultural, and theoretical considerations. In P. M. Crittenden & A. H. Claussen (Eds.), *The organization of attachment relationships: Maturation, culture, and context* (pp. 358–384). New York, NY: Cambridge University Press.

Crittenden, P. M. (2005). Attachment theory, psychopathology, and psychotherapy: The dynamic-maturational approach. *Psicoterapia, 30,* 171–182. Retrieved from http://familyrelationsinstitute.org/include/docs/attachment_theory_2005.pdf

Crittenden, P. M. (2007). *Modified Adult Attachment Interview.* Unpublished manuscript, Miami, FL.

Crittenden, P. M. (2008). *Raising parents: Attachment, parenting and child safety.* New York, NY: Routledge.

Crittenden, P. M. (2015). *Raising parents: Attachment, representation, and treatment* (2nd ed.). London, England: Routledge.

Crittenden, P. M., & Ainsworth, M. D. S. (1989). Child maltreatment and attachment theory. In D. Cicchetti & V. Carlson (Eds.), *Handbook of child maltreatment* (pp. 432–463). New York, NY: Cambridge University Press.

Crittenden, P. M., & Dallos, R. (2014). An attachment approach to treatment: DMM-FST integrative treatment. *Child and Family Clinical Psychology Review, 2,* 53–61.

Crittenden, P. M., Dallos, R., Landini, A., & Kozlowska, K. (2014). *Attachment and family therapy.* Berkshire, England: Open University Press.

Crittenden, P. M., & Landini, A. (2011). *Assessing adult attachment: A dynamic-maturational approach to discourse analysis.* New York, NY: W. W. Norton.

Crittenden, P. M., & Newman, L. (2010). Comparing models of borderline personality disorder: Mother's experience, self-protective strategies, and dispositional representations. *Clinical Child Psychology and Psychiatry, 15*(3), 433–451.

Crowell, J. A., Fraley, R. C., & Shaver, P. R. (1999). Measurement of individual differences in adolescent and adult attachment. In J. Cassidy & P. R. Shaver (Eds.), *Handbook of attachment: Theory, research, and clinical applications* (pp. 434–465). New York, NY: Guilford Press.

Crowell, J. A., & Owens, G. (1998). *Manual for the Current Relationship Interview and scoring system, Version 4.0.* Unpublished manuscript, State University of New York at Stony Brook.

Crowell, J. A., & Treboux, D. (1995). A review of adult attachment measures: Implications for theory and research. *Social Development, 4*(3), 294–327.

Crowell, J. A., Treboux, D., & Waters, E. (1999). The Adult Attachment Interview and the Relationship Questionnaire: Relations to reports of mothers and partners. *Personal Relationships, 6*(1), 1–18.

Crowell, J. A., & Waters, E. (1995, March 30–April 2). *Is the parent–child relationship prototype of later love relationships? Studies of attachment and working models of attachment.* Poster symposium presented at the Society for Research in Child Development, Indianapolis, IN.

Csikszentmihalyi, M. (1990). *Flow: The psychology of optimal experience.* New York, NY: Harper & Row.

Cyranowski, J. M., Bookwala, J., Feske, U., Houck, P., Pilkonis, P., Kostelnik, B., & Frank, E. (2002). Adult attachment profiles, interpersonal difficulties, and response to interpersonal psychotherapy in women with recurrent major depression. *Journal of Social and Clinical Psychology, 21*(2), 191–217.

Dawson, T. L. (2004). Assessing intellectual development: Three approaches, one sequence. *Journal of Adult Development, 11,* 71–85.

Dawson, T. L., & Wilson, M. (2004). The LAAS: A computerized developmental scoring system for small- and large-scale assessments. *Educational Assessment, 9,* 153–191.

DeJong, M. L. (1992). Attachment, individuation, and risk of suicide in late adolescence. *Journal of Youth and Adolescence, 21*(3), 357–373.

Dennett, D. (1978). *Brainstorms.* Cambridge, MA: MIT Press.

Dennett, D. (1987). *The intentional stance.* Cambridge, MA: MIT Press.

Depue, R. A., & Lenzenweger, M. F. (2001). A neurobehavioral dimensional model. In W. J. Livesley (Ed.), *Handbook of personality disorders: Theory, research and treatment* (pp. 136–176). New York, NY: Guilford Press.

Derryberry, D., & Rothbart, M. K. (1988). Arousal, affect and attention as components of temperament. *Journal of Personality and Social Psychology, 55*(6), 958–966.

de Young, M., & Lowry, J.A. (1992). Traumatic bonding: Clinical implications in incest. *Child Welfare, 71*(2), 165–176.

Dickinson, K. A, & Pincus, A. L. (2003). Interpersonal analysis of grandiose and vulnerable narcissism. *Journal of Personality Disorders, 17,* 188–207.

Diehl, M., Elnick, A. B., Bourbeau, L. S., & Labouvie-Vief, G. (1998). Adult attachment styles: Their relations to family context and personality. *Journal of Personality and Social Psychology, 74*(6), 1656–1669.

Dimaggio, G., Semerari, A., Carcione, A., Nicolò, G., & Procacci, M. (2007). *Psychotherapy of personality disorders: Metacognition, states of mind and interpersonal cycles.* New York, NY: Routledge.

Doron, G., Moulding, R., Kyrios, M., Nedeljkovic, M., & Mikulincer, M. (2009). Adult attachment insecurities are related to obsessive-compulsive phenomena. *Journal of Social and Clinical Psychology, 28,* 1022–1049.

Dozier, M. (1990). Attachment organization and treatment use for adults with serious psychopathological disorders. *Development and Psychotherapy, 2*(1), 47–60.

Dozier, M., & Kobak, R. R. (1992). Psychophysiology in attachment interviews: Converging evidence for deactivating strategies. *Child Development, 63*(6), 1473–1480.

Dozier, M., & Lee, S. W. (1995). Discrepancies between self- and other-report of psychiatric symptomatology: Effects of dismissing attachment strategies. *Development and Psychopathology, 7*(1), 217–226.

Dozier, M., Stevenson, A. L., Lee, S. W., & Velligan, D. I. (1991). Attachment organization and familial over-involvement for adults with serious psychopathological disorders. *Development and Psychopathology, 3*(4), 475–489.

Dozier, M., Stovall-McClough, K. C., & Albus, K. E. (2008). Attachment and psychopathology in adulthood. In J. Cassidy & P. R. Shaver (Eds.), *Handbook of attachment: Theory, research, and clinical applications* (2nd ed., pp. 718–744). New York, NY: Guilford Press.

Durrett, M. E., Otaki, M., & Richards, P. (1984). Attachment and the mother's perception of support from the father. *International Journal of Behavioral Development, 7*(2), 167–176.

Dutton, D. G., & Painter, S. L. (1981). Traumatic bonding: The development of emotional attachments in battered women and other relationships of intermittent abuse. *Victimology, 6*(1–4), 139–155.

Eagle, M. N. (2013). *Attachment and psychoanalysis: Theory, research, and clinical implications.* New York: Guilford.

Ehlers, W., & Plassmann, R. (1994). Diagnosis of narcissistic self-esteem regulation in patients with factitious illness (Munchausen syndrome). *Psychotherapy and Psychosomatics, 62*(1–2), 69–77.

Ein-Dor, T., & Doron, G. (2015). Attachment and psychopathology. In J. A. Simpson and W. S. Rholes (Eds.), *Attachment, theory and research: New directions and emerging themes* (pp. 346–373). New York, NY: Guilford Press.

Ein-Dor, T., Doron, G., Solomon, Z., Mikulincer, M., & Shaver, P. (2010). Together in pain: Attachment-related dyadic processes and posttraumatic stress disorder. *Journal of Clinical and Counseling Psychology, 57*(3), 317–327.

Eisendrath, S. J. (1984). Factitious illness: A clarification. *Psychosomatics, 25*(2), 110–117.

Emmons, R. A. (1999). *The psychology of ultimate concerns: Motivation and spirituality in personality.* New York, NY: Guilford Press.

Engler, J. (1986). Therapeutic aims in psychotherapy and meditation. In K. Wilber, J. Engler, & D. Brown (Eds.), *Transformations of consciousness* (pp. 17–51). Boston, MA: Shambhala.

Erickson, E. H. (1979). *Identity and the life cycle.* New York, NY: W. W. Norton.

Farber, B. A., & Metzger, J. A. (2009). The therapist as a secure base. In J. H. Obegi and E. Berant (Eds.), *Attachment theory and research in clinical work* (pp. 46–70). New York, NY: Guilford Press.

Farina, B., Speranza, A. M., Ditoni, S., Gnoni, V., Trentini, C., Vergano, C. M., . . . Della Marca, G. M. (2014). Memories of attachment hamper EEG cortical connectivity in dissociative patients. *European Archives of Psychiatry and Clinical Neuroscience, 264*(5), 449–458.

Farnfield, S., Hautamäki, A., Nørbech, P., & Sahhar, N. (2010). DMM assessments of attachment and adaptation: Procedures, validity, and utility. *Clinical Child Psychology and Psychiatry, 15*, 313-328.

Feeney, J. A. (2008). Adult romantic attachment: Developments in the study of couple relationships. In J. Cassidy and P. R. Shaver (Eds.), *Handbook of attachment: Theory, research, and clinical applications* (2nd ed., pp. 456–481). New York, NY: Guilford Press.

Feeney, J. A., & Noller, P. (1990). Attachment style as a predictor of adult romantic relationships. *Journal of Personality and Social Psychology, 58*(2), 281–291.

Feeney, J. A., Noller, P., & Callan, V. J. (1994). Attachment style, communication, and satisfaction in the early years of marriage. In K. Bartholomew & D. Perlman (Eds.), *Advances in personal relationships: Vol. 5. Attachment processes in adulthood* (pp. 269–308). London, England: Jessica Kingsley.

Feeney, J. A., Noller, P., & Hanrahan, M. (1994). Assessing adult attachment. In M. B. Sperling & W. H. Berman (Eds.), *Attachment in adults: Clinical and developmental perspectives* (pp. 128–152). New York, NY: Guilford Press.

Field, T. M. (1978). The three R's of infant–adult interactions. *Journal of Pediatric Psychology, 3,* 131–136.

First, M. B., Gibbon, M., Spitzer, R. L., Williams, J. B. W., & Benjamin, L. S. (1997). *Structured Clinical Interview for DSM-IV Axis II Personality Disorders, (SCID-II)* Personality Questionnaire. SCID-II Scoring Booklet. Washington, DC: American Psychiatric Press.

First, M., Spitzer, R., Gibbon, M., & Williams, J. (1997). *User's guide for the Structured Clinical Interview for DSM-IV Axis I Disorders: Clinician Version.* Washington, DC: American Psychiatric Press.

Flavell, J. H. (1979). Metacognition and cognitive monitoring: A new area of cognitive-developmental inquiry. *American Psychologist, 34*(10), 906–911.

Flavell, J. H. (1986). The development of children's knowledge about the appearance–reality distinction. *American Psychologist, 41*(4), 418–424.

Flavell, J. H., Flavell, E. R., & Green, F. L. (1983). Development of the appearance–reality distinction. *Cognitive Psychology, 15,* 95–120.

Flores, P. J. (2004). *Addiction as an attachment disorder.* New York, NY: Jason Aronson.

Folks, D. G., & Freeman, A. M. (1985). Munchausen's syndrome and other factitious illness. *Psychiatric Clinics of North America, 8*(2), 263–278.

Fonagy, P. (2013). Commentary on "Letters from Ainsworth: Contesting the 'organization' of attachment. *Journal of the Canadian Academy of Child and Adolescent Psychiatry, 22,* 178-179.

Fonagy, P., & Bateman, A. W. (2006). Mechanisms of change in mentalization-based treatment of BPD. *Journal of Clinical Psychology, 62,* 411–430.

Fonagy, P., Gergely, G., Jurist, E. L., & Target, M. (2002). *Affect regulation, mentalization, and the development of the self.* New York, NY: Other Press.

Fonagy, P., Leigh, T., Steele, M., Steele, H., Kennedy, R., Mattoon, G., Target, M., & Gerber, A. (1996). The relation of attachment status, psychiatric classification, and response to psychotherapy. *Journal of Consulting and Clinical Psychology, 64*(1), 22–31.

Fonagy, P., Steele, H., & Steele, M. (1991). Maternal representations of attachment during pregnancy predict the organization of infant–mother attachment at one year of age. *Child Development, 62,* 891–905.

Fonagy, P., Steele, M., Steele, H., Leigh, T., Kennedy, R., Mattoon, G., & Target, M. (1995). Attachment, the reflective self, and borderline states: The predictive specificity of the Adult Attachment Interview and pathological emotional development. In S. Goldberg, R. Muir, & J. Kerr (Eds.), *Attachment theory: Social, developmental and clinical perspectives* (pp. 233–278). New York, NY: Analytic Press.

Fonagy, P., Steele, M., Steele, H., Moran, G. S., & Higgitt, A. C. (1991). The capacity for understanding mental states: The reflective self in parent and child and its significance for security of attachment. *Infant Mental Health Journal, 12*(3), 201–218.

Fonagy, P., & Target, M. (1997). Attachment and reflective function: Their role in self-organization. *Development & and Psychopathology, 9,*, 679–-700.

Fonagy, P., Target, M., Steele, H., & Steele, M. (1998). *Reflective functioning manual (Version 5).* Unpublished manuscript. University College, London.

Fonagy, P., Target, M., Steele, M., Steele, H., Leigh, T., Levinson, A., & Kennedy, R. (1997). Morality, disruptive behavior, borderline personality disorder, crime, and their relationship to security of attachment. In L. Atkinson & K. Zucker (Eds.), *Attachment and psychopathology* (pp. 223–274). New York, NY: Guilford Press.

Fosha, D. (2000). *The transforming power of affect.* New York, NY: Basic Books.

Fosha, D. (2003). Dyadic regulation and experiential work with emotion and relatedness in trauma and disorganized attachment. In M. F. Solomon & D. J. Siegel (Eds.), *Healing trauma* (pp. 221–281). New York, NY: W. W. Norton.

Fosha, D. (2008). Transformance, recognition of self by self, and effective action. In K. J. Schneider (Ed.), *Existential-integrative psychotherapy: Guideposts to the core of practice* (pp. 290–320). New York, NY: Routledge.

Fosha, D. (2009a). Emotion and recognition at work: Energy, vitality, pleasure, truth, desire and the emergent phenomenology of transformational experience. In D. Fosha, D. J. Siegel, & M. F. Solomon (Eds.), *The healing power of emotion: Affective neuroscience, development, and clinical practice* (pp. 172–203). New York, NY: W. W. Norton.

Fosha, D. (2009b). Healing attachment trauma with attachment (and then some!). In M. Kerman (Ed.), *Clinical pearls of wisdom: 21 leading therapists offer their key insights* (pp. 43–56). New York, NY: W. W. Norton.

Fosha, D. (2014, October). *AEDP: Undoing aloneness and the transformation of emotional suffering.* Workshop given in Stockholm, Sweden.

Fraley, R. C., & Davis, K. E. (1997). Attachment formation and transfer in young adults' close friendships and romantic relationships. *Personal Relationships, 4*(2), 131–144.

Fraley, R. C., Fazzare, D. A., Bonanno, G. A., & Dekel, S. (2006). Attachment and psychological adaption in high exposure survivors of the September 11, attack on the World Trade Center. *Personality and Social Psychology Bulletin, 32*(4), 538–551.

Fraley, R. C., Garner, J. P., & Shaver, P. R. (2000). Adult attachment and the defensive regulation of attention and memory: Examining the role of preemptive and postemptive defensive processes. *Journal of Personality and Social Psychology, 79*(5), 816–826.

Fraley, R. C., & Shaver, P. R. (1997). Adult attachment and the suppression of unwanted thoughts. *Journal of Personality and Social Psychology,* 73(5), 1080–1091.

Fraley, R. C., & Waller, N. G. (1998). Adult attachment patterns: A test of the typological model. In J. A. Simpson & W. S. Rholes (Eds.), *Attachment theory and close relationships.* (pp. 77–114). New York, NY: Guilford Press.

Fraley, R. C., Waller, N. G., & Brennan, K. A. (2000). An item response theory analysis of self-report measures of adult attachment. *Journal of Personality and Social Psychology, 78*(2), 350–365.

Frank, J. D. (1963). *Persuasion and healing: A comparative study of psychotherapy.* New York, NY: Schocken.

French, T. M. (1952). *The integration of behavior: Vol. 1. Basic postulates.* Chicago, IL: University of Chicago Press.

Frodi, A., Dernevik, M., Sepa, A., Philipson, J., & Bragesjo, M. (2001). Current attachment representations of incarcerated offenders varying in degree of psychopathy. *Attachment & Human Development, 3*(3), 269–283.

Geisen-Bloo, J., van Dyck, R., Spinhoven, P., van Tilburg, W., Dirksen, C., van Asselt, T., . . . Arntz, A. (2006). Outpatient psychotherapy for borderline personality disorder. *Archives of General Psychiatry, 63,* 649–658.

Geller, J. D., Behrends, R., Hartley, D., Farber, B. A., & Rohde, A. (1992). *The therapist representation inventory II.* Unpublished manuscript, Yale University, New Haven, CT.

Geller, J., & Farber, B. (1993). Factors influencing the process of internalization in psychotherapy. *Psychotherapy Research, 3*(3), 166–180.

Gendlin, E. T. (1982). *Focusing* (2nd Rev. ed.). New York, NY: Bantam Books.

Gendlin, E. T. (1997). *Experiencing and the creation of meaning: A philosophical and psychological approach to the subjective.* Chicago, IL: Northwestern University Press.

George, C., Kaplan, N., & Main, M. (1996). *Adult Attachment Interview protocol* (3rd ed.). Unpublished manuscript, University of California, Berkeley.

George, C., & Solomon, J. (1996). Representational models of relationships: Links between caregiving and attachment. *Infant Mental Health Journal, 17,* 198-216.

George, C., & Solomon, J. (1999). Attachment and caregiving: The caregiving behavioral systems approach. In J. Cassidy & P. R. Shaver (Eds.), *Handbook of attachment: Theory, research, and clinical applications* (pp. 649–670). New York, NY: Guilford Press.

George, C., & Solomon, J. (2008). The caregiving system: A behavioral systems approach to parenting. In J. Cassidy & P. R. Shaver (Eds.), *Handbook of attachment: Theory, research, and clinical applications* (2nd ed., pp. 833–856). New York, NY: Guilford Press.

George, C., & West, M. L. (2012). *The adult attachment projective picture system.* New York, NY: Guilford Press.

Gergely, G., & Watson, J. S. (1996). The social biofeedback model of parental affect-mirroring. *International Journal of Psychoanalysis, 77*(6), 1181–1212.

Gilbert, P. (1989). *Human nature and suffering.* East Sussex, England: Erlbaum.

Goossens, F. A., & van IJzendoorn, M. H. (1990). Quality of infants' attachments to professional caregivers: Relation to infant–parent attachment and day-care characteristics. *Child Development, 61*(3), 832–837.

Gopnik, A., & Astington, J. W. (1988). Children's understanding of representational change and its relation to the understanding of false belief and the appearance–reality distinction. *Child Development, 59,* 26–37.

Gopnik, A., & Graf, P. (1988). Knowing how you know: Young children's ability to identify and remember the sources of their beliefs. *Child Development, 59*(1), 1366–1371.

Greenspan, S., & Lourie, R. S. (1981). Developmental structuralist approach to the classification of adaptive and pathological personality organizations. *American Journal of Psychiatry, 138*(6), 725–735.

Grice, H. P. (1975). Logic and conversation. In P. Cole & J. L. Moran (Eds.), *Syntax and semantics: Vol. 3. Speech acts* (pp. 41–58). New York, NY: Academic Press.

Grice, H. P. (1989). *Studies in the way of words.* Cambridge, MA: Harvard University Press.

Griffin, D. W., & Bartholomew, K. (1994). Models of self and other: Fundamental dimensions underlying measures of adult attachment. *Journal of Personality and Social Psychology, 67*(3), 430–445.

Grossmann, K. (1989, September). *Avoidance as a communicative strategy in attachment relationships.* Paper presented at the fourth world congress of the World Association of Infant Psychiatry and Allied Disciplines, Lugano, Switzerland.

Grossmann, K. E., & Grossmann, K. (1991). Attachment quality as an organizer of emotional and behavioral responses in a longitudinal perspective. In C. M. Parkes, J. Stevenson-Hinde, & P. Marris (Eds.), *Attachment across the life cycle* (pp. 93–114). New York, NY: Tavistock/Routledge.

Grossmann, K. E., Grossmann, K., & Waters, E. (Eds.) (2005). *Attachment from infancy to adulthood: The major longitudinal studies.* New York, NY: Guilford Press.

Gudjonsson, G. H. (1984). A new scale of interrogative suggestibility. *Personality and Individual Differences, 5,* 303–314.

Gunnar, M. R., Brodersen, L., Nachmias, M., Buss, K., & Rigatuso, J. (1996). Stress reactivity and attachment security. *Developmental Psychobiology, 29*(3), 191–204.

Haft, W., & Slade, A. (1989). Affect attunement and maternal attachment: A pilot study. *Infant Mental Health Journal, 10*(3), 157–172.

Hamilton, C. (2000). Continuity and discontinuity of attachment from infancy through adolescence. *Child Development, 71*(3), 690–694.

Hare, R. D. (1991). *Hare Psychopathy Checklist–Revised (PCL-R).* Toronto, Ontario, Canada: Multi-Health Systems.

Harlow, H. (1958). The nature of love. *American Psychologist, 3*(12), 673–685.

Harris, P. L., Donnelly, K., Guz, G. R., & Pitt-Watson, R. (1986). Children's understanding of the distinction between real and apparent emotion. *Child Development, 57*(4), 895–909.

Hart, S. D., Cox, D., & Hare, R. (1997). *Hare Psychopathy Checklist: Screening Version (PCL:SV).* Toronto, Ontario, Canada: Multi-Health Systems.

Hassan, S. (2000). *Releasing the bonds: Empowering people to think for themselves.* Newton, MA: Freedom of Mind Press.

Hassan, S. (2009). *Freedom of mind: Helping loved ones leave controlling people, cults, and beliefs.* Newton, MA: Freedom of Mind Press.

Havens, L. (1986). *Making contact: Uses of language in psychotherapy.* Cambridge, MA: Harvard University Press.

Hazen, C., & Shaver, P. R. (1987). Romantic love conceptualized as an attachment process. *Journal of Personality and Social Psychology, 52*(3), 511–524.

Hazen, C., & Shaver, P.R. (1990). Love and work: An attachment- theoretical perspective. *Journal of Personality and Social Psychology, 59*(2), 270–280.

Hazen, C., & Zeifman, D. (1999). Pair bonds as attachments. In J. Cassidy & P. R. Shaver (Eds.), *Handbook of attachment: Theory, research, and clinical applications* (pp. 336–354). New York, NY: Guilford Press.

Heard, D., Lake, B., & McCluskey, U. (2009). *Attachment therapy with adolescents and adults: Theory and practice post Bowlby.* London, England: Karnac Books.

Hedges, L. (1994). *Remembering, repeating, and working through childhood trauma.* Northvale, NJ: Aronson.

Henderson, A. J. Z., Bartholomew, K., & Dutton, D. G. (1997). He loves me; he loves me not: Attachment and separation resolution of abused women. *Journal of Family Violence, 12*(2), 169–191.

Hendrix, H. (1988). *Getting the love you want: A guide for couples.* New York, NY: Henry Holt.

Herman, J. L. (1992). *Trauma and recovery.* New York, NY: Basic Books.

Hesse, E. (1999). The Adult Attachment Interview: Historical and current perspectives. In J. Cassidy & P. R. Shaver (Eds.), *Handbook of attachment: Theory, research, and clinical applications* (pp. 395–433). New York, NY: Guilford Press.

Hesse, E. (2008). The Adult Attachment Interview: Protocol, methods of analysis, & empirical studies. In J. Cassidy & P. R. Shaver (Eds.), *Handbook of attachment: Theory, research, and clinical applications* (2nd ed., pp. 552–598). New York, NY: Guilford Press.

Hesse, E., & van IJzendoorn, M. H. (1999). Propensities towards absorption are related to lapse in the monitoring of reasoning or discourse during the Adult Attachment Interview: A preliminary investigation. *Attachment & Human Development, 1,* 67–91.

Holmes, J. (1994). Clinical implications of attachment theory. *British Journal of Psychotherapy, 11,* 62–76.

Holmes, J. (1996). *Attachment, intimacy, autonomy: Using attachment theory in adult psychotherapy.* Northvale, NJ: Jason Aronson.

Holmes, J. (2004). Disorganized attachment and borderline personality disorder: A clinical perspective. *Attachment & Human Development, 6*(2), 181–190.

Holmes, J. (2010). *Exploring in security: Towards an attachment-informed psychoanalytic psychotherapy.* New York, NY: Routledge.

Horowitz, L. M., Rosenberg, S. E., & Bartholomew, K. (1993). Interpersonal problems, attachment styles, and outcome in brief dynamic psychotherapy. *Journal of Consulting and Clinical Psychology, 61*(4), 549–560.

Horowitz, M., Wilner, N., & Alvarez, W. (1979). Impact of Event Scale: A measure of subjective stress. *Psychosomatic Medicine, 41*(3), 209–218.

Horvath, A. O., & Greenberg, L. S. (1989). Development and validation of the Working Alliance Inventory. *Journal of Counseling Psychology, 36*(2), 223–233.

Howes, C. (1999). Attachment relationships in the context of multiple caregivers. In J. Cassidy & P. R. Shaver (Eds.), *Handbook of attachment: Theory, research, and clinical applications* (pp. 671–687). New York, NY: Guilford Press.

Hu, P., & Meng, Z. (1996). *An examination of infant–mother attachment in China.* Poster presented at the meeting of the International Society for the Study of Behavioral Development, Quebec City, Quebec, Canada.

Hudson, W. W. (1997). *The WALMYR Assessment Scales scoring manual.* Tallahassee, FL: WALMYR.

Hyler, S. E., & Spitzer, R. L. (1978). Hysteria split asunder. *American Journal of Psychiatry, 135*(12), 1500–1504.

Illing, V., Tasca, G. A., Balfour, L., & Bissada, H. (2010). Attachment insecurity predicts eating disorder symptoms and treatment outcomes in a clinical sample of women. *Journal of Nervous and Mental Disease, 198*(9), 653–659.

Inagaki, K. (1989). Developmental shift in biological inference processes. *Human Development, 32*(2), 79–87.

Ivarsson, T. (2008). Obsessive-Compulsive Disorder in Adolescence: An AAI Perspective. In H. Steele & M. Steele (Eds.), *Clinical Applications of the Adult Attachment Interview* (pp. 213-235). New York: Guilford.

Iyengar, U., Sohye, K., Martinez, S., Fonagy, P., & Strathearn, L. (2014). Unresolved trauma in mothers: Intergenerational effects and the role of organization. *Frontiers in Psychology, 5,* 966.

Izard, C. E. (1971). *The face of emotion.* New York, NY: Appleton-Century-Crofts.

Izard, C. E., Porges, S. W., Simons, R. F., & Hayes, O. M. (1991). Infant cardiac activity. *Developmental Psychology, 27*(3), 432–439.

Jacobvitz, D., Curran, M., & Moller, N. (2002). Measurement of adult attachment: The place of self-report and interview methodologies. *Attachment & Human Development, 4*(2), 207–215.

Jacobvitz, D., Hazen, N., & Riggs, S. (1997, April). Disorganized mental processes in mothers, frightening/frightened caregiving, and disoriented/disorganized behavior in infancy. In D. Jacobvitz (Chair), *Caregiving correlates and longitudinal outcomes of disorganized attachments in infants.* Symposium conducted at the biennial meeting of the Society for Research in Child Development, Washington, DC.

Jaffe, J., Beebe, B., Feldstein, S., Crown, C. L., & Jasnow, M. D. (2001). Rhythms of dialogue in infancy: Coordinated timing in development. *Monographs of the Society for Research in Child Development, 66*(2), 1–132.

Joffe, W. G., & Sandler, J. (1966). Notes on pain, depression and individuation. *Psychoanalytic Study of the Child, 20,* 394–424. New York, NY: International University Press.

Johnson, S. C., Dweck, C. S., & Chen, F. S. (2007). Evidence for infant's internal working models of attachment. *Psychological Science, 18*(6), 501–502.

Kagan, J. (1978). On emotion and its development. In M. Lewis & L. A. Rosenblum (Eds.), *The development of affect* (pp. 11–42). New York, NY: Plenum Press.

Kagan, J. (1984). *The nature of the child.* New York, NY: Basic Books.

Karen, R. (1998). *Becoming attached: First relationships and how they shape our capacity to love.* New York, NY: Oxford University Press.

Kassel, J., Wardle, M., & Roberts, J. (2007). Adult attachment security and college student substance use. *Addictive Behaviors, 32*(6), 1164–1176.

Katz, J. (1984). *The silent world of doctor and patient.* Baltimore, MD: Johns Hopkins University Press.

Kegan, R. (1982). *The evolving self: Problem and process in human development.* Cambridge, MA: Harvard University Press.

Kermoian, R., & Leiderman, P. H. (1986). Infant attachment to mother and child caretaker in an East African community. *International Journal of Behavioral Development, 9*(4), 455–469.

Kerns, K. A. (2008). Attachment in middle childhood. In J. Cassidy & P. R. Shaver (Eds.), *Handbook of attachment: Theory, research, and clinical applications* (2nd ed., pp. 366–383). New York, NY: Guilford Press.

Kihlstrom, J. F. (1994). One hundred years of hysteria. In S. J. Lynn & J. W. Rhue (Eds.), *Dissociation: Clinical and theoretical perspectives* (pp. 365–394). New York, NY: Guilford Press.

Kjellander, C., Bongar, B., & King, A. (1998). Suicidality in borderline personality disorder. *Journal of Crisis Intervention and Suicide Prevention, 19*(3), 125–135.

Kobak, R. R. (1989/1993). *The Adult Attachment Interview Q-Set.* Unpublished manuscript, University of Delaware.

Kobak, R. R., Cole, H. E., Ferenz-Gillies, R., Fleming, W. S., & Gamble, W. (1993). Attachment and emotional regulation during mother–teen problem-solving: A control theory analysis. *Child Development, 64*(1), 231–245.

Kobak, R. R., & Sceery, A. (1988). Attachment in late adolescence: Working models, affect regulation, and representations of self and others. *Child Development, 59*(1), 135–146.

Kobak, R. R., Sudler, N., & Gamble, W. (1991). Attachment and depressive symptoms during adolescence: A developmental pathways analysis. *Development and Psychopathology, 3*(4), 461–474.

Kohlberg, L. (1981). *The philosophy of moral development.* New York, NY: Harper & Row.

Kohut, H. (1971). *The analysis of the self.* New York, NY: International Universities Press.

Kohut, H. (1977). *Restoration of the self.* New York, NY: International Universities Press.

Konner, M. (1977). Infancy among the Kalahari Desert San. In P. H. Leiderman, S. R. Tulkin, & A. Rosenfeld (Eds.), *Culture and infancy: Variation in the human experience* (pp. 287–328). New York, NY: Academic Press.

Kozlowska, K., & Williams, L. M. (2009). Self-protective organization in children with conversion and somatoform disorders. *Journal of Psychosomatic Research, 67*(3), 223–233.

Kuzendorf, R. (1980). Imagery and consciousness: A scientific analysis of the mind-body problem. *Dissertation Abstracts International: Section B. Sciences and Engineering, 40,* 3448–3449.

Labouvie-Vief, G. (1982). Dynamic development and mature autonomy: A theoretical prologue. *Human Development, 25,* 161–191.

Labouvie-Vief, G. (1990). Modes of knowledge and the organization of development. In M. L. Commons, C. Armon, L. Kohlberg, F. A. Richards, T. A. Grotzer, & J. D. Sinnott (Eds.), *Adult development: Vol. 2. Models and methods in the study of adolescent and adult thought* (pp. 43–62). New York, NY: Praeger.

Lamb, M. E. (1997). Fathers and child development: An introductory overview and guide. *The Role of the Father in Child Development, 3*(1), 1–18.

Lamb, M. E., Thompson, R. A., Gardner, W. P., Charnov, E. L., & Estes, D. (1984). Security of infantile attachment as assessed in the "Strange Situation." *Behavioral and Brain Sciences, 7*(1), 127–171.

Landa, S. & Duschinsky, R. (2013). Letters from Ainsworth: Contesting 'organization' of attachment. *Journal of the Canadian Academy of Adolescent Psychiatry*, 22, 172–177.

Landenburger, K. (1989). A process of entrapment in and recovery from an abusive relationship. *Issues in Mental Health Nursing, 10*(3–4), 209–227.

Leech, G. (1983). *Principles of pragmatics.* London, England: Longman.

Levinson, A., & Fonagy, P. (2004). Offending and attachment: The relationship between interpersonal awareness and offending in a prison population with psychiatric disorder. *Canadian Journal of Psychoanalysis, 12*, 225-251.

Levy, D. (1937). Primary affect hunger. *American Journal of Psychiatry, 94*, 643–652.

Levy, K. N. (2005). The implications of attachment theory and research for understanding borderline personality disorder. *Development and Psychopathology, 17*(4), 959–986.

Levy, K. N., Meehan, K. B., Clarkin, J. F., Kernberg, O. F., Kelly, K. M., Reynoso, J. S., & Weber, M. (2006). Change in attachment patterns and reflective function in a randomized control trial of transference-focused psychotherapy for borderline personality disorder. *Journal of Consulting and Clinical Psychology, 74*(6), 1027–1040.

Levy, M. B., & Davis, K. E. (1988). Lovestyles and attachment styles compared: Their relations to each other and to various relationship characteristics. *Journal of Social and Personality Relationships, 5*(4), 439–471.

Lewis, M. (1971). A developmental study of the cardiac response to stimulus onset and offset during the first year of life. *Psychophysiology, 8*(6), 689–698.

Lewis, M., & Brooks, J. (1978). Self-knowledge and emotional development. In M. Lewis & L. A. Rosenblum (Eds.), *The development of affect* (pp. 205–226). New York, NY: Plenum.

Lichtenberg, J. (1975). The development of a sense of self. *Journal of the American Psychoanalytic Association, 23*(3), 453–484.

Linehan, M. M. (1993). *Cognitive-behavioral treatment of borderline personality disorder.* New York, NY: Guilford Press.

Liotti, G. (1992). Disorganized/disoriented attachment in the etiology of dissociative disorders. *Dissociation, 5*, 196–204.

Liotti, G. (1999). *Attachment and metacognition in borderline patients.* Retrieved November 24, 2015, from http://www.psychomedia.it/pm/modther/probpsiter/liotti-2.htm

Liotti, G. (2005, December 2–3). *The role of parallel integrated treatments in the psychotherapy of complex trauma-related disorders.* Presentation at Harvard Medical School, Boston, MA.

Liotti, G., Cortina, M., & Farina, B. (2008). Attachment theory and multiple integrated treatments of borderline patients. *Journal of the American Academy of Psychoanalysis and Dynamic Psychiatry, 36*(2), 295–315.

Liotti, G., & Gilbert, P. (2011). Mentalizing, motivation, and social mentalities: Theoretical considerations and implications for psychotherapy. *Psychology and Psychotherapy: Theory, Research and Practice, 84*(1), 9–25.

Lipman, R. S., Covi, L., & Shapiro, A. K. (1977). The Hopkins Symptom Checklist (HSCL): Factors derived from the HSCL-90. *Psychopharmacology Bulletin, 13*(2), 43–45.

Loevinger, J. (1976). *Ego development: conceptions and theories.* San Francisco: Jossey-Bass.

Loevinger, J., & Wessler, R. (1970). *Measuring ego development: Vol. 1. Construction and use of a sentence completion test.* San Francisco, CA: Jossey-Bass.

Lopez, F. G. (2009). Clinical Correlates of adult attachment organization. In J. H. Obegi and E. Berant (Eds.), *Attachment theory and research in clinical work* (pp. 94–120). New York, NY: Guilford Press.

Lorenz, K. (1937). The companion in the bird's world. *Archival Journals, 54*(3), 245–273.

Luborsky, L. (1977). Measuring a pervasive psychic structure in psychotherapy: The core conflictual relationship theme. In N. Freedman & S. S. Grand (Eds.), *Communicative structures and psychic structures* (pp. 367–395). New York, NY: Plenum Press.

Luborsky, L. (1984). *Principles of psychoanalytic psychotherapy: A manual for supportive-expressive treatment.* New York, NY: Basic Books.

Luborsky, L., & Crits-Christoph, P. (1998). *Understanding transference: The core conflictual relationship theme method.* Washington, DC: American Psychological Association.

Lyons-Ruth, K. (1999). The two-person unconscious: Intersubjective dialogue, enactive relational representation, and the emergence of new forms of relational organization. *Psychoanalytic Inquiry, 19*(4), 576–617.

Lyons-Ruth, K., Alpern, L., & Repacholi, B. (1993). Disorganized infant attachment classification and maternal psychosocial problems as predictors of hostile-aggressive behavior in the preschool classroom. *Child Development, 64*(2), 572–585.

Lyons-Ruth, K., Bronfman, E., & Parsons, E. (1999). Atypical attachment in infancy and early childhood among children att developmental risk. IV. Maternal frightened, frightening, or atypical behavior and disorganized infant attachment patterns. *Monographs of the Society for Research in Child Development, 64*(3), 67–96.

Lyons-Ruth, K., & Jacobvitz, D. (1999). Attachment disorganization: Unresolved loss, relational violence, and lapses in behavioral and attentional strategies. In J. Cassidy & P. R. Shaver (Eds.), *Handbook of attachment: Theory, research, and clinical applications* (pp. 520–554). New York, NY: Guilford Press.

Lyons-Ruth, K., & Jacobvitz, D. (2008). Attachment disorganization: Genetic factors, parenting contexts, and developmental transformation from infancy to adulthood. In J. Cassidy & P. R. Shaver (Eds.), *Handbook of attachment: Theory, research, and clinical applications* (2nd ed., pp. 666–697). New York: Guilford Press.

Lyons-Ruth, K., Melnick, S., Patrick, M., & Hobson, R. P. (2007). A controlled study of hostile-helpless states of mind among borderline and dysthymic women. *Attachment & Human Development, 9*(1), 1–16.

Mahler, M. S., Pine, F., & Bergman, A. (1975). *The psychological birth of the human infant: Symbiosis and individuation.* New York, NY: Basic Books.

Main, M. (1973). *Exploration, play and cognitive functioning as related to child–mother attachment.* Unpublished doctoral dissertation, Johns Hopkins University, Baltimore, MD.

Main, M. (1977). Analysis of a peculiar form of behavior seen in some daycare children: Its history and sequelae in children who are home-reared. In R. Webb (Ed.), *Social development in daycare* (pp. 33–78). Baltimore, MD: Johns Hopkins University Press.

Main, M. (1979a). *Scale for disordered/disoriented infant behavior in response to the Main and Weston Clown Session.* Unpublished manuscript, University of California, Berkeley.

Main, M. (1979b). The ultimate causation of some infant attachment phenomena: Further answers, further phenomena and further questions. *Brain Sciences, 2,* 640–643.

Main, M. (1991). Metacognitive knowledge, metacognitive monitoring, and singular (coherent) vs. multiple (incoherent) models of attachment. In C. M. Parkes, J. Stevenson-Hinde, & P. Harris (Eds.), *Attachment across the life cycle* (pp. 127–159). London, England: Routledge.

Main, M. (1995). Attachment: Overview with implications for clinical work. In S. Goldberg, R. Muir, & J. Kerr (Eds.), *Attachment theory: Social, developmental and clinical perspectives* (pp. 467–474). Hillsdale, NJ: Analytic Press.

Main, M., & Cassidy, J. (1988). Categories of response to the reunion with the parent at age six:

Predicted from infant attachment classifications and stable over a one-month period. *Developmental Psychology, 24*(3), 415–426.

Main, M., & George, C. (1985). Responses of abused and disadvantaged toddlers to distress in agemates: A study in the daycare setting. *Developmental Psychology, 21*(3), 407–412.

Main, M., & Goldwyn, R. (1984a). *Adult attachment scoring and classification system.* Unpublished manuscript, University of California, Berkeley.

Main, M., & Goldwyn, R. (1984b). Predicting rejection of her infant from mother's representation of her own experience: Implications for the abused–abusing intergenerational cycle. *International Journal of Child Abuse and Neglect, 8*(2), 203–217.

Main, M., & Goldwyn, R. (1994). *Adult attachment rating and classification system, Manual in Draft: Version 6.0* . Unpublished manuscript, University of California, Berkeley.

Main, M., & Goldwyn, R. (1998). *Adult attachment scoring and classification system, Version 6.0.* Unpublished manuscript, University of California, Berkeley.

Main, M., Goldwyn, R., & Hesse, E. (2002). *Adult attachment scoring and classification system, Manual in Draft: Version 7.1.* Unpublished manuscript, University of California, Berkeley.

Main, M., & Hesse, E. (1990). Parents' unresolved traumatic experiences are related to infant disorganized attachment status: Is frightened and/or frightening parental behavior a linking mechanism? In M. T. Greenberg, D. Cicchetti, & E. M. Cummings (Eds.), *Attachment in the preschool years: Theory, research and intervention* (pp. 161–182). Chicago, IL: University of Chicago Press.

Main, M., & Hesse, E. (1992). Disorganized/disoriented infant behavior in the Strange Situation, lapses in the monitoring of reasoning and discourse during the parent's Adult Attachment Interview, and dissociative states (translated into Italian). In M. Ammaniti & D. Stern (Eds.), *Attaccamento e psicoanalisi* (pp. 86–140). Rome, Italy: Laterza.

Main, M., Kaplan, N., & Cassidy, J. (1985). Security in infancy, childhood, and adulthood: A move to the level of representation. In I. Bretherton & E. Waters (Eds.), *Growing points in attachment theory and research. Monographs of the Society for Research in Child Development, 50*(1–2), 66–104.

Main, M., & Morgan, H. (1996). Disorganization and disorientation in infant Strange Situation behavior: Phenotypic resemblance to dissociative states. In L. K. Michelson & W. J. Ray (Eds.), *Handbook of dissociation: Theoretical, empirical, and clinical perspectives* (pp. 107–138). New York, NY: Plenum.

Main, M., & Solomon, J. (1986). Discovery of an insecure disorganized/disoriented attachment pattern: Procedures, findings, and implications for the classification of behavior. In T. B. Brazelton & M. Yogman (Eds.), *Affective development in infancy* (pp. 95–124). Norwood, NJ: Ablex.

Main, M., & Solomon, J. (1990). Procedures for identifying infants as disorganized/disoriented during the Ainsworth Strange Situation. In M. T. Greenberg, D. Cicchetti, and E. M. Cummings (Eds.), *Attachment in the preschool years* (pp. 121–160). Chicago, IL: Chicago University Press.

Main, M., & Weston, D. (1981). The quality of the toddler's relationship to mother and to father: Related to conflict behavior and the readiness to establish new relationships. *Child Development, 52*(3), 932–940.

Malatesta, C. Z., & Haviland, J. M. (1982). Learning display rules. *Child Development, 53*(4), 991–1003.

Mallinckrodt, B., Daly, K., & Wang, C-C.D.C. (2009). An attachment approach to adult psychotherapy. In J. H. Obei & E. Berant (Eds.), *Attachment theory and research in clinical work with adults* (pp. 234–268). New York, NY: Guilford Press.

Mallinckrodt, B., Gantt, D. L., & Coble, H. M. (1995). Attachment patterns in the psychotherapy relationship: Development of the Client Attachment to Therapist Scale. *Journal of Counseling Psychology, 42*(3), 307–317.

Mallinckrodt, B., & Jeong, J. (2015). Meta-analysis of client attachment to therapist: Associations with working alliance, and client pretherapy attachment. *Psychotherapy, 52*(1), 134–139. doi: 10.1037/a0036890

Mallinckrodt, B., Porter, M. J., & Kivlighan, D. M., Jr. (2005). Client attachment to therapist, depth of in-session exploration, and object relations in brief psychotherapy. *Psychotherapy: Theory, Research, Practice, Training, 42*(1), 85–100.

Mallinckrodt, B., & Wei, M. (2005). Attachment, social competencies, social support, and psychological distress. *Journal of Counseling Psychology, 52*(3), 358–367.

Manassis, K., Bradley, S., Goldberg, S., Hood, J., & Swinson, R. P. (1994). Attachment in mothers with anxiety disorders and their children. *Journal of the American Academy of Child and Adolescent Psychiatry, 33*(8), 1106–1113.

Marks, I. M. (1987). The development of normal fear: A review. *Journal of Child Psychology and Psychiatry, 28*(5), 667–697.

Marvin, R. S. (1972). *Attachment and cooperative behavior in two-, three-, and four-year-olds.* Unpublished doctoral dissertation, University of Chicago, Chicago, IL.

Marvin, R. S. (1977). An ethological-cognitive model for the attenuation of mother–child attachment behavior. In T. M. Alloway, L. Krames, & P. Pliner (Eds.), *Advances in the study of communication and effect: Attachment behavior* (Vol. 3, pp. 25–60). New York, NY: Plenum Press.

Marvin, R. S., & Britner, P. A. (2008). Normative development: The ontogeny of attachment. In J. Cassidy & P. R. Shaver (Eds.), *Handbook of attachment: Theory, research, and clinical applications* (2nd ed., pp. 269–294). New York, NY: Guilford Press.

Marvin, R. S., VanDevender, T. L., Iwanaga, M., LeVine, S., & LeVine, R. A. (1977). Infant–caregiver attachment among the Hausa of Nigeria. In H. M. McGurk (Ed.), *Ecological factors in human development* (pp. 247–260). Amsterdam, Netherlands: North-Holland.

Maunder, R. G., & Hunter, J. J. (2009). Assessing patterns of attachment in medical patients. *General Hospital Psychiatry, 31*(2), 123–130.

McClellan, A. C., & Kileen, M. R. (2000). Attachment theory and violence toward women by male intimate partners. *Journal of Nursing Scholarship, 32*(4), 353–360.

McGlashan, T. (1986). The Chestnut Lodge follow-up study: III. Long-term outcome of borderline personalities. *Archives of General Psychiatry, 43,* 20-30.

Meins, E. (1997). *Security of attachment and the social development of cognition.* East Sussex, England: Psychology Press.

Meltzoff, A. N. (1985). The roots of social and cognitive development: Models of man's original nature. In T. Field & N. Fox (Eds.), *Social perception in infants* (pp. 1–30). Norwood, NJ: Ablex.

Meltzoff, A. N. (1990). Foundations for developing a concept of self: The role of imitation in relating self to other and the value of social mirroring, social modeling, and self practice in infancy. In D. Cicchetti & M. Beeghley (Eds.), *The self in transition: Infancy to childhood* (pp. 139–164). Chicago, IL: University of Chicago Press.

Meltzoff, A. N., & Gopnik, A. (1993). The role of imitation in understanding persons and developing a theory of mind. In S. Baron-Cohen, H. Tager-Flusberg, & D. Cohen (Eds.), *Understanding other minds: Perspectives from autism* (pp. 335–365). New York, NY: Oxford University Press.

Meltzoff, A. N., & Moore, M. K. (1977). Imitation of facial and manual gestures by human neonates. *Science, 198*(4312), 75–78.

Meltzoff, A. N., & Moore, M. K. (1998). Infant intersubjectivity: Broadening the dialogue to include imitation, identity and intention. In S. Bråten (Ed.), *Intersubjective communication and emotion in early ontogeny* (pp. 47–62). Cambridge, England: Cambridge University Press.

Meyer, B., & Pilkonis, P. A. (2005). An attachment model of personality disorders. In M. F. Lenzenweger & J. F. Clarkin (Eds.), *Major theories of personality disorder* (2nd ed., pp. 231–281). New York, NY: Guilford Press.

Mickelson, K. D., Kessler, R. C., & Shaver, P. R. (1997). Adult attachment in a nationally representative sample. *Journal of Personality and Social Psychology, 73*(5), 1092–1106.

Mikulincer, M. (1995). Attachment style and the mental representation of the self. *Journal of Personality and Social Psychology, 69*(6), 1203–1215.

Mikulincer, M. (1998). Adult attachment style and affect regulation: Strategic variations in self-appraisals. *Journal of Personality and Social Psychology, 75*(2), 420–435.

Mikulincer, M., Dolev, T., & Shaver, P. R. (2004). Attachment-related strategies during thought suppression: Ironic rebounds and vulnerable self-representation. *Journal of Personality and Social Psychology, 87*(6), 940–956.

Mikulincer, M., & Florian, V. (1998). The relationship between adult attachment styles and emotional and cognitive reactions to stressful events. In J. A. Simpson & W. S. Rholes (Eds.), *Attachment theory and close relationships* (pp. 143–165). New York, NY: Guilford Press.

Mikulincer, M., Florian, V., & Tolmacz, R. (1990). Attachment style and fear of personal death: A case study of affect regulation. *Journal of Personality and Social Psychology, 58*(2), 273–280.

Mikulincer, M., & Horesh, N. (1999). Adult attachment style and the perception of others: The role of projective mechanisms. *Journal of Personality and Social Psychology, 76*(6), 1022–1034.

Mikulincer, M., & Nachshon, O. (1991). Attachment styles and patterns of self-disclosure. *Journal of Personality and Social Psychology, 61*(2), 321–331.

Mikulincer, M., & Orbach, I. (1995). Attachment styles and repressive defensiveness: The accessibility and architecture of affective memories. *Journal of Personality and Social Psychology, 68*(5), 917–925.

Mikulincer, M., & Shaver, P. R. (2003). The attachment behavioral system in adulthood: Activation, psychodynamics, and interpersonal process. In M. P. Zanna (Ed.), *Advances in experimental social psychology* (Vol. 35, pp. 53–152). New York, NY: Academic Press.

Mikulincer, M. & Shaver. P. R. (2007). *Attachment in adulthood: Structure. dynamics, and change.* New York: Guilford Press.

Mikulincer, M., & Shaver, P. R. (2008). Adult development: The ontogeny of attachment. In J. Cassidy & P. R. Shaver (Eds.), *Handbook of attachment: Theory, research, and clinical applications* (2nd ed., pp. 503–531). New York, NY: Guilford Press.

Mikulincer, M., & Shaver, P. R. (2012). An attachment perspective on psychopathology. *World Psychiatry, 11*(1), 11–15.

Mikulincer, M., Shaver. P. R. Cassidy. J. & Berant, E. (2009). Attachment-related defensive processes. In J. H. Obegi and E. Berant (Eds.), *Attachment theory and research in clinical work* (pp. 293–327). New York, NY: Guilford Press.

Mikulincer, M., Shaver, P. R., & Pereg, D. (2003). Attachment theory and affect regulation: The dynamics, development, and cognitive consequences of attachment-related strategies. *Motivation and Emotion, 27*(2), 77–102.

Millon, T. (1987). *Manual for the Millon clinical multiaxial inventory-II (MCMI-II).* Minneapolis, MN: National Computer Systems.

Morelli, G. A., & Tronick, E. Z. (1991). Efe multiple caretaking and attachment. In J. L. Gewirtz & W. M. Kurtines (Eds.), *Intersections with attachment* (pp. 41–52). Hillsdale, NJ: Erlbaum.

Nadelson, T. (1985). False patients/real patients: A spectrum of disease presentation. *Psychotherapy and Psychosomatics, 44*(4), 175–184.

Nagy, E., & Molnar, P. (1994). "Homo imitans" or "Homo provocans"? *International Journal of Psychophysiology, 18*(2), 128.

Nelson, S. M. (2009). An attachment perspective on crying in psychotherapy. In J. H. Obegi and E. Berant (Eds.), *Attachment theory and research in clinical work* (pp. 328–350). New York. NY: Guilford Press.

Neumann, E., Nowacki, K., Roland, I. C., & Kruse, J. (2011). Attachment and somatoform disorders: Low coherence and unresolved states of mind related to chronic pain. *Psychotherapie, Psychosomatik, Medizinische Psychologie, 61*(6), 254–261.

New, A. (2015, September). *Neurobiology, hormones and attachment.* Paper presented at the Harvard Medical School and McLean Hospital Conference on Attachment and Borderline Personality Disorder, Boston, MA.

Nijenhuis, E. R. S., Spinhoven, P., van Dijck, R., van der Hart, O., & Vanderlinden, J. (1996). The development and psychometric characteristics of the Somatoform Dissociation Questionnaire (SDQ-20). *Journal of Nervous and Mental Disease, 184,* 688–694.

Nijenhuis, E. R. S., van der Hart, O., & Steele, K. (2002). The emerging psychobiology of trauma-related dissociation and dissociative disorders. In H. A. H. D'haenen, H. den Boer, P. Westenberg, & P. Wilner (Eds.), *Textbook of biological psychiatry* (Vol. 2, pp. 1079–1098). London, England: Wiley.

Nilsson, D., Holmqvist, R., & Jonson, M. (2011). Self-reported attachment style, trauma exposure and dissociative symptoms among adolescents. *Attachment & Human Development, 13*(6), *579–595.*

Obegi, J. H., & Berant, E. (2009). *Attachment theory and research in clinical work with adults.* New York, NY: Guilford Press.

Ogawa, J. R., Sroufe, L. A., Weinfield, N. S., Carlson, E. A., & Egeland, B. (1997). Development and the fragmented self: Longitudinal study of dissociative symptomatology in a nonclinical sample. *Development and Psychopathology, 9*(4), 855–879.

Pajuhinia, S., & Faraji, R. (2014). Explanation of vulnerability to somatization and anxiety based on attachment styles. *Neuroscience Journal of Shefaye Khatam, 2*(3, Suppl. 1).

Parish, M., & Eagle, M. (2003). Attachment to the therapist. *Psychoanalytic Psychology, 20*(2), 271–286.

Patrick, M., Hobson, R. P., Castle, P., Howard, R., & Maughan, B. (1994). Personality disorder and mental representation of early social experience. *Development and Psychopathology, 6*(2), 375–388.

Pence, E., & Paymer, M. (1993). *Power and control: Tactics of men who batter.* Duluth, MN: Minnesota Program Development.

Piaget, J. (1963). *The origins of intelligence in children.* New York, NY: W. W. Norton.

Piaget, J. (1981). *Intelligence and affectivity: Their relationship during child development.* Palo Alto, CA: Annual Reviews.

Pianta, R. C., Egeland, B., & Adam, E. K. (1996). Adult attachment classification and self-reported psychiatric symptomatology as assessed by the Minnesota Multiphasic Personality Inventory–2. *Journal of Consulting and Clinical Psychology, 64*(2), 273–281.

Pielage, S., Gerlsma, C., & Schaap, C. (2000). Insecure attachment as a risk factor for psychopathology: The role of stressful events. *Clinical Psychology and Psychotherapy, 7*(4), 296–302.

Pierrehumbert, B., Miljkovitch, R., Plancherel, B., Halfon, O., & Ansermet, F. (2000). Attachment and temperament in early childhood: Implications for later behavior problems. *Infant and Child Development, 9*(1), 17–32.

Pillemer, D. B., & White, S. H. (1989). Childhood events recalled by children and adults. In H. V. Reese (Ed.), *Advances in child development and behavior* (Vol. 21, pp. 297–340). New York, NY: Academic Press.

Plassmann, R. (1994). Munchausen syndromes and factitious diseases. *Psychotherapy and Psychosomatics, 62*(1–2), 7–26.

Pleshkova, N. L., & Muhamedrahimov, R. J. (2010). Quality of attachment in St Petersburg (Russian Federation): A sample of family-reared infants. *Clinical Child Psychology and Psychiatry, 15*(3), 355–362.

Pocock, D. (2010, August). Debating truth, error, and distortion in systemic psychotherapy: A contribution from the DMM. *Context,* pp. 1–6.

Posner, M. I., Rothbart, M. K., Visueta, N., Thomas, K. M., Levy, K. N., Fossella, J., . . . Kernberg, O. (2003). An approach to the psychobiology of personality disorders. *Development and Psychopathology, 15*(4), 1093–1106.

Prunetti, E., Bosio, V., Bateni, M., & Liotti, G. (2013). Three-week inpatient Cognitive Evolutionary Therapy (CET) for patients with personality disorders: Evidence of effectiveness in symptoms reduction and improved treatment adherence. *Psychology and Psychotherapy, 86*(3), 262–279.

Prunetti, E., Framba, R., Barone, L., Fiore, D., Sera, F., & Liotti, G. (2008). Attachment disorganization and borderline patients' metacognitive responses to therapists' expressed understanding of their states of mind: A pilot study. *Psychotherapy Research, 18*(1), 28–36.

Putnam, F. W. (1998, March 20). *Developmental pathways in sexually abused girls.* Presentation at the Psychological Trauma: Maturational Processes and Psychotherapeutic Interventions conference, Harvard Medical School, Boston MA.

Reis, S., & Grenyer, B. F. S. (2004). Fearful attachment, working alliance, and treatment response for individuals with major depression. *Clinical Psychology and Psychotherapy, 11*(6), 414–424.

Riggs, S. A., & Jacobvitz, D. (2002). Expectant parents' representations of early attachment relationships: Associations with mental health and family history. *Journal of Consulting and Clinical Psychology, 70*(1), 195–204.

Robertson, J. (1953). *A two-year-old goes to hospital* [Film]. University Park, PA: Penn State Audio Visual Services.

Robertson, J. (1962). *Hospitals and children: A parent's eye view.* New York, NY: Gollancz.

Rogers, R., Bagby, M., & Dickens, S. E. (2002). *Structured interview of reported symptoms.* Lutz, FL: Psychological Assessment Resources.

Roisman, G. I., Fraley, R. C., Holland, A., Fortuna, K., Clausell, E., & Clarke, A. (2007). The Adult Attachment Interview and self-reports of attachment style: An empirical rapprochement. *Journal of Personality and Social Psychology, 92,* 678–697.

Rosenstein, D. S., & Horowitz, H. A. (1996). Adolescent attachment and psychopathology. *Journal of Counseling and Clinical Psychology, 64*(2), 244–253.

Rosenzweig, D. L., Farber, B. A., & Geller, J. D. (1996). Clients' representations of their therapists over the course of psychotherapy. *Journal of Clinical Psychology, 52*(2), 197–207.

Roth, S., Newman, E., Pelcovitz, D., van der Kolk, B., & Mandel, F. S. (1997). Complex PTSD in victims exposed to sexual and physical abuse: Results from the DSM-IV field trial for posttraumatic stress disorder. *Journal of Traumatic Stress, 10*(4), 539–555.

Sable, P. (2000). *Attachment and adult psychotherapy.* Northvale, NJ: Jason Aronson.

Sable, P. (2004). Attachment, ethology and adult psychotherapy. *Attachment & Human Development,* 6, 3–19.

Safran, J. D., Muran, J. C., Samstag, L. W., & Stevens, C. (2001). Repairing alliance ruptures. *Psychotherapy, 38*(4), 406–412.

Sagi, A., Lamb, M. E., Lewkowicz, K. S., Shoham, R., Dvir, R., & Estes, D. (1985). Security of infant–mother, –father, and –metapelet attachments among kibbutz-reared Israeli children. In I. Bretherton & E. Waters (Eds.), *Growing points in attachment theory and research. Monographs of the Society for Research in Child Development, 50*(1–2), 257–275.

Sagi, A., van IJzendoorn, M. H., Aviezer, O., Donnell, F., Karie-Korem, N., Joels, T., & Harel, Y. (1995). Attachments in a multiple-caregiver and multiple-infant environment: The case of the Israeli kibbutzim. In E. Waters, B. E. Vaughn, G. Posada, & K. Kondo-Ikemura (Eds.), Caregiving, cultural, and cognitive perspectives on secure-base behavior and working models: New growing points of attachment theory and research [Special issue]. *Monographs of the Society for Research on Child Development, 60*(2–3), 71–91.

Sander, L. W. (1975). Infant and caretaking environment: Investigation and conceptualization of adaptive behavior in a system of increasing complexity. In E. G. Anthony (Ed.), *Explorations in child psychology* (pp. 126–166). New York, NY: Plenum.

Sander, L. W., & Julia, H. L. (1966). Continuous interactional monitoring in the neonate. *Psychosomatic Medicine, 28*(6), 822–835.

Savov, S., & Atanassov, N. (2013, January). Deficits of affect mentalization in patients with drug addiction: Theoretical and clinical aspects. *ISRN Addiction,* pp. 1–6. doi: 10.1155/2013/250751

Scheidt, C. E., Waller, E. H., Schock, C. H., Becker-Stoll, F., Zimmermann, P., Lücking, C. H., & Wirsching, M. (1999). Alexithymia and attachment representation in idiopathic spasmodic torticollis. *Journal of Nervous and Mental Disease, 187*(1), 47–52.

Schore, A. N. (1996). *Affect regulation and the origin of the self: The Neurobiology of emotional development.* New Jersey: Lawrence Erlbaum Associates.

Schuengel, C., Bakermans-Kranenburg, M. J., & van IJzendoorn, M. H. (1999). Frightening maternal behavior linking unresolved loss and disorganized infant attachment. *Journal of Consulting and Clinical Psychology, 67*(1), 54–63.

Schuengel, C., & van IJzendoorn, M. H. (2001). Attachment in mental health institutions: A critical review of assumptions, clinical implications, and research strategies. *Attachment & Human Development, 3*(3), 304–323.

Schur, M. (1955). Comments of the metapsychology of somatization. *Psychoanalytic Study of the Child, 10,* 119–164.

Searle, B., & Meara, N. M. (1999). Affective dimensions of attachment styles: Exploring self-reported attachment style, gender, and emotional experience among college students. *Journal of Counseling Psychology, 46*(2), 147–158.

Semerari, A., Carcione, A., Dimaggio, G., Falcone, M., Nicolò, G., Procacci, M., & Alleva, G. (2003). How to evaluate metacogntive functioning in psychotherapy? The Metacognition Assessment Scale and its applications. *Clinical Psychology and Psychotherapy, 10*(4), 238–261.

Shanmugam, V., Jowett, S., & Meyer, C. (2012). Eating psychopathology amongst athletes: Links to current attachment styles. *Eating Behaviors, 13,* 5–12.

Shaver, P. R., & Clark, C. L. (1994). The psychodynamics of adult romantic attachment. In J. M. Masling & R. F. Bornstein (Eds.), *Empirical perspectives on object relations theories* (pp. 105–156). Washington, DC: American Psychological Association.

Shaver, P. R., & Mikulincer. M. (2009). An overview adult attachment theory. In J. H. Obegi and E. Berant (Eds.), *Attachment theory and research in clinical work* (pp. 17–45). New York, NY: Guilford Press.

Sierra, M., & Berrios, G. E. (1998). Depersonalization: Neurobiological perspectives. *Biological Psychiatry, 44*(9), 898–908.

Sierra, M., & David, A. S. (2011). Depersonalization: A selective impairment of self-awareness. *Consciousness and Cognition, 20*(1), 99–108.

Silverman, A. B., Reinherz, H. Z., & Giaconia, R. M. (1996). The long-term sequelae of child and adolescent abuse: A longitudinal community study. *Child Abuse and Neglect, 20*(8), 709–723.

Silverton, L., & Gruber, C. (1998). *Malingering probability scale (MPS).* Los Angeles, CA: Western Psychological Services.

Simeon, D., Gross, S., Guralnik, O., Stein, D. J., Schmeidler, J., & Hollander, E. (1997). Feeling unreal: 30 cases of DSM-II-R depersonalization disorder. *American Journal of Psychiatry, 154*(8), 1107–1113.

Simonelli, A., & Vizziello, G. F. (2002). La qualita delle rappresentazioni di attaccamento in madri tossicodipendenti come fattore de rischio per lo sviluppo affettivo del bambino (Internal working models of attachment in drug-addicted mothers as a risk factor in infant affective development). *Ea Evolutiva, 72,* 54–60.

Simpson, J. A. (1990). Influence of attachment styles on romantic relationships. *Journal of Personality and Social Psychology, 59*(5), 971–980.

Simpson, J. A., & Rholes, W. S. (1998). *Attachment theory and close relationships.* New York, NY: Guilford Press.

Simpson, J. A., Rholes, W. S., & Nelligan, J. S. (1992). Support seeking and support giving within couples in an anxiety-provoking situation: The role of attachment styles. *Journal of Personality and Social Psychology, 62*(3), 434–446.

Slade, A. (1999). Attachment theory and research: Implications for the theory and practice of individual psychotherapy with adults. In J. Cassidy & P. R. Shaver (Eds.), *Handbook of attachment: Theory, research, and clinical applications* (pp. 575–594). New York, NY: Guilford Press.

Slade, A. (2008). The implications of attachment theory and research for adult psychotherapy: Research and clinical perspectives. In J. Cassidy & P.R. Shaver (Eds.). *Handbook of attachment: Theory, research, and clinical applications* (2nd ed., pp. 762-782). New York, NY: Guildford Press.

Slade, P. D. (1982). Towards a functional analysis of anorexia nervosa. *British Journal of Clinical Psychology,* 21, 167–179.

Solomon, J., & George, C. (1999). *Attachment disorganization.* New York, NY: Guilford Press.

Solomon, J., & George, C. (2008). The measurement of attachment security and related constructs in infancy and early childhood. In J. Cassidy & P. R. Shaver (Eds.), *Handbook of attachment: Theory, research, and clinical applications* (2nd ed., pp. 383–416). New York, NY: Guilford Press.

Spangler, G., & Grossmann, K. E. (1993). Biobehavioral organization in securely and insecurely attached infants. *Child development, 64*(5), 1439–1450.

Sperling, M. B., & Lyons, L. S. (1994). Representations of attachment and psychotherapeutic change. In M. B. Sperling & W. H. Berman (Eds.), *Attachment in adults: Clinical and developmental perspectives* (pp. 331–349). New York, NY: Guilford Press.

Spiro, H. R. (1968). Chronic factitious illness. *Archives of General Psychiatry, 18*(5), 569–579.

Spitz, R. (1945). Hospitalism: An inquiry into the genesis of psychiatric conditions in early childhood. *Psychoanalytic Study of the Child, 1,* 53–74.

Spitz, R. (1947). *Grief: A peril in infancy* [Film]. University Park, PA: Penn State Audio Visual Services.

Spitzer, R. L., Williams, J. B. W., Gibbon, M. S. W., & First, M. B. (1993). The Structured Clinical Interview for DSM-III-R (SCID): I. History, rationale, and description. *Archives of General Psychiatry, 49*(8), 624–629.

Sroufe, L. A. (2005). Attachment and development: A prospective, longitudinal study from birth to adulthood. *Attachment & Human Development, 7*(4), 349–367.

Sroufe, L. A., Egeland, B., Carlson, E. A., & Collins, W. A. (2005). *The development of the person: The Minnesota study of risk and adaptation from birth to adulthood.* New York, NY: Guilford Press.

Sroufe, L. A., & Fleeson, J. (1986). Attachment and the construction of relationships. In W. W. Hartup & Z. Rubin (Eds.), *Relationships and development* (pp. 51–71). Hillsdale, NJ: Erlbaum.

Sroufe, L. A., & Waters, E. (1997). Attachment as an organizational construct. *Child Development, 48*(4), 1184–1199.

Stalker, C. A., & Davies, F. (1995). Attachment organization and adaptation in sexually-abused women. *Canadian Journal of Psychiatry, 40*(5), 234–240.

Stechler, G., & Carpenter, G. (1967). A viewpoint on early affective development. In J. Hellmath (Ed.), *The exceptional infant* (Vol. 1). New York, NY: Brunner/Mazel.

Steele, H. (2003). Unrelenting catastrophic trauma within the family: When every secure base is abusive. *Attachment & Human Development, 5*(4), 353–366.

Steele, H., & Steele, M. (2008a). *Clinical applications of the Adult Attachment Interview.* New York, NY: Guilford Press.

Steele, H., & Steele, M. (2008b). On the origins of reflective functioning. In F. N. Busch (Ed), *Mentalization: Theoretical considerations, research findings, and clinical implications* (pp. 133–158). New York, NY: Analytic Press.

Steinberg, M. (1993). *Revised Structured Clinical Interview for DSM-IV Dissociative Disorders (SCID-D):* Scoring sheet. Interviewer's guide. Washington, DC: American Psychiatric Press.

Stern, D. (1971). A microanalysis of the mother–infant interaction. *Journal of the American Academy of Child Psychiatry, 10,* 501–507.

Stern, D. (1985). *The interpersonal world of the infant.* New York, NY: Basic Books.

Stern, D. (2010). *Partners in thought: Working with unformulated experience, dissociation, and enactment.* New York, NY: Taylor & Francis.

Sternberg, R. (1984). Higher-order reasoning in postformal operational thought. In M. L. Commons, F. A. Richards, & C. Armon (Eds.), *Beyond formal operations: Late adolescence and adult cognitive development* (pp. 74–91). New York, NY: Praeger.

Stevenson-Hinde, J., & Marshall, P. J. (1999). Behavioral inhibition, heart period, and respiratory sinus arrhythmia: An attachment perspective. *Child Development, 70*(4), 805–816.

Stovall-McClough, K. C., & Cloitre, M. (2006). Unresolved attachment, PTSD, and dissociation in women with childhood abuse histories. *Journal of Consulting and Clinical Psychology, 74,* 219–228.

Stovall-McClough, K. C., Cloitre, M., & McClough, J. F. (2008). Adult attachment and posttraumatic stress disorder in women with histories of childhood abuse. In H. Steele & M. Steele (Eds.), *Clinical applications of the Adult Attachment Interview* (pp. 320–340). New York, NY: Guilford.

Strentz, T. (1979). The Stockholm syndrome. In F. M. Ochberg & D. A. Soskis (Eds.), *Victims of terrorism* (pp. 149–163). Boulder, CO: Westview.

Strupp, H. H., & Binder, J. L. (1984). *Psychotherapy in a new key: A guide to time-limited psychotherapy.* New York, NY: Basic Books.

Sullivan, H. S. (1953). *The interpersonal theory of psychiatry.* New York, NY: W. W. Norton.

Symonds, M. (1982). Victim's response to terror: Understanding and treatment. In F. M. Ochberg & D. A. Soskis (Eds.), *Victims of terrorism* (pp. 95–103). Boulder, CO: Westview.

Takahashi, S. (1986). Examining the strange-situation procedure with Japanese mothers and 12-month-old infants. *Developmental Psychology, 22*(2), 265–270.

Terr, L. (1994). *Unchained memories: True stories of traumatic memories, lost and found.* New York, NY: Basic Books.

Teti, D., Gelfand, D. M., Messinger, D. S., & Isabella, R. (1995). Maternal depression and the quality for early attachment: An examination of infants, preschoolers, and their mothers. *Developmental Psychology, 31*(3), 364–376.

Teyber, E., & McClure, F. H. (2011). *Interpersonal process in therapy: An integrative model.* Belmont, CA: Brooks/Cole.

Thalhuber, K., Jacobvitz, D., & Hazen, N. L. (1998, March). *Effects of mothers' posttraumatic experiences on mother–infant interactions.* Paper presented at the biennial meeting of the Southwestern Society for Research in Human Development, Galveston, TX.

Timmerman, I. G. H., & Emmelkamp, P. M. G. (2006). The relationship between attachment styles and Cluster B personality disorders in prisoners and forensic inpatients. *International Journal of Law and Psychiatry, 29,* 48–56.

Tolmacz, R. (2009). Transference and attachment. In J. H. Obegi and E. Berant (Eds.), *Attachment theory and research in clinical work* (pp. 269–292). New York, NY: Guilford Press.

Tolpin, M. (1971). On the beginnings of a cohesive self. *Psychoanalytic Study of the Child, 26,* 316–352.

Tomasello, M. (2009). *Why we cooperate: Based on the 2008 Tanner Lectures on Human Values at Sanford.* Cambridge, MA: MIT Press.

Tomasello, M. (2010). *Origins of human communication.* Cambridge, MA: MIT Press.

Tomkins, S. S. (1962). *Affect, imagery, consciousness* (Vol. 1). New York, NY: Springer.

Tomkins, S. S. (1968). Affects: Primary motives of man. *Humanitas, 3,* 321–345.

Trevarthen, C. (1979). Communication and cooperation in early infancy: A description of primary intersubjectivity. In M. M. Bullowa (Ed.), *Before speech: The beginning of human communication* (pp. 321–347). New York, NY: Cambridge University Press.

Trevarthen, C. (1998). The concept and foundations of infant intersubjectivity. In S. Bråten (Ed.), *Intersubjective communication and emotion in early ontogeny* (pp. 15–46). Cambridge, MA: Cambridge University Press.

Tronick, E., Adamson, L. B., Als, H., & Brazelton, T. B. (1975). *Infant emotions in normal and pertubated interactions.* Paper presented at the biennial meeting of the Society for Research in Child Development, Denver, CO.

True, M. M. (1994). *Mother–infant attachment and communication among the Dogon of Mali (West Africa).* Unpublished doctoral dissertation, University of California, Berkeley.

Turton, P., McGauley, G., Marin-Avellan, L., & Hughes, P. (2001). The Adult Attachment Interview: Rating and classification problems posed by non-normative samples. *Attachment & Human Development, 3*(3), 2284–2303.

van der Hart, O., Nijenhuis, E., Steele, K., & Brown, D. (2004). Trauma-related dissociation: Conceptual clarity lost and found. *Australian and New Zealand Journal of Psychiatry, 38*(11–12), 906–914.

van der Kolk, B.A. (1989). The compulsion to repeat the Trauma: Re-enactment, revictimization, and masochism. *Psychiatric Clinics of North America, 12*(2), 389-411.

van der Kolk, B. A., & Courtois, C. A. (2005). Editorial comments: Complex developmental trauma. *Journal of Traumatic Stress, 18*(5), 385–388.

van der Kolk, B. A., Roth, S., Pelcovitz, D., Sunday, S., & Spinazzola, J. (2005). Disorders of extreme stress: The empirical foundation of a complex adaptation to trauma. *Journal of Traumatic Stress, 18*(5), 389–399.

Vanderlinden, J., & Vandereycken, W. (1997). *Trauma, dissociation, and impulse dyscontrol in eating disorders.* New York, NY: Brunner/Mazel.

van IJzendoorn, M. (1995). Adult attachment representations, parental responsiveness, and infant attachment: A meta-analysis on the predictive validity of the Adult Attachment Interview. *Psychological Bulletin, 117*(3), 387–403.

van IJzendoorn, M., & Bakermans-Kranenburg, M. (1996). Attachment representations in mothers, fathers, adolescents, and clinical groups: A meta-analytic search for normative data. *Journal of Clinical and Counseling Psychology, 64*(1), 8–21.

van IJzendoorn, M. H., & Sagi, A. (1999). Cross-cultural patterns of attachment: Universal and contextual dimensions. In J. Cassidy & P. R. Shaver (Eds.), *Handbook of attachment: Theory, research, and clinical applications* (pp. 713–734). New York, NY: Guilford Press.

van IJzendoorn, M. H., Sagi, A., & Lambermon, M. W. E. (1992). The multiple caregiver paradox: Data from Holland and Israel. In R. C. Pianta (Ed.), *New directions for child development: No. 57. Beyond the parent: The role of other adults in children's lives* (pp. 5–24). San Francisco, CA: Jossey-Bass.

van IJzendoorn, M. H., Feldbrugge, J. T. T. M., Derks, F. C. H., de Ruiter, C., Verhagen, M. F. M., Phillipse, M. W. G., . . . Riksen-Walraven, J. M. A. (1997). Attachment representations of personality-disordered criminal offenders. *American Journal of Orthopsychiatry, 67*(3), 440–459.

Vaughn, B. E., & Waters, E. (1990). Attachment behavior at home and in the laboratory: Q-sort observations and Strange Situation classifications of one-year-olds. *Child Development, 61*(6), 1965–1973.

Vondra, J. I., Hommerding, K. D., & Shaw, D. S. (1996). *Stability and change in infant attachment in a low income sample.* Unpublished manuscript.

Vygotsky, L. S. (1978). *Mind and society: The development of higher psychological processes.* Cambridge, MA: Harvard University Press.

Waldinger, R. J., Schulz, M. S., Barsky, A. J., & Ahern, D. K. (2006). Mapping the road from childhood trauma to adult somatization: The role of attachment. *Psychosomatic Medicine, 68*(1), 129–135.

Waldinger, R. J., Seiman, E. L., Gerber, A. J., Leim, J. H., Allen, J. P., & Hauser, S. T. (2003). Attachment and core relational themes: Wishes for autonomy and closeness in the narratives of securely and insecurely attached adults. *Psychotherapy Research, 13*(1), 77–98.

Waller, E., Scheidt, C. E., Endorf, K., Hartmann, A., & Zimmermann, P. (2015, April 30). Unresolved trauma in fibromyalgia: A cross-sectional study. *Journal of Health Psychology.* doi: 10.1177/1359105315580460

Waller, E., Scheidt, C. E., & Hartmann, A. (2004). Attachment representation and illness behavior in somatoform disorders. *Journal of Nervous and Mental Disease, 192,* 200–209.

Wallin, D. J. (2007). *Attachment in psychotherapy.* New York, NY: Guilford Press.

Wallis, P., & Steele, H. (2001). Attachment representations in adolescence: Further evidence from psychiatric residential settings. *Attachment & Human Development, 3*(3), 259–268.

Ward, A., Ramsay, R., Turnull, S., Steele, M., Steele, H., & Treasure, J. (2001). *British Journal of Medical Psychology, 74,* 497–505.

Warren, S. L., Huston, L., Egeland, B., & Sroufe, L. A. (1997). Child and adolescent anxiety disorders and early attachment. *Journal of the Academy of Child and Adolescent Psychiatry, 36*(5), 637–644.

Wartner, U. G., Grossmann, K., Fremmer-Bombik, E., & Suess, G. (1994). Attachment patterns at age six in South Germany: Predictability from infancy and implications for preschool behavior. *Child Development, 65*(4), 1014–1027.

Waters, E. (1978). The reliability and stability of individual differences in infant–mother attachment. *Child Development, 49*(2), 483–494.

Waters, E., & Deane, K. (1985). Defining and assessing individual differences in attachment relationships: Q-methodology and the organization of behavior in infancy and early childhood. In I. Bretherton & E. Waters (Eds.), *Growing pains of attachment theory and research. Monographs of the Society for Research in Child Development, 50*(1–2), 41–65.

Waters, E., Merrick, S., Treboux, D., Crowell, J., & Albersheim, L. (2000). Attachment security in infancy and early adulthood: A twenty-year longitudinal study. *Child Development, 71*(3), 684–689.

Watkins, J. G., & Watkins, H. H. (1978). *The therapeutic self: Developing resonance—key to effective relationships.* New York, NY: Human Sciences.

Watson, D., & Freind, R. (1969). Measurement of social-evaluative anxiety. *Journal of Consulting and Clinical Psychology, 33,* 448–457.

Wei, M., Heppner, P. P., & Mallinckrodt, B. (2003). Perceived coping as a mediator between attachment and psychological distress: A structural equation modeling approach. *Journal of Counseling Psychology, 50*(4), 438–447.

Wei, M., Heppner, P. P., Russell, D. W., & Young, S. K. (2006). Maladaptive perfectionisms and ineffective coping as mediators between attachment and future depression: A prospective analysis. *Journal of Counseling Psychology, 53*(1), 67–79.

Wei, M., Mallinckrodt, B., Larson, L. M., & Zakalik, R. A. (2005). Adult attachment, depressive symptoms, and validation from self versus others. *Journal of Counseling Psychology, 52*(3), 368–377.

Wei, M., Vogel, D. L., Ku, T.-Y., & Zakalik, R. A. (2005). Adult attachment, affect regulation, negative mood, and interpersonal problems: The mediating roles of emotional reactivity and emotional cutoff. *Journal of Counseling Psychology, 52*(1), 14–24.

Weinfield, N., Whaley, G., & Egeland, B. (2004). Continuity, discontinuity, and coherence in attachment from infancy to late adolescence: Sequelae of organization and disorganization. *Attachment & Human Development, 6*(1), 73–97.

West, M., & Keller, A. (1994). Psychotherapy strategies for insecure attachment in personality disorders. In M. B. Sperling & W. H. Berman (Eds.), *Attachment in adults: Clinical and developmental perspectives* (pp. 313–330). New York, NY: Guilford Press.

Whiffen, V. E., Judd, M. E., & Aube, J. A. (1999). Intimate relationships moderate the association between childhood sexual abuse and depression. *Journal of Interpersonal Violence, 14,* 940–954.

Widiger, T. A., & Trull, T. J. (2007). Plate tectonics in the classification of personality disorder: Shifting to a dimensional model. *American Psychologist, 62*(2), 71.

Widom, C. S. (1999). Posttraumatic stress disorder in abused and neglected children grown up. *American Journal of Psychiatry, 156*(8), 1223–1229.

Widom, C. S., Ireland, T. O., & Glynn, P. J. (1995). Alcohol abuse and neglected children followed-up: Are they at increased risk? *Journal of the Study of Alcohol, 56*(2), 207–217.

Wilber, K. (2000). *Integral psychology: Consciousness, spirit, psychology, therapy.* Boston, MA: Shambhala.

Wilber, K. (2007). *Integral spirituality: A startling new role for religion in the modern and postmodern world.* Boston, MA: Integral Books.

Winnicott, D. W. (1953). Transitional objects and transitional phenomena. *International Journal of Psycho-analysis, 34*(2), 89–97.

Winnicott, D. W. (1957). *The child and the family.* London, England: Tavistock.

Winnicott, D. W. (1960). The theory of the parent–infant relationship. In *The maturational processes and the facilitating environment* (pp. 37–55). New York, NY: International Universities Press.

Winnicott, D. W. (1965). The maturational process and the facilitating environment:; Studies in the theory of emotional development. *The International Psycho-aAnalytical Library, 64,* 1--26. London, England: The Hogarth Press and the Institute of Psycho-aAnalysis.

Winnicott, D. W. (1971). *Playing and reality.* London, England: Tavistock.

Wishnie, H. (1977). *The impulsive personality: Understanding people with destructive character disorders.* New York, NY: Plenum Press.

Wolff, P. H. (1969). The causes, controls, and organization of behavior in the neonate. In G. S. Klein (Ed.), *Psychological issues* (Monograph 17). New York, NY: International Universities Press.

Woodhouse, S. S., Schlosser, L. Z., Crook, R. E., Ligiéro, D. P., & Gelso, C. J. (2003). Client attachment to therapist: Relations to transference and client recollections of parental caregiving. *Journal of Counseling Psychology, 50*(4), 395–408.

Young, J. E., & Brown, G. (2001). *Young schema questionnaire: Special edition.* New York, NY: Schema Therapy Institute.

Young, J. E., Klosko, J. S., & Weishaar, M. E. (2003). *Schema therapy: A practitioner's guide.* New York, NY: Guilford Press.

Zachrisson, H. D., & Kulbotten, G. R. (2006). Attachment in anorexia nervosa: An exploration of associations with eating disorder psychopathology and psychiatric symptoms. *Eating and Weight Disorders, 11*(4), 163–170.

Zeijlmans van Emmichoven, I. A., van IJzendoorn, M. H., de Ruiter, C., & Brosschot, J. F. (2003). Selective processing of threatening information: Effects of attachment representation and anxiety disorder on attention and memory. *Development and Psychopathology, 15*(1), 219–237.

Contributors

Daniel P. Brown, PhD, is Associate Clinical Professor of Psychology at Harvard Medical School, where he teaches courses on performance excellence for health professionals and judges. He is the author or co-author of 16 books, including *Hypnotherapy and Hypnoanalysis* (with Erika Fromm), *Hypnosis and Behavioral Medicine* (with Erika Fromm); *Transformations of Consciousness* (with Ken Wilber and Jack Engler), and a book on Tibetan meditation, *Pointing Out the Great Way.* He is the senior author of *Memory, Trauma-Treatment, and the Law* (with Alan Scheflin and Cory Hammond), winner of the Guttmacher award for the best contribution to forensic psychiatry.

David S. Elliott, PhD, is a clinical psychologist and former president of the Rhode Island Psychological Association. He is on the faculty of the International School for Psychotherapy, Counseling, and Group Leadership, in St. Petersburg, Russia, and teaches internationally on attachment, personality, and psychotherapy process.

Paula Morgan-Johnson, LICSW, a former instructor and senior clinical supervisor at Bessel van der Kolk's Trauma Center, has expertise in the treatment of complex PTSD and maintains a private practice in Boston.

Paula Sacks, LICSW, is a psychotherapist at a nonprofit clinic in Cambridge and maintains a private practice in Chestnut Hill, Massachusetts, specializing in adult attachment disturbances and hypnotherapy.

Caroline R. Baltzer, PhD, is a Lecturer in Psychology in the Department of Psychiatry at Harvard Medical School and is an affiliate of McLean Hospital. Her private practice is in Cambridge, Massachusetts.

James Hickey practices in Brighton, Massachusetts. After receiving his PsyD from Antioch University New England, he worked for years with prisoners, witnessing the enduring effects of trauma and disordered attachment.

Andrea Cole, PhD, is a clinical psychologist in private practice in Northampton, Massachusetts. She specializes in the treatment of attachment disorders and depression.

Jan Bloom, PhD, earned degrees from Tufts, Harvard, and the University of Minnesota. She currently consults with physicians and schools and works with parents and children, adolescents, and adults in her private practice.

Deirdre Fay, LICSW, has a private practice in Arlington, Massachusetts. Founder of the Becoming Safely Embodied Skills, she integrates trauma and attachment therapy with yoga for safe embodiment.

Author Index

Subject Index

Note: Italicized page locators indicate figures; tables are noted with *t*.